LAW AND PRACTICE
OF
INTERNATIONAL
COMMERCIAL ARBITRATION

AUSTRALIA
Law Book Co.
Sydney

CANADA and USA
Carswell
Toronto

HONG KONG
Sweet & Maxwell Asia

NEW ZEALAND
Brookers
Wellington

SINGAPORE and MALAYSIA
Sweet & Maxwell Asia
Singapore and Kuala Lumpur

LAW AND PRACTICE
OF
INTERNATIONAL
COMMERCIAL ARBITRATION

FOURTH EDITION

By

ALAN REDFERN
Barrister, One Essex Court,
Temple, London, FCIArb

MARTIN HUNTER
Barrister, London; Professor of
International Dispute Resolution
Nottingham Law School, FCIArb

With

NIGEL BLACKABY
Partner, Freshfields Bruckhaus
Deringer

CONSTANTINE PARTASIDES
Partner, Freshfields Bruckhaus
Deringer

LONDON
SWEET & MAXWELL
2004

Published in 2004 by
Sweet & Maxwell Limited of
100 Avenue Road, London NW3 3PF
www.sweetandmaxwell.co.uk
Computerset by
Interactive Sciences Ltd,
Gloucester.

Printed and bound in England
by Bath Press, UK

First Edition 1986
Second Edition 1991
Reprinted 1993, 1996, 1997, 1998
Third Edition 1999
Reprinted 2001, 2003
Fourth Edition 2004
Reprinted 2006

**A CIP record for this book is available from the
British Library**

ISBN 0–421–892–900
ISBN 978-0–421–892–903

FOREWORD

Looking back at the prefaces to earlier editions of this book, it is clear that we saw our primary mission to be the creation of a *practitioners' guide*. We signed our first publishing agreement with Sweet & Maxwell in early 1984, and shortly afterwards started the two-year labour of preparing our text for publication in 1986.

In those days we had no thought of writing a text for *students* in the usual sense of the word. A handful of institutions, such as the Chartered Institute of Arbitrators, were providing training courses for budding *arbitrators* in the field of domestic arbitration; but, so far as we are aware, no training was on offer for lawyers and others whose ambition was to start their careers in international arbitration by representing clients. Aspirants simply had to "learn on the job", as we did.

How things change! Since the mid-1980s the volume of global trade has steadily increased. The practice of international arbitration has become a substantial service industry that has attracted the attention of large and small law firms in many countries, either as a service to their existing clientele or as a useful means of establishing a presence in overseas jurisdictions.

Competition has brought with it a need for young graduates and practitioners with high levels of skill in the field (note that we use the word "skill", rather than "knowledge"). This has in turn promoted a need for degrees, diplomas and other programmes for post-graduate and post-qualification students. This need has been addressed by universities and arbitral institutions, and to our own knowledge literally hundreds of courses are offered to aspiring practitioners in many different jurisdictions.

For several years we have been bombarded with pleas from professors from universities around the world to let them have an affordable version of our book that could realistically be prescribed as the "course book" for masters level students. We considered various solutions, in discussion with our publishers, including the preparation of an abbreviated "nutshell" version along the lines of the series published by Sweet & Maxwell's sister company Westlaw. In the end we decided to offer the existing edition to *bona fide* students, unaltered, but with a number of cost-saving features. These include a paperback cover, slightly different paper and the omission of the appendices—because our market research showed that students routinely have access to the appendix materials on websites created for their courses.

The first student edition published in September 2003 was well received; we would welcome comments and suggestions for improvement from users so that we can continue the development of student versions of future editions of the work.

Alan Redfern and Martin Hunter
London, September 2004

PREFACE

We embarked upon the task of writing the first edition of this book just over twenty years ago. When published it was a slim volume of some 400 pages, with just six appendices of which the most important were the New York Convention of 1958 and the UNCITRAL Arbitration Rules. They have now been joined by the Model Law, which is a benchmark for any modern law of arbitration, as well as some of the other international materials that are referred to most frequently in the text. However, following the structure of the third edition, we have not included any examples of national arbitration laws. This is partly because they are easily accessible on various websites, and partly because—taking account of the remarks of friends and colleagues concerning the size of the second edition, which was rather fat—we have jealously guarded our resolve to remain relatively slim (at least so far as the book is concerned!).

When the first edition appeared, we were pleased with the response from reviewers, practitioners and students—and particularly perhaps with the reaction of our overseas colleagues, who were surprised that two English lawyers could adopt a genuinely "internationalist" approach, whilst maintaining what they regarded as "typically English pragmatism". We do not know whether it is typically English or not, but we have endeavoured to keep the book both clear and practical in its treatment of a subject which the late Sir Robert Jennings described in his foreword to the first edition as "a great body of practice, precedent and experience taking shape as a new and elaborate kind of international mercantile law."

Sir Robert, having had the doubtful pleasure of teaching international law to us and to generations of other Cambridge law students, moved on—perhaps with some relief—to the International Court of Justice, where he was subsequently elected to the presidency of the Court. In the same foreword, he referred to commercial arbitration as "uncommonly well adapted to developing new rules and practices better suited to the conditions of the modern world, and to finding new and reasonable accommodations between the reasonable needs of both host state and foreign investor." Written twenty years ago, this was prescient indeed. The expansion of global trade and the need for foreign investment in the less developed countries of the world in order to help them generate wealth through their own resources—including their people, as well as natural resources such as agriculture, oil, gas and other minerals—underline the need for a just and acceptable method of dispute resolution, so as to ensure a fair balance between protecting the investor and preventing exploitation.

The recent "explosion", as it has been described, of Bilateral Investment Treaties, with their provision for the resolution of disputes by arbitration, is designed to achieve this goal. But there is still much to be done. Potential investors have to be reasonably assured of a proper return on investment and of protection from expropriation and other unfair treatment that is contrary to international standards. Host states for their part need to be protected from damage to their countries' resources by exploitation—and over all is the shadow of corruption. International arbitrators are limited in what they can achieve by the terms of the contract in which business has been done; perhaps more use should be made of hardship clauses and even equity clauses so that arbitrators have more freedom to achieve what they perceive to be the right decision in all the circumstances of the case?

The importance of foreign investment, including the role of investment treaties, led us to include a further chapter in this fourth edition devoted to investment arbitrations. This is in line with another of our aims, which has been to ensure that each new edition of this book is not a mere update with a few new cases thrown in for good measure, but a reassessment of what is important and what is not, so that material which has lost its relevance is taken out to make way for what is new. At the same time, we have tried to maintain the basic structure of the book, which seems to have worked well since it was first written down on one sheet of paper.

What of the future? We very much hope to see the book continue as a standard work of value to practitioners and students alike—and indeed to those international arbitrators and judges from different countries who from time to time are good enough to cite a particular passage with approval. With this in mind, we looked for younger lawyers who might be prepared to take over from us, English speaking but for preference practising in a civil law jurisdiction so as to retain a truly internationalist outlook for the book. It took time, but as we looked around it became clear that two lawyers in the Paris office of the firm where we had spent the major part of our professional life were emerging in their own right, not simply as practitioners of international commercial arbitration but as authors too. We were very pleased when Nigel Blackaby and Constantine Partasides, who are both now partners in Freshfields Bruckhaus Deringer's Paris office, agreed to take over gradually during the five-year cycle covering the fourth and fifth editions; and we were even more pleased when it became apparent that they would bring to the venture not only continuity, knowledge and skills from a different perspective (that of counsel, rather than of arbitrators), but also a freshness of approach that we have greatly valued during the preparation of this edition.

Nigel and Constantine have written their own preface, which appears below. We wish them well and assure them of our support for as long as they wish to have it—which we hope may be a long time!

Preface

The title page for this edition, as our readers will see, is:

Law and Practice of International Commercial Arbitration *by* Alan Redfern and Martin Hunter *with* Nigel Blackaby and Constantine Partasides.

The working title for the fifth edition is:

Redfern and Hunter on International Commercial Arbitration, *by* Nigel Blackaby and Constantine Partasides.

It is time now to express our grateful thanks to those who have helped us in so many ways in the preparation of this book. First, we take the opportunity to thank our wives, Marie-Louise and Linda, who have not only put up with the inevitable lost weekends, late nights and interrupted holidays (coupled with promises they never believed that it would all be different next time), but who have also become actively involved in many very practical ways—photocopying, scanning, typing, translating, proof-reading and so forth. Next we gratefully acknowledge the contribution of Pat Allan, who recently retired as a senior secretary and personal assistant at the firm formerly known as Freshfields. She has been closely involved with the book since the first edition. We interrupted what she had planned as a well-deserved retirement in the English countryside and prevailed upon her to co-ordinate the work of all four authors, attend meetings in Paris and London, liaise with the publishers and generally get the show on the road.

Others who have been helped us from the beginning include Judy Freedberg, head of the editorial staff of ICCA publications located at the PCA offices in the Peace Palace, who continues to be the fountain of all published materials and unpublished knowledge in the field of international commercial arbitration, and Robert Spicer, a freelancer retained by Sweet & Maxwell to prepare the index and cross-references for all four editions. Many others have provided invaluable help for this edition. Fred Bennett and his team of international arbitration specialists at the Los Angeles based law firm Quinn Emanuel sent us materials and explanatory memoranda concerning the latest developments in the USA, which have proved to be very useful in evaluating and explaining developments in that important jurisdiction. Several busy people from the world's premier arbitration institutions have provided statistics and other valuable assistance. These include Bill Slate, president of the AAA, Anne-Marie Whitesell, secretary-general of the ICC's International Court of Arbitration, Antonio Parra, of ICSID, Adrian Winstanley, director-general and registrar of the LCIA, and Brooks Daly of the PCA. Finally, newcomers for the fourth edition have included Lucy Reed of Freshfields Bruckhaus Deringer's New York office and Alexander Luetgendorf, an Austrian *rechsanwalt* on assignment at Essex Court Chambers.

Best efforts have been made to update the text by reference to materials published by May 1, 2004.

Alan Redfern and Martin Hunter
London, August 2004

As for many practitioners of our generation, Redfern & Hunter was the first text on international arbitration that either of us ever opened. As a recently qualified lawyer, Nigel remembers Martin handing him a copy of Redfern and Hunter to read over the weekend as preparation for an arbitration involving cruise lines in Miami. It was not a difficult task. Beautifully written and illustrated with real examples from the professional lives of two of the pioneers in this field of law, it was a revelation. After more than a decade of practice as counsel, it has remained our first port of call when confronted with tricky questions of arbitration law or practice. The reason for this is simple. Of the many learned texts that enrich our chosen field, none have explained the issues with greater practicality of perspective, or clarity of expression.

So when Alan and Martin invited us for dinner a little over two years ago, and asked us to co-author this edition and eventually take over future editions of the book, we were both honoured and daunted: honoured to be involved in one of the great works in our field, and daunted by the prospect of maintaining Alan's and Martin's exacting standards in the years to come.

In addition to being two of the world's leading international arbitrators, Alan and Martin are the founding fathers of the Freshfields' arbitration practice in which we both learnt our trade. Working with them as co-authors for this edition has therefore been a special privilege. It has also been an education. As we expected, they have accumulated countless insights into the practice of international arbitration. They also have the ability to communicate those insights with rare style and clarity. But what perhaps we might not have expected from two individuals who have already achieved so much in the field, is the great energy and affection that they continue to maintain for the study and practice of international arbitration.

In this edition, Alan and Martin have looked to the future. It cannot be easy to hand over to others a work that has been crafted and re-crafted with love and sweat over twenty years. We thank them for the faith they have shown in us, and we hope to justify it in the years to come. Our apprenticeship has begun in this edition, but it is not yet finished. Readers will be reassured to know (as are we) that Alan and Martin will continue to be closely involved in the preparation of the next edition.

As to this edition, in addition to Lucy Reed of Freshfields Bruckhaus Deringer's New York office (who is acknowledged by Alan and Martin above), we have benefited from the invaluable assistance of a number of talented members of the Freshfields Bruckhaus Deringer international arbitration group based in Paris, London, Amsterdam and Frankfurt. Of the many who have assisted us, we would like to give special thanks to Jonathan Sutcliffe, a senior associate in London, whose erudition and energy facilitated and simplified our work immeasurably.

Last but not least we thank the ladies in our lives, Maria, Patricia and Nayeli, for their support, patience and understanding—past and future.

Nigel Blackaby and Constantine Partasides

ACKNOWLEDGMENTS

Grateful acknowledgment is made for permission to reproduce from the under-mentioned works:

American Arbitration Association
AAA International Arbitration Rules, 1997 edition

London Court of International Arbitration
LCIA Arbitration Rules, 1998 edition

International Chamber of Commerce
ICC Rules of Arbitration, 1998 edition. ICC publication No 581–ISBN 92.842.1239.1(E). Published in its official English version by the International Chamber of Commerce. Copyright © 1997—International Chamber of Commerce (ICC), Paris. Available from: The ICC International Court of Arbitration, 38 Cours Albert 1er, 75008 Paris, France.

International Bar Association
IBA Ethics for International Arbitrators 1987; IBA Rules on the Taking of Evidence in International Commercial Arbitration, 1999 edition

Southwestern Legal Foundation's Institute for Transnational Arbitration
Scoreboard of Adherances to International Treaties as of December 1998
Copyright 1999 by the Southwestern Legal Foundation. Reprinted with kind permission of the Southwestern Legal Foundation's Institute for Transnational Arbitration, which produces the *Scoreboard*

United Nations Publications
UNCITRAL Arbitration Rules 1976; UNCITRAL Model Law 1985; New York Convention on the Recognition and Enforcement of Awards 1958; and UNCITRAL Notes on Organizing Arbitral Proceedings 1996.

WIPO
WIPO Arbitration Rules 1994

Acknowledgments

The World Bank
ICSID Rules of Procedure for the Institution of Concilation and Arbitration Rules 1965

Whilst every care has been taken to establish and acknowledge copyright, and contact the copyright owners, the publishers tender their apologies for any accidental infringement. They would be pleased to come to a suitable arrangement with the rightful owners in each case.

TABLE OF CONTENTS

Table of Contents

Table of Contents

Table of Contents

CHAPTER 5—POWERS, DUTIES AND JURISDICTION OF AN ARBITRAL TRIBUNAL

Table of Contents

CHAPTER 11—ARBITRATION UNDER INVESTMENT TREATIES

Table of Contents

ABBREVIATIONS

AAA	American Arbitration Association
ABA	American Bar Association
ADR	Alternative Dispute Resolution
AAA International Rules	AAA's International Arbitration Rules, as amended, effective from April 1, 1997
Arb. Int.	Arbitration International, published by the LCIA
CEDR	Centre for Dispute Resolution, established in London in 1990
CIETAC	China Economic and Trade Arbitration Commission. CIETAC Arbitration Rules, October 1995 edition
CMEA	Council for Mutual Economic Assistance
CPR Rules	The Rules of the Centre for Public Resources for Non-administered Arbitration of International Disputes
Delvolvé Report	Commission on International Arbitration "Final Report on Multi-Party Arbitrations", Paris, June 1994, by the Working Group under the Chairmanship of M. Jean-Louis Delvolvé
European Convention 1961	European Convention on International Commercial Arbitration 1961
FIDIC	Federation Internationale des Ingenieurs-Conseils
Final Report – ICC Clause	Final Report of the Working Group on the ICC Standard Arbitration Clause, document 420/318, October 21, 1991
GAFTA	Grain and Feed Trade Association
GAFTA Arbitration Rules	The arbitration rules adopted by GAFTA, January 31, 1997 edition
Geneva Convention	Geneva Convention on the Execution of Foreign Arbitral Awards, September 26, 1927
Geneva Protocol	Geneva Protocol on Arbitration Clauses, 1923
Hague Convention 1899	Hague Convention on the Pacific Settlement of International Disputes 1899
Hague Convention 1907	Hague Convention on the Pacific Settlement of International Disputes 1907

Handbook Commercial Arbitration	ICCA handbook on International Commercial Arbitration, consisting of national reports and basic legal texts. Published by Kluwer
IACAC	Inter-American Commercial Arbitration Commission
IBA	International Bar Association
IBA Rules	IBA Rules on the Taking of Evidence in International Commercial Arbitration, adopted June 1999
ICC	International Chamber of Commerce, located in Paris
ICCA	International Council for Commercial Arbitration
ICC Court	International Court of Arbitration of the ICC, established in Paris in 1923
ICC Rules	ICC Rules of Arbitration, June 1, 1998 edition
ICDR	International Centre for Dispute Resolution
ICJ	International Court of Justice, located at The Hague
ICSID	International Centre for the Settlement of Investment Disputes
ICSID Rules	ICSID Rules of Procedure for Arbitration Proceedings, 1984 edition
ILM	International Legal Materials, published by The American Society of International Law
Iran–US C.T.R.	Iran–US Claims Tribunal Reports, published by Grotius
J.Int'l Arb	Journal of International Arbitration
LCIA	London Court of International Arbitration
LCIA Rules	LCIA Arbitration Rules, January 1, 1998 edition
LMAA	The London Maritime Arbitrators Association
LMAA Terms	These terms, effective from January 31, 1997, govern the basis upon which members of the LMAA accept appointment
LQR	Law Quarterly Review
Model Law	Model Law on International Commercial Arbitration, adopted by UNCITRAL on June 21, 1985
Moscow Convention	Convention on the Settlement by Arbitration of Civil Law Disputes Resulting from Economic, Scientific and Technological Co-operation, 1972
NAFTA	North American Free Trade Agreement

New York Convention	Convention on the Recognition and Enforcement of Foreign Arbitral Awards, 1958
Panama Convention	Inter-American Convention on International Commercial Arbitration, 1975
PCA	Permanent Court of Arbitration, at The Hague
PCIJ	Permanent Court of International Justice; predecessor of the ICJ
SCC	Stockholm Chamber of Commerce
Strasbourg Uniform Law	European Convention providing a Uniform Law on Arbitration, done at Strasbourg on June 20, 1966
Swiss PIL Act	Swiss Private International Law Act of December 18, 1987, Chapter 12: International Arbitration
UNCITRAL	United Nations Commission on International Trade Law
UNCITRAL Arbitration Rules	UNCITRAL Arbitration Rules, adopted on December 5, 1976
UNCITRAL Conciliation Rules	UNCITRAL Conciliation Rules, adopted in July 1980
UNCITRAL Model Law	See under "Model Law"
UNCITRAL Notes	UNCITRAL Notes on Organizing Arbitral Proceedings, adopted in Vienna in 1996
Vienna Rules	Rules of Arbitration and Conciliation of the International Arbitral Centre of the Federal Economic Chamber, Vienna
Washington Convention	Convention on the Settlement of Investment disputes between States and nationals of other States 1965
WIPO	World Intellectual Property Organization
WIPO Rules	WIPO Rules on Organizing Arbitrations, October 1, 1994 edition
Yearbook Commercial Arbitration	ICCA's Yearbook of commercial Arbitration (published by Kluwer).

TABLE OF CASES

Table of Cases

Table of Cases

Table of Cases

Table of Cases

Table of Cases

Table of Cases

TABLE OF ARBITRATION AWARDS

Table of Arbitration Awards

Table of Arbitration Awards

Table of Arbitration Awards

Table of Arbitration Awards

TABLE OF STATUTES

1. United Kingdom

2. United States

3. Europe

Germany

Ireland

4. Other Jurisdictions

TABLE OF MAJOR ARBITRATION CONVENTIONS

1

TABLE OF INTERNATIONAL ARBITRATION RULES

Table of International Arbitration Rules

TABLE OF CIVIL CODES

TABLE OF TREATIES

Bilateral Investment Treaties

TABLE OF DIRECTIVES

TABLE OF EUROPEAN REGULATIONS

TABLE OF CIVIL PROCEDURE RULES

Chapter 1

INTRODUCTION

1. Key Elements of International Arbitration

(a) Generally

International arbitration has become the established method of determining **1–01** international commercial disputes.[1] All over the world, states have modernised their laws of arbitration to take account of this fact. New arbitral centres have been established and the rapidly evolving law and practice of international commercial arbitration is a subject for study in universities and law schools alike.

Yet at its core, international commercial arbitration remains much as it always was. It is a private method of dispute resolution, chosen by the parties themselves as an effective way of putting an end to disputes between them, without recourse to the courts of law. It is conducted in different countries and against different legal and cultural backgrounds, with a striking lack of formality. There are no national flags or other symbols of state authority. There are no ushers, wigs or gowns—simply a group of people seated around a row of tables, in a room hired for the occasion. To an outsider, it would look as if a conference or business meeting was in progress. It does not look like a legal proceeding at all.

Yet the appearance conceals the reality. It is true that the parties themselves choose to arbitrate, as an alternative to litigation or to other methods of dispute resolution. It is true too that, to a large extent, the arbitrators and the parties may choose for themselves the procedures to be followed. If they want a "fast-track" arbitration,[2] they may have one. If they want to dispense with the disclosure of documents or the evidence of witnesses, they may do so. Indeed, they may even dispense with the hearing itself if they wish.[3] Nonetheless, the practice of

---

[1] Arbitral institutions generally keep a record of the number of requests for arbitration they receive each year. One of the leading institutions, the International Chamber of Commerce ("the ICC") recorded 344 requests for arbitration in 1986, when the first edition of this book was published. In 2003, the ICC recorded 580 requests, with the amount in dispute ranging from US$10,000 to US$2,500,000,000. Other arbitral institutions report an increasing number of cases—and this does not tell the whole story, since many international arbitrations are conducted in different parts of the world without the involvement of an arbitral institution.

[2] Fast-track arbitration is discussed in Ch.6, paras 6–43—6–45.

[3] The Rules of Arbitration of the ICC provide in Art.20.6 that the arbitral tribunal may make a decision based on documents only "unless any of the parties requests a hearing". Other institutions have similar rules.

resolving disputes by international commercial arbitration only works because it is held in place by a complex system of national laws and international treaties.[4] Even a comparatively simple international commercial arbitration may require reference to as many as four different national systems or rules of law.[5] First, there is the law that governs recognition and enforcement of the agreement to arbitrate. Then there is the law that governs, or regulates, the actual arbitration proceedings themselves. Next—and in most cases, most importantly—there is the law or the set of rules that the arbitral tribunal has to apply to the substantive matters in dispute before it. Finally, there is the law that governs recognition and enforcement of the award of the arbitral tribunal.

1–02   These laws may well be the same. The law that governs the arbitral proceedings (which will usually be the national law of the place of arbitration) may also govern the substantive matters in issue. But this is not necessarily so. The substantive law—that is, the law which governs the matters in issue (and which may also be known as the applicable law, the governing law or the proper law) may be an entirely different system of law. For example, an arbitral tribunal sitting in England, governed (or regulated) by English law as the law of the place of arbitration, may well be required to apply the law of New York as the applicable or substantive law of the contract.[6] Moreover, the applicable or substantive law of the contract may not necessarily be a given national system of law. It may be international law; or a blend of national law and international law; or even an assemblage of rules of law known as international trade law, transnational law, the "modern law merchant" (the so-called *lex mercatoria)* or by some other convenient title.[7] Finally, because most international arbitrations take place in a "neutral" country—that is to say, a country which is not that of the parties—the system of law which governs recognition and enforcement of the award of the arbitral tribunal will usually be different from that which governs the arbitral proceedings themselves.

This dependence of the international commercial arbitral process upon different, and sometimes conflicting, rules of national and international law is one of the major themes of this book. First, however, it is necessary to consider the arbitral process itself and to understand what is meant by "international commercial arbitration".

---

[4] As will be seen, the support of international treaties, such as the New York Convention of 1958 on the Recognition and Enforcement of Foreign Awards, is essential to the effectiveness of arbitration internationally.

[5] See, for instance, the comment of Richard Kreindler: "Increasingly, the body or rules of law as agreed by the parties are different from those at the situs, from those at the place of principal or characteristic performance and in turn, from those at the place or places of likely enforcement", in "Approaches to the Application of Transnational Public Policy by Arbitrators", *Journal of World Investment*, Geneva, April 2003, Vol.4, No.2, p.239; this echoes the statement by Lord Mustill: "It is by now firmly established that more than one national system of law may bear upon an international arbitration": *Channel Tunnel Group Ltd v Balfour Beatty Construction Ltd* [1993] A.C. 334 at 357.

[6] See, for instance, *XL Insurance v Owens Corning* [2000] 2 Lloyd's Rep. 500.

[7] The different systems or rules of law which may constitute the substantive law of an international commercial contract are discussed in Ch.2.

(b) A brief historical review

In its origins, the concept of arbitration as a method of resolving disputes was **1–03** a simple one:

> "The practice of arbitration therefore, comes, so to speak, naturally to prim-
> itive bodies of law; and after courts have been established by the state and a
> recourse to them has become the natural method of settling disputes, the
> practice continues because the parties to a dispute want to settle it with less
> formality and expense than is involved in a recourse to the courts."[8]

A distinguished French lawyer wrote of arbitration as an "apparently rudimen-
tary method of settling disputes, since it consists of submitting them to ordinary
individuals whose only qualification is that of being chosen by the parties."[9] He
added that, traditionally, countries of the civil law were hostile to arbitration as
being "too primitive" a form of justice.

It is not difficult to visualise the "primitive" nature of the arbitral process in
its early history. Two traders, in dispute over the price or quality of goods
delivered, would turn to a third whom they knew and trusted for his decision. Or
two merchants, arguing over damaged merchandise, would settle their dispute by
accepting the judgment of a fellow merchant. And they would do so not because
of any legal sanction, but because this was expected of them within the community in which they carried on business.

> "Looking first at its history, the origins of contemporary private arbitration lie
> in mediaeval Western Europe. A comprehensive account of second millennial
> arbitration, focused in a way which would enable the vigorous assertions made
> about the juristic basis of current mega-arbitrations to be checked against
> recorded facts, has yet to appear. Nevertheless, it can be said with some
> confidence that the dispute resolution mechanisms of the post-classical mer-
> cantile world were conducted within, and drew their strengths from, commu-
> nities consisting either of participants in an individual trade or of persons
> enrolled in bodies established under the auspices and control of geographical
> trading centres. Such communities gave birth to the implicit expectations and
> peer-group pressures which both shaped and enforced the resolution of dis-
> putes by an impartial and often prestigious personage. Within such commu-
> nities external sanctions would have been largely redundant, even if a legal
> framework had been available to bring them into play, which in the main it was
> not."[10]

This happy picture of arbitration in the old days, as a self-regulated system of **1–04**
dispute resolution with no need for legal sanctions, is perhaps seen through rose-

---

[8] Holdsworth, *History of English Law* (1964), Vol.XIV, p.187.
[9] Fouchard, *L'Arbitrage Commercial International* (1965), pp.1, 30 and 31 (translation by the
authors).
[10] Michael Mustill, "Is it a bird . . . " in Claude Reymond, *Liber Amicorum* (Editions du Juris-
Classeur, Paris, 2004), p.209.

tinted spectacles; but it was seen in much the same way by one of the most distinguished French commentators on arbitration:

"Arbitration was mainly conceived of in the past as an institution of peace, the purpose of which was not primarily to ensure the rule of law but rather to maintain harmony between persons who were destined to live together. It was recognised that in some cases the rules and procedures provided by the law were too rigid. The law was therefore willing to give effect to an arbitration agreement entered into by the parties to settle their disputes. Parties were authorised to submit a dispute to an arbitrator only after this dispute had arisen. The arbitrator was chosen *intuitu personae*, because the parties trusted him or were prepared to submit to his authority; he was a squire, a relative, a mutual friend or a man of wisdom, of whom it was expected that he would be able to devise a satisfactory solution for the dispute. The Italian Code of Procedure of 1865 significantly treated arbitration in a preliminary chapter 'On Conciliation and Arbitration.'"[11]

Within a small local community, the authority of the squire in an English county, or of a Sheikh in one of the territories of the Arabian Gulf,[12] may well have been sufficient to ensure that the parties accepted and carried out the decision of "their" arbitrator. In the same way, within a particular trade or market, a trader's concern for his reputation—or the risk of sanctions being imposed by a trade association[13]—would probably be sufficient to ensure compliance. But it is plain that in a wider, more general context, something more is needed if a system of "private justice" is to be truly effective—and that is the support of the legal system within which the process of private dispute resolution operates.

In theory, such a legal system might have remained indifferent to the private settlement of disputes, in much the same way as it would not concern itself with enforcing the private rules of a tennis or sailing club. Roman law did in fact adopt an attitude of indifference to private arbitration. An arbitration agreement was not illegal and was not unknown, but neither the arbitration agreement nor any arbitral award had any legal effect. To get round this problem, parties would make a double promise (a *"com-promissum"*) to which a term was added that a penalty would be payable if a party failed to honour the arbitration agreement or the arbitral award. In such an event, the court would not enforce the arbitration agreement or the award, but it would enforce the promise to pay a penalty.[14]

---

[11] René David, *Arbitration in International Trade* (Kluwer, 1985), p.29.

[12] "Disputes in pre-Islamic Arabia were resolved under a process of arbitration (of sorts) . . . This was voluntary arbitration, an essentially private arrangement that depended on the goodwill of the parties." Nudrat Majeed, "Good Faith and Due Process: Lessons from the Shari'ah", (2004) 20 Arbitration International 104.

[13] *cf.* the power of commodity trade associations, such as the Grain and Feed Trade Association, to punish a member who fails to comply with an arbitration award by "posting" the defaulter—that is to say, by giving notice of the default to all members, thus warning members against doing further business with the defaulter.

[14] See David, *Arbitration in International Trade, op.cit.*, pp.84 and 85.

Yet no modern state could stand back and allow a system of private justice, **1–05** which depended on the goodwill of the participants, to regulate commercial activities which were of increasing importance; and so it was to be expected that at some stage, the national state would step in and regulate matters.[15]

But international commercial arbitration does not stay within national boundaries. On the contrary, it crosses them. For example, a corporation based in the USA might contract with another corporation based in Germany, for the construction of a power plant in Egypt, with any disputes being resolved by arbitration in London. How is the arbitration agreement to be enforced, if a dispute arises and one of the parties refuses to arbitrate? And if there is an arbitration which leads to an award of damages, how is that award to be enforced against the assets of the losing party, if that party refuses to carry out the award voluntarily? The national law of one state alone could not deal with problems of this kind. Plainly what was needed was an international treaty or convention which would link together national laws and provide a uniform solution.

In time, as will be seen later in this chapter, such treaties came into being. There was, notably, the Geneva Protocol of 1923, which went some way to provide for the international enforcement of arbitration agreements and arbitral awards. This was followed by the Geneva Convention of 1927, which widened the scope of the Geneva Protocol; and then by the New York Convention of 1958, which further strengthened the process of the international enforcement of arbitration agreements and arbitral awards. The influence of arbitral institutions in the establishment of these international treaties was considerable. The London Court of International Arbitration ("LCIA") is one of the oldest of these institutions, having been founded on November 23, 1892 as the London Chamber of Arbitration. At the time, with a rhetoric which no doubt exceeded the reality, it was said:

"This Chamber is to have all the virtues which the law lacks. It is to be expeditious where the law is slow, cheap where the law is costly, simple where the law is technical, a peace-maker instead of a stirrer-up of strife."[16]

The Swedish Chamber of Commerce's Committee for the Settlement of **1–06** Disputes in Commerce, Industry and Shipping was founded in 1917; but it was the Court of Arbitration of the International Chamber of Commerce in Paris,

---

[15] The first English statute was the Arbitration Act of 1698, although in *Vynior's Case* ((1609) 8 Co. Rep. 80a, 81b) the court ordered the defendant to pay the agreed penalty for refusing to submit to arbitration as he had agreed to do. In France, an edict of Francis II promulgated in August 1560 made arbitration compulsory for all merchants in disputes arising from their commercial activity. Later this edict came to be ignored. During the French Revolution, arbitration came back into favour as "the most reasonable device for the termination of disputes arising between citizens" and in 1791, judges were abolished and replaced by "public arbitrators". However, this proved to be a step too far and the French Code of Civil Procedure, in 1806, effectively turned arbitration into the first stage of a procedure which would lead to the judgment of a court. See David, *op.cit.*, pp.89 and 90.

[16] Manson (1893) IX L.Q.R. 86 cited by Veeder and Dye, "Lord Bramwell's Arbitration Code" (1992) 8 Arbitration International 330.

5

founded in 1923, which played a major role in the promulgation of the Geneva treaties and of the New York Convention and which has been at the forefront of developments since.

The modern arbitral process has lost its early simplicity. It has become more complex, more legalistic, more institutionalised. Yet in its essentials it has not changed. There is still the original element of two or more parties, faced with a dispute that they cannot resolve for themselves, agreeing that one or more private individuals will resolve it for them. And if the arbitration runs its full course (that is to say, if the dispute is not settled in the course of the proceedings) it will be resolved *not* by a negotiated settlement or by mediation or by some other form of compromise, but by a decision which is binding on the parties and which they may be compelled by law to carry out, if they do not carry it out voluntarily.

In the modern arbitral process, this decision is made by an arbitral tribunal composed of one or more arbitrators chosen by or on behalf of the parties. The task of this tribunal is to consider the case put forward by each party and then to arrive at a decision on the dispute. The tribunal's decision is made in writing in the form of an award and usually[17] sets out the reasons on which it is based. The award binds the parties (subject to any right of appeal or challenge that may exist[18]) and represents the final word on the dispute. If it is not carried out voluntarily, the award may be enforced by legal process against the assets of the losing party.[19]

(c) Significant features of arbitration

1–07   Four significant features of international commercial arbitration are singled out for mention now, although they will be the subject of more detailed comment later. These features are:

- the agreement to arbitrate;
- the choice of arbitrators;
- the decision of the arbitral tribunal;
- the enforcement of the award.

The agreement to arbitrate

1–08   An agreement by the parties to submit to arbitration any disputes or differences between them is the foundation stone of modern international commercial arbitration. If there is to be a valid arbitration, there must first be a valid agreement to arbitrate. This is recognised both by national laws and by international treaties.

---

[17] Both institutional and international rules of arbitration usually require the arbitral tribunal to state the reasons upon which the tribunal bases its decision, although under some rules the parties may agree that this is not necessary: see, *e.g.*, the UNCITRAL Arbitration Rules, Art.32, r.3.
[18] See Ch.9.
[19] See Ch.10.

For example, under both the New York Convention[20] and the Model Law,[21] recognition and enforcement of an arbitral award may be refused if the parties to the arbitration agreement were under some incapacity, or if the agreement was not valid under its own governing law.[22]

An arbitration agreement is usually spelt out in the main contract, as an "arbitration clause"; or it may be set down in a separate "submission to arbitration". Exceptionally, however, there may be what might be called a "standing offer" to arbitrate disputes, as with the bilateral investment treaties that are discussed later[23]; a claimant may then take advantage of this offer by commencing arbitral proceedings.

Whichever way it is done, there must be an agreement. If there is no agreement, there can be no valid arbitration. Moreover, for all practical purposes, and in particular for the purposes of enforcement internationally, there must be *written* evidence of the agreement to arbitrate.[24] The requirement of writing is to be found both in international treaties and in domestic law. The New York Convention, for example, will only give recognition and enforcement to an arbitration agreement if it is "in writing". The Convention defines this by stating:

"The term 'agreement in writing' shall include an arbitral clause in a contract or an arbitration agreement, signed by the parties or contained in an exchange of letters or telegrams."

The rapid development of modern methods of communication has left this definition looking distinctly old-fashioned,[25] when many contracts are concluded by telex, fax or email.[26] The Model Law, which was adopted in 1985 (almost 30 years after the New York Convention), maintains the requirement for an arbitration agreement to be "in writing", but sets out a more modern definition of this term. It includes agreements made by any means of telecommunication "which

1–09

---

[20] "The Convention on the Recognition and Enforcement of Foreign Arbitral Awards" done at New York on June 10, 1958, *United Nations Treaty Series* (1954) Vol.330, No.4739, p.38.

[21] "The Model Law on International Commercial Arbitration" as adopted by the United Nations Commission on International Trade Law in June 1985.

[22] New York Convention, Art.V(1)(a); Model Law Art.36(1)(a)(i).

[23] See Ch.11.

[24] See the discussion in Ch.3, paras 3–07—3–09.

[25] See Kaplan "Is the need for writing in the New York Convention and the Model Law out of step with commercial practice?" (1996) 12 Arbitration International 27. It may be out of step, but it is still a strict requirement in some jurisdictions: see, *e.g.*, the decision of the US Court of Appeals for the Second Circuit in *Kahn Lucas Lancaster Inc v Lark International Ltd* [1999] 186 F.3d 210.

[26] The reference to modern methods of communication, in the second edition of this book, led Dr Richard Hill to point out to the authors that "telex produces a weak form of authentication (proof of origin) whereas fax cannot be authenticated. It is becoming easier and easier to forge faxes because of widespread availability of fax cards and software for PCs and the development of bit-image manipulation software for the PC". A party relying upon an agreement by fax, the existence of which is challenged by the other party, may have a difficult burden of proof, as may indeed be the case with email.

Introduction

provides a record of the agreement"[27]; an exchange of statements of claim and defence in which "the existence of an agreement is alleged by one party and not denied by another"[28]; and reference in a written contract to a document which "contains an arbitration clause".[29]

Most modern laws of arbitration are concerned to define the requirements for "writing" as widely as possible—to the point where it has been suggested that in the English Arbitration Act of 1996, "writing" has now been so defined[30] as to include an agreement made orally.

The requirement for an arbitration agreement to be "in writing" and to be "signed by the parties" has created problems. It has been the subject of considerable discussion; and it is considered in more detail in Ch.3 of this book.

The point has already been made that an agreement to arbitrate may be contained either in an arbitration clause or in a separate form of agreement. An arbitration clause (or *clause compromissoire*, as it is known in the civil law) relates to disputes that might arise between the parties at some time in the future. It will generally be short and to the point. An exchange of telexes stating that "Any dispute is to be settled by arbitration in London" would constitute a valid arbitration agreement—although in practice so terse a form is not to be recommended.[31]

1–10   An arbitration agreement which is drawn up to deal with disputes that have *already* arisen between the parties is generally known as a submission agreement, a *compromis*, or a *compromiso*. It is usually a fairly detailed document, dealing with the constitution of the arbitral tribunal, the procedure to be followed, the issues to be decided, the substantive law and other matters. At one time, it was the *only* type of arbitration agreement recognised by the law of many states,[32] since recourse to arbitration was only permitted in respect of *existing* disputes. In some states, this is still the position.[33]

Most states, however, are prepared to recognise the validity of arbitration clauses that relate to future disputes. In fact, almost all international commercial

[27] Model Law, Art.7(2).
[28] *ibid.*
[29] *ibid.*
[30] This is because under the Act "writing" includes an agreement made orally, provided that there is reference to a written form which itself contains an agreement to arbitrate. When this Act was being drafted, there was concern within the shipping community that it should include towage and salvage agreements, which are commonly made orally (or by VHF radio) by reference to Lloyd's Open Form or some other standard form of contract containing an agreement to arbitrate. The master of a ship that is being driven onto the rocks in a force nine gale is generally not in a position to sign a written contract, but the master of the tug which is coming to his rescue will want to be sure that if the reward for his services is not agreed, it will be determined by experienced maritime arbitrators in accordance with established principles. The Act provides, in s.5(3), that an *oral* agreement to written terms that contain an arbitration agreement is sufficient.
[31] For a similar short form of arbitration clause, see, *e.g.*, *Arab African Energy Corp Ltd v Oliepro-ducten Nederland BV* [1983] 2 Lloyd's Rep. 419; and more generally, see the discussion in Ch.3.
[32] This point, and in particular the distinction between existing and future disputes, is discussed below at paras 1–37 *et seq.*
[33] A submission agreement is still required (whether or not a valid arbitration agreement already exists), *e.g.* in Argentina and Uruguay: see Ch.3.

8

arbitrations take place pursuant to an arbitration clause. Such a clause is often one of the standard clauses of the standard forms of contract that are internationally accepted in such diverse activities as shipping, insurance, commodity trading and major civil engineering projects.

The importance of the arbitration agreement

In an international commercial arbitration, the arbitration agreement fulfils **1–11** several important functions. The most important of these in the present context is that it shows that the parties have consented to resolve their disputes by arbitration. This element of consent is essential. Without it, there can be no valid arbitration.[34] The fact that international commercial arbitration rests on the agreement of the parties is given particular importance by some continental jurists. The arbitral proceedings are seen as an expression of the will of the parties and, on the basis of party autonomy (*l'autonomie de la volonté*) it is sometimes argued that international commercial arbitration should be freed from the constraints of national law and treated as denationalised or delocalised.[35]

Once parties have validly given their consent to arbitration, this consent cannot be unilaterally withdrawn. Even if the arbitration agreement forms part of the original contract between the parties and that contract comes to an end, the obligation to arbitrate survives. It is an independent obligation separable from the rest of the contract.[36]

Enforcement of the arbitration agreement

An agreement to arbitrate, like any other agreement, must be capable of being **1–12** enforced at law. Otherwise, it will be a mere statement of intention which, whilst morally binding, is without legal effect. However, an agreement to arbitrate is a contract of imperfect obligation. If it is broken, an award of damages is unlikely to be a practical remedy, given the difficulty of quantifying the loss sustained; and an order for specific performance is equally impracticable, since a party cannot be compelled to arbitrate if it does not wish to do so. As the saying goes, "you can lead a horse to water, but you cannot make it drink".

In arbitration this problem has been met, both nationally and internationally, by a policy of *indirect* enforcement. Rules of law are adopted which provide that, if one of the parties to an arbitration agreement brings proceedings in a national court in breach of that agreement, those proceedings will be stopped at the request of any other party to the arbitration agreement (unless there is good reason why they should not be). This means that if a party wishes to pursue its

---

[34] There are circumstances in which arbitration may be a compulsory method of resolving disputes, *e.g.* in domestic law, arbitrations may take place compulsorily under legislation governing agricultural disputes or labour relations. The growth of court-annexed arbitration (discussed later in this chapter) may perhaps be said to constitute a form of compulsory arbitration.

[35] An early mention of this revolutionary theory appears in Fouchard, above, para.1–03, especially pp.22–27, although the presence of serious obstacles to the theory is noted. The theory is discussed in more detail in Ch.2, para.2–25.

[36] The issue of separability is discussed in Ch.3, para.3–60.

claim, it must honour the agreement it has made and do so by arbitration, since this is the only legal course of action open to it.[37]

It would be of little use to enforce an obligation to arbitrate in one country if it could be evaded by commencing legal proceedings in another. Therefore, as far as possible, an agreement for international commercial arbitration must be given effect *internationally* and not simply in the place where the agreement was made. As already mentioned, this fact was recognised in the Geneva Protocol of 1923,[38] one of the first multilateral conventions on arbitration. The Protocol provides that the courts of the contracting state, on being seized of a dispute to which an arbitration agreement covered by the Protocol applies, "shall refer the parties on the application of either of them to the decision of the arbitrators".[39]

Powers conferred by the arbitration agreement

1–13 An arbitration agreement does not merely serve to evidence the consent of the parties to arbitration and to establish the obligation to arbitrate. It is also a basic source of the powers of the arbitral tribunal. In principle, an arbitral tribunal may exercise such powers as the parties are entitled to confer and do confer upon it, whether expressly or by implication, together with any additional or supplementary powers that may be conferred by the law governing the arbitration.[40] Parties to an arbitration are masters of the arbitral process to an extent impossible in proceedings in a court of law. For example, the parties may decide (within limits which will be considered later) the number of arbitrators to comprise the arbitral tribunal, how this tribunal should be appointed, what powers it should possess, and what procedure it should follow.

Finally, it is the arbitration agreement that establishes the jurisdiction of the arbitral tribunal. The agreement of the parties is the only source from which this jurisdiction can come. In the ordinary legal process whereby disputes are resolved through the public courts, the jurisdiction of the relevant court may come from several sources, of which an agreement by the parties to submit to the jurisdiction will be only one. In the arbitral process, which is a private method of resolving disputes, the jurisdiction of the arbitral tribunal is derived simply and solely from the agreement of the parties.

The choice of arbitrators

1–14 One of the features that distinguishes arbitration from litigation is the fact that the parties to an arbitration are free to choose their own tribunal. Sometimes, it is true, this freedom is unreal, because the choice may be delegated to a third

---

[37] Of course, the party concerned may decide to abandon its claim, and is free to do so.
[38] League of Nations Treaty Series (1924), Vol.XXVII, No.678, p.158.
[39] Geneva Protocol of 1923, Art.4. The New York Convention extends similar recognition to the international force and effect of arbitration agreements in Art.II(3). Both the Geneva Protocol of 1923 and the New York Convention are discussed in more detail later in this chapter.
[40] See Ch.2.

party such as an arbitral institution.[41] However, where the freedom exists, each party should make sensible use of it. A skilled and experienced arbitrator is one of the key elements of a fair and effective arbitration.

The choice of a suitable arbitrator involves many considerations. These are discussed in detail later.[42] At this stage, however, perhaps all that needs to be stressed is that an international commercial arbitration demands different qualities in an arbitrator from those required for a purely national, or domestic, arbitration. This is not only because of the different systems of law and the different rules that will apply, but also because the parties will almost invariably be of different nationalities and the arbitration itself will often take place in a country that is "foreign" to them. Indeed, the place of arbitration will usually have been chosen precisely because it *is* foreign, so that no party has the advantage of playing at home, so to speak. If the arbitral tribunal consists of three arbitrators (as is normally the case in any major dispute), each of the arbitrators may be of a different nationality, with each of them (if they are lawyers) perhaps having been brought up in a different legal environment—whether of the civil law, the common law or the Shari'ah.[43]

This means that there is almost inevitably a difference of legal (and often of cultural) background amongst those involved in an international commercial arbitration. A good international arbitrator will be aware of this and will try hard to avoid misunderstandings which may arise because of this difference of background or simply because of different nuances of language.[44]

Choosing the right arbitrator for a particular dispute is a matter of great importance.[45] Most, if not all, experienced practitioners would agree with the comment by a distinguished lawyer with many years' experience of international commercial arbitration when he wrote:

1–15

> "The choice of the persons who compose the arbitral tribunal is vital and often the most decisive step in an arbitration. It has rightly been said that arbitration is only as good as the arbitrators."[46]

The decision of the arbitral tribunal

It is not uncommon for a settlement to be reached between the parties in the course of arbitral proceedings. In recognition of this fact, institutional rules of

1–16

---

[41] In ICC arbitrations, *e.g.*, where the dispute is to be referred to a sole arbitrator, that person will be chosen by the ICC itself, unless (as is sensible) the parties agree on a suitable candidate: ICC Arbitration Rules, Art.8.3.

[42] See Ch.4, para.4–12.

[43] In the well-known *Aminoil* arbitration, in which the original authors took part as counsel, the members of the arbitral tribunal were respectively French, British and Egyptian and the registrar was Swiss; the parties, lawyers and experts were American, Swiss, Kuwaiti, British, Egyptian and Lebanese. The seat of the arbitration was France.

[44] A German industrialist, in charge of a major British industrial company, was quoted as saying that when one of his British foremen said that there was "a small problem", he knew something was seriously wrong!

[45] This is discussed in more detail in Ch.4, para.4–12.

[46] J.-F. Lalive, "Mélanges en l'honneur de Nicolas Valticos" in *Droit et Justice* (Editions Pédone, 1989), p.289.

arbitration generally make provision for this. The UNCITRAL Rules, for example, state:

> "If, before the award is made, the parties agree on a settlement of the dispute, the arbitral tribunal shall either issue an order for the termination of the arbitral proceedings or, if requested by both parties and accepted by the tribunal, record the settlement in the form of an arbitral award on agreed terms. The arbitral tribunal is not obliged to give reasons for such an award."[47]

However, if the parties cannot resolve their dispute, the task of the arbitral tribunal is to resolve the dispute for them by making a decision, in the form of a written award. An arbitral tribunal does not have the powers or prerogatives of a court of law,[48] but it has a similar function to that of the court in this respect, namely that it is entrusted by the parties with the right and the obligation to reach a decision which will be binding upon them.

1–17 The power to make binding decisions is of fundamental importance. It distinguishes arbitration as a method of resolving disputes from other procedures, such as mediation and conciliation,[49] which aim to arrive at a negotiated settlement. The *procedures* that must be followed in order to arrive at a binding decision by way of arbitration may be described as judicial. An arbitral tribunal is bound to "act fairly and impartially as between the parties, giving each party a reasonable opportunity of putting his case and dealing with that of his opponent". The quotation is from the English 1996 Act,[50] but the obligation is one of general application.[51]

There is no similar requirement governing the procedures to be followed where parties are assisted in arriving at a negotiated settlement by mediation, conciliation or some other process of this kind.[52]

The enforcement of the award

1–18 Once an arbitral tribunal has made its award, it has fulfilled its function and its existence comes to an end.[53] The tribunal's award, however, gives rise to important and lasting legal consequences. Although it is the result of a private arrangement and is made by a private arbitral tribunal, the award constitutes a

---

[47] UNCITRAL Arbitration Rules, Art.34.1.

[48] For a scholarly discussion of the differences between a judge and an arbitrator, see Serge Lazareff, "L'arbitre est-il un juge?" in Claude Reymond, *Liber Amicorum* (Litec, Editions du Juris-Classeur, 2004), p.173.

[49] For further discussion of these topics see below, paras 1–76—1–77.

[50] English Arbitration Act 1996, s.33(1)(a).

[51] *e.g.* Model Law, Art.18.

[52] The arbitral process also produces a different *result* from that which might have been reached by the parties through negotiation, with or without the help of a mediator or conciliator, since a negotiated agreement must necessarily be in the form of a compromise acceptable to both parties.

[53] Save possibly for incidental matters such as the interpretation of its award or correction of obvious errors; and those rare cases in which the tribunal may be required by a court to reconsider its decision: see Ch.9.

binding decision on the dispute between the parties. If it is not carried out voluntarily, the award may be enforced by legal proceedings—both locally (that is to say, in the place in which it was made) and internationally.

Important regional and international treaties and conventions relate to the recognition and enforcement of foreign arbitral awards. The most important and widely used is the New York Convention. It sets out the procedure to be followed for recognition and enforcement of foreign arbitral awards, whilst specifying limited grounds on which recognition and enforcement of such awards may be refused by a contracting state. This Convention was the first of a series of major steps[54] taken by the United Nations since its inception to aid the development of international commercial arbitration.[55] Most of the major trading nations of the world have become parties to the New York Convention. At the time of writing, the Convention has more than 130 signatories, including less-developed as well as developed countries. In particular, several Latin American states (such as Argentina, Colombia, Mexico and Venezuela) and Arab states (such as Egypt, Kuwait and Saudi Arabia) are parties to the Convention.

The provisions of the New York Convention are considered in more detail later, as are the provisions of other conventions dealing with the recognition and enforcement of foreign arbitral awards.[56] At this stage it is sufficient simply to note that there is in place an effective international network of treaties and conventions which governs the recognition and enforcement of foreign arbitral awards. These conventions are instruments of international law; but their application with respect to any particular award will be a matter for the national (or local) law and the national (or local) courts of the place of enforcement. The exact procedure to be followed, the time-limits to be observed, the way in which the conventions are to be interpreted and other relevant factors are all matters which fall to be determined by the law of the country in which recognition and enforcement of a particular award is sought.[57]

Summary

International commercial arbitration is a hybrid. It begins as a private agree- **1–19**
ment between the parties. It continues by way of private proceedings, in which the wishes of the parties are of great importance. Yet it ends with an award that has binding legal force and effect and which, on appropriate conditions, the courts of most countries of the world will recognise and enforce. The private

---

[54] The second major step was the promulgation of the UNCITRAL Arbitration Rules, which are considered later; and the third and latest is the promulgation of the Model Law, which is considered throughout the text.

[55] The United Nations was established by Charter on June 26, 1945.

[56] See Ch.10.

[57] For a comprehensive review of the operation of the New York Convention, and cases in national courts relating to interpretation of the Convention, see van den Berg, *The New York Arbitration Convention of 1958* (Kluwer, 1981) and his later report to the ASA Conference in Zurich (ASA Special Series No.9, August 1996); see also the Yearbooks of Commercial Arbitration (Kluwer) and the Kluwer website *www.kluwerarbitration.com*.

process has a public effect, implemented with the support of the public authorities of each state and expressed through its national law. This interrelationship between international commercial arbitration, national law and international treaties and conventions is considered in more detail later. In this introduction, it is appropriate to consider the basic concepts that form part of the day-to-day practice of international commercial arbitration.

Having looked briefly at the agreement to arbitrate, the choice of arbitrators, the decision of the arbitral tribunal and the enforcement of that decision, the next step is to consider what is usually meant by the terms "international" and "commercial", before going on to analyse a typical arbitration agreement.

(d) The meaning of "international"

1–20   Terms in common use may elude definition. "When I use a word," said a well-known literary character, "it means just what I choose it to mean—neither more nor less."[58] It would be a little unfair to say the same of those who speak or write about international commercial arbitration, but there is nonetheless a certain (and perhaps inevitable) ambiguity in the use of the terms "international" and "commercial". One state's definition differs from another's. Nevertheless, an attempt at definition must be made.

International and domestic arbitrations contrasted

1–21   The term "international" is used to mark the difference between arbitrations which are purely national or domestic and those which in some way transcend national boundaries and so are international or, in the terminology adopted by Judge Jessup, "transnational".[59]

It is sometimes said that *every* arbitration is a "national" arbitration, in the sense that it must be held at a given place and is accordingly subject to the national law of that place.[60] Whilst this may be an interesting topic for debate, it is customary in practice to distinguish between arbitrations which are purely "domestic" and those which are "international" (because of the nature of the dispute, the nationality of the parties or some other relevant criteria).

There are good reasons for doing this. First, an international arbitration will usually have no connection with the state in which the arbitration takes place, other than the fact that it is taking place on the territory of that state. Secondly, the parties will usually be corporations or state entities, rather than private individuals. Accordingly, the state concerned can afford to take a more relaxed

---

[58] Attributed to Humpty Dumpty in Lewis Carroll's *Alice Through the Looking Glass*.

[59] Judge Jessup used this term to describe those rules of law, whether local, national or international, which govern cross-border relationships and transactions: see Jessup, "Transnational Law", *Storrs Lectures on Jurisprudence* (Yale Law School, 1956).

[60] See, for instance, Mann "Lex facit arbitrum" in (1986) 2 Arbitration International 241 at 244; however, this statement is not true in respect of ICSID arbitrations, which are governed by international law as discussed later in this chapter.

attitude towards such arbitrations. By contrast, domestic arbitrations will usually involve claims by private individuals that may be small in amount,[61] but are of considerable importance to those concerned.

An element of consumer protection is involved.[62] Many years ago, the English **1–22** appellate court proclaimed that there would be "no Alsatia in England where the King's Writ does not run".[63] Its concern was that powerful trade associations would otherwise impose their own "law" on traders and citizens less powerful than they. For this reason, some control (and even "supervision") of the arbitral process by the local courts was considered desirable.

By contrast, one of the major features of the Model Law (which was expressly designed to provide for *international* commercial arbitration) is that it imposes strict limits on the extent to which a national court may intervene in the arbitration proceedings.[64] Many states, including Belgium, Brazil, Colombia, France, Hong Kong, Nigeria, Singapore, Switzerland and others, have adopted a separate legal regime to govern international commercial arbitrations—recognising that different considerations may apply to such arbitrations.

Another reason for distinguishing between "international" and "domestic" **1–23** arbitrations is that in some states, the state itself (or in some cases, entities of the state) may only enter into an arbitration agreement in respect of international transactions. Accordingly, it is necessary to know how such transactions are defined and whether an arbitration in respect of them would be considered as "international" by the state concerned.

A further reason, which in practice is perhaps the most significant, is that different nationalities, different legal backgrounds and cultures, different legal systems and different principles will almost certainly be encountered in international commercial arbitrations. It is important that those concerned, and particularly the members of the arbitral tribunal, should understand this. At the end of this chapter, reference is made to the emergence of what has been called "a common procedural pattern in international arbitration". In order to develop and to work with such a system, it is necessary to abandon narrow, parochial concepts of how an arbitration should or should not be conducted. This in itself calls for a different and truly "internationalist" approach to such arbitrations.

---

[61] Of course, there is no reason in principle why domestic arbitrations may not involve considerable sums of money or important issues of law, or both. The only point made here is that a state will generally wish to regulate domestic arbitrations more extensively than international arbitrations.

[62] In Sweden, for example, consumers who enter into an arbitration agreement prior to a dispute with a business enterprise (for instance, in a standard form contract) are not bound by that agreement, "unless the international obligations of Sweden provide otherwise"; and a challenge to an arbitrator's fees may be made in the District Court: 1999 Swedish Arbitration Act, ss.6 and 41 respectively.

[63] *per* Scrutton L.J. in *Czarnikow v Roth, Schmidt & Co* [1922] 2 K.B. 478 at 488. The reference to Alsatia was not a reference to the province of Alsace, but to the Whitefriars area of London, near Fleet Street, now occupied by lawyers and accountants but once a well-known sanctuary for criminals.

[64] The Model Law states, in Art.5: "In matters governed by this Law, no court shall intervene except where so provided in this Law."

One final point should be made. Even states that make no formal distinction between "domestic" and "international" arbitrations in their legislation[65] are compelled to recognise the distinction when it comes to the enforcement of arbitral awards. This is an important topic, which is discussed later,[66] but, to put it briefly, there are a series of international conventions (of which easily the most important is the New York Convention) which provide for the enforcement of arbitration awards in most of the major countries of the world, provided that these are "foreign" or "international" awards. Such awards are defined, in the New York Convention, as being "made in the territory of the State other than the State where the recognition and enforcement of such awards are sought".[67]

(e) The relevant criteria

1–24   Two main criteria are used, either alone or in conjunction, to define the term "international" in the context of an international commercial arbitration. The first requires analysing the *nature of the dispute,* so that an arbitration is treated as international if it "involves the interests of international trade".[68] The second focuses on the *parties.* It will look at either their nationality or habitual place of residence or, if (as is usually the case) the party is a corporate entity, the seat of its central control and management. On this criterion, to take a simple example, an arbitration between a British company and a French company would be an international arbitration, much as the annual Six Nations rugby match involving England and France is an "international" match. Some national systems of law have adopted the first approach.

Some have adopted the second. Others have followed the Model Law in selecting a mixture of the two.

The international nature of the dispute

1–25   The International Chamber of Commerce established its Court of Arbitration in Paris in 1923.[69] It was quick to adopt the *nature* of the dispute as its criterion for deciding whether or not an arbitration was an international arbitration under

---

[65] It is interesting to note that there was provision in the English Arbitration Act 1996 for a distinction to be made for some purposes between "domestic" and "non-domestic" (or "international") arbitration. However, these provisions (in ss.85–87 of the Act) were not brought into effect. One major reason for this was that it was considered that to draw a distinction between British nationals and nationals of other countries in the EU would be a breach of Community law: see Saville "The Arbitration Act 1996 and its effect on International Arbitration in England" (1997) 63(2) Arbitration 104 at 112.

[66] Ch.10.

[67] This definition is extended to include arbitral awards which are "not considered as domestic awards" by the enforcement state. (The significance of these additional words is reviewed later.)

[68] This is the definition used in Art.1492 of the French Code of Civil Procedure, Decree Law No.81-500 of May 12, 1981.

[69] The court is now known as the International Court of Arbitration of the ICC. It is not a court in the generally accepted sense. It is, rather, a council that, *inter alia*, supervises the administration of arbitral tribunals constituted under the ICC Arbitration Rules and approves the draft awards of these tribunals, whilst leaving the tribunals themselves in full charge of the cases before them.

its rules. Although at first it only considered business disputes as "international" if they involved nationals of different countries, the ICC altered its rules in 1927 to cover disputes that contained a foreign element, even if the parties were nationals of the same country.

The present Rules define the function of the International Court of Arbitration of the ICC as being "to provide for the settlement by arbitration of business disputes of an international character" in accordance with these Rules.[70] There is no definition in the Rules of what is meant by "business disputes of an international character" but the explanatory booklet issued by the ICC used to state:

" . . . the international nature of the arbitration does not mean that the parties must necessarily be of different nationalities. By virtue of its object, the contract can nevertheless extend beyond national borders, when for example a contract is concluded between two nationals of the same State for performance in another country, or when it is concluded between a State and a subsidiary of a foreign company doing business in that State."[71]

This wide interpretation of the term "international" is also to be found in the French law on international arbitration. By a Decree Law of May 12, 1981, a separate legal regime was created for "international" arbitrations conducted in France.[72] The definition given in the Decree Law itself is sparse. Article 1492 of the French Code of Civil Procedure simply provides that "an arbitration is international when it involves the interests of international trade".[73] In using this language, the Code has adopted the definition given by the highest French court (the Cour de Cassation) in several previous decisions:

1–26

"It is generally recognised that this definition covers the movement of goods or money from one country to another, with significant regard being paid to other elements such as the nationality of the parties, the place of the conclusion of the contract, etc."[74]

---

[70] ICC Arbitration Rules, Art.1(1).

[71] *The International Solution to International Business Disputes*—ICC Arbitration, ICC Publication No.301 (1977), p.19 (copyright ICC 1983).

[72] The Decree Law No.81–500 of May 12, 1981 is conveniently set out in French, English and German in Delvolvé, *Arbitration in France, The French Law of National and International Arbitration* (1982).

[73] This definition looks to the subject matter of the dispute, rather than the nationality of the parties.

[74] Delvolvé, "France as a forum for international arbitration—the decree of May 12, 1981 (Arts 1492 to 1507 of the French Code of Civil Procedure)" *The International Contract Law and Finance Review*, Vol.2, No.7, 421 at 422; see also Craig, Park & Paulsson, "French Codification of a Legal Framework for International Commercial Arbitration: the Decree of May 12, 1981" (1982) VII Yearbook Commercial Arbitration 407; and Delvolvé, Rouche & Pointon, *French Arbitration Law and Practice*, Kluwer Law International, 2003.

Former French colonies, such as Djibouti and the Côte d'Ivoire and, to a lesser extent, Algeria and Tunisia, also follow this approach in defining what is meant by an "international" arbitration.

The nationality of the parties

1–27   An alternative approach is to focus attention on the parties. This involves reviewing the nationality, place of residence or place of business of the parties to the arbitration agreement. It is an approach that was adopted in the European Convention of 1961,[75] which, although little used, contains several useful definitions, including a definition of the agreements to which it applies as:

> "Arbitration agreements concluded for the purpose of settling disputes arising from international trade between physical or legal persons having, when concluding the agreement, their habitual place of residence or their seat in different Contracting States."[76]

Before 1996, English law[77] distinguished between "domestic" and "international" arbitrations by defining what was meant by a "domestic arbitration agreement" (namely, an agreement which did not provide expressly or by implication for arbitration outside the UK and to which no foreign resident or corporation was a party). Everything else was treated as a foreign or "international" arbitration agreement. A similar definition was adopted in the Arbitration Act 1996, but it was not brought into effect.[78] Accordingly, there is now no distinction between domestic and international arbitration in English law—except when it comes to enforcement of a foreign or international award under one of the relevant international treaties, when special provision is made.

1–28   Switzerland is an example of a country in which the nationality of the parties determines whether or not an arbitration is "international". Arbitration in Switzerland used to be governed by the law of the canton in which the arbitration was based (the place or "seat" of arbitration). Since January 1, 1989, international arbitrations that are located in Switzerland are governed by Switzerland's law on international arbitration. Under this law an arbitration is "international" where, at the time the arbitration agreement was concluded, at least one of the parties was not domiciled or habitually resident in Switzerland.[79]

---

[75] European Convention on International Commercial Arbitration, done at Geneva, April 21, 1961, *United Nations Treaty Series* (1963–64), Vol.484, No.7041, p.364. For further discussion of this Convention, see para.1–149.

[76] European Convention of 1961, Art.I.1(a).

[77] English Arbitration Acts 1975 and 1979.

[78] See para.1–123.

[79] In such cases, the parties may opt for Cantonal law, but are unlikely to do so. For a commentary on Switzerland's law on International Arbitration (Ch.12 of Swiss Private International Law (PIL) Act 1987) see, *e.g.*, Bucher & Tschanz, "International Arbitration in Switzerland", Helbing & Lichtenhahn, 1989, Basle and Frankfurt; Reymond, "La nouvelle Loi Suisse et le droit d'arbitrage international: Réflexions de droit comparé" (1989) 3 Revue de l'Arbitrage 385; P. Lalive, "The New Swiss Law on International Arbitration" (1998) 4 Arbitration International 2.

The "nationality" test is also used by the US for the purposes of the New York Convention, but arbitration agreements between US citizens or corporations are excluded from the scope of the Convention unless their relationship "involves property located abroad, envisages performance or enforcement abroad or has some reasonable relation with one or more foreign states."[80]

The Model Law criteria: a combined approach

The lack of an internationally agreed definition of "international" in the context of international commercial arbitration may pose problems. Each state has its own test for determining whether an arbitration award is "domestic" or *"foreign"*. This is recognised by the New York Convention which, as we have seen, defines "foreign" awards as awards which are made in the territory of a state *other* than the state in which recognition and enforcement is sought, but adds to this definition awards which are "not considered as domestic awards" by the enforcement state. The consequence is that an award which one country considers to be "domestic" (because it involves parties who are nationals of that state) might well be considered by the enforcement state as *not* being domestic (because it involves the interests of international trade). **1–29**

The Model Law was specifically designed to apply to *international* commercial arbitration. Accordingly, some definition of the term "international" was essential. The official Report on the Model Law stated that, in considering the term "international" it would appear to be:

"necessary, though difficult, to define that term since the Model Law is designed to provide a special legal regime for those arbitrations where more than purely domestic interests are involved."[81]

The definition adopted in the Model Law[82] is as follows: **1–30**

"1(3) An arbitration is international if:

(a) the parties to an arbitration agreement have, at the time of the conclusion of that agreement, their places of business in different States; or
(b) one of the following places is situated outside the State in which the parties have their places of business:

(i) the place of arbitration if determined in, or pursuant to, the arbitration agreement;
(ii) any place where a substantial part of the obligations of the commercial relationship is to be performed or the place with which the subject-matter of the dispute is most closely connected; or

---

[80] US Code, Title 9 (Arbitration), s.202.
[81] Report of the Secretary-General, 14th Session of UNCITRAL, June 19–26, 1981, UN Doc. A/CN 9/207, para.32.
[82] UNCITRAL Model Law on International Commercial Arbitration.

(c) the parties have expressly agreed that the subject-matter of the arbitration agreement relates to more than one country."[83]

This definition combines the two criteria mentioned earlier. The first criterion of internationality is related to the *parties*, arising from their having places of business in different states.[84] But there is also the alternative criterion of the internationality of the *dispute* itself in that, for instance, the place with which the subject-matter of the dispute is most closely connected may be foreign to the parties.[85] Finally, there is the element of internationality that may arise from the choice of a foreign place of arbitration or, it would seem, from an agreement between the parties that the subject-matter of the arbitration agreement is international.[86]

For the purposes of this work, the authors adopt a wide definition and consider as "international" an arbitration that involves parties of different nationalities (in the sense of Art.1(3)(a) of the Model Law); an arbitration that takes place in a country which is "foreign" to the parties (Art.1(3)(b)(i) of the Model Law); or finally, an arbitration that involves an international dispute (in the sense of French law and of Art.1(3)(b)(ii) or Art.1(3)(c) of the Model Law).[87] Nonetheless, a *caveat* must be entered to the effect that such arbitrations will not necessarily be universally regarded as international. If a question arises as to whether or not a particular arbitration is "international", the answer will depend upon the provisions of the relevant national law.

(f) The meaning of "commercial"

1–31   It is generally agreed that arbitration is a particularly suitable method for the resolution of disputes arising out of business relationships (as opposed, for instance, to domestic relationships).[88] Indeed, in civil law countries, a distinction is generally made between contracts which are "commercial" and those which are not. A commercial contract is, in broad terms, the kind of contract made by merchants or traders in the ordinary course of their business—whether their business is to buy and sell office equipment or to rent motor cars. Such contracts are usually governed by a special code of commercial law apart from the general law of obligations; and it is notable that in many civil law countries arbitral institutions are associated with a Chamber of Commerce, such as the Belgian Chamber of Commerce, the Geneva and Zurich Chambers of Commerce,[89] the

---

[83] Art.1.(3).
[84] *ibid.*, Art.1(3)(a).
[85] *ibid.*, Art.1(3)(b)(ii).
[86] *ibid.*, Art.1(3)(b)(i) and (c).
[87] It is interesting to note that Spain has adopted this wide definition in the Spanish Arbitration Act 2003, at Art.3.
[88] It will be recalled that the Edict of Francis II of France, promulgated in 1560, made arbitration compulsory for all merchants *in disputes arising from their commercial activity*.
[89] Six Chambers of Commerce in Switzerland, including those of Geneva and Zurich, have adopted uniform rules based on the UNCITRAL Arbitration Rules, with effect from January 2004.

Stockholm Chamber of Commerce and, of course, the International Chamber of Commerce in Paris.

The concept of a commercial contract is of importance in the civil law as regards arbitration, since in some countries only disputes arising out of commercial contracts may be submitted to arbitration. Thus it would be permissible to hold an arbitration between two merchants over a contract that they had made in the course of their business but not, for example, in respect of a contract for the division of property made on the marriage of their children.

The fact that in some countries arbitration is only permissible in respect of commercial contracts, whilst in others there is no such limitation, was given international recognition many years ago. The Geneva Protocol of 1923 obliged each contracting state to recognise the validity of an arbitration agreement concerning disputes that might arise from a contract "relating to commercial matters or to any other matter capable of settlement by arbitration". The words quoted indicate recognition of the distinction between "commercial" and other matters. The implication is that commercial matters are *necessarily* capable of being settled by arbitration under the law of the state concerned, in the sense that the state allows them to be settled by arbitration, whilst it may (or may not) allow other matters to be settled in that way.

Further emphasis is added to the distinction between "commercial matters" and "any other matter" by the stipulation in the Protocol that each contracting state may limit its obligations "to contracts that are considered as commercial under its national law".[90] This is the so-called "commercial reservation", and it appears again in the New York Convention.[91]

Both the Geneva Protocol and the New York Convention allow a contracting   **1–32** state that enters the commercial reservation to decide for itself what is meant by "commercial". At first sight, this seems to rule out any prospect of establishing a uniform custom and practice as to what matters are or are not "commercial". Yet the term has now become part of the language. It serves, for instance, to distinguish international arbitrations concerning business or trade disputes from international arbitrations between states over boundary disputes and other political issues. It also serves to distinguish them from arbitrations (which are usually but not necessarily domestic) regarding such matters as property tenure, employment and family law.

It may be important to know whether the legal relationship out of which the arbitration arose was or was not a commercial relationship. The question arises, for example, if it becomes necessary to seek recognition or enforcement of a foreign arbitral award in a state that has adhered to the New York Convention, but has entered the commercial reservation. It is necessary to look at the law of the state concerned to see what definition it adopts of the term "commercial".

Problems occasionally arise because courts of particular countries adopt a narrow definition of "commercial",[92] but the general approach internationally is

---

[90] Geneva Protocol of 1923, Art.1.
[91] New York Convention, Art.1.3.
[92] See paras 10–28 *et seq.*

to define "commercial" so as to embrace all types of trade or business transactions. The Model Law does not define the word but states:

> "The term 'commercial' should be given a wide interpretation so as to cover matters arising from all relationships of a commercial nature, whether contractual or not. Relationships of a commercial nature include, but are not limited to, the following transactions: any trade transaction for the supply or exchange of goods or services; distribution agreement; commercial representation or agency; factoring; leasing; construction of works; consulting; engineering; licensing; investment; financing; banking; insurance; exploitation agreement or concession; joint venture and other forms of industrial or business co-operation; carriage of goods or passengers by air, sea, rail or road."[93]

1–33   In this book, the authors follow this wide interpretation of the term "commercial", so as to include all aspects of international business. However, in doing so, they again add the *caveat* that if it becomes necessary to decide whether or not a particular contract is "commercial" (for instance, for purposes of enforcement under the New York Convention) reference must be made to the relevant national law.

(g) Anatomy of a simple arbitration clause

1–34   There are many choices to be made in drawing up an agreement to arbitrate. Should the agreement provide for ad hoc arbitration or arbitration according to the rules of an arbitral institution—and if the latter, what institution? How many arbitrators should there be—one or three? Where should the arbitration take place? What law should the arbitral tribunal apply to the substantive matters that are in issue between the parties?

These are important questions with important consequences. They will be considered later. For the present, it may be helpful to look at some of the basic concepts that form part of the day-to-day practice of international commercial arbitration and to do so by looking at a very simple form of arbitration clause providing for an ad hoc arbitration. Such a clause might read as follows:

> "Any dispute or difference arising out of or in connection with this agreement shall be referred to and determined by a sole arbitrator in [place of arbitration]".[94]

---

[93] The definition appears as a footnote to Art.1(1), which states that the Model Law applies to "international commercial arbitration".

[94] This clause of itself is sufficient to constitute an ad hoc arbitration agreement, but in case of difficulty—*e.g.* over the appointment of the arbitral tribunal—it would be necessary to call in aid the law of the place of arbitration, the *lex arbitri*. Accordingly, a fuller form is recommended: see Ch.3.

Arbitrability

The clause set out above provides that "any" dispute or difference shall be **1–35** referred to arbitration. However, there are some disputes which, in the words of the New York Convention, concern a subject-matter which is not "capable of settlement by arbitration". The concept of a dispute which is not "capable of settlement by arbitration" has already been encountered in considering the Geneva Protocol of 1923, which refers to commercial matters and "any other matter capable of settlement by arbitration". The words "capable of settlement by arbitration" are not meant as an adverse reflection on arbitrators or on the arbitral process. Arbitrators are—or should be—as "capable" of determining a dispute as anyone else. But, for public policy reasons, national laws will regard certain matters as more suitable for settlement by the courts than by a private system of dispute resolution. For instance, a dispute over matrimonial status may be regarded by the law of a particular state as not being "capable" of settlement by arbitration—although a better term would be "not permitted" to be settled by arbitration.

It is important to know which disputes are not "arbitrable" in this sense[95] and the question is discussed more fully in Ch.3.

Is there any need for a dispute?

At first glance, this may seem to be an unnecessary question. Surely, it might **1–36** be said, if the parties are not in dispute, there is nothing to resolve?

The problem arises when one party has what it regards as an "open and shut" case, to which there is no real defence. For example, a party who is faced with an unpaid cheque or bill of exchange may take the view that there cannot be any *genuine* dispute about liability and that, if legal action has to be taken to collect the money which is due, he or she should be entitled to go to court and ask for summary judgment. Such a claim may be met, however, by the argument that there was an arbitration clause in the underlying agreement with the debtor and that the remedy is accordingly to go to arbitration, rather than to the courts. The problem is that, in the time it may take to establish an arbitral tribunal, a judge with summary powers could well have disposed of the case.

The expedient adopted in certain countries, including England, when legislating for the enactment of the New York Convention was to add words that were not in that Convention, so as to allow the court to deal with the case if the judge was satisfied "that there is not in fact any dispute between the parties with regard to the matter agreed to be referred".[96] Thus it was possible to avoid a reference

---

[95] In an inappropriate and confusing use of language, some writers (and indeed some judges, particularly in the USA) will describe a dispute as not being "arbitrable" when what they mean is that it falls outside the jurisdiction of the arbitral tribunal, because of the limited scope of the arbitration clause or for some other reason. *E.g.* the US Court of Appeals for the Tenth Circuit considered that a dispute was not "arbitrable" because the reference to arbitration was made after the relevant time-limit: see *Howsam v Dean Witter Reynolds Inc* 537 U.S. 79, 123 S.Ct. 588, decided December 10 2002.

[96] Arbitration Act 1975, s.1(i). This Act was repealed by the Arbitration Act 1996, although the New York Convention continues to be part of English law.

to arbitration and to obtain summary judgment if the court was satisfied that there was no arguable defence. English law has now followed the strict wording of the New York Convention.[97] It can no longer be argued in England that there is not a genuine dispute, so that the matter should not be referred to arbitration; but such an argument may still remain sustainable in other countries.

Existing and future disputes

1–37   A distinction is sometimes drawn between existing and future disputes. This is seen in the international conventions on arbitration. For instance, there is a provision in the Geneva Protocol of 1923, under which each of the contracting states agrees to recognise the validity of an arbitration agreement, "whether relating to existing or *future* differences."[98] Similarly, in the New York Convention each contracting state recognises the validity of an agreement under which the parties undertake to submit to arbitration: "all or any differences which have arisen or *which may arise between them.*"[99]

This distinction is principally of historical importance. Most states in the civil law tradition which did not enforce agreements for future disputes to be referred to arbitration[1] now do so.

The reason for the traditional civil law view is that, by agreeing to arbitrate, the parties agree to accept something less than their full entitlement, which is to have recourse to the established courts of the land. Such recourse was regarded as the sovereign remedy—in some cases literally so, since the courts were the Sovereign's courts and justice was the Sovereign's justice. On this view, an agreement to arbitrate represented a compromise on the part of the parties; and this is perhaps reflected in the language of the civil law that refers to a submission agreement as a *compromis*[2] and to an arbitration clause as a *clause compromissoire*.[3]

In the common law systems, fewer difficulties were placed in the way of referring future disputes to arbitration.[4] Even so, states that follow common law traditions often find it convenient for other reasons to differentiate between existing disputes and future disputes. An arbitration clause is a blank cheque

---

[97] Arbitration Act 1996, s.9. Lord Saville, stated: "The action of the Courts in refusing to stay proceedings where the defendant has no defence is understandable. It is, however, an encroachment on the principle of party autonomy which I find difficult to justify. If the parties have agreed to arbitrate their disputes, why should a Court ignore that bargain, merely because with hindsight one party realises that he might be able to enforce his rights faster if he goes to Court?" "Arbitration and the Courts", The Denning Lecture 1995, p.13.

[98] Geneva Protocol of 1923, Art.1 (emphasis added).

[99] New York Convention, Art.II.1 (emphasis added).

[1] These states included France which, as the country in which the ICC is based, is an important centre for arbitration.

[2] In Robert, *Dictionnaire de la langue Française* the secondary meaning of *compromis* is given as "an agreement under which the parties make mutual concessions".

[3] It was not until 1925, two years after acceding to the Geneva Protocol of 1923, that France altered its law to allow the arbitration of future disputes, in line with the Protocol.

[4] Although in the US it was not until 1920 that the State of New York recognised arbitration clauses as valid and enforceable; and it was the first state to do so: see Coulson "Commercial Arbitration in the United States" (1985) 51 Arbitration 367.

which may be cashed for an unknown amount at a future, and as yet unknown date. It is hardly surprising that states adopt a more cautious attitude towards allowing future rights to be given away than they do towards the relinquishment of existing rights.

Arising out of or in connection with this agreement

There is an increasing tendency for a party to an arbitration agreement to attempt to resile from that agreement when a dispute actually arises. An arrangement that seemed sensible at the time looks much less attractive to the defending party when a request for arbitration is actually made. It may then become a matter of trying to avoid the bargain, so that at best the claimant will not be able to proceed at all and at worst the claimant will have to proceed in the respondent's national courts, with all the trouble, expense and uncertainty that such a course of action is likely to entail. This means that the precise words used in arbitration clauses have come under increasing scrutiny, as the argument is put forward that the particular dispute which has arisen is *not* one that falls within the scope of the agreement to arbitrate. To avoid this kind of problem, particular care needs to be taken in drafting the arbitration clause. This topic is discussed in more detail in Ch.3. **1–38**

It might be added that, whilst almost all disputes which go to arbitration are contractual in origin, it is possible (given an appropriate arbitration agreement) for the matters in dispute to be governed by principles of delictual or tortious liability. Both the New York Convention and the Model Law refer to an agreement to submit to arbitration disputes "whether contractual or not".[5] Again, this is a matter that is discussed in more detail in Ch.3.

Shall be referred to and determined by arbitration

The meaning and effect of these words has already been touched upon. When parties agree that a dispute shall be determined by arbitration, they cut themselves off from recourse to the courts of law. They have agreed to a *private* method of dispute resolution and they will be held to this agreement by the courts of law, both nationally and internationally, in accordance with national legislation and with international treaties. **1–39**

Other matters

The appointment of arbitrators, the place of arbitration, the choice between ad hoc and institutional arbitration, the procedures to be followed and other matters of importance in the conduct of an international commercial arbitration are discussed later. For the present, enough has been said to indicate some of the basic concepts that underlie an agreement to arbitrate. However, one even more basic question needs to be considered. Why go to the trouble and expense of putting an arbitration clause into a commercial contract? Or the even greater **1–40**

---

[5] New York Convention, Art.II.(1); Model Law, Art.7(1).

trouble and expense of drawing up an ad hoc submission to arbitration, when there are other methods of resolving disputes, including the courts of law which have been established expressly for that purpose? In other words, why arbitrate?

2. WHY ARBITRATE?

(a) The principal reasons

1–41   The principal alternative to arbitration is to submit the dispute to a national court of law. Indeed it may well be argued that if parties wish a dispute to be decided in a binding way, they should normally have recourse to the established courts of law, rather than to a specially created arbitral tribunal. Why then should parties to an international commercial dispute choose to go to arbitration, rather than to an established national court? Why has arbitration become established worldwide as the usual method of resolving international commercial disputes?

There are two principal reasons. First, arbitration gives the parties an opportunity to choose a "neutral" forum and a "neutral" tribunal. Secondly, arbitration—if carried through to the end—leads to a decision which is enforceable against the losing party not only in the place where it is made but also internationally, under the provisions of such treaties as the New York Convention.

A choice of a "neutral" forum and a "neutral" tribunal

1–42   Parties to an international commercial contract almost always come from different countries. The "home court" of one party will be a foreign court to the other party. And it will be "foreign" in the sense that not only will it have its own procedures, which may or may not be suitable for the trial of an international dispute, but also in the sense that it will have its own language—which may or may not be the language of the contract—and its own bench of judges and lawyers. A party to an international contract which does not contain an agreement to arbitrate is likely to find, if a dispute arises, that it is obliged to commence proceedings in a foreign court, to employ lawyers other than those who are accustomed to its business and to embark upon the time-consuming and expensive task of translating the contract, the correspondence between the parties and other relevant documents into the language of that court.

By contrast, a reference to arbitration means that the dispute is likely to be determined in a neutral forum (or place of arbitration) rather than on the home ground of one party or the other. This is a particularly important consideration in the context of *international* commercial disputes and is discussed in more detail in a later section of this chapter.

The choice of arbitration as a method of resolving disputes also gives each party an opportunity to participate in the selection of a "neutral" tribunal. One or more arbitrators may be chosen for their special skill and expertise in commercial law, intellectual property, civil engineering or some other relevant discipline. An experienced arbitral tribunal should be able to grasp quickly the salient issues of fact or law in dispute and so save the parties both time and money, as well as offering them the prospect of a sensible award. Moreover, there is a continuity of role in an arbitration, since the arbitral tribunal is appointed to deal with one particular case and follows it throughout. This enables the arbitral tribunal to get to know the parties, their advisers *and* the case as it develops through the pleadings.

An enforceable decision

At the end of the arbitration (if no settlement has been reached between the parties before that stage is reached) the arbitral tribunal will issue its decision in the form of an award. As to this, three points need to be made. First, the end result of the arbitral process will be a binding decision and not (as in mediation) a recommendation which the parties are free to accept or reject as they please. Secondly, and within limits that will be discussed later, the award will be final. It will not, as is the case with some court judgments, be the first step on a ladder of appeals. Thirdly, once the award has been made, it will be directly enforceable by court action, both nationally and internationally.   **1–43**

In this respect an award differs from an agreement entered into as a result of mediation or some other form of "alternative dispute resolution", which is only binding contractually. In its *international* enforceability, an award *also* differs from the judgment of a court of law, since the international treaties that govern the enforcement of an arbitral award (such as the New York Convention) have much greater acceptance internationally than treaties for the reciprocal enforcement of judgments. Indeed, the only major multilateral treaty for the recognition and enforcement of court judgments is contained in European Council Regulation No.44/2001 (formerly the Brussels and Lugano Conventions) in relation to judgments made in the Member States of the European Union and Switzerland.[6] The Hague Conference on Private International Law has been struggling in recent years to produce an "interim" draft of a "Convention on Jurisdiction and the Recognition and Enforcement of Foreign Judgments in Civil and Commercial Matters". However, agreement on such a Convention was still a long way off at the time of preparation of this edition.

(b) Subsidiary reasons

There are other reasons that make arbitration an attractive alternative to litigation. In particular, the flexibility of arbitral proceedings and the "confidentiality" of the arbitration process.   **1–44**

---

[6] The Mercosur common market (Argentina, Brazil, Paraguay and Uruguay) has also etablished the Las Leñas Protocol for the mutual recognition and enforcement of judgments from Mercosur states within the region.

The flexibility of the arbitral process will be addressed later in this book. However, the point that needs to be made here is that there is no standard book containing detailed procedural rules which have to be followed in the conduct of an arbitration. Parties and arbitrators are free to work out for themselves the procedures which will best be suited to the particular circumstances of the particular dispute in which they are involved.

As to the "confidentiality" of arbitration, developments in the law and practice of arbitration over recent years have been such that the old certainties no longer exist and a fresh look has to be taken.[7]

(c) Perceived disadvantages of arbitration

1–45   Not everything in the garden is lovely. Arbitration has its critics. A glance at the arbitration journals will show that amongst the matters which are most criticised are: costs; the limited powers of arbitrators; a general inability to bring multi-party disputes before the same tribunal; and conflicting awards. These are now discussed in turn.

Costs

1–46   Arbitration is not necessarily a cheaper method of resolving disputes than litigation. First, the fees and expenses of the arbitrators (unlike the salary of a judge) must be paid by the parties; and in international commercial arbitrations of any significance, these charges may be substantial.[8] Secondly, it may be necessary to pay the administrative fees and expenses of an arbitral institution, and these too can be substantial, particularly when they are assessed by reference to the amounts in dispute.[9] If the services of a specialised arbitral institution are not used, it may be necessary (in a particularly heavy case) to appoint a secretary or registrar to administer the proceedings. Once again, a fee must be paid. Finally, it will be necessary to hire rooms for meetings and hearings, rather than making use of the public facilities of the courts of law.[10]

This means that arbitration, particularly in international commercial disputes, is unlikely to be cheaper than proceedings in court, unless there is a conscious effort to make it so. One of the objectives of this book is to consider ways in which this may be done. Additionally it should not be forgotten that arbitration is a form of "one-stop shopping", so that although its cost may not be less than that of proceedings in court (and may indeed be more) the award of the arbitrators is unlikely to be followed by a series of costly appeals to superior courts.

---

[7] See paras 1–53 *et seq.*
[8] See Ch.4.
[9] See Ch.4.
[10] The fees and expenses of the arbitral tribunal, and of any arbitral institution, together with such expenses as the hire of rooms, may add up to a considerable sum of money; but in any major arbitration they are likely to be dwarfed by the fees and expenses of the parties' lawyers and experts, which may easily exceed US$1,000,000 for each party.

Limited powers of arbitrators

An arbitral tribunal must depend for its full effectiveness upon an underlying **1–47** national system of law. Sometimes arbitrators may exercise greater powers than those accorded to judges. For example, in many jurisdictions an arbitral tribunal may have the power to order the payment of *compound* interest at such rates and with such rests as it considers meet the justice of the case: where this power exists, it is likely to make arbitration a particularly attractive prospect for businessmen.

In an article which in part traces the history of awarding interest by arbitrators, an English commentator concludes:

> " . . . Where compound interest would provide a fair and reasonable element of compensation to the innocent victim of a contract breaker, it is increasingly awarded by international commercial arbitrators . . . "[11]

In general, however, the powers accorded to arbitrators, whilst usually adequate for the purpose of resolving the matters in dispute, fall short of those conferred upon a court of law. For example, the power to require the attendance of witnesses under penalty of fine or imprisonment, or to enforce awards by the attachment of a bank account or the sequestration of assets, are powers which form part of the prerogative of the state. They are not powers that any state is likely to delegate to a private arbitral tribunal, however eminent or well intentioned that arbitral tribunal may be. In practice, if it becomes necessary for an arbitral tribunal to take coercive action in order to deal properly with the case before it, such action must usually be taken indirectly, through the machinery of the local courts, rather than directly, as a judge himself can do.[12]

No joinder of parties

Another perceived drawback of the arbitral process lies in the fact that, in **1–48** general, it is not possible to bring multi-party disputes together before the same arbitral tribunal. Unlike a national court of law, an arbitral tribunal generally has no power to order consolidation of actions. There are many cases in which at least one of the parties to an arbitration is content that this should be so, since the intervention of third parties is not always welcome; but leaving such cases aside, an arbitral tribunal cannot usually order consolidation of actions, even if this would seem to be necessary or desirable in the interests of justice.

The position is discussed in more detail in Ch.3, but the classic example is an international construction project in which the employer has entered into a contract with a main contractor, who in turn has contracted with various sub-contractors and suppliers. If the employer has any complaints regarding the work

---

[11] Veeder, "Whose Arbitration Is It Anyway?" in *The Leading Arbitrators' Guide to International Arbitration*, Juris Publishing Inc, 2004, p.366.
[12] For further discussion of this topic, see Ch.5.

done or materials supplied, then (unless all parties concerned agree to consolidation) the employer must arbitrate against the main contractor, who in turn must seek to recover from the sub-contractors or suppliers by way of separate arbitrations. In court proceedings, all the relevant parties would usually be joined in one action; and so any liability owed to the employer would be passed down the chain of contracts and sub-contracts to the party or parties ultimately responsible.

Conflicting awards

1–49   Finally, there is the problem of conflicting awards. There is no system of precedents in arbitration—that is to say, no rule which means that an award on a particular issue, or a particular set of facts, is binding on arbitrators confronted with similar issues or similar facts. Each award stands on its own; and it may well happen that an arbitral tribunal which is required, for example, to interpret a policy of reinsurance will arrive at a different conclusion from another tribunal faced with the same problem. The award of the first tribunal, if it is known—and it may not be known, because of confidentiality—may be of persuasive effect, but no more.

The problem is a real one. In *CME v Czech Republic*, for instance, a single investment dispute involving virtually undisputed facts produced conflicting awards from arbitral tribunals in London and Stockholm, as well as giving rise to litigation in the Czech Republic, the US and Sweden.[13]

It has been suggested that one solution would be to create a new international court for resolving disputes over the enforcement of arbitral awards; but the commentator described this as "the impossible dream"[14]; and in a case such as *CME v Czech Republic* such a court would need to function as, in effect, a court of appeal rather than simply as an enforcement court. This would no doubt suit lawyers and arbitrators, who would welcome consistency of decisions, but it might not suit businessmen, who are looking for the solution to a particular dispute with which they are faced, rather than for the opportunity to contribute, at their own expense, to the development of the law.

International arbitration or national litigation?

1–50   The comparative advantages and disadvantages of arbitration as opposed to litigation used to be well rehearsed.[15] If, as it appears, the debate is now over, it is because opinion has shifted strongly in favour of international arbitration for the resolution of disputes involving international commerce.

1–51   In purely domestic disputes, the question of whether to arbitrate or to litigate may be finely balanced. In the final analysis, much may depend upon the

---

[13] See Charles Brower I, Charles Brower II & Jeremy Sharpe, "The Coming Crisis in the Global Adjudication System" (2003) 19 Arbitration International 424.

[14] *ibid.*, p.436.

[15] For one of the most effective, and certainly the most entertaining, critiques of arbitration see Kerr, "Arbitration v Litigation, the Macao Sardine Case", reproduced as an annexe to Kerr, *As far as I remember* (Hart Publishing, 2002).

circumstances of each particular case and the reputation and procedures of the local courts. However, where the question arises in an international transaction, the balance comes down firmly in favour of arbitration.

In a domestic context, parties who are looking for a binding decision on a dispute will usually have an effective choice between a national court and national arbitration. In an international context there is no such choice. There is no international court to deal with international commercial disputes.[16] In effect, the real choice is between recourse to a *national* court and recourse to *international* arbitration.

A claimant who decides to take court proceedings will, in the absence of any agreed submission to the jurisdiction of a particular court, usually be obliged to have recourse to the courts of the defendant's home country, place of business or residence.[17] To the claimant, this court (as already stated) will be "foreign" in every sense of that word—in nature, character and origin. The claimant will generally not be able to be represented by lawyers of his own nationality, with whom the claimant is accustomed to dealing, but instead will have to use the services of foreign lawyers. The claimant may well find that the language of the court is not that of the contract, so that essential documents and evidence will have to be translated, with all the attendant costs, delay and opportunities for misunderstanding to which that may give rise. Finally, the claimant may find that the court is unaccustomed to international commercial transactions and that its laws and practices are not adequate to deal with them. When viewed against this background, the prospect of bringing a claim arising out of an international business transaction before a foreign court is unattractive.

If one of the parties to the contract is a state or state entity, the prospect is likely to be even less attractive. The private party to the contract will be reluctant to have its dispute submitted to the national courts of the state party. The private party will usually have little or no knowledge of the law and practice of that court and will be afraid of encountering judges predisposed to find in favour of the government to which they owe their appointment. For its part, the state (or state entity) concerned will not wish to submit to the national courts of the private party. Indeed, it will probably object to submitting to the jurisdiction of *any* foreign court.

1–52

In situations of this kind, recourse to international arbitration, in a convenient and neutral forum, is generally seen as more acceptable than recourse to national courts as a way of solving any dispute that cannot be settled by negotiation. It is plainly more attractive to set up a carefully chosen tribunal of experienced arbitrators, with knowledge of the language and commercial intentions of the

---

[16] Unless these disputes are between states, in which case the states concerned may by agreement submit their case to the International Court of Justice at The Hague. The European Court of Justice in Luxembourg may deal with disputes between private parties under EU law, but disputes of this kind are outside the scope of this book.

[17] A national court may allow service abroad of its proceedings, but this so-called extra-territorial jurisdiction is unlikely to be exercised if the foreign defendant has no connection with the country concerned. In any event, difficult problems of enforcement may arise, particularly if a judgment is obtained by default.

disputed contract, who will sit in a neutral country and do their best to carry out the reasonable expectations of the parties, than to entrust the resolution of the dispute to an unknown and perhaps commercially inexperienced foreign court, with its own particular, national procedural rules and regulations.

It is for such reasons as these that international commercial arbitration has come to be the accepted method of resolving international business disputes.[18]

(d) Confidentiality

1–53   The confidentiality of arbitral proceedings is often taken to be one of the important advantages of arbitration. Unlike proceedings in a court of law, where press and public are generally entitled to be present, an international commercial arbitration is not a public proceeding. It is essentially a *private* process. A former Secretary-General of the ICC stated:

> "It became apparent to me very soon after taking up my responsibilities at the ICC that the users of international commercial arbitration, *i.e.* the companies, governments and individuals who are parties in such cases, place the highest value upon confidentiality as a fundamental characteristic of international commercial arbitration. When enquiring as to the features of international commercial arbitration which attracted parties to it as opposed to litigation, confidentiality of the proceedings and the fact that these proceedings and the resulting award would not enter into the public domain was almost invariably mentioned."[19]

It has been suggested, following some research, that in fact "privacy"[20] does not rank very highly on the scale of factors which lawyers and business people value in arbitration, coming well below a "fair and just result", cost and finality of decision. It is understandable that people should want a "fair and just result"—by which, no doubt, they have in mind a decision in their favour—but it is perhaps surprising that they do not value more highly the confidentiality of the proceedings.[21]

Allegations of bad faith, of misrepresentation, of incompetence and worse are often made in the course of commercial disputes. It would be understandable if the disputants preferred such mud slinging to take place in private rather than in public, where business reputations might be irreparably—and unjustly—damaged. However, if parties *do* wish the airing of their disputes to take place in

---

[18] See para.1–01, n.1.
[19] Expert report of Stephen Bond in *Esso/BHP v Plowman* (1995) 11 Arbitration International 273.
[20] See Naimark & Keer "International Private Commercial Arbitration—Expectations and Perceptions of Attorneys and Business People" *International Business Lawyer*, May 2002, pp.203–208. It would seem that in this context, although the word "privacy" is used, it is intended to cover what is usually referred to as the "confidentiality" of the proceedings.
[21] For research which points to confidentiality as one of the reasons for choosing arbitration, see the references in Michael Pryles, "Confidentiality" in *The Leading Arbitrators' Guide to International Arbitration* (Juris Publishing Inc, 2004), p.415.

private, rather than in public, how confident can they be that an arbitration will satisfy their wish?

In attempting to answer this question, it is helpful to distinguish between the **1–54** hearing of the dispute and the eventual award of the arbitral tribunal.

So far as the hearing is concerned, the major institutional rules are in agreement: the hearing is private. The ICC Arbitration Rules state:

> *"Article 21—Hearings*
> . . .
> 3. The Arbitral Tribunal shall be in full charge of the hearings, at which all the parties shall be entitled to be present. Save with the approval of the Arbitral Tribunal and the parties, persons not involved in the proceedings shall not be admitted."

The rules of the ICDR, ICSID, LCIA and WIPO contain similar provisions, as do the rules of such commercial arbitration organisations as the Austrian Federal Economic Chamber, the China International Economic and Trade Arbitration Commission ("CIETAC") and the Japanese Commercial Arbitration Association ("JCAA").[22]

The UNCITRAL Arbitration Rules spell out the position in similar terms:

> *"Article 25.4*
> Hearings shall be held *in camera* unless the parties agree otherwise. The arbitral tribunal may require the retirement of any witness or witnesses during the testimony of other witnesses. The arbitral tribunal is free to determine the manner in which witnesses are examined."

If the hearing is to be held in private, it would seem to follow that the documents disclosed and the evidence given at that hearing should also be—and should remain—private. In principle, there would seem to be no point in excluding non-participants from an arbitration hearing if they can later read all about it, in printed articles or on an authorised website.

The classical position

A general principle of confidentiality in arbitrations under English law, which **1–55** might be said to represent the classical view, was spelt out by the English Court of Appeal in *Dolling-Baker v Merrett*.[23] Subsequently, in *Hassneh Insurance Co of Israel v Mew*,[24] the court recognised the existence of an implied duty of confidentiality as the natural extension of the undoubted privacy of the hearing in an international commercial arbitration:

---

[22] See "Report on Confidentiality as a Purported Obligation of the Parties in Arbitration", ICC Forum, April 2002.
[23] *Dolling-Baker v Merrett* [1991] 2 All E.R. 890.
[24] *Hassneh Insurance Co of Israel v Mew* [1993] 2 Lloyd's Rep. 243.

"If it be correct that there is at least an implied term in every agreement to arbitrate that the hearing shall be held in private, the requirement of privacy must in principle extend to documents which are created for the purpose of that hearing. The most obvious example is a note or transcript of the evidence. The disclosure to a third party of such documents would be almost equivalent to opening the door of the arbitration room to that third party. Similarly witness statements, being so closely related to the hearing, must be within the obligation of confidentiality. So also must outline submissions tendered to the arbitrator. If outline submissions, then so must pleadings be included."[25]

In *Ali Shipping Corporation v "Shipyard Trogir"*, the English Court of Appeal reaffirmed this classical position. The court stated that the confidentiality rule was founded on the privacy of arbitral proceedings and that an implied term as to the confidentiality of arbitration was "[a term] which arises as the nature of the contract itself implicitly requires" which the law would imply as a necessary incident of a definable category of contractual relationship.[26]

The Court acknowledged, however, that "the boundaries of the obligations of confidence which thereby arise have yet to be delineated."[27]

This echoes what is a constant theme in English decisions on the implied duty of confidentiality, namely that it exists, but is subject to limitations that remain to be determined on a case-by-case basis.

The current trend

1–56   The current trend in international arbitration is to distinguish between the unquestioned privacy of the hearing and the confidentiality of the arbitral proceedings as a whole. This trend seems to have been considerably influenced by arbitrations in which there was a genuine public interest—in the sense that the decision of the arbitral tribunal would in some way affect the general public. For example, in *Esso Australia Resources Ltd v The Honourable Sidney James Plowman*,[28] the Australian court concluded that whilst the privacy of the hearing should be respected, confidentiality was not an essential attribute of a private arbitration. Specifically, the court found that a requirement to conduct proceedings *in camera* did not translate into an obligation prohibiting disclosure of documents and information provided in, and for the purpose of, the arbitration. The court then concluded that although a certain degree of confidentiality might arise in certain situations, it was not absolute. In the particular case before the court, "the public's legitimate interest in obtaining information about the affairs of public authorities" prevailed.[29]

---

[25] *Hassneh Insurance Co of Israel v Mew* [1993] 2 Lloyd's Rep. 243 at 247, *per* Colman J.
[26] [1998] 1 Lloyd's Rep. 643 at 651.
[27] *ibid.*
[28] *Esso Australia Resources Ltd v The Honourable Sidney James Plowman* (1995) 183 CLR 10. The case is also set out in (1995) 11 Arbitration International 235.
[29] (1995) 11 Arbitration International 235 at 249.

In respect of this final point, one of the judges discussed the standards for disclosure in respect of information that is of legitimate interest to the public, and held:

"The courts have consistently viewed governmental secrets differently from personal and commercial secrets. As I stated in *The Commonwealth of Australia v John Fairfax and Sons Ltd*, the judiciary must view the disclosure of governmental information 'through different spectacles'. This involves a reversal of the onus of proof: the government must prove that the public interest demands non-disclosure."[30]

In another Australian case,[31] the appellate court decided that an arbitrator had no power to make a procedural direction imposing an obligation of confidentiality which would have had the effect of preventing the government from disclosing to a state agency, or to the public, information and documents generated in the course of the arbitration which ought to be made known to that authority or to the public. It was said that public health and environmental issues were involved:

"Whilst private arbitration will often have the advantage of securing for the parties a high level of confidentiality for their dealing, where one of those parties is a government, or an organ of government, neither the arbitral agreement nor the general procedural powers of the arbitrator will extend so far as to stamp on the governmental litigant a regime of confidentiality or secrecy which effectively destroys or limits the general governmental duty to pursue the public interest."[32]

In the US, neither the Federal Arbitration Act nor the Uniform Arbitration Act **1–57** contains a provision requiring the parties or the arbitrators to keep secret arbitration proceedings in which they are involved. As a consequence, unless the parties' agreement or applicable arbitration rules provide otherwise, the parties are not required by US law to treat as confidential the arbitration proceedings and what transpires in them.[33]

In *United States v Panhandle Eastern Corp*,[34] Panhandle brought a motion before a US Federal District Court for a protective order, preventing the disclosure of documents relating to arbitration proceedings between it and Sonatrach, the Algerian national oil and gas company. In support of its motion, Panhandle argued that disclosure to third parties of documents related to the

---

[30] (1995) 11 Arbitration International 235 at 247, *per* Chief Justice Mason.
[31] *Commonwealth of Australia v Cockatoo Dockyard Pty Ltd* [1995] 36 N.S.W.L.R. 662.
[32] *ibid.*, 682, *per* Kirby P.
[33] See *Industrotech Constructors Inc v Duke University* (1984) 67 N/C/App. 741, 314 S.E. 2d 272; *Giacobassi Grandi Vini SpA v Renfield Corp* (1987) US Dist.; Lexis 1783.
[34] *United States v Panhandle Eastern Corp* (D.Del. 1988) 118 F.R.D. 346.

arbitration would severely prejudice Panhandle's ongoing business relationship with both Sonatrach and the Algerian Government.

The court denied the motion on the grounds that Panhandle had failed to satisfy the "good cause" requirements of r.26(c) of the Federal Rules of Civil Procedure, and that the filing was untimely, but it proceeded to address the question of confidentiality and, having rejected the existence of an express confidentiality agreement between the parties, gave no credence to the existence of an implied obligation.[35]

The award

1–58   Some institutional rules of arbitration, including those of ICSID, provide that the award may only be made public with the consent of the parties; and a provision to the same effect is set out in the UNCITRAL Arbitration Rules.

It has always been recognised, however, that there are circumstances in which an award may need to be made public—for instance, for the purpose of enforcement by a national court. In *Hassneh Insurance v Mew*—a case mentioned earlier—the judge concluded that an award and the reasons contained in that award were different in character from the other elements of the arbitration proceedings (*e.g.* notes and transcripts of evidence, witness statements, submissions and pleadings, all of which were, in his view, covered by the principle of privacy stemming from the fact that arbitration hearings were held in private). He found that the award was "potentially a public document for the purposes of supervision by the courts or enforcement in them" and therefore ruled that the award could be disclosed without the consent of the other party or the permission of the court if, but only if, the party seeking disclosure needed to do so in order to assert or protect its legal rights *vis-à-vis* a third party.[36]

In addition to the disclosure of awards where required by law, disclosure of a kind takes place when an arbitral institution—such as the ICC—publishes "edited and redacted" copies of arbitral awards, as a guide for the benefit of lawyers and arbitrators.[37]

1–59   The ICDR's International Arbitration Rules provide[38] that an award may be made public "only with the consent of all parties or as required by law". Those rules provide that, unless otherwise agreed by the parties, selected awards may be made publicly available, with the names of the parties and other identifying features removed. If the award has become publicly available through enforcement proceedings or otherwise, then the names need not be removed.

---

[35] It would seem that the decision of the court was *obiter*. Moreover, it has been suggested that too much should not be read into this decision. Panhandle was seeking a "protective order" to shield the arbitration documents from disclosure and the onus of establishing "good cause" is a heavy one: see Patrick Neill, "Confidentiality in Arbitration" (1996) 12 Arbitration International 303.

[36] The LCIA Arbitration Rules mirror this position, as pointed out by Rawding & Seeger in "*Aegis v European Re* and the Confidentiality of Arbitration Awards" (2003) 19 Arbitration International 483.

[37] The ICC has no specific rule as to the confidentiality of awards, although the internal rules of its court stress the "confidential character" of the work of the court.

[38] In Art.27.

In Sweden it appears that there is no implied duty of confidentiality in relation to either the arbitral proceedings or the award, although it is accepted that arbitration is fundamentally a private process and that this is one of its perceived advantages.[39]

In England, the Privy Council had to consider whether an arbitration award in one arbitration under a reinsurance agreement could be relied upon by the winning party in another arbitration under the same agreement, despite an express confidentiality agreement in respect of the first arbitration. The case came to the Privy Council on appeal from the Court of Appeal of Bermuda and disclosure of the award was allowed. The Privy Council said that the legitimate use of an earlier award in a later, also private, arbitration between the same parties was *not* the kind of mischief against which the confidentiality agreement was directed. This decision has been rightly described as "eminently sensible in the circumstances of the case. The private and, in theory, confidential nature of arbitration should not mean that the parties can go on arbitrating the same point *ad infinitum* until they get the result they prefer."[40]

At the other end of the scale from the Swedish disregard for confidentiality **1–60** was the decision of the Paris Cour d'Appel in *Aita v Ojjeh*,[41] in which the court ruled that the mere bringing of court proceedings to challenge an arbitration award violated the principle of confidentiality in that it caused "a public debate of facts which should remain confidential". The judgment also contains *dicta* to the effect that it is in "the very nature of arbitral proceeding that they ensure the highest degree of discretion in the resolution of private disputes, as the two parties had agreed".[42]

Confidentiality in investor-state arbitrations

In the *Cockatoo Dockyard* case, to which reference has already been made, the **1–61** Australian court concluded that whilst there was a "high level of confidentiality" in arbitral proceedings, this should not prevent disclosure where the public interest was concerned. It is this concern for the public interest—and for the public's "right to know"—that has led to the erosion of the principle of confidentiality in arbitral proceedings. The need to balance the *private* interest in confidentiality against the possible *public* interest in disclosure may be seen in arbitrations that have taken place under the treaty that established the North American Free Trade Agreement.

---

[39] *A.I. Trade Finance Inc v Bulgarian Foreign Trade Bank Ltd*, Supreme Court of Sweden, October 27, 2000, *Mealey's International Arbitration Report*, Vol.15, No.12, p.A-1. It seems odd to accept that arbitration is a private process, if nothing is done to protect that privacy.

[40] Rawding & Seeger, *op.cit.*, pp.488, 489.

[41] (1986) Revue de l'Arbitrage 583.

[42] Some commentators argue that the reasoning of the French court is unsatisfactory, and that the extreme position advanced must be seen in the context of the court's determination to punish what it evidently viewed as a hopeless and tactically motivated attempt to set aside an English award in the French courts: see Paulsson & Rawding, "The Trouble with Confidentiality" (1994) ICC International Court of Arbitration Bulletin 48.

In the early 1980s, an international arbitral tribunal applying the ICSID Rules in *Amco v The Republic of Indonesia* held that:

"as to the 'spirit of confidentiality' of the arbitral procedure, it is right to say that the Convention and the Rules do not prevent the parties from revealing their case . . . "[43]

Balanced against this finding, the *Amco* tribunal nonetheless referred to a general duty existing under international law not to exacerbate disputes, and relied on the existence of this duty to recommend to the parties that they should ensure that their public statements about cases in which they were involved were both short and accurate.

1–62   In the years since *Amco v The Republic of Indonesia*, tribunals applying the ICSID Rules, including NAFTA tribunals, have striven to achieve the same balance. For example, in *Metalclad Corporation v United Mexican States*, Mexico made an application for a confidentiality order, pursuant to Art.1134 of NAFTA ("interim measures of protection") and Art.28 of the (then) ICSID Additional Facility Rules ("procedural orders"). The Tribunal dismissed the application, finding as follows:

"There remains nonetheless a question as to whether there exists any general principle of confidentiality that would operate to prohibit discussion of the arbitration proceedings by either party. *Neither the NAFTA nor the ICSID (Additional Facility) Rules contain any express restriction on the freedom of the parties in this respect.* Though it is frequently said that one of the reasons for recourse to arbitration is to avoid publicity, unless the agreement between the parties incorporates such a limitation, each of them is still free to speak publicly of the arbitration. . . . Indeed, as has been pointed out by the Claimant in its comments, under US security laws, the Claimant, as a public company traded on a public stock exchange in the US, is under a positive duty to provide certain information about its activities to its shareholders, especially regarding its involvement in a process the outcome of which could perhaps significantly affect its share value.

The above having been said, it still appears to the Arbitral Tribunal that it would be of advantage to the orderly unfolding of the arbitral process and conducive to the maintenance of working relationships between the Parties if during the proceedings they were both to limit public discussion of the case to a minimum, subject only to any externally imposed obligation by which either of them may be legally bound."[44]

In another NAFTA arbitration, *R. Loewen and Loewen Corporation v United States of America*, the US Government requested that all filings, as well as the

---

[43] *Amco Corporation v The Republic of Indonesia* (1983) 1 ICSID Reports 410 at 412, Decision on Request for Provisional Measures, December 9, 1983.
[44] *Metalclad Corporation v United Mexican States*, Final Award, September 2, 2000 at para.13 (emphasis added).

minutes of oral proceedings, be treated as open and available to the public. Loewen did not oppose public disclosure, but requested that the disclosure take place only after the conclusion of the arbitration. The tribunal rejected the US Government's request, referring to Art.44(2) of the ICSID Additional Facility Rules, which provide that minutes of hearings should not be published without the consent of the parties.[45]

Although the tribunal rejected the US Government's request, it did not recog- **1–63** nise any general duty of confidentiality. Rather, it rejected Loewen's submission that each party is under an obligation of confidentiality in relation to the proceedings. In its award on jurisdiction, the tribunal summarised its conclusions as follows:

"In its Decision the Tribunal rejected the Claimants' submission that each party is under a general obligation of confidentiality in relation to the proceedings. The Tribunal stated that in an arbitration under NAFTA, it is not to be supposed that, in the absence of express provision, the Convention or the Rules and Regulations impose a general obligation on the parties, the effect of which would be to preclude a Government (or the other party) from discussing the case in public, thereby depriving the public of knowledge and information concerning government and public affairs. The decision concluded by repeating the comment made by the *Metalclad* Tribunal, namely that it would be of advantage to the orderly unfolding of the arbitral process if during the proceedings, the parties were to limit public discussion to what is considered necessary."[46]

Revisions to rules of arbitration

The increasing number of arbitrations in which there is a legitimate public **1–64** interest, such as the NAFTA arbitrations which have been discussed and the ICSID arbitrations which are discussed later, has led to an erosion of the concept of confidentiality, with pleadings and awards being publicly available on the internet and elsewhere.

Some rules of arbitration have been amended to impose a duty of confidentiality upon the parties, but this may be overridden if it is judged that the public interest so requires.[47]

LCIA Rules

Article 30 of the LCIA Rules, introduced in January 1998, imposes an express **1–65** duty of confidentiality on the parties to the arbitration as follows:

---

[45] *R. Loewen and Loewen Corp v United States of America*, Award on Jurisdiction, January 5, 2001 at para.25. (Although Art.44 has since been excluded from the Additional Facility Rules, pursuant to the amendments that came into force on January 1, 2003, reg.22 of the ICSID Administrative and Financial Regulations imposes the same prohibition.)

[46] *ibid.*

[47] *e.g.* the Swiss Rules which came into effect on January 1, 2004 contain a general provision for the confidentiality of awards and orders, as well as material submitted in the course of the arbitral proceedings, unless there is a legal duty of disclosure.

"30.1 Unless the parties expressly agree in writing to the contrary, the parties undertake as a general principle to keep confidential all awards in their arbitration, together with all materials in the proceedings created for the purpose of the arbitration and all other documents produced by another party in the proceedings not otherwise in the public domain—save and to the extent that disclosure may be required of a party by legal duty, to protect or pursue a legal right or to enforce or challenge an award in bona fide legal proceedings before a state court or other judicial authority.

30.2 The deliberations of the Arbitral Tribunal are likewise confidential to its members, save and to the extent that disclosure of an arbitrator's refusal to participate in the arbitration is required of the other members of the Arbitral Tribunal under Articles 10, 12 and 26.

30.3 The LCIA Court does not publish any award or any part of an award without the prior written consent of all parties and the Arbitral Tribunal."

This rule recognises the importance of confidentiality in arbitral proceedings, which may well involve the disclosure of commercial or financial information, proprietary "know-how" and other so-called "trade secrets" which the parties may not wish to be made publicly available.

The WIPO Arbitration Rules

1–66 The WIPO Rules carry the protection of "trade secrets" much further, as might be expected from an organisation concerned with the protection of intellectual property rights. Article 52 of the Rules defines "confidential information" as any information, regardless of the medium in which it is expressed, "which is (i) in the possession of a party, (ii) not accessible to the public, (iii) of commercial, financial or industrial significance and (iv) treated as confidential by the person possessing it."

On application by the relevant party, the tribunal may classify such information as "confidential",[48] thus in effect restricting its disclosure to the tribunal and the parties. In exceptional circumstances, the tribunal may delegate this duty to a "confidentiality advisor" who will determine whether the information is to be so classified and if so, to whom it may be disclosed, in whole or in part.[49] As an additional safeguard, the tribunal may appoint the "confidentiality advisor" as an expert to report on specific issues on the basis of the confidential information, without disclosing that information either to the other party or to the tribunal itself.[50]

For completeness, it should be noted that the WIPO Arbitration Rules extend the protection of confidentiality to the very existence of the arbitration[51]; to

[48] r.52(c).
[49] r.52(d).
[50] r.52(e).
[51] Art.73.

disclosures made during the arbitration[52]; and to the award.[53] The duty of confidentiality is also, of course, imposed upon the tribunal and the WIPO centre itself.[54]

Not all rules of arbitration contain provisions governing confidentiality. The **1–67** UNCITRAL Arbitration Rules, for example, provide for hearings to be held in private (unless the parties otherwise agree)[55] and for the award to be made public only if the parties agree,[56] but they do not contain any general provisions for confidentiality. Nor do the ICC Rules of Arbitration. This is left either to the law governing the arbitration[57] or to the agreement of the parties.

Conclusion

One of the advantages of arbitration is that it is a private proceeding, in which **1–68** the parties may air their differences and grievances and discuss their financial circumstances, their proprietary "know-how" and so forth, without exposure to the gaze of the public and the reporting of the media. The fact that arbitral hearings are held in private still remains a constant feature of arbitration. However, to ensure the confidentiality of the entire proceedings, it is increasingly necessary to rely on an express provision of the relevant rules (for instance, those of the LCIA or of WIPO) or to enter into a specific confidentiality agreement[58] (and it seems that this may be overridden in some jurisdictions if the relevant court considers it to be in the public interest that it should be).

(e) Alternative dispute resolution

Introduction

There are many ways of settling a commercial dispute. The simplest is by **1–69** negotiations between the parties or their advisers. The parties themselves are (or should be) in the best position to know the strengths and weaknesses of their respective cases. If they need advice on points of difficulty or controversy, they can always seek it from lawyers, accountants, engineers or other experts as required. The problem is that negotiation is unlikely to succeed unless those involved are capable of a certain degree of detachment and objectivity, qualities which are sometimes hard to find. Indeed, sometimes they only emerge after a certain amount of blood has been spilt (or money spent), whether by way of

---

[52] Art.74.
[53] Art.75.
[54] Art.76.
[55] UNCITRAL Arbitration Rules Art.25(4).
[56] *ibid.*, Art.32(5).
[57] The Spanish Arbitration Act 2003, *e.g.*, contains an express provision as to the confidentiality of information disclosed in the course of the arbitral proceedings: Art.24(2).
[58] See the concluding comments of Rawding & Seeger, *op.cit.*: "In the meantime, given the prevailing sense of confusion amongst practitioners as to the precise nature and scope of any implied duty of confidentiality in arbitration, and as to the exceptions to any such duty, parties would be well advised not to take anything for granted and to continue including express confidentiality provisions in their arbitration agreement or in procedural directions at the outset of the case".

litigation or arbitration. It should be remembered, however, that a settlement by negotiation is always possible, even after other methods of resolving the dispute have been set in motion.[59]

If direct negotiations between the parties or their advisers fail, the intervention of a disinterested third party may be helpful. Indeed, as dispute resolution in international commerce becomes more sophisticated, it is becoming increasingly common for parties to an international contract to stipulate that, before embarking upon an arbitration, the parties will endeavour to settle any dispute by negotiation or some other form of alternative dispute resolution (or "ADR", as it has come to be known).

1–70   One formula often found in long-term agreements is a provision that, in the event of a dispute arising, the parties will first endeavour to settle their differences by negotiations "in good faith". An obligation to negotiate "in good faith" is a somewhat nebulous obligation. Who is to open negotiations? How long are they to last? How far does a party need to go in order to show "good faith"? Is a party obliged to make concessions, even on matters of principle, in order to demonstrate good faith? It was uncertainties of this kind that led a senior English judge to say:

> "an agreement to negotiate, like an agreement to agree, is unenforceable . . . because it lacks the necessary certainty. A duty to negotiate in good faith is as unworkable in practice as it is inherently inconsistent with the position of the negotiating party."[60]

In the third edition of this book, the view was expressed that English law might come to take a more positive view of an obligation to negotiate in good faith and indeed this is what is happening. As will be seen below, the English judicial system, in common with those of other countries such as Australia and the USA, now recognises the value of negotiation as a method of resolving disputes, particularly when the negotiations take place in a formalised manner, as part of a process of ADR.

What is meant by ADR?

1–71   The growing cost of litigation in the US (a cost not only of lawyers' fees and expenses, but also of management and executive time, made worse by procedural delaying tactics, overcrowded court lists and the jury trial of civil cases, often leading to the award of hugely excessive damages against major corporations (and their insurers)) gave rise to a search for quicker and cheaper methods of dispute resolution. These methods tend to be grouped together under the general heading of ADR. Some of them, as will be seen, come close to arbitration in its conventional sense. Others—in particular mediation and conciliation—are seen

---

[59] One major construction dispute in which one of the authors took part was settled by negotiation after an arbitration hearing which had lasted for 80 days, but before the award was issued (unpublished ad hoc arbitration before a sole arbitrator in England).

[60] Lord Ackner in *Walford v Miles* [1992] 2 A.C. 128 at 138.

as first steps in the settlement of a dispute to be followed, if unsuccessful, by arbitration or litigation. Accordingly, it is appropriate to describe briefly what is meant by ADR; how it works; and why it has developed as a method of resolving disputes.

It might be thought that the term "alternative dispute resolution" would be used to describe any methods of resolving disputes, other than those adopted by the courts of law as part of the system of justice established and administered by the state. On this view, arbitration would itself be classified as a method of alternative dispute resolution—since it is a very real alternative to the courts of law. However, the term ADR is not always used in this wide (or, it might be said, precise) sense. Accordingly, for the purpose of this section, arbitration is not included. As has been said:

> "Arbitration presents an alternative to the judicial process in offering privacy to the parties as well as procedural flexibility. However, it is nonetheless fundamentally the same in that the role of the arbitrator is judgmental. The function of the judge and the arbitrator is not to decide how the problem resulting in the dispute can most readily be resolved so much as to apportion responsibility for that problem."[61]

It is tempting to suggest that one distinction between ADR on the one hand and litigation and arbitration on the other is that, whilst litigation and arbitration are compulsory,[62] ADR is a *non-compulsory* method of resolving disputes:

> "ADR, like litigation and arbitration, will often involve an independent third party but his function is fundamentally different from that of a judge or arbitrator and is best described as a neutral facilitator. He does not impose a decision on the parties but, on the contrary, his role is to assist the parties to resolve the dispute themselves. He may give opinions on issues in dispute but his primary function is to assist in achieving a negotiated solution."[63]

It is doubtful, however, that a valid distinction between a "compulsory" and **1–72** a non-compulsory, or "consensual", process can be maintained. There are various forms of dispute resolution, as will be seen, which come under the general heading of ADR but which are compulsory and lead to a binding decision which can be enforced, on ordinary contractual principles. Perhaps the most workable definition is to describe ADR as a method of resolving, or attempting to resolve, disputes without resort to the courts (or to arbitration) by procedures which are informal.

---

[61] Carroll & Dixon, "Alternative Dispute Resolution Developments in London" (1990) 4 International Construction Law Review 436 at 437.

[62] Assuming, as to litigation, that the court has jurisdiction and, as to arbitration, that there is a valid and enforceable agreement to arbitrate.

[63] Carroll & Dixon, *loc. cit.*

How does ADR work?

1–73   It would be out of place to attempt to list all the different forms that ADR may take.[64] However, the examples that follow will give an indication of how the process works, in some of the many different forms of ADR.

Mediation

1–74   Mediation lies at the heart of ADR. Parties who have failed to resolve a dispute for themselves may turn to an independent third person, or mediator, who will listen to an outline of the dispute and then meet each party separately—often "shuttling" between them[65]—and try to persuade the parties to moderate their respective positions.[66] The task of the mediator is to attempt to persuade each party to focus on its real interests, rather than on what it conceives to be its contractual or legal entitlement. One illustration of the process is that of a dispute over a consignment of oranges, to which both parties claim title.[67] In this modern Aesop's fable, it transpires (after careful enquiry by the mediator) that one party needs the oranges for their juice and the other for their peel—and so an amicable solution to the dispute is happily found.[68]

Conciliation

1–75   The terms "mediation" and "conciliation" are generally used as if they are interchangeable; and there is no general agreement as to how they should be defined. Historically, in private dispute resolution, a conciliator was seen as someone who went a step further than the mediator, so to speak, in that the conciliator would draw up and propose the terms of an agreement that he or she considered represented a fair settlement. In practice, the two terms seem to have merged, although common lawyers tend to speak of "mediation", whilst civil lawyers speak of "conciliation".

The UNCITRAL Conciliation Rules

1–76   There are various international or institutional rules designed to provide for conciliation, including those of the ICC, ICSID and UNCITRAL. The UNCITRAL Conciliation Rules, which were recommended by the General Assembly

---

[64] It may be of interest to note that a White Book on ADR is to be issued by the ICC in the autumn of 2004.
[65] "He moves backwards and forwards between the parties: the Chinese word for conciliator is said to be a 'go-between who wears out a thousand sandals' ", Donaldson "ADR" (1992) 58 J.C.I. Arb. 102.
[66] These separate meetings are known as "caucuses".
[67] An example for which acknowledgment is due to Dr Richard Hill, at a conference in London, December 1995.
[68] This is what the proponents of ADR describe as a "win-win situation", with each side obtaining a favourable result. There is here, perhaps, an unconscious echo of the Caucus Race in *Alice's Adventures in Wonderland*, in which everyone "began running when they liked and left off when they liked, so that it was not easy to know when the race was over" but at last the Dodo said: "Everybody has won and all must have prizes".

of the United Nations in December 1980, may be taken as an example of how the process works. First, the parties need to agree that they will try to settle any dispute by conciliation. This may be done ad hoc—that is to say, once a dispute has arisen. Or it may be done by prior agreement, by inserting a provision for conciliation or mediation in their contract. The model clause recommended by UNCITRAL states:

> "Where, in the event of a dispute arising out of or relating to this contract, the parties wish to seek an amicable settlement of that dispute by conciliation, the conciliation shall take place in accordance with the UNCITRAL Conciliation Rules as at present in force."[69]

The UNCITRAL Conciliation Rules deal not only with the conciliation process itself, but also with important provisions such as the admissibility in subsequent litigation or arbitration of evidence or documents put forward in the conciliation process.[70] Under the UNCITRAL Conciliation Rules, there is normally only one conciliator unless the parties agree otherwise. The role of the conciliator is to make proposals for a settlement. The proposals need not be in writing, and need not contain reasons.

> "The conciliator assists the parties in an independent and impartial manner in their attempt to reach an *amicable* settlement of their dispute."[71]

Conciliation under the UNCITRAL Conciliation Rules is both simple and flexible. The parties may be represented or assisted by lawyers or any other persons of their choice. Each party sends to the conciliator (and to the other side) a brief written statement describing the general nature of the dispute and the points at issue. If necessary, the conciliator requests further written statements, or additional information.[72] The conciliator may meet the parties, either together or separately, and may arrange for administrative assistance by a suitable institution or person. **1–77**

One important issue in any conciliation proceedings is the extent to which the conciliator is free to disclose to one party information given to him or her in private by the other party. Suppose, for instance, that the conciliator is told that

---

[69] The model clause appears at the end of the UNCITRAL Conciliation Rules. The Rules themselves may be accessed on the UNCITRAL website, *www.uncitral.org.*

[70] It is obviously important to know, for instance, whether evidence produced or admissions made by a party in the course of the conciliation proceedings can be used if conciliation fails and is followed by litigation or arbitration. In its International Arbitration Legislation, Bermuda has introduced statutory provisions for conciliation that deal with the issue by making it an implied term of the conciliation agreement that unless otherwise agreed in writing, the parties will not introduce in evidence in subsequent proceedings any opinion, admissions or proposals for settlement made in the course of the conciliation proceedings. See Rawding, "ADR: Bermuda's International Conciliation and Arbitration Act 1993" (1994) 10 Arbitration International 99.

[71] UNCITRAL Conciliation Rules, Art.7.1 (emphasis added).

[72] UNCITRAL Conciliation Rules, Arts 5.2 and 5.3.

a claimant would be prepared to settle for a third of its claim, but considers itself entitled to more: is the conciliator free to pass on this information?

1–78   The UNCITRAL Conciliation Rules provide[73] that a conciliator may disclose the substance of any *factual* information he or she receives, "in order that the other party may have the opportunity to present any explanation which he considers appropriate". However, it also provides that a party may give information to the conciliator subject to a specific condition as to confidentiality, in which case the conciliator is bound by that condition.

Either the conciliator or the parties themselves may at any time during the course of the proceedings propose a settlement. If no initiative for settlement is taken during the course of the proceedings, then at the end the conciliator may formulate the terms of a possible settlement and submit them to the parties for their observations. The process comes to an end either when a settlement is achieved or when it appears that no settlement is possible.[74]

Another form of conciliation is provided under the ICC Rules. These Rules are less comprehensive than those of UNCITRAL and they may lead to a less formal approach to conciliation although the intervention of the institution in relation to costs and other matters perhaps make the proceedings appear to be more formalised than they need to be.

The UNCITRAL Model Law on Conciliation

1–79   In 2002, UNCITRAL published its Model Law on International Commercial Conciliation.[75] Like the UNCITRAL Model Law on International Commercial Arbitration, this is intended as a guide for states that wish to implement legislation—but this time, in relation to conciliation. It remains to be seen whether it will achieve the outstanding success of the Model Law on International Commercial Arbitration.

Since conciliation is essentially a voluntary process, there are no sanctions in the Model Law on Conciliation, so that it reads like a code of good conduct for international conciliators, with useful provisions as to the extent to which information disclosed by the parties must be kept confidential, a prohibition on the conciliator subsequently acting as an arbitrator (unless agreed by the parties) and so forth. However, in Art.14, the Model Law on Conciliation does envisage that a state enacting the Model Law may wish to add provisions for the enforcement of any settlement agreement that is reached through the conciliation process.

Dispute Resolution Centres

1–80   The development of ADR has led to the growth of organisations devoted to this method of resolving disputes (as opposed to organisations such as the ICC

---

[73] Art.10.

[74] As a safeguard, it would be sensible to couple a conciliation agreement with an agreement to arbitrate.

[75] This may be accessed on the UNCITRAL website, above.

which are primarily concerned with arbitration, but which offer conciliation as an additional service). In the US, for example, there are various centres, including the Center for Public Resources in New York. In Europe, one of the best-known organisations is the Centre for Dispute Resolution ("CEDR") which is based in London and was established in 1990 with the backing of industrial and professional firms.

Mini-trial

Probably the most structured form of mediation is the so-called "mini-trial", **1–81** found primarily in the USA. The purpose of a mini-trial is to put two high-level executives, one from each party, into an environment in which the strengths and weaknesses of their respective cases are drawn to their attention. The theory is that, confronted in this way, the businessmen will focus on the risks involved in taking the dispute to litigation; and that this, together with the time and costs likely to be involved in litigation, will induce them to reach a compromise.

There is no hard and fast procedure in a mini-trial. Often a hearing of one or two days, sometimes called an "information exchange", follows a limited form of disclosure of documents and an exchange of briefs. Lawyers for each party make a brief presentation outlining the evidence they would call in the event of a trial. The hearing is presided over by a "neutral adviser" (generally, a retired judge or senior lawyer, who gives a preliminary opinion as to how a court would be likely to react). This "information exchange" is followed by negotiations between the two principals, either with or without the intervention of the "neutral adviser".

If a settlement is not reached, the parties may ask the neutral adviser to give a non-binding opinion as to the likely result of litigation. This in itself may well lead to a settlement.

Mediation/Arbitration (Med/Arb)

In this process, the parties agree that if mediation does not produce a nego- **1–82** tiated agreement, the mediator will change identity and adopt the role of arbitrator to decide the dispute. Although the process is used in the US (for instance, in labour disputes), to a lawyer it raises many questions. For example, how open are the parties likely to be in their discussions with the mediator (including letting him know what settlement proposals they would be prepared to accept) if they know that he might be called upon to act as arbitrator in the same dispute? And how can the arbitrator satisfy or appear to satisfy the requirements of "impartiality" and "a fair hearing" if he has previously held private discussions with the parties separately and indicated his views to them?

The neutral listener agreement

This is, in effect, a variation of the mediation process. Each party submits its **1–83** best offer in settlement to a neutrally selected third party. This "neutral listener" then informs the parties whether their offers are:

- substantially similar or overlapping; or

- within a range which looks negotiable.

If the neutral listener considers the position to be negotiable he may, with the agreement of the parties, try to bridge the gap.

"Last offer" or "baseball" arbitration

1–84   "Last offer" arbitration is a format under which each disputant submits to the arbitral tribunal its best offer, leaving the tribunal to pick (and to award) the one which comes nearest to its own assessment. This technique of dispute settlement is prominently used in the negotiation of professional athletes' contracts in the US (and is sometimes known as "baseball arbitration"). The parties are compelled to narrow their demands in recognition of the fact that an overstated claim will almost certainly result in the award going to their opponent.

Court-annexed ADR

1–85   In the US, many district courts will order the parties to submit their dispute first to arbitration or to mediation. Similarly, in England parties are encouraged "to use an alternative dispute resolution procedure".[76] This recognition of the value of ADR has led the courts to enforce obligations to negotiate. For example, in *Dunnett v Railtrack plc* the defendant was denied its costs in the Court of Appeal for refusing to accept an invitation to mediate (notwithstanding the fact that it won its case). The court said:

> "Skilled mediators are now able to achieve results satisfactorily to both parties in many cases which are quite beyond the power of lawyers and courts to achieve . . . A mediator may be able to provide solutions which are beyond the powers of the court to provide."[77]

In another English case, *Hurst v Leeming*,[78] the judge described ADR as being "at the heart of today's civil justice system" and although, on the particular facts, it was held that the defendant's refusal to mediate was reasonable, the hurdle which this case established for refusing an offer to mediate was a high one— namely, that the court has to be satisfied that the mediation has no real prospect of success. In *Cable & Wireless v IBM*,[79] the English court enforced an ADR clause without hesitation. The parties had entered into a 10-year agreement which contained the following ADR provision:

> "If the matter is not resolved through negotiation, the parties shall attempt in good faith to resolve the dispute or claim through an alternative dispute

---

[76] Civil Procedure Rules, Pt 1.4(2).
[77] [2002] 1 W.L.R. 2434 at 2436–2437.
[78] [2002] C.P. Rep. 59.
[79] [2002] EWHC 2059 (Comm Ct).

resolution (ADR) procedure as recommended to the parties by the Centre for Dispute Resolution. However, an ADR procedure which is being followed shall not prevent any party from issuing proceedings."

A dispute arose and C&W commenced judicial proceedings without first attempting an ADR procedure. IBM applied for a stay of the action in order to enforce the ADR procedure. The judge ordered a stay of judicial proceedings pending ADR. In enforcing the ADR clause, he drew a clear distinction between an agreement merely to negotiate in good faith, which was not binding, and the ADR clause before him, which he judged went "further than that by identifying a particular procedure, namely an ADR procedure as recommended to the parties by the Centre for Dispute Resolution (CEDR) . . . " The judge added that his decision would have been the same without any reference to an institutional procedure, provided that "the obligation to negotiate was expressed in unqualified and mandatory terms".

In Australia too, the courts have enforced ADR clauses in recent years. The **1–86** Supreme Court of New South Wales did so in *Aiton Australia Pty Ltd v Transfield Pty Ltd*.[80] As the Judge stated: "It is trite to observe that parties ought to be bound by their freely negotiated contracts".

Expert determination (including adjudication and Dispute Review Boards)

Most of the methods of ADR that have been discussed are aimed at bringing **1–87** the parties to an agreed settlement of their differences, involving—almost certainly—a measure of "give and take" by the disputants. There are, however, methods of dispute resolution which fall short of proceedings in court, or before an arbitral tribunal, and yet which may result in a decision which the parties accept as binding. The most prominent of these methods is that of "expert determination".[81]

The traditional role of an expert lies in the area of valuation or assessment. An expert may be asked to assess the worth of a house or a block of flats; or to put a price on shares in a private company or a professional partnership; or to certify the value of work done by a building or engineering contractor. However, the role of the expert, whether he or she is an accountant, an architect, a surveyor, an engineer or a lawyer, has developed beyond this point. The work of valuation continues, but increasingly the expert is seen as a "decision maker"—someone whose determination of a dispute may well put an end to it.

When the expert becomes an adjudicator, then the process of expertise itself begins to resemble more closely that of arbitration. Nonetheless, there is a difference and it is an important difference. There are two main reasons why this

---

[80] Einstein J. in [1999] N.S.W.S.C. 996. The case contains a useful examination of relevant Australian and English authorities and also stands as the Australian *locus classicus* for what constitutes good faith in an ADR clause. It has since been followed in other Supreme Court of New South Wales decisions, such as *Morrow v Chinadotcom Corp* [2001] N.S.W.S.C. 209.

[81] For a comprehensive and helpful review of the role of the expert as decision maker, see Kendall, *Expert Determination* (2nd ed., FT Law & Tax, 1996).

is so. First, an arbitrator, unlike an expert, is generally regarded as being immune from liability for negligence in the carrying out of his or her functions.[82] Secondly, the award of an arbitrator is directly enforceable, both nationally and internationally, under such treaties as the New York Convention of 1958. The decision of an expert, however, is only binding contractually and will need to be enforced by proceedings in court, if it is not carried out voluntarily.

1–88   The increasing use of experts to resolve disputes once they have arisen can be seen in some of the major international construction projects carried out in recent years. In the Channel Tunnel project, for example, any dispute had to be referred to the Panel of Experts and then, if either party so requested, to arbitration under the ICC Rules. In the Boston Central Artery/Tunnel project—one of the most complex highway projects ever undertaken, involving many hundreds of contracts and sub-contracts—it was provided that any disputes were to be resolved first by "partnering" (a form of mediation) by an "authorised representative", who would give a decision. If this proved unsuccessful, disputes were to be resolved by a Dispute Review Board, which by agreement with the parties could refer the dispute to any form of ADR that was acceptable to them, before going on, if necessary, to issue its findings and recommendations. Again, in the Hong Kong Airport Core programme, four steps were contemplated. These were the submission of any dispute for decision by the engineer, followed (if either party was dissatisfied at any stage) by mediation, adjudication and then arbitration. Although complex, these procedures, consisting, like a wedding cake, of three or four tiers, are a reflection of the amounts of money likely to be at stake in major projects—and of reluctance to trust in one decision maker.

In earlier and simpler times, the "engineer" under a construction contract would give a decision that would be binding unless reversed by subsequent arbitration. The engineer was well placed to do this, since he and his staff would be familiar with the project and likely to be aware of problems as soon as they arose. However, the engineer, who is appointed by the employer, has come to be regarded as lacking the necessary independence to make important decisions.

Panels of Experts and Dispute Review Boards are generally regarded as forming part of ADR, but there is nothing voluntary or consensual in the procedures they adopt. Once parties have agreed to refer their disputes to a Review Board or Panel, they are contractually bound to go this route, if one party insists upon it (in the same way as a party must arbitrate, if there is a valid and binding arbitration agreement which the other party is not prepared to waive). Once the Review Board or Panel has given its decision, this decision is usually binding and must be carried out, unless or until it is reversed by subsequent arbitration.

1–89   One of the problems involved in setting up a panel or a committee of experts is that of deciding what specialist qualifications are required of the experts who

---

[82] See the discussion in Ch.5.

are to constitute the panel. In a major construction project, it is easy to suggest that the experts should be engineers. But from what precise disciplines should they be drawn? In a project for the construction of a major airport, an expert who is highly qualified in one discipline (for instance, runway construction) would be the wrong expert for a dispute over the air traffic control system. It may be that, for long-term engineering projects involving different disciplines, there should be a list of experts from whom to draw, rather than a permanent "Panel" as in the Channel Tunnel project. In this way, it would be possible to establish a suitably qualified panel for each particular dispute as it arose.

The enforceability of agreements for expert determination

Are such agreements enforceable, even if they are not arbitration agreements **1–90**
stricto sensu? The highest court in England was in no doubt that they were:

"This is not the case of a jurisdiction clause, purporting to exclude an ordinary citizen from his access to a court and featuring inconspicuously in a standard printed form of contract. The parties here were large commercial enterprises, negotiating at arm's length in the light of a long experience of construction contracts . . . [A]ll concerned must have recognised the potential weaknesses of the two-stage procedure and concluded that despite them there was a balance of practical advantage over the alternative of proceedings before the national courts of England and France. Having made this choice I believe that it is in accordance, not only with the prescription exemplified in the English cases above that those who make agreements for the resolution of disputes must show good reasons for departing from them, but also with the interests of the orderly regulation of commerce that having promised to take their complaints to the experts and if necessary to the arbitrators, that is where the appellants should go."[83]

Why has ADR developed as it has?

Business and cultural considerations
It may be said that ADR is simply old wine in a new bottle, with a new label. **1–91**
As one commentator has said:

"In my view, modern dispute resolution techniques, although couched in the language of sociology—and indeed often in a jargon of their own—reflect

---

[83] *per* Lord Mustill, *Channel Tunnel Group Ltd v Balfour Beatty Construction Ltd* [1993] A.C. 334 at 353; [1993] 1 Lloyd's Rep. 291 at 300–301. To resolve any possible doubts, the English Arbitration Act 1996, in s.9(2), now provides that an application to enforce an arbitration agreement by staying court proceedings may be made "notwithstanding that the matter is to be referred to arbitration only after the exhaustion of other dispute resolution procedures".

techniques used by successful outsiders for centuries in settling disputes in many cultures and legal systems."[84]

Certainly, there is nothing new about trying to settle a dispute by negotiation. It is what every sensible businessman and politician[85] should do. Nor is there anything new in turning to an independent third party to see if, from a different perspective, he or she can resolve a dispute which the parties themselves have failed to resolve. This is probably how resort to arbitration itself began, "with mediation no doubt merging into adjudication".[86] What is new is the different form, structure and impetus which ADR has given to the negotiating and decision-making process; and what is clear is that these new methods have struck a chord not only with businessmen, but with lawyers, judges and even governments.

Why should this be? There are at least two important, and distinct, reasons. The first is a question of time and money—of searching for a solution that is relatively quick and inexpensive. The second is a question of approach—of wishing to avoid confrontation, if possible. This wish may spring from a simple desire to maintain friendly relations (as, perhaps, in a partnership dispute) or to maintain a potentially profitable business relationship (as in a joint venture, for instance). However, the wish may have deeper roots than this—it may be part of a tradition that dislikes confrontation:

" . . . arbitration has a striking cultural drawback in an increasingly important sub-set of disputes—those between Asian and Western parties. The traditions of many Asian trading nations abhor such a confrontational form of dispute resolution. They prefer face-saving mutually agreeable compromises to awards proclaiming one party's rights. Consequently, Asian parties may resist clauses that send disputes straight to arbitration."[87]

1–92   Countries in the common law tradition, led notably by the US but including England, Australia and New Zealand, have shown themselves ready to adopt ADR. So have countries with a civil law tradition.[88]

---

[84] Holtzmann, workshop on "The Peaceful Settlement of International Disputes in Europe: Future Prospects", Hague Academy of International Law, September 1990.

[85] Consider, *e.g.*, the Churchillian phrase that "Jaw-jaw is better than war-war".

[86] Mustill, "Arbitration: History and Background" (1989) 6 Journal of International Arbitration 43.

[87] Burton, "Combining Conciliation with Arbitration of International Commercial Disputes" (1995) 18 Hastings International & Comparative Law Review 636 at 637. Thus, it is said, parties may prefer, in the tradition of Confucius, to conduct business and to settle their differences within the cultural ethic of "Li" (peace, harmony and conciliation) rather than "Fa" (the strict application of legal rules).

[88] See, *e.g.*, the Report by Maître Jean-Claude Goldsmith at the ICC Institute Seminar, Paris and Brussels 1995.

ADR—future perspectives

For some of its protagonists, ADR is a way of resolving disputes which will **1-93** make existing conventional techniques as outmoded as the coach and horses. This is probably going too far. There are useful practices to be learnt from ADR (including strict limits upon the extent of disclosure and time-limits for hearings) which can be readily adopted to reduce the time and expense of more conventional methods of resolving disputes, such as arbitration.[89] However, there are certain limits to the ADR process.

- First, ADR is likely to work better where the parties, and the mediator, have the same (or a similar) national background. It is easy to see how, for example, a well respected former judge of a US appeals court may be able to persuade two US corporations to settle their differences. It is less easy if the parties are of different nationalities and backgrounds and the mediator is of a third nationality.

- Secondly, the aim of ADR is compromise—and there are some disputes which cannot, or should not, be compromised. An obvious example is where the dispute concerns the interpretation of a clause in a standard form contract. The interpretation given to that clause may affect hundreds, or thousands, of other contracts. What is needed by the insurers, bankers, shipowners or others who rely on the document is a decision, not a compromise solution.

- Thirdly, there are cases where, to put it starkly, one party is wholly right and the other is wholly wrong. Why should the party that is wholly right take 50 per cent or less of its entitlement? Humanity's sense of justice (and injustice) is strong, as anyone with children will know. Although this is perhaps a moral rather than a material point, it is probably unwise to go too far in creating a situation where points of principle are no longer important and all that matters is to "do a deal".

- Fourthly, one party may find it better to delay and not agree to any meaningful resolution of the dispute—particularly if the business relationship has broken down and there is no prospect of its being renewed. In such a case, any attempt at mediation is likely to be a waste of time and money; what is needed is an enforceable decision, not a suggested compromise solution that is simply ignored.

- Finally, it has to be accepted that the mediation process may fail, in which case it will only have added to the delay and expense of reaching a resolution of the dispute.

---

[89] The original authors were proponents of such practices for both litigation and arbitration long before ADR came into fashion.

The need for judicial control

1–94   If ADR does develop as a widely accepted method of resolving commercial disputes, there will almost certainly be abuses, which means that there will be a need for judicial control, much as the arbitral process is subject to control to ensure that the parties are treated "with equality" (to use the words of the Model Law) and that the arbitral tribunal is impartial. There may be corrupt or dishonest mediators; or there may be defendants who (as is reported to be the case in California) use the process in order to find out the strengths and weaknesses of the claimant's case—and, in particular, what is the least that he or she will accept—and then make use of this knowledge to fight the case in the courts. Judicial control may be needed, as a measure of consumer protection; but the risk then is that the process will lose the speed and flexibility which is one of its major attractions.

ADR and arbitration combined

1–95   The mediation process may fail, in which case the parties will still be left with an unresolved dispute. If this happens, what is to be done? Med/Arb, as it is called in an unattractive but convenient abbreviation, has already been described.[90] It contemplates that there will be a move from mediation, if unsuccessful, to arbitration. However, the fact that the same person may be called upon to fulfil both the role of mediator and arbitrator may well give rise to serious problems.[91] What would be sensible, it is suggested, is to combine a mediation clause (if this is what the parties wish) with a clause providing for arbitration, if mediation fails.

A "two-tier" system of dispute resolution has long been common in major construction contracts, as already noted,[92] and some form of mediation could well constitute the first tier. If this is to be done, the appropriate clause or agreement needs to be carefully drafted, so as to ensure that the mediation process is not allowed to drag on interminably, putting at risk the prospects of an effective arbitration.

Amiable compositeur, *equity clauses,* "ex aequo et bono"

1–96   Arbitration agreements sometimes specify that the arbitrators are to act as "*amiable compositeurs*" or, if the agreement has been drafted by public international lawyers or scholars,[93] that the arbitrators will decide *ex aequo et bono*. Such clauses are likely to become more usual, given the influence of the Model Law which specifically permits an arbitral tribunal to decide in accordance with equity if the parties authorise it to do so.[94]

---

[90] Above at para.1–82.

[91] *ibid.*

[92] *e.g.* in the discussion of expert determination.

[93] The terms are not meant to be mutually exclusive.

[94] Model Law, Art.28(3); and see, for instance, the English Arbitration Act 1996, which (in s.46) allows the parties to agree what "considerations" should govern the substance of the dispute.

3. WHAT KIND OF ARBITRATION?

(a) Introduction

The simple form of arbitration clause which is set out earlier in this chapter **1–97**
provides for a reference to ad hoc arbitration before a sole arbitrator. Since the
clause does not specify any particular set of rules for the conduct of the
arbitration, this will have to be worked out either by the parties or, in default of
agreement, by a decision of the arbitrator. A more usual clause for ad hoc
arbitration would include a reference to the rules which were to be applicable (for
instance, the UNCITRAL Arbitration Rules or if it was a trade or commodity
arbitration, the rules of the relevant association). It would also probably specify
a reference to a tribunal of three arbitrators, unless the amounts at stake were not
likely to be large.

The alternative to an ad hoc arbitration is an arbitration conducted under the
rules of a named arbitral institution. It is helpful first to consider the distinction
between ad hoc and institutional arbitration and then to look at some of the more
important arbitral institutions operating in the field of international commercial
arbitration.

An ad hoc arbitration is one which is conducted pursuant to rules agreed by the
parties themselves or laid down by the arbitral tribunal. Parties are free to work
out and establish rules of procedure for themselves, so long as these rules treat
the parties with equality and allow each party a reasonable opportunity of
presenting its case. Alternatively, and more usually, the relevant arbitration
clause will provide for the arbitration to be conducted according to an established
set of rules, such as the UNCITRAL Arbitration Rules.

But this is not the only way in which ad hoc arbitrations may be conducted. If **1–98**
the case is important enough, and, in particular if a state entity is involved, the
arbitration may take place under the provisions of a "tailor-made" submission
agreement. This submission agreement will usually be a detailed document,
negotiated and agreed between the parties and the arbitral tribunal and, amongst
other things, confirming the establishment of the tribunal and setting out the
substantive law, the place (or "seat") of arbitration and the procedural rules upon
which the parties have agreed.

(b) Institutional and ad hoc arbitration

In contrast to an ad hoc arbitration, an "institutional" arbitration is one that is **1–99**
administered by a specialist arbitral institution under its own rules of arbitration.[95] There are many such institutions. Amongst the better known are ICDR—-

---

[95] As a further refinement, it should be mentioned that an administered arbitration may be wholly
administered or semi-administered. An example of wholly-administered arbitration is that of
ICSID, where the Centre provides a full service to the arbitral tribunal. An example of semi-
administered arbitration is that of certain arbitrations conducted in England under the Rules of the
Chartered Institute of Arbitrators: in these cases, the Institute collects the initial advance on costs
from the parties, appoints the arbitral tribunal and then leaves it to the arbitral tribunal to
communicate with the parties, arrange meetings and hearings and so on.

which is a division of the American Arbitration Association (AAA)—the IACAC, ICSID, the ICC and LCIA. There are also regional arbitral institutions, such as those in Singapore and the Chambers of Commerce of Switzerland, Stockholm and Vienna.

The rules of these arbitral institutions tend to follow a similar pattern. They are expressly formulated for arbitrations that are to be administered by the institution concerned and they generally come into play under an institutional arbitration clause in the agreement between the parties. The clause recommended by the ICC, for instance, states:

> "All disputes arising in connection with the present contract shall be finally settled under the Rules of Conciliation and Arbitration of the International Chamber of Commerce by one or more arbitrators appointed in accordance with the said Rules."

In common with other institutional clauses, this clause is a convenient short-form method of incorporating into the agreement between the parties a detailed book of rules that will govern any arbitration that may take place in the future. An obvious advantage of such a clause is that even if, at some future stage, one party proves reluctant to go ahead with arbitration proceedings, it will never-theless be possible to arbitrate effectively, because a set of rules exists to regulate the way in which the arbitral tribunal is to be appointed and the arbitration is to be administered and conducted.

(c) Institutional arbitration—advantages and disadvantages

1–100   Rules laid down by established arbitral institutions (and most notably those of the ICC, ICSID and the LCIA) will generally have proved to work well in practice; and they will have undergone periodic revision in consultation with experienced practitioners to take account of new developments in the law and practice of international commercial arbitration.

As already mentioned, the rules themselves are generally set out in a small booklet. Parties who agree to submit any dispute to arbitration in accordance with the rules of a named institution effectively incorporate that institution's book of rules into their arbitration agreement.

Advantages

1–101   Automatic incorporation of a book of rules is one of the principal advantages of institutional arbitration. Suppose, for instance, that there is a challenge to an arbitrator, on the grounds of lack of independence and impartiality; or suppose that the arbitration is to take place before an arbitral tribunal of three arbitrators and the defending party is unwilling to arbitrate and fails or refuses to appoint an arbitrator? The book of rules will provide for this situation.

It will also contain provisions under which the arbitration may proceed in the event of any other default by one of the parties. The ICC Rules, for instance, stipulate that:

"If any of the parties, although duly summoned, fails to appear without valid excuse, the Arbitral Tribunal shall have the power to proceed with the hearing."[96]

In a default situation, such rules are of considerable value.

Another important advantage of institutional arbitration is that most arbitral **1–102** institutions provide trained staff to administer the arbitration. They will ensure that the arbitral tribunal is appointed, that advance payments are made in respect of the fees and expenses of the arbitrators, that time-limits are kept in mind and, generally, that the arbitration is run as smoothly as possible. If an arbitration is not administered in this way the work of administering it will have to be undertaken by the arbitral tribunal itself. With the agreement of the parties it may delegate some of its tasks (such as the selection and reservation of rooms for the hearing) to one of the parties, usually the claimant, or to a secretary or registrar specially appointed to take care of financial and administrative arrangements.[97]

An additional advantage of institutional arbitration is where the institution itself reviews the arbitral tribunal's award in draft form, before it is sent to the parties. Such a review, which is undertaken notably by the ICC, serves as a measure of "quality control". The institution does not comment on the substance of the award, or interfere in any way with the decision of the arbitral tribunal, but it does ensure that the tribunal has dealt with all the issues before it and that its award covers such matters (which are sometimes forgotten) as interest and costs.

Disadvantages

Under some institutional rules,[98] the parties pay a fixed fee in advance for the **1–103** costs of the arbitration—that is to say, the fees and expenses of the institution and of the arbitral tribunal. This fixed fee is assessed on an *ad valorem* basis. If the amounts at stake are considerable, and the parties are represented by advisers experienced in international commercial arbitration, it may be worthwhile to consider conducting the arbitration ad hoc rather than under institutional rules.[99] On the other hand, the ability to pay a fixed fee for the arbitration may work to the parties' advantage (and to the disadvantage of the arbitrators, in terms of their fees).

A further disadvantage is the delay which results from the need to process certain steps in the arbitral proceedings through the machinery of the arbitral institution involved. Conversely, the time-limits imposed by institutional rules are often unrealistically short. A claimant is unlikely to be troubled by this, since

---

[96] ICC Arbitration Rules Art.21.2.
[97] See Ch.4.
[98] *e.g.* those of the ICC.
[99] This may be done by agreement of the parties, even if the arbitration clause in the original agreement provided for institutional arbitration; however, to sound a cautionary note, such a course can lead to complete disaster, leaving the claimant without any effective remedy; see, *e.g.*, ICC Case No.3383, reported in (1982) VII Yearbook Commercial Arbitration 119.

he usually has plenty of time in which to prepare his case before he delivers it to the respondent, or to the relevant arbitral institution, and so set the clock running. However, a respondent is likely to find himself pressed for time, particularly in a case (such as a dispute under an international construction contract) which involves consideration of voluminous documents and where the claim which is put forward may, in fact, prove to be a whole series of claims on largely unrelated matters.

Although extensions of time will usually be granted, either by the institution concerned or by the arbitral tribunal, the respondent is placed in the invidious position of having to seek extensions of time from the very outset of the case: he starts on the wrong foot, so to speak. If the respondent is a state or state entity, the problem is worse. The time-limits laid down in institutional rules usually fail to take account of the time which a state or state entity needs to obtain approval of important decisions, through its own official channels. In the ICC Rules for example, the time-limit for rendering a final award is six months, although this may be (and frequently is) extended by the ICC's International Court of Arbitration.[1]

(d) Ad hoc arbitration—advantages and disadvantages

Advantages

1–104   One distinct advantage of ad hoc arbitration is that it may be shaped to meet the wishes of the parties and the facts of the particular dispute. It needs the co-operation of the parties and their advisers for this to be done efficiently and effectively; but if such co-operation is forthcoming, the difference between an ad hoc arbitration and an institutional arbitration is like the difference between a tailor-made suit and one that is bought "off-the-peg".

It is, however, a time-consuming process to draft special rules for an ad hoc arbitration. Time and money can be saved by adopting, or adapting, rules of procedure which have been specially formulated for the purpose. There are various sets of rules which are suitable, of which the best known are the UNCITRAL Rules. It is not advisable to try to adopt or adapt institutional rules (such as those of the ICC) for use in an ad hoc arbitration, since such rules make repeated references to the institution concerned and will not work properly or effectively without it.

The greater flexibility offered by ad hoc arbitration means that many important arbitrations involving a state party are conducted on this basis. Many of the well-known arbitrations under oil concession agreements (including the *Sapphire*, *Texaco*, *BP* and *Liamco* arbitrations) were ad hoc arbitrations.[2]

---

[1] One commentator has quoted with approval the authors' suggestion that institutional time-limits "are often unrealistically short" and has added that, although speed may be an undoubted good in standard commercial arbitrations, "rules which cater to that desideratum may not be appropriate in cases involving difficult issues of public policy": Toope, *Mixed International Arbitration* (Grotius Publications Ltd, 1990), p.204.

[2] These cases are considered in more detail in Ch.2.

In the *Aminoil* arbitration between the Government of Kuwait and the American Independent Oil Company, the inherent flexibility of ad hoc proceedings was a considerable advantage in a dispute involving legal issues of great importance. These issues were defined in a way that considerably shortened the time spent in dealing with the case.[3] Moreover, certain practices that are common in arbitrations between states were followed to advantage in this arbitration. For example, the parties each appointed an agent[4] to represent it for the purposes of the proceedings. The day-to-day presentation of the Government's case was left in the hands of the external lawyers retained by the Government. The agent alone had authority to make immediate decisions on behalf of the Government on the many practical and logistical questions that necessarily arise during the conduct of a major arbitration; and, of course, it was the agent who was in touch with his Government on any issues of policy that arose. The procedure adopted also provided that the parties should file their pleadings at the same time, which they did over a period of months in an exchange of memorials, counter-memorials and replies. By this simple device, neither party was labelled as respondent—an appellation that is sometimes resented, when each party considers that it has justifiable claims against the other. In the same spirit, the arbitral tribunal ordered that the Government should lead on some issues (where it was, so to speak, the claimant and had to discharge the burden of proof) and that Aminoil should lead on others.

1–105

There is much to be said in favour of ad hoc arbitration where the sums at stake are large—and in particular, perhaps, where a state or state entity is involved and issues of public policy and sovereignty are likely to arise.[5] In ad hoc arbitration, it is possible to devise a procedure which is fair to both parties, whilst being sensitive to the particular needs of the state party.

1–106

Disadvantages

The principal disadvantage of ad hoc arbitration is that it depends for its full effectiveness on co-operation between the parties and their lawyers, backed up by an adequate legal system in the place of arbitration. It is easy to delay arbitral proceedings by refusing to appoint an arbitrator, or by challenging the impartiality of one of the arbitrators, or by raising jurisdictional issues; and if one of the parties proves difficult or recalcitrant at the outset of the proceedings, there will be no arbitral tribunal in existence and no book of rules available to deal with the situation. It will then be necessary to rely on such provisions of law as may be

1–107

---

[3] For an account of the *Aminoil* arbitration, in which the original authors took part on behalf of the Kuwaiti Government, see Redfern, "The arbitration between the Government of Kuwait and Aminoil" [1985] B.Y.I.L. 65.

[4] The practice of appointing agents to represent governments in international arbitrations was codified in The Hague Convention of 1907, which (in Art.62) provided: "The parties are entitled to appoint special agents to attend the Tribunal to act as intermediaries between themselves and the Tribunal. They are further authorised to retain for the defence of their rights and interests before the Tribunal counsel or advocates appointed by them for this purpose."

[5] To this effect, see in particular Toope, *Mixed International Arbitration* (Grotius Publications Ltd, 1990), pp.212–217.

available to offer the necessary support.[6] Only when an arbitral tribunal is in existence, and a proper set of rules has been established, will an ad hoc arbitration proceed as smoothly as an institutional arbitration if one of the parties fails or refuses to play its part in the proceedings.

(e) Arbitral institutions

1–108   There are numerous institutions around the world which exist to administer international arbitrations. Some, such as the Hong Kong Arbitration Centre or the Cairo Regional Centre for Arbitration, are directed primarily towards a particular country or region. Some, such as the maritime associations in Paris or London,[7] serve a particular trade or industry, whilst others, such as WIPO, offer their services for a particular type of dispute.

Each arbitral centre tends to have its own set of rules, although in the more recent centres these are often (sensibly) based on the UNCITRAL Rules. Each centre also usually has its own model form of arbitration clause. It is usual (but not essential) to use one of these model forms if institutional arbitration is to be adopted. No fee is payable to the institution for referring to it in an arbitration agreement. Payment only starts if it becomes necessary to make use of the institution's services, either for the appointment of an arbitrator or for the conduct of an arbitration.

In view of the great number of arbitral institutions, or centres, in the world and the fact that new ones continue to come into existence, it is not practicable to list them all. What is proposed is, first, to set out the type of considerations which the parties (or their lawyers) should have in mind in choosing an arbitral institution; and, secondly, to review briefly some of the better known institutions.

What to look for in an arbitral institution

1–109   An arbitral institution will, of necessity, charge fees for its services to cover the expenses of its premises, its staff, its publications and so on. Since these fees will add to the cost of arbitration (in some cases substantially), parties and their lawyers should have some concept of what to look for in any given arbitral institution. It is suggested that the basic requirements should include the following.

A degree of permanency

1–110   Disputes frequently arise many years after the making of the original commercial agreement, particularly in long-term contracts. It is important that the institutions named in the arbitration clause should still be in existence when the dispute arises, otherwise, the arbitration agreement may prove to be "inoperative

---

[6] See Ch.4.

[7] The London Maritime Arbitration Association receives literally thousands of requests for arbitration per year—although not all of these cases proceed to arbitration, and others may be resolved on the basis of documents only.

or incapable of being performed", in the words of the New York Convention, and the only recourse will be to national courts. It might be said, with some justice, that this comment militates against the creation of new arbitral institutions in developing parts of the world and so is unfairly biased in favour of established institutions. There is truth in this; but a lawyer who advises his or her client to select a particular arbitration centre will need to be confident that the advice is good. It is easier to have such confidence if the institution or centre that is chosen has an established track record or, if it is a recent creation, has some reasonable guarantee of permanency.[8]

Modern rules of arbitration

The practice of international commercial arbitration changes as new laws and **1–111** procedures come into existence, both nationally and internationally. It is important that the rules of the arbitral institutions should be altered to reflect these changes[9] and not rest in some comfortable time warp. It is difficult to conduct an effective, modern arbitration under rules designed for a different era. Parties are entitled to expect that institutional rules will be reviewed, and if necessary, revised at regular intervals.[10]

Qualified staff

One of the main objects of an arbitral institution is to assist arbitrators and the **1–112** parties in the conduct of an arbitration. This assistance may extend not only to explaining the rules, making sure that time-limits are observed, collecting fees, arranging visas and reserving accommodation, but also to advising on appropriate procedures by reference to past experience. It is a task that requires a combination of qualities—tact and diplomacy as well as legal knowledge and experience. It is an area in which the ICC sets the standard, with each arbitration being under the supervision of a designated "counsel", drawn from the ICC's staff of experienced and multilingual lawyers.

Reasonable charges

Some arbitral institutions assess their own administrative fees and expenses, **1–113** and the fees payable to the arbitrator, by reference to a sliding scale which is based on the amounts in dispute (including the amount of any counterclaim). This has the advantage of certainty, in that the parties can find out at a reasonably early stage what the total cost of the arbitration is likely to be. However, it operates as a disincentive to experienced arbitrators if the amounts in dispute are not substantial. Other institutions, such as the LCIA, assess their administrative costs and expenses, and the fees of the arbitrators, by reference to the time spent

---

[8] As with WIPO, which is an agency of the United Nations.
[9] As happened in England, following the Arbitration Act 1996.
[10] After some hesitation, the ICC published new rules effective from January 1, 1998, the last minor revision to the Rules having been made 10 years earlier. The LCIA also published new rules, effective from the same date.

on the case (with an upper and lower limit, so far as the fees of the arbitrators are concerned).

Some well-known institutions

The International Chamber of Commerce

1–114 The International Court of Arbitration of the International Chamber of Commerce was established in Paris in 1923. The ICC has played an important role in promoting international laws on arbitration (such as the New York Convention) and is one of the world's leading organisations in the arbitration of international commercial disputes.[11] It should be noted, however, that the so-called "International Court of Arbitration", as already mentioned, is not a "court" in the sense of a court of law. It is, in effect, the administrative body of the ICC, with representatives from many different countries.

ICC arbitrations are conducted by an arbitral tribunal established for each particular case. If the parties have agreed that there is to be a sole arbitrator, they may wish to nominate a suitable person and simply ask the court to confirm their choice. Otherwise, the appointment will be made by the court itself. If the parties have agreed that there should be three arbitrators, the parties each nominate one arbitrator for confirmation by the court and the third arbitrator will be appointed directly by the court, unless the parties agree otherwise. Where there is no agreement as to the number of arbitrators, the ICC will decide whether there should be one or three, its decision depending upon the size and nature of the dispute.

The day-to-day work of the ICC is carried out by the Secretary-General and other counsel who, as already mentioned, besides being multilingual, provide administrative guidance and assistance to the arbitral tribunals whose cases are assigned to them.[12] The latest version of the ICC Rules came into effect on January 1, 1998. They provide an effective modern code for the conduct of an international commercial arbitration, whilst still leaving considerable freedom of action to the parties and their arbitral tribunal.

1–115 Two features of these Rules call for particular comment, as they are not always properly understood. The first is the provision for Terms of Reference; the second is the provision for scrutiny of awards by the ICC's court.

Once the arbitral tribunal receives the file of documents from the Secretariat of the ICC, it is required[13] to draw up Terms of Reference which set out, *inter alia,* the names and addresses of the parties and their representatives, a summary of

---

[11] Since its inception in 1923 to the end of 2003—a period of some 80 years—the ICC has received a total of 13,101 requests for arbitration. More than half of these were filed in the 15 years between 1988 and 2003.

[12] There is an abundance of literature on the work of the ICC. The leading authority is Craig, Park & Paulsson, *International Chamber of Commerce Arbitration* (3rd ed., Oceana Publications, 1997). For a commentary on the 1998 Rules of Arbitration, in English and French, see Verbist & Imhoos, "The New 1998 ICC Rules of Arbitration" (1997) 8 Revue de Droit des Affaires Internationales (International Business Law Journal) 991.

[13] ICC Arbitration Rules, Art.18.

their claims, the place of arbitration and, unless the arbitral tribunal considers it inappropriate, a list of the issues to be determined.

It is a useful discipline for an arbitral tribunal to draw up such a document at the outset of an arbitration. Indeed, many arbitrators will go through a similar exercise even if not obliged to do so by the rules under which they are operating. In particular, if the "issues to be determined" can be defined, this helps to focus the attention of both the parties and the arbitrators on what is really at stake. But it is not always easy to determine the issues at a relatively early stage of the proceedings and so this is no longer a mandatory requirement, as it was under previous editions of the ICC Rules.

When the arbitral tribunal is ready to deliver its award, the tribunal is required[14] to submit it in draft form for "scrutiny" by the ICC's court. As already stated, the court does not interfere with the arbitrators' decision—and it would be wrong to do so. However, the court does check the formal correctness of the award, to ensure that it deals with all the matters with which it is required to deal (including costs) and that there are no obvious misprints or arithmetical errors.   **1–116**

The LCIA

The LCIA owes its origins to the London Chamber of Arbitration, which was founded in 1892. The LCIA aims to provide a comprehensive service for disputes arising out of commercial transactions, irrespective of the nationality of those involved. Its "Arbitration Court" consists of arbitration practitioners drawn from the major trading nations, including China and Japan. It has its own book of rules, revised in 1998, which are designed to take the arbitral tribunal step by step through the procedural stages of the arbitration, from the initial Request for Arbitration to the eventual award. These rules are drawn in more detail than those of other institutions and so provide particularly useful guidance to both parties and tribunals. The LCIA is also prepared to act as an appointing authority and as arbitration administrator under the UNCITRAL Arbitration Rules.   **1–117**

The American Arbitration Association

The AAA was established in 1926 to study, promote and administer procedures for the resolution of disputes of all kinds through the use of arbitration and other private techniques of dispute settlement.   **1–118**

The considerable growth in international commercial arbitration over recent years has led the AAA to establish a separate division. Its first centre was opened in New York in 1996 and a European centre was opened as the ICDR in Dublin, in the Republic of Ireland, in June 2001.

In addition to administering arbitrations under its own rules, the AAA also administers IACAC arbitrations and makes its services available, if required, in arbitrations conducted under the UNCITRAL Arbitration Rules, whether those arbitrations are held inside or outside the US.

[14] ICC Arbitration Rules, Art.27.

The WIPO Arbitration Centre

1–119   The WIPO Arbitration Centre was established in 1994, under the auspices of the World Intellectual Property Organisation which, in various forms, has been in existence as an intergovernmental agency for over 100 years, since the conclusion of the Paris Convention for the Protection of Industrial Property in 1883.

The WIPO Arbitration Centre, based in Geneva, has an excellent modern set of rules, both for mediation and for arbitration. The Centre maintains a list of arbitrators and when called upon to appoint an arbitrator, makes use of the "list procedure": each party is sent an identical list of potential arbitrators and is asked to strike out anyone to whom it objects, and to mark the remaining names in order of preference.

Domain names

1–120   The internet revolution has given birth to a new category of intellectual property dispute relating to domain names. In December 1999, the Internet Corporation for Assigned Names and Numbers ("ICANN") adopted the Uniform Domain Name Dispute Resolution Policy ("UDRP"), which is incorporated by reference into the registration agreement for any internet domain name. The UDRP provides for mandatory dispute resolution before a limited number of approved dispute resolution service providers. The WIPO Arbitration and Mediation Centre is the leading such service provider (others include the CPR Institute for Dispute Resolution and e-Resolution), which has administered over 20,000 domain name disputes since the UDRP came into effect. These disputes are subjected to online procedures, are generally resolved within two months of the filing of a request and only very rarely involve oral hearings.

(f) Arbitrations involving a state or state entity

1–121   Disputes between states belong to the realm of public international law. However, where the state exercises a commercial function, either by itself or through a state entity, and enters into a business relationship with a private party, any disputes which arise are likely to be referred either to the courts of the state concerned or to international commercial arbitration. Almost invariably, the private party to such a contract will prefer to submit to arbitration as a "neutral" process, rather than to the courts of the state with which it is in dispute.

At one time, there was almost a tidal wave of state ownership, as newly developing nations, following the example of the former socialist states, emerged as owners and operators of airlines, merchant fleets, oilfields, oil companies, refineries and process plants—as well as banking, investment and trading corporations. This trend to state ownership was encouraged by resolutions of the United Nations directed to the establishment of a New International Economic Order, in which the state was seen as taking the dominant role in the control both of its own resources and of transnational corporations operating on its territory. However, as the tide once came in, it has now gone out: "privatisation" has replaced nationalisation.

In consequence, state ownership has diminished in importance. Nevertheless, there are still many arbitrations in which a state or state entity is concerned. Many factors must be weighed in the balance when a state or state entity considers whether or not to submit to arbitration. There are political considerations, such as the effect which a refusal to go ahead with arbitration might have on relations with the state to which the foreign claimant belongs. There are also economic considerations, such as the loss of foreign investment which a refusal to arbitrate might bring about. There are legal considerations such as the effect of an award being granted *in absentia*, as happened in the Libyan oil nationalisation arbitrations.[15] In addition, questions of national prestige are involved, in being seen as a state that is prepared to honour its commitments. It is sometimes said that the right of a state to claim immunity from legal proceedings forms part of its sovereign dignity. However, one might prefer to agree with a well-known English judge who said: "It is more in keeping with the dignity of a foreign sovereign to submit himself to the rule of law than to claim to be above it."[16]

Arbitrations in which one of the parties is a state or state entity may take place **1–122** under the rules of institutions such as those already discussed.[17] However, there are two international institutions that are usually concerned only with disputes where one of the parties is a state or state entity. These are the International Centre for the Settlement of Investment Disputes (ICSID) in Washington and the Permanent Court of Arbitration (the PCA) at The Hague.

ICSID

ICSID was established by the Washington Convention of 1965.[18] This conven- **1–123** tion, which is formally known as the "Convention on the Settlement of Investment Disputes between States and Nationals of Other States," or less formally as "the ICSID Convention", entered into force on October 14, 1966. It was formulated by the executive directors of the International Bank for Reconstruction and Development (the World Bank) and was submitted by them to the governments of the Member States of the Bank in 1965.

The Washington Convention broke new ground. It gave both private individuals and corporations who were "investors" in a foreign state the right to bring legal proceedings against that state, before an international arbitral tribunal. It was no longer necessary for such investors to ask their own government to take up their case at an inter-state level: the so-called method of "diplomatic protection". They now had the right of direct recourse against the foreign state in their

[15] The three major international arbitrations arising out of the nationalisation by the Libyan Government of oil concession agreements with foreign corporations which still had many years to run are discussed in Ch.2. The Libyan Government declined to take part in the arbitrations and so its case went, if not unconsidered, at least unargued.

[16] Lord Denning in *Rahimtoola v The Nizam of Hyderabad* [1958] A.C. 379 at 418.

[17] A considerable number of arbitrations involving states or state entities take place under the ICC Rules, for example.

[18] Convention on the Settlement of Investment Disputes between States and Nationals of Other States, done at Washington, March 18, 1965. United Nations Treaty Series (1966), Vol.575, No.8359, p.160. For a more detailed review of ICSID arbitrations, see Ch.11.

own name and on their own behalf. This was a significant development. As a distinguished commentator pointed out:

> "At the time the Convention was concluded, some of its most important features represented significant new developments, though in the light of subsequent advances in international law they now appear almost common-place. For the first time a system was instituted under which non-State entities—corporations or individuals—could sue States directly; in which State immunity was much restricted; under which international law could be applied directly to the relationship between the investor and the host State; in which the operation of the local remedies rule was excluded; and in which the tribunal's award would be directly enforceable within the territories of the State's parties.
>
> The system was at first limited to cases where both the national State of the investor and the State party to the case were Parties to the Convention. This meant that if one party to the dispute did not meet this requirement, the matter could not be submitted to ICSID, even if both parties so wished. This problem was solved in 1978 by the creation by the Bank of the 'Additional Facility' which permits recourse—albeit imperfect—to the main elements of the ICSID system even if only one party meets the requirements, provided that both have given their consent.
>
> Consent to jurisdiction under the system was originally foreseen as deriving principally from express references to it in the arbitration clauses of invest-ment contracts. However, the sources of consent have been significantly widened by the development of recourse to ICSID on the basis of provisions in inter-State bilateral investment protection and investment guarantee agree-ments as well as by multilateral arrangements such as the North American Free Trade Agreement."[19]

1–124   The Washington Convention was indeed a significant development towards establishing a system under which individuals and corporations could demand redress directly against a foreign state, by way of conciliation or arbitration. The impact of the Convention is studied in more detail in Ch.11, which relates to investor-state disputes.

ICSID procedures

1–125   ICSID is based at the principal office of the World Bank in Washington. It helps to promote the settlement of investment disputes by means of two different procedures—conciliation and arbitration. These procedures are available on four conditions: the parties must have agreed to submit their dispute to ICSID; the dispute must be between a contracting state (or one of its subdivisions or

---

[19] Sir Elihu Lauterpacht, in his foreword to Christoph Schreuer, *The ICSID Convention: A commen-tary* (Cambridge University Press, 2001), pp.xi-xii.

agencies) and a national of *another* contracting state; it must be a legal dispute; and it must arise directly out of an investment.[20]

The term "investment" is not defined in the Washington Convention, but in practice it has been taken to cover the investment of services and technology, as well as more traditional forms of capital investment. ICSID has full international legal personality; and persons appointed to act as conciliators or arbitrators enjoy immunity from all legal process with respect to acts performed by them in the exercise of their functions, unless ICSID has waived this immunity.[21]

The Washington Convention provides that each contracting state shall recognise an award rendered pursuant to it as binding and shall enforce the pecuniary obligations imposed by that award within its territories as if it were a final judgment of a court in that state.[22] An ICSID award is enforceable in a contracting state without any possibility of revision or review under the law of that state.[23]

ICSID—an international institution

Because it is governed by an international treaty, rather than by a national law, **1–126** an ICSID arbitration[24] is truly delocalised or denationalised. The exclusion of national law from any control of an ICSID arbitration is made plain in the provisions of the Washington Convention governing challenge, recognition and enforcement of an ICSID award. Under Art.53 of the Convention, the award of ICSID arbitrators is stated to be binding on the parties and not subject to any appeal or any other remedy, except those provided for in the Convention itself. These remedies are as to interpretation of the meaning or scope of the award[25]; revision on the ground of discovery of a previous unknown fact of decisive importance[26]; and annulment by an ad hoc committee.[27]

This last provision for annulment creates a situation in which the award of a tribunal of three arbitrators appointed by or on behalf of the parties may be set aside by another (ad hoc) committee of arbitrators of equal status, whose own

---

[20] Washington Convention, Art.25(1). For an authoritative review of the Convention, see Christoph Schreuer, *The ICSID Convention: A Commentary* (Cambridge University Press, 2001).

[21] Washington Convention, Art.21.

[22] In the UK, for instance, special provisions for the enforcement of ICSID awards are laid down in the Arbitration (International Investment Disputes) Act 1966 (amended, but not in this respect, by the Arbitration Act 1996).

[23] Washington Convention, Art.54(1). This offers the intriguing possibility that an award rendered *ex aequo et bono* in an ICSID arbitration would have to be recognised and enforced in a contracting state which did not allow arbitral tribunals to decide *ex aequo et bono* under its own law.

[24] ICSID arbitrations are more fully discussed in Ch.11.

[25] *ibid.*, Art.50.

[26] *ibid.*, Art.51.

[27] Washington Convention, Art.52: either party may request annulment of an award on specific limited grounds, which are set out in the article, including lack of jurisdiction, violation of due process and failure to give reasons for the award. Such a request is referred to an ad hoc committee of three arbitrators who have power to annul the award.

views are not binding on the next, new tribunal that may then be set up to determine the dispute.[28] This process, an expensive version of the childhood game of snakes and ladders, may go on for years, as is illustrated by the well-known case of *Klockner v The United Republic of Cameroon and SOCAME*. The case arose out of a project by the Klockner group of companies to construct and manage (for a period of at least five years) a fertiliser factory in the Republic of Cameroon. The project failed and Klockner claimed to be owed a substantial sum of money and referred the dispute to ICSID arbitration. The first award of the ICSID tribunal was made in October 1983. It was annulled by an ad hoc committee in May 1985. The dispute was re-submitted to a new tribunal, which made its award in January 1988. Both parties then requested annulment, which was refused by an ad hoc committee in June 1990. This was nine years since the first request for arbitration had been submitted[29] and after consideration of the case by no less than four separate tribunals.

There were similar requests for annulment in the *Amco*[30] case; in *MINE*[31]; and in the closing drama of the *Pyramids* arbitration, which concerned a project to develop two international tourist projects, one of which was to be at the site of the famous Pyramids of Giza, near Cairo.[32] Since then, there have been three more cases in which requests for annulment have been made. This is not the place to review the chequered history of these arbitrations. It is sufficient to indicate that they have led to severe (and it may be thought justified) criticism of the ICSID annulment procedure.[33] At one time, one commentator went so far as to say:

---

[28] See Feldman, "The annulment proceedings and the finality of ICSID Arbital Awards" 19 ICSID Review 85 at 97. The writer adds that the doubts to which this is likely to give rise, for the users of ICSID arbitration, "may be compounded by the fact that, while the tribunal may be appointed by the parties . . . the ad hoc Committee is appointed by the Chairman of ICSID's Administrative Council from the ICSID Panel of Arbitrators. The number of competent arbitrators available from the Panel is more limited than it should be because the Contracting States sometimes nominate persons who are not independent (such as government officials) or who lack experience in arbitration." It would seem, however, that ad hoc committees are now being more cautious about overturning ICSID awards: see, *e.g.*, the carefully considered appraisal by Williams, "Review and Recourse against Awards Rendered under Investment Treaties" *The Journal of World Investment*, Geneva, April 2003, pp.251 *et seq.*

[29] See Williams, *op. cit.*, p.270.

[30] *Amco Asia Corp v Republic of Indonesia (Merits)*, ICSID Award of November 21, 1984, published in (1985) 24 I.L.M. 1022.

[31] *Maritime International Nominees Establishment v Republic of Guinea* (Annulment Proceedings); see ICSID Annual Report (1989). The Annulment Proceedings were discontinued; see ICSID Annual Report (1991).

[32] *The Arab Republic of Egypt v Southern Pacific Properties*, Cour d'Appel de Paris, July 12, 1984; published in English in (1984) 23 I.L.M. 1048. For additional comment, see Redfern, "Jurisdiction Denied: The Pyramid Collapses", 1986, Journal of Business Law, p.15; see also (1984) IX Yearbook Commercial Arbitration 487; Delaume, "The Pyramid Stands" (1993) 8 ICSID Review 231.

[33] See, *e.g.*, Feldman, *op. cit.*, para.1–126; Redfern, "ICSID—Losing its Appeal?" (1987) 3 Arbitration International 98; Reisman, "The Breakdown of the Control Mechanism in ICSID Arbitration" (1989) 4 Duke Law Journal 739; Craig, "Uses and Abuses of Appeal from Awards" (1998) 4 Arbitration International 174.

"ICSID of course has lost much of its credibility as a consequence of the annulments of arbitral awards which have added another negative feature to the massive complexity of its constitution and rules."[34]

It has been suggested, however, that "after a difficult start, the system of **1–127** annulment has now found its proper balance".[35] Indeed, the ad hoc committee in *Vivendi* recognised that "the Committee must take great care to ensure that the reasoning of an arbitral tribunal is clearly understood, and must guard against the annulment of awards for trivial cause".[36]

ICSID's Additional Facility

Under ICSID's "Additional Facility", the ICSID Secretariat may administer **1–128** arbitration or conciliation proceedings between a state and a national of another state, which do not fall within the provisions of the Washington Convention. This facility is available, for example, where one of the parties is not a contracting state or the national of a contracting state.

This is a useful service. It should be emphasised, however, that since proceedings under the Additional Facility are, by definition, outside the provisions of the Washington Convention, they must depend on national (rather than international) law for their efficacy. Indeed, the relevant rules provide that proceedings may *only* be held in countries that are signatories to the New York Convention. This is because the award, not being governed by the Washington Convention, is not enforceable under the extremely effective provisions of that Convention. In these circumstances, an award that qualifies for recognition and enforcement under the New York Convention is regarded as the best alternative. Such awards are outside ICSID's internal review procedures and are thus open to challenge in national courts, as discussed in Ch.11.

The Permanent Court of Arbitration ("the PCA")

The PCA was established by the Convention for the Pacific Settlement of **1–129** International Disputes, concluded at The Hague in 1899, and revised in 1907. It was the product of the first Hague Peace Conference, which was convened on the initiative of Tsar Nicholas II of Russia "with the object of seeking the most effective means of ensuring to all peoples the benefits of a real and durable peace."[37] Sadly, the creation of the PCA did not avert the great conflicts of the twentieth century, but a number of major inter-state disputes were arbitrated there

---

[34] Wetter, "Arbitration in The New Europe" *Mealey's International Arbitration Report*, Vol.5, Issue 11, No.1990, p.15; moreover, the ICSID Rules, which the late Dr Wetter also criticises here, seem to many (including the present authors) to be excellent.

[35] Schreuer, *The ICSID Convention: A Commentary* (Cambridge University Press, 2001), p.903; and Williams, "Review and Recourse against Awards Rendered under Investment Treaties", *op. cit.*, p.270.

[36] *Compania de Aguas del Aconquija SA & Vivendi Universal v Argentina Republic*, ICSID Case No.Arb/97/3, Decision on Annulment, at para.63.

[37] Frederick W. Holls, *The Peace Conference at The Hague* (Macmillan, 1900), pp.8–9.

in its early years,[38] and in 1935 it administered its first commercial arbitration between a private party and a state.[39]

Nowadays, arbitrations involving disputes in which at least one party is a state, a state entity, or an intergovernmental organisation, may be held at the PCA. The parties can choose the procedural rules that will apply, from either the rules of The Hague Conventions of 1899 or 1907; the PCA Optional Rules[40] or other appropriate rules such as the UNCITRAL Arbitration or Conciliation Rules. In several recent cases, ad hoc rules tailored to the specific dispute have been adopted.[41] The fact that the parties are allowed such a broad choice shows a great deal of modernity and forward thinking by the PCA. Arbitrations held under the auspices of the PCA are not required to take place in The Hague, but many parties choose to take advantage of the excellent facilities of the Peace Palace, including hearing and meeting rooms, which are made available for PCA arbitrations. The PCA can also provide the services of the International Bureau for a moderate charge.[42] Given the time and expense involved in conducting a major international commercial arbitration,[43] the PCA's facilities and the staff of the International Bureau have much to commend themselves to parties.[44] By the end of 2003, more than 100 states had become a party to one or other of the two Hague Conventions. Recent growth in membership bodes well for the future of this historic institution.[45]

---

[38] See J.G. Merrills, "The Contribution of the Permanent Court of Arbitration to International Law and to the Settlement of Disputes by Peaceful Means" in *The Permanent Court of Arbitration: International Arbitration and Dispute Resolution, Summaries of Awards, Settlement Agreements and Reports* (P. Hamilton *et al.* eds, Kluwer, 1999) pp.3–27.

[39] *Radio Corporation of America v China* (1941) 8 I.L.R. 26.

[40] There are five different sets of PCA Optional Rules that may be adopted for arbitration. They are the PCA Optional Rules for: (1) arbitrating disputes between two states (1992); (2) arbitrating disputes between two parties of which only one is a state (1993); (3) arbitration involving international organisations (1996); (4) arbitration between international organisations and private parties; and (5) arbitration of disputes relating to natural resources and the environment (2001). The PCA has helpfully produced a single publication, which contains all the relevant documents, except the new environmental rules, and is appropriately entitled "Permanent Court of Arbitration Basic Documents—Conventions, Rules, Model Clauses and Guidelines" (1998).

[41] See, *e.g.*, *Bank of International Settlements Partial Award* (2003) XXVIII Yearbook Commercial Arbitration 100 at 102.

[42] The International Bureau provides administrative support, such as holding documents, deposits, arranging hearings and meetings, and can also provide secretarial, language and communication services. The PCA's Secretary-General heads the International Bureau; his function under the UNCITRAL Arbitration Rules is discussed in Ch.4.

[43] *e.g.* rooms must be hired, and it may prove necessary to appoint a secretary or registrar, as well as translators and stenographers, to assist the arbitral tribunal (and the parties). These matters are discussed further in para.4–86.

[44] The first arbitration between a state and a private party held at the Peace Palace under the PCA's (old) 1962 Rules was *Turriff Construction (Sudan) Ltd v Government of the Republic of Sudan* (discussed in Ch.3). The original authors took part in the arbitration on behalf of Turriff and can testify to the excellence of the facilities at the Peace Palace.

[45] In the last decade, over 20 states have joined the PCA. Recent signatories of one of The Hague Conventions include Belize (2003), Estonia (2003), Ethiopia (2003), Ireland (2002), Kuwait (2003) and Saudi Arabia (2002). (The authors wish to express their thanks to Mr Brooks W. Daly, Special Counsel at the PCA, for his help and information.)

4. Claims Commissions and Tribunals

The Jay Treaty of 1794,[46] between the UK and the US, is generally regarded **1–130** as the new starting point for the development of arbitrations between states. The three disputes that were left unresolved by the Jay Treaty were referred to arbitration, with a "mixed commission" of arbitrators, some of whom were party appointed, whilst the rest were "neutrals". This system of mixed commissions became the usual method of settling claims by one government against another and by the nationals of one government against another.[47]

In more recent years, similar claims tribunals have been set up to determine claims by individuals and corporations. Amongst the most significant of these are the Iran–United States Claims Tribunal, the United Nations Compensation Commission, and the Claims Resolution Tribunal for Dormant Accounts in Switzerland.

The work of each of these tribunals is almost over. Accordingly, there is no longer any need to describe it as fully as was done in the previous edition of this book. Instead, a few brief notes should suffice.

(a) The Iran–United States Claims Tribunal

The Iran–United States Claims Tribunal was established as the central element **1–131** of the arrangements under which the American hostages held in Iran were released in January 1981, in return for the release of Iranian assets frozen in the US.[48] The hundreds of commercial lawsuits pending in the US relating to Iran were suspended by Presidential Order[49] and a fund of $1 billion was released by the US to a "depository bank" to be held in escrow. This account was used for the payment of sums awarded to US claimants by the Tribunal.

The work of the Iran–US Claims Tribunal has been of great significance in the development of international commercial arbitration. This is so for two main reasons. First, the rules governing the Tribunal's operations are based on the UNCITRAL Arbitration Rules[50] and so considerable experience has been gained in the practical, day-to-day operation of these Rules. Secondly, decisions and awards of the Tribunal are published. This published jurisprudence, as well as the substantial analytical literature to which it has given rise, provides a valuable

---

[46] This was a General Treaty of Friendship, Commerce and Navigation and was called the "Jay Treaty" after John Jay, the American Secretary of State.

[47] For a full account of the Jay Treaty and of mixed commissions, see Simpson & Fox, *International Arbitraton* (Stevens, London, 1959).

[48] The full text of the Algiers Declarations of January 19, 1981 is set out at (1982) VII Yearbook Commercial Arbitration 256; and at 1 Iran–US C.T.R. 3.

[49] Suspension of Litigation Against Iran (Executive Order 12294 of February 24, 1981), reproduced in (1982) VII Yearbook Commercial Arbitration 260. More than 4,000 cases have been filed with the Tribunal. As of April 14, 2003, the Tribunal had finalised 3,934 cases by award, decision or order (including the agreed lump-sum settlement of 2,884 "small claims" of less than $250,000 filed by US nationals through the US Government); awarded around $3 billion; and issued over 20,000 orders.

[50] The Final Tribunal Rules of Procedure were adopted on May 3, 1983 and are reprinted in 2 Iran–US C.T.R. 405.

insight into the way in which arbitral tribunals composed of members of different nationalities apply the UNCITRAL Rules and resolve disputes in international trade.[51] As already stated, most of the work of the Iran–US Claims Tribunal has been completed.[52]

(b) The United Nations Compensation Commission

1–132   The United Nations Compensation Commission was established in Geneva by the United Nations Security Council in 1991 to resolve the millions of individual, corporate and state claims against Iraq resulting from Iraq's invasion and occupation of Kuwait.[53]

Although the magnitude of the work of the UNCC dwarfs that of the Iran–US Claims Tribunal,[54] the impact of the UNCC on international commercial arbitration has been less direct. Commercial claims are a comparatively small percentage of the claims before the UNCC, which cover personal injury, death, evacuation and environmental damage. Furthermore, the UNCC did not resolve all cases with individual, reasoned awards. Instead, fundamental factual and legal issues were framed for consideration by the panels of commissioners named for the various claims categories. Test cases were then held and reports and recommendations made, which when adopted were applied to similar cases.

The "mass production" approach to claims enabled the UNCC to work much faster than the Iran–US Claims Tribunal: almost 1,500,000 individual small claims were dealt with on a priority basis.[55] The use of advanced computer technology, with sophisticated databases for claims management, processing, verification and valuation, was another useful first step in the resolution of huge numbers of claims; and the publication of decisions on issues such as depreciation values in the calculation of damages has added to the store of knowledge of lawyers and arbitrators everywhere.[56]

As already stated, most of the work of UNCC has been completed.

---

[51] Among the major books published on the Tribunal and its jurisprudence are: C. Brower & J. Brueschke, *The Iran–United States Claims Tribunal* (Kluwer, 1998); G. Aldrich, *The Jurisprudence of the Iran–United States Claims Tribunal: An Analysis of the Decisions of the Tribunal* (Oxford University Press, 1996); S. Baker & M. Davis, *The UNCITRAL Arbitration Rules in Practice: The Experience of the Iran–United States Claims Tribunal* (Kluwer, 1992); J. van Hoff, *Commentary on the UNCITRAL Arbitration Rules: The Application by the Iran–United States Claims Tribunal* (Kluwer, 1991).

[52] The last commercial case was decided in 2003.

[53] United Nations Security Council Resolution 687. For detailed background on the UNCC, see *The United Nations Compensation Commission* (13th Sokol Colloquium) (R. Lillich ed., 1995). See also (1998) 32 The International Lawyer 502; (1997) 31 The International Lawyer 602.

[54] Over 2,500,000 claims were filed with the UNCC. The UN provided extensive headquarters in Geneva for the UNCC which at one time had a staff of approximately 200 professional and support personnel.

[55] All claims in Category A have been resolved, with awards totalling over US$3.2 billion; all claims in Category B have been resolved, with over US$13 million being awarded; and in Category C, only a few claims remain outstanding.

[56] UNCC decisions may be found in *Mealey's International Arbitration Report* and the International Law Institute's *Gulf War Claims Reporter*.

(c) The Holocaust Tribunals

The late 1990s witnessed the beginning of worldwide efforts to locate and return assets to Holocaust victims and their heirs. Amongst other initiatives, the "Claims Resolution Tribunal for Dormant Accounts in Switzerland" was established in 1997 to resolve claims to Swiss bank accounts that had been opened by non-Swiss customers before the end of the Second World War and remained dormant thereafter. This Claims Resolution Tribunal was supervised by the "Independent Committee of Eminent Persons" and the Swiss Federal Banking Commission, and funded by the Swiss Bankers Association.[57] The task of the Claims Resolution Tribunal was to resolve approximately 10,000 claims to 5,000 dormant bank accounts in an equitable and expeditious manner. It has now been accomplished.

1–133

The focus of the Claims Resolution Tribunal was necessarily a narrow one, but its reliance upon arbitral procedures showed how widespread these have become in the resolution of disputes. It also showed the flexibility of the arbitral process. The Tribunal's rules of procedure included a special provision, entitled "Relaxed Rules of Proof"[58] to help in overcoming the obvious difficulty of proving long-delayed claims.

Other Holocaust tribunals and processes have been established, including a Second Claims Resolution Tribunal ("CRT-II"), the German Forced Labour Compensation Programme and the International Commission on Holocaust Era Insurance Claims. In broad terms, these all share the same basic features, including: a limited period for making claims; "plausibility" as the standard of proof; and the promise of a final settlement and future amnesty for the "defendant" parties.

5. Regulation of International Arbitration

(a) Generally

An arbitration between nationals of the same country, which takes place in that country, will generally involve only the law of the country in which it takes place. It is that law which will usually govern the matters in dispute, the conduct of the arbitration and, if necessary, the enforcement of the award by a court of law. An international commercial arbitration is different. By its very nature—the different nationalities of the parties, the place of arbitration, the place of enforcement of the award and so forth—international commercial arbitration crosses national

1–134

---

[57] General information about the Claims Resolution Tribunal is available in *Mealey's International Arbitration Report.*

[58] Art.22 of the Tribunal's Rules of Procedure provided that the claimant need only show that it was "plausible" that he was entitled to the dormant account. Moreover, the arbitrators had at all times to bear in mind both the difficulties in proving a claim after the destruction of the Second World War and the Holocaust, and that a long time had elapsed since the accounts were opened. The personal circumstances of the claimant and his family had also to be taken into account.

boundaries. As Sir Robert Jennings, a former judge of the International Court of Justice, said in the preface to the first edition of this book:

"International commercial disputes do not fit into orthodox moulds of dispute procedures—they lie astraddle the frontiers of foreign and domestic law and raise questions that do not fit into the categories of private international law either. Not least they raise peculiar problems of enforcement.

Yet it is because this institution of the international commercial contract crosses back and forth between what were supposed only recently to be wholly different and even barely related systems of law that it is able to fulfil a role that, judging only from the sheer volume of international commercial arbitration in modern times, is of great importance to international trade and the movement of investment and skills across international frontiers . . . "

International arbitration, in the sense of arbitrations between states, was a frequent method of settling disputes in medieval times, but fell into disuse with the rise of the modern state. It was born again, so to speak, with the Jay Treaty, which, as previously mentioned, was concluded between the UK and the USA in 1794 and:

"provided a new starting point for the development of international arbitrations after the process, in the preceding century or more, had come to be regarded as virtually in desuetude."[59]

1–135   Various commissions were set up under the provisions of the Jay Treaty to resolve boundary and shipping disputes between the two countries, each commission consisting of one or two commissioners nominated by each party, with the third or fifth commissioner being chosen by agreement or by drawing lots. However, it was the *Alabama Claims* arbitration, which took place in Geneva in 1871–72, which may be said to have paved the way for modern international arbitration. The dispute between the two countries arose because the UK had permitted *Alabama* and her supply ship, *Georgia*, to be built in a British yard and delivered to the Southern States during the American Civil War. The US claimed that this was a breach of neutrality. A new type of tribunal was established to determine the dispute—one member from each side, with "neutral" members being appointed by the King of Italy, the President of the Swiss Confederation and the Emperor of Brazil: "Thus, a collegiate international court, which was to set the pattern for many others, had emerged".[60]

1–136   The Hague Peace Conferences led to the establishment of the Permanent Court of Arbitration—a panel of names from which arbitrators might be selected as

---

[59] Simpson & Fox, *International Arbitration* (Stevens, 1959), p.1; see also generally: Brierley, *The Law of Nations* (6th ed., Oxford University Press, 1963) and Merrills, *International Dispute Settlement* (2nd ed., Cambridge University Press, 1996).
[60] Simpson & Fox, *op. cit.*, p.8.

required—and to which states might refer to settle their differences. The Hague Convention of 1899 stated, in Art.16, that:

"In questions of a legal nature, and especially in the interpretation or application of International Conventions, arbitration is recognised by the Signatory Powers as the most effective, and at the same time the most equitable, means of settling disputes which diplomacy has failed to settle."

The Conference of 1907 more cautiously added:

"Consequently, it would be desirable that, in disputes regarding the above-mentioned questions, the Contracting Powers should, if the case arise, have recourse to arbitration, in so far as circumstances permit."[61]

This cautionary note underlined the fact that, for states, arbitration is a voluntary method of dispute settlement. A state could not be compelled to arbitrate if it did not wish to do so. The position was the same with the Permanent Court of International Justice which was established as part of the peace settlement, following the First World War. Submission by states to the jurisdiction of the court was not compulsory; and this remains the position with the International Court of Justice ("ICJ"), which was founded in 1945 as the principal judicial organ of the United Nations and as the successor to the Permanent Court of Justice.

The ICJ, which is based at the Peace Palace at The Hague, is commonly known **1–137** as the "World Court". Article 38(1) of the Statute of the ICJ is a guide both for the ICJ and for other tribunals in ascertaining the applicable rules of public international law. Article 38(1) states:

"1. The Court, whose function is to decide in accordance with international law such disputes as are submitted to it, shall apply:

(a) international conventions, whether general or particular, establishing rules expressly recognised by the contesting States;
(b) international custom, as evidence of a general practice accepted as law;
(c) the general principles of law recognised by civilised nations;
(d) subject to the provisions of Article 59, judicial decisions and the teachings of the most highly qualified publicists of the various nations, as subsidiary means for the determination of rules of law.

2. This provision shall not prejudice the power of the Court to decide a case *ex aequo et bono,* if the parties agree thereto."

The reference to "international law" in Art.38(1) is a reference to what is generally called "public international law" which traditionally regulated the

---

[61] Simpson & Fox, *op. cit.,* p.14.

relationship between states. It might be thought that international commercial arbitrations would be governed (or regulated) by international law; and indeed, from time to time this is so. For example, an arbitration between two sovereign states, even if the matters in dispute are concerned with commercial rather than with the more usual political issues, would be governed by international law.[62] The same is true of arbitrations relating to investment disputes held under the provisions of the Washington Convention, where only one of the parties is a state and the other is a private investor.

For the most part, however, international commercial arbitration depends for its full effectiveness upon the support of different systems of law and in particular the law of the place (or "seat") of arbitration, which might be a local law (as in Florida) or a national law (as in France). This may lead to some apparently strange consequences, with a process that is directed to the solution of *international* commercial disputes being subject to the vagaries of a particular national or local law. The validity or otherwise of a major international arbitral award may depend, for example, on the procedural law of a province or canton within a federal state. Alternatively, a local court may decide that a dispute that is regarded as "commercial" elsewhere is not so regarded under its own law.[63] Or again it may decide that an award of interest that was valid in the place where the award was made is too high and offends the public policy of the country of enforcement.

(b) The role of national law

1–138   An understanding of the necessary interchange between the arbitral process and national systems of law is fundamental to a proper appreciation of international commercial arbitration. Such an interchange may take place at any phase of the arbitral process. At the beginning of an arbitration, it may be necessary to ask a court to enforce the arbitration agreement (if a party seeks to circumvent it by commencing legal proceedings) or to appoint the arbitral tribunal (if this cannot be done under the arbitration agreement) or the relevant rules of arbitration. After an award has been made, national courts may once again be asked by the parties to intervene. The losing party, for example, may seek to challenge the award before the courts of the place in which it was made, on the basis that the arbitral tribunal exceeded its jurisdiction; or that there was a substantial miscarriage of justice in the course of the proceedings; or on some other legally recognised ground. If this challenge succeeds, the award will either be amended or set aside completely.[64] By contrast, the winning party may need to apply to national courts for recognition and enforcement of the award.[65]

---

[62] See Simpson, "The diverted cargoes arbitration" (1956) 5 I.C.L.Q. 471; and the "Free Zones" arbitrations between France and Switzerland.
[63] See the discussion about the commercial reservation to the New York Convention at paras 10–26 *et seq.*
[64] See Ch.9.
[65] See Ch.10.

State participation in the arbitral process

States that recognise international commercial arbitration as a valid method of **1–139** resolving disputes are, in general, prepared to give their assistance to the arbitral process. Indeed, in many cases they are bound to do so by the international conventions to which they are parties. It is generally recognised that, in return, states are entitled to exercise a degree of control over the arbitral process. Such control is usually exercised on a territorial basis, first, over arbitrations conducted in the territory of the state concerned, and secondly, over awards brought into the territory of the state concerned for the purpose of recognition and enforcement.

As to the first of these propositions, it would be somewhat unusual for a state to lend its support to arbitral tribunals operating within its jurisdiction *without* claiming some degree of control over the conduct of those arbitral tribunals, to ensure that certain minimum standards of justice are met, particularly in procedural matters:

> " . . . there is virtually no body, tribunal, authority or individual in this country whose acts or decisions give rise to binding legal consequences for others, but who are altogether immune from judicial review in the event of improper conduct, breaches of the principles of natural justice, or decisions which clearly transcend any standard of objective reasonableness."[66]

As to the second of the propositions, it is similarly accepted that states which may be called upon to recognise and enforce an international arbitral award are entitled to ensure that certain minimum standards have been observed in the making of that award. They are further entitled to insist that the subject-matter of the award should be "arbitrable" in terms of their own laws and that the award itself should not offend public policy.[67]

The dependence of the international arbitral process upon national systems of **1–140** law must be recognised, but not exaggerated. The modern tendency is for a coming together of the different systems of law which govern the procedural aspects of international commercial arbitration and the recognition and enforcement of international awards. International conventions such as the New York Convention have played an important role in this process of assimilation, and it has been given considerable further impetus by the Model Law. In addition, there is increasing recognition of the importance of international commercial arbitration, both in terms of the economic life of the international community and in terms of the business that such arbitrations can bring to a country. Arbitration centres have been set up in many parts of the world. Whilst some of them may

---

[66] Kerr, "Arbitration and the Courts: the UNCITRAL Model Law" (1984) 50 Arbitration 14.
[67] For further discussion of "arbitrability" and public policy see Ch.3.

have only a nominal existence, taken as a whole they represent a potential source of revenue (and perhaps of prestige) to a country.

(c) The role of international conventions and the Model Law

1–141   The most effective method of creating an international system of law governing international commercial arbitration has been through international conventions (and, more recently, through the Model Law). International conventions have served to link national systems of law into a network of laws which, although they may differ in their wording, have as their objective the international enforcement of arbitration agreements and of arbitral awards.

Bilateral Investment Treaties

1–142   States which wished to do business with each other would frequently enter into so-called "Treaties of Friendship, Commerce and Navigation". In order to encourage trade and investment, the states concerned would grant each other favourable trading conditions and agree that any disputes would be resolved by arbitration.

A later and more significant development is that of Bilateral Investment Treaties, or "BITs" as they are known.[68] Many of these instruments contain an agreement on the part of the states concerned to arbitrate any dispute between the host state and investors of another state. The definition of "investors" is often sufficiently broad to include nationals and public legal entities of the host state. There has been what has been described as an "explosion" in the number of BITs over recent years, with more than 2,000 being recorded by the end of 2001.

The classic agreement to arbitrate is one that is made between the parties at a given time, either in an arbitration clause or in a subsequent clause, or in a subsequent submission to arbitration. In a BIT, however, the position is different. The state party makes, as it were, a standing offer to arbitrate any dispute that might arise in the future; but it is only when a dispute actually arises and the private investor accepts this offer to arbitrate, that an "agreement to arbitrate" is formed. An experienced commentator has described this situation as "arbitration without privity",[69] a situation which is far removed from the usual concept of arbitration. Certainly, the concept of a "standing offer" to arbitrate is different from the conventional model. Once the offer has been accepted, however, there comes into existence an effective agreement to arbitrate, to which both the state (or the state entity) and the private investor are parties:

> "In view of the huge and still rapidly growing number of such treaty consents in particular, it is increasingly likely that any given investor will, in accordance with the terms of such a consent, be able to resort to arbitration in respect of a dispute with a host state despite the absence of an earlier arbitration

[68] BITs are discussed in more detail in Ch.11.
[69] Jan Paulsson, "Arbitration without Privity" (1995) 10 Foreign Investment Law Journal 232.

agreement with the state—or, in many instances, despite the existence of an earlier agreement describing a different method for settling the dispute".[70]

Other treaties, too, demonstrate the importance of arbitration as a method of resolving disputes. In 1993, for example, the North American Free Trade Agreement (NAFTA) was finalised, followed in 1994 by the Energy Charter Treaty.[71] As Paulsson notes: **1–143**

"By allowing direct recourse by private complainants with respect to [such] a wide range of issues, those treaties create a dramatic extension of arbitral jurisdiction in the international realm."[72]

Indeed, so dramatic has been the growth and importance of arbitrations between states and "investors" that it is now the subject of a separate chapter in this book.[73]

International conventions generally

The point has already been made that, to have an effective international arbitration system, it is necessary to link up national systems of law; and to do so by means of a treaty or convention, which will provide for the enforcement of arbitration agreements and arbitral awards by the national courts of those countries which are parties to that treaty or convention.   **1–144**

There have been several such treaties. The first, in modern times, was the Montevideo Convention.[74] This was made in 1889 and provided for the recognition and enforcement of arbitration agreements between certain Latin American states.[75] It was, therefore, essentially a regional convention. The first modern and genuinely *international* convention was the Geneva Protocol of 1923, which was drawn up on the initiative of the ICC and under the auspices of the League of Nations. It was quickly followed by the Geneva Convention of 1927.

The Geneva Protocol of 1923

The Geneva Protocol of 1923 had two objectives. Its first and main objective was to ensure that arbitration clauses were enforceable *internationally*, so that parties to any arbitration agreement would be obliged to resolve their disputes by arbitration, rather than through the courts. Its second and subsidiary objective   **1–145**

---

[70] Antonio Parra, "Provisions on the Settlement of Investment Disputes in Modern Investment Laws, Bilateral Investment Treaties and Multilateral Instruments on Investment" (1997) 12 Foreign Investment Law Journal 287.
[71] The text of the treaty appears in (1995) 10 Foreign Investment Law Journal 258.
[72] Paulsson, *op. cit.*, p.233.
[73] Ch.11.
[74] Treaty concerning the Union of South American States in respect of Procedural Law, signed at Montevideo, January 11, 1889. The Treaty is published, in an English translation, in *Register of Texts of Conventions and other Instruments concerning International Trade Law, Volume II* (1973), United Nations, p.5.
[75] Montevideo Convention, Arts 5, 6 and 7.

was to ensure that arbitration *awards* made pursuant to such arbitration agreements would be enforced in the territory of the states in which they were made. (These two objectives of the Geneva Protocol of 1923—the enforceability both of arbitration agreements and of arbitral awards—are also to be found in a more modern version in the New York Convention.)

The Geneva Protocol of 1923 was limited in its range and effect. It applied only to arbitration agreements made "between parties subject respectively to the jurisdiction of different contracting states"[76]; and it could be further limited by states availing themselves of the "commercial reservation", which has already been discussed.

So far as enforcement of arbitral awards was concerned, each contracting state agreed to ensure the execution under its own laws of awards *made in its own territory* pursuant to an arbitration agreement which was covered by the Protocol.[77]

The Geneva Convention of 1927

1–146 On September 26, 1927 a convention on the execution of foreign arbitral awards was drawn up in Geneva, again under the auspices of the League of Nations.[78] The purpose of this convention was to widen the scope of the Geneva Protocol by providing for the recognition and enforcement of Protocol awards within the territory of contracting states (and not merely within the territory of the state in which the award was made).[79]

A number of problems were encountered in the operation of the Geneva treaties. There were limitations in relation to their field of application[80] and, under the Geneva Convention of 1927, a party seeking enforcement had to *prove* the conditions necessary for enforcement. This led to what became known as the problem of "double *exequatur*". In order to show that the award had become final in its country of origin, the successful party was often obliged to seek a declaration in the courts of the country where the arbitration took place to the effect that the award was enforceable in that country, before it could go ahead and enforce the award in the courts of the place of enforcement.[81]

Despite their limitations, the Geneva treaties have a well-deserved place in the history of international commercial arbitration. They represent a first step on the

---

[76] Geneva Protocol of 1923, Art.1. The meaning of this provision, which gave rise to many difficulties in practice, is considered in Ch.10.
[77] Many European countries became parties to the Geneva Protocol of 1923. These included Belgium, Czechoslovakia, Denmark, Finland, France, Germany, Greece, the Netherlands, Norway, Poland, Portugal, Spain and the UK. One Latin American country, Brazil, became a party to the Protocol; and so did India, Japan, Thailand and New Zealand.
[78] Convention for the Execution of Foreign Arbitral Awards signed at Geneva, September 26, 1927, *League of Nations Treaty Series* (1929–30), Vol.XCII, p.302.
[79] The states which have adhered to the Geneva Convention are substantially those which adhered to the Geneva Protocol (with some notable omissions, such as Brazil, Norway and Poland).
[80] In particular, the parties had to be subject to the jurisdiction of different contracting states.
[81] These points are considered in greater detail in Ch.10.

road towards international recognition and enforcement of international arbitration agreements and awards.

The New York Convention of 1958

It was again the ICC that, in 1953, promoted a new treaty to govern international commercial arbitrations.[82] The ICC's proposals were taken up by the United Nations Economic and Social Council (ECOSOC) and resulted in the New York Convention, which was adopted in 1958. **1–147**

The New York Convention is the most important international treaty relating to international commercial arbitration. Indeed, it may be regarded as a major factor in the development of arbitration as a means of resolving international trade disputes. However, the operation of the Convention has not been without practical difficulties. This is not only because there has not been a uniform approach on the interpretation of the Convention by the courts of various contracting states,[83] but also because the Convention itself is now beginning to show its age.[84]

The New York Convention is plainly a considerable improvement upon the Geneva Convention of 1927. It provides for a much more simple and effective method of obtaining recognition and enforcement of foreign arbitral awards; and it replaces the Geneva Convention of 1927 as between states that are parties to both conventions.[85] Although the title of the Convention does not suggest it, the Convention also gives much wider effect to the validity of arbitration agreements than the Geneva Protocol of 1923 does; and again the Convention replaces the Protocol, as between states which are bound by both.[86] In order to enforce arbitration agreements, the New York Convention adopts the technique found in the Geneva Protocol of 1923. In Art.II.3, the Convention requires the courts of contracting states to refuse to allow a dispute that is subject to an arbitration agreement to be litigated before its courts, if an objection to such litigation is raised by any party to the arbitration agreement.

Unlike the Geneva Protocol of 1923, the New York Convention does not provide that the parties to an arbitration agreement to which the Convention applies shall be "subject respectively to the jurisdiction of different contracting states". Plainly, however, the New York Convention is intended to apply to *international* arbitration agreements, rather than to purely domestic arbitration **1–148**

---

[82] The draft document produced by the ICC gave an early indication of the debate that has continued ever since concerning the feasibility of a truly international award. However, the ICC's proposal for an *international* award, which would not be subject to control by the law of the place in which it was made, was then unacceptable to the majority of states, as it has also proved to be in more modern times when the Model Law was being formulated.

[83] A comprehensive study of the operation of the New York Convention has been undertaken by van den Berg, *The New York Arbitration Convention of 1958* (1981).

[84] As, for instance, in the definition of an "agreement in writing" which has already been discussed.

[85] New York Convention, Art.VII.2. In fact, at the time of preparation of this book the Geneva treaties were only relevant for arbitral awards made in Portugal or Mauritius.

[86] *ibid.*

agreements; and it is in this sense that the Convention has been interpreted by national laws implementing the Convention, such as those of the US and the UK and by the reported decisions of national courts, when called upon to apply the Convention.[87] The New York Convention also deals with the recognition and enforcement of foreign arbitral awards. Indeed, as its full title suggests, this is the primary objective of the Convention. These provisions of the Convention, which are effective in many countries of the world,[88] are discussed in Ch.10.

Conventions after 1958

1–149   The New York Convention represents a vital stage in the shaping of modern international commercial arbitration. No convention since 1958 has had the same impact. Yet later conventions are worthy of brief examination for the direction of development they indicate and the approach they reveal.

The European Convention of 1961 was made in Geneva under the aegis of the Trade Development Committee of the UN Economic Commission for Europe. It applies to international arbitrations to settle trade disputes between parties from different states, whether European or not.[89] Amongst its useful provisions is an express recognition of the capacity of the state or other public body to enter into an arbitration agreement, although the Convention also allows a state, on becoming a party to the Convention, to limit this faculty to such conditions as may be stated in its declaration.[90] Otherwise, however, the European Convention of 1961 failed to meet its objectives. First, its approach was theoretical rather than practical. More importantly, it did not deal with the recognition and enforcement of awards. This was left to other conventions such as the New York Convention to which the European Convention may fairly be seen as a supplement.[91]

The Washington Convention of 1965, which gave rise to ICSID, has been discussed earlier. The next development was a brave but unsuccessful attempt to unify the national arbitration laws of the member states of the Council of Europe in the Strasbourg Uniform Law of 1966.[92] Only Austria and Belgium signed the Convention and it has only been implemented in Belgium. It is, therefore, of little practical interest.

---

[87] The ICCA Yearbook Commercial Arbitration reports each year court decisions made in different countries on the interpretation and application of the New York Convention translated into English.

[88] The major trading nations of the world have become parties to the New York Convention, including the US, the Russian Federation, Japan, France, Switzerland, Germany, Canada and the UK, as well as African countries such as Nigeria and Ghana, Arab countries such as Kuwait and Egypt and Latin American countries such as Chile, Cuba and Mexico.

[89] European Convention on International Commercial Arbitration, done at Geneva, April 21, 1961, *United Nations Treaty Series* (1963–1964) Vol.484, No.7041, p.364. For a note on the background and objectives of the Convention, see Benjamin, "The European Convention on International Commercial Arbitration" (1961) B.Y.I.L. 478. Nineteen countries have ratified or acceded to the European Convention. For a useful comment on the Convention see the article by Hascher in (1990) XV Yearbook Commercial Arbitration 624.

[90] European Convention of 1961, Art.II.2.

[91] van den Berg, above, para.1–18; (1984) IX Yearbook Commercial Arbitration 396.

[92] European Convention providing a Uniform Law on Arbitration, done at Strasbourg, January 20, 1966, *European Treaty Series*, No.56.

Regional conventions

There are also regional conventions on arbitration, such as the Panama Con-   **1–150**
vention and the Amman Convention, which may need to be consulted in relation
to arbitration agreements or awards that touch those regions. Some of these (such
as the Panama Convention, to which the US is a party, as are many South
American states) may be of particular importance in terms of enforcing an
arbitral award.[93]

The Model Law

The Model Law began with a proposal to reform the New York Convention.   **1–151**
This led to a report from UNCITRAL[94] to the effect that harmonisation of the
arbitration laws of the different countries of the world could be achieved more
effectively by a model or uniform law. The final text of the Model Law was
adopted by resolution of UNCITRAL at its session in Vienna in June 1985; and
a recommendation of the General Assembly of the United Nations commending
the Model Law to Member States was adopted in December 1985.[95]

The Model Law has been a major success.[96] The text goes through the arbitral
process from beginning to end, in a simple and readily understandable form. It is
a text that many states have adopted, either as it stands or with minor changes;
and it is a text that any state proposing to adopt a modern law of arbitration
should regard as a baseline.

(d) Practice—national or international

There is no established and universally accepted international *practice* of   **1–152**
international commercial arbitration.

The international conventions touch only indirectly on the practice that should
be followed during the course of an arbitration; and they do so *negatively,* by
stipulating that if the correct practice is *not* followed, recognition and enforcement of the ensuing award may be denied. It is possible to distil positive
procedural obligations from the international conventions, but the result is not
particularly illuminating. The New York Convention, for instance, simply
requires that a party should be given proper notice of the appointment of the
arbitrator or of the arbitral proceedings; that the arbitral procedure should be in
accordance with the agreement of the parties or the law of the country in which
the arbitration takes place; and that a party should be able to present its case.[97]
Although these provisions are admirable as far as they go, they provide little or

---

[93] See the discussion in Ch.10.
[94] This report was entitled "Study on the Application and Interpretation of the Convention on the
Recognition and Enforcement of Foreign Arbitral Awards", UN Doc. A/CN 9/168.
[95] For a full account of the origins and aims of the Model Law, see the second edition of this book,
pp.508 *et seq.*
[96] Many states have modernised their laws governing international arbitration in recent years and in
doing so they have either adopted the Model Law as it stands or at least taken very careful account
of it.
[97] New York Convention, Art.V.1(b) and (d).

no guidance on the way in which an arbitration should actually be conducted—and, to be fair, they are not intended to do so.

The Model Law goes a little further. It provides directly, in connection with the conduct of the arbitral proceedings, that "[t]he parties shall be treated with equality and each party shall be given a full opportunity of presenting his case". Even so, this falls a long way short of specifying how an arbitration should be conducted. Should there be written submissions and, if so, what kind? Should evidence be called from witnesses and, if so, in what manner and under what rules? If written witness statements are submitted, what status do they have? Are they only to be taken into account if the witness subsequently appears at the hearing or do they have some weight, even if the person who made the statement does not attend a subsequent hearing? Is the lawyer representing a party to the arbitration allowed to interview potential witnesses or is this a breach of professional rules? Where a witness appears at a hearing, should he or she be cross-questioned and if so, by whom—the representatives of the parties, the tribunal or both? Should experts be appointed and, if so, by whom—the parties themselves or the tribunal? How should arguments of law be presented—orally, in writing, or both?

1–153   There is no detailed and internationally accepted book of rules to provide an answer to these questions. Each arbitration is different; and with parties and arbitrators generally coming from different legal and cultural backgrounds it would be unreasonable to expect otherwise. Anyone who takes part in an international commercial arbitration, whether as counsel or expert or arbitrator, must be prepared to accept this. No doubt a lawyer who is used to appearing before his or her own local court would be much happier—or at least, more at home—if the arbitration was conducted in accordance with the procedural rules of that court. But the proper comparison is not with what that lawyer might have wished, but with what the alternative might have been—an appearance (if permitted by the rules of the local bar) before a court whose language, rules and custom might well be as foreign as Brobdingnag was to Gulliver during his travels.

This is not to say, however, that there are no guidelines to assist the travelling lawyer or arbitrator. There are—and plenty. Where the arbitration is being conducted under the rules of an arbitral institution, or under the UNCITRAL Arbitration Rules, there will be a book of rules to provide guidance. They will be expressed in broad terms, but they will usually contain provisions governing the place of arbitration (if this has not already been chosen by the parties), the appointment of the arbitral tribunal, challenges to any of the arbitrators or to their jurisdiction, the exchange of written submissions, the appointment of experts, the holding of a hearing and so forth. Even if the arbitration is to be conducted ad hoc, and without reference to any particular set of rules, an experienced tribunal will have well in mind the provisions of such rules, which are designed to ensure orderly and fair proceedings, leading to a reasoned award.

In addition, the practitioner will need to keep in mind any mandatory rules which the law of the place of arbitration may lay down, governing the conduct of arbitrations on its territory. This topic is covered in more detail in the next chapter.

How procedure is determined

What happens in practice is that the parties and the arbitral tribunal generally **1–154** work out for themselves the details of the procedure to be followed. The starting point is often the desire of each party to adopt its own national procedures, on the basis of familiarity. Indeed, many lawyers seem to assume that the proceedings will *naturally* be conducted in a manner that is familiar to them—even if it is totally unfamiliar to their opponents. It has been said that:

> "The large American law firms continue to consider international arbitrations as but one kind of 'litigation' (or, more recently, 'dispute resolution') among others. As a partner in a leading New York law firm observed, 'Arbitration is considered by us to be an adjunct to litigation—litigation in the courts. It's simply a different forum'."[98]

Where the parties to the arbitration have conflicting views as to what constitutes a fair and proper way of proceeding, there are two key requirements. The first is an experienced arbitral tribunal which understands what is going on and what needs to be done. The second is a procedural meeting between the arbitral tribunal and the representatives of the parties, so that the procedure to be followed can be discussed, determined and set down in writing.

In a comparatively small case, it may be possible to work out the rules to be followed up to and including any hearing of the dispute and the issue of the award. In most cases, however, experience tends to indicate that it is better to lay down procedures only to a certain stage (for instance, the exchange of witness statements) and then to hold a further procedural meeting (or pre-trial review) to determine what further steps need to be taken to ensure that the hearing can be conducted as fairly and as expeditiously as possible.

In effect, each international commercial arbitration sets a new problem for **1–155** those engaged in it—namely, how is this particular arbitration to be conducted, given that there is no set pattern or formula to follow? In one sense, it is appropriate that this should be so. One of the advantages of arbitration, as opposed to litigation, is its flexibility. An arbitration, which comes into existence only to deal with disputes between the parties should be "tailor-made" to fit the facts of that dispute; and so the arbitral tribunal and the parties should seek out and adopt "procedures suitable to the circumstances of the particular case, avoiding unnecessary delay or expense, so as to provide a fair means for the resolution of the matters falling to be determined".[99]

It may be said that this is rather like reinventing the wheel, with the arbitral tribunal and the parties spending time and money in laying down rules and

---

[98] Dezalay & Garth, *Dealing in Virtue* (University of Chicago Press, 1996), p.55.
[99] The quotation is from s.33(1)(b) of the English Arbitration Act 1996.

establishing procedures which could readily be drawn from a data bank of previous cases. It would certainly be possible for legislators to draw up a set of detailed rules for the conduct of arbitration (national or international) but this would be a retrograde step,[1] depriving the arbitral process of flexibility.

If more detailed guidance is needed in formulating an appropriate procedure for a particular arbitration, there are two authoritative sources from which this may be obtained—the International Bar Association's "Rules on the Taking of Evidence in International Commercial Arbitration" and the UNCITRAL "Notes on Organizing Arbitral Proceedings" ("the UNCITRAL Guidelines").

1–156   The IBA first formulated a set of rules to govern the presentation of evidence in international commercial arbitration in 1983. Although they were not intended to provide a complete code for the conduct of arbitration, but only for the presentation of evidence, they were less successful than had been hoped. They have since been completely rewritten by lawyers from various jurisdictions. These rules, entitled "The IBA Rules on the Taking of Evidence in International Commercial Arbitration (1999)" may be adopted (or adapted) in whole or in part, with the agreement of the parties and the tribunal. They are particularly useful in dealing with witness evidence and document production and it is becoming increasingly common for these sections of the Rules to be adopted or at least referred to as part of the rules governing the arbitration.

The UNCITRAL Guidelines are helpful in identifying the type of procedural issues that may have to be resolved, particularly in an ad hoc arbitration, and in suggesting solutions to such issues. They also operate as a checklist of points to bear in mind.

These and other procedural matters are discussed in more detail later in this book.[2]

1–159   In practice most experienced international arbitrators have their own checklists and precedents. On the basis of such documents, and in consultation with the parties or their representatives, a form of procedure is tailored to the particular issues in dispute. Where experienced arbitrators and parties are involved, there tends to be a blending of different national practices, with the best of each being selected and the worst rejected. As an experienced arbitrator (and former judge) expressed it:

> "It is a cliché that the objective of the users of arbitration is to achieve speedy finality with fairness and economy of costs. But, like all clichés, it is true. The

---

[1] The idea of a special code of procedure to deal with the arbitration of small claims was considered but rejected by the Departmental Advisory Committee on Arbitration Law in the preparation of the English Arbitration Act 1996. It was considered that it would be wrong for the Act "to lay down a rigid structure for any kind of case": see their Report and Supplementary Report, February 1996 and January 1997, at paras 167 and 168. Note also the comment of Professor Reymond: "The reaction of certain people has been to propose the adoption of more and more detailed rules of procedure, which would deprive arbitration of one of its main advantages, subtlety and adaptability" (authors' translation) (see "L'Arbitration Act 1996, Convergence et Originalité" (1997) 1 Revue de l'Arbitrage 45 at 54).

[2] Particularly in Ch.6.

essence of the emerging common procedural pattern in international arbitration is designed to achieve these objectives by a system of checks and balances in the form of mainly written proceedings which concentrate on the important issues, avoid becoming bogged down in unnecessary detail, and curtail oral hearings as much as possible. General discovery on traditional English lines, let alone pre-trial depositions as under the American system, are never used. Pleadings should be replaced by full written submissions covering both fact and law, with each side referring to, and exhibiting, all documents relied upon. Requests for the disclosure of further documents should not be excluded, but also not encouraged. All witness statements should be supplied in writing and refer to and exhibit any documents relied upon. The emphasis should be in favour of dealing with some predominant issues before others in the hope of promoting settlement before the main hearing, and issues of quantum should always be hived off from liability. Oral cross-examination of witnesses should be permitted upon request, but only under the control of the tribunal. This may involve advance notice of the issues on which it is desired to cross-examine each witness, whereupon the tribunal may impose limits on the number of witnesses, on the issues which it considers to be relevant, and on the time available for cross-examination. In preparing for the main hearing, the joint production of an agreed, chronologically paged bundle, and a core bundle if necessary, is now also accepted in civil law venues as an indispensable tool. Finally, since the arbitrators are likely to be busy professional people and often from different countries, the oral hearings will usually be remarkably short by English standards. Their main purpose is to hear the cross-examination of the witnesses, bracketed by short opening and closing remarks from both sides, which are then often supplemented by written post-hearing submissions."[3]

6. Summary

International conventions on arbitration, together with the growing inter- **1–158** national recognition of the commercial importance of arbitration, have helped to modernise the many different national laws that govern the process of international commercial arbitration in different parts of the world.

The various conventions relating to international commercial arbitration (apart from the Washington Convention) operate through the national law of those states that have agreed to be bound by them. It is true that these conventions may be adopted with reservations as to "reciprocity" and as to the "commercial nature" of the dispute; and it is also true that states may apply their own criteria as to the "arbitrability" of a dispute and as to public policy grounds for refusing recognition of an arbitration agreement or award. Nevertheless, the principal conventions represent a compelling force for unification of national laws on

[3] Sir Michael Kerr's Keating Lecture, "Concord and Conflict in International Arbitration" (1997) 13 Arbitration International 121. Again, the IBA Arbitration Rules on the Taking of Evidence in International Commercial Arbitration (1999) are useful in this context.

arbitration. Indeed, when considering these different local or national laws, it is generally possible to see through the detailed drafting to a framework derived from a particular treaty or convention.

The Model Law has added its own significant impetus to this movement towards the convergence of national laws on international arbitration. Many countries which have sought to modernise their laws on international arbitration have simply adopted the Model Law—sometimes just as it is and sometimes with minor modifications. Even those countries which have decided to adopt a more detailed, or more sophisticated, code of law have tended to use the Model Law as their baseline; and so, an experienced practitioner has an immediate sense of familiarity with that law, even though he or she may be seeing it for the first time.[4]

1–159 People involved in international commercial arbitration, whether as arbitrators, parties or advisers, need to be aware of this continuous interplay between national and international laws. They should also be capable of abandoning a parochial view of the law, as constituted by the particular national system with which they happen to be familiar, in favour of a wider and more international outlook. In particular, they must be prepared to accept that there are other systems of law which may, in some respects, be better than their own and which must in any event be taken into account.

Similar considerations apply to the *practice* of international commercial arbitration. There is no uniform or standard method of procedure. What happens (or should happen) is that the arbitrators, the parties and their advisers will tailor a procedure to fit the dispute with which they are confronted. International commercial disputes take on myriad different forms. Any attempt to design a uniform arbitral procedure would be fraught with problems. It would also run the risk of defeating the purpose of international commercial arbitration, which is to offer both a binding and *flexible* means of resolving disputes.

In approaching each new arbitration, probably the most that can be done, as already indicated, is to maintain a "checklist" of points that need to be considered.[5] To go further is to risk depriving international commercial arbitration of its adaptability, which is (or should be) one of its principal advantages. The different methods of ADR, which have been discussed earlier in this chapter, show how procedures can be adopted to save time and money. The arbitral process may itself be adapted to similar effect. Whilst general guidance can be offered as to ways of arbitrating international commercial disputes speedily and effectively, the need for initiative and open-mindedness in adopting, adapting and developing the appropriate procedures to deal with the particular dispute cannot be overstated. This is part of the continuing challenge of the practice of international commercial arbitration.

---

[4] Consider, *e.g.*, the German Arbitration Act 1998 and the Irish Arbitration (International Commercial) Act 1998.

[5] See, for instance, the UNCITRAL Notes on Organizing Arbitral Proceedings.

Chapter 2

APPLICABLE LAWS

1. Introduction

(a) Generally

Many disputes that are referred to arbitration are determined by arbitral **2–01** tribunals with no more than a passing reference to the law. They turn on matters of fact: what was said and what was not said; what was promised and what was not promised; what was done and what was not done. A plant for the manufacture of glass pharmaceutical bottles is erected and put into operation on a turnkey basis, but fails to produce bottles of the right quality and quantity and the plant operates at a loss. Was this because of some defect in the plant, for which the supplier is responsible; or was it due to mismanagement by the owner in the operation of the plant? A major bank is involved in a financial scandal and the bank's institutional shareholders agree to compensate depositors for their loss. Are these payments recoverable under a policy of insurance, or reinsurance, or are they not covered?

In such cases the arbitral tribunal first needs to resolve the issues of fact, as best it can. Once this has been done, only issues of contractual interpretation remain and if the words of the contract are plain enough, no reference to any underlying system of law is likely to be required. As an experienced arbitrator has said:

"While we find many writings and meetings dealing with general or specific aspects of determining the applicable substantive law in international arbitrations, in practical cases, I have found that this issue plays much less of a role, because, at least in larger arbitrations, the contracts have been drafted by sophisticated businessmen and lawyers trying to deal with all foreseeable difficulties in great detail. Thus, it is my experience that in most cases the contract and its interpretation play a much larger role for the outcome of the case than the applicable substantive law. I would expect this to continue to be so in the future."[1]

Just as an arbitral tribunal frequently reaches its decision on the merits of a dispute without detailed reference to the law applicable to those merits, so an

[1] K.H. Böckstiegel, "Perspectives of Future Development in International Arbitration" in *The Leading Arbitrators' Guide to International Arbitration* (Juris Publishing Inc, 2004), p.505.

arbitral tribunal may well pay little or no attention to the law that governs its own existence and proceedings as an arbitral tribunal. Indeed, it may not even give more than fleeting recognition to the fact that such a law exists—any more than the average purchaser of a motor car gives at best fleeting recognition to the law of contract that underpins the transaction.

(b) No legal vacuum

2–02   It would be wrong to deduce from this, however, that international commercial arbitration exists in a legal vacuum. That would be like suggesting that there is no need for a law of contract, since parties to a contract make their own law. Millions of contracts, most of them made orally rather than in writing, are made every day throughout the world. They may be as simple as the purchase of a bus ticket or the hire of a taxi, or they may be as complex as the purchase of a car on credit terms. Most are made, performed—and forgotten. Disputes are rare, the involvement of lawyers rarer still. Yet law governs each of these situations. The apparent simplicity of the purchase of a bus ticket or the hire of a taxi is deceptive. They are transactions that involve a contractual relationship and such relationships are underpinned by complex rules of law. These may not be referred to expressly, but they exist nonetheless:

> "It is often said that the parties to a contract make their own law, and it is, of course, true that, subject to the rules of public policy and *ordre public,* the parties are free to agree upon such terms as they may choose. Nevertheless, agreements that are intended to have a legal operation (as opposed to a merely social operation) create legal rights and duties, and legal rights and duties cannot exist in a vacuum but must have a place within a legal system which is available for dealing with such questions as the validity, application and interpretation of contracts, and, generally, for supplementing their express provisions."[2]

Like a contract, an arbitration does not exist in a legal vacuum. It is regulated first by the rules of procedure that have been agreed or adopted by the parties and the arbitral tribunal. Secondly, it is regulated by the law of the place of arbitration. It is important to recognise at the outset—as even distinguished judges and commentators sometimes fail to do—that this dualism exists.

For the most part, modern laws of arbitration are content to leave parties and arbitrators free to decide upon their own particular, detailed rules of procedure, so long as the parties are treated equally. Under these modern laws, it is accepted that the courts of law should be slow to intervene in an arbitration, if they

---

[2] Lord McNair, former President of the International Court of Justice, "The General Principles of Law Recognised by Civilised Nations" (1957) 33 B.Y.I.L. 1 at 7.

intervene at all.[3] Nevertheless, rules need the sanction of law if they are to be effective; and in this context the relevant law is the law of the place or seat of the arbitration. This is occasionally referred to as the "curial law", generally by English lawyers, but is much more commonly known as the "*lex arbitri*".

This is an important—and frequently misunderstood—topic, to which it will **2–03** be necessary to return later in this chapter.

(c) A complex interaction of laws

International commercial arbitration, unlike its domestic counterpart, usually **2–04** involves more than one system of law or of legal rules. Indeed it is possible, without undue sophistication, to identify at least five different systems of law which in practice may have a bearing on an international commercial arbitration. These are:

(i) the law governing the parties' capacity to enter into an arbitration agreement;

(ii) the law governing the arbitration agreement and the performance of that agreement;

(iii) the law governing the existence and proceedings of the arbitral tribunal— the *lex arbitri*;

(iv) the law, or the relevant legal rules, governing the substantive issues in dispute—generally described as the "applicable law", the "governing law", "the proper law of the contract" or "the substantive law";

(v) the law governing recognition and enforcement of the award (which may, in practice, prove to be not one law, but two or more, if recognition and enforcement is sought in more than one country in which the losing party has, or is thought to have, assets).[4]

This chapter deals with the law governing the arbitration itself (the *lex arbitri*); the law governing the substantive matters in dispute (the substantive law); the law governing the main agreement between the parties; and the law governing the agreement to arbitrate. The law governing the parties' *capacity* to enter into an arbitration agreement is dealt with in Ch.3; and issues relating to the

---

[3] The lead is given by the Model Law which states categorically (in Art.5) that "In matters governed by this Law, no court shall intervene except where so provided in this Law". Even states that have not adopted the Model Law *per se* have thought it appropriate to make a similar statement—for instance, Swiss law states that its courts will "decline jurisdiction" where there is an agreement to arbitrate, except in limited circumstances: Art.7 of Swiss Private International Law Act 1987. The Swedish Arbitration Act 1999 contains a similar provision, at s.4, although ss.5 and 6 contain exceptions to this rule; and the Spanish Arbitration Act 2003, which is based on the Model Law with significant changes, states unequivocally that "In matters governed by this Act, no court shall intervene except where so provided in this Act" (Art.7).

[4] See Ch.10.

laws governing the arbitral award (including challenge, recognition and enforcement) are dealt with in Chs 9 and 10.

2. THE LAW GOVERNING THE ARBITRATION

(a) Introduction

2–05   An international commercial arbitration usually takes place in a country that is "neutral", in the sense that none of the parties to the arbitration has a place of business or residence there. This means that in practice the law of the country in whose territory the arbitration takes place, the *lex arbitri*, will generally be different from the law that governs the substantive matters in dispute. An arbitral tribunal with its seat in France, for example, may be required to decide the substantive issues in dispute between the parties in accordance with the law of Switzerland or the law of the State of New York or some other law, as the case may be. Nevertheless, the arbitration itself, and the way in which it is conducted, will be governed (if only in outline) by the relevant French law on international arbitration.

This difference between the *lex arbitri* (the law of the place or "seat" of the arbitration) and the law governing the substance of the dispute, was part of the juridical tradition of continental Europe, but is now firmly established in international commercial arbitration.[5]

It is right that there should be a distinction between the *lex arbitri* and the substantive law of the contract. Where parties to an international arbitration agreement choose for themselves a seat of arbitration, they usually choose a place that has no connection with either themselves or their commercial relationship. They choose a "neutral" place.[6] By doing so, they do not necessarily intend to choose the law of that place to govern their relationship.[7] Indeed, as well as choosing a place of arbitration, they may well choose a substantive law that has no connection with that place.

2–06   If the parties do not make an express choice of the place of arbitration, the choice will have to be made for them, either by the arbitral tribunal itself or by a designated arbitral institution. The UNCITRAL Rules, for instance, state:

> "Unless the parties have agreed upon the place where the arbitration is to be held, such place shall be determined by the arbitral tribunal, having regard to the circumstances of the arbitration."[8]

---

[5] *Fouchard Gaillard Goldman on International Commercial Arbitration* (E. Gaillard & J. Savage eds, Kluwer Law International, 1999), para.1428. Early recognition of this principle in English law may be seen in *Compagnie Tunisienne de Navigation SA v Compagnie d'Armament Maritime SA* [1971] A.C. 572 at 604.

[6] For choice of place, see para.2–06.

[7] For choice of law, see para.2–38.

[8] UNCITRAL Arbitration Rules, Art.16(1).

The ICC Rules leave the choice to the ICC's own Court of Arbitration:

"The place of arbitration shall be fixed by the Court unless agreed upon by the parties."[9]

If the ICC is called upon to choose a place of arbitration under this provision of the Rules, it generally selects the country of the sole or presiding arbitrator. The arbitrator is usually of a different nationality from that of the parties.[10] In doing so the ICC does its best to ensure that the country chosen is one which favours arbitration.

It will be seen that in cases of this kind, which are not uncommon both in   **2–07**
institutional and in ad hoc arbitration, the choice of the place of arbitration has little or nothing to do with the parties or with the contract under which the dispute arises. It is, so to speak, an unconnected choice. In these circumstances, it would be illogical to hold that the *lex arbitri*, the law of the place of arbitration, was *necessarily* the law applicable to the issues in dispute. (Occasionally, it may be otherwise if the parties have chosen a place of arbitration but not chosen a law to govern their contractual relationship.[11])

(b) What is the *lex arbitri*?

It is appropriate, at this stage, to consider what is meant by the *lex arbitri*. The   **2–08**
question was posed rhetorically by a distinguished English judge:

"What then is the law governing the arbitration? It is, as the present authors trenchantly explain,[12] a body of rules which sets a standard external to the arbitration agreement, and the wishes of the parties, for the conduct of the arbitration. The law governing the arbitration comprises the rules governing interim measures (*e.g.* Court orders for the preservation or storage of goods), the rules empowering the exercise by the Court of supportive measures to assist an arbitration which has run into difficulties (*e.g.* filling a vacancy in the composition of the arbitral tribunal if there is no other mechanism) and the rules providing for the exercise by the Court of its supervisory jurisdiction over arbitrations (*e.g.* removing an arbitrator for misconduct)."[13]

(c) The content of the *lex arbitri*

Each state will decide for itself what laws it wishes to lay down to govern the   **2–09**
conduct of arbitrations within its own territory. Some states will wish to build an element of consumer protection into their law, so as to protect private individuals.

---

[9] ICC Arbitration Rules, Art.14.1.
[10] ICC Arbitration Rules, Art.9.5.
[11] Under s.48 of the Swedish Arbitration Act 1999, *e.g.*, where parties have not chosen a substantive law to govern their contract, it will be governed by the law of the seat of the arbitration. This situation is discussed later in this chapter.
[12] The reference was to the second edition of this book.
[13] *per* Steyn J., *Smith Ltd v H&S International* [1991] 2 Lloyd's Rep. 127 at 130.

For example, the Swedish Arbitration Act 1999 provides[14] that an arbitration agreement with a consumer involving goods or services for private use is invalid if made before a dispute arises. Again, for example, the Swedish Act provides that the arbitral tribunal must set out in its award its decision as to the fees payable to each of the arbitrators[15]; and the arbitral tribunal must notify the parties of the steps that may be taken to appeal to the district court against this decision.[16]

In recognition of the distinction between domestic arbitration and international arbitration—where the sums at issue are likely to be larger and the parties are judged better able to look after themselves—some states have (sensibly, it may be thought) introduced a code of law specifically designed for international commercial arbitrations. Such a code of law is usually fairly short—the Swiss Code, for example, contains only 23 articles,[17] some of which consist of a single sentence, and the French Code, containing only 16 articles,[18] is even more concise. Indeed, some states (such as Colombia) have enacted short laws which simply define the concept of international arbitration and clarify that such arbitrations are to be governed by the international treaties signed by that state rather than by codes applicable to domestic arbitration.[19]

Reference has already been made to the UNCITRAL Model Law ("the Model Law") which the authors have described as the baseline for any state wishing to modernise its law of arbitration.[20] The point needs to be made, however, that this is a model law for use in international commercial arbitration. Although the Model Law contains more provisions than those to be found in the comparable Swiss or French laws, these provisions are drawn in relatively broad terms. They do not purport to lay down any detailed procedural rules as to the actual conduct of an arbitration—such rules, for example, as the submission and exchange of witness statements, the order in which witnesses are to be called, the time to be allotted for the questioning and cross-questioning of witnesses and so forth. Indeed, the Model Law expressly provides that:

"(1) Subject to the provisions of this Law, the parties are free to agree on the procedure to be followed by the arbitral tribunal in conducting the proceedings.

---

[14] Swedish Arbitration Act 1999, s.6. (For an English translation of the Act, see (2001) 17 Arbitration International 426; and for commentaries on the Act, *ibid.*, throughout.)

[15] Swedish Arbitration Act 1999, s.37.

[16] Swedish Arbitration Act 1999, s.41. It is an unattractive proposition for arbitrators whose work has been accomplished and whose role is over, to face a possible challenge before the local courts in relation to their fees.

[17] Swiss Private International Law Act 1987.

[18] French Code of Civil Procedure, Book IV, Title V—International Arbitration.

[19] Law 315 of September 12, 1996 on International Arbitration (now consolidated in Decree 1818/98) consists of just five articles and states at Art.2: "All matters relating to international arbitration shall be governed by this Law and, in particular, by the provisions of treaties, conventions and protocols and other international agreements signed and ratified by Colombia, which shall prevail over the provisions of the Code of Civil Procedure".

[20] Refer to Ch.1.

(2) Failing such agreement, the arbitral tribunal may, subject to the provisions of this Law, conduct the arbitration in such manner as it considers appropriate. The power conferred upon the arbitral tribunal includes the power to determine the admissibility, relevance, materiality and weight of any evidence."[21]

It may be helpful at this point to give examples of the matters with which the   **2–10**
lex arbitri might be expected to deal, although the exact position under the relevant *lex arbitri* should be checked, particularly where these legal provisions are mandatory. With this qualification, the *lex arbitri* is likely to extend to:

- the definition and form of an agreement to arbitrate;

- whether a dispute is capable of being referred to arbitration (that is to say, whether it is "arbitrable" under the *lex arbitri*);

- the constitution of the arbitral tribunal and any grounds for challenge of that tribunal;

- the entitlement of the arbitral tribunal to rule on its own jurisdiction;

- equal treatment of the parties;

- freedom to agree upon detailed rules of procedure;

- interim measures of protection;

- statements of claim and defence;

- hearings;

- default proceedings;

- court assistance if required;

- the powers of the arbitrators, including any powers to decide as *"amiable compositeurs"*;

- the form and validity of the arbitration award; and the finality of the award, including any right to challenge it in the courts of the place of arbitration.

These are all important aspects of international commercial arbitration. They may well arise in practice and all are addressed later in this chapter. Three essential points should be made now.

First, there is an obvious prospect of conflict between the *lex arbitri* and a different system of law that may be equally relevant. Consider, for example, the question of arbitrability, that is to say, whether or not the subject-matter of the

---

[21] Model Law, Art.19.

dispute is "capable" of being resolved by arbitration. The concept of arbitrability is basic to the arbitral process. Both the New York Convention and the Model Law refer explicitly to disputes that are "capable of being resolved by arbitration".

2–11   It may be said that, if a dispute is capable of being resolved by litigation in the courts, which will lead to a decision that (subject to any appeal) puts an end to that dispute, surely the same dispute is equally capable of being resolved by arbitration? Theoretically, this may well be correct. In practice, however, as already mentioned in Ch.1 and as discussed in more detail later,[22] every state reserves for itself, as a matter of public policy, what might perhaps be called a "state monopoly" over certain types of dispute. Accordingly, whether or not a particular dispute—for instance, over the disposal of assets belonging to a bankrupt company—is legally "capable of being resolved by arbitration" is a matter which each state will decide for itself. It is a matter on which states may well differ, with some taking a more restrictive attitude than others. Thus, a claim may be arbitrable under the law governing the arbitration agreement and under the *lex arbitri* but not under the law of the place of enforcement. An award on such a dispute, although validly made under the *lex arbitri,* might prove to be unenforceable under the New York Convention.

Secondly, the effective conduct of an international commercial arbitration may depend upon the provisions of the law of the place of arbitration. One way of illustrating this dependence is by reference to any provisions of the local law for judicial assistance in the conduct of the arbitration. Even if the arbitrators have the power to order interim measures of protection, such as orders for the preservation and inspection of property, they are unlikely to have the power to enforce such orders—particularly if the property in question is in the possession of a third party. For this, it is necessary to turn to national courts for assistance.[23]

Thirdly, the choice of a particular place of arbitration may have important and unintended consequences. This is because the law of that place may confer powers on the courts or on the arbitrators that were not expected by the parties. An example of this is the power to consolidate arbitrations. Whether or not a court or arbitral tribunal has the power to consolidate two or more arbitrations that involve the same basic issues of fact or law is a controversial question which is discussed further in Ch.3. In the present context, it is only necessary to note

---

[22] See Ch.3.

[23] See, *e.g.*, the Swiss Private International Law Act 1987, Ch.12, Art.183 which provides that the arbitral tribunal may request the assistance of the court where a party does not voluntarily comply with a protective measure; the Netherlands Arbitration Act 1986, Art.1022(2), which provides for a party to request a court to grant interim measures of protection; the English Arbitration Act 1996, s.44(1) and (2), which gives the court the same powers to order the inspection, photocopying, preservation, custody or detention of property in relation to an arbitration as it has in relation to litigation; and the Model Law, Art.9, which allows a party to seek interim measures of protection from a court.

that such a power may exist under the *lex arbitri*[24]; and this may come as a disagreeable surprise to a party who does not wish to have other parties joined in its arbitration.

(d) Procedural rules and the *lex arbitri*

The preceding discussion about the content of the *lex arbitri* indicates that **2–12** most, if not all, national laws governing arbitration deal with general propositions, such as the need to treat each party equally, rather than with detailed rules of procedure, such as the time for exchange of witness statements or the submission of pre-hearing briefs.

Nevertheless, at some stage in the conduct of an arbitration—and indeed, at a fairly early stage—the parties will need to know where they stand in terms of the detailed procedure to be followed. There are many points to be clarified. For example, will the claimant's statement of claim simply outline the facts supporting the claim or will it be accompanied by the documents that are relied upon and perhaps by legal submissions? When the respondent has submitted its defence, will the claimant have the right to put in a reply or is that the end of the written statements? What about the evidence of witnesses? Are there to be written statements of witnesses and if so, in what order, within what time-limits and with what (if any) right of reply?

It is plainly necessary for the parties and the arbitral tribunal to know what procedural rules they are to follow, particularly in an international arbitration where the parties will usually come from different backgrounds, with a different approach to such questions as the interviewing of witnesses, the disclosure of documents and so forth.

All that needs to be understood at this point is that there is a great difference **2–13** between the general provisions of the law governing the arbitration (the *lex arbitri*) and the detailed procedural rules that will need to be adopted, or adapted, for the fair and efficient conduct of the proceedings. The rules of the arbitral institutions, such as the ICC and the LCIA, provide an overall framework within which to operate, as do the UNCITRAL Arbitration Rules. However, it is important to note that even these rules will need to be supplemented by more detailed provisions.

It is sometimes suggested that parties to an arbitration are free to choose between the law governing the arbitration (the *lex arbitri*) and a set of procedural rules. Thus, having stated (correctly, it may be thought) that by comparing various institutional rules such as those of UNCITRAL, the LCIA and the ICC,

---

[24] The Netherlands Arbitration Act 1986 provides in Art.1046 that related arbitral proceedings before another arbitral tribunal in the Netherlands may be consolidated by order of the court notwithstanding the objection of one of the parties unless the parties have agreed otherwise. British Columbia has adapted the Model Law, in s.27(2) of the International Commercial Arbitration Act 1996, to allow court-ordered consolidation where the parties to two or more arbitration agreements have agreed to consolidate the arbitrations arising out of those agreements.

"a core of 'international' procedural rules may emerge". One commentator goes on to say:

> "For present purposes, the key point is simply that the procedural law of an international arbitration is not *necessarily* governed by the *lex loci arbitri* but may be regulated by another system of rules chosen or designed by the parties or, in the absence of choice, by the arbitrators."[25]

This cannot be right. The key point is that of dualism. An international arbitration is governed not only by the rules adopted (or adapted) by the parties and the arbitral tribunal, but also by the *lex arbitri.* It may well be that the *lex arbitri* will govern with a very free rein, but it will govern nonetheless. The only exception is the particular case of arbitration between investors and states under the ICSID Convention, which is almost entirely insulated from the place of arbitration. Interim measures may only be sought from the tribunal itself (unless there is an express agreement otherwise) and any review of the award is the exclusive domain of an ad hoc committee appointed by the institution itself rather than the courts of the place of arbitration (see ICSID Arbitration rr.50 *et seq.*).[26]

(e) The seat theory

2–14   The concept that an arbitration is governed by the law of the place in which it is held, which is the "seat" (or "forum" or "*locus arbitri*") of the arbitration, is well established in both the theory and practice of international arbitration.[27] It has influenced the wording of international conventions from the Geneva Protocol of 1923 to the New York Convention of 1958. The Geneva Protocol states:

> "The arbitral procedure, including the constitution of the arbitral tribunal, shall be governed *by the will of the parties* and *by the law of the country* in whose territory the arbitration takes place."[28]

The concept of dualism could hardly be more clearly expressed: the will of the parties and the law of the country where the arbitration takes place. Nor should

---

[25] Stephen Toope, *Mixed International Arbitration* (Grotius Publications Ltd, 1990), p.41 (emphasis added).

[26] See Ch.9 at para.9–09.

[27] See, for instance, Park, "The Lex Loci Arbitri and International Commercial Arbitration" (1983) 32 I.C.L.Q. 21; Jarvin, "Le Lieu de l'arbitrage" (1993) ICC Bulletin, Vol.4, No.2, p.7; Born, *International Commercial Arbitration* (Transnational Publishers Inc and Kluwer International, 2001), p.573; and G. Kaufmann-Kohler, "Identifying and Applying the Law Governing the Arbitral Procedure—the role of the place of arbitration" in ICCA Congress Series No.9, 1999, entitled "Improving the Efficiency of Arbitration Agreements and Awards: 40 Years of Application of the New York Convention", p.336, who states " . . . to identify the law applicable to the arbitration procedure, one must define the place of arbitration . . . "

[28] Geneva Protocol of 1923, Art.2 (emphasis added).

this pose any problem, at least in theory. In modern arbitral practice, the "will of the parties" is recognised by the considerable degree of autonomy which is given to the parties as to the way in which the arbitration is conducted, with the parties being free to adopt almost any procedural rules they wish, subject to each party being given equal treatment. The "law of the country in whose territory the arbitration takes place"—the *lex arbitri*—is increasingly likely to be supportive of the arbitral process and to intervene in that process as little as possible.

The New York Convention[29] maintains the reference to "the law of the country where the arbitration took place"[30] and, synonymously, to "the law of the country where the award is made".[31] This continues the clear territorial link between the place of arbitration and the law governing that arbitration, the *lex arbitri*. This territorial link is again maintained in the Model Law:

"The provisions of this Law, except articles 8, 9, 35 and 36, apply only if the place of arbitration is in the territory of this State."[32]

Amongst modern laws on arbitration, those of Switzerland and of England are **2–15** perhaps particularly clear on the link between the seat of the arbitration and the *lex arbitri*. Swiss law states:

"The provisions of this chapter shall apply to any arbitration *if the seat of the arbitral tribunal is in Switzerland* and if, at the time when the arbitration agreement was concluded, at least one of the parties had neither its domicile nor its habitual residence in Switzerland."[33]

In English law, certain provisions of the 1996 Act apply only where the seat of the arbitration is in England, Wales or Northern Ireland, whereas other provisions (for instance, for the stay of court proceedings commenced in breach of an arbitration agreement) apply even if the seat of the arbitration is not in those countries or no seat has been designated.[34] The "seat of the arbitration" is defined as "the juridical seat of the arbitration" designated by the parties, or by an arbitral institution or the arbitrators themselves, as the case may be.[35] Unless the parties agree otherwise, the seat of the arbitration must be stated in the award of the arbitrators.[36]

---

[29] Which, by Art.VII.2, replaces the Geneva Protocol of 1923 to the extent that contracting states become bound by the New York Convention.

[30] New York Convention, Art.V.1(d).

[31] *ibid.*, Art.V.1(a) and (e).

[32] Model Law, Art.1(2); Arts 8 and 9 are concerned with enforcing the arbitration agreement and interim measures of protection respectively; Arts 35 and 36 are concerned with recognition and enforcement of the award.

[33] Swiss Private International Law Act 1987, Ch.12, Art.176(1) (emphasis added).

[34] English Arbitration Act 1996, s.2.

[35] *ibid.*, s.3.

[36] *ibid.*, s.52(5).

As this introduction tries to make clear, the place or seat of the arbitration is not merely a matter of geography. It is the territorial link between the arbitration itself and the law of the place in which that arbitration is legally situated:

"When one says that London, Paris or Geneva is the place of arbitration, one does not refer solely to a geographical location. One means that the arbitration is conducted within the framework of the law of arbitration of England, France or Switzerland or, to use an English expression, under the curial law of the relevant country. The geographical place of arbitration is the factual connecting factor between that arbitration law and the arbitration proper, considered as a nexus of contractual and procedural rights and obligations between the parties and the arbitrators."[37]

2–16 The seat of an arbitration is thus intended to be its central point or its centre of gravity. This does not mean that *all* the proceedings of the arbitration have to take place there, although preferably some should do so:

"Although the choice of a 'seat' also indicates the geographical place for the arbitration, this does not mean that the parties have limited themselves to that place. As is pointed out[38] in a passage approved by the Court of Appeal in *Naviera Amazonia Peruana SA v Compania Internacional de Seguros del Peru* [1988] 1 Lloyd's Rep. 116 at 121, it may often be convenient to hold meetings or even hearings in other countries. This does not mean that the 'seat' of the arbitration changes with each change of country. The legal place of the arbitration remains the same even if the physical place changes from time to time, unless of course the parties agree to change it."[39]

Arbitrators and the parties to an international commercial arbitration come from many different countries. It may not always be convenient for everyone concerned to travel to the country which is the seat of the arbitration for the purpose of a meeting or a hearing. Or it may simply be easier and less expensive to meet elsewhere. In recognition of this reality, the ICC Rules of Arbitration were amended to allow hearings and meetings to be held other than at the place (or seat) of the arbitration. The relevant rule reads as follows[40]:

"1. The place of the arbitration shall be fixed by the Court unless agreed upon by the parties.

---

[37] Reymond, "Where is an Arbitral Award made?" (1992) 108 L.Q.R. 1 at 3. As indicated earlier, there is no such "curial" law in ICSID arbitration proceedings. In accordance with Art.62 of the ICSID Convention, the place of the proceedings is the seat of the centre unless otherwise agreed but this does not impose the curial law of Washington DC.
[38] By the present authors, in the 2nd edition of this book.
[39] Saville J. in *Union of India v McDonnell Douglas Corp* [1993] 2 Lloyd's Rep. 48. (The Peruvian case referred to in this citation is generally known as "the *Peruvian Insurance* case".)
[40] Art.14.

2. The Arbitral Tribunal may, after consultation with the parties, conduct hearings and meetings at any location it considers appropriate unless otherwise agreed by the parties.

3. The Arbitral Tribunal may deliberate at any location it considers appropriate."

The LCIA has a similar rule[41]:

"The Arbitral Tribunal may hold hearings, meetings and deliberations at any convenient geographical place in its discretion; and if elsewhere than the seat of the arbitration, the arbitration shall be treated as an arbitration conducted at the seat of the arbitration and any award as an award made at the seat of the arbitration for all purposes."

The Model Law also allows the arbitral tribunal to meet at any place it **2–17** considers appropriate for its deliberations or to hear witnesses, unless the parties object.[42]

These are sensible provisions. They recognise the realities of international commercial arbitration, with parties, lawyers and arbitrators likely to be based in different parts of the world. They give flexibility to the tribunal and to the parties in selecting a convenient location for procedural meetings, hearings and deliberations. It may be, for example, that although the seat of the arbitration is Vancouver, the arbitral tribunal will find it convenient to meet from time to time in a European city, in order to discuss procedural matters or to review the case so far. In international construction disputes it is often necessary for an arbitral tribunal sitting in one country to visit the site of the project in another country to carry out an inspection. Equally, it may be more convenient for an arbitral tribunal sitting in one country to conduct a hearing in another country—for instance, for the purpose of taking evidence.

An arbitral tribunal which visits another country must, of course, respect the law of that country. For example, if the purpose of the visit is to take evidence from witnesses, the arbitral tribunal should respect any provisions of the local law that govern the taking of evidence.[43] However, each move of the arbitral tribunal does not of itself mean that the seat of the arbitration changes. The seat of the arbitration remains the place initially agreed by or on behalf of the parties.[44]

---

[41] Art.16.
[42] Model Law, Art.20(2). The Netherlands Arbitration Act 1986, Art.1037(3) is to like effect. But contrast the law in the US that requires that hearings be conducted in the place of the arbitration unless the parties agree otherwise: *Spring Hope Rockwool v Industrial Clean Air Inc*, 504 F.Supp.1385 (1981); *Snyder v Smith* 736 F.2d 409 (7th Cir.1984), cert. denied, 469 US 1037 (1984); *Jain v de Méré* 51 F.3d (7th Cir. 1995), pp.686, 692.
[43] The local law, *e.g.*, may not permit arbitrators to take evidence from witnesses on oath.
[44] The preceding two paras were cited with approval by Kerr L.J. in the *Peruvian Insurance* case, which is referred to at n.39.

2–18   What is the legal position if, as sometimes happens, the arbitral tribunal—having consulted the parties and perhaps against the objection of one of them—holds all meetings, hearings and deliberations in a place which is not the seat of the arbitration?[45] To proceed in this manner reduces the seat of the arbitration to a legal fiction: a place of arbitration in which nothing takes place. In the light of the provisions set out above, this would seem to be permissible. It conforms with the letter, if not the spirit, of the law or the applicable rules. But there is perhaps a risk that such conduct on the part of the arbitral tribunal would be seen as going beyond what was contemplated—in which case, the award might be challenged on the basis that the arbitral procedure did not conform to the real agreement of the parties.[46]

(f) Is the *lex arbitri* a procedural law?

2–19   In some countries, the law governing arbitration, including international arbitration, is part of the Code of Civil Procedure. This is so, for example, in France and in Germany; and it is sometimes said that the *lex arbitri* is a law of procedure, as if that is all that it is. It is true, of course, that the *lex arbitri* may deal with procedural matters—such as the constitution of an arbitral tribunal where there is no relevant contractual provision—but the authors suggest that the *lex arbitri* is much more than a purely procedural law. It may stipulate that a given type of dispute—over patent rights, for instance, or (as in Belgium and some Arab states) over a local agency agreement—is not capable of settlement by arbitration under the local law. This is surely not simply a matter of procedure.[47] Or again, by way of example, an award may be set aside on the basis that it is contrary to the public policy of the *lex arbitri*. Once more, this would not seem to be merely a matter of procedure.

It is also sometimes said that parties have selected the procedural law that will govern their arbitration, by providing for arbitration in a particular country.[48] This is too elliptical. What the parties have done is to choose a place of arbitration in a particular country. That choice brings with it submission to the laws of that country, including any mandatory provisions of its law on arbitration. To say that the parties have "chosen" that particular law to govern the arbitration is rather like saying that an English woman who takes her car to France has "chosen" French traffic law, which will oblige her to drive on the right-hand side of the road, to give priority to vehicles approaching from the right and generally

---

[45] In ICC Case No.10623 the tribunal held all meetings, etc. in Paris, although the seat of the arbitration was in Ethiopia and the government of that country protested at the tribunal's action.

[46] New York Convention, Art.V.1(d).

[47] Another good reason for not labelling the *lex arbitri* as "procedural" is that different countries have different notions of what is a matter of procedure and what is a matter of substance: *cf.* the treatment of time-limits in English law, discussed in Ch.4, para.4–04.

[48] See, for instance, the reference of Lord Diplock to the "selection" of a particular *lex arbitri* by the choice of a place of arbitration, in the *Compagnie Tunisienne* case cited at n.5.

to obey traffic laws to which she may not be accustomed. But it would be an odd use of language to say that this notional motorist had opted for "French traffic law". What she has done is to choose to go to France. The applicability of French law then follows automatically. It is not a matter of choice.

Parties may well choose a particular place of arbitration precisely because its *lex arbitri* is one which they find attractive.[49] Nevertheless, once a place of arbitration has been chosen, it brings with it its own law. If that law contains provisions that are mandatory so far as arbitrations are concerned[50] those provisions must be obeyed. It is not a matter of choice, any more than the notional motorist is free to choose which local traffic laws to obey and which to disregard.

(g) Choice of a foreign procedural law

The concept of subjecting an arbitration in one state to the procedural law of   **2–20** another has been the subject of much theoretical discussion. Thus, for example, an arbitration could be held in Switzerland but, by agreement between the parties, made subject to the procedural law of Germany. Swiss law provides that the parties to an arbitration may "subject the arbitral procedure to the procedural law of their choice".[51]

It is not easy to understand why parties might wish to complicate the conduct of an arbitration in this way (unless, as is possible, they do not understand what they are doing). It means that the parties and the arbitral tribunal would need to have regard to two procedural laws. That of Germany, as the chosen procedural law, and that of Switzerland, to the extent that the provisions of Swiss law (such as the requirement of equality of treatment of the parties[52]) are mandatory. Nor is this all. If it becomes necessary during the course of the arbitration to have recourse to the courts—for example, on a challenge of one of the arbitrators—to which court would the complainant go? The Swiss court would presumably be reluctant to give a ruling on German procedural law; the German court might well prove unwilling to give a ruling on a procedural matter which it could not directly enforce, since the arbitration was not within its territorial jurisdiction.

It is tempting to suggest that if the procedural law of a particular country is either so attractive or so familiar to the parties that they wish to adopt it, they would do better to locate their arbitration in that country. It is only necessary to look at the difficulties that a party would face in obtaining a *subpoena* against a

---

[49] See Ch.6.
[50] *e.g.* consolidation under Dutch law; and the mandatory provisions of other national laws governing arbitration, such as the mandatory provisions of the English Arbitration Act 1996.
[51] Swiss Private International Law Act 1987, Ch.12, Art.182; there are provisions in Dutch and Italian law to the same effect and in the French New Civil Code at Art.1494(1). However, non-compliance with public policy rules would be a ground for setting an award aside, even if another procedural law was chosen.
[52] Swiss Private International Law Act 1987, Ch.12, Art.182(3).

reluctant witness to realise the problems inherent in a choice of foreign procedural law.[53]

2–21   In the *Peruvian Insurance* case,[54] the English Court of Appeal considered a contract that had been held by the court of first instance to provide for an arbitration to be located in Peru but subject to English procedural law. The Court of Appeal construed the contract as providing for arbitration in London under English law but noted that a situation (such as that contemplated by the Florida International Arbitration Act) involving a choice of foreign procedural law was theoretically possible. However, practical difficulties were foreseen:

> "There is equally no reason in theory which precludes parties to agree that an arbitration shall be held at a place or in country X but subject to the procedural laws of Y. The limits and implications of any such agreement have been much discussed in the literature, but apart from the decision in the instant case there appears to be no reported case where this has happened. This is not surprising when one considers the complexities and inconveniences which such an agreement would involve. Thus, at any rate under the principles of English law, which rest upon the territorially limited jurisdiction of our courts, an agreement to arbitrate in X subject to English procedural law would not empower our courts to exercise jurisdiction over the arbitration in X."[55]

(h) Where an award is made

2–22   From time to time, it may become necessary to determine where an award is made. The point is an important one. For example, recognition and enforcement of an award may be refused on the basis that the arbitration agreement was not valid "under the law of the country where the award was made"[56]; or on the basis that the award itself had been "set aside or suspended" by a court of the country in which it was made.[57]

Some arbitration rules and some national laws deal expressly with the place at which an award is "made". For example, the ICC Rules provide that an award is deemed to be made at the place (or seat) of the arbitration and on the date stated therein.[58] This is a sensible provision when arbitrators who live in different countries may well have agreed on the final terms of the award by telephone, fax

---

[53] In many countries an arbitrator has no power to issue a *subpoena* and the parties must rely upon the relevant court for such process. See, *e.g.*, the Model Law, Art.27. The US does allow for an arbitrator to summon a witness to attend and to bring any material documents or evidence. But the local Federal District Court must be called in aid to assist in compelling a reluctant witness to attend or to punish a witness who fails to attend (Federal Arbitration Act 1925, s.7). See Ch.7.

[54] *Naviera Amazonia Peruana SA v Compania Internacional de Seguros de Peru* [1988] 1 Lloyd's Rep. 116.

[55] *ibid., per* Kerr L.J. at 120.

[56] New York Convention, Art.V.1(a); Model Law, Art.36(1)(a)(i).

[57] New York Convention, Art.V.1(e); Model Law, Art.36(1)(a)(v). Note that these provisions are discretionary: recognition and enforcement *may* be refused: see Ch.10.

[58] ICC Arbitration Rules, Art.25.3.

or email. The Model Law contains a similar provision,[59] as does, for instance, the Netherlands 1986 Act[60] and the English 1996 Act.[61]

But what happens when there is no provision in the rules of arbitration or in the *lex arbitri* as to where the award is made? Is this then a question of fact or is there some relevant legal presumption? In an international commercial arbitration, with a tribunal of three arbitrators, the award in its final form may well be signed in three different countries, each member of the tribunal adding his or her signature in turn. There is a strong argument that, in such circumstances, the award should be deemed to have been made at the seat of the arbitration: **2–23**

> "The award, it is submitted, is no more than a part, the final and vital part of a procedure which must have a territorial, central point or seat. It would be very odd if, possibly without the knowledge of the parties or even unwittingly, the arbitrators had the power to sever that part from the preceding procedure and thus give a totally different character to the whole."[62]

This analysis appears to be correct, but it does assume, of course, that the "central point or seat" was real, in the sense that the arbitral proceedings (or most of them) actually took place there. **2–24**

An alternative view is that an award is "made" at the place where it is signed. This was the view taken by the English court,[63] but the ruling was reversed by the 1996 Arbitration Act.[64] Nevertheless, it is a view which may still prevail elsewhere in the world. The question is important and is discussed in more detail in Ch.6.

(i) Delocalisation

So far as international commercial arbitration is concerned, it would save considerable time, trouble and expense if the laws governing arbitrations were the same throughout the world, so that there was—so to speak—a universal *lex arbitri*. There would then be a "level playing field" for the conduct of international commercial arbitrations wherever they took place. An arbitral tribunal would not have to enquire whether there were any special provisions governing arbitration which were peculiar to the law of the country which was the seat of the arbitration. On this aspect of the arbitral process, all laws would be the same. **2–25**

In practice, however, the idea of a universal *lex arbitri* is as illusory as that of universal peace. Each state has its own national characteristics, its own interests

---

[59] Model Law, Art.31(3).
[60] Netherlands Arbitration Act 1986, Art.1037(1).
[61] English Arbitration Act 1996, ss.52(5) and 53.
[62] Mann, "Where is an award 'made'?" (1985) 1 Arbitration International 107 at 108. However, the view of Dr Mann that an award is "made" at the arbitral seat and not necessarily at the place where it is signed was not accepted in *Hiscox v Outhwaite* [1992] A.C. 562.
[63] In *Hiscox v Outhwaite* [1992] A.C. 562 at 594, where the arbitration was conducted in London, but the award was signed in Paris.
[64] s.3.

to protect and its own concepts of how arbitrations should be conducted on its territory. Even states which adopt the Model Law cannot resist adding their own particular provisions to it.[65] Indeed, states with a long history of arbitration and a highly developed law and practice are particularly unlikely to adopt simplified models, which may, in themselves, create fresh problems.[66] Nevertheless, it is inconvenient (to put it no higher) that the regulation of international commercial arbitration should differ from one country to another; and this has led to the search for an escape route.

In this connection, two separate developments are seen. The first (which no doubt should not properly be characterised as an "escape route") is for the state to loosen considerably the control which it seeks to exercise over international commercial arbitrations conducted on its territory. This is the route taken by modern laws of arbitration. These laws take careful note of the theme of the Model Law, which is that their courts should not intervene in arbitrations, unless authorised to do so. The role of the courts should be supportive not inter-ventionist.

2–26 The second development is to detach an international commercial arbitration from control by the law of the place in which it is held. This is the so-called "delocalisation" theory, the idea being that instead of a dual system of control, first by the *lex arbitri* and then by the courts of the place of enforcement of the award, there should be only one point of control—that of the place of enforce-ment. In this way, the whole world (or most of it) would be available for international commercial arbitrations; and international commercial arbitration itself would be "supra-national", "a-national", "transnational", "delocalised" or even "expatriate". More poetically, such an arbitration would be a "floating arbitration", resulting in a "floating award".[67]

The delocalisation theory[68] took as its starting point the autonomy of the parties—the fact that it was their agreement to arbitrate which brought the proceedings into being—and rested upon two basic (yet frequently confused)

---

[65] Egypt, *e.g.*, has adopted the Model Law but has added a provision which provides for annulment if the award fails to apply the law agreed by the parties—thus opening the way for the Egyptian courts to review awards on issues of law, which is not permitted under the Model Law. For an authoritative commentary on the Egyptian Code see Borham Atallah, "The 1994 Egyptian Arbitration Law Ten Years On", ICC Bulletin, Vol.14, No.2, Autumn 2003, pp.16 and 17.

[66] This was the view of the Mustill Committee, which recommended that the Model Law should not be adopted, but that the English law of arbitration should nevertheless take careful account of it—as has been done, in the Arbitration Act 1996.

[67] See in particular Fouchard, *L'Arbitrage Commercial International* (1965), pp.22–27; Paulsson, "Arbitration Unbound: Award Detached from the Law of its Country of Origin" (1981) 30 I.C.L.Q. 358; and Paulsson, "Delocalisation of International Commercial Arbitration: When and Why it Matters" (1983) 32 I.C.L.Q. 53.

[68] In this discussion, "delocalisation" is used (as it originally was) to signify the detachment of international commercial arbitration from control by the law of the place of arbitration. Somewhat confusingly, the term is now sometimes used to indicate not only detachment from the *lex arbitri* but also the replacement of a national law governing the *substance* of the dispute by general principles or some other non-national concept: see, for instance, Toope, *Mixed International Arbitration* (Grotius Publications Ltd, 1990) who, at p.19, states: "Some [specialists] would preclude the delocalisation of procedure, but allow delocalisation of the substantive law, through the application of 'general principles', 'a *lex mercatoria*' or international law *per se*".

arguments. The first assumed that international commercial arbitration was sufficiently regulated by its own rules, which were either adopted by the parties[69] (as an expression of their autonomy) or drawn up by the arbitral tribunal itself. The second assumed that control should only come from the law of the place of enforcement of the award.

The arguments considered

The first argument was, in effect, that an international commercial arbitration **2–27** is self-regulating and that this was, or should be, sufficient. It is true that the parties to an international commercial arbitration will generally (but not always) have a set of procedural rules to follow, whether they are those of an arbitral institution or formulated ad hoc. It is also true that the arbitral tribunal will generally (but again not always) have the power to fill any gaps in these rules by giving procedural directions; and this set of rules, whether agreed by the parties or laid down by the arbitral tribunal, may perhaps be said to constitute "the law of the arbitration", in the same way as a contract may be said to constitute "the law of the parties". Finally, when the arbitration is being administered by an arbitral institution (such as the ICC) that institution may be said to have taken over the state's regulatory functions, by itself laying down rules for the confirmation or removal of arbitrators, terms of reference, time-limits, scrutiny of awards and so on.[70]

Most arbitrations are conducted without any reference to the law that governs them. Nonetheless, to repeat a point that has already been made, this law—the *lex arbitri*—exists.[71] Its support may be needed not only to fill any gaps in the arbitral process (such as the appointment of arbitrators) but also to give the force of law to orders of the arbitral tribunal that reach beyond the parties themselves—for instance, for the "freezing" of a bank account or for the detention of goods. More crucially, this law will confer its nationality on the award of the arbitral tribunal, so that it is recognised, for example, as a Swiss award or a Dutch award and may benefit from any international treaties (such as the New York Convention) to which its country of origin is a party.

The second argument in support of the delocalisation theory is that any control of the process of international commercial arbitration should come only at the place of enforcement of the award. If this were the position, it would mean that the place of arbitration was, in legal terms, irrelevant. This may or may not be a desirable solution; but it is significant that one state, Belgium, which had compulsorily "delocalised" international arbitrations has now changed its mind.[72] For the rest the prevailing emphasis, both nationally and internationally,

---

[69] For instance, by a standard arbitration clause.
[70] See Fouchard, *op. cit.*
[71] The point is no doubt so obvious as to need no comment, but the statement of Professor Weil seems particularly apt in this context: "The principle of *pacta sunt servanda* and that of party autonomy do not float in space; a system of law is necessary to give them legal force and effect" (Weil, "Problèmes relatifs aux contrats passés entre un état et un particulier" (1969) 128 Hague Recueil 95 at 181 (authors' translation)).
[72] See n.75.

is on a necessary connection between the place of arbitration and the law of that place. This may be seen, as has already been demonstrated, in the New York Convention[73] and in the Model Law.[74]

The position in reality

2–28   The delocalisation theory has attracted powerful and eloquent advocates, but the reality is that the delocalisation of arbitrations (other than those, like ICSID, which are governed directly by international law) is only possible if the local law (the *lex arbitri*) permits it.

One country that opted in favour of a substantial degree of delocalisation was Belgium. By its law of March 27, 1985, a provision was added to Art.1717 of the Belgian Code Judiciaire which meant that a losing party was not permitted to challenge in the Belgian courts an award made in an international arbitration held in Belgium, unless at least one of the parties had a place of business or other connection with Belgium. However, it appears that this legal provision discouraged parties from choosing Belgium as the seat of the arbitration; and the law has since been changed.[75]

(j) The "seat" theory and the *lex arbitri*

2–29   The strength of the seat theory is that it gives an established legal framework to an international commercial arbitration so that, instead of "floating in the transnational firmament, unconnected with any municipal system of law",[76] the arbitration is firmly anchored in a given legal system. Just as the law of contracts will help to ensure that contracts are performed as they should be, and are not mere social engagements, so the *lex arbitri* will help to ensure that the arbitral process works as it should. The necessity for such support for (and control of) the arbitral process is, of course, recognised by the Model Law, which allows for certain functions (such as the appointment of arbitrators, where there is a vacancy) and for certain sanctions (such as the setting aside of an award) to be exercised by the courts of the place of arbitration.[77]

The fact that different states have different laws governing international commercial arbitration and that some of these laws may not be well suited to this task has two practical consequences. First, it means that wherever an international commercial arbitration is held, the provisions of the local law should be checked to see whether there are any particular mandatory rules which must be observed in order to obtain a valid award. Secondly, it means that not every

[73] Art.V.1(a) and (e).
[74] Art.36.1(a)(i) and (v).
[75] The authors commented, in the second edition of this book, that claimants would no doubt welcome the "hands-off" attitude of the Belgian legislature but that respondents were likely to be less enthusiastic and their lawyers might be expected to advise against Belgium as a suitable place for arbitration. This has proved to be the case. Belgian law now allows parties to an international arbitration to opt out of local control if they wish, but no longer provides for compulsory delocalisations: Law of May 19, 1998.
[76] *Bank Mellat v Helliniki Techniki SA* [1984] Q.B. 291, [1983] 3 All E.R. 428 (CA)
[77] See the Model Law, Art.6 (which allocates various functions to the local courts) and Art.34 (which allows the local court to set aside awards made in its territory, on certain limited grounds).

country is a suitable *situs* for international commercial arbitration; a certain amount of "forum shopping" is advisable.

The first point is almost self-evident. For example, if the local law requires an award to be made within a defined period of time or to be lodged with a local court for it to be valid, then the necessary action must be taken to conform to this requirement. The second point is less evident, but equally important. Since the law and practice of international commercial arbitration differs from one state to the next (and may even differ from place to place within the same state), care should be taken to choose a place of arbitration in a state that is favourable rather than in one that is unfavourable. This is a matter of considerable practical importance; as such it is considered in more detail in Ch.3.

One final comment is necessary before leaving the discussion of delocalisation **2–30** and the *lex arbitri*. It seems that the movement in favour of total delocalisation, in the sense of freeing an international arbitration from control by the *lex arbitri*, has run into the ground. As the Belgian experiment showed, delocalisation is only possible to the extent that it is permitted by the *lex arbitri*; and parties to an arbitration may well prefer an arbitral tribunal which is subject to some legal control, rather than risk a runaway tribunal. However, there is still discontent amongst practitioners at the impact of local laws which are seen to operate unfairly and, at times, almost arbitrarily and so there have been cases of what may perhaps be described as "delocalisation by a side door".

In *Chromalloy*, for example, the Egyptian court annulled an arbitral tribunal's award made in Cairo in favour of a US corporation. Despite this annulment by the courts of the place of arbitration, the award was granted recognition and enforcement by the US District Court in Washington DC—"to the advantage of the home team" in the words of certain distinguished US commentators.[78] *Chromalloy* is only one example of national courts enforcing awards that have been annulled by the courts of the place of arbitration.

Then there are the problems caused by local courts which issue injunctions at the seat of the arbitration to prevent arbitral tribunals carrying out their task. Some tribunals continue with the arbitral proceedings despite the injunction (even when they are within the territorial jurisdiction of the court concerned) on the basis that the injunction is not justified. In effect, these arbitrators "delocalise" their arbitration by refusing to accept the rulings of the local court under the *lex arbitri*: again, this is discussed in more detail in Ch.7.

3. THE LAW APPLICABLE TO THE SUBSTANCE

(a) Generally

When questions of procedure have been settled, the principal task of the **2–31** arbitral tribunal is to establish the material facts of the dispute. It does this by

---

[78] Charles Brower I, Charles Brower II & Jeremy Sharpe, "The Coming Crisis in the Global Adjudication System" (2003) 19 Arbitration International 424.

examining the agreement between the parties, by considering other relevant documents (including correspondence, minutes of meetings and so on) and by hearing witnesses if necessary. The arbitral tribunal then builds its award on this foundation of facts, making its decision either on the basis of the relevant law or exceptionally, and then only if expressly authorised by the parties, on the basis of what seems to be fair and reasonable in all the circumstances.

Once the relevant facts have been established, the arbitral tribunal may not need to go outside the confines of the agreement originally made between the parties in order to determine the dispute. This agreement, particularly in international commercial transactions, will generally be quite detailed. For example, international construction contracts run to many hundreds of closely printed pages accompanied by detailed drawings and specifications. Properly understood, such an agreement will generally make clear what the parties intended, what duties and responsibilities they each assumed and, in consequence, which of them must be held liable for any failure of performance that has occurred.

But, as already stated, an agreement intended to create legal relations does not exist in a legal vacuum. It is supported by a system of law which is generally known as "the substantive law", "the applicable law" or "the governing law" of the contract.[79] These terms all denote the particular system of law that governs the interpretation and validity of the contract, the rights and obligations of the parties, the mode of performance and the consequences of breaches of the contract.[80]

2–32 Changes in the law applicable to the contract may bring about changes in the contract itself. For instance, a country may enact currency regulations. These regulations will then apply to contracts that are governed by the law of that country. This happened in a case where the delivery of bearer bonds to their lawful owner was refused because, under the law of Czechoslovakia, it had become illegal for the bonds to be delivered without the consent of the Central Bank. The Central Bank refused consent. The owner of the bonds sued for their delivery, but was unsuccessful:

"If the proper law of the contract is the law of Czechoslovakia, that law not merely sustains but, because it sustains, may also modify or dissolve the contractual bond. The currency law is not part of the contract, but the rights and obligations under the contract are part of the legal system to which the currency law belongs."[81]

Accordingly, it is not enough to know what agreement the parties have made. It is also essential to know what law is applicable to that agreement. In a purely

[79] In private international law, it is also known as the "proper law" of the contract.
[80] *Compagnie d'Armement Maritime SA v Compagnie Tunisienne de Navigation SA* [1971] A.C. 572 at 603, *per* Lord Diplock.
[81] *per* Lord Radcliffe in *Kahler v Midland Bank Ltd* [1950] A.C. 24 at 56. Similar problems have arisen in Argentine investments where obligations payable in foreign currency were forcibly redenominated in Argentine pesos at a rate of one dollar to one peso. This applied only to contracts governed by Argentinian law.

domestic contract, the applicable law will usually be that of the country concerned. If a French woman purchases a dress in a Paris boutique, French law will
be the applicable or substantive law of that contract. However, where the contract
is in respect of an international transaction, the position is more complicated.
There may then be two or more different national systems of law capable of
qualifying as the substantive law of the contract; and (although it is important not
to exaggerate the possibilities) these different national systems may contain
contradictory rules of law on the particular point or points in issue.

Crossing national frontiers

An individual who crosses a national frontier on foot or by car, passport in   **2–33**
hand, realises that he or she is moving from one country to another. After a
moment's thought the traveller would realise that he or she was transferring from
one legal system to another; and that indeed what is lawful in one country is not
necessarily so in another.

This transition from one legal system to another is less apparent, or at least
more easily forgotten, when national frontiers are crossed by electronic signals
from telephones, telexes, faxes or email. For example, an oil company in New
York may enter into an agreement by fax to buy crude oil on the spot market in
Rotterdam, for shipment to a refinery in Germany. A bullion dealer in London
may buy gold over the telephone from Zurich for delivery to a bank in Italy, on
the basis that payment is to be made by an irrevocable letter of credit drawn on
a bank in Chicago. These transactions cross national frontiers as unmistakably as
travellers by road or train. Although there are no frontier posts to go through,
complex questions of law may still arise because of the crossing of national
boundaries. Transactions such as those mentioned take place constantly throughout the year. Rules of law govern each transaction. Yet problems still arise, first,
in identifying what law applies, and, secondly, in dealing with any conflict
between the applicable laws.

(b) The autonomy of the parties

It is generally recognised that parties to an international commercial agreement   **2–34**
are free to choose for themselves the law (or the legal rules)[82] applicable to that
agreement. The doctrine of party autonomy, which was first developed by
academic writers and then adopted by national courts, has gained extensive
acceptance in national systems of law:

---

[82] The point as to "relevant rules", by which is meant something other than a national system of law,
is developed below. The Model Law (and the UNCITRAL Arbitration Rules) allows the parties to
choose the "rules of law" applicable to their contract (which may include, for instance, the *lex
mercatoria*) but stipulates that if the parties fail to make such a choice, the arbitral tribunal shall
apply "the law" applicable to the dispute (which would not include the *lex mercatoria*). This same
dichotomy is to be found in national systems of law, including English and Swiss (the latter being
helpfully discussed in Bucher & Tschanz, *International Arbitration in Switzerland* (Helbing &
Lichtenhahn, 1989), pp.117 *et seq.*). However, French law does allow an arbitrator to choose
"appropriate" rules of law.

" . . . despite their differences, common law, civil law and socialist countries have all equally been affected by the movement towards the rule allowing the parties to choose the law to govern their contractual relations. This development has come about independently in every country and without any concerted effort by the nations of the world; it is the result of separate, contemporaneous and pragmatic evolutions within the various national systems of conflict of laws."[83]

The doctrine has also found expression in international conventions, such as the Rome Convention. The Rome Convention,[84] which is applicable to contractual obligations within the European Union, accepts as a basic principle the right of parties to a contract to choose, expressly or by implication,[85] the law which is to govern their contractual relationship.

If national courts are prepared, as most of them are, to recognise the principle of party autonomy in the choice of the law applicable to a contract, an arbitral tribunal should also be prepared to do so. An international arbitral tribunal owes its existence to the agreement of the parties and in applying the law chosen by the parties, an arbitral tribunal is simply carrying out their agreement.

Recognition by international conventions

2–35   Both the international conventions and the model rules on international commercial arbitration confirm that the parties are free to choose for themselves the law applicable to their contract.

For example, the Washington Convention provides:

"The Tribunal shall decide a dispute in accordance with such rules of law as may be agreed by the parties."[86]

The UNCITRAL Rules provide:

"The arbitral tribunal shall apply the law designated by the parties as applicable to the substance of the dispute."[87]

Amongst the rules of arbitral institutions, the ICC Rules provide:

"The parties shall be free to agree upon the rules of law to be applied by the arbitral tribunal to the merits of the dispute . . . "[88]

---

[83] Lew, *Applicable Law in International Commercial Arbitration* (1978), p.75.

[84] The Rome Convention on the Law Applicable to Contractual Obligations may be found in [1980] Official Journal of the European Union, No.L266/1.

[85] *ibid.*, Art.3, para.1. The Convention does not apply to arbitration agreements, but the subject under discussion here is not that of arbitration agreements but of the contract between the parties under which a dispute has arisen.

[86] Washington Convention, Art.42.

[87] UNCITRAL Arbitration Rules, Art.33.1.

[88] ICC Arbitration Rules, Art.17.1. The reference to "rules of law" marks a shift in thinking from the previous (1988) version of the ICC Arbitration Rules, which referred simply to the "law" to be applied.

As one experienced commentator has stated:

"There are few principles more universally admitted in private international law than that referred to by the standard terms of the 'proper law of the contract'—according to which the law governing the contract is that which has been chosen by the parties, whether expressly or (with certain differences or variations according to the various systems) tacitly."[89]

Time of choice

At its origin, the rule of party autonomy related to the freedom of the parties **2–36** to choose the applicable law at the time of making their contract. It now extends (under the international conventions and rules cited) to the right of the parties to choose the law as it is to be applied at the time of the dispute.

It is logical to allow the parties to choose the law that is to govern their contract at the time when they make it. In their contract, the parties set out the rights and duties they undertake towards each other. It is appropriate that they should, at the same time, refer to the system of law by which that contract is to be governed because that law forms an essential element of the bargain between them.

There is less logic in allowing the parties to choose the applicable law once a dispute has arisen and yet, in practice, it seems that parties may do this, even if their choice of law differs from what they had chosen previously. Indeed, the Rome Convention makes express provision for this.[90] If any justification for this delayed choice (or even change) of law is sought in legal philosophy, it appears to lie in the concept of the autonomy of the parties. Parties are generally free to vary the terms of their contract by agreement; in the same way, they should be free to vary by agreement the law applicable to a dispute arising out of that contract.

Restrictions on party autonomy

For lawyers who practise in the resolution of international trade disputes, and **2–37** who are accustomed to wending their way through a maze of national laws, the existence of a general transnational rule of law supporting the autonomy of the parties is almost too good to be true. The natural inclination is to ask whether there are any restrictions on the rule, and if so, what?

The answer is that there may be limited restrictions on the rule, designed to ensure that the choice of law is bona fide and is not contrary to public policy. Thus, the Rome Convention, for example, does not allow the choice of a foreign law to override the mandatory rules of law of a country to which all the factual elements of the contract point—so that, for example, the choice of a foreign law for the purposes of tax evasion would not be permissible. And the relevant court

---

[89] Lalive, cited in Lew, p.87, above, para.2–32.
[90] The Rome Convention, Art.3, provides that a choice of law, or a variation of a choice, can be made at any time after the conclusion of the contract by agreement between the parties.

may apply its own national rules of public policy or *ordre public*. Thus in *Soleimany v Soleimany*,[91] the English Court of Appeal refused to enforce an award where the transaction was not illegal under the applicable law, but was illegal under English law.

The case concerned a contract between a father and son, which involved the smuggling of carpets out of Iran in breach of Iranian revenue laws and export controls. The father and son had agreed to submit their dispute to arbitration by the Beth Din, the Court of the Chief Rabbi in London, which applied Jewish law. Under the applicable Jewish law, the illegal purpose of the contract had no effect on the rights of the parties and the Beth Din proceeded to make an award enforcing the contract. In declining to enforce the award, the English Court of Appeal stated:

"The Court is in our view concerned to preserve the integrity of its process, and to see that it is not abused. The parties cannot override that concern by private agreement. They cannot by procuring an arbitration conceal that they, or rather one of them, is seeking to enforce an illegal contract. Public policy will not allow it."[92]

The choices

2–38   Subject only to the qualifications of bona fides, legality and no public policy objection, the conventions and rules on arbitration which have been mentioned make it plain that the parties may choose for themselves the law applicable to the dispute. Parties to an international commercial agreement should make full and proper use of this freedom and insert a "choice of law" clause into their contract. If this is not done, it will almost certainly be a matter for regret if a dispute should arise, since (as will be seen) the search for the proper law can be a long and expensive process.

A choice of law clause may be drawn in very simple terms. It is usually sufficient to say: "This agreement shall in all respects be governed by the law of England" (or of Singapore, or of the State of New York, or of any other state which has in place a modern law of contract).

The question that then arises is, given a free choice, what system of law should the parties choose as the law applicable to the dispute? Is their choice limited to the choice of a national system of law or may it extend beyond this, perhaps to rules of law such as those of the law merchant (*lex mercatoria*)? Indeed, are the parties limited to a choice of law or of legal rules? May they not, for instance, agree that the dispute should be decided according to considerations of equity and good conscience?

[91] [1999] Q.B. 785.
[92] *ibid.*, at 800.

It is to these questions that attention must now be turned. The choices that may   **2–39** be available to the parties include:

- national law;

- public international law (including the general principles of law);

- concurrent laws (and combined laws—the *tronc commun* doctrine);

- transnational law (including international development law; the *lex merca-toria*; codified terms and practices; and trade usages);

- equity and good conscience.

(c) National law

In most international commercial contracts, including those where a state or   **2–40** state entity is one of the parties, it is usual for a given system of law to be chosen as the law applicable to the contract itself. There is much sense in such a choice. Parties who choose a law to govern their contract, or any subsequent dispute between them, will generally choose an autonomous system of law. Such a system[93] is not merely a set of general principles or of isolated legal rules. It is an interconnecting, interdependent collection of laws, regulations and ordinances, enacted by or on behalf of the state and interpreted and applied by the courts. It is a complete legal system, designed to provide an answer to any legal question that might be posed. Furthermore, a national system of law will in principle be a known and existing system, capable of reasonably accurate interpretation by experienced practitioners.

In law, as in life, there is no certainty. However, a national system of law provides a known (or at least, determinable) legal standard, against which the rights and responsibilities of the parties can be measured. In the event of a dispute, the parties can be advised with reasonable confidence as to their legal position; or, at the very least, they can be given a broad indication of their chances of success or failure. If, for example, parties to a dispute which is to be heard in Switzerland agree that the arbitral tribunal shall apply the law of France, then all concerned (arbitrators, parties and advisers alike) know where they stand. The arbitrators will know to what system of law they have to refer, if such reference becomes necessary. The parties and their advisers will be able to evaluate their prospects of success against the known content of French law. They will know, too, what sort of legal arguments they will have to present; and what sort of legal arguments (as to fault, compensation and so on) they may be required to address.

---

[93] Which in this context will be referred to as a "national" system of law, the term being intended to cover not merely a "national law" properly so called, such as that of France, but also the law of a "state" within a federal system such as New York or California.

Choice of a system of national law

2–41   The standard arbitration clauses recommended by arbitral institutions, such as the ICC, are usually followed by a note pointing out that in addition to incorporating the arbitration clause in their agreement, the parties should also add a "choice of law" clause. In-house lawyers and others who are concerned with the drafting of contracts will invariably do this, so that in most commercial contracts it is usual to find an arbitration clause, followed by a "choice of law" clause.

Almost invariably, the law chosen is a national law. This may be because of that law's connection with the parties to the contract; or it may simply be because the parties regard it as a system of law which is well suited to govern their commercial relations. Indeed, many contracts incorporate the choice of a particular country's law, although they have no connection with that country. For example, commodity contracts, shipping and freight contracts and contracts of insurance often contain a choice of English law, because the commercial law of England is considered to reflect and to be responsive to the needs of modern international commerce. For similar reasons, many major reinsurance contracts contain a choice of the law of New York.

In an ideal world, almost any national system of law should be suitable, so long as that law had been drawn up, or has developed, in a manner which suits the requirements of modern commerce. In the real world, some national systems of law will be found to contain outdated laws and regulations which make them unsuitable for use in international contracts.

2–42   Indeed, even well-developed and modern codes of law are not necessarily best suited to the needs of international (as opposed to purely domestic) commerce. The law of a country reflects the social, economic and, above all, the political environment of that particular country. If a country habitually controls the import and export trade (perhaps permitting such activities only through state corporations) and prohibits the free flow of currency across the exchanges, these restrictions will permeate the national law. This may or may not benefit the country concerned, but it is not an environment in which international trade and commerce is likely to flourish. A national law that does not permit the free flow of goods and services across national frontiers is probably not the most suitable law to govern international commercial contracts and the disputes that may arise from them.

Parties to an international commercial contract will need to bear these kinds of considerations in mind in choosing a given system of law to govern their contractual relationships. Even in countries which favour international trade and development, problems may arise, particularly where the contract is made with the state itself or with a state agency. The problem, shortly stated, is that the state (as legislator) may change the law and so change the terms of the contract, lawfully but without the agreement of the other party to the contract. The state may, for instance, impose labour or import restrictions, which render performance of the contract more expensive. Unless the contract has been drafted with such possible contingencies in mind—and they may be difficult to foresee—it is the private party who will suffer from this change in the equilibrium of the contract.

The problem of protecting a party from changes in the local law was considered in the *Sapphire* arbitration:

"Under the present agreement, the foreign company was bringing financial and technical assistance to Iran, which involved it in investments, responsibilities and considerable risks. It therefore seems normal that they should be protected against any legislative changes which might alter the character of the contract and that they should be assured of some legal security. This would not be guaranteed to them by the outright application of Iranian law, which it is within the power of the Iranian State to change."[94]

Precluding unfair treatment

Various devices have been borrowed from private law contracts, in an attempt **2–43** to maintain the balance of the contract. These include revision clauses, hardship clauses and *force majeure* clauses, all of which have a part to play in helping to maintain the balance of the contractual relationship. In some long-term economic development agreements, the national law has been "frozen" by the parties agreeing that the law of the state party will be applied as it was on a given date. Strictly speaking, the state law does not then operate as the applicable law, but as an immutable code of law incorporated into the contract. It will not change no matter what amendments are made to the state law itself. The problem, however, (apart from the lack of flexibility that this device introduces into the contract) is that the state party may still introduce a law avoiding such clauses in its own territory. In other words, the problem of entrenching such clauses has to be faced; and whilst initially attractive, the "freezing" solution may fly in the face of political, social and economic realities.

Stabilisation clauses

Another method that has been tried, particularly in oil concession agreements, **2–44** is the inclusion of stabilisation clauses. These are undertakings on the part of the contracting state that it will not change the terms of the contract by legislative action, without the consent of the other party to the contract. In one of the arbitrations which arose out of the Libyan oil nationalisations, the arbitrator held that the Libyan Government's act of nationalisation was in breach of certain stabilisation clauses and was accordingly an illegal act under international law, entitling the companies to restitution of their concessions.[95] This decision is generally criticised as going too far, not only in its rejection of Libyan law as a basic ingredient of the governing law clause, and in its so-called "internationalisation" of the oil concession agreement, but also in its decision in favour of

[94] *Sapphire International Petroleum Ltd v The National Iranian Oil Company* (1964) 13 I.C.L.Q. 1011 at 1012.
[95] *Texaco* arbitration, below, para.2–50.

restitutio in integrum.[96] In any event, restitution was obviously impracticable. The only purpose it could serve was to indicate the basis on which damages should be paid for the allegedly illegal expropriation.[97] In another of the Libyan oil nationalisation arbitrations, where the facts were almost identical, the sole arbitrator did *not* regard the stabilisation clauses as preventing the Government's act of nationalisation. He held that this nationalisation was a legitimate exercise of sovereign power, as long as it was accompanied by "equitable compensation".[98] In the *Aminoil* arbitration, the arbitral tribunal held by a majority (with a separate opinion attached to the award) that, properly interpreted, the stabilisation clause in the concession agreement (which was to run for a period of 60 years) did not prevent the Kuwaiti Government's act of nationalisation.[99]

Stabilisation clauses, like provisions that seek to freeze the law, attempt to maintain a particular legal regime in existence, often for a considerable period of time, irrespective of any changes which may occur in the political, social and economic environment of the country concerned.[1] Such clauses attempt, unrealistically, to create the cobwebbed palace of the sleeping beauty—"La Belle au Bois Dormant"—in which time has come to a stop.[2] They are likely to be accorded less and less efficacy by arbitral tribunals. In this sense, *Aminoil* marked a turning point in the treatment of long-term contracts for the exploitation of national resources.[3]

Summary

2–45   In most of the international commercial disputes that are referred to arbitration, there is a choice of law clause, in addition to the arbitration clause. As already indicated, the law chosen will generally be that of a given country—the

---

[96] See, in particular, Rigaux, *"Des dieux et des héros: Réflexions sur une sentence arbitrale"* (1978) Revue Critique de droit international privé, p.435; and Brigitte Stern, *"Trois arbitrages, un même problème, trois solutions"* (1980) 1 Revue de l'Arbitrage 2.

[97] See para.8–15.

[98] The *Liamco* arbitration (1981) VI Yearbook Commercial Arbitration 89 at 104 and 113. For further discussion of the three Libyan oil nationalisation arbitrations see Greenwood, "State Contracts in International Law—The Libyan Oil Arbitrations" (1982) 53 B.Y.I.L. 27.

[99] *Aminoil* arbitration [1982] 21 I.L.M. 976, separate opinion of Sir Gerald Fitzmaurice Q.C. at 1027.

[1] For further discussion of stabilisation clauses see, *e.g.*, Wetter, *The International Arbitral Process: Public and Private* (1979), Vol.1, p.407; Toope, *Mixed International Arbitration* (Grotius Publications Ltd, 1990), pp.52 *et seq.*; Nagla Nassar, *The Sanctity of Contracts Revisited* (Martinus Nijhoff, 1994). For an example of a stabilisation clause in an LNG contract which worked against the party it was intended to protect, see Gaillard, "The role of the arbitrator in determining the applicable law" in *The Leading Arbitrators' Guide to International Arbitration* (Juris Publishing Inc, New York, 2004), p.186.

[2] It could be argued that, particularly in developing countries, stabilisation clauses help to create a secure and favourable legal regime and thereby encourage investment. See, *e.g.*, the Nigerian Liquefied Natural Gas Venture, discussed by Rawding, "Protecting Investments under State Contracts; Some legal and ethical issues" 99 Arbitration International 341. Rawding also suggests that stabilisation clauses should not be viewed as literally freezing the law, but as placing a financial restriction on, or defining, the financial consequences of the state's exercise of its right to nationalise.

[3] *American Independent Oil Company Inc (Aminoil) v Government of the State of Kuwait* [1982] 21 I.L.M. 976.

law of England, or of Switzerland, or whatever the case may be. The same is true of arbitrations that are commenced under the terms of a submission agreement.

Where the choice of law is left to the arbitrators—a situation which is discussed in more detail below—the position is perhaps less clear-cut. The arbitrators will look for the law with which the contract has the closest connection, but may balk at selecting this if it is also the national law of one of the parties, for fear of appearing biased. They may then look for one of the other possible options, which are about to be considered.

In the same way, a party to a contract with a state or state entity may well insist, or try to insist, upon one of these options. The state concerned would almost certainly not agree to subject its contracts to the law of another state; and the private party might well be unwilling to accept the national law of the state with which it was contracting, for fear of adverse changes in that law.

(d) Public international law and general principles of law

Public international law is concerned primarily with states, but not exclusively so.[4] As Dame Rosalyn Higgins, a judge of the ICJ, has contended, international law is a dynamic (not static) decision-making process, in which there are a variety of participants:

2–46

> "Now, in this model, there are no 'subjects' and 'objects', but only *participants*. Individuals *are* participants, along with states, international organizations (such as the United Nations, or the International Monetary Fund (IMF) or the ILO), multinational corporations, and indeed private non-governmental groups."[5]

Amongst the "participants" to whom Judge Higgins referred are those individuals and corporations who brought claims before the Iran-US Claims Tribunal and those "investors" who seek to protect their investment through the machinery of ICSID.[6] This has brought public international law into sharper focus so far as private individuals and corporations—and their lawyers—are concerned. Increasingly, "international law" may be specified as the substantive law of a contract, particularly where that contract is with a state or state agency. The reference may be to "international law" on its own; or it may be—as discussed below—used in conjunction with a national system of law.

Reference has already been made to the freedom which parties (generally) have in selecting the law or the legal rules applicable to their contract. There is no reason in principle why they should not select public international law, or

---

[4] Rosalyn Higgins, *Problems & Process: International Law and How We Use It* (Clevedon Press, Oxford, 1994), p.39.

[5] Higgins, *op.cit.*, p.50.

[6] See Ch.11 in relation to the applicable law in disputes under investment treaties.

alternatively the general principles of law, as the law which is to govern their contractual relationship.[7] To quote again from Judge Higgins:

> "The increasing importance of international arbitration is an area that we should perhaps be watching. It is now commonplace for a foreign private corporation and a state who have entered into contractual relations to agree to international arbitration in the event of a dispute. (And, in principle, the private party could be an *individual*, though as such he will probably have less leverage than a foreign corporation and may well have to accept the local legal system rather than reference to international arbitration). The applicable law clause may designate a national legal system, but more usually it will refer to 'general principles of law' or 'the law of country X and the relevant principles of general international law', or some such similar formula. At one bound, therefore, the private party has escaped the need to have his claim brought by his national government, and can invoke international law. Thus, if State X and Mr Y have a contract, State X's ability to vary the terms of that contract will be interpreted by reference to the relevant principles of international law; and compensation due to Mr Y will likewise be appraised by reference to international law ... Arbitral clauses which refer to international law as the applicable law effectively remove the alleged inability of individuals to be the bearer of rights under international law. This is being done by mutual consent, of course—but the point is that there is *no inherent reason* why the individual should not be able directly to invoke international law and to be the beneficiary of international law."[8]

2–47   There are many sources of international law, including international conventions and international custom, but probably the most relevant, so far as non-state parties are concerned, are "the general principles of law recognised by civilised nations."[9]

However, the problem of adopting international law, or alternatively "the general principles of law", as the system of law which is to govern a commercial relationship is not a problem of principle, but of practice. International law, being concerned primarily with the relationship between states, is not particularly well equipped to deal with detailed contractual issues—such as mistake, misrepresentation, time of performance, the effect of bankruptcy or liquidation, *force*

---

[7] *cf.* the observation of Megaw J. in a case brought many years ago: "Thus, it may be, though perhaps it would be unusual, that the parties could validly agree that a part, or the whole, of their legal relations should be decided by the arbitral tribunal on the basis of a foreign system of law, or perhaps on the basis of principles of international law; *e.g.*, in a contract to which a Sovereign State was a party." See *Orion Compania Espanola de Seguros v Belfort Maatschappij Voor Algemene Verzekgringeen* [1962] 2 Lloyd's Rep. 257 at 264.

[8] Higgins, *op. cit.*, p.54.

[9] Art.38 of the Statute of the ICJ (which was established in 1945 and is generally known as "the World Court") states that in applying international law to the disputes before it, the court is to apply, *inter alia*, those general principles of law.

majeure or the measure of damages and so forth. The same criticism may be directed at the "general principles of law" as the governing law of a commercial contract. The problem with the general principles is they are just that. They deal with such topics as the principle of good faith in treaty relations, abuse of rights, the concept of state and individual responsibility. They are excellent as generalisations, but lack sufficient detail.[10] That is why the authors suggest that if they are to be used in a contract, they should be used as a concurrent law, rather than on their own.

(e) Concurrent laws, combined laws and the *tronc commum* doctrine

As already indicated in the discussion of contracts to which a state or state   **2–48**
entity is a party, one of the main anxieties of commercial organisations engaged in trading or other business relationships with a sovereign state is that, after the bargain has been struck and the contract has been signed, the state may change its own law to the disadvantage of the private party.

One established safeguard against unfair or arbitrary action by the state party to the contract is to stipulate that the state's own law will apply only insofar as it accords with either public international law, the general principles of law or some other system with accepted minimum standards.

The Washington Convention, which established ICSID, makes use of this system of concurrent laws. The Convention[11] provides for the resolution of disputes between a state (or a state entity) and a private party[12]; it stipulates that if a dispute arises and there has been no express choice of law by the parties, the arbitral tribunal will apply the law of the contracting state and "such rules of international law as may be applicable". Thus, honour is satisfied. The state's own law is given proper recognition. Yet some fetter is imposed upon possibly unfair or arbitrary action, by the reference to public international law.[13]

This is a system of concurrent laws. For example, a state that terminated a   **2–49**
long-term investment contract by an act of nationalisation would presumably do so in a way that was valid under its own law. However, such an act of nationalisation would not be valid under international law unless it was shown to be non-discriminatory and to serve a public purpose, with proper compensation being offered. In this way, international law would be brought into play to set a minimum standard, which the arbitral tribunal would be empowered to uphold in its award.[14]

---

[10] For an excellent (and, it must be admitted, detailed) work on this topic see Bin Cheng, *General Principles of Law as Applied by International Courts and Tribunals* (Grotius Publications Ltd, 1987).

[11] See the discussion of this Convention in Ch.1.

[12] So long as the state has adopted the Washington Convention.

[13] Rawding (above) describes this option as subjecting national law to "international quality control". The issue of applicable law in cases brought under investment treaties is addressed in Ch.11.

[14] For a discussion of compensation, see Ch.11, paras 11–31—11–36.

The Libyan oil nationalisation arbitrations

2–50   The coupling of national law with international law is seen in the three arbitrations that arose out of the Libyan oil nationalisations,[15] although it only worked effectively in one of them. In the others, the tribunal either misread or misapplied the choice of law clause.

This choice of law clause was the same in the different concession agreements that came before three different arbitrators. It read as follows:

> "This concession shall be governed by and interpreted in accordance with the principles of law of Libya common to the principles of international law and, in the absence of such common principles, then by and in accordance with the general principles of law, including such of those principles as may have been applied by international tribunals."[16]

On a plain reading of this clause, it seems clear that the intention was that the concession agreement should be governed primarily by the principles of the law of Libya, to the extent that these were in accordance with the principles of international law, and that the role of Libyan law should only be ignored or overridden to the extent that it failed to comply with those established principles. However, if this was the intention, it was not fulfilled. In the *Texaco* arbitration the sole arbitrator held that the clause was primarily a choice of *public international law,* whereas in the *BP* arbitration, the sole arbitrator appears to have regarded it as a choice of the general principles of law.[17] Neither arbitrator gave proper weight to the law of Libya, which is the system of law mentioned first in the choice of law clause.

2–51   The sole arbitrator in the *Liamco* arbitration[18] was closer to the intended meaning of the clause. He held that the governing law of the contract was the law of Libya but that the clause excluded any part of that law which was in conflict with the principles of international law.[19]

The arbitral tribunal in the *Aminoil* arbitration arrived at a similar conclusion in respect of a concession agreement that had been brought to an end by an act of nationalisation, coupled with an offer of "fair compensation". The Government of Kuwait and Aminoil agreed in the submission agreement that their

---

[15] The *Texaco* arbitration, the *BP* arbitration and the *Liamco* arbitration (1981) VI Yearbook Commercial Arbitration 89. See also Greenwood, "State Contracts in International Law—The Libyan Oil Arbitrations" (1982) 17 I.L.M. 14; Rigaux, "Des dieux et des héros, Réflexions sur une sentence arbitrale" (1978) 67 Rev. Crit. 435–459; and Stern, "Trois arbitrages, un même problème, trois solutions" (1980) 3 Revue de l'arbitrage 43.

[16] For this text, see the *Texaco* arbitration.

[17] "The governing system of law is what that clause expressly provides, *viz.* in the absence of principles common to the law of Libya and international law, the general principles of law, including such of those principles as may have been applied by international tribunals", Judge Lagergren in the *BP* arbitration, above.

[18] *Liamco v Libya* (1982) 62 I.L.R. 140 at 143.

[19] The fact that three different arbitrators could arrive at three different conclusions on the meaning of the same choice of law clause highlights one of the weaknesses of the arbitral system, which is the possibility of conflicting awards on the same basic problem: see Stern, *op.cit.*, n.114.

dispute should be settled by arbitration "on the basis of law", but left the choice of law to the tribunal with the stipulation that the tribunal should have regard to "the quality of the parties, the transnational character of their relations and the principles of law and practice prevailing in the modern world".[20] On this basis, Aminoil argued that the concession agreement was governed by transnational law, which it equated with the general principles of law, including the principles of *pacta sunt servanda*; reparation for injury; respect for acquired rights; the prohibition of unjust enrichment; and the requirement of good faith (including the prohibition against abuse of rights and estoppel or preclusion). The Government, for its part, argued for the application of the law of Kuwait, of which public international law formed part.

It is useful to look at the tribunal's decision on the applicable law for two reasons. First, the *Aminoil* arbitration—in which the state took part, unlike Libya in the Libyan arbitrations—marked a decisive turning point in the treatment of state contracts. Secondly, the dramatic increase in the work of ICSID[21] has focused attention on concurrent law clauses.

The tribunal in *Aminoil* stated that the question of the law applicable to the   **2–52** substantive issues in dispute before it was a simple one. The law of Kuwait applied to many matters over which it was directly involved; but, as the Government had argued, established public international law was part of the law of Kuwait; and the general principles of law were part of public international law.[22] The tribunal concluded:

> "The different sources of the law thus to be applied are not—as least in the present case—in contradiction with one another. Indeed, if, as recalled above, international law constitutes an integral part of the law of Kuwait, the general principles of law correspondingly recognize the rights of the State in its capacity of supreme protector of the general interest. If the different legal elements involved do not always and everywhere blend as successfully as in the present case, it is nevertheless on taking advantage of their resources, and encouraging their trend towards unification, that the future of a truly international economic order in the investment field will depend."[23]

The tribunal's respect for the law of the host state may have marked the end of the so-called "internationalisation" of state contracts, with its cavalier disregard for the law of the state concerned.

The use of a system of concurrent laws, such as that envisaged by the Washington Convention in the absence of an express choice of law, seems to be the way forward for international contracts to which a state or state entity is a party. The reference to the law of the state concerned gives proper importance to the sovereign position of the state party; yet the reference to international law, or

---

[20] *The Government of Kuwait v Aminoil* (1982) 21 International Legal Materials 976 at 980.
[21] See Chs 2, 3 and 5.
[22] *The Government of Kuwait v Aminoil* (1982) 21 International Legal Materials 976 at 1000.
[23] *ibid.*, at 1001.

possibly to the general principles of law, provides a measure of protection to the private party to the contract. There is a balance to be struck between state law and international law. It is important that arbitral tribunals should be prepared to give due weight to both.[24]

2–53   The previous discussion has shown where the search for a "neutral" law may lead, particularly in relation to state contracts.[25] However, the search for such a law is not confined to state contracts. One solution, which has been canvassed in theory, and occasionally adopted in practice, is to choose the national laws of both parties and so obtain the best (or possibly the worst) of both worlds. This *tronc commun* doctrine is based on the proposition that, if free to do so, each party to an international commercial transaction would choose its own national law to govern that transaction. If this proves unacceptable, why not go some way towards achieving this objective by identifying the common parts of the two different systems of law and applying these common parts to the matters in dispute?[26]

The *Sapphire* arbitration has already been mentioned as an illustration of the problem of affording protection to the private party to a state contract against changes in the national law enacted by the state party. There was no express choice of law in the contract. There were, however, choice of law clauses in similar concession agreements previously made by the respondent, the National Iranian Oil Company, which were in the following terms:

"In view of the diverse nationalities of the parties to this Agreement, it shall be governed by and interpreted and applied in accordance with the principles of law common to Iran and the several nations in which the other parties to this Agreement are incorporated, and in the absence of such common principles then by and in accordance with principles of law recognised by civilised nations in general, including such of those principles as may have been applied by international tribunals."

This choice of law clause appears to be an adoption of the *tronc commun* solution to the choice of law problem. What the arbitrator was required to do was to find out what principles existed in the law of Iran, which were also to be found in the national laws of the other parties to the agreement, and apply those common principles to the matters in dispute before him. However, the arbitrator failed to do this. Instead, he read the clause as entitling him to disregard the law

---

[24] Distrust of the awards of international arbitral tribunals, which have concentrated on "internationalising" state contracts so as to exclude the role of the state's own law, has had some influence in the formulation of the New International Economic Order: *e.g.* Art.2(2)(c) of the Charter of Economic Rights and Duties of States provides that any controversy over compensation on the nationalisation of foreign property should be settled under the domestic law of the state concerned.

[25] See para.2–48 *et seq.*

[26] The *tronc commun* doctrine was first elaborated by Rubino-Sammartano in 1987: see his article "Le Tronc Commun des lois nationales en présence. Réflexions sur le droit applicable par l'arbitre international" (1987) Revue de l'Arbitrage 133; and, by the same author, in *International Arbitration Law* (Kluwer, 1990), p.274.

of Iran (although this was specifically mentioned in the choice of law clause) and
to apply the general principles of law. What the arbitrator said was:

"It is quite clear from the above that the parties intended to exclude the
application of Iranian law. But they have not chosen another positive legal
system and this omission is on all the evidence deliberate. All the connecting
factors cited above point to the fact that the parties therefore intended to
submit the interpretation and performance of their contract to principles of law
generally recognised by civilised nations, to which article 37 of the agreement
refers, being the only clause which contains an express reference to an
applicable law."

Accordingly, if the choice of law clause was intended to operate as a choice of **2–54**
combined laws (or more correctly, as a choice of combined legal principles), it
failed in its objective.

Many years after the *Sapphire* arbitration, another important example of
combined laws (or again, more correctly, of combined legal principles) came to
be generally reported (and sometimes misreported). In the Channel Tunnel
project,[27] the concessionnaires, Eurotunnel, entered into a construction contract
with a group of Anglo-French companies, known as Trans-Manche Link. Surprisingly,[28] this agreement between two private entities referred not to the
national law of either party, nor indeed to any national system of law, but instead
to the common principles of both systems of law. The relevant clause provided
that the contract would:

" . . . in all respects be governed by and interpreted in accordance with the
principles common to both English law and French law, and in the absence of
such common principles by such general principles of international trade law
as have been applied by national and international tribunals."

A dispute under the construction contract[29] went to the English court and this
choice of law clause was considered both by the Court of Appeal and by the
highest court in England, the House of Lords. In the Court of Appeal, one of the
judges said:

"Since both Eurotunnel and the contractors were partly French and partly
English, I wonder why they did not choose either English law or French law
exclusively—and for that matter why they chose Brussels as the seat of any
arbitration. The hybrid system of law which they did choose has a superficial

---

[27] See n.129.
[28] It is surprising in that the *tronc commun* is generally chosen as the "politically correct" choice of
law in cases involving a foreign state, not cases involving only private parties.
[29] When Eurotunnel sought an injunction to prevent Trans-Manche from carrying out a threat to cease
work on part of the project.

attraction, but I suspect that it will lead to lengthy and expensive dispute."[30]

2–55 This comment turned out to be accurate.[31] The search for common principles of English and French law meant that for each dispute that arose under the construction contract—and there were many—teams of French and English lawyers on each side had to determine what the answer was likely to be under the applicable principles of their own law and then work out to what extent, if at all, these principles were common to both systems of law. As one of the construction group's external counsel has commented:

"The main reason for the difficulty in applying a clause providing for the application of common principles between English and French law is that although both systems tend to produce the same or very similar results, they fall short of providing the set of common principles which is necessary to cover all contractual disputes."[32]

Although the Court of Appeal was, in passing, critical of this choice of law clause—as a hybrid system of law—it did not suggest that it was anything other than a binding and enforceable agreement. This emerges even more strongly in the decision of the House of Lords:

"The parties chose an indeterminate 'law' to govern their substantive rights; an elaborate process for ascertaining those rights; and a location for that purpose outside the territories of the participants. This conspicuously neutral, 'a-national' and extra-judicial structure may well have been the first choice for the special needs of the Channel Tunnel venture. But whether it was right or wrong, it is the choice which the parties have made."[33]

---

[30] *Channel Tunnel Group Ltd v Balfour Beatty Construction Ltd* [1992] 1 Q.B. 656 at 675.

[31] Rubino-Sammartano, in "The Channel Tunnel and the Tronc Commun Doctrine" (1993) 10 Journal of International Arbitation 59 at 61, states: "The Channel Tunnel contract is an example of an express choice by the parties and as such it does not seem to leave the door open to possible argument. The view expressed by Staughton L.J., 'I suspect it will lead to lengthy and expensive dispute' cannot consequently be shared." In fact, as stated in the text above, it was entirely accurate, in that two teams of lawyers, French and English, had to be engaged by each of the parties in order to advise on the many disputes that arose. It is true that the choice of law clause was clear. This is not the issue. What was *not* clear was what were the "common principles" of French and English law which were applicable to the various different disputes which arose— including, *e.g.*, disputes as to whether a particular claim was or was not barred (or extinguished) by lapse of time.

[32] Duval, "English and French Law: The Search for Common Principles" (1997) 25 International Business Lawyer 181 at 182.

[33] *Channel Tunnel Group Ltd v Balfour Beatty Construction Ltd* [1993] A.C. 334 at 368. In the same judgment, Lord Mustill said (at 353): " . . . having promised to take their complaints to the experts and if necessary to the arbitrators, that is where the appellants should go."

The Channel Tunnel project was one of the major international construction contracts of the twentieth century.[34] Of course, even if only one system of law had been chosen as the applicable law, both French and English lawyers would have been needed to deal with the financing of the project, as well as "domestic" issues such as staff accommodation on either side of the Channel, labour relations and so on; but the dispute resolution process itself would have been simpler, less expensive and, it is suggested, much more predictable.

There are many large international projects in which lawyers from different   **2–56** countries are likely to be needed. In such major projects, the expense involved in searching for the common principles of two national systems of law, or for "the common part"[35] of these two national laws, may perhaps be justified (particularly if the two systems are known to have much in common). However, in ordinary trading contracts, of the kind that constitute the day-to-day substance of international commerce, it must be doubtful whether the additional trouble and expense can be justified.

In summary, it is suggested that in ordinary international commercial contracts, including construction contracts, the parties would do well to try to agree upon a given national law as the law of the contract. It may take time to reach agreement, but it would be time well spent. Where one of the parties to the contract is a state or a state agency it may be necessary to adopt a system of concurrent laws (which may not be easy to operate, but which will probably be better than a system of combined laws).

(g) Transnational law (including *lex mercatoria*; the UNIDROIT Principles; the Shari'ah; international development law and trade usages)

Introduction

The reference to "such rules of international law as may be applicable" (as, for   **2–57** example, in the Washington Convention),[36] or to "the relevant principles of international law" (as in the Channel Tunnel Treaty) serve to remind us that it is not the whole *corpus* of law, but only certain specific rules of law that are likely to be relevant in any given dispute. For example, an international contract for the sale of goods governed by the law of Austria will usually bring into consideration only those provisions of Austrian law which deal with the sale of goods. An international construction project that is governed by the law of England will principally involve consideration of that special area of law which is concerned with construction contracts. This breaking down of the whole body of the law into specific, discrete sections is reflected by increased specialisation within the

---

[34] For further comment on the House of Lords decision see Reymond, "The Channel Tunnel Case and the Law of International Arbitration" (1993) 109 L.Q.R. 337; and Veeder, "L'Arrêt Channel Tunnel de la Chambre des Lords" (1993) 4 Revue de l'arbitrage 705.

[35] Rubino-Sommartano, "The Channel Tunnel and the Tronc Commun Doctrine", *op. cit.*, p.61: "the common part of these two national laws must be treated as that chosen by the parties".

[36] Washington Convention, Art.42.

legal profession itself. Thus, for example, within an association of lawyers such as the International Bar Association, there are specialist groups whose primary expertise is in energy law or intellectual property or construction law—and so forth.[37]

In these circumstances, it seems appropriate to ask whether or not a particular group of bankers, or merchants, or traders, may develop their own special rules of conduct which gradually acquire the force of law, either by themselves or by incorporation into national law or international treaty. Experience suggests that the answer to this question is a cautious "yes". Indeed, in the past this is how much of our law developed. Colombus,[38] for example, tells of the early maritime codes such as the Rhodian Sea Law which dated from the second or third century B.C. and which was "of great authority in the Mediterranean, for its principles were accepted by both Greeks and Romans and its memory lasted for a thousand years". This was an early form of transnational law, as indeed was the celebrated Consolato des Mare which, again according to Colombus:

> "throughout the Middle Ages, reigned supreme in the Mediterranean until the advent of sovereign states, national legislation superseding the customary laws of the sea, so often incorporating many of its rules".[39]

It is significant that, within time, the "customary laws of the sea" were superseded by legislation. As states evolve, this is almost inevitable. In the present day world of sovereign states and complex legislation, it may be questioned whether there is still room for the crystallisation of customary practices into rules of law. Even if there is, it is likely to be confined to particular usages and to particular trades—and to grow, so to speak, in the interstices of existing laws, rather than to form one vast *corpus* of law.

2–58 There are many different communities carrying on activities which may be as diverse (and have as little in common) as the transport of goods or the establishment of an international telecommunications network. The rules of law that are relevant to these different commercial activities are in themselves likely to be very different. They may share certain basic legal concepts—such as the sanctity of contracts (*pacta sunt servanda*)—but even here different considerations are likely to apply. For example, an international contract for the sale of goods will be performed within a comparatively short timescale. Compare this to a major infrastructure project that will take many years to perform and during the course of which the basis on which the original bargain was struck may change dramatically.

Given these words of caution, the approach adopted in this book is pragmatic rather than theoretical. This is probably the most useful approach, since in practice lawyers and arbitrators are concerned with a particular dispute or series

---

[37] The same division into specialist groups may be seen within law firms where, increasingly, specialist advice or expertise in a particular area of law is what the clients are seeking.
[38] Colombus, *International Law of the Sea*.
[39] *ibid.*

of disputes rather than with some "general theory" of law. A Report on Transnational Rules by the International Law Association put it as follows:

"The Committee's approach in its continuing study of transnational law has been to step back from the highly contentious issues that arise from any theoretical consideration of transnational law, or *lex mercatoria*, as a discrete body of principles and to examine, in a pragmatic way, the application of individual identifiable principles at least as a phenomenon of international commercial arbitration, which it undoubtedly is."[40]

The lex mercatoria

Probably the most important development in the field of transnational law is **2–59** that of the *lex mercatoria*. This new law draws on the sources of law which have already been mentioned, including public international law and the general principles of law. It also draws on the UNIDROIT Principles of International Commercial Law ("the UNIDROIT Principles") and the 1998 Principles of European Contract Law, which are discussed later.

This modern version of a "law merchant" is taken to consist of rules and practices which have evolved within the international business communities. The late Professor Goldman, who named this new "law" and who contributed greatly to its development,[41] refers to it as having had "an illustrious precursor in the Roman *jus gentium*",[42] which he describes as "an autonomous source of law proper to the economic relations (*commercium*) between citizens and foreigners (*peregrine*)".[43]

The advantage of such a code of law is obvious. It would be adapted to the needs of modern international commerce and it would be of uniform application. The problem is whether such a system of law, which might have existed in Roman times or in the Middle Ages, can arise spontaneously—as it were—amongst states which already possess in full measure their own laws, orders and regulations. Amongst some commentators, the new *lex mercatoria* has been

[40] Bowden, "Transnational Rules in International Commercial Arbitration" (1993) ICC Publication No.480/4, p.127.
[41] See Goldman, "*Lex Mercatoria*", Forum Internationale, No.3 (Nov. 1983). The late Professor Goldman, having referred to the codification of international commercial practices, such as the ICC "Uniform Customs and Practices for Documentary Credits" and the INCOTERMS, as evidence of the emergence of an *international* business practice stated, at p.5: "Commentators in the early 1960s began to take note of this evolution. Clive Schmithoff was the first in England to salute the new Law Merchant; in France, Philippe Kahn, with respect to international sales, Philippe Fouchard, with respect to international commercial arbitration and Jean Stoufflet, with respect to documentary credits, undertook to study this law. As for myself, I concluded that a place could be acknowledged for the *lex mercatoria*—a name which stuck—within the boundaries of the law".
[42] Goldman, *op. cit.*, p.3.
[43] *ibid.*

greeted with approval.[44] Others have been politely sceptical[45] or (in the context of state contracts) have dismissed it as an idea whose time has passed, since more sophisticated laws and rules now exist.[46] Others still have been openly hostile.[47] What then is this new "law" which has aroused so much controversy and which, from time to time, has made its appearance in arbitral awards and in court proceedings?

2–60   For Professor Goldman, the distinguishing features of the *lex mercatoria* were its "customary" and "spontaneous" nature.[48] It was his view that international commercial relationships:

" . . . may perfectly well be governed by a body of specific rules, including transnational custom, general principles of law and arbitral case law. It makes no difference if this body of rules is not part of a legal order[49] comporting its own legislative and judicial organs. Within this body of rules, the general principles of law are not only those referred to in Article 38(a) of the Statute of the International Court of Justice; there may be added to it principles progressively established by the general and constant usage of international trade."[50]

It is not difficult to envisage rules developing in a particular area of international trade—such as documentary credits—and eventually being codified, either in national legislation or by international treaty, so as to attain the force of law.[51] But the custom in question is usually that of a particular trade or industry. The point has already been made that international traders do not constitute one

---

[44] Goldman, "La Lex Mercatoria dans les contrats d'arbitrage internationaux: Réalité et Perspectives" (1979) Clunet Journal du Droit International 475; Lalive, "Transnational (or Truly International) Public Policy and International Arbitration", ICC Congress Series No.3 (New York, 1986), p.257; Gaillard, "Transnational Rules in International Arbitration 1993" ICC Publication No.480/4 (a very helpful review of aspects of transnational law by distinguished contributors).

[45] See, for instance, Mustill, "The New Lex Mercatoria: the First Twenty-five Years" (1997) 4 Arbitration International 86, where he notes that: "The *Lex Mercatoria* has sufficient intellectual credentials to merit serious study, and yet is not so generally accepted as to escape the sceptical eye".

[46] See, *e.g.*, Delaume, "The Proper Law of State Contracts and the *Lex Mercatoria*: A Reappraisal" (1988) 3 ICSID Review—Foreign Investments Law Journal 79, where (at 106) this experienced international practitioner suggests that the risk of changes in state law to the detriment of the private party to a state contract may be insured under the Convention Establishing the Multilateral Investment Guarantee Agency ((1985) 24 I.L.M. 1589) and that this is far more adapted to the commercial realities "than the *Lex Mercatoria* which remains, both in scope and in practical significance, an elusive system and a mythical view of a transnational law of State Contracts whose sources are elsewhere."

[47] See, for instance, Mann, "The Proper Law in the Conflict of Laws" (1987) 36 I.C.L.Q. 437 at 448; and Toope, *Mixed International Arbitation* (Grotius Publications Ltd, 1990), particularly at p.96 where the author concludes: "It would appear that the so-called *lex mercatoria* is largely an effort to legitimise as 'law' the economic interests of Western corporations".

[48] Goldman, *op. cit.*, p.6.

[49] Although Professor Goldman himself contended that it *was* part of a legal order.

[50] Goldman, *op.cit.*, p.21.

[51] Both the ICC Arbitration Rules (Art.17.2) and the UNCITRAL Arbitration Rules (Art.33.3) require arbitrators to take account of relevant trade usages.

single homogeneous community. Instead they constitute a myriad of communities, each with their own different customary rules. How are these very different and specific rules to evolve into universal rules of international trade law?

Rather than pose these theoretical questions, it is perhaps more useful to ask: what is this new law? What principles does it embody? What specific rules does it lay down? In short, what is its content?

There appear to be two alternative approaches towards assessing the content of the new *lex mercatoria*: the "list" method and the functional method.

The list method

So far as the "list" method is concerned, various lists of rules or principles   **2–61**
have been prepared over the past decade,[52] drawing amongst other things upon the UNIDROIT Principles and the 1998 Principles of European Contract Law.[53] The list process has been criticised as lacking flexibility. To counter that criticism, Professor Berger has proposed "creeping codification":

"Creeping codification is to be distinguished from more formalized techniques for defining the *lex mercatoria* (UNIDROIT and Lando Principles): it is intended to avoid the 'static element' characteristic of other approaches and to provide the openness and flexibility required in order to take account of the rapid development of international trade and commerce."[54]

"Creeping codification" is intended to ensure that a list of transnational commercial principles is capable of being rapidly and continually revised and updated. Berger has established the Central Transnational Law Database[55] as the institutional framework within which to develop and update the list.[56]

The functional method

The alternative approach involves identifying a particular rule of the *lex*   **2–62**
mercatoria when a specific question arises. This so-called "functional approach" regards *lex mercatoria* as a method for determining the appropriate rule or principle. Professor Gaillard is a leading exponent of this approach.[57] He

---

[52] See, *e.g.*, K.P. Berger, *The Creeping Codification of Lex Mercatoria* (Kluwer Law International, 1999), p.212; Mustill, "The New Lex Mercatoria: the First Twenty-five Years" (1997) 4 Arbitration International 185—although he thought the results "a modest haul for twenty-five years of international arbitration"; and Paulsson, "La lex mercatoria dans l'arbitrage de la CCI" (1990) Revue de l'Arbitrage 55.

[53] Prepared by the Lando Commission and sometimes called the "Lando Principles".

[54] Berger, *op. cit.*, at n.192.

[55] See Berger, "Lex Mercatoria Online, The Central Transnational Law Database at *www.tldb.de*" (2002) 18 Arbitration International 83.

[56] Fortier, "The new, new *lex mercatoria*, or back to the future" (2001) 17 Arbitration International 126.

[57] Gaillard, "Transnational law: a legal system or a method of decision-making" (2001) 17 Arbitration International 62.

emphasises that the controversy, which initially focused on the existence of transnational rules, has shifted. It is now:

" . . . concentrating more recently on the establishment in further detail of the *content* of those rules or the more systematic assessment of the means to do so. As a result, very significant differences of opinion on how such goals may be achieved have emerged."[58]

According to Gaillard, the functional approach presents the advantage that any claim made by a party in a given case would necessarily find an answer, which may not be the position under the list approach.[59] It is suggested that when arbitrators seek to identify the content of the *lex mercatoria*, they draw increasingly on the UNIDROIT Principles:

"If the Unidroit Principles embody concepts already in the *lex mercatoria*, . . . these Principles would seem to provide a point of explicit reference for arbitral tribunals. And this is exactly what appears to be happening: the Unidroit Principles have already been referred to in about thirty ICC cases, it is recently reported, in order to identify general legal principles."[60]

The usefulness of the UNIDROIT Principles and of the Lando Principles (which set out rules common to the main legal systems surveyed) has also been recognised by Yves Fortier:

"The result—a concrete, usable list of principles and rules—addresses head-on the traditional concern of practitioners that the *lex* is too abstract and impractical to be of any use in the real world."[61]

2–63   Fortier refers to this set of rules as the "new, new *lex mercatoria*". The fact that the UNIDROIT Principles embody concepts within the *lex mercatoria*, but are not a source of it, has similarly been stressed by Professor Mayer, who has published a useful survey of ICC awards on the issue[62]:

"Each arbitral award stands on its own. There is no doctrine of precedence or of *stare decisis* as between different awards; and in general there is no appellate court to sort the wheat from the chaff. There is, in this sense, no formal control of the arbitral process.[63] Arbitrators are free to decide as they

---

[58] Gaillard, *op.cit.*, p.60; and see also Fortier, *op. cit.*
[59] Gaillard, *op cit.*, p.64.
[60] Molineaux, "Applicable law in arbitration—The coming convergence of civil and Anglo-Saxon law via Unidroit and *lex mercatoria*" (2000) 1 Journal of World Investment 130.
[61] Fortier, *op. cit.*, pp.124–125.
[62] Mayer, "The UNIDROIT Principles in Contemporary Contract Practice" in ICC Bulletin—Special Supplement: UNIDROIT Principles of international commercial contracts—Reflections on their use in international arbitration (2002), p.111.
[63] Except on procedural matters, which are not under consideration here.

choose. Conscientious arbitrators will obviously do their utmost to ensure that their decision is made in accordance with the law governing the contract. Their professional conscience will demand no less; and they will not decide *ex aequo et bono* without the express authorisation of the parties. But if the law governing the contract consists of those rules or principles which the arbitrators consider most appropriate, and which may conveniently be labelled as part of the *lex mercatoria*, those arbitrators are in effect free to decide in accordance with what they consider to be just and equitable, whilst purporting to decide in accordance with legal rules."

This is a pertinent observation. Under the guise of applying the *lex mercatoria*, an arbitral tribunal may in effect pick such rules as seem to the tribunal to be just and reasonable—which may or may not be what the parties intended when they made their contract.

The *lex mercatoria* has made an impact upon the law of international commercial arbitration.[64] It has also served to remind both the parties to international commercial arbitration and the arbitral tribunals who are called upon to resolve their disputes, that they are operating at an international level and that different considerations may come into play from those to be found in purely national, or domestic, arbitrations.

Where the *lex mercatoria* is said to govern the parties' contract, either by **2–64** agreement of the parties themselves or by a decision of the tribunal, will a court enforce that choice of law, if called upon to do so? Secondly, will such a court enforce an award made in conformity with the *lex mercatoria*, if called upon to do so?

In principle, the answer to both questions appears to be "yes". If the parties have agreed upon a particular method of dispute resolution, the court should be prepared to enforce that agreement on normal contractual principles. Having made their choice of a dispute resolution method, the parties should implement it.[66] Again, if the arbitral tribunal has carried out the mission entrusted to it, and has decided the case in accordance with the rules of law chosen by the parties, there would seem to be no reason why a court should refuse to enforce the award. The tribunal has simply done what the parties empowered it to do. So far as concerns enforcement of the award, the resolution adopted by the International Law Association[66] expresses the position that should sensibly be taken:

"The fact that an international arbitrator has based an award on transnational rules (general principles of law, principles common to several jurisdictions,

---

[64] For instance, in authorising arbitrators to choose the governing law of the contract, where the parties have not done so, without necessarily following the conflict rules of the place of arbitration.

[65] *cf.* the statement of Mustill in the *Channel Tunnel* case (above): "having promised to take their complaints to the experts and if necessary to the arbitrators, that is where the appellants should go".

[66] At its conference in Cairo, April 1992.

international law, usages of trade, etc.) rather than on the law of a particular State should not itself affect the validity or enforceability of the award:

(1) where the parties have agreed that the arbitrator may apply transnational rules; or

(2) where the parties have remained silent concerning the applicable law."[67]

This position has been adopted in practice by various national courts, including the French Court de Cassation, the Austrian Supreme Court and the English Court of Appeal.[68]

UNIDROIT Principles

2–65   The influence of codified terms and practices in the concept and development of a new *lex mercatoria* has already been noted. For example, the Uniform Custom and Practice for Documentary Credits, formulated as long ago as 1933,[69] has helped significantly in moving towards a single, uniform international standard for the interpretation of documentary credits—those valuable pieces of paper upon which much of international trade depends. Similarly, the INCOTERMS or "International Rules for the Interpretation of Trade Terms"[70] are intended to give a consistent, uniform meaning to terms which are in frequent use in international trade—so that expressions such as "ex works", "CIF" and "FOB" should mean the same to businessmen and traders in São Paulo as they do in London or New York.

Reference has already been made to the UNIDROIT Principles of International Commercial Contracts. They are, in nature, a restatement of the general principles of contract law. The principles are comprehensive.[71] They cover not only the interpretation and performance of contractual obligations, but also the conduct of negotiations leading to the formation of a contract. The emphasis is, not surprisingly, on good faith and fair dealing.[72] The aim of the UNIDROIT Principles is to establish a neutral set of rules that may be used throughout the world, without any particular bias to one system of law over another:

---

[67] "Transnational Rules in International Commercial Arbitration", *op. cit.* Note, however, that if no choice of law has been made by the parties, the arbitral tribunal may not be free to choose anything other than national law: see below.

[68] *Banque de Proche-Orient v Société Fougerolle*, Cour de Cassation, Civ. 2ème, December 9, 1981; judgment of the French Cour de Cassation, Civ. 1ère, October 3, 1984. Judgment of the Austrian Supreme Court, November 18, 1982, reproduced in (1984) Yearbook Commercial Arbitration 161. *Deutsche Schachtbau und Tiefbohrgesellschaft GmbH (F/Germ) v R'as Al Khaimah National Oil Co (Ras Al Khaimah, UAE) & Shell International Petroleum Co Ltd (UK)* [1987] 3 W.L.R. 1027 (reversed on other grounds: [1990] 1 A.C. 295). See also D. Rivkin, "Enforceability of awards based on *lex mercatoria*" (1993) 19 Arbitration International 47.

[69] ICC Publication No.400.

[70] ICC Publication No.350. Both INCOTERMS and documentary credits are discussed with trade usages, below.

[71] The UNIDROIT Principles were revised in April, 2004. They may be accessed on the UNIDROIT website *www.unidroit.org*.

[72] Art.1.7 states: "Each party must act in accordance with good faith and fair dealing in international trade. The parties may not exclude or limit this duty."

"They were not drafted in the interest of a specific party or lobbying group. They will strike a fair balance between the rights and obligations of all parties to the contract."[73]

The UNIDROIT Principles "represent a system of rules of contract law".[74] They apply only when the parties choose to apply them to their contract,[75] so that in this sense they supplement (but do not replace) the substantive law of the contract. However, in practice, arbitral tribunals may themselves decide to refer to the UNIDROIT Principles as an aid to the interpretation of contract terms and conditions; or even as a standard to be observed—for instance, in the negotiation of a contract.

Indeed, in one recent case, a European claimant had concluded a contract for **2–66** technology exchange with a Chinese counterparty without incorporating a governing law clause. The European claimant argued in favour of Swedish law, basing itself on the choice of Sweden as a place of arbitration. The Chinese party argued in favour of Chinese law, because China had the closest connection with the contract. The tribunal relied on Art.24(1) of the rules of the Arbitration Institute of the Stockholm Chamber of Commerce, which permitted it to apply "the law or rules of law which the tribunal considers to be most appropriate". Having decided that no common intention as to a particular national system of law could be found, the tribunal decided as follows:

"In the Tribunal's view, it is reasonable to assume that the contracting parties expected that the eventual law chosen to be applicable would protect their interest in a way that any normal business man would consider adequate and reasonable, given the nature of the contract and any breach thereof, and without any surprises that could result from the application of domestic laws of which they had no deeper knowledge. This leads the Tribunal to conclude that the issues in dispute between the parties should primarily be based, not on the law of any particular jurisdiction, but on such rules of law that have found their way into international codifications or suchlike that enjoy a widespread recognition among countries involved in international trade . . . the only codification that can be considered to have this status is the UNIDROIT Principles of International Commercial Contracts . . . The Tribunal determines that the rules contained therein shall be the first source employed in reaching a decision on the issues in dispute in the present arbitration."[76]

---

[73] See van Houtte, "The UNIDROIT Principles of International Commercial Contracts" (1995) 11 Arbitration Internation 374.

[74] A commentary on the revised principles has been published by UNIDROIT entitled: "UNIDROIT Principles of International Commercial Contracts, 2004".

[75] The opening words to the preamble to the Principles states: "These Principles set forth general rules for international commercial contracts. They shall be applied when the parties have agreed that their contract be governed by them. They may be applied when the parties have agreed that their contract be governed by 'general principles of law', the *lex mercatoria*' or the like".

[76] See Stockholm Arbitration Report 2002 at 59, with commentary by Fernandez-Armesto.

One example will indicate how the UNIDROIT Principles are intended to work. In many forms of contract, the party that bears the major responsibility for performance will seek either to limit its liability or even to exclude liability altogether. Thus a clause in a construction contract may, for example, stipulate that the contractor has no liability for loss of profit arising out of any breach of the contract, whether caused by negligence or any other breach of duty. The question then arises as to the scope of this clause and, in particular whether in specific circumstances it may be set aside altogether.[77] In relation to such a claim, the UNIDROIT Principles state[78]:

"A clause which limits or excludes one party's liability for non-performance or which permits one party to render performance substantially different from what the other party reasonably expected may not be invoked if it would be grossly unfair to do so, having regard to the purpose of the contract."

The effect of such a clause, in a dispute to which the UNIDROIT Principles are applicable, is to permit an arbitral tribunal to disregard the exemption clause in appropriate circumstances. In each case, it will be for the tribunal to decide what was the purpose of the contract and whether, in all the circumstances, it would be "grossly unfair" to apply the exemption clause.

The Shari'ah

2–67   This Islamic law, which applies across a broad swathe of Muslim countries,[79] embodies not only the Quran but also the other sources of Islamic law.[80] Modern codes of law in Islamic countries take account of the Shari'ah, often as a principal source of law[81]; and the Shari'ah itself contains general principles, which are basic to any civilised system of laws, such as good faith in the performance of obligations and the observance of due process in the settlement of disputes.[82]

In a case which came before the English court,[83] a financial transaction had been structured in a manner (an "Estisna form") which ensured that the transaction conformed with orthodox Islamic banking practice. There was provision for any disputes to be settled by arbitration in London under the ICC Rules of

---

[77] *e.g.* as an exemption clause might be disregarded under domestic legislation to protect consumers.

[78] Art.7.1.6.

[79] These range from Arab countries such as Saudi Arabia, UAE, Kuwait, Oman, Bahrain, Syria, Yemen and Iraq, to African states such as Egypt, Tunisia, Sudan, Morocco and Algeria; and to Asian states such as Pakistan, Bangladesh, Malaysia and Indonesia.

[80] Namely, the *Sunnah* (the sayings and practices of Muhammad), *Ijma* (consensus among recognised religious authorities) and *Qiyas* (inference by precedent).

[81] The constitutions of Yemen, Qatar and Egypt, *e.g.*, state that the Shari'ah is a primary source of law.

[82] See Nudrat Majeed, "Good Faith and Due Process: Lessons from the Shari'ah" (2004) 20 Arbitration International 97.

[83] *Sanghi Polyesters Ltd (India) v The International Investor KCFC (Kuwait)* [2000] 1 Lloyd's Rep. 480.

Arbitration; and there was a choice of law clause which provided for any dispute to be "governed by the Law of England except to the extent it may conflict with Islamic Shari'ah, which shall prevail". A dispute arose and the ICC appointed as sole arbitrator Mr Samir Saleh, an experienced lawyer and expert on Shari'ah law. The arbitrator's award was challenged by the losing party, but this challenge was rejected by the English court which held that the award was a clear and full evaluation of the issues and had all the appearances of being right.

International development law

At one time, it seemed possible that a particular code of law which might be described as "international development law" would evolve so as to govern relationships between states and foreign investors. On May 1, 1974, the General Assembly of the United Nations adopted two Resolutions that were respectively entitled "Declaration on the Establishment of a New International Economic Order"[84] and "Programme of Action on the Establishment of a New International Economic Order".[85] These two Resolutions, the "Declaration" and the "Programme of Action", together with the "Charter of the Economic Rights and Duties of States"[86] are the basic documents relating to the so-called New International Economic Order. The Declaration reads more like a political manifesto than a statement of legal rules or principles but it does set out certain principles on which the New International Economic Order was to be founded, including:

2–68

- sovereign equality of states;

- full permanent sovereignty of every state over its natural resources and all economic activities;

- regulation and supervision of the activities of transnational corporations; and

- a "just and equitable relationship" between the prices of raw materials and other products exported by developing countries and the prices of goods imported by them.[87]

The two Resolutions were adopted by consensus—that is to say, without a vote and by a simple decision of the President of the General Assembly to the effect that there was no opposition to their adoption.[88] Certain elements of these

---

[84] UN Resolution 3202 (S-VI), UN Doc.A/RES/3202 (S-VI), May 16, 1974.

[85] UN Doc.A/RES/3281 (XXIX), December 12, 1974.

[86] For discussion of this point see, *e.g.*, Sloan, "The binding force of a Recommendation of the General Assembly of the United Nations" (1948) 25 BYIL 1 at 32; Johnson, "The effect of Resolutions of the General Assembly of the United Nations" (1955–6) 32 B.Y.I.L. 97; Virally "La valeur juridique des recommandations des organisations internationales" (1956) A.F.D.I. 66.

[87] Declaration on Establishment of a New International Economic Order, Art.4.

[88] Certain states, including the US, deny that the Resolutions were expressive of a true consensus.

Resolutions represent established international law.[89] For the most part, however, both are permeated by statements indicating the opinions of certain developing states as to what the law should be, rather than what it is.

The Charter of Economic Rights and Duties of States is different.[90] Opinion remains divided as to the legal effect of the Charter. Some commentators are decisive. They say that it has *no* legal binding effect.[91] Others consider that a recommendation of the General Assembly is:

" . . . A judgment made by an organ of the world community and supported by many of the same considerations which support positive international law . . . [which has] a twilight existence hardly distinguishable from morality or justice until the time when the imprimatur of the world community will attest its jural quality."[92]

2–69   Certain principles laid down in the Charter are established principles of public international law.[93] Other statements of principle set out in the Charter do not form part of established international law, but may come to do so. However, the balance of power has now swung in favour of investors and potential investors, as may be seen from the increasing numbers of bilateral investment treaties. It is these treaties, and the arbitral awards issued under them, that are likely to play a leading role in the growth of international development law.[94]

Trade usages

2–70   As already mentioned, institutional rules (such as those of the ICC) and international arbitration rules (such as those of UNCITRAL) require an arbitral tribunal to take account of relevant trade usage.[95] A similar requirement is to be found in the Model Law[96] and in some national legislation, such as the Netherlands Arbitration Act 1986.[97]

The relevant trade usages will have to be established by evidence in any given case (unless the arbitrators are familiar with them and make this clear to the parties). However, organisations such as the ICC have been prominent in

---

[89] For instance, the Declaration of Full Permanent Sovereignty of a State over its Natural Resources.

[90] It was adopted by the United Nations on December 12, 1974, with 120 votes in favour, 6 against and 10 abstentions. For a summary of the historical and procedural background to the Charter, see Brower & Tepe, "The Charter of Economic Rights and Duties of States: a Reflection or Rejection of International Law" (1975) 9 International Lawyer 295; see also White, "A New International Economic Order" (1975) 24 I.C.L.Q. 542.

[91] See, *e.g.*, Brower & Tepe, *op.cit.*

[92] Sloan, *op. cit.*

[93] *e.g.* Ch.1 of the Charter includes such generally accepted principles as: (i) the sovereign equality of states; (ii) the peaceful settlement of disputes; (iii) fulfilment in good faith of international obligations; and (vi) respect for human rights and fundamental freedoms.

[94] See Ch.11 of this book.

[95] ICC Arbitration Rules, Art.17.2; UNCITRAL Arbitration Rules, Art.33.3.

[96] Art.28(4).

[97] Art.1054.

attempting to establish a commonly understood meaning for expressions that are in frequent use in international trade contracts. Terms such as "ex works", "CIF", "FOB" and so forth are expressions which are in common use and which are intended to set out, in an abbreviated form, the rights and obligations of the parties. It is obviously important that they should have the same meaning worldwide. To this end, the precise extent of these rights and obligations is spelt out as INCOTERMS (or "International Rules for the Interpretation of Trade Terms").[98] In much the same way, the Uniform Customs and Practice for Documentary Credits (formulated as long ago as 1933)[99] have proved valuable in moving towards a single international standard for the interpretation of these important instruments of world trade.

Standard form contracts are commonplace in the shipping trade, in the commodity markets, in the oil industry and so forth. It is a small but important step from the establishment of international terms and conditions to the establishment of uniform rules for the interpretation of these terms and conditions. Such uniform rules only apply within the ambit of a national system of law; but if the same rules are uniformly applied by different national courts, or by arbitral tribunals, the basis is laid for the establishment of a customary law which has been created by merchants and traders themselves (rather than by lawyers) and which may achieve international recognition.

Authority to apply non-national law

The authority of an arbitral tribunal to apply a non-national system of law **2–71** (such as the general principles of law or the *lex mercatoria*) will depend upon (a) the agreement of the parties and (b) the provisions of the applicable law.

The Washington Convention, for example, is clear on this point. It states: "The Tribunal shall decide a dispute in accordance with such *rules of law* as may be agreed by the parties".[1] The reference to "rules of law", rather than to "law" or "a system of law" is a coded reference to the applicability of appropriate legal rules, even though these may fall short of being an established and autonomous system of law.

Within different states, different positions are adopted. France and Switzer- **2–66** land, for example, allow arbitrators to decide according to rules of law.[2] By contrast, the Model Law, whilst leaving it to the parties to make an express choice of such "*rules of law*" as they wish, requires an arbitral tribunal, if the choice is left to the tribunal, to apply "the *law* determined by the conflict of law rules which it considers applicable".[3] As already mentioned, English law follows this lead. The arbitral tribunal has to decide the dispute (a) in accordance with the

---

[98] ICC Publication No.350.
[99] ICC Publication No.400.
[1] Art.42 (emphasis added).
[2] Art.1496 of the Code of Civil Procedure, Decree No.81–500 of May 12, 1981; Swiss Private International Law Act 1987, Ch.12, Art.187. The ICC Arbitration Rules also now refer to "the rules of law" (in Art.17) rather than to "the law" to be applied.
[3] Model Law, Art.28 (emphasis added).

law chosen by the parties or (b) if the parties agree, in accordance with "such other considerations as are agreed by them or determined by the tribunal". If there is no choice or agreement by the parties, the tribunal must apply "the law", which must be determined by the appropriate conflict rules.[4]

2–72   The ICC Rules[5] go further than the Model Law. They not only allow the parties to choose the application of "rules of law" to govern the dispute, but they also allow the arbitral tribunal, in the absence of an agreement by the parties, to apply "the rules of law which it determines to be appropriate". Thus, by confirming their ability to choose rules of law other than those of a single state,[6] the rules confer greater flexibility on both the arbitrators and the parties.

(i) Equity and good conscience

2–73   Arbitrators may from time to time be required to settle a dispute by determining it on the basis of what is "fair and reasonable", rather than on the basis of law. Such power is conferred upon them by so-called "equity clauses" which state, for example, that the arbitrators shall "decide according to an equitable rather than a strictly legal interpretation" or, more simply, that they shall decide as *amiable compositeurs*.

This power to decide "in equity", as it is sometimes expressed, is open to several different interpretations. It may mean, for instance that the arbitral tribunal:

- should apply relevant rules of law to the dispute, but may ignore any rules which are purely formalistic (for example, a requirement that the contract should have been made in some particular form); or

- should apply relevant rules of law to the dispute, but may ignore any rules which appear to operate harshly or unfairly in the particular case before it; or

- should decide according to general principles of law; or

- may ignore completely any rules of law and decide the case on its merits as these strike the arbitral tribunal.

Commentators generally reject this fourth alternative. To the extent that they do agree, the commentators seem to suggest that even an arbitral tribunal that decides "in equity" must act in accordance with some generally accepted legal principle. In many (or perhaps most) cases this means, as indicated at the outset of this chapter, that the arbitral tribunal will reach its decision based largely on a consideration of the facts and on the provisions of the contract, whilst trying to ensure that these provisions do not operate unfairly to the detriment of one or the other of the parties.

---

[4] English Arbitration Act 1996, s.46.
[5] ICC Arbitration Rules, Art.17(1).
[6] *e.g.* general principles of law, or the *lex mercatoria*, or the UNIDROIT Principles.

French law, for example, allows the arbitrators to act as *amiables composi-* **2–74** *teurs*, but requires them to satisfy certain standards.[7] The Paris Cour d'Appel has held that "arbitrators acting as *amiable compositeurs* have an obligation to ensure that their decision is equitable or else they would betray their duty and give rise to a cause for annulment."[8]

For an "equity clause" to be effective, there are in principle two basic requirements. First, that the parties *expressly* agree to it and, secondly, that it should be permitted by the applicable law. Both requirements are seen in such provisions as the UNCITRAL Rules that provide:

"The arbitral tribunal shall decide as amiable compositeur or *ex aequo et bono* only if the parties have expressly authorised the arbitral tribunal to do so and if the law applicable to the arbitral procedure permits such arbitration."

The arbitration laws of some states nevertheless assume that the arbitrators will decide in equity unless it is expressly stated that they must decide in law. This recalls the time when arbitration was considered a "friendly" method of dispute resolution, rather than the law-based process it has become. If the arbitration is to take place in such a state, parties should take care to specify if they do not want the arbitrators to decide in accordance with principles of equity.[9]

4. CONFLICT RULES AND THE SEARCH FOR THE APPLICABLE LAW

(a) Generally

As the previous discussion has endeavoured to make clear, parties to a contract **2–75** are entitled to choose the law which is to govern their contractual relationship; and parties should exercise this entitlement with proper care and consideration, in any international commercial contract into which they may enter. In the event of a dispute, it may prove to be very valuable indeed.

The choices generally open to parties have been set out above. Clearly there is a strong bias in favour of a modern, national system of commercial law. If disputes arise, and no choice of law has been agreed, it is difficult to make a

---

[7] See E. Loquin, *L'amiable compositeur en droit comparé et international. Contribution à l'étude du non-droit dans l'arbitrage international* (Litec, 1980).

[8] Paris, January 11, 1996, p.351; see also n. E. Loquin (1996) Rev. Arb. 100.

[9] See, *e.g.*, Ecuador's Law of Arbitration (145/1997) which states at Art.3: "The parties will decide whether the arbitrator shall decide in law or in equity. Unless otherwise agreed, the award shall be in equity." Other countries reverse this presumption—see Chile's Judicial Code, Art.235: "If the parties have not indicated the type of arbitrator, the law presumes that he will be an arbitrator at law."

proper assessment of the rights and obligations of the parties because there is no known legal framework within which to make this assessment.

If arbitration proceedings are commenced, one of the first tasks of the arbitral tribunal will be to do what the parties have failed to do, that is to establish what law *is* applicable to the contract. This may be a time-consuming and expensive process. The following section indicates how arbitrators are likely to approach the task, if obliged to do so.

(b) Implied or tacit choice

2–76   In the absence of an express choice of law, the arbitral tribunal will usually look first for the law that the parties are be presumed to have intended to choose. This is often referred to as a *tacit* choice of law. It may also be known as an implied, inferred or implicit choice. There is a certain artificiality involved in selecting a substantive law for the parties and attributing it to their *tacit* choice, where (as often happens in practice) it is apparent that the parties themselves have given little or no thought to the question of the substantive law which is applicable to their contract.

The Rome Convention, which was referred to earlier, recognises this artificiality when it provides that a choice of law must be "expressed or *demonstrated with reasonable certainty* by the terms of the contract or the circumstances of the case".[10] The Report by Professors Guiliano and Lagarde,[11] which was published with the Convention, has a special status in the interpretation of the Convention. The Report states that the parties may have made a real choice of law, although not expressly stated in their contract, but that the court is not permitted to infer a choice of law that the parties might have made, *where they had no clear intention of making a choice.*[12]

In such an event, the court—or the arbitral tribunal—will generally decide that the contract is to be governed by the law of the country with which it is most closely connected. It will be presumed that this is the country which is the place of business or residence of the party that is to effect the performance characteristic of the contract. However, this presumption does not apply if the place of characteristic performance cannot be determined. Indeed, it will be disregarded altogether if it appears that the contract is more closely connected with another country.[13]

2–77   In practice, as already indicated, parties to an international commercial contract would do well to make a specific choice of law, rather than leave the matter to be determined by a court or arbitral tribunal.

---

[10] Rome Convention, Art.3(1) (emphasis added).
[11] [1980] Official Journal of the European Union No.C282, p.1.
[12] *ibid.*, p.17; and see Dicey & Morris, *The Conflict of Laws* (13th ed., Sweet & Maxwell, 2000), pp.1198 *et seq.* (emphasis added).
[13] Rome Convention, Art.4; and see Dicey & Morris, *op. cit.*, pp.1236 *et seq.* for a commentary on this provision of the Convention, which is based on Swiss and, subsequently, Dutch law.

Choice of forum as choice of law

One criterion for attributing a choice of law to the parties, in the absence of   **2–78**
any express choice, is that based on a choice of forum by the parties. If the parties
make no express choice of law, but agree that any disputes between them shall
be litigated in a particular country, it is generally assumed that they intend the law
of that country to apply to the substance of their disputes. This assumption is
expressed in the maxim *qui indicem forum elegit jus*: a choice of forum is a
choice of law.

The assumption makes sense when the reference is to a court of law. For
instance, if the parties fail to put a choice of law clause into their contract but
provide for the resolution of any disputes by the courts of New York, it would
seem to be a reasonable assumption that they intended those courts to apply their
own law—that is to say, the law of New York. The assumption is less compelling,
however, when the dispute resolution clause provides for arbitration in a particular country, rather than litigation in the courts of that country. A place of
arbitration may be chosen for many reasons, unconnected with the law of that
place. It may be chosen because of its geographical convenience to the parties;
or because it is a suitably neutral venue; or because of the high reputation of the
arbitration services to be found there; or for some other, equally valid reason. In
one case before the Arbitration Institute of the Stockholm Chamber of Commerce, the tribunal highlighted the fallacy of the principle that a choice of forum
is a choice of law in the context of arbitration in the following terms:

> "[I]t is highly debatable whether a preferred choice of the *situs* of the
> arbitration is sufficient to indicate a choice of governing law. There has for
> several years been a distinct tendency in international arbitration to disregard
> this element, chiefly on the ground that the choice of the place of arbitration
> may be influenced by a number of practical considerations that have no
> bearing on the issue of applicable law."[14]

Nevertheless, where the parties have not made an express choice of the
substantive law of their contract, but have included a reference to arbitration and
have chosen the place of arbitration, that choice may influence the decision as to
what the substantive law of the contract should be. First, the choice of a particular
place of arbitration is sometimes taken as an implied choice of the law governing
the contract.[15] Secondly, the choice of a place of arbitration may be taken as an
indicator that the arbitration clause itself is to be governed by the law of that
place, irrespective of the law which governs the contract containing the arbitration clause. Thus, in a case where the choice of the substantive law of the contract
was unenforceable, because it was too uncertain, but the arbitration clause was

---

[14] See Stockholm Arbitration Report 2002, p.59, with commentary by Fernandez-Armesto.
[15] See, for instance, the English case of *Egon Oldendorff v Liberia Corporation* [1995] 2 Lloyd's
Rep. 64; *(No.2)* [1996] 2 Lloyd's Rep. 380. The fact that the contract was in the English language
may also have played some part in the court's decision. The law governing an arbitration clause
is discussed later in this chapter.

clear in its provision for arbitration in London, it was held that the arbitration agreement was a valid agreement and was governed by English law.[16]

(c) Conflict rules

2–79   In the absence of an express choice by the parties, an arbitral tribunal is faced with the problem of choosing a system of law or a set of legal rules to govern the contract. It must first decide whether it has a free choice or whether it must follow the conflict of law rules of the seat of the arbitration—the conflict rules of the *lex fori*. Every developed national system of law contains its own rules for the conflict of laws (sometimes called private international law, in the narrower sense of that phrase). These conflict rules usually serve to indicate what law is to be chosen as the law applicable to a contract.

To carry out this role, the relevant conflict rules generally select particular criteria that serve to link or connect the contract in question with a given system of law. These criteria are often referred to as "connecting factors". However, they differ from country to country. Accordingly, the answer to the question "What is the applicable law?" will also differ from country to country. Some of the rules that are applied to connect a particular contract with a particular national law or set of legal rules now look decidedly out of date. Under the conflict rules of some states, for instance, the applicable law (in the absence of an express or tacit choice) is likely to be the law of the place where the contract was concluded (the *lex locus contractus*). The place of conclusion of a contract may at one time have been a factor of some significance, since it would usually be the place of business or residence of one of the parties and might well also have been the place in which the contract was to be performed. However, with contracts being concluded nowadays by email or by fax, or by meetings at an airport or some other location, the place in which the contract is finally concluded is often a matter of little or no significance.

The modern conflict rule is that adopted in the Rome Convention,[17] which has already been discussed and which, in the absence of an express choice by the parties, looks to the law of the country with which the contract is most closely connected.

Does an international arbitral tribunal have a *lex fori*?

2–80   As already stated, conflict of law rules differ from one country to another. A judge or arbitral tribunal in one country may select the applicable law by reference to the place where the contract was made, whereas in another country it may be selected by reference to the law with which the contract has the closest connection. In short, the same question may produce different answers, depending upon where the judge or arbitral tribunal happens to be sitting.

---

[16] *Sonatrach Petroleum v Ferrell International* [2002] 1 All E.R. 637.
[17] It is worth noting that arbitral agreements are expressly excluded from the scope of the Convention by Art.1(2)(d); but the discussion in the present section is about contracts as a whole and not about a separate (or separable) agreement to arbitrate.

In the context of international commercial arbitration, this is plainly unsatisfactory. The seat of the arbitration is invariably chosen for reasons that have nothing to do with the conflict rules of the law of the place of arbitration. This has led to the formulation of a doctrine that has found support both in the rules of arbitral institutions and in the practice of international arbitration, namely that, unlike the judge of a national court, an international arbitral tribunal is not bound to follow the conflict of law rules of the country in which it has its seat.

A leading commentator has spoken of "the almost total abandonment of the application of the rules of conflict of the so-called arbitral forum"[18]; and the point is emphasised by the comment that, unlike the judge of a national court, an international arbitral tribunal has no *lex fori*:

> "Contrary to a State judge, who is bound to conform to the conflict law rules of the State in whose name he metes out justice, the arbitrator is not bound by such rules. He must look for the common intention of the parties, and use the connecting factors generally used in doctrine and in case law and must disregard national peculiarities."[19]

This was an early enunciation of what has come to be known as the "direct **2–81** choice" (*"voie directe"*) method of choosing the substantive law, which in reality gives arbitrators the freedom to choose as they please.

(d) International conventions, rules of arbitration and national laws

The Washington Convention states that, in the absence of any choice of the **2–82** applicable or governing law of the contract by the parties, the arbitral tribunal must apply the law of the contracting state which is a party to the dispute, together with such rules of international law as may be applicable.[20] The Washington Convention, however, is necessarily concerned with states or state entities. Accordingly, it follows the traditional practice of giving considerable weight to the law of the *state* party to a contract, in the absence of any choice of law.

Other conventions are content to leave the choice to the arbitral tribunal. The European Convention of 1961, for instance, provides that: "Failing any indication by the parties as to the applicable law, the arbitrators shall apply the proper law under the rules of conflict that the arbitrators deem applicable".[21] Although the European Convention refers to "rules of conflict", it will be seen that these are *not* necessarily the rules of conflict of the country in which the arbitration has its seat. On the contrary, the reference is to the conflict rules that the arbitrators deem applicable.

A similar approach is adopted in the UNCITRAL Rules, which state that failing any designation of the applicable law by the parties the arbitral tribunal

---

[18] Goldman, "La lex mercatoria dans les contrats et l'arbitrage internationaux: réalité et perspectives" [1979] Journal du Droit International 475 at 491.
[19] The *Sapphire* arbitration, above, at n.94.
[20] Washington Convention, Art.42(1).
[21] European Convention of 1961, Art.VII.

shall apply "the law determined by the conflict of laws rules which it considers applicable."[22]

2–83   The Model Law adopts the same terminology.[23] The intention is to make it clear that the arbitral tribunal is entitled to choose the governing law of the contract, in the absence of any express or implied choice of law by the parties themselves. In doing this, the arbitrators proceed objectively. But should they still be obliged to proceed by way of particular conflict rules? The point may be academic, since in practice an arbitral tribunal will seek to apply the law (or if permitted, the rules of law) which it considers to be appropriate. Whether this choice is reached through conflict rules, or more directly, may not matter. It should be noted, however, that French law omits any reference to conflict rules. This is both logical and sensible. French law states that:

> "The arbitrator shall settle the dispute in accordance with the rules which the parties have chosen, and in the absence of such a choice, in accordance with those rules which he considers to be appropriate."[24]

It will be seen that this provision contains two propositions. First, that an international arbitral tribunal is not obliged to proceed to its choice of law by the adoption of any national conflict of laws rules. Secondly, that it is not obliged to choose a *system* of law as the substantive law of the contract. It may, instead, choose such *rules* of law as it considers appropriate for the resolution of the dispute. The trail blazed by French law has been followed by other countries, including the Netherlands.[25]

(e) Conclusion

2–84   In reaching its decision on the law to be applied in the absence of any choice by the parties, an arbitral tribunal is entitled (unless otherwise directed by the applicable rules or the *lex arbitri*) to select any of the systems or rules of law upon which the parties themselves might have agreed, if they had chosen to do so.

When it comes to determining how an arbitral tribunal should proceed to its decision, then once again (as so often in international commercial arbitration) no universal rule can be identified. Some systems of law insist that, in making its choice, an arbitral tribunal should follow the rules of conflict of the seat of the arbitration. This attitude looks increasingly anachronistic. The modern tendency is for international conventions and rules of arbitration to give considerable latitude to arbitral tribunals in making their choice of law, whilst still requiring them to do so by way of appropriate or applicable conflict rules. Some national laws (including the French, the Swiss and the Dutch) carry the matter to its

---

[22] UNCITRAL Arbitration Rules, Art.33.

[23] Model Law, Art.28(2).

[24] Art.1496 of the Code of Civil Procedure, Decree Law No.81-500 of May 12, 1981.

[25] The Netherlands Arbitration Act 1986, Art.1054; Swiss law comes close to the same position, in Art.187 of the Swiss Private International Law Act 1987.

logical conclusion: by abandoning the reference to conflict rules altogether they allow an arbitral tribunal to decide for itself what law (or rules of law) the tribunal considers appropriate to settle the dispute.

This is an approach to be commended. If an arbitral tribunal can be trusted to decide a dispute, presumably it can be trusted to determine the set of legal rules by which it will be guided in reaching its decision. If the parties do not wish the arbitral tribunal to have such freedom of action, the remedy is in their own hands. They should agree upon the applicable law or set of legal rules, preferably in their contract but, if not, then at any time after the dispute has arisen. If this is not done, it will fall to the arbitral tribunal to make a decision that is likely to impact on the outcome of the arbitration. In order to reach this decision (which may be given as a ruling on a preliminary issue by way of an interim or partial award) the arbitral tribunal will usually have to consider detailed arguments of law and fact. This is an expense which could readily have been avoided, if the parties had taken the time and the trouble to agree on one of the many choices open to them.

5. The Law Governing the Agreement to Arbitrate

An agreement to arbitrate, as already discussed, may be set out in a purpose-made submission agreement or, much more frequently, in an arbitration clause. Both submission agreements and arbitration clauses are considered in detail in the following chapter. It is appropriate, however, to finish this present chapter with a note on the law governing arbitration agreements. **2–85**

A submission to arbitration, which is drawn up after the dispute between the parties has arisen, should address all the principal aspects of the proposed arbitration, including choice of the arbitral tribunal and choice of the law which that tribunal is to apply. Thus, the submission agreement may say, for example: "The law governing the substantive issues in dispute shall be the law of France." This makes it clear that the arbitral tribunal must decide the matters in issue before it in accordance with French law.

But what if there is a dispute about the submission agreement itself? If, for instance, there is an issue as to whether or not a party was legally capable of entering into such an agreement, this would in principle fall to be determined under the law applicable to that party.[26] If, on the other hand, the issue concerned the validity or scope of the submission agreement itself, this would fall to be determined under the law applicable to the submission agreement.

It might be assumed that this is the same law as that which the parties had chosen to govern the substantive issues in dispute. But this is not necessarily a safe assumption. The applicable law clause set out above refers expressly to the "substantive issues in dispute". It does not refer in terms to disputes that might arise in relation to the submission agreement itself; and it would be sensible, in **2–86**

---

[26] New York Convention, Art.V(1)(a); but see the discussion on capacity in Ch.3.

drafting a submission agreement, to make clear what law is to apply to that agreement.

An arbitration clause, which is drawn up as part of the contract between the parties to provide for any dispute that may arise in the future, will usually be set out towards the end of the contract and, as a matter of good practice, and for the reasons already given, it should be preceded—or followed—by a choice of law clause. Since the arbitration clause is only one of many clauses in a contract, it would seem reasonable to assume that the law chosen by the parties to govern the contract will also govern the arbitration clause.[27] If the parties expressly choose a particular law to govern their agreement, why should some other law—which the parties have *not* chosen—be applied to one of the clauses in the agreement, simply because it happens to be the arbitration clause? It seems reasonable to say, as Professor Lew has said:

> "There is a very strong presumption in favour of the law governing the substantive agreement which contains the arbitration clause also governing the arbitration agreement. This principle has been followed in many cases. This could even be *implied* as an agreement of the parties as to the law applicable to the arbitration clause".[28]

The presumption that the arbitration clause is governed by the same law as the underlying contract was reaffirmed by the English court in *Sonatrach Petroleum Corporation (BVI) v Ferrell International Ltd*[29]:

> "Where the substantive contract contains an express choice of law, but the agreement contains no separate choice of law, the latter agreement will normally be governed by the body of law expressly chosen to govern the substantive contract."

2–87   A distinguished French commentator has written:

> "The autonomy of the arbitration clause and of the principal contract does not mean that they are totally independent one from the other, as evidenced by the fact that acceptance of the contract entails acceptance of the clause, without any other formality."[30]

---

[27] *e.g.* in *Union of India v McDonnell Douglas Corp* [1993] 2 Lloyd's Rep. 48, the court stated: "An arbitration clause in a commercial contract like the present one is an agreement inside an agreement . . . The parties may make an express choice of law to govern their commercial bargain and that choice may also be made of the law to govern the agreement to arbitrate. In the present case it is my view that by Art.11 the parties have chosen the law of India not only to govern the rights and obligations arising out of their commercial bargain but also the rights and obligations arising out of their agreement to arbitrate."

[28] Lew, "The Law Applicable to the Form and Substance of the Arbitration Clause", ICCA Congress Series No.14, 1998, Paris, para.136. It could also be seen as an *express* choice, if the arbitration clause is considered as simply one of the rights and obligations assumed by the parties in their contract, to be governed by the law which governs that contract.

[29] [2002] 1 All E.R. (Comm) 627.

[30] Derains, The ICC International Court of Arbitration Bulletin, Vol.6, No.1, p.10, at pp.16–17.

This supports the view that the arbitration clause is generally governed by the same law as the rest of the contract; but the reference to the "autonomy" of the arbitration clause, in this citation, points to the problem that may arise. An arbitration clause is taken to be autonomous and to be separable from other clauses in the agreement.[31] If necessary, it may stand alone. In this respect, it is comparable to a submission agreement. It is this separability of an arbitration clause that opens the way to the possibility that it may be governed by the different law from that which governs the main agreement.

If it becomes necessary to determine what law is to govern an agreement to arbitrate, whether contained in an arbitration clause or a submission agreement, what are the choices? The law of the place where the agreement was made would appear to have little or no relevance.[32] There are other possibilities, but the real choice—in the absence of any express or implied choice by the parties—appears to be between the law of the seat of the arbitration and the law which governs the contract as a whole.

The New York Convention[33] points to the same conclusion. In the provisions **2–88** relating to enforcement, the Convention stipulates that the agreement under which the award is made must be valid "under the law to which the parties have subjected it" *or* failing any indication thereon, "under the law of the country where the award was made" (which will be the law of the seat of the arbitration).

As a US commentator has expressed it:

"At the end of the day, selecting the law governing the parties' arbitration agreement (absent an express agreement) usually requires choosing between two principal alternatives—the substantive law of the parties' underlying contract or the law of the place where the arbitration has its seat (assuming this is different from the law governing the underlying contract)".[34]

There are a number of cases, in different jurisdictions, in which a court or **2–89** arbitral tribunal has taken the law of the seat of the arbitration as the appropriate law to govern the parties' arbitration agreement. The following examples illustrate this:

(1) In ICC Case No.6162,[35] the main contract contained an arbitration clause providing for arbitration in Geneva under the ICC Arbitration Rules. It also provided that "Egyptian laws will be applicable". The respondent submitted that, as the arbitrators were not designated by the arbitration clause nor by a separate agreement, the arbitration clause was void under

---

[31] Separability is discussed in Ch.3.
[32] Lew, *op.cit.*
[33] New York Convention, Art.V.1(a). There is a similar provision in the Model Law, at Art.34(2)(a).
[34] Gary Born, *International Commercial Arbitration* (2nd ed., Transnational Publishers Inc and Kluwer Law International, 2001), p.111, n.(d).
[35] See Lew, *op.cit.*, p.27, para.116.

Art.502(3) of the Egyptian Law of Civil and Commercial Procedures. As a matter of Egyptian law, this argument appears to have been well founded; but it would have brought the arbitral proceedings to an end. The tribunal decided that the law of Switzerland, as the law of the place of arbitration, was the law applicable to the form and validity of the arbitration agreement—and not the law that had been chosen by the parties to govern their contract.

(2) In the *Bulbank* case,[36] the Bulgarian Foreign Trade Bank (Bulbank) concluded a contract with an Austrian bank. The contract contained an arbitration clause that expressed a choice of Austrian law. When a dispute arose between the two parties, arbitral proceedings were initiated under the UNECE rules in Stockholm. The award was challenged by Bulbank in the Swedish courts on the basis that the arbitration agreement was void. The Supreme Court of Sweden held that the arbitration agreement was valid under the law of the seat of arbitration, Swedish law, stating:

" . . . no particular provision concerning the applicable law for the arbitration agreement itself was indicated [by the parties]. In such circumstances the issue of the validity of the arbitration clause should be determined in accordance with the law of the state in which the arbitration proceedings have taken place, that is to say, Swedish law."

The Supreme Court thus ignored the choice of Austrian law, requiring an express choice of law to be made in relation to the arbitration agreement, not merely in relation to the whole contract.

(3) In *XL Insurance Ltd v Owens Corning*,[37] English law was applied to an insurance policy containing a New York applicable law clause and a London arbitration clause, which referred specifically to the Arbitration Act 1996.

(i) the applicable law clause stated that the policy as a whole should be construed in accordance with the internal laws of the State of New York "except in so far as such laws: . . . are inconsistent with any provision of this Policy". The arbitration clause, however, provided that any dispute as to the policy or its breach, termination or invalidity was to be determined "in London . . . under the provisions of the Arbitration Act 1996";

---

[36] *Bulgarian Foreign Trade Bank Ltd v Al Trade Finance Inc* (2001) XXVI Yearbook Commercial Arbitration 291, Swedish Supreme Court, October 27, 2000, Case No.T1881-99. It should be noted that the Swedish Arbitration Act 1999 provides, in s.48, that where an arbitration agreement has an international connection, and the parties have not agreed upon a choice of law, the arbitration agreement will be governed by the law of the seat of the arbitration.
[37] [2000] 2 Lloyd's Rep. 500.

   (ii) when a dispute arose between the parties as to the meaning of the policy, Owens Corning began proceedings in Delaware, USA, arguing that the arbitration agreement was not valid under US law; XL sought an anti-suit injunction against Owens Corning on the grounds that there *was* a valid arbitration agreement and the dispute should be resolved by arbitration in London;

   (iii) the English court stated that "it is by now firmly established that more than one national system of law may bear upon an international arbitration . . . [T]here is the proper law which regulates the substantive rights and duties of the parties . . . Exceptionally, this may differ from the national law governing the interpretation of the agreement to submit the dispute to arbitration." The court held that by stipulating for arbitration in London under the provisions of the Arbitration Act 1996, the parties had chosen English law to govern the matters falling within those provisions. These included not only those matters arising under the Act, but also issues concerning the formal validity of the arbitration clause and the jurisdiction of the arbitral tribunal.

(4) In a Belgian case, *Matermaco v PPM Cranes*,[38] the law of the place of arbitration, Belgium, was applied to questions of arbitrability, despite the laws of the State of Wisconsin having been chosen by the parties to apply to the underlying contract. The Brussels Tribunal de Commerce considered Arts II.1 and V.2(a) of the New York Convention, stating that their similarity:

> "and a consistent interpretation of the Convention require that the arbitrable nature of the dispute be determined, under the said Articles II and V, under the same law, that is, the *lex fori*. Hence it is according to Belgian law that the arbitrable nature of the present dispute must be determined."

In the first three of these four cases, it is plain that the effect of the decision **2–90** of the relevant court or tribunal was to validate the arbitration agreement. The parties had agreed to arbitrate disputes but when the time came to do so, one party sought to renege on that agreement. In choosing the law of the place of arbitration as the law governing the arbitration agreement, the court or tribunal may be seen as having decided to give effect to the parties' agreement. And in all four cases, the court or tribunal acted consistently with the choice of law principles which are generally applicable where there is no express choice of law, since an agreement to arbitrate is usually more closely connected with the country of the seat of the arbitration than any other country.[39]

---

[38] *Matermaco SA v PPM Cranes Inc* (2000) XXV Yearbook Commercial Arbitration, September 20, 1999, Tribunal de Commerce, Brussels.
[39] See Dicey & Morris, *The Conflict of Laws* (13th ed., Sweet & Maxwell, 2000), p.598.

The importance of the law of the seat of arbitration, in considering the law applicable to an arbitration agreement, is particularly marked in the USA. The Federal Arbitration Act of 1925 ("the FAA") controls arbitrations involving interstate or foreign commerce and maritime transactions; and it also implements the New York Convention. One commentator has written[40]:

"The FAA creates a body of federal substantive law of arbitrability and pre-empts contrary state law policies. Hence, once the dispute is covered by the FAA, federal law applies to all questions of interpretation, construction, validity, revocability and enforceability."

2–91   The scope of the FAA is therefore such that it appears of itself to constitute the law governing the arbitration agreement. This analysis is confirmed by recent US cases focusing on the relationship between the FAA and state (or even foreign) law. These emphasise its pre-eminence as the law governing the arbitration, even where there is an express choice of state (or foreign law) in relation to the arbitration clause or agreement itself. The following examples illustrate this:

(1) In *Pedcor Mgt Co Inc Welfare Benefit Plan v N. Am. Indemnity*,[41] which concerned a class arbitration, and where the arbitration agreement expressed a choice of Texan law, the court stated:

"it is well established that the FAA pre-empts state laws that contradict the purpose of the FAA by 'requiring a judicial forum for the resolution of claims which the contracting parties agreed to resolve by arbitration'."

(2) In *Milos Sovak v Chugai Pharmaceutical Co*[42] there was a motion to vacate an arbitration award on the grounds that the successful party had waived its right to compel arbitration under Illinois state law, which governed the arbitration provision. The US Court of Appeals for the Ninth Circuit stated:

"the strong default presumption is that the FAA, not state law, supplies the rules of arbitration . . . a general choice of law clause within an arbitration provision does not trump the presumption that the FAA supplies the rules for arbitration . . . "

(3) In the *Chloe Z Fishing v Odyssey Re*[43] the FAA was given pre-eminence even though the parties had chosen a foreign forum and foreign law (as opposed to a state forum and state law) to govern their disputes:

---

[40] Zekos, "Problems of Applicable Law in Commercial and Maritime Arbitration" (1999) 16(4) Journal of International Arbitration 173.

[41] *Pedcor Mgt Co Inc Welfare Benefit Plan v N. Am. Indemnity*, August 13, 2003, Federal Court of Appeals for the Fifth Circuit.

[42] *Milos Sovak and Biophysica Inc v Chugai Pharmaceutical Co*, April 10, 2002, US Court of Appeals for the Ninth Circuit.

[43] *Chloe Z Fishing Co Inc v Odyssey Re*, US District Court, Southern District of California, April 26, 2000, No.99-2521—IEG RBB.

(i) the plaintiffs, US commercial fishing companies, purchased marine insurance coverage from Odyssey Re. The policies contained an arbitration clause providing for arbitration of disputes in London under English law. A dispute arose between the parties as to the handling of claims by Odyssey Re, and the plaintiffs filed an action in a Californian court. Odyssey Re removed the action to the US District Court for the Southern District of California and filed a motion to compel arbitration and stay the proceedings;

(ii) the court referred the parties to arbitration in London and stayed court proceedings, holding that the arbitral clause in the policies constituted a valid arbitration agreement under the New York Convention and the FAA. It held that, despite the English choice of law (and forum), where the New York Convention and the FAA applied to an arbitration clause:

> " . . . they provide an 'overriding basis' for why the law under which the case 'arises'—the Convention and its implementing legislation—must apply to the question of whether these parties agreed to arbitrate their disputes . . . once a dispute is covered by the [Federal Arbitration] Act, federal law applies to all questions of [the arbitration agreement's] interpretation, construction, validity, revocability and enforceability".

The court's conclusion was that notwithstanding its request for supplemental briefing on the parties' intent to be bound by English law, the choice of law provision in the policies, and the express provision for arbitration in London, federal law applied to the court's preliminary inquiry as to the scope of the arbitration clauses.

Summary

The New York Convention, as already stated, requires an arbitration agreement **2–92** to be valid "under the law to which the parties have subjected it or, failing any indication thereon, under the law of the country where the award was made".[44] As the previous discussion has shown, the country where the award is made is generally deemed to be the country which is the seat of arbitration. In other words, under the New York Convention, an arbitration agreement is valid if it is judged to be so either by the law chosen by the parties to govern that agreement or, failing any such choice, by the law of the place of arbitration.

Where the agreement to arbitrate is set out in a specially drawn submission **2–93** agreement, the parties should choose a law to govern that agreement and should set out their choice in an appropriate clause. This is what the parties would normally do in any other kind of international agreement; and in this respect a submission agreement is no different. If no express choice of law is made, and

---

[44] New York Convention, Art.V.1(a).

a question arises as to the law governing the submission agreement, the general principles as to the choice of law will apply but, in the absence of any contrary indication, the law of the place of arbitration chosen by the parties will generally be regarded as the applicable law.

Where the agreement to arbitrate is set out in an arbitration clause, the position is different. It is not customary to set out expressly the law which is to govern the arbitration clause. It is generally assumed, as the previous discussion shows, that the arbitration clause is governed by the same law, or set of legal rules, as the parties choose to govern the totality of the agreement.[45] It should be stressed, however, that even where there is an express choice of law by the parties, this choice may be overridden by a court or tribunal in determining the law applicable to the arbitration clause. This is likely to occur where particular attention is focused on the parties' agreement to arbitrate—for instance, where the choice of law may impact upon the validity of that agreement. It is also likely to occur where (as in the US cases considered above) the law of the place of arbitration claims to override any choice of law the parties may have made, so far as the arbitration clause is concerned.

2–94   Where there has been no choice of law in the contract containing the arbitration clause, the general principles as to choice of law will apply but again—as with a submission agreement—the law of the place of arbitration chosen by the parties will generally prevail.

---

[45] It would not be a major exercise to make express provision for the arbitration clause, in drafting a choice of law clause. It should be sufficient, *e.g.*, to say: "This agreement, including the arbitration clause, is governed by the law of X", where X represents the chosen law. It may become necessary to do this, as a precautionary measure, if the usual assumption is consistently disregarded by courts or tribunals.

CHAPTER 3

ARBITRATION CLAUSES AND SUBMISSION AGREEMENTS

1. BACKGROUND

(a) Generally

The agreement to arbitrate is the foundation stone of international commercial **3–01** arbitration.[1] It records the consent of the parties to submit to arbitration—a consent which is indispensable to any process of dispute resolution outside national courts. Such processes depend for their very existence upon the agreement of the parties. Continental European jurists in particular attach great importance to the wishes of the parties—*l'autonomie de la volonté.* Indeed, they sometimes appear to suggest that this consent, together with an appropriate set of rules, is sufficient to turn international arbitration into an autonomous, delocalised process that takes place independently of national law. For many, this goes too far.[2] It attaches too much importance to the wishes of the parties, and not enough to the framework of national laws within which the arbitral process must take place. Nevertheless, the consent of the parties remains the essential basis of a voluntary system of international commercial arbitration.[3]

(b) Categories of arbitration agreements

There are two basic types of arbitration agreement: the arbitration clause and **3–02** the submission agreement. An arbitration clause looks to the future, whereas a submission agreement looks to the past. The first, which is most common, is usually contained in the principal agreement between the parties and is an agreement to submit *future* disputes to arbitration. The second is an agreement to submit *existing* disputes to arbitration.

---

[1] See Ch.1, para.1–08.

[2] Except for arbitrations which genuinely take place under international law (such as ICSID arbitrations); for further discussion of delocalised arbitration, see Ch.2, para.2–25.

[3] Compulsory arbitration does exist. Nationally, it is used as a supposedly cheap and informal method of resolving disputes in particular areas. Internationally, the most striking example of compulsory arbitration was in the socialist countries of Central and Eastern Europe, where it was employed as the method of settling disputes under the provisions of the Moscow Convention of 1972. However, compulsory arbitration is outside the scope of this book, which is concerned with the mainstream of international commercial arbitration—that is to say, with arbitration as a consensual process, taking place pursuant to an arbitration agreement.

In this book, the terms "arbitration clause" and "submission agreement" are used according to these descriptions. Arbitration clauses are usually short, whilst submission agreements are usually long. This is not because of any particular legal requirement. It is simply a reflection of the practicalities of the situation. An arbitration clause that deals with disputes which may arise in the future does not usually go into too much detail, since it is not known what kind of disputes will arise and how they should best be handled. Indeed, although the parties to a contract may agree to an arbitration clause, they hope that there will be no need to invoke it. Usually they insert a short model clause, recommended by an arbitral institution, as a formality. By contrast, a submission agreement deals with a dispute that *has* in fact already arisen; and so it can be tailored to fit precisely the circumstances of the case. In addition to indicating the place of arbitration and the substantive law, it generally names the arbitrators, sets out the matters in dispute and even, if thought appropriate, provides for the exchange of written submissions and other procedural matters.[4]

Most international commercial arbitrations take place pursuant to an arbitration clause in a commercial contract.[5] These clauses are often "midnight clauses", *i.e.* the last clauses to be considered in contract negotiations, sometimes late at night or in the early hours of the morning. Insufficient thought is given as to how disputes are to be resolved (possibly because the parties are reluctant to contemplate falling into dispute) and an inappropriate and unwieldy compromise is often adopted.[6] For example, there may be a wrong choice (or no choice at all) of the substantive law or of the place of arbitration. If a dispute arises, and arbitration proceedings begin, these matters must be dealt with before any progress can be made with the real issues.

3–03 Later, this chapter deals separately with arbitration clauses and submission agreements, since different considerations apply to each. First however, some general observations should be made. They apply equally to both types of arbitration agreement, and derive from the international conventions governing arbitration. In this regard, the important point to note is that the international conventions and the Model Law all recognise the validity of arbitration agreements that deal with future disputes, as well as those dealing with existing disputes.

---

[4] This is not a universal rule. A submission agreement may take the form of a brief agreement to submit an existing dispute to the procedures of an arbitral institution. Conversely, an arbitration clause providing for ad hoc arbitration could identify the procedure to be followed in detail, as well as means of establishing the arbitral tribunal, filling vacancies and so forth.

[5] It should be noted, however, that in some Latin American states, *e.g.*, Argentina and Uruguay, a clause to submit future disputes to arbitration is not operative until a submission agreement (or "*compromiso*") has also been executed (the same is also true of Brazil unless the arbitration clause incorporates a mechanism to constitute the arbitral tribunal, which it may do by reference to a set of institutional rules). In these jurisdictions, the ICC Arbitration Rules may be preferred as they provide for a functional equivalent to the *compromiso* (the Terms of Reference), which are not included in other institutional rules. See Blackaby, Lindsey & Spinillo, *International Arbitration in Latin America* (2002), pp.12, 31–32 and 73.

[6] For a step-by-step guide to drafting arbitration clauses, see: *The Freshfields Guide to Arbitration and ADR Clauses in International Contracts* (2nd ed., Kluwer, 1999).

(c) International conventions

The Geneva treaties

Although this topic is considered in Ch.1, it is worth repeating a brief summary **3–04** here. The first international convention on commercial arbitration was the Geneva Protocol of 1923. Its main purpose was to secure recognition of the validity of international arbitration agreements[7] and to ensure that, if a party commenced litigation, the courts would refer the parties to arbitration.[8] The Geneva Protocol of 1923 was followed by the Geneva Convention of 1927 which applied to the execution of foreign arbitral awards.[9] Various regional conventions followed,[10] and eventually the most important convention in the field of international commercial arbitration, the New York Convention, was promulgated in 1958.

The New York Convention continued where the Geneva treaties left off.[11] Its title as a "Convention on the Recognition and Enforcement of Foreign Arbitral Awards" is something of a misnomer. The Convention's starting point is the recognition and enforcement of arbitration agreements.[12] Having provided for recognition of the validity and enforceability of arbitration agreements, it also provides for the international enforcement of awards that comply with the specified criteria.[13]

Closely modelled[14] on the New York Convention, the 1975 Panama Convention[15] was signed by a significant number of Latin American states[16] and marked another step forward in the recognition of arbitration as an established method of resolving disputes in a regional context.

(d) International standards

The effect of these and other conventions on arbitration,[17] whether inter- **3–05** national or regional, has been to establish what is usually required for a valid international arbitration agreement and to indicate the parameters within which such an agreement will operate.

---

[7] Geneva Protocol 1923, Art.1. This was at a time when many states did not recognise agreements to refer future disputes to arbitration. However, recognition was limited to *international* arbitration agreements, where the parties were subject to the jurisdiction of different states. Additionally, recognition could be (and frequently was) limited to commercial disputes. See Ch.1.

[8] Geneva Protocol 1923, Art.4.

[9] See Ch.10.

[10] *e.g.* the Bustamante Code of 1928, and the European Convention of 1961.

[11] The New York Convention replaces the Geneva treaties between states that became bound by it: Art.VII.2.

[12] New York Convention, Arts II.1 and II.3.

[13] The Model Law follows a similar pattern.

[14] It too recognises the validity of an agreement that submits existing and future disputes to arbitration: Panama Convention, Art.1.

[15] Its formal title is "The Convention on the Settlement of Civil Law Disputes Resulting from Economic, Scientific and Technological Co-operation". The text of the Convention appears in (1978) III Yearbook Commercial Arbitration 15.

[16] Including Brazil, Chile, Columbia, El Salvador, Panama and Uruguay.

[17] Such as the European Convention of 1961 and the Washington Convention of 1965.

Unlike Venus, these Conventions did not arise fully formed from the sea.[18] Instead they reflect the provisions to be found in developed arbitration laws and in the practice of arbitral institutions such as the ICC. In turn, they—together with the Model Law—have played an important part in modernising and harmonising state laws governing arbitration. An arbitration agreement that provides for international commercial arbitration must take account of these international requirements. If it fails to do so, the arbitration agreement, and any award made under it, may not qualify for international recognition and enforcement.

In seeking to establish the "international requirements", the starting point has to be the New York Convention. This has been described as "the single most important pillar on which the edifice of international arbitration rests"[19] and one which "perhaps could lay claim to be the most effective instance of international legislation in the entire history of commercial law".[20] Under the Convention each contracting state undertakes to recognise and give effect to an arbitration agreement when the following requirements are fulfilled:

- the agreement is in writing;

- it deals with existing or future disputes;

- these disputes arise in respect of a defined legal relationship, whether contractual or not; and

- they concern a subject matter capable of settlement by arbitration.

3–06   These are the four positive requirements of a valid arbitration agreement, laid down in Art.II.1 of the New York Convention.[21] Another two requirements are, in effect, added by the provisions of Art.V.1(a).[22] This Article stipulates that recognition or enforcement of an award may be refused if the party requesting refusal is able to prove that the arbitration agreement was made by a person under incapacity, or that the agreement was invalid under the applicable law. If these requirements are expressed positively,[23] they represent additional requirements to the effect that:

- the parties to the arbitration agreement must have legal capacity under the law applicable to them;

- the arbitration agreement must be valid under the law to which the parties have subjected it or, failing any indication thereon, under the law of the

---

[18] As in Botticelli's painting "The Birth of Venus".
[19] Wetter, "The Present Status of the International Court of Arbitration of the ICC: An Appraisal" (1990) 1 American Review of International Arbitration 91 at 93.
[20] Mustill "Arbitration: History and Background" (1989) 6 Journal of International Arbitration 43.
[21] The first three are also contained in the Model Law, Art.7(1), and the fourth in Arts 34(2)(b) and 36(2)(b)(i).
[22] They are also to be found in the Model Law, Arts 34(2)(a) and 36(1)(a)(i).
[23] Although it should be noted that the burden of proof is on the party opposing recognition or enforcement, who must prove lack of capacity or invalidity.

country where the award was made. In the words used earlier in the New York Convention (in Art.II.3), the agreement must not be "null and void, inoperative or incapable of being performed".

2. THE VALIDITY OF AN ARBITRATION AGREEMENT

(a) Formal validity—the need for writing

All the international conventions on arbitration that have already been men-   **3–07**
tioned, as well as the Model Law, require that an agreement to arbitrate shall be "in writing". The reason for imposing this requirement is self-evident. A valid agreement to arbitrate excludes the jurisdiction of the national courts[24] and means that any dispute between the parties must be resolved by a private method of dispute resolution, namely arbitration. This is a serious step to take, albeit one that is becoming increasingly commonplace. There exist good reasons, therefore, for ensuring that the existence of such an agreement should be clearly established. This is best done by producing evidence in writing, although as already noted in Ch.1, the trend in modern national legislation appears to be moving towards the relaxation of this formal requirement.[25]

In the New York Convention, the definition of "writing" is as follows:

"The term 'agreement in writing' shall include an arbitral clause in a contract or an arbitration agreement, signed by the parties or contained in an exchange of letters or telegrams."[26]

The requirement for signature by the parties has given rise to problems in some states[27]; but the general view is that a signature is not necessary, provided that the arbitration agreement is in writing.[28]

There has, however, been a revolution in communications since the New York   **3–08**
Convention was drawn up in 1958. Telegrams, which were a frequent method of

---

[24] See the discussion in Ch.1, para.1–08.

[25] In this regard, see Landau, "The requirement of a written form for an arbitration agreement. When 'written' means 'oral' ", 16th ICCA Congress, May 12–15, 2002, London.

[26] New York Convention, Art.II.2. See Kaplan, "Is the need for writing as expressed in the New York Convention and Model Law out of step with commercial practice?" (1996) 12 Arbitration International 27. See also Landau, *op. cit.*

[27] See, *e.g.*, the cases cited in Cohen, "Agreements in writing: Notes in the margin of the Sixth Goff Lecture" (1997) 13 Arbitration International. This article is a response to the earlier article by Kaplan (cited at para.3–07 above).

[28] See "Obergericht of Basle, June 3, 1971" (1979) IV Yearbook Commercial Arbitration 309; *Miserecchi v Agnesi*, Corte di Cassazione, Dec. 13, 1971, No.3620, with comment by Barone in *Riv. di Dir. Internaz, Priv. e Proc.*, 1972, p.563; also reported in (1976) I Yearbook Commercial Arbitration 190.

communicating an urgent message in writing, were largely replaced by telex, and later by fax and now email. This change in methods of communication is reflected in the Model Law, which goes much further than the New York Convention in its definition of "writing". The Model Law provides that:

"The arbitration agreement shall be in writing. An agreement is in writing if it is contained in a document signed by the parties or in an exchange of letters, telex, telegrams or other means of telecommunication which provides a record of the agreement, or in an exchange of statements of claim and defence in which the existence of an agreement is alleged by one party and not denied by another. The reference in a contract to a document containing an arbitration clause constitutes an arbitration agreement provided that the contract is in writing and the reference is such as to make that clause part of the contract."[29]

Thus, for the purposes of the Model Law, the requirement for writing may be satisfied by any means of telecommunication that provides "a record of the agreement". Where a party takes part in an arbitration without denying the existence of an arbitration agreement,[30] what has been called an "implied consent" to arbitration may be sufficient.

How is this long-established international requirement for an "agreement in writing" translated into practice, in national legislation and court decisions? In some systems of law no particular form is required for an arbitration agreement. Indeed, as has been seen, an exchange of telexes between two firms of brokers in Paris containing the simple statement "English law—arbitration, if any, London according ICC Rules" has been held to be a valid arbitration agreement, providing for arbitration in London under the ICC Rules with English law as the substantive law of the contract.[31]

3–09   However, whilst there may be no requirement of form, there *is* almost inevitably a requirement for writing or at least a permanent record (such as a disk or an electronic tape) from which a written transcription can be made. For example, the Netherlands 1986 Act requires that the arbitration agreement shall be proven by an instrument in writing expressly or impliedly accepted by the parties.[32] Swiss

---

[29] Model Law, Art.7(2).

[30] See Sanders, "Arbitration" in *Encyclopaedia of International and Comparative Law*, Vol.XIV, Ch.12 , para.106. See also Kaplan, *op. cit.*

[31] *Arab African Energy Corp Ltd v Olieprodukten Nederland BV* [1983] 2 Lloyd's Rep. 419; however, such a form is not recommended.

[32] Netherlands Arbitration Act 1986, Art.1021; see the commentary on this article in Sanders & van den Berg, *The Netherlands Arbitration Act 1986* (Kluwer, 1987), English Text and Notes, p.12, where it is said that the Act abolishes the possibility, which existed under the old Act, that an arbitration agreement could be concluded orally but that an arbitration agreement is deemed to be concluded if the parties appear before the arbitral tribunal without invoking the lack of an agreement prior to raising any defence.

Law requires an agreement to be made in writing or by means of communication that allows it to be evidenced by a text. The statute states simply:

> "As regards its form, an arbitration agreement shall be valid if made in writing, by telegram, telex, telecopier or any other means of communication which permits it to be evidenced by a text."[33]

In the New York Convention, the emphasis is on a *signed* agreement. In the modern laws of arbitration this requirement has largely disappeared. All that is required is some *written* evidence of an agreement to arbitrate. In some systems of law an oral agreement to arbitrate will be regarded as being "in writing" if it is made "by reference to terms which are in writing"[34]; or if an oral agreement "is recorded by one of the parties, or by a third party, with the authority of the parties to the agreement".[35] In these modern arbitration laws, there has in effect been a triumph of substance over form. As long as there is some written evidence of an agreement to arbitrate, the form in which that agreement is recorded is immaterial.[36]

However, a degree of caution is necessary. First, even courts in jurisdictions familiar with international arbitration still sometimes refuse to enforce arbitration agreements that are not in a written document signed by the parties or otherwise contained in an exchange of letters or telegrams.[37] Secondly, an arbitration agreement that is regarded as valid by an arbitral tribunal or court in one country may not be so regarded by the courts of the country where the award falls to be enforced.[38] By way of example, the Norwegian Court of Appeal refused recognition of an award rendered in London because an exchange of emails did not, in its view, satisfy the writing requirement of Art.II.2 of the New York Convention. Although such an electronic exchange was valid and sufficient to evidence the existence of an arbitration agreement as a matter of the law of the place of arbitration, *i.e.* English law, the court held that the validity of the arbitration agreement was to be separately assessed by the local enforcement authority and that: "it should not be sufficient for enforcement that the arbitral award is valid

---

[33] Swiss Private International Law Act 1987, Ch.12, Art.178(1).

[34] See, *e.g.*, the English Arbitration Act 1996, s.5(3).

[35] *ibid.*, s.5(4). The "implied consent" provisions of the Model Law are also to be found in s.5(5).

[36] A useful illustration of this point can be found in two decisions of the Hong Kong Supreme Court. See: *Oonc Lines Ltd v Sino-American Trade Advancement Co Ltd*, summarised in (1994) Arbitration and Dispute Resolution Law Journal 291; *Aster-Reiniger Joint Venture v Argos Engineering Co Ltd* (1995) The Arbitration and Dispute Resolution Law Journal 41. At the time of preparation of this edition, UNCITRAL had resolved to undertake a comprehensive review of the writing requirement.

[37] See, *e.g.*, the decision of the Second Circuit Court of Appeals in *Kahn Lucas Lancaster Inc v Lark International Ltd* 186 F.3d 210 (1999). The Second Circuit's decision in *Kahn Lucas* has been applied by a number of other US courts, who have arrived at varying interpretations (some liberal; some less so) of an "exchange of letters and telegrams". See, *e.g.*, the US District Court of the Southern District of California decision in *Chloe Z Fishing Co Inc v Odyssey Re (London) Ltd* 109 F.Supp. 2d 1048 (2000) and the US District Court of the Western District of Washington decision in *Bothell & Bothell v Hitachi Zosen Corp* 97 F.Supp. 2d 1048 (2000).

[38] See the discussion in Ch.2 on the law governing the arbitration agreement.

according to the law of the country in question" (*i.e.* in this case England, the place of arbitration).[39]

Finally, there remain states in which special requirements of form *are* imposed in respect of agreements to arbitrate.[40] Accordingly, the relevant national law must be examined if there is reason to believe that the formal validity of an arbitration agreement is likely to be questioned under that law. Where any special requirements are not followed, the validity of the arbitration agreement may fall to be determined under the law of the country that imposes these requirements. However, such formalities may be disregarded elsewhere (for instance, if the question is first raised on an application for recognition and enforcement of an award) on the basis that they are simply matters of form, rather than of substance.

(b) A defined legal relationship

3–10   Almost all international commercial arbitrations arise out of contractual relationships between the parties. However, for the purposes of both the New York Convention and the Model Law, it is sufficient that there should be a "defined legal relationship" between the parties, whether contractual or not. Plainly there has to be some contractual relationship between the parties, since there must be an arbitration agreement to form the basis of the arbitral proceedings. Given the existence of such an agreement, the dispute submitted to arbitration may be governed by principles of delictual or tortious liability rather than (as is usually the case) by the law of contract.

Thus, in *Kaverit Steel & Crane Ltd v Kone Corporation*,[41] Kaverit commenced court proceedings alleging that Kone had breached certain licence and distribution agreements. Kone sought a stay and a reference to arbitration pursuant to the arbitration clause in the agreements. The clause stated that all disputes "arising out of or in connection with this contract" would be referred to arbitration. The Alberta Queen's Bench Division refused the stay on the grounds that some of the claims by Kaverit contained allegations that went beyond breach of contract; for example, conspiracy and inducing breach of contract. The court held that these tort-based claims fell outside the scope of the arbitration clause.

However, the Alberta Court of Appeal held that the wording of the arbitration clause was wide enough to bring within its scope any claim that relied on the existence of a contractual relationship, even if the claim itself was a claim in tort.[42] To give an example: because the claim alleging "conspiracy by unlawful means to harm [Kaverit]" relied upon a breach of contract as the source of the

---

[39] Decision of the Halogaland Court of Appeal (Norway), August 16, 1999 (2002) XXVII Yearbook Commercial Arbitration 519.
[40] Including particularly the requirement in some jurisdictions, *e.g.*, Argentina and Paraguay, that an arbitration clause is not operative until a submission agreements has also been executed: see para.3–02, above.
[41] 87 D.L.R. 4th 129; (1994) XVII Yearbook Commercial Arbitration 346.
[42] The court held that a dispute "arises out of or in connection with a contract" if the "existence of the contract is germane either to the claim or the defence".

"unlawfulness", that dispute should be referred to arbitration. However, those claims that were not based on the existence of a contract should proceed to trial, not arbitration.[43]

Thus, subject to any provisions of the relevant applicable law, the terms of an arbitrator's jurisdiction and powers in any particular case depends on a proper construction of the arbitration agreement. The arbitral tribunal must consider the dispute in question and then elicit from the arbitration agreement whether or not the parties intended a dispute of the kind in question to be resolved by arbitration.[44] **3–11**

(c) Arbitrability

Arbitrability, in the sense in which it is used both in this book and generally,[45] involves determining which types of dispute may be resolved by arbitration and which belong exclusively to the domain of the courts. Both the New York Convention and the Model Law are limited to disputes that are "capable of settlement by arbitration".[46] **3–12**

In principle, *any* dispute should be just as capable of being resolved by a private arbitral tribunal as by the judge of a national court. Article 2059 of the French Civil Code, for example, provides that "all persons may enter into

---

[43] Courts around the world have adopted even wider interpretations of similar clauses, although the underlying principles are similar. See *ABI Group Contractors Pty v Transfield Pty Ltd Mealey's International Arbitration Report* (1999), Vol.14, No.1 pp.G-1–G-10; summary in (1999) XXIV Yearbook Commercial Arbitration 591; *Multistar Leasing Ltd v Twinstar Leasing Ltd*, US District Court, Eastern District of Louisiana, August 28, 1998, Civil Action Case No.98-1330; summary in (2000) XXV Yearbook Commercial Arbitration 871; *American Bureau of Shipping v Tencara SpA*, Italian Corte di Cassazione, Plenary Session, June 26, 2001, No.8744; summary in (2002) XXVII Yearbook Commercial Arbitration 509. See also the decision of the German court in *Landgericht Hamburg* (1979) IV Yearbook Commercial Arbitration 261 and the commentary by van den Berg, "Scope of the Arbitration Agreement" (1996) XXI Yearbook Commercial Arbitration 415.

[44] English cases give further guidance. In *Ashville Investments Ltd v Elmer Contractors* [1988] Lloyd's Rep. 73, an arbitration clause which referred to "any matter or thing of whatsoever nature arising thereunder or in connection therewith" was sufficiently wide to cover claims based on alleged mistake and misrepresentation. Similarly in *Ethiopian Oilseeds and Pulses Export Corp v Rio del Mar Foods Inc* [1990] 1 Lloyd's Rep. 86, the words "arising out of" were held to cover disputes concerning rectification. But in *Fillite (Runcorn) Ltd v Aqua-lift (a firm)* (1989) 45 B.L.R. 27, disputes arising under a contract was not wide enough to include disputes as to misrepresentation, or negligent misstatements since it referred exclusively to obligations created by or incorporated into that contract. See also *Hi-Fert v Kiukiang Maritime Carriers* [1999] 2 Lloyd's Rep. 782.

[45] In the US and elsewhere, there is sometimes discussion by judges and others as to whether a particular dispute is "arbitrable", in the sense that it falls within the scope of the arbitration agreement. The concern in such cases is with the court's jurisdiction over a particular dispute rather than a more general enquiry as to whether the dispute is of the type that comes within the domain of arbitration. See Zekos, "Courts' Intervention in Commercial and Maritime Arbitration under US Law" (1997) 14 Journal of International Arbitration 99. For a general discussion of "arbitrability" in the sense of "legally capable of settlement by arbitration", see Sanders, "The Domain of Arbitration" in the "Arbitration" section of *Encyclopaedia of International and Comparative Law* (Martinus Nijhoff), Vol.XVI, Ch.12, pp.113 *et seq.*; see also Hanotiau, "The Law Applicable to the Issue of Arbitrability" ICCA Congress, Series No.14, Paris, 1998.

[46] New York Convention, Arts II.1 and V.2(a); Model Law, Arts 34(2)(b)(i) and 36(1)(b)(i).

arbitration agreements relating to the rights that they may freely dispose of". Although Art.2060 further provides that parties may not agree to arbitrate disputes in a series of particular fields (*e.g.* family law), and "more generally in all matters that have a public interest" (*"plus généralement dans toutes les matières qui intéressent l'ordre public"*), this limitation has been construed in a very restrictive way by French courts. Similarly, s.1030(1) and (2) of the German Code of Civil Procedure provide that any claim involving an economic interest (*Vermögensrechtlicher Anspruch*) can be subject to arbitration, as can claims not involving an economic interest of which the parties may freely dispose.

However, it is precisely because arbitration is a private proceeding with public consequences[47] that some types of dispute are reserved for national courts, whose proceedings are generally in the public domain. It is in this sense that they are not "capable of settlement by arbitration".

3–13 National laws establish the domain of arbitration, as opposed to that of the local courts. Each state decides which matters may or may not be resolved by arbitration in accordance with its own political, social and economic policy. In some Arab states, for example, contracts between a foreign corporation and its local agent are given special protection by law and, to reinforce this protection, any disputes arising out of such contracts may only be resolved by the local courts. The legislators and courts in each country must balance the domestic importance of reserving matters of public interest to the courts against the more general public interest in promoting trade and commerce and the settlement of disputes. In the international sphere, the interests of promoting international trade as well as international comity have proved important factors in persuading the courts to treat certain types of dispute as arbitrable.[48]

If the issue of arbitrability arises, it is necessary to have regard to the relevant laws of the different states that are or may be concerned. These are likely to include the law governing the party involved, where the agreement is with a state or state entity; the law governing the arbitration agreement; the law of the seat of arbitration; and the law of the place of enforcement of the award.

Whether or not a particular type of dispute is "arbitrable" under a given law is in essence a matter of public policy for that law to determine. Public policy varies from one country to the next, and indeed changes from time to time.[49] The most that can be done here is to indicate the categories of dispute that may fall outside the domain of arbitration.

---

[47] For instance, in the recognition and enforcement of the award.

[48] See the *Mitsubishi* case, discussed below. However, the opposite is often argued in the context of less developed countries. In that situation, it is suggested that the state should impose very strict limits on arbitrability, especially in respect of disputes involving state entities. The reason for such a policy is that this is the only way for these states to retain control over foreign trade and investment, where more economically powerful traders may have an unfair advantage. See Sornarajah, "The UNCITRAL Model Law: A Third World Viewpoint" (1989) 6 Journal of International Arbitration 7 at 16.

[49] The concept of so-called "international public policy" which may impose limits on the arbitrability of certain agreements—for instance, an agreement to pay bribes (below, para.3–20)—is considered later, in Ch.10, in the context of challenging recognition and enforcement of arbitral awards.

Reference has already been made in passing to contracts of agency, for which **3–14**
special provision may be made in some states as a matter of public policy. More
generally, criminal matters and those which affect the status of an individual or
a corporate entity (such as bankruptcy or insolvency) are usually considered as
not arbitrable. In addition, disputes over the grant or validity of patents and trade
marks may not be arbitrable under the applicable law. These various categories
of dispute are now considered.

Patents, trade marks and copyright

Whether or not a patent or trade mark should be granted is plainly a matter for **3–15**
the public authorities of the state concerned, these being monopoly rights that
only the state can grant. Any dispute as to their grant or validity is outside the
domain of arbitration. However, the owner of a patent or trade mark frequently
issues licences to one or more corporations or individuals in order to exploit the
patent or trade mark; and any disputes between the licensor and the licensee may
be referred to arbitration. Indeed, disputes over such intellectual property rights
are commonly referred to international arbitration. First, because this gives the
parties an opportunity to select for themselves a tribunal of arbitrators experienced in such matters, and secondly, and perhaps more importantly, because of
the confidentiality of arbitral proceedings, which helps to provide a safeguard for
trade secrets.[50]

Unlike patents or trade marks, copyright is an intellectual property right which
exists independently of any national or international registration, and may be
freely disposed of by parties. There is, therefore, generally no doubt that disputes
relating to such private rights may be referred to international arbitration.

Antitrust and competition laws

Adam Smith, writing in the eighteenth century, said: **3–16**

"People of the same trade seldom meet together, even for merriment and
diversion, but the conversation ends in a conspiracy against the public, or in
some contrivance to raise prices."[51]

This early distrust of monopolies and cartels finds its modern echo in increasingly wide-ranging antitrust legislation across the world. Amongst national
legislators, the US has been prominent, beginning with the celebrated Shearman
Act in 1890. Similarly, in 1958 the European Community adopted rules of law
that were to be directly applicable in all Member States, and which prohibit
agreements and arrangements having as their object or effect the prevention,
restriction or distortion of competition (Art.81 of the EU Treaty), as well as any
abuse of a dominant position (Art.82), within what is now the European Union.

---

[50] See generally, Lew, "Intellectual Property Disputes and Arbitration", Final Report of the Commission on International Arbitration (ICC Publication, 1997), especially pp.7–15.
[51] Adam Smith, *The Wealth of Nations* (1776) Book 1, Ch.10, Pt 2.

Articles 81 and 82 have historically been enforced primarily by the European Commission, which has the power to investigate, prohibit behaviours, impose heavy fines, and also to grant exemptions pursuant to Art.81(3) where appropriate in the light of the wider benefits of the activity or agreement that infringes Art.81.[52]

What can an arbitral tribunal do when confronted with an allegation that the contract under which the arbitration is brought is itself an illegal restraint of trade or in some other way a breach of antitrust law? For example, in disputes between the licensor of a patent and the licensee, it has become almost standard practice for the licensor to allege, amongst a series of defences, that in any event the licence agreement is void for illegality. In general, an allegation of illegality should not prevent an arbitral tribunal from adjudicating on the dispute, even if its finding is that the agreement in question is indeed void for illegality. This is because under the doctrine of separability,[53] the arbitration clause in a contract constitutes a separate agreement and survives the contract of which it forms part. More specifically, it is now widely accepted that antitrust issues are arbitrable. In France, the arbitrability of competition law issues was acknowledged in the *Mors/Labinal* case in 1993,[54] and reaffirmed by the Cour de Cassation in 1999.[55] Likewise, in Switzerland, the arbitrability of EU competition law was recognised by a decision of the Federal Tribunal in 1992, in which the court found that:

"Neither Article 85 of the [EU] Treaty nor Regulation 17 on its application forbid a national court or an arbitral tribunal to examine the validity of that contract."[56]

3–17   The US Supreme Court had already adopted this approach in the well-known *Mitsubishi* case.[57] At one time, it was held in the US that claims under the antitrust laws were not capable of being resolved by arbitration, but had to be referred to the courts. In the *American Safety* case,[58] the reaction of the court was that:

---

[52] Agreements which offend against Art.81 are void under Art.81(2), unless an exemption is granted under Art.81(3). Until May 1, 2004 the power to grant exemptions fell to the European Commission alone. Since then, pursuant to Council Regulation No.1/2003, the power has been extended to national courts and competition authorities. The Regulation makes no mention of arbitral tribunals, and it remains to be seen how, if at all, the Regulation will impact upon their work. In this regard, see Pinsolle, "Private Enforcement of European Community Competition Rules by Arbitrators" [2004] Int. A.L.R. 14. See also Derains "L'arbitre, la Commission et la cour: questions de procédure" [2003] Gazette du Palais 45.

[53] Under this doctrine, the arbitration clause in a contract is regarded as separate from, and independent of, the contract of which it forms part: see below, para.3–60.

[54] See the decision of the Cour d'Appel de Paris of May 19, 1993 [1993] Rev. Arb. 645, n. Jarrosson.

[55] See the decision of the Cour de Cassation of January 5, 1999.

[56] Decision of the Tribunal Fédéral, April 28, 1992 [1992] A.SA Bull. 368. The same court reaffirmed this position in its decision of November 13, 1998 [1999] A.SA Bull. 529 and 455.

[57] *Mitsubishi Motors Corp v Soler Chrysler Plymouth Inc*, 473 US 614, 105 S.Ct.3346 (1985). And see generally: "Competition and Arbitration", Dossier of the Institute of International Business Law and Practice, ICC (1993).

[58] *American Safety Equipment Corp v J.P. Maguire & Co*, 391 F.2d 821(2nd Cir. 1968).

"A claim under the antitrust laws is not merely a private matter . . . Antitrust violation can affect hundreds of thousands, perhaps millions, of people and inflict staggering economic damage. We do not believe Congress intended such claims to be resolved elsewhere than the Courts."[59]

However, in *Mitsubishi* the US Supreme Court, by a majority of five to three, decided that antitrust issues arising out of international contracts were arbitrable under the Federal Arbitration Act. This was so despite:

- the public importance of the antitrust laws;

- the significance of private parties seeking treble damages as a disincentive to violation of those laws; and

- the complexity of such cases.

In its judgment, the court stated:

" . . . we conclude that concerns of international comity, respect for the capacities of foreign and transnational tribunals and sensitivity to the need of the international commercial system for predictability in the resolution of disputes require that we enforce the parties' agreement, even assuming that a contrary result would be forthcoming in a domestic context."

However, the court went on to point out that the public interest in the **3–18** enforcement of antitrust legislation could be asserted, if necessary, when it came to enforcement of any award made by the arbitral tribunal. The court stated:

"Having permitted the arbitration to go forward, the national courts of the United States will have the opportunity at the award enforcement stage to ensure that the legitimate interest in the enforcement of the antitrust laws has been addressed. The [New York Convention] reserves to each signatory country the right to refuse enforcement of an award where the 'recognition or enforcement of the award would be contrary to a public policy of that country'."[60]

Rather than question whether antitrust issues are arbitrable, later decisions tend to indicate that—at least in the EU—international tribunals are duty bound to address such issues. In its landmark decision in *Eco Swiss China Time Ltd v Benetton International NV,*[61] the European Court of Justice identified Art.81 of the EU Treaty as a matter of public policy that would justify the annulment or refusal of enforcement of an award that ignores it. In the context of a challenge

---

[59] *ibid.*, at 826.
[60] *Mitsubishi Motors Corp v Soler Chrysler Plymouth Inc,* 473 US 614, 105 S.Ct.3346 (1985) at 628.
[61] Case C-126/97 (1999) XXIV Yearbook Commercial Arbitration 629.

to an award that gave effect to a licence agreement that was alleged, only after the award was rendered, to violate Art.81 of the EU Treaty, the ECJ ruled:

"A national court to which application is made for annulment of an arbitration award must grant that application if it considers that the award in question is in fact contrary to Article 81 EC (ex Art.85), where its domestic rules of procedure require it to grant an application for annulment founded on failure to observe national rules of public policy."[62]

Although the ECJ did not explicitly rule on whether arbitrators have a duty to apply Art.81 *ex officio* if the parties themselves made no reference to it, this decision is generally seen—at the very least—as implying that arbitrators should do so or risk the annulment of their award on grounds of a violation of public policy.[63]

Securities transactions

3–19   An earlier ruling by the Supreme Court in a dispute under the US Securities Act 1933 foreshadowed the decision in *Mitsubishi.* In 1953, the Supreme Court had held that disputes under the Securities Act were not arbitrable.[64] In 1974, however, the court held that such disputes *were* arbitrable in an international commercial arbitration. This was in *Scherk v Alberto-Culver*[65] where the Supreme Court said that a "parochial refusal by the courts of one country to enforce an international arbitration agreement" would not only frustrate the purpose of the agreement but would "damage the fabric of international commerce and trade and imperil the willingness and ability of businessmen to enter into international commercial agreements".[66] In subsequent cases, the court went on to accept the arbitrability of securities disputes in US domestic arbitration.[67]

Bribery and corruption

3–20   Issues of bribery or corruption in the procurement or performance of a contract raise important questions of public policy. In its 2000 Interim Report on public

[62] *ibid.,* at 631. The decision arose from a preliminary reference made to the ECJ under Art.234 (ex Art.177) of the EU Treaty by the Supreme Court of the Netherlands.
[63] See Pinsolle, *op. cit.,* p.18.
[64] *Wilko v Swan* 346 US 427 (1953). See, generally, McCormack, "Recent US Legal Decisions on Arbitration Law" (1994) 11 Journal of International Arbitration 73.
[65] *Scherk v Alberto-Culver,* 417 US 506 (1974).
[66] *ibid.*
[67] See, *e.g., Shearson v McMahon,* 482 US 220, 107 S.Ct.2332 (1987). See also: McCormack, *op. cit.;* Ebenroth & Dillon "Arbitration Clauses in International Finance Agreements" (1993) 10 Journal of International Arbitration 5.

policy as a bar to the enforcement of international arbitral awards, the Committee on International Arbitration of the International Law Association reviewed the development of the concept of public policy during the latter part of the twentieth century, and referred to "an international consensus that corruption and bribery are contrary to international public policy".[68]

On an international level, there is general agreement that corruption should be stamped out.[69] However, the practice of states does not always match up to their preaching.[70] States that are quick to condemn bribery and corruption may nevertheless be prepared to allow national companies to claim tax relief in respect of the money spent on commissions and other inducements so as to procure export orders. As one distinguished commentator has written:

"Virtuous proclamations which raise the fight against corruption to the level of a principle of international public policy (*l'ordre public véritablement international*) live side-by-side with fiscal rules which from the point of view of taxation confer a benefit on the practice."[71]

What is an arbitral tribunal to do if there is a dispute as to the performance of an international commercial agreement and it is said, as an excuse for non-performance, that the agreement had for its object the payment of bribes or some other fraudulent inducement? This issue was first raised in 1963 before a distinguished Swedish jurist, Judge Largegren, who was acting as sole arbitrator in ICC arbitration No.1110.[72]

This well-known arbitration involved a dispute as to whether an agreement **3–21** entered into in 1950 for the payment to Mr X of a 10 per cent commission on the value of industrial equipment then required for a particular public energy project in Argentina also covered the sale of equipment in 1958 for another similar project. Testifying before Judge Lagergren, Mr X stated that he ceded certain "participations" to "influential personalities" among a "clique of people which had a controlling influence upon the Government's economic policy." Witnesses for the respondent (a foreign supplier) testified that they understood that most of

---

[68] ILA Committee on International Arbitration, "Interim Report on Public Policy as a bar to enforcement of international arbitral awards" (London Conference, 2000), p.22.

[69] See, for instance, the OECD Convention on Combating Bribery of Foreign Public Officials in International Business Transactions adopted by the negotiating conference of the OECD on November 21, 1997; and ICC Document No.315, "Extortion and Bribery in Business Transactions".

[70] To this effect, see, *e.g.*, Knoepfler, *Corruption et arbitrage international* (Publication CEDIDAC, Lausanne, 1998), pp.359 *et seq.*

[71] Knoepfler, *op. cit.*, p.377 (translation by the authors); see also Oppetit, "Le paradoxe de la corruption à l'épreuve du droit de commerce international" (1987) Journal du Droit International 5.

[72] G. Wetter, "Issues of Corruption before International Tribunals: The Authentic Text and True Meaning of Judge Gunnar Largegren's 1963 Award in ICC Case No.1110" (1994) 10 Arbitration International 277.

the money was for "Peron and his boys" as the only way to "get business of any scale in Argentina."

Finding the contract to be "condemned by public decency and morality" because it "contemplated the bribing of Argentine officials for the purpose of obtaining the hoped-for business", Judge Largegren found that such a dispute was not arbitrable, stating that the parties to such a contract had "forfeited the right to ask for assistance of the machinery of justice."[73]

The modern approach, based on the concept of separability[74] that has now received widespread acceptance both nationally and internationally, is that an allegation of illegality does not in itself deprive the arbitral tribunal of jurisdiction.[75] On the contrary, it is generally held that the arbitral tribunal is entitled to hear the arguments and receive evidence and to determine for itself the question of illegality. Thus, in Switzerland, in a case involving a consultancy agreement, the Swiss Federal Tribunal decided that even if a consultancy agreement was in effect an agreement to pay a bribe (and this was not alleged, still less proved), the arbitration agreement would survive.[76]

3–22   Rather than raising questions of arbitrability, allegations of corruption made in an arbitration now raise the rather more substantive questions of proof, and if proved, the consequences of such impropriety under the relevant law. Accepting without question the arbitrability of allegations of impropriety, an ad hoc arbitral tribunal acting under the UNCITRAL Arbitration Rules addressed allegations of corruption put before it thus:

"The members of the Arbitral Tribunal do not live in an ivory tower. Nor do they view the arbitral process as one which operates in a vacuum divorced from reality. The arbitrators are well aware of the allegations that commitments by public sector entities have been made with respect to major projects in Indonesia without adequate heed to their economic contribution to public welfare, simply because they benefited a few influential people. The arbitrators believe that cronyism and other forms of abuse of public trust do indeed exist in many countries, causing great harm to untold millions of ordinary people in

---

[73] Early commentators on this award criticised this approach as failing to give effect to the principle of the autonomy of the arbitration clause. However, as Dr Wetter's publication of the award 30 years later revealed, there was no such contractual arbitration clause. The dispute had been the subject of a manifestly autonomous submission agreement. Judge Largegren's decision was founded simply on the grounds of non-arbitrability.

[74] See paras 3–60 *et seq.*

[75] See Kreindler, "Aspects of illegality in the formation and performance of contracts" 16th ICCA Congress, London, May 2002. See also Kosheri & Leboulanger, "L'arbitrage face à la corruption et aux trafics d'influence" (1984) Revue de l'Arbitrage 3; Lalive "Ordre public transnational et arbitrage international" (1986) Revue de l'Arbitrage 329; Oppetit, above, at pp.5–21. See also Knoepfler, above, p.371; and Derains, "Les Commissions Illicites" ICC Publication No.480/2 (1992), pp.65–68.

[76] Decision of the Tribunal Fédéral, September 2, 1993, in *National Power Corporation (Philippines) v Westinghouse (USA)*, ATF 119 II 380.

a myriad of insidious ways. They would rigorously oppose any attempt to use the arbitral process to give effect to contracts contaminated by corruption.

But such grave accusations must be proven . . . Rumours or innuendo will not do."[77]

If an allegation of corruption is made in plain language in the course of the arbitration proceedings, the arbitral tribunal is clearly under a duty to consider the allegation and to decide whether or not it is proved. It remains less clear, however, whether an arbitral tribunal has a duty to assume an inquisitorial role and to address the question of corruption on its own initiative, where none is alleged. Initiating its own investigation, and rendering a decision on the outcome of such a self-initiated investigation, might leave a tribunal open to charges of straying into territory that is *ultra petita*.[78] Conversely, a failure to address the existence of such illegality may threaten the enforceability of an award, and thus may sit uncomfortably with an arbitral tribunal's duty under some modern rules of arbitration to use its best endeavours to ensure that its award is enforceable.[79] Striking the right balance between these competing considerations may not be easy. At the time of the preparation of this edition, the extent of an arbitral tribunal's duty—if any—to probe matters of illegality of its own motion remains unclear.

Fraud

Where allegations of fraud in the procurement or performance of a contract are **3–23** alleged, there appears to be no reason for the arbitral tribunal to decline jurisdiction. Indeed, in the heat of battle such allegations are frequently made, although much less frequently proved. Where a claim put forward in the course of an arbitration is found to be fraudulent, it will be for the arbitral tribunal to dismiss it. However, problems may arise, as they did in *Fougerolle*, if the alleged fraud is not discovered until an award has been made. An ICC tribunal rejected a claim by *Fougerolle*, the sub-contractor under a turnkey contract, to the effect that it had encountered unexpected ground conditions; in a partial award the arbitrators ordered *Fougerolle* to repay moneys to its main contractor. Some months later, it became known that the main contractor was relying on the same grounds as had been put forward by *Fougerolle* (which the main contractor had denied and which had been rejected by the tribunal arbitrators) in support of its own claims against the engineer. The arbitral tribunal refused to review their award, on the basis that it had been made and could not be reversed at that stage, the award having been approved by the ICC's Court. The Paris Cour d'Appel stated that the

---

[77] *Himpurna California Energy Ltd v PT (Persero) Perusahaan Listruik Negara*, Final Award dated May 4, 1999, extracts of which are published in (2000) XXV Yearbook Commercial Arbitration.

[78] See Kreindler, *op. cit.*, n.75.

[79] See, *e.g.*, Art.35 of the ICC Rules and Art.32.1 of the LCIA Rules.

award could be annulled, if fraud was proved; but in the event it was decided that there had been no fraud.[80]

Conclusion

3–24   The significance of "arbitrability" should not be exaggerated. It is important to be aware that it may be an issue, but in broad terms most commercial disputes are arbitrable under the laws of most countries.[81]

3. THE PARTIES TO AN ARBITRATION AGREEMENT

(a) Capacity

3–25   Parties to a contract must have legal capacity to enter into that contract, otherwise it is invalid. The position is no different if the contract in question happens to be an arbitration agreement. The general rule is that any natural or legal person who has the capacity to enter into a valid contract has the capacity to enter into an arbitration agreement. Accordingly, the parties to such agreements include individuals, as well as partnerships, corporations, states and state agencies.

If an arbitration agreement is entered into by a party who does not have the capacity to do so, the provisions of the New York Convention (or the Model Law, where applicable) may be brought into operation, either at the beginning or at the end of the arbitral process. At the beginning, the requesting party asks the competent court to stop the arbitration, on the basis that the arbitration agreement is void, inoperative or incapable of being performed.[82] At the end of the arbitral process, the requesting party asks the competent court to refuse recognition and enforcement of the award, on the basis that one of the parties to the arbitration agreement is "under some incapacity"[83] under the applicable law.

The rules governing capacity to contract can be found in the standard text-books on the law of contract. They vary from state to state. Thus, in the context of an arbitration agreement it is generally necessary to have regard to more than one system of law. In practice, the issue of capacity rarely arises in international commercial arbitration. Nevertheless, lack of capacity is a ground for objection to an arbitration agreement or to an arbitration award. Accordingly, it may be helpful to look briefly at the kind of questions that may arise; first in relation to

---

[80] For a fuller account of this case, see de Boisséson, "L'arbitrage et la fraude" (1993) Revue de l'Arbitrage 3. In the same article Maître de Boisséson also reviews the *Beltronic* case, which came before a French court of appeal. This was a somewhat unusual case, in that the arbitral process itself was fraudulent. A fake arbitration centre was set up, with the arbitrator and the fake centre sharing the damages awarded by the arbitrator against the unfortunate Canadian defendant!

[81] See Kirry, "Arbitrability: current trends in Europe" 12 Arbitration International 373; van den Berg, "Arbitrability" (1996) XXI Yearbook Commercial Arbitration 450.

[82] New York Convention, Art.II.3; Model Law, Art.8(1).

[83] New York Convention, Art.V.1(a); Model Law, Art.36(1)(a).

individuals and corporate entities and, secondly, more importantly perhaps, in relation to states and state entities.

Natural persons

The New York Convention and the Model Law, where applicable, require the   **3–26** parties to an arbitration agreement to have the capacity to enter into that agreement "under the *law* applicable to them".[84] More correctly, this should perhaps refer to the law "or laws" applicable to them. The capacity of an individual to enter into a contract within the state of his place of domicile and residence will depend upon the law of that state; but in the context of an international contract it may become necessary to have regard also to the law of the contract. For instance, a person aged 20 may well have the capacity to enter into an agreement under his own law, but not under the law governing the transaction in question. If that transaction turned out badly, a party who lacked capacity under one or other of the two systems of law might rely upon this as a reason for not carrying out the contract (or any agreement to arbitrate contained within it). However, there may be an applicable rule of law that defeats such sophistry. For instance, the Rome Convention provides:

> "In a contract concluded between persons who are in the same country, a natural person who would have capacity under the law of that country may invoke his incapacity resulting from another law only if the other party to the contract was aware of his incapacity at the time of the conclusion of the contract or was not aware thereof as a result of negligence."[85]

Corporations

The capacity of a corporation to enter into a contract is governed primarily by   **3–27** its constitution and the law of its place of incorporation. However, as with an individual, in the context of an international commercial agreement it may well be necessary to consider the law governing that agreement. For example, a corporation may be prevented under its own law and constitution from dealing in securities anywhere in the world, but allowed to do so in a particular country by a local law.

A corporation is required to act through its directors and officers in accordance with its constitution and its own governing law. If a corporation enters into a transaction that goes beyond its power (in other words, a transaction which is *ultra vires)* and the transaction turns out badly, it would be open to the corporation to contend that the agreement was not binding on it and that it was not obliged to arbitrate any dispute. To guard against this possibility, it is not unusual

---

[84] Otherwise, the agreement will be regarded as invalid and accordingly unenforceable: see the provisions of the New York Convention and the Model Law cited above.

[85] The Rome Convention on the Law Applicable to Contractual Obligations was concluded in 1980 by the then Member States of the European Community. The uniform rules of this Convention do not apply to questions involving the status or legal capacity of natural persons, except as stated above.

for states to have specific rules of law that restrict or abrogate the doctrine of *ultra vires*, so as to protect persons dealing in good faith with corporations.[86]

States and state agencies

3–28   It would be unusual to encounter a corporation whose constitution insisted that any disputes should be referred to the courts, rather than to arbitration. As stated previously, arbitration is now almost always the preferred method of resolving international commercial disputes. It is more usual, however, to find states or state agencies that are not permitted to refer disputes between themselves and a private party to arbitration. In France, for example, under Art.2060 of the Civil Code, disputes concerning public collectives and public establishments and all matters involving public policy may not be referred to arbitration. However, certain industrial and commercial public entities may be authorised by decree to enter into arbitration agreements. In addition, disputes arising out of industrial or commercial activities may be referred to *international* arbitration.[87] In Belgium, public law entities were at one time prohibited from concluding arbitration agreements. This prohibition has now been abolished,[88] but some restrictions remain.[89] In other countries, such as Saudi Arabia, the state or state agency must obtain the approval of the relevant authorities before entering into an agreement for international commercial arbitration.

This means that before entering into an arbitration agreement with a foreign state or state entity it is advisable to check that the persons entering into the contract on behalf of the state or state agency have the necessary authority to do so. It is also wise to check that any necessary procedures for obtaining consent to an arbitration agreement are obtained. It is sensible to include a statement in the contract to this effect.[90]

It is plainly unsatisfactory for a state or state agency to be entitled to rely on its own law to defeat an agreement that it has freely entered into. A praiseworthy attempt to deal with this problem was made in the European Convention of 1961. This provided that persons considered by the law applicable to them to be "legal persons of public law" should have the right to conclude valid arbitration agreements. Also that if a state wished to limit this facility in some way, it should say so on signing, ratifying or acceding to the Convention.[91] Although the European Convention has met with only limited success, progressive states have dealt with the problem by adopting a similar approach. Swiss law, for example, provides that:

---

[86] See, *e.g.*, within the EU, the First Directive on Company Law [1968] Official Journal of the European Union No.L65/7.

[87] See the decision of the French Supreme Court in the *Galakis* case, Cass. Civ. May 2, 1966, D.S. 1966, 575.

[88] Law of May 19, 1998, Art.1676.2.

[89] The arbitration agreement must relate to the settlement of disputes regarding the formation or the performance of an agreement: *ibid.*

[90] It would also be advisable to ensure that, under the relevant state law, the subject matter of the contract is "arbitrable", in the sense discussed below.

[91] European Convention 1961, Art.II.1 and 2.

"If a party to the arbitration agreement is a state or enterprise or organisation controlled by it, it cannot rely on its own law in order to contest its capacity to be a party to an arbitration or the arbitrability of a dispute covered by the arbitration agreement."[92]

This is a provision that all states would do well to follow. One of the judges of the Swedish Court of Appeal stated, in relation to a plea of state immunity: **3–29**

"It has become even more common during recent years that States and State-owned organs act as parties to agreements of a commercial nature. If such agreements provide for arbitration, it is shocking *per se* that one of the contracting parties later refuses to participate in the arbitration or to respect a duly rendered award. When a State party is concerned, it is therefore a natural interpretation to consider that said party, in accepting the arbitration clause, committed itself not to obstruct the arbitral proceedings or their consequences, by invoking immunity."[93]

Some writers[94] have argued that restrictions imposed by a state on its capacity to enter into an arbitration agreement should not be qualified as issues of capacity, but rather as issues of arbitrability. It is argued that the restriction is self-imposed and could be waived at any time by the state concerned. It is not a true limitation on capacity, such as the protection of persons under mental disability. Accordingly, it should be treated as a matter of "subjective arbitrability", rather than as a matter of capacity.[95]

In practice, the important point is that there may be restrictions on the power of a state or state entity to enter into an arbitration agreement, whether these restrictions are qualified as matters of capacity or of subjective arbitrability. Legal advisers and others dealing with a state or state entity should be aware of this point.

(b) Third parties to the arbitration agreement

Party consent is a prerequisite for arbitration. Such consent is embodied in an arbitration agreement which, as discussed above,[96] will generally be concluded "in writing" and signed by the parties. The requirement of a signed agreement in **3–30**

---

[92] Art.177(2) of the Swiss Private International Law Act 1987. Presumably, however, the state concerned might try to rely on its own law to defeat recognition or enforcement outside Switzerland of any arbitration award against it.

[93] Court of Appeal, Stockholm, June 19, 1980 (1981) 20 International Legal Materials 893.

[94] See, *e.g.*, *Fouchard Gaillard Goldman on International Commercial Arbitration* (E. Gaillard & J. Savage eds, Kluwer Law International, 1999), para.539; Paulsson, "May a state invoke its internal law to repudiate consent to international commercial arbitration?" (1986) 2 Arbitration International.

[95] It is interesting to note in this context that the Swiss law to which reference has been made above refers in the same section both to "capacity" and to "arbitrability", so that—at the very least—the two concepts may merge.

[96] See para.3–07.

writing, however, does not altogether exclude the possibility of an arbitration agreement concluded in proper form between two or more parties also binding other parties. Third parties to an arbitration agreement have been held to be bound by (or entitled to rely on) such an agreement in a variety of ways: first, by operation of the "group of companies" doctrine pursuant to which the benefits and duties arising from an arbitration agreement may in certain circumstances be extended to other members of the same group of companies; and, secondly, by operation of general rules of private law, principally on assignment, agency, and succession. Thus, by way of example, the affiliate of a signatory to an arbitration clause may find itself as a co-respondent in arbitration proceedings; an assignee of an insurance contract may be able to commence arbitration against the insurer of the original insured party; a principal may find itself bound by an arbitration agreement signed by its agent; and a merged entity may continue to prosecute arbitral proceedings commenced by one of its original constituent entities.

Piercing the corporate veil within groups of companies

3–31   A number of arbitral tribunals and national courts have been called upon to consider whether an arbitration agreement concluded by a company may be binding on its group affiliates or even a natural person who is the group's ultimate controlling shareholder.[97] Such attempts to pierce the corporate veil are often motivated by the stated aim to find the "true" party in interest; and, of greater practical importance, to target a more creditworthy member of the relevant group of companies.

Although an objection of principle may readily be made—namely that corporate personality is created precisely in order to contain liability within a particular corporate entity—in practice much will depend on the construction of the arbitration agreement in question, as well as the circumstances surrounding the entry into, and performance of, the underlying contract.[98]

The leading authority on the "group of companies" doctrine is the *Dow Chemical* case,[99] in which a claim was brought before an ICC tribunal not only

---

[97] See generally: Yves Derains, "L'extension de la clause d'arbitrage aux non-signataires—la doctrine des groupes de sociétés" (1994) 8 ASA Special Series 241; Charles Jarosson, "Conventions d'arbitrage et groupes de sociétés", *ibid.*, 209; Yves Derains & Sylvie Schaf, "Clauses d'arbitrage et groupes de sociétés" [1985] Revue de Droit des Affaires Internationales 231; Ibrahim Fadlallah, "Clauses d'arbitrage et groupes de sociétés" [1984–1985] Travaux du Comité français de droit international privé 105; *Fouchard Gaillard Goldman on International Commercial Arbitration* (E. Gaillard & J. Savage eds, Kluwer, 1999), paras 500 *et seq.*

[98] Otto Sandrock, "Arbitration agreements and groups of companies" in *Etudes Pierre Lalive* (1993), p.625 and "The Extension of Arbitration Agreements to Non-Signatories: An Enigma Still Unresolved" in *Corporations, Capital Markets and Business in the Law* (Theodor Baums *et al.* eds, Liber Amicorum Richard M. Buxbaum, 2000) p.461, has argued that all of the cases usually discussed in connection with the "group of companies" theory ought to be regarded (or to have been decided) on theories of agency, such as the theory of the undisclosed principal (or, in some legal systems, indirect representation), the reverse construction of *mandat apparent*, or principles of good faith and estoppel.

[99] ICC 4131/1982 (Interim Award) in *Dow Chemical France v ISOVER Saint Gobain (France)* (1983) 110 Journal du Droit International 899, n. Derains, (1984) 9 Yearbook Commercial Arbitration 131.

by the companies that had signed the relevant agreements but also by their parent company, a US corporation, and a French subsidiary in the same group. Examining the circumstances in which the underlying contract had been entered into, a distinguished international tribunal chaired by Professor Sanders found that the parent, Dow Chemical Company (USA), exercised "absolute control over its subsidiaries having either signed the relevant contracts or, like Dow Chemical France, effectively and individually participated in their conclusion, their performance, and their termination". In particular, a term according to which "deliveries could be made by any wholly owned subsidiary of [Dow Chemical Company (USA) demonstrated that it] was the pivot of the contractual relationship finally established between certain entities of its group and the distributors".[1] On this basis, and apparently relying on trade usages rather than French law as the substantive law of the contract, the tribunal considered the group of companies to be "one and the same economic reality (*une réalité économique unique*)" of which the arbitral tribunal should take account in determining that it had jurisdiction over all of the named parties.[2]

The Paris Cour d'Appel subsequently refused to set aside the interim award on jurisdiction, holding: **3–32**

> "[F]ollowing an autonomous interpretation of the agreements and the documents exchanged at the time of their negotiation and termination, the arbitrators have, for pertinent and non-contradictory reasons, decided, in accordance with the intention common to all companies involved, that Dow Chemical France and The Dow Chemical Company (USA) have been parties to these agreements although they did not actually sign them, and that therefore the arbitration clause was also applicable to them".[3]

The "group of companies" doctrine, and related principles producing similar results, have found expression in the decisions of tribunals and national courts in a variety of jurisdictions. An ICC tribunal accepted jurisdiction over the owner of a group of companies on the grounds that "in the eyes of third parties, all the companies owned by Mr Z undoubtedly form a group of companies dependent on Mr Z" and that he could not "in good faith argue the contrary [having] entertained a total confusion between the different companies in the eyes of third

---

[1] *ibid.*, at 903.

[2] *ibid.*, at 904. The tribunal looked carefully at the parties' intentions in concluding the relevant arbitration clauses and said that the negotiating record showed that "neither the 'Sellers' nor the 'Distributors' attached the slightest importance to the choice of the company within the Dow Group that would sign the contracts"; and, further, that "the arbitration clause expressly accepted by certain of the companies of the group should bind the other companies which, by virtue of their role in the conclusion, performance, or termination of the contracts containing said clauses, and in accordance with the mutual intention of all parties to the proceedings, appear to have been veritable parties to these contracts or to have been principally concerned by them and the disputes to which they may give rise".

[3] Cour d'Appel, Paris, October 22, 1983, *Société Isover-Saint-Gobain v Société Dow Chemical France* [1984] Revue de l'Arbitrage 98 at 100–101, n. Chapelle.

parties".[4] Similarly, New York courts have found non-signatories bound by an agreement to arbitrate where the signatories are their *alter egos*.[5] A number of US courts have also held, on estoppel principles, that when an agreement as a whole confers a "direct benefit" (as opposed to an incidental benefit[6]) upon a third party, such third party may be estopped from contesting the binding effect of an arbitration clause within that agreement,[7] provided that it had sufficient notice of the arbitration clause and failed to object to it.[8]

However, the "group of companies" doctrine has not been universally accepted. Some jurisdictions, for example Switzerland, have refused to recognise the doctrine[9]; while others have been equivocal. Although French,[10] US[11] and English[12] courts have on occasion permitted the piercing of the corporate veil so as to recognise third party group affiliates as non-signatory parties to arbitration agreements, courts in the same jurisdictions have also shown themselves ready to refuse to recognise the "group of companies" doctrine. Thus, while the doctrine was discussed at length in *amicus curiae* briefs submitted to the US Supreme Court in *Ruhrgas AG v Marathon Oil Co*,[13] US courts have generally relied on more traditional principles such as *alter ego*, agency, estoppel and third-party beneficiaries to find jurisdiction over non-signatories.[14] In England, the court set aside an award rendered by an arbitral tribunal in London in which the "group

---

[4] ICC 5730/1988, (1990) 117 Journal du Droit International 1029. But see ICC 4972/1989 (1989) 116 Journal du Droit International 1100, which refused to apply the group of companies doctrine (*réelle unité économique*) to permit a natural person to be sued, when that person had signed the relevant contract in his capacity as the managing director of a company of which he was the controlling shareholder.

[5] See, *e.g.*, *Wm Passalacqua Builders v Resnick Developers* 933 F.2d 131 (2nd Cir. 1991).

[6] See *Cargill Int'l SA v M/T Pavel Dybenko*, 991 F.2d 1012 at 1019 (2nd Cir. 1993): "To allow a plaintiff to claim the benefit of the contract and simultaneously avoid its burdens would both disregard equity and contravene the purpose underlying enactment of the Arbitration Act."

[7] *American Bureau of Shipping v Société Jet Flint SA*, 170 F.3d 349 at 353 (2nd Cir. 1999).

[8] *Avila Group Inc v Norma J of California*, 426 F.Supp. 537 at 542 (D.C.N.Y. 1977): "To allow a plaintiff to claim the benefit of the contract and simultaneously avoid its burdens would both disregard equity and contravene the purpose underlying enactment of the Arbitration Act."

[9] See, *e.g.*, ICC 4504/1985–1986, (1986) 113 *Journal du Droit International* 1118.

[10] See, *e.g.*, Cour d'Appel, Paris, November 26, 1986, *Sponsor AB v Ferdinand Louis Lestrade* [1988] Revue de l'Arbitrage 153, n. Chapelle; Cour d'Appel, Paris, November 30, 1988, *Korsnas Marma v Durand-Auzias* [1989] Revue de l'Arbitrage 697, n. Tschanz; Cour d'Appel, Paris, February 14, 1989, *Société Ofer Brothers v The Tokyo Marine and Fire Insurance Co Ltd, ibid.*; Cass. Civ. 1re, June 25, 1991, *Cotunav v Comptoir Commercial André* [1991] Revue de l'Arbitrage 453, n. Mayer.

[11] See, *e.g.*, *Smith Enron v Smith Cogeneration International*, 198 F.3d 88 at 97–98 (2nd Cir. 1999), a case partly decided on estoppel principles.

[12] See *Roussel-Uclaf v GD Searle & Co* [1978] 1 Lloyd's Rep. 225, (1979) 4 Yearbook Commercial Arbitration 317 (non-signatory subsidiary seeking a stay of an action brought in breach of an arbitration agreement: "the two parties are so closely related on the facts of this case that it would be right to hold that the subsidiary can establish that it is within the purview of the arbitration clause on the basis that it is claiming through or under the parent to do what it is in fact doing, whether ultimately held to be wrongful or not"). But Mustill & Boyd, *Commercial Arbitration* (2nd ed., 1989) p.137, regard this as a possible case of agency.

[13] 526 US 574 (1999).

[14] See, *e.g.*, *Bridas v Government of Turkmenistan* 345 F.3d 347, 354 (5th Cir. 2003), *Dupont v Rhone Poulenc* 269 F.3d 187, 190–91 (3rd Cir. 2001) and *TWS Holdings Inc v MKT Securities Corp*, 680 N.Y.S. 2d 891.

of companies" doctrine was recognised, finding inter alia that the doctrine "forms no part of English law".[15]

Significant doubts thus remain as to the existence and parameters of the **3–33** doctrine. Many still hold the view, reflected in the preparatory materials of the UNCITRAL Model Law, that "trade usages" are too vague a basis upon which to impose an arbitration agreement on a non-signatory party.[16] More established principles of private law—such as assignment, agency and succession—thus remain the surest way in which to bind a third party to an arbitration agreement.

Assignment, agency and succession

Assignment

The effect of an assignment of a contract on an arbitration clause contained **3–34** therein will be determined principally by reference to the law governing the assignment in question as well as the law governing the arbitration agreement. If the arbitration agreement is assignable under the relevant laws, there will be a further question as to the particular form, if any, which the assignment must take. This requirement must not be confused with the writing requirement that applies to the arbitration agreement itself.

Different laws take differing positions on whether an arbitration agreement should be presumed as having been assigned along with the main contract. Some laws, for example German law, make this presumption.[17] For others, for example French law and (it would appear) New York law, an arbitration agreement will be considered as producing mostly duties—rather than rights—and consequently requires express agreement on the part of the assignee in order to produce effects for that party.[18] The Swedish Supreme Court appears to have adopted a middle position, namely that an arbitration clause will be presumed to be assignable if the parties have not expressly agreed otherwise, but once assigned it will operate *vis-à-vis* the assignee only if that party has actual or constructive knowledge of the arbitration clause.[19]

---

[15] *Peterson Farms Inc v C&M Farming Ltd* [2004] All E.R. (D) 50 (Feb.).

[16] Howard Holtzmann & Joseph Neuhaus, *The UNCITRAL Model Law on International Commercial Arbitration* (1994), p.300.

[17] See Bundesgerichtshof decision (1978) 71 BGHZ 162 at 164–165.

[18] French law (Arts 1166 and 1275 of the *Code Civil*) makes a distinction between perfect and imperfect novation, of which only the former discharges the original debtor of his obligations, but requires the original creditor's consent to that effect: see ICC 6962/1991, (1994) 19 Yearbook Commercial Arbitration 184. See further Cass. Civ. 1re, November 6, 1990, *Fraser v Compagnie Européenne des Pétroles* [1991] Revue de l'Arbitrage 73 at 74 ("an arbitration clause remains subject to the principles of privity of contracts and cannot therefore circulate in a chain of contracts, unless the parties have expressly provided otherwise"); and Cour d'Appel, Paris, March 22, 1995, *SMABTP v Statinor* [1997] Revue de l'Arbitrage 550 at 552 (the assumption of obligations requires knowledge of such obligations on the part of the assignee). On New York law see *Lachmar v Trunkline LNG Co*, 753 F.2d 8 at 9–10 (2nd Cir. 1985); but see *Hosiery Mfg Corp v Goldston*, 238 N.Y. 22 at 28 (1924); and *Banque de Paris v Amoco Oil*, 573 F.Supp. 1465 at 1472 (S.D.N.Y. 1983).

[19] Supreme Court of Sweden, October 15, 1997, *Ms Emja Braack Shiffahrts KG v Wärtsilä Diesel AB* [1998] Revue de l'Arbitrage 431 at 433, nn. Hansson Lecoanet and Jarvin.

Arbitration agreements concluded by agents

3–35   The binding effect of an arbitration agreement concluded by an agent on behalf of a principal involves questions of authority (*i.e.* the agent's ability to bind the principal to such agreements) and allied questions of necessary form.[20] Thus, an ICC tribunal invited to determine whether a principal was bound by an arbitration agreement concluded by its agent distinguished between the law governing the arbitration agreement (in that case, the law of the seat of the arbitration), the laws which governed the agent's capacity to conclude an arbitration agreement on behalf of the principal (the law of the principal's registered office) and the form in which such capacity should have been conferred on the agent (the law of the jurisdiction in which the agreement between the agent and the principal was concluded).[21]

National laws feature substantial differences on questions of necessary form (*i.e.* whether the principal's written authorisation is required) and content (*i.e.* whether the principal's authorisation need expressly envisage the conclusion of an arbitration agreement). For example, both Swiss and Austrian law require the principal expressly to authorise an agent to enter into an arbitration agreement on its behalf in order for a principal to be bound by such an agreement, but only Austrian law requires such express authorisation to be in writing.[22] Under Italian,[23] French[24] and German[25] law no particular form of authorisation is required.

Succession and novation

3–36   Questions of succession in international commercial arbitration arise most often in connection with companies, rather than natural persons.[26] The general

---

[20] See Andreas Reiner, "The Form of the Agent's power to sign an Arbitration Agreement and Art.II(2) of the New York Convention", ICCA Congress Series No.9 (1999), p.82.
[21] ICC 5832/1988, (1988) 115 Journal du Droit International 1198. Applying Austrian law, which requires authorisation to be given in writing by a principal to an agent in order for the latter validly to conclude an arbitration agreement ("to provide clear and simple evidence and to protect the parties against the waiver of procedural guarantees"), the tribunal refused to regard the principal as bound by the purported arbitration agreement. The conflict of laws rules on these different aspects of agency are notoriously complex. See further Dicey & Morris *The Conflict of Laws* (Lawrence Collins ed., 13th ed., Sweet & Maxwell, 2000), pp.1464 *et seq.*
[22] On Austrian law see s.1008 of the Civil Code and note above; and on Swiss law see Art.396(3) of the Swiss Federal Code of Obligations.
[23] See Corte di Cassazione Judgment No.6915/1982, *Rocco Giuseppe e Fli v Federal Commerce and Navigation Ltd* (1985) 10 Yearbook Commercial Arbitration 464.
[24] See Code civil, Art.1985 and Code de Commerce, Art.L110-3 (formerly Art.109) (in respect of the contract of mandate or mandat); and Corte di Cassazione, Judgment No.361/1977, *Total v Achille Lauro* (1977) 17 Rassegna dell'Arbitrato 94 at 95. However, under Art.1989 of the Code Civil the conclusion of an arbitration agreement requires specific authorisation.
[25] See Landesgericht Hamburg, Judgment December 19, 1967 [1968] Arbitrale Rechtspraak 138 at 140 (in respect of a commercial broker or *Handelsmakler*, under s.75h(2) of the German Commercial Code). Sandrock, in "The Extension of Arbitration Agreements to Non-Signatories: An Enigma Still Unresolved", *op. cit.*, p.467, believes that an arbitration agreement concluded by an agent or representative without the principal's written authorisation would bind that principal only if in the circumstances third parties' legitimate expectations required protection.
[26] On natural persons see s.8(1) of the English Arbitration Act 1996: "Unless otherwise agreed by the parties, an arbitration agreement is not discharged by the death of a party and may be enforced by or against the personal representatives of that party."

rule is that arbitration agreements, like other contracts, enure to the benefit of universal successors of companies[27]; that is, the entities that succeed them as a result, for example, of a voluntary merger,[28] or by operation of law.[29] Such questions involve the status of a company and are thus generally to be resolved by reference to the law of its incorporation (or, in respect of natural persons, by reference to the law of succession).

4. ANALYSIS OF AN ARBITRATION AGREEMENT

(a) Scope

An arbitration agreement confers a mandate upon an arbitral tribunal to decide **3–37** any and all of the disputes that come within the ambit of that agreement. It is important that an arbitrator should not go beyond this mandate.[30] If he does, there is a risk that his award will be refused recognition and enforcement under the provisions of the New York Convention. Art.V.1(c) provides that recognition and enforcement may be refused:

"If the award deals with a difference not contemplated by or not falling within the terms of the submission to arbitration, or if it contains decisions on matters beyond the scope of the submission to arbitration . . . "

The Model Law contains an almost identical provision to the effect that an award may be set aside by the competent court, as well as being refused recognition and enforcement, if it:

" . . . deals with a dispute not contemplated by or not falling within the terms of the submission to arbitration or contains decisions on matters beyond the scope of the submission to arbitration."[31]

---

[27] See ICC 2626/1977, (1977) 2 Yearbook Commercial Arbitration 153, where an Italian limited liability company (SAS) had been succeeded—as was evident on the companies register—by a public limited company (SpA). The SpA was held to be a proper respondent on the basis of universal succession under Italian law.

[28] See ICC 3281/1981, (1982) 109 Journal du Droit International 990; ICC 3742/1983, (1984) 111 Journal du Droit International 910; and *cf.* the ad hoc award in *Starways Ltd v UN*, (1969) 44 I.L.R. 433 (where the claimant had ceased to exist as a separate legal entity).

[29] Mustill & Boyd, *op. cit.*, at 137 observe that in cases of statutory novation "the claimant has replaced the person originally named as a party, who therefore has ceased to have any rights or duties under the contract".

[30] The poet's reflection that "a man's reach should exceed his grasp, or what's a heaven for?" seems not to be apposite for an international arbitrator (Robert Browning, *Andrea del Sarto*, line 97).

[31] Model Law, Arts 34(2)(iii) and 36(i)(a)(iii). The reference to a "submission to arbitration" would include an arbitration clause and, for instance, the Terms of Reference in an ICC arbitration (as to which, see Ch.1). There is a saving provision under both the Convention and the Model Law to the effect that if it is possible to separate the matters which *were* submitted to arbitration from those that were not, the award may be saved in respect of the matters that were submitted.

Forms of wording

3–38   It is important to ensure that the wording adopted in an arbitration agreement is adequate to fulfil the intentions of the parties. Usually, when parties agree to resolve any disputes between them by arbitration, they intend to resolve *all* disputes between them by this method (unless a specific exception is made). Accordingly, the arbitration agreement should be drafted in broad, inclusionary terms, rather than referring only certain categories of dispute to arbitration and leaving others to the jurisdiction of national courts.[32]

Fortunately, most national courts now regard arbitration as an appropriate way of resolving international commercial disputes and accordingly seek to give effect to arbitration agreements wherever possible,[33] rather than seeking to narrow the scope of the agreement so as to preserve the court's jurisdiction. Thus, an English court held that a provision for the arbitration of disputes arising "in connection with" the contract was sufficient to give the arbitral tribunal the power to rectify the contract so as to achieve its true meaning.[34] Similarly, a US court interpreted the same words as giving arbitrators broad powers to rule on disputes, thus enabling the court to stay litigation in favour of a referral to arbitration, even though the claim had been framed in terms of tort (libel, conspiracy and violation of legislation concerning unfair trading practices). The court held:

> "The International Chamber of Commerce recommended clause which provides for arbitration of 'all disputes arising in connection with the present contract' must be construed to encompass a broad scope of arbitrable issues. The recommended clause does not limit arbitration to the literal interpretation or performance of the contract. It embraces every dispute between the parties having a significant relationship to the contract regardless of the label attached to the dispute."[35]

3–39   Where an issue *does* arise as to the scope of an arbitrator's jurisdiction the issue may fall to be determined by the arbitrator (possibly at the outset of the

---

[32] See the recommendations of the Final Report of the Working Group on the ICC Standard Arbitration Clause, Document 420/318, October 21, 1991 (hereinafter "Final Report-ICC clause").

[33] A striking illustration of this policy can be seen in the decision of the US Federal District Court in *Warnes SA v Harvic International Ltd*, summarised in (1994) Arbitration and Dispute Resolution Law Journal 65. The arbitration clause referred to the "New York Commercial Arbitration Association", a non-existent association. The court held that it was clear that the parties intended to arbitrate and that an agreement on a non-existent forum was the equivalent of an agreement to arbitrate which does not specify a forum. Accordingly, the parties were directed to arbitrate in the AAA system.

[34] *Ashville Investments Ltd v Elmer Contractors Ltd* (1997) 37 B.L.R. 60 at 81 (CA); see also *Ethiopian Oilseeds & Pulses Export Corp v Rio Del Mar Foods Inc* [1990] 1 Q.B. 86: Hirst J. (at 97) held that "arising out of" should be given a wide interpretation covering a claim for rectification of the contract; and G. Wetter, "The Importance of Having a Connection" (1987) 3 Arbitration International 329.

[35] *J.J. Ryan & Son Inc v Rhone Poulenc* 863 F.2d 315 (4th Cir. 1988).

arbitration) or by a competent court (for instance, where enforcement of the award is sought). There is a chance that the answer will differ, according to the tribunal before which it is raised. In general, arbitrators are likely to take a less restrictive approach than the courts. This is understandable. An arbitrator is likely to consider that as there *are* disputes between the parties, it would be sensible to try, so far as possible, to resolve them all in the same set of proceedings. A national court would no doubt be sympathetic to this approach; but it would nevertheless have it in mind that, unlike an arbitral award, its judgment might set a precedent for the future.[36] Whatever the tribunal, its decision will depend upon its interpretation of the words of the arbitration agreement and the intention of the parties, in the light of the law that governs that agreement.

It has been suggested that the precise wording used in an arbitration agreement is likely to be subjected to closer analysis by common law jurisdictions than by civil law jurisdictions.[37] Be that as it may, the case law raises a number of issues. First, general words such as "claims", "differences", and "disputes" have been held by the English courts to encompass a wide jurisdiction in the context of the particular agreement in question.[38] In the US the words "controversies or claims" have similarly been held to have a wide meaning; and if other words are used, it may be considered that the parties intended some limitation on the kind of disputes referred to arbitration.[39]

Linking words such as "in connection with", "in relation to", "in respect of", "with regard to", "under"[40] and "arising out of"[41] are also important in any dispute as to the scope of an arbitration agreement. For example, English courts have given a wide meaning to the phrase "arising out of", and this form of words will usually embrace all disputes capable of being submitted to arbitration.[42] By contrast, the use of the words "under this contract" may be interpreted as

---

[36] Or even worse, might be overruled on appeal!

[37] Final Report—ICC clause, see n.32 above.

[38] See, *e.g.*, *Woolf v Collis Removal Service* [1948] 1 K.B. 11 at 18; *F. & G. Sykes (Wessex) v Fine Fare Ltd* [1967] 1 Lloyds Rep. 53; *The Angelic Grace* [1995] 1 Lloyd's Rep. 87 (CA).

[39] In the case of *Prima Paint Corp v Conklin Mfg Co* 388 US 395, 87 S.Ct. 1801, 18 L.Ed.2d 1270 (1967), the words "any controversy or claim arising out of or relating to this agreement" were described as a broad arbitration clause, and in the *Scherk* case, above, "any controversy or claim" was held to include statutory claims under the Securities Exchange Act.

[40] *e.g.* in *Onex Corp v Ball Corp*, the Ontario Court of Justice held that a claim for rectification was a dispute arising "under" the contract: summarised in (1996) The Arbitration and Dispute Resolution Law Journal 193 and (1995) XX Yearbook Commercial Arbitration 275.

[41] A similarly wide interpretation was given to the term "concerning" in *Fletamentos Maritimos SA v Effjohn International BV* [1996] 2 Lloyd's Rep. 304.

[42] In *Ethiopian Oilseeds & Pulses Export Corp v Rio Del Mar Foods Inc* [1990] 1 Q.B. 86, Hirst J. (at 97) held that "arising out of" should be given a wide interpretation covering a claim to rectification of the contract. See also *The Angelic Grace* [1995] 1 Lloyd's Rep. 87, (CA). In the US, a decision of the Fifth Circuit Court of Appeals on May 13, 1998 evidenced an equally broad approach to the construction of a clause which referred to arbitration "any dispute, controversy or claim arising out of or in relation to or in connection with 'the agreement' ": *Pennzoil Exploration and Production Co v Ramco Energy Ltd*, Case 96-20497. The approach of the German courts appears to be much the same: see Oberlandesgericht, Frankfurt, September 24, 1985, summarised in (1990) XV Yearbook Commercial Arbitration 666, concerning the expression "arising out of".

excluding any claims other than those when the cause of action is contractual.[43]

3–40   The model arbitration clause recommended in the UNCITRAL Rules probably owes its origin to a mixture of English and US practice:

> "Any dispute, controversy or claim arising out of or relating to this contract, or the breach, termination or invalidity thereof, shall be settled by arbitration in accordance with the UNCITRAL Rules as at present in force."

The second point that emerges from the case law is that there are, in general, three categories of claim that are potentially within the scope of an arbitration agreement. These are:

- contractual claims (including claims incidental to the contract, such as *quantum meruit*);

- claims in tort; and

- statutory claims.

The first two are self-explanatory. The third relates to those claims that arise out of legislation which might bind the parties, such as securities and antitrust legislation. In all three categories of claim, it is necessary to determine whether a particular claim or defence has a sufficient connection with the contract to be covered by the arbitration agreement. In a claim for libel, for instance, it is unlikely that the claim would be covered even by a broad arbitration clause, since there is not likely to be any connection between the complaint and the contract. Likewise, in relation to statutory claims, the arbitral tribunal or a judge may need to examine a claim or defence in relation to the wording of the arbitration agreement, in order to decide whether there is a sufficiently close connection.

3–41   In South Africa, New Zealand and Australia the case law is generally consistent with that of the US and England. Thus, a widely drawn arbitration clause will encompass claims for rectification as well as claims such as the alleged existence of a collateral oral agreement, which are outside the written contract.[44]

When considering the scope of the arbitration agreement, the parties, by their conduct in referring a matter to arbitration, may be taken as impliedly agreeing to confer on the arbitrator jurisdiction beyond that which would have existed pursuant to the arbitration clause. Accordingly, a claim in tort that may not be

---

[43] *Ashville Investments Ltd v Elmer Contractors Ltd* [1989] Q.B. 488, 508. In *Fillite (Runcorn) Ltd v Aqua-lift (a firm)* (1989) 45 B.L.R. 27, it was held that use of the word "under" excluded tortious claims for negligent misstatement from the scope of the arbitration clause. See also *Hi-Fert v Kiukiang Maritime Carriers* [1999] 2 Lloyd's Rep. 782, in which it was held that an arbitration clause referring to "any dispute arising from" the contract excluded claims for negligent misrepresentations that arose from pre-contractual representations.

[44] *Kathmer Investments Pty Ltd v Woolworths Pty Ltd* (1970) 2 S.A. 498; *Roose Industries Ltd v Ready Mixed Concrete Ltd* [1974] 2 N.Z.L.R. 246; *Drennan v Pickett* [1983] 1 Qd. R. 445.

within the scope of the arbitration clause, may nevertheless come within an arbitrator's jurisdiction where the parties address that claim in the arbitral proceedings, without reservation as to jurisdiction.[45]

(b) Basic elements

There is no shortage of learned commentaries on the drafting of an arbitration **3–42** agreement.[46] They are of very little importance or relevance, except to specialists in arbitration who may be called upon to draft a particularly complicated arbitration clause for use, for example, in a complex long-term contract or in a multi-tiered dispute resolution process,[47] or who may be asked to prepare a detailed submission agreement for use in a major arbitration.[48]

International commercial arbitrations usually take place pursuant to a standard form arbitration clause, recommended either by the arbitral institution to which they refer (such as the ICDR, ICC or the LCIA) or by UNCITRAL. Any subsequent arbitration takes place according to the rules of either the institution concerned or of UNCITRAL and these rules will generally be adequate to guide the process from beginning to end, including (if necessary) the constitution of the arbitral tribunal, the filling of any vacancies, the exchange of written submissions and so on. Where the parties wish to provide for ad hoc arbitration, but not to make use of the UNCITRAL Rules, it will generally be sufficient to adopt a clause that makes it clear that all disputes are to be referred to arbitration. Also, the clause should specify that this is to take place in a state which has a modern law of arbitration which, if necessary, will provide for the appointment of arbitrators, the filling of vacancies and so on. In France, for example, a simple clause such as "Resolution of disputes: arbitration, Paris" whilst not recommended, would be held as a valid submission to arbitration in an international

---

[45] See, for instance, *The Almare Prima* [1989] 2 Lloyd's Rep. 376.
[46] See, in particular, the report of Gélinas on *The elements of an effective arbitration clause* (hereinafter Gélinas) at the ICCA Congress Series No.14, Paris 1998. An impressive list of articles and talks is cited in this paper, including Stephen R. Bond "How to Draft an Arbitration Clause" in (1989) 6 Journal of International Arbitration 66; revisited in (1990) 1 ICC International Court of Arbitration Bulletin 14; Craig, Park & Paulsson, *International Chamber of Commerce Arbitration* (3rd ed., Oceana, 2000), pp.85–126; Ulmer, "Drafting the International Arbitration Clause" (1986) 20 The International Lawyer 4; "Guide de rédaction des clauses d'arbitrage et de droit applicable dans les contrats commerciaux internationaux", Pierre Bienvenue, *Revue du Barreau du Québec* (1996) Tome 56, No.1, Avril-Mai, 39; *The Freshfields Guide to Arbitration and ADR* (Kluwer, 1999); William W. Park, "When and Why Arbitration Matters" in *The Commercial Way to Justice* (1997), pp.73–99, at p.96; and Derains, "Rédaction de la clause d'arbitrage", *Le Droit des Affaires Propriété Intellectuelle* (Henri-Desbois, Librairies Techniques), p.15. Also worth mentioning is Bernadini, "The Arbitration Clause of an International Contract" (1992) 9 Journal of International Arbitration 45; Ball, "Just do it. Drafting the Arbitration Clause in an International Agreement" (1993) 10 Journal of International Arbitration 29, and Debevoise & Plimpton's *Annotated Model Arbitration Clauses for International Contracts* (1996).
[47] See Ch.1.
[48] In one arbitration between a state and a private corporation in which two of the authors took part as counsel, the negotiation and agreement of the detailed submission agreement took 18 months and involved consideration of several different systems of law and of transnational rules.

commercial contract.[49] The French law on international arbitration would then give such support to the arbitral process as required, including appointment of the arbitral tribunal under Art.1493 of the French Code of Civil Procedure.

Arbitration clauses are usually drawn in wide terms, to ensure that all disputes which arise out of or in connection with a particular contract or contractual relationship are referred to arbitration. It is possible to limit arbitration to certain disputes, leaving others to the courts, but this is not generally desirable.[50] If a dispute does arise, there may well be a threshold issue as to whether or not it is a dispute which is covered by the arbitration clause—in other words, a dispute about what kind of dispute it is.

3–43   As already indicated, where parties agree to put an arbitration clause into their contract, they will usually select a standard form or "model" clause, either from one of the arbitral institutions or from an internationally recognised authority such as UNCITRAL. These model clauses are widely drawn. The UNCITRAL model, as has been seen, refers to:

> "Any dispute, controversy or claim arising out of or relating to this contract, or the breach, termination or invalidity thereof . . . "

Similar language is used in the ICC and LCIA model forms.

Where a model clause is used it is sensible to supplement it by reference to the number of arbitrators, the place of arbitration, the law or laws governing the arbitration clause and the contract of which it forms part, the language of the arbitration and so on. Otherwise any problems which arise in these respects, and on which the parties cannot agree, will have to be resolved by the relevant arbitral institution or by the arbitral tribunal itself.

3–44   There follows a note of the key elements of an arbitration clause, including those that may usefully supplement a model clause. Since these key elements have already been discussed, either in this chapter or in the preceding chapters, the note is brief.

A valid arbitration agreement

3–45   First, there must be a valid arbitration agreement. In particular it must be made clear, as it is in the model clauses, that the parties intend that any and all disputes between them shall be finally resolved by *arbitration*. Examples of defective clauses, in which such an intention was not made clear, are given later in this chapter.

---

[49] *Fouchard Gaillard Goldman on International Commercial Arbitration* (E. Gaillard & J. Savage eds, Kluwer Law International, 1999), para.486; *cf.* the decision to similar effect in *Arab African Energy Corp Ltd v Olieprodukten Nederland BV* [1983] 2 Lloyd's Rep. 419.

[50] Gélinas, *op. cit.*, p.15, states: "Unless the parties want to exclude from arbitration certain controversies . . . or to limit the arbitration procedure to precisely identified areas of conflict a broad clause is to be recommended over one that will attempt to list every possible type of dispute". He points out that most modern judges are now prepared to give effect to broad wording such as that found in the standard ICC arbitration clause and adds that "if no limitation is intended to the scope of the arbitration agreement, a broad clause must be preferred . . . "

The number of arbitrators

As already discussed, in an international commercial arbitration[51] there should **3–46** be an uneven number of arbitrators; and it is suggested that, in general, three at most will be sufficient. The system of appointing only two arbitrators, with an "umpire" or "referee" to adjudicate between them if they cannot agree, may be appropriate for arbitrations within a defined trade or commodity association, but is impracticable for the generality of international commercial arbitrations.[52]

Establishment of the arbitral tribunal

This is dealt with in Ch.4.   **3–47**

Ad hoc or institutional arbitration

This is one of the most important decisions that has to be taken; and of course, **3–48** it has to be taken at the wrong time. In an ideal world, it would be possible to wait until any disputes had arisen and then decide, according to their importance and complexity, how they should best be handled. Would a simple ad hoc agreement, backed by a modern system of arbitration law, be sufficient to dispose of the disputes without involving a national court[53] or an arbitral institution?[54] If not, would it be sensible to enlist the help and support (and the rules) of one of the arbitral institutions and, if so, which institution—the ICC, the LCIA or the ICDR? Or would it be better, given the complexity of the dispute, the amount of money involved, the expertise likely to be required and the importance of the issues to be resolved, to negotiate a detailed submission agreement?

These questions would be best answered when a dispute arises. But the reality is that by this stage the parties, like a divorcing couple, may not be talking to each other—or at most will only be doing so through their lawyers. Accordingly, good sense dictates that the agreement to arbitrate should be negotiated and concluded at the same time as the contract to which it relates. As one commentator has expressed it:

---

[51] See Ch.1, paras 1–14 *et seq.*
[52] English law, *e.g.*, provides that where there is to be an even number of arbitrators and an umpire, unless the parties agree otherwise the umpire should attend the proceedings and receive all the pleadings and other documents. Any orders or decisions should be made by the arbitrators unless they cannot agree, when the umpire will replace them as the tribunal: Arbitration Act 1996, s.21. This raises certain practical questions such as: how is the umpire to be chosen; which of the arbitrators is to take the lead in organising the proceedings, drawing up orders and so on, until the umpire takes over; what is the point of having the umpire present, if the arbitrators agree upon all matters relating to the arbitration; what is the point of having arbitrators present and taking part in the proceedings, if at some stage they are to be replaced as a tribunal and the decisions, orders and awards are to be made by a single individual? "Umpire" arbitrations may be suitable for a small group of arbitrations in particular trades; but in general the authors do not recommend them.
[53] For instance, to appoint the arbitrator or arbitrators.
[54] To provide a set of rules and to assist in the administration of the arbitration.

"The primary objective, in inserting an arbitration clause in a contract, is to ensure that when the time comes—that is, when a dispute parts the parties—neither one will be able to escape arbitration . . . "[55]

The choice between ad hoc and institutional arbitration has already been considered in Ch.1,[56] and need not be repeated here. The criteria by which an arbitral institution should be judged are also considered in that chapter.[57]

Filling vacancies in the tribunal

3–49 During the course of an arbitration it may sometimes be necessary to replace an arbitrator, whether because his or her appointment has been successfully challenged or because he or she has died or for some other reason, such as incapacity. The rules of the established arbitral institutions contain detailed provisions to cover such contingencies,[58] as do modern laws of arbitration.[59]

It was customary for institutional rules of arbitration to provide for the replacement of an arbitrator by the same method by which he or she was appointed.[60] In the late 1990s, however, both the ICC and the LCIA adopted rules under which their courts have complete discretion as to whether or not to follow the original procedure.[61]

Where there is a submission agreement that is intended, so far as possible, to be self-contained,[62] provisions for filling any vacancies in the tribunal must be spelt out in some detail. One problem that then arises is, how is a "vacancy" to be determined and who is to determine it? Death and resignation are unambiguous. But it would also be sensible to provide for incapacity. And in the absence of an arbitral institution or a national court, who is to determine when an arbitrator is incapacitated? Should incapacity be limited to ill health, or should it extend to refusal to act due to other commitments, which may cause unacceptable delay in the fixing of hearings? For the determination of incapacity, there are no realistic alternatives in the case of ad hoc arbitration, between leaving this to agreement between the parties (which may not be forthcoming) or to a decision by the other members of the arbitral tribunal. Leaving it to the tribunal is not satisfactory since it is undoubtedly difficult, if not invidious, for two members of an arbitral tribunal to declare that their colleague is incapacitated.

3–50 As to failure or refusal to act, the arbitrator concerned should be called upon to withdraw from the arbitration in order that an alternative appointment may be made. If he or she refuses to do so, it may well be necessary to apply to a national court at the place of arbitration for his or her removal.

---

[55] Gélinas, *op. cit.*, p.4.
[56] paras 1–99 *et seq.* and 1–104 *et seq.*
[57] paras 1–109 *et seq.*
[58] See, for instance, the ICC Arbitration Rules, Art.12; LCIA Arbitration Rules, Arts 10 and 11.
[59] See, for instance, the English Arbitration Act 1996, s.27.
[60] See, for instance, the previous (1988) version of the ICC Arbitration Rules, Art.2.12.
[61] ICC Arbitration Rules, Art.12.4; LCIA Arbitration Rules, Art.11.1; see also the ICSID Arbitration Rules, Art.11.2(a).
[62] In the sense that it will not need to be supplemented by the applicable law.

Place of arbitration

This is another decision of major importance. The place of arbitration con- **3–51** stitutes the seat of the arbitration and the law of that place governs the arbitral proceedings. This has already been fully considered in Ch.2. It is advisable for the parties themselves to choose a suitable place of arbitration, rather than leaving the choice to others.[63] In doing so, they should take account of practical matters such as distance, availability of adequate hearing rooms, back-up services and so on. However, they should also locate their arbitration in a state whose laws are adapted to the needs of modern international commercial arbitration and which is a party to the New York Convention.

Governing law

Again, this topic has already been fully discussed.[64] All that need be stated is **3–52** that the main contract should contain a choice of law clause and, if the arbitration agreement is to be governed by a different law, what law.

Default clauses

It is important that the failure or refusal of one of the parties to take part should **3–53** not frustrate an arbitration. The defaulting party usually is the respondent, who sees that it has nothing to win and may have much to lose by taking part in proceedings that are likely to lead to an award against it. Exceptionally, however, a claimant may lose heart in the face of a substantial counterclaim. It may then be the respondent who wishes to proceed. The rules of the arbitral institutions usually contain adequate default provisions; so too do the UNCITRAL Rules which provide:

"1. If, within the period of time fixed by the arbitral tribunal, the claimant has failed to communicate his claim without showing sufficient cause for such failure, the arbitral tribunal shall issue an order for the termination of the arbitral proceedings. If, within the period of time fixed by the arbitral tribunal, the respondent has failed to communicate his statement of defence without showing sufficient cause for such failure, the arbitral tribunal shall order that the proceedings continue.

2. If one of the parties, duly notified under these Rules, fails to appear at a hearing, without showing sufficient cause for such failure, the arbitral tribunal may proceed with the arbitration.

3. If one of the parties, duly invited to produce documentary evidence, fails to do so within the established period of time, without showing sufficient

---

[63] The ICC's statistics indicate a growing awareness by the parties to an arbitration agreement of the importance of choosing a suitable place of arbitration. In each of the five years up to and including 2003, the place of arbitration has been chosen by the parties in over 80 per cent of all new cases filed with the ICC.

[64] See Ch.2.

cause for such failure, the arbitral tribunal may make the award on the evidence before it."[65]

Where there is no default clause in the relevant rules of arbitration, it is sensible to include one in the arbitration clause.

Language

3–54   It is both customary and logical for the language of the arbitration to be the language of the contract. This will be the usual position in an institutional arbitration, although the arbitral tribunal usually has discretion to direct that other languages may be used or that documents may be admitted in their original language without the need for a translation.

Sometimes a contract is made in two languages, each to be of equal authenticity.[66] In such cases, simultaneous translations at the hearing of the arbitration may be unavoidable (although it slows down the proceedings and is not inexpensive).

Entry of judgment and rule of court clauses

3–55   In the US many arbitration agreements contain an express provision to the effect that judgment may be entered upon the award in any court of competent jurisdiction.

Such provision seeks to reinforce arbitration, by making it clear that a national court that has jurisdiction may enforce the arbitration agreement and the award. Although the court may well have this power irrespective of the agreement of the parties, the use of an "entry of judgment" clause is recommended where the arbitration is likely to take place in the US, in order to avoid an argument that its omission indicates that the parties intended to exclude any court procedure on the award.[67]

Other procedural matters

3–56   Other procedural matters need to be covered only in a clause providing for ad hoc arbitration, or where the parties wish to deviate in certain respects from the rules adopted by them in their arbitration clause. An example is where the parties adopt the UNCITRAL Rules, but wish the presiding arbitrator to make an award as if he or she was sole arbitrator, in the event that a majority award is not possible.[68]

The parties may also wish to confer special powers on the arbitral tribunal that do not normally exist under the law governing the arbitration or under the rules

---

[65] UNCITRAL Arbitration Rules, Art.28. Where the respondent has a counterclaim on which it wishes to proceed, even if the claimant fails to do so, the tribunal would presumably allow this, subject to payment of any advance on fees.

[66] As in the *Channel Tunnel* arbitration, discussed in Ch.2.

[67] Domke, *The Law and Practice of Commercial Arbitration* (revised ed., 1985), p.76.

[68] See the UNCITRAL Arbitration Rules, Art.31; only in relation to questions of procedure may the presiding arbitrator decide on his own in the absence of a majority.

of the relevant arbitral institution, if any.[69] These additional powers may enable the arbitral tribunal to grant remedies that otherwise might not be available under the applicable law. For example, power may be given to order a party to provide security in relation to an amount in dispute, either by paying it into a special account established in the name of the arbitral tribunal, or into some other blocked escrow account.[70]

(c) Submission agreements

Generally

The position of the parties and their advisers in dealing with a submission **3–57** agreement is radically different from the position that exists when an arbitration clause is being written into a contract. First, a dispute has actually arisen, and usually this means that there will be a hostile element in the relationship. Secondly, from a technical point of view, the legal advisers know what kind of dispute they are facing, and they will wish to structure the arbitration to deal with it efficiently and appropriately. Thirdly, the interests of the parties may conflict, in that the claimant usually wants a speedy resolution, whereas the respondent often considers that it will be to his advantage to create delay.[71] For all these reasons, the negotiation of a submission agreement may be a lengthy process. However, the importance of "getting it right" cannot be overemphasised.[72]

Drafting a submission agreement

The submission agreement should contain many, if not all of the basic ele- **3–58** ments of an arbitration agreement as set out above.[73] In addition, it should contain a definition, or at least an outline, of the disputes that are to be arbitrated; provision for a possible site inspection; provision for appointment of experts by the arbitral tribunal; provision for interim awards; provision for the costs of the proceedings; and provisions concerning the award, including a provision covering what is to happen if the arbitrators fail to reach agreement; and, finally, an agreement that the award of the arbitral tribunal is to be final and binding upon the parties.

It is also possible to include in the submission agreement procedural arrangements, such as for production of documents, exchange of written submissions and witness statements, the timetable to be followed and other matters. On

---

[69] For the powers of an arbitral tribunal, see Ch.5.
[70] Such an express power is contained, *e.g.*, in the LCIA Arbitration Rules, Art.25.1(a).
[71] Although it should of course be borne in mind that the claimant may be compensated for the delay by an award of interest, and that delay is usually only achieved by the expenditure of costs—*e.g.* the determination of a preliminary issue. Ultimately, the respondent may be directed to pay the costs of the arbitration, particularly if it is considered that its conduct has contributed to the delay. See Ch.8.
[72] See, for instance, the discussion of the arbitration between Turriff Construction (Sudan) Ltd and the Government of the Republic of the Sudan, below, para.3–59.
[73] See para.3–42.

balance, however, it is probably better to deal with such questions in a separate document, once the submission agreement has been concluded.

An illustration

3–59   The importance of ensuring that the submission agreement deals with all these matters emerges clearly from the *Turriff* arbitration, which took place at the Peace Palace in The Hague.[74] During the course of the proceedings two of the three arbitrators originally appointed resigned and the respondent withdrew, leaving the arbitration to proceed as a default arbitration.[75] The resignation of the presiding arbitrator on grounds of ill health was dealt with by agreement; the Canadian chairman was replaced by a Dutch judge. The withdrawal of the Government from the arbitration could *not* be dealt with by agreement, since by then all co-operation between the parties had ceased. However, the arbitral tribunal had express power under the submission agreement to proceed in default (that is to say, in the absence of one of the parties). It decided to do this and a date was fixed for an adjourned hearing. A third crisis prevented this. The Sudanese arbitrator failed to attend the adjourned hearing. One of the arbitrators, who had been delegated by the arbitral tribunal to deal with procedural matters, fixed a new date for the hearing. He ordered that, in the absence of the Sudanese arbitrator, Turriff's oral argument and evidence should be presented before two members of the arbitral tribunal and should be fully recorded, authenticated and preserved.[76]

Under the submission agreement, it was for the Government to appoint a new arbitrator[77] within 60 days. When it failed to do this, Turriff asked the President of the ICJ to make the appointment, which he did. Thereupon, the remaining two arbitrators were deemed to have been reappointed. In this way a new arbitral tribunal was constituted; and the hearing then continued *ex parte* as before, with the new arbitrator reading the transcript of the previous days' proceedings, in order to acquaint himself with the facts. In April 1970, the arbitral tribunal issued an award under which the Government was ordered to pay a sum of over £6 million, together with an additional sum to cover Turriff's legal costs and the costs, fees and expenses of the arbitral tribunal.[78]

---

[74] See above, para.3–57.

[75] The case is briefly noted in Stuyt, *Survey of International Arbitrations 1794–1970* (1976), App.I, Case No.A31; and more fully by Erades, "The Sudan Arbitration" (1970) N.T.I.R. 2 at 200–222. Dr Erades became presiding arbitrator on the resignation of his predecessor. It is also commented upon by Schwebel in *International Arbitration: three salient problems* (Grotius Publications Ltd, 1987).

[76] Erades, *loc. cit.*, p.209.

[77] Although this was not known at the time, the Government had in fact made an order revoking or purporting to revoke the Sudanese judge's appointment as an arbitrator.

[78] Erades, *loc. cit.*, p.222. To complete the story, negotiations took place between the Government and Turriff after the issue of the award and the company accepted in settlement a substantial part of the sum awarded.

(d) Separability

The concept of the separability of the arbitration clause,[79] is both interesting in theory and useful in practice. It means that the arbitration clause in a contract is considered to be separate from the main contract of which it forms part and, as such, survives the termination of that contract. Indeed, it would be entirely self-defeating if a breach of contract or a claim that the contract was voidable was sufficient to terminate the arbitration clause as well; this is one of the situations in which the arbitration clause is most needed. **3–60**

As those who drafted the Model Law observed in relation to the principle of separability:

"The main practical advantage of this principle is that it constitutes a serious bar, for a party who desires delay or wishes to repudiate his arbitration agreement, to subvert the arbitration clause by questioning in court the existence or validity of the arbitration agreement [by questioning the validity of the main contract]."[80]

Separability thus ensures that if, for example, one party claims that there has been a total breach of contract by the other, the contract is not destroyed for all purposes. Instead:

"It survives for the purpose of measuring the claims arising out of the breach, and the arbitration clause survives for determining the mode of their settlement. The purposes of the contract have failed, but the arbitration clause is not one of the purposes of the contract."[81]

Another method of analysing this position is that there are in fact two separate contracts. The primary or main contract concerns the commercial obligations of the parties; the secondary or collateral contract contains the obligation to resolve any disputes arising from the commercial relationship by arbitration. This secondary contract may never come into operation; but if it does, it will form the basis for the appointment of an arbitral tribunal and for the resolution of any dispute arising out of the main contract. **3–61**

The doctrine of separability is endorsed by institutional and international rules of arbitration, such as those of UNCITRAL, which state in the context of pleas as to the jurisdiction of an arbitral tribunal:

" . . . an *arbitration clause* which forms part of a contract and which provides for arbitration under the Rules shall be treated as an *agreement independent of the other terms of the contract.*"[82]

---

[79] This concept is known in some systems of law as the autonomy of the arbitration clause— *l'autonomie de la clause compromissoire.*
[80] Szurski, *op. cit.*, p.76.
[81] *per* Lord MacMillan in *Heyman v Darwins Ltd* [1942] A.C. 356 at 374.
[82] UNCITRAL Arbitration Rules, Art.21.2 (emphasis added).

Following the provisions of the UNCITRAL Rules, the Model Law provides that:

"The arbitral tribunal may rule on its own jurisdiction, including any objections with respect to the existence or validity of the arbitration agreement. For that purpose, an arbitration clause which forms part of a contract shall be treated as an agreement independent of the other terms of the contract. A decision by the arbitral tribunal that the contract is null and void shall not entail *ipso jure* the invalidity of the arbitration clause."[83]

3–62   Similarly, the LCIA rules stipulate that for the purpose of a ruling on jurisdiction:

"[A]n arbitration clause which forms or was intended to form part of another agreement shall be treated as an arbitration agreement independent of that other agreement. A decision by the Arbitral Tribunal that such other agreement is non-existent, invalid or ineffective shall not entail *ipso jure* the non-existence, invalidity or ineffectiveness of the arbitration clause."[84]

In the *Gosset* case, the French Cour de Cassation recognised the doctrine of separability in very broad terms as follows:

"In international arbitration, the agreement to arbitrate, whether concluded separately or included in the contract to which it relates, is always save in exceptional circumstances . . . completely autonomous in law, which excludes the possibility of it being affected by the possible invalidity of the main contract."[85]

Five years later, the US Supreme Court also recognised the separability of the arbitration clause in the *Prima Paint* case[86]; and modern laws on arbitration confirm the concept. Swiss law, for example, provides that:

"The validity of an arbitration agreement cannot be contested on the ground that the main contract may not be valid . . . "[87]

3–63   An increasing number of countries[88] have made their position clear by making the separability of the arbitration clause part of their laws on arbitration.[89] The

---

[83] Model Law, Art.16(1).
[84] LCIA Arbitration Rules, Art.23.1.
[85] Cour de Cassation, 1re Civil Chamber, May 7, 1963 (Dalloz, 1963, p.545).
[86] *Prima Paint Co v Flood & Conklin Manufacturing Corp*, 388 US 395 at 402 (1967).
[87] Swiss Private International Law Act 1987, Art.178(3).
[88] For instance: the Netherlands in the Arbitration Act 1986, Art.1903; England in the Arbitration Act 1996, s.7; and states that either adopt the Model Law or adapt their legislation to it.
[89] See: Marrella "International Business Law and International Commercial Arbitration: the Italian Approach" (1997) Arbitration and Dispute Resolution Law Journal 25; Rogers & Launders, "Separability—The Indestructible Arbitration Clause" (1994) 10 Arbitration International 71; Svernlou "What Isn't, Ain't: The Current Status of the Doctrine of Separability" (1991) 8 Journal of International Arbitration 37.

number of states in which the concept has not yet been accepted is steadily diminishing.[90]

An independent (or autonomous) arbitration clause thus gives the arbitral tribunal a basis to decide on its own jurisdiction, even if it is alleged that the main contract has been terminated by performance or by some intervening event. Some laws and rules go further and establish that the arbitration clause will survive even if the main contract that contains it proves to be null and void.[91] However, this must depend on the reason for which the contract is found to be null and void (*i.e.* is it a reason that will also affect the "separate" arbitration agreement?), and whether it is void *ab initio*.

While the doctrine of separability is now accepted in principle in all developed arbitral jurisdictions, application of the doctrine continues to vary—even within jurisdictions—in circumstances in which the main contract is argued never to have come into existence at all.

In France, the courts will not stay court proceedings in circumstances in which **3–64** the arbitration agreement is "*manifestement nul*" (manifestly void), although in practice it is very rare for French courts to deny an arbitral tribunal the opportunity to rule on its own jurisdiction.[92] In England, the Arbitration Act 1996 provides that an arbitration agreement contained in another agreement "shall not be regarded as invalid, non-existent or ineffective because that other agreement . . . *did not come into existence*", although recent case law suggests that for some English judges the fate of an arbitration agreement remains inextricably linked to the initial existence of the main contract.[93]

It will be appreciated from what has been said that there is a direct connection between the autonomy of the arbitration clause and the power (or competence) of an arbitral tribunal to decide upon its own jurisdiction (or competence). This power (that of competence/competence, as it is sometimes known) is discussed in Ch.5, which deals with jurisdiction and other issues.

(d) Summary

As already stated, most arbitrations take place pursuant to an arbitration clause **3–65** in a "contract". Where the parties decide that any dispute between them will be submitted to arbitration under the rules of a particular arbitral institution, the model clause recommended by that institution should be incorporated into the contract. Where the parties decide that the services of an arbitral institution are unlikely to be required, but that they would nevertheless like to adopt an existing

---

[90] See Sanders, *Arbitration*, Ch.12, paras 107–112; it should be noted, however, that, as Sanders observes, a "comparative study can only be made on the basis of the current situation" and "situations change rapidly" (*ibid.*, para.102).

[91] The UNCITRAL Arbitration Rules, Art.21.2 state that a decision by the arbitral tribunal that the contract is null and void "shall not entail *ipso jure* the invalidity of the arbitration clause"; and as has been seen, the Model Law itself adopts this terminology, Art.16(1).

[92] See Gaillard "The negative effect of competence-competence", International Arbitration Report, No.1, January 1, 2002.

[93] s.7 of the English Arbitration Act 1996; but see Shackleton, "Arbitration without a Contract", *Mealey's International Arbitration Report*, Vol.17, No.9, September 2002.

set of rules, they should incorporate the recommended UNCITRAL arbitration clause into the contract.

Where such arbitration clauses are adopted, most national courts will recognise and give effect to the parties' wishes to arbitrate any disputes between them. These model clauses bring with them a set of rules that are self-sufficient, and which should be enough to guide the arbitral tribunal and the parties from the beginning to the end of the arbitral process.

Nonetheless it would be advisable to add to the model clause at least three of the basic elements of an arbitration agreement, discussed above, namely, the number of arbitrators, the place of arbitration and the governing law of the contract. It may also be—or become—necessary to identify the law governing the arbitration agreement.[94]

3–66   If the parties do not require the services of an arbitral institution and do not wish to adopt the UNCITRAL Rules, a simple submission to arbitration— adapted from one of the model clauses—would be sufficient in theory. In practice however, it is sensible to provide not only for the number of arbitrators, the place of arbitration and the governing law but also to consider such provisions as those relating to the establishment of the arbitral tribunal, the filling of vacancies and the failure or refusal of a party to take part in the arbitration.

The fact that the parties have agreed in their arbitration clause to an arbitration under institutional rules does not prevent them from agreeing, when a dispute has arisen, to a different method of resolving the dispute. Thus they may switch from, say, an ICC arbitration to an ad hoc arbitration or vice versa; but if they do so, a new arbitration agreement should be made, so as to avoid problems. It is not practicable, for example, to conduct an arbitration under the ICC Rules without the involvement of the ICC.

5. Defective Arbitration Clauses

3–67   The principal defects found in arbitration clauses are those of inconsistency, uncertainty and inoperability. The argument as to whether an arbitration clause suffers from one or more of these defects is likely to be raised where, for example, a party takes action in a national court in relation to a dispute and the defendant seeks a stay of the proceedings on the basis of the existence of the arbitration clause. In such circumstances, the application for a stay may be opposed on the basis that the arbitration agreement was "inoperative or incapable of being performed".[95]

---

[94] See the discussion in Ch.2, para.2–05.
[95] These terms are used in the New York Convention, Art.II.3 and in the Model Law, Art.8(1). For further discussion of defective arbitration clauses see Schmitthoff, "Defective Arbitration Clauses" [1975] J.B.L. 9.

(a) Inconsistency

Where there is an apparent inconsistency in the clause, most national courts **3–68** usually attempt to give a meaning to it, in order to give effect to the general intention of the parties, which was to submit disputes to arbitration. This is the case in England where the courts uphold a clause and strike out an inconsistent provision, if it is clear that the "surviving clause" carries into effect the real intention of the parties and the "discarded clause" would defeat the object of the agreement.[96]

(b) Uncertainty

Similarly, as regards uncertainty, the courts of most countries generally try to **3–69** uphold an arbitration provision,[97] unless the uncertainty is such that it is difficult to make sense of it. The same is true of institutions. By way of example, the ICC has in the past accepted the following vague and imprecise formulations as references to the ICC International Court of Arbitration: "the official Chamber of Commerce in Paris, France"; "the Arbitration Commission of the Chamber of Commerce and Industry of Paris"; and "a Commission of Arbitration of French Chamber of Commerce, Paris".[98]

From time to time, however, courts and institutions are confronted with clauses which simply fail for lack of certainty. Examples are:

"In the event of any unresolved dispute, the matter will be referred to the International Chamber of Commerce."

"All disputes arising in connection with the present agreement shall be submitted in the first instance to arbitration. The arbitrator shall be a well-known Chamber of Commerce (like the ICC) designated by mutual agreement between both parties."

"Any and all disputes arising under the arrangements contemplated here-under . . . will be referred to mutually agreed mechanisms or procedures of international arbitration, such as the rules of the London Arbitration Association."

"For both parties is a decision of Lloyd or Vienna stock exchange binding and both will subjugate to the International Chamber of Commerce."

The problem with the first example is that, even if the broad reference to the International Chamber of Commerce is taken to be a reference to the ICC's

---

[96] See: *Central Meat Products Ltd v J.V. McDaniel Ltd* [1952] 1 Lloyd's Rep. 562 and note *E.J.R. Lovelock Ltd v Exportles* [1968] 1 Lloyd's Rep. 163, where inconsistencies and uncertainties were exposed in the clause itself. See also *Mangistaumunaigoz Oil v United World Trade Inc* [1995] 1 Lloyd's Rep. 617, where the arbitration clause provided that "arbitration, if any, by ICC Rules in London". The words "if any" could be rejected as surplus usage.
[97] See: *Star Shipping AS v China National Foreign Trade Transportation Corp* [1993] 2 Lloyd's Rep. 445 (CA); *Nokia Maillefer SA v Mosser*, Tribunal Cantonal (Court of Appeal) March 30, 1993, (1996) XXI Yearbook Commercial Arbitration 681; and *ASA Bulletin* (1995) No.1, p.64.
[98] Y. Derains & E. Schwartz, *A Guide to the New ICC Rules of Arbitration* (1st ed., 1998).

International Court of Arbitration in Paris, the clause by itself does not stipulate whether the unresolved dispute is to be settled by arbitration or by conciliation or by some other procedure. The second example provides for arbitration, but fails to provide for the appointment of an arbitral tribunal. Even if the parties agreed upon "a well-known Chamber of Commerce" as arbitrator, this would be of no avail, since arbitrators must be individuals. Moreover, it is unclear in this clause what is meant by "in the first instance". The third example requires the future agreement of the parties on "mutually agreed mechanisms or procedures". The fourth is simply meaningless.

3–70   Further examples of what have been referred to as "pathological arbitration clauses" are to be found in Craig, Park & Paulsson's commentary on ICC Arbitration.[99] Two of the more flagrant examples include:

"In case of dispute (*contestation*), the parties undertake to submit to arbitration but in case of litigation the Tribunal de la Seine shall have exclusive jurisdiction."[1]

and:

"Disputes hereunder shall be referred to arbitration, to be carried out by arbitrators named by the International Chamber of Commerce in Geneva in accordance with the arbitration procedure set forth in the Civil Code of Venezuela and in the Civil Code of France, with due regard for the law of the place of arbitration."[2]

The latter clause is given as an example of a "disastrous compromise" which might lead to extensive litigation (unrelated to the merits of the dispute) to sort out any contradictions in the various laws stated to be applicable.[3]

(c) Inoperability

3–71   The New York Convention states:

"The court of a Contracting State, when seized of an action in a matter in respect of which the parties have made an agreement within the meaning of this article, shall, at the request of one of the parties, refer the parties to arbitration, unless it finds that the said agreement is null and void, inoperative or incapable of being performed."[4]

---

[99] Craig, Park & Paulsson, *International Chamber of Commerce Arbitration* (3rd ed., Oceana, 2000), pp.127–135.

[1] *ibid.*, p.128.

[2] *ibid.*, pp.132–133.

[3] *ibid.*

[4] New York Convention, Art.II.3; similar words are contained in the Model Law, Art.8(1).

The reference to the agreement being "null and void" refers to the arbitration agreement itself since, as seen in the discussion of the principle of separability, in most countries the nullity of the main contract does not necessarily affect the validity of the arbitration agreement. At first sight it is difficult to see a distinction between the terms "inoperative" and "incapable of being performed". However, an arbitration clause is inoperative where it has ceased to have effect as a result, for example, of a failure by the parties to comply with a time-limit, or where the parties have by their conduct impliedly revoked the arbitration agreement.[5] By contrast, the expression "incapable of being performed" appears to refer to more practical aspects of the prospective arbitration proceedings. It applies, for example, if for some reason it is impossible to establish the arbitral tribunal.[6]

Lack of the ability to make payment of an award should not mean that an arbitration clause is incapable of being performed.[7] However, in India it has been held that a stay of court proceedings should be refused on the grounds that exchange control regulations would prevent payments in foreign currency to the arbitrators and other overseas expenses of those participating in a foreign arbitration.[8]

(d) Repudiation and waiver of arbitration agreements

A related question arises where the claimant is said to have abandoned or waived by conduct its right to proceed with arbitration against the respondent. This raises the question of whether an arbitral tribunal has the power to strike out a claim as a result of delay by the claimant in pursuing the arbitration. For this purpose, legislation appears to be required.   **3–72**

In Hong Kong, for instance, the Arbitration Ordinance was amended in 1982 to give the arbitral tribunal or any of the parties an opportunity to apply to the court for an arbitration to be terminated for want of prosecution. In England, legislation provides for the *arbitral tribunal* to have the power to dismiss a claim, on broadly the same grounds as a national court may strike out claims in litigation.[9] The English 1996 Act provides that, unless otherwise agreed by the parties, the tribunal may dismiss the claim if it is satisfied that there has been inordinate and inexcusable delay on the part of the claimant in pursuing its claim and that the delay either gives rise, or is likely to give rise, to a "substantial risk" that a fair resolution of the dispute is not possible or that it has caused, or is likely to cause, serious prejudice to the respondent.

---

[5] *Corcoran v Ardra Insurance Company Ltd* 842 F.2d 31 (2nd Cir. 1988); also reported in (1989) XIV Yearbook Commercial Arbitration 773. For the continuation of the saga, see: (1991) XVI Yearbook Commercial Arbitration 663 and (1992) XVII Yearbook Commercial Arbitration 666.

[6] In *Aminoil v Government of Kuwait* (1982) XXI I.L.M. 976 the original arbitration clause provided that the third arbitrator was to be appointed by the British Political Resident in the Gulf, an official whose post had ceased to exist at the time the dispute arose; this defect was in the event cured by the conclusion of a new submission agreement.

[7] See, *e.g.*, *The Rena K* [1979] Q.B. 377; [1978] 1 Lloyd's Rep. 545.

[8] See van den Berg, *The New York Arbitration Convention of 1958* (1981), p.160.

[9] This provision was incorporated into the Arbitration Act 1950 by the Courts and Legal Services Act 1990; it was later incorporated into the English Arbitration Act 1996, s.41(3).

6. MULTI-PARTY ARBITRATIONS

(a) Generally

3–73   When several parties are involved in a dispute, it is usually considered desirable that the issues should be dealt with in the same proceedings, rather than in a series of separate proceedings. In general terms, this saves time and money. More importantly, it avoids the possibility of conflicting decisions on the same issues of law and fact, since all issues are determined by the same tribunal at the same time. In national courts it is generally possible to join additional parties, or to consolidate separate sets of proceedings. In arbitration, however, it is difficult and sometimes impossible to achieve this, because the arbitral process is based upon the agreement of the parties:

> "The difficulties of multi-party arbitrations all result from a single cause. Arbitration has a contractual basis; only the common will of the contracting parties can entitle a person to bring a proceeding before an arbitral tribunal against another person and oblige that other person to appear before it. The greater the number of such persons, the greater the degree of care which should be taken to ensure that none of them is joined in the proceeding against its will." [10]

Where there is a multi-party arbitration, it may be because there are several parties to one contract; or it may be because there are several contracts with different parties that have a bearing on the matters in dispute. It is helpful to distinguish between the two.

Several parties to one contract

3–74   It is increasingly common, particularly in international trade and commerce, for individuals, corporations or state agencies to join together in a joint venture or consortium or in some other legal relationship of this kind, in order to enter into a contract with another party or parties. Where such a contract contains an arbitration clause and a dispute arises, the members of the consortium or joint venture may decide that they would each like to appoint an arbitrator. This is what happened in *Dutco*.[11] Dutco had entered into a contract with a consortium of two German companies and, when disputes arose, brought arbitral proceedings under the ICC Arbitration Rules against those two companies. Each of the companies claimed to be entitled to appoint an arbitrator. This created problems, because the ICC Rules do not contemplate an arbitral tribunal of more than three

---

[10] Commission on International Arbitration, Final Report on Multi-party Arbitrations, Paris, June 1994, by the Working Group under the Chairmanship of M. Jean-Louis Delvolvé (published in (1995) 6 ICC Bull. 26 (hereinafter the "Delvolvé Report")), para.5.
[11] French Cass. Civ. 1re, January 7, 1992 *(BKMI and Siemens v Dutco)* (1992) 1 Bull. Civ.; (1992) 119 Journal du Droit International 707, 2nd document; (1992) Revue de l'Arbitrage 470, comment by Bellet at 473–482; excerpts in *ICCA Year Book* (1993), 140–142.

arbitrators.[12] The ICC requested the two German companies to make a joint nomination of an arbitrator. They did so, but reserved their right to challenge the ICC's decision, which they regarded as depriving each of them of the right to nominate an arbitrator. The French Cour de Cassation agreed with the German companies. The court regarded the principle of equality in the appointment of arbitrators as a matter of public policy.

The 1998 edition of the ICC Arbitration Rules seeks to deal with this situation by providing that:

"1. Where there are multiple parties, whether as Claimant or as Respondent, and where the dispute is to be referred to three arbitrators, the multiple Claimants, jointly, and the multiple Respondents, jointly, shall nominate an arbitrator for confirmation pursuant to Article 9.

2. In the absence of such a joint nomination and where all the parties are unable to agree to a method for the constitution of the Arbitral Tribunal, the Court may appoint each member of the Arbitral Tribunal and shall designate one of them to act as chairman. In such a case, the Court shall be at liberty to choose any person it regards as suitable to act as arbitrator, applying Article 9 when it considers this appropriate".[13]

The 1998 edition of the LCIA Arbitration Rules adopts a similar position: **3–75**

"8.1. Where the Arbitration Agreement entitles each party howsoever to nominate an arbitrator, the parties to the dispute number more than two and such parties have not all agreed in writing that the disputant parties represent two separate sides for the formation of the Arbitral Tribunal as Claimant and Respondent respectively, the LCIA Court shall appoint the Arbitral Tribunal without regard to any party's nomination.

8.2. In such circumstances, the Arbitration Agreement shall be treated for all purposes as a written agreement by the parties for the appointment of the Arbitral Tribunal by the LCIA Court."[14]

Each of these rules recognises the right of the parties to nominate a member of the arbitral tribunal, if they are able to agree, but takes this right away from them and vests it in the institution if they cannot do so. This is a sensible solution to the problem of constituting an arbitral tribunal where there are three or more parties who are unable to agree amongst themselves. However, there may be difficulties when it comes to obtaining recognition and enforcement of an award made by a tribunal that has been established *for* the parties, rather than *by* the parties. The New York Convention, in Art.V.1(d), states that recognition and enforcement of an award may be refused on proof that:

---

[12] ICC Arbitration Rules, Art.8.4.
[13] ICC Arbitration Rules, Art.10.
[14] LCIA Arbitration Rules, Art.8.

"The composition of the arbitral authority or the arbitral procedure was not in accordance with the agreement of the parties, or, failing such agreement, was not in accordance with the law of the country where the arbitration took place".

3–76   The Model Law contains a similar provision.[15]

If a losing party in an arbitration asked the competent court to refuse recognition or enforcement of an award on these grounds, the party seeking enforcement would presumably argue that the composition of the arbitral tribunal *was* in accordance with the agreement of the parties, since by adopting the institutional rules they had agreed, *inter alia*, to this particular provision. The only question that might then arise would be whether such an agreement, made before the arbitration proceedings began, was permitted by the *lex arbitri*—that is, the law of the state where the arbitration took place.

Several contracts with different parties

3–77   A different problem arises where there are several contracts with different parties, each of which has a bearing on the issues in dispute. Again, this is a situation that is not uncommon in modern international trade and commerce. A major international construction project is likely to involve not only the employer and the main contractor (which itself may be a consortium of companies), but also a host of specialised suppliers and sub-contractors. Each of them will be operating under different contracts, often with different choice of law and arbitration clauses; and yet any dispute between, say, the employer and the main contractor is likely to involve one or more of the suppliers or sub-contractors.

What happens when a dispute between the employer and the main contractor is referred to arbitration, and the main contractor wishes to join the sub-contractor in the proceedings, on the basis that if there is any liability, it is a liability the main contractor is entitled to pass on to the sub-contractor? This was the issue raised in the *Adgas* case.[16] Adgas[17] was the owner of a plant that produced liquefied natural gas in the Arabian Gulf. The company started an arbitration in England against the main contractors under an international construction contract, alleging that one of the huge tanks that had been constructed to store the gas was defective. The main contractor denied liability but added that, if the tank was defective, it was the fault of the Japanese sub-contractor. Adgas brought ad hoc arbitration proceedings against the main contractor before a sole arbitrator in London. The main contractor then brought separate arbitration proceedings, also in London, against the Japanese sub-contractor.

---

[15] In Art.36(1)(a)(iv).

[16] *Abu Dhabi Gas Liquefaction Co Ltd v Eastern Bechtel Corp* [1982] 2 Lloyd's Rep. 425, CA; (1982) XXI International Legal Materials 1057; [1983] Revue de l'arbitrage 119 (with comment by Paulsson); and (1984) IX Yearbook Commercial Arbitration 448.

[17] The Abu Dhabi Gas Liquefaction Co Ltd, which itself was owned by a consortium consisting of the Abu Dhabi National Oil Corporation and several international corporations.

There is little doubt that if the matter had been litigated in an English court, the Japanese company would have been joined as a party to the action. However, Adgas did not agree that the Japanese sub-contractor should be brought into its arbitration with the main contractor, since this would have lengthened and complicated the proceedings.[18] Nor did the Japanese sub-contractor agree to be joined. It preferred to await the outcome of the main arbitration, to see whether or not there was a case to answer.

Lord Denning, giving judgment in the English Court of Appeal, plainly wished **3–78** that an order could be made consolidating the two sets of arbitral proceedings, so as to save time and money and to avoid the risk of inconsistent awards:

"As we have often pointed out, there is a danger in having two separate arbitrations in a case like this. You might get inconsistent findings if there were two separate arbitrators. This has been said in many cases ... it is most undesirable that there should be inconsistent findings by two separate arbitrators on virtually the self-same question, such as causation. It is very desirable that everything should be done to avoid such a circumstance."[19]

However, the court recognised that it was powerless to order consolidation without the consent of all parties:

"There is no power in this court or any other court to do more upon an application such as this than to appoint an arbitrator or arbitrators, as the case may be; we have no powers to attach conditions to that appointment, and certainly no power to inform or direct an arbitrator as to how he should thereafter conduct the arbitration or arbitrations".[20]

However, the court was able to go some way towards meeting the problem of conflicting decisions. The case had come before the court on an application for the appointment of an arbitrator; and the court decided that it could appoint the *same* arbitrator in each case, if that arbitrator was ready to accept the appointment (as indeed he was). Lord Denning said:

"It seems to me that there is ample power in the court to appoint in each arbitration the same arbitrator. It seems to me highly desirable that this should be done so as to avoid inconsistent findings."[21]

This was one practical solution to the problem of conflicting decisions; but it **3–79** still meant that there would be two separate arbitrations arising out of the same dispute.

---

[18] There was also a different choice of law clause in the two contracts.
[19] *Abu Dhabi Gas, op.cit.* at 427.
[20] *ibid., per* Watkins L.J.
[21] *ibid.*, at 427, *per* Lord Denning.

Other solutions have been adopted, as will be seen; but none is entirely satisfactory. As a former Secretary-General at the ICC Court of Arbitration pointed out:

> "No generally acceptable solution to the manifold issues arising from multi-party arbitrations has yet been found by either the ICC or any of the dozens of other scholars, lawyers and arbitral institutes working on this issue."[22]

Various solutions have, however, been put into practice in commodity and shipping arbitrations, and other general solutions have been put forward. It is useful to consider them to see whether, and if so how, they work.

(b) "String" arbitrations

3–80   In the commodity markets, the seller may make a contract with a purchaser who then passes the product down a line of intermediaries, until it reaches the last buyer in the chain or "string". If a dispute then arises as to the quality and condition of the product, it would obviously be wasteful for the dispute to be litigated or arbitrated at each stage; accordingly, the practice has developed within certain commodity markets of holding a single arbitration between the seller and the last buyer, on the basis that the award will be binding on *all* parties and enforceable, if necessary, by each contracting party against his co-contractant.

A similar technique has been developed in maritime arbitrations.[23] For instance, a shipowner may charter his vessel to a company that then charters it to a sub-charterer and so on down the line. If the same dispute (such as to the vessel's suitability for purpose) arises under each sub-contract, the parties may agree to appoint the same arbitrator and to accept that his award will be binding on all parties.

Procedures of this kind are sensible; but they are only likely to work effectively as between members of the same trade who are accustomed to the practice, used to dealing with each other, and have a common interest in the quick and efficient settlement of disputes.

(c) Concurrent hearings

3–81   Another possible solution to the problem is to appoint the same arbitrator to both arbitrations. As mentioned earlier, this may be possible where, for instance, a national court appoints the arbitrator.[24] If it is done, the procedures to be

---

[22] Stephen Bond, *Recent Developments in International Chamber of Commerce Arbitration* (Practising Law Institute, ed., International Commercial Arbitration: Recent Developments, New York, 1988) 55–101, p.89.

[23] Bernstein's *Handbook of Arbitration and Dispute Resolution Practice* (4th ed., Sweet & Maxwell, London, 2003) contains a section on "Maritime Arbitrations" by Bruce Harris, which describes "string" or "chain" arbitrations at para.11–078.

[24] It was the solution adopted by the English Court of Appeal in *Abu Dhabi Gas Liquefaction Co Ltd v Eastern Bechtel Corporation* [1982] 2 Lloyds Rep. 425 (above, para.3–77).

followed need to be considered carefully. The arbitrator may direct that (subject to any necessary provisions as to confidentiality) documents disclosed in one arbitration should be made available to the parties in the other[25]; and that a transcript of the witness evidence should be made, so that evidence given in one arbitration may be used in the other (with the parties being given the opportunity to question or comment upon it).

There is no reason in principle why this practice should not be adopted by the parties themselves, without any need for the court to intervene. It would depend upon the agreement of *all* the parties concerned; and once again appropriate procedural rules would have to be worked out. This could no doubt be done more easily in an ad hoc arbitration than in one that is subject to institutional rules.[26]

(d) Court-ordered consolidation

A solution that has been adopted in different parts of the world has been to **3–82** enact legislation which enables the relevant national court to order consolidation of arbitrations. In the Netherlands, for example, under the 1986 Arbitration Act, the President of the District Court in Amsterdam may order the whole or partial consolidation of two or more connected arbitrations in the Netherlands, unless the parties agree otherwise.[27] Similarly in Hong Kong, the Arbitration Ordinance regulating domestic arbitration allows the local court, if it thinks fit, to order consolidation of two or more arbitrations in which common questions of law or fact arise without any need for the consent of all the parties.[28]

There is no provision in the Model Law for the consolidation of arbitrations, but nevertheless several states which have adopted the Model Law have added a provision providing for court-ordered consolidation. In any given case, it is necessary to consider the relevant legislation of the state concerned to see exactly what provision is made, but two examples illustrate what might be expected. Under Florida's International Arbitration Act, a single arbitral tribunal may determine disputes, provided that all the affected parties agree and it is seen to be in the interests of justice and the speedy resolution of the disputes.[29] In California, the court may order consolidation on such terms as the court considers just and necessary. If the parties cannot agree upon the arbitrators, the court will

---

[25] In this regard, see *Aegis v European Re* [2003] 1 W.L.R. 1041, and Rawding & Seeger's commentary thereon in (2003) 4 Arbitration International 483.

[26] However, the Rules of the London Maritime Arbitrators Association contain provisions enabling arbitrators to order concurrent hearings of arbitrations, even where the tribunals are not identical.

[27] Code of Civil Procedure 1986, Art.1046. However, this provision only applies where both sets of proceedings are in the Netherlands.

[28] The Hong Kong Arbitration Act 1982, s.6B. Although there is a different system for international cases, based on the Model Law which was introduced in Hong Kong in 1990, parties may adopt the rules for domestic arbitration and accordingly contract into the possibility of court-ordered consolidation. See Sanders (*op. cit.*) p.86.

[29] Florida International Arbitration Act 1988, s.684.12.

appoint them; the court will also determine any other matters on which the parties cannot agree and which are necessary for the conduct of the arbitration.[30]

At first sight, court-ordered consolidation seems to be the ideal solution to the problem of ensuring consistent decisions, when the same or similar issues of law and fact would otherwise come before different arbitral tribunals. There are likely to be practical and legal problems, however. The different arbitration agreements may differ in their provisions as to number and method of appointment of arbitrators, as to the relevant rules of arbitration, as to the power to issue interim awards and so on. They may also differ[31] as to the law governing the merits of the dispute. Finally, there may be a problem in obtaining recognition and enforcement for such awards. Reference has already been made to the requirement of Art.V.1(d) of the New York Convention to the effect that the composition of the arbitral authority, and the arbitral procedure, must be in accordance with the agreement of the parties. Where an arbitral tribunal which has been imposed upon the parties makes an award, it may be argued that the award should be refused recognition and enforcement under this provision of the Convention.[32] There is strong support, however, for the view that where a court *has* ordered a consolidated arbitration, the award *would* be enforceable under the New York Convention, provided that the parties have at least agreed to arbitration and to the same arbitral jurisdiction.[33]

3–83   In England, when the 1996 Arbitration Act was being drafted, it was proposed that there should be a provision in the Act that would empower either the arbitral tribunal or the court (or both) to order consolidation or concurrent hearings. These proposals were considered carefully by the Advisory Committee[34] but rejected. The Committee wrote:

> "In our view it would amount to a negation of the principle of party autonomy to give the tribunal or the Court power to order consolidation or concurrent hearings. Indeed it would to our minds go far towards frustrating the agreement of the parties to have their own tribunal for their own disputes. Further difficulties could well arise, such as the disclosure of documents from one arbitration to another. Accordingly we would be opposed to giving the tribunal or the Court this power. However, if the parties agree to invest the tribunal with such a power, then we would have no objection."[35]

---

[30] California Code of Civil Procedure, s.1297.272. For a note of other states that adopted the Model Law, but added a provision for consolidation of arbitrations, see Sanders, above, p.45. See also: Leboulanger, "Multi-Contract Arbitrations" (1996) 13 Journal of International Arbitration 43.

[31] As in *Adgas*, above, para.3–77.

[32] See Hascher, "Consolidation of Arbitration by American Courts: Fostering or Hampering International Commercial Arbitration?" (1984) 1 Journal of International Arbitration 127.

[33] See van den Berg, "Consolidated Arbitrations and the 1958 New York Arbitration Convention" (1986) 2 Arbitration International 367; see also Jarvin, "Consolidated Arbitrations, the New York Arbitration Convention and the Dutch Arbitration Act 1986—a critique of Dr van den Berg" (1987) Arbitration International 254; and van den Berg, "A replique to Mr Jarvin" (1987) 3 Arbitration International 259.

[34] This was the Departmental Advisory Committee on Arbitration Law.

[35] Report on the Arbitration Bill by the Departmental Advisory Committee on Arbitration Law, February 1996, para.180.

The Committee went on to state that it appreciated the common sense behind the proposal for compulsory consolidation, but nevertheless they were of the opinion that the problem would best be solved by agreement of the parties. It was suggested that arbitration agreements could be drafted so as to permit consolidation or concurrent hearings; and by way of example, reference was made to the Rules of the London Maritime Arbitrators Association.[36] In order to make it plain that such procedures are permissible under English law, the 1996 Act provides that:

"(1) The parties are free to agree—

    (a) that the arbitral proceedings shall be consolidated with other arbitral proceedings, or
    (b) that concurrent hearings shall be held,
       on such terms as may be agreed.

(2) Unless the parties agree to confer such power on the tribunal, the tribunal has no power to order consolidation of proceedings or concurrent hearings."[37]

Provisions such as this emphasise the consensual nature of arbitration. They make it clear that in principle it is right to allow the parties themselves to decide whether there should be a consolidated arbitration or concurrent hearings in any given dispute.

(e) Consolidation by consent

Under an arbitration agreement

The ICC Commission on International Arbitration's Final Report on multi-party arbitrations summarised its work as follows: **3–84**

"Reaching the end of its investigations, the Working Group has come to the conclusion that it is improper to deal with multi-party arbitration as if it were susceptible of simple and uniform treatment. International trade gives rise to situations which have become extremely complex."[38]

The Working Group suggested that the problem posed called for "a wide range of solutions". One was for the parties to agree in advance that any dispute between them would be referred to a multi-party arbitration.[39] The Report stated:

---

[36] Mentioned above, para.3–81.
[37] s.35.
[38] The Delvolvé Report, para.114.
[39] *ibid.*

"In a multilateral relationship, whether involving a single contract or separate related contracts, it may be appropriate or necessary to have a multi-party arbitration clause."[40]

Drafting such a clause is not easy. It requires a close understanding of the nature of the relationship between the different parties, and of the type of disputes that may conceivably arise; and it calls for careful and detailed drafting. It is miles away from the standard or model form of arbitration clause under which most arbitrations are conducted. The Report contains examples of multi-party arbitration agreements that have been drawn from various sources and these are included in the annexe to the Report.[41]

Under institutional rules

3–85 Neither the Model Law nor the UNCITRAL Rules[42] contain any provision for the consolidation of different arbitrations. However, the problem is a real one; and it is a problem to which arbitral institutions such as the ICC and the LCIA have given long and careful consideration. The ICC *has* provided, however, that where it receives a Request for Arbitration in connection with a legal relationship in respect of which arbitration proceedings between the same parties are already pending, the ICC may "at the request of a party" decide to include the claims contained in the Request in the pending arbitration. This at least avoids the prospect of two separate arbitrations, with two different tribunals, proceeding between the same parties in connection with the same legal relationship. However, once Terms of Reference have been signed or approved by the ICC, additional claims may only be included in the pending proceedings if authorised by the arbitral tribunal.[43]

The LCIA Rules, in a provision conferring additional powers on the arbitral tribunal,[44] give the tribunal the power, on the application of a party, to join one or more third persons in the arbitration, provided that the third person or persons and the applicant have consented in writing. Thereafter, the arbitral tribunal may make a single final award, or separate awards, in respect of all parties "so implicated in the arbitration".[45] This rule does not require the consent of *all* the parties to the arbitration, but it does require at least the consent of the party making the application and of the party or parties who are to be joined in the proceedings.

In an appropriate case, a provision such as this should prove useful in bringing everyone concerned before the same arbitral tribunal. However, the provision

---

[40] *ibid.*, para.113.
[41] They are not, however, to be regarded as approved by the Working Group.
[42] In their current Rules, effective as from January 1, 1998.
[43] ICC Arbitration Rules, Art.4, r.6; and for the addition of new claims, see Art.19.
[44] LCIA Arbitration Rules, Art.22(h).
[45] *ibid.*

only operates with the consent of at least one party to the arbitration and all of the parties who are to be joined.[46] The procedure to be followed in the conduct of such a consolidated arbitration would also have to be carefully worked out, so as to ensure that each party is given a proper opportunity to present its case. Otherwise, any award may be refused recognition or enforcement.[47]

---

[46] Accordingly, it would not work in circumstances such as the *Adgas* case, where the Japanese sub-contractor would have refused to join in the arbitration, even if the main contractor had agreed.

[47] Under the provisions of the New York Convention, Art.V.1(b) or the Model Law, Art.36-(1)(a)(ii).

CHAPTER 4

THE ESTABLISHMENT AND ORGANISATION OF AN ARBITRAL TRIBUNAL

1. BACKGROUND

(a) Generally

4–01   Once the decision to start an arbitration has been taken, and the appropriate form of notice or request for arbitration has been delivered, the next step is to establish the arbitral tribunal.

A national court of law is a standing body to which an application may be made at almost any time, but an arbitral tribunal must be brought into existence before it can exercise any jurisdiction over the dispute and the parties. The contrast between the two is seen most clearly when a dispute has arisen, attempts at settlement have failed, and one of the parties decides that the time has come to pursue its legal rights. If the dispute is to be taken to court, the procedure is simple. The claimant need only issue a writ, file a complaint or initiate whatever form of originating process is appropriate to set the machinery of justice into operation.

It is different if the dispute is to be referred to arbitration. The claimant cannot bring his case before an arbitral tribunal or seek any measures of relief or other directions[1] from that tribunal until it has been established. It usually takes time to establish an arbitral tribunal, particularly if this has to be done by agreement or if the appointment has to be approved by an arbitral institution. Under the ICC Rules, for example, arbitrators who are nominated by the parties have to be confirmed in their appointments by the ICC's Secretary-General.[2] Accordingly, once the decision to arbitrate has been made, the arbitral tribunal should be appointed without delay.

4–02   There are three main reasons for this. First, no procedural orders or directions can be made and no useful steps can be taken in the arbitration until an arbitral tribunal has been appointed. Secondly, as discussed immediately below, the need to comply with time-limits must be considered. Thirdly, there is the question of costs. Costs incurred in the course of arbitral proceedings may be recoverable by

---

[1] Exceptionally, some arbitral institutions provide mechanisms where urgent action is required; *e.g.* the ICC has a "pre-arbitral referee" procedure; adopting a slightly different philosophy, the LCIA Rules provide for expedited formation of the tribunal in appropriate cases (LCIA Rules, Art.9). See also Ch.6, para 6–39.
[2] ICC Arbitration Rules, Arts 8.3 and 8.4.

the successful party,[3] but it is not usually possible to recover legal or other costs incurred *before* arbitration proceedings are commenced.

(b) Commencement of an arbitration

The commencement of an arbitration[4] tends to go hand in hand with the establishment of the arbitral tribunal. It is a significant step, not merely as evidence of a real conflict between the parties, but also in terms of any time-limits for the presentation of claims. **4–03**

Time-limits

Time-limits in litigation or arbitration must always be considered with care. Failure to observe them may be fatal. Time usually starts to run against a claim from the date on which the cause of action arises. It may well be necessary to take some positive step towards the appointment of an arbitral tribunal (such as the notification of a claim to arbitration or the service of a notice requiring the appointment of an arbitrator) in order to prevent a claim failing through lapse of time. Prescriptive time-limits are generally imposed by legislation. In addition, there may be contractual time-limits, which appear in many standard forms of contract—whether for the charter of a ship or for the carrying out of a major civil engineering project. **4–04**

The generally accepted purpose of time-limits is to ensure that claims are made while events are reasonably fresh in the minds of those concerned; and to provide "some limit to the uncertainties and expense of arbitration and litigation".[5] This is a reasonable aim. Documentary or other evidence may be lost or destroyed; witnesses may move to another job or to another country; memories fade and recollections of what happened become less reliable as time passes.

Statutory time-limits

Time-limits for bringing legal proceedings by way of arbitration or litigation are imposed by the law of most, if not all, countries. It is said that the interest of the state is that litigation should be started within a reasonable time of the events that gave rise to it occurred. Whereas contractual time-limits are often short, generally a matter of months, those imposed by law are longer, generally a number of years. This in itself creates no special problem. In principle it is right that a claimant should have adequate time in which to prepare and bring a claim. **4–05**

---

[3] See Ch.8, para.8–91 for discussion of claims in respect of costs.

[4] This inelegant phrase is used since it tends to have a specific and important meaning both in national legislation and in the rules of some arbitral institutions.

[5] Mocatta J. in *A/S Det Dansk-Franske Dampskibselskab v Compagnie Financiere D'Investisse-ments Transatlantiques SA (Compafina) (The Himmerland)* [1965] 2 Lloyd's Rep. 353 at 360; although this is a relatively old case the principle is unchanged by the 1996 Act and is still valid.

Most problems arise in the area of conflict of laws. In particular, there may be a difference in both the length and the nature of the time-limits laid down by different national systems of law. One system of law, for example, may provide that claims under a contract are to be brought within three years, whilst another system of law may allow five years. More importantly, one system of law may classify time-limits as matters of procedure, to be governed by the law of the place of arbitration, while another system may classify time-limits as matters of substance, governed by the same law as that which governs all the other substantive matters in issue.

If a claim is referred to arbitration four years after the cause of action has arisen, which time-limit should prevail? In the example given above, if it is the substantive law of the contract, the three-year limit imposed by the law of the place of arbitration does not apply; but if the procedural law of the place of arbitration is to be applied, the arbitral proceedings may be barred by lapse of time. This example indicates that, if time is running out, it is advisable to look carefully at the intended place or places of arbitration and to choose one that will give the most favourable result for the claimant; this is one aspect of what is sometimes known as "forum shopping".

4–06   Civil law countries tend to classify provisions relating to time-limits as substantive, while the approach of common law countries until the second half of the twentieth century was to treat questions relating to time-limits as procedural. However, the modern tendency in common law countries is to classify "foreign" laws governing time-limits as matters of substance. Where there is likely to be a problem over time-limits, the provisions contained in the relevant legal systems (usually those of the substantive law of the contract and the law of the place of arbitration) must be reviewed to find out what time-limits they impose and whether those limits are classified as substantive or procedural.[6]

Contractual time-limits

4–07   Contractual time-limits are sometimes drawn so tightly that they may be disregarded by some (but by no means all) systems of law on the basis that they offend public policy. When imposed, they vary both in the length of time allowed and in their legal effect. Some clauses simply limit the time within which claims must be brought, whilst others provide that if claims are not brought within a certain time, the right to make a claim at all is extinguished.

Provisions of the first kind are said to "bar the remedy"; provisions of the second kind are said to "bar the right". The practical difference is slight, since a right for which there is no remedy is scarcely better than a right which has been

---

[6] Although the subject of time-limits for commencing arbitral proceedings is one of great practical importance, a detailed account of the varying rules in different national systems of law is outside the scope of this book. The subject is usually treated in some detail in the leading textbooks on private international law or conflict of laws—see, *e.g.*, Dicey & Morris, *The Conflict of Laws* (13th ed., Sweet & Maxwell, 2001), Ch.7, p.172.

extinguished.[7] Where a time-limit is contained in a contract, the precise words used must be studied against the background of the applicable law to determine their meaning and effect.

Two examples, one found in standard forms of shipping contract and the other in a standard form of construction contract, demonstrate this point. Many shipping contracts contain a *Centrocon* clause, which provides for the reference of disputes to arbitration and then states:

"Any claim must be made in writing and claimant's arbitrator appointed within three months of final discharge and where this provision is not complied with the claim should be deemed to be waived and absolutely barred."[8]

Two steps must therefore be taken within the short time-limit fixed by the clause. First, a claim must be made in writing; secondly, the claimant must appoint an arbitrator.

The second example is found in the FIDIC suite of Model Conditions, some **4–08** of which are widely used for international construction projects—either as they stand or with amendments agreed by the parties.[9] Clause 20 of the Conditions of Contract for Construction of Building and Engineering Works Designed by the Employer, introduced in 1999, deals with the settlement of disputes. It is a complicated clause, but in essence it provides that the contractor must submit claims to the engineer within 28 days of becoming aware of the circumstance giving rise to the claim. This is followed by provisions relating to a determination by the engineer and/or adjudication by a Dispute Adjudication Board and then, eventually, ICC arbitration—all within specified time-limits.

It has been suggested that in English law this clause has the effect of barring recourse to the courts, as well as to arbitration, if the specified time-limits are not observed. However, the position may be different in other legal systems. For example, it was argued in an ICC arbitration that a former version of the clause was against the public policy of the law governing the contract, since its effect was to limit the claimant's right to arbitration and to deny the claimant any right of recourse. In a preliminary award, the arbitral tribunal dealt with the public policy argument by distinguishing between the right of recourse to arbitration

---

[7] A difference may exist, in that if the *remedy* is barred the arbitrator may not have jurisdiction to decide whether or not the claim is time-barred, whereas if the *right* is barred the arbitrator may have jurisdiction; see (1977) II Yearbook Commercial Arbitration 242.

[8] The period of three months is often extended by agreement, but usually to only 6 or 12 months. The clause began life as a standard clause in a standard form contract for the charter of a ship for a single voyage. In such circumstances, it was not unreasonable that the parties should have only three months from final discharge of the ship within which to bring claims. However, the clause is sometimes found in time charters, consecutive voyage charters (which may last for years) and bills of lading. The period for commencing an arbitration may be extended by the court in cases where injustice would occur, under the Arbitration Act 1996, s.12.

[9] See Conditions of Contract for Construction for Building and Engineering Works Designed by the Employer (1st ed., 1999) in which some of the engineer's dispute resolution functions are replaced by a Dispute Adjudication Board.

and the right of recourse to the courts. The arbitral tribunal stated in its award:

> "Finally, we have considered whether there is any substance in the Claimants' submission that under [the substantive] law the provisions as to timing in Clause 67 [the version of the clause in the previous edition] of the Contract are null and void, and we have concluded that this point is without substance. We are persuaded by the cogent arguments of the defendants' Counsel that the law in question is concerned with time-limits in litigation. What we are concerned with here is arbitration, an entirely alternative procedure in regard to which the parties are their own legislators in the contracts which they make."[10]

(c) Commencement of an arbitration under the applicable law

4–09   It is for the claimant to ensure that his claim is brought within the time-limit imposed by the contract or by the applicable law or both.[11] Where the time-limit is contained in a contract, the contract itself usually indicates what needs to be done, whether by notification of claim or by request for arbitration, in order to comply with the contractual provisions. Where the time-limit is imposed by law, it is necessary to look at the detailed provisions of that law in order to see what is required in order to stop time running against the claimant.

If the dispute resolution clause refers only to arbitration, without referring to an arbitral institution, the relevant legislation usually provides that the "commencement of arbitration proceedings" is sufficient to stop time running. Some positive action is required to mark the commencement of proceedings, but the form of action required differs from one arbitration clause to another and from country to country. It may be necessary:

- to lodge a claim with the arbitral tribunal, if an arbitral tribunal is designated in the arbitration agreement; or

- to call upon the opposing party to submit the dispute to the arbitral tribunal, if an arbitral tribunal is designated in the arbitration agreement; or

- to commence the procedure for designation of the arbitral tribunal, as provided in the arbitration agreement; or

- to require the opposing party to appoint or to concur in the appointment of an arbitrator.

For example, the Swiss 1987 Act provides that:

---

[10] ICC Arbitration No.4620, Interim Award, April 18, 1984.
[11] It may be possible to agree an extension of time with the respondent, or in some legal systems it may be possible to obtain an extension of time in special circumstances (*e.g.* in England under the Arbitration Act 1996, s.12); but it would be unwise to rely on these possibilities.

"The arbitral proceedings shall be pending from the time when one of the parties submits its request to the arbitrator or arbitrators designated in the arbitration agreement or, in the absence of such designation, from the time when one of the parties initiates the procedure for the constitution of the arbitral tribunal." [12]

(d) Commencement of an arbitration under institutional rules

In order to stop time running, arbitration proceedings must be commenced in accordance with the relevant applicable law (as discussed above). If there is any difference between this law and any institutional rules of arbitration adopted by the parties, the applicable law prevails. For example, the ICC Rules require a party wishing to have recourse to arbitration to submit a "Request for Arbitration" which must contain, *inter alia*, a statement of the claimant's case and particulars concerning the number and choice of arbitrators. The ICC Rules state that: **4–10**

"The date on which the Request is received by the Secretariat shall, for all purposes, be deemed to be the date of commencement of the arbitral proceedings." [13]

This means that under the ICC Rules, an arbitration is commenced when a Request for Arbitration is received by the ICC Secretariat, and not when it is received by the other party (to whom it will in due course be sent by the Secretariat). The date designated under the ICC Rules of Arbitration as being "for all purposes" the date of commencement of the arbitral proceedings may well be the same date under a particular national system of law. This is the case in French law, where time will stop running if and when a Request for Arbitration is made in conformity with the relevant arbitration clause; and the position is the same in English law.

In other cases, the institutional requirements for the "commencement of an arbitration" may go beyond what is required by national systems of law. For example, an ICSID arbitration is deemed to have commenced only when the Secretary-General notifies the parties that all the arbitrators have accepted their respective appointments.[14] However, many national systems of law regard an arbitration as having commenced well before this date.

In summary: **4–11**

- institutional rules providing for the date when an arbitration shall be deemed to commence are valid for the purposes of the institution concerned;

---

[12] Swiss Private International Law Act 1987, Ch.12, Art.181. In England the parties may agree upon when the proceedings are to be regarded as commenced for limitation purposes; failing agreement it is when one party gives a written notice to the other party or the appointing authority seeking the establishment of the tribunal; Arbitration Act 1996, s.14.

[13] ICC Arbitration Rules, Art.4.1.

[14] ICSID Arbitration Rules, r.6(1).

- institutional rules may also mark the "commencement of an arbitration" for the purpose of any time-limit contained in the contract, where the contract refers disputes to arbitration in accordance with the rules of that particular institution;

- institutional rules may mark "the commencement of an arbitration" for the purpose of legislative time-limits, *but only if* the provisions of the relevant legislation coincide with the rules of the institution or in some way treat those rules as an agreement of the parties that overrides the statutory limits;

- the provisions of the relevant legislation determine the "date of commencement of the arbitration" for the purpose of any statutory time-limits that must be observed.

(e) Selecting an arbitral tribunal

4–12   Once a decision to refer a dispute to arbitration has been made, nothing is more important than choosing the right arbitral tribunal. It is an important choice not only for the parties to the particular dispute, but also for the reputation and standing of the arbitral process itself. It is, above all, the quality of the arbitral tribunal that makes or breaks the process.[15]

It is difficult to choose a suitable arbitrator (or arbitrators) for a dispute which has not arisen. In an ideal world, each of the relevant factors would be considered by the parties and their legal advisers *after* the dispute had arisen, so that the most suitable arbitrator or arbitrators could be chosen to deal with that particular dispute. Is the claim large or small? Is it essentially a legal problem or does it turn mostly on the facts? Is particular expertise required to evaluate the facts quickly and correctly? These are the kind of questions which need to be answered before the most suitable arbitrator or arbitrators can be chosen; "horses for courses" is a rule that applies beyond the race track.

In principle, the parties should be free to choose their own arbitrators, so that the dispute may be resolved by "judges of their own choice".[16] Often, however, parties to an arbitration will find that they do not have a completely free choice—indeed, sometimes they may find that they have no effective choice at all. The number of arbitrators may have been settled in advance, in the arbitration clause, when the parties could only guess at the kind of dispute that might arise between them.

This is not likely to have any disastrous consequences since in an international commercial arbitration the choice is generally between one arbitrator and three, and it is possible to argue convincingly for either choice. But, more seriously, the qualifications of the arbitrator may have been designated in advance of any

---

[15] For a comprehensive review of the complex criteria involved in the selection of arbitrators, see Lalive, "Requirements of International Arbitration, The selection of Arbitrators" and "On The Neutrality of Arbitrators and The Place of Arbitration" in *Swiss Essays on International Arbitration* (Zurich, 1984), pp.23–33.
[16] This phrase comes from The Hague Convention of 1907.

conflict. For example, it may be provided that he should be a lawyer of "not less than five years' standing" or that he should be a "commercial man". This may cause delay in ascertaining whether or not a particular arbitrator comes within the qualification; and in any event, it is often not possible to define the type of arbitrator required until disputes arise.

A more common example of the surrender by the parties of their right of **4–13** choice is seen when they agree that, in the event of a dispute proceeding to arbitration, the arbitral tribunal will be selected by an appointing authority. In this case, the choice will devolve upon that appointing authority. Although it may know more about particular arbitrators than the parties, it will certainly know less about the dispute than they do and it is not certain that the right kind of arbitrators will be appointed.

Nevertheless in many arbitrations (particularly ad hoc arbitrations) the parties are free to choose their own arbitral tribunal after a dispute has arisen. Even where this freedom is restricted (for example, as to qualifications) there are still important matters to take into account in the establishment of an arbitral tribunal. The first of these concerns the number of arbitrators to be appointed.

(f) Sole arbitrators and multi-arbitrator tribunals

The establishment of an arbitral tribunal involves many considerations. There **4–14** is first, the question of numbers. Should there be more than one arbitrator and, if so, how many? Is there any general rule as to the number of arbitrators that should be appointed or does this depend upon the circumstances of the particular dispute? The answer is that an arbitral tribunal may consist of one or more arbitrators, depending on what the parties have agreed.

The laws of some countries sensibly provide that the number of arbitrators must be uneven,[17] but the drafters of modern arbitration clauses should bear this in mind too. Clauses providing for two arbitrators and an "umpire", used principally (but not exclusively) in shipping and commodities disputes, are unsuitable for modern international arbitration. This is discussed in more detail below. Tribunals of five (or more) arbitrators are best reserved for arbitrations between states.[18] Thus an important consideration in the drafting of an arbitration clause or a submission agreement is the number of arbitrators to be appointed. In commercial cases, the choice in practice is between one and three.

---

[17] See Ch.3, paras 3–46 *et seq.* The Supreme Court of India held in that an agreement that provides for the appointment of an umpire by both the appointed arbitrators satisfies the requirement of an uneven number of arbitrators stipulated by law; *M.M.T.C. Ltd (India) v Sterlite Industries Ltd* JT (1996) 10 S.C. 390; see also (1997) XXII Yearbook Commercial Arbitration 273.

[18] *e.g.* in NAFTA state-to-state arbitrations under NAFTA Ch.20, under which five arbitrators are appointed. See, *e.g.*, *Mexico v USA* (Cross-Border Trucking), in which one of the authors was the chairman of the tribunal (USA-98-2008-01, February 6, 2001), found at *www.nafta-sec-alena.org/*; other examples may be found at the PCA website, *www.pca-cpa.org/*, *e.g. Ireland v United Kingdom* (Mox Plant), an arbitration pursuant to Annexe VII of the 1982 United Nations Convention on the Law of the Sea.

Sole arbitrators

4–15   The ICC Rules provide that where the parties have not agreed upon the number of arbitrators, a sole arbitrator will be appointed, unless "the dispute is such as to warrant the appointment of three arbitrators".[19] Following the same policy, the LCIA Rules state:

> "A sole arbitrator shall be appointed unless the parties have agreed in writing otherwise, or unless the LCIA Court determines that in view of all the circumstances of the case a three-member tribunal is appropriate."[20]

There is much to be said for such a provision on grounds of speed and economy. The advantages of referring a dispute to a sole arbitrator are self-evident. Appointments for meetings or hearings can be more easily arranged with a sole arbitrator than with an arbitral tribunal of three arbitrators, if only because there will be a smaller number of people to consult. The interests of economy are also served, since the parties will only have to bear the fees and expenses of one arbitrator rather than three. Moreover, the arbitral proceedings should be completed more quickly, since a sole arbitrator does not need to "deliberate" with others, without having to spend time in consultation with colleagues in an endeavour to arrive at an agreed or majority determination of the matters in dispute. If the parties to an international commercial arbitration are able to agree upon the appointment of a sole arbitrator in whom they both have confidence, it makes sense for them to do so.

Nevertheless, in the practice of international commercial arbitration, there is a clear preference for the appointment of three arbitrators in all but the smallest cases. The UNCITRAL Rules reflect this preference by providing that, if the parties have not previously agreed otherwise, three arbitrators will be appointed.[21] A similar provision is contained in the Model Law.[22]

Two arbitrators

4–16   In certain trades and specialised markets the practice is to submit disputes to an arbitral tribunal of two arbitrators, with a subsequent reference to an umpire if the two party-nominated arbitrators cannot agree between themselves. This practice derives from the concept of arbitration as a "friendly" method of settling disputes; and within the context of a defined trade or market, it is a system that no doubt works reasonably well. However, it is not a practice to be recommended in international commercial arbitrations. It is important, particularly in a highly contentious dispute, that there should be someone who can take the lead within the arbitral tribunal. If there is only one arbitrator, there is no problem; a sole arbitrator is unmistakably in charge of the proceedings. The position is the same

---

[19] ICC Arbitration Rules, Art.8.2.
[20] LCIA Arbitration Rules, Art.5.4.
[21] UNCITRAL Arbitration Rules, Art.5.
[22] Model Law, Art.10 (2).

with a tribunal of three arbitrators, where the presiding arbitrator is plainly in charge. However, if there are two arbitrators, which of them is to lead? How much time are they required to spend on such discussions, before deciding (if such is the case) that they cannot agree? If they cannot agree, whose responsibility is it to inform the parties and to ensure that steps are taken to appoint an umpire?

Within the confines of a trade association, these kind of problems rarely arise or, if they do, they may be dealt with relatively easily by trade practice. However, where the arbitrators come from different countries, which may be thousands of miles apart and separated by different time zones, much time may be wasted in trying—and failing—to select a suitable umpire. Once the arbitration has started, with the umpire taking a back seat, which of the two arbitrators presides over the hearings?

In mainstream international arbitration it is preferable to avoid such problems by avoiding altogether the "two arbitrator" system.

Three arbitrators

As already indicated, modern preference is for international commercial dis-   **4–17** putes to be referred to an arbitral tribunal of three arbitrators, unless the amount in dispute is small. This preference has much to commend it. If the dispute is to be determined by a sole arbitrator, and the parties cannot agree who this should be, an arbitrator is "imposed" upon them; that is to say, an arbitrator will be chosen by a national court or by a designated appointing authority, such as the president of a professional body or one of the specialised arbitral institutions.[23] The arbitrator so chosen may or may not be suitable for the task. What is certain is that he or she will not have been chosen by the parties; but by someone else on their behalf. In contrast, where the arbitral tribunal consists of three arbitrators, each of the parties will usually have the right to nominate one arbitrator, leaving the third arbitrator to be chosen in some other manner.

The advantage to a party of being able to nominate an arbitrator is that it gives the party concerned a feeling of confidence in the arbitral tribunal. Each party will have at least one "judge of his choice" to listen to its case. This is particularly important in an international commercial arbitration where, in addition to the matters formally in issue, there may well be differences of language, tradition and culture between the parties and, indeed, between the members of the arbitral tribunal themselves. An arbitrator nominated by a party will be able to make sure that the case of the appointing party is properly understood by the arbitral tribunal. In particular, such an arbitrator should be able to ensure that any misunderstandings that may arise during the deliberations of the arbitral tribunal (for instance, because of difficulties of legal practice, culture or language) are resolved before they lead to injustice.

It may appear to be difficult in practice, but it is possible for an arbitrator to fulfil a useful role in representing the interests of due process of the party who

---

[23] The procedure for the appointment of arbitrators is discussed below at paras 4–21 *et seq.*

nominated him or her without stepping outside the bounds of independence and impartiality. In the context of arbitrations between states it has been suggested that:

"One function of the national or ad hoc member is to ensure that the contentions and arguments of the party which appointed him are fully understood by the tribunal as a whole. That this is an essential function will be apparent to those familiar with the workings of international tribunals. The task of presenting a complicated case to a Bench composed wholly of lawyers who differ in language, legal training and general culture not only from counsel appearing before them, but also from each other, would be formidable. The task becomes manageable with the help of the national or ad hoc member, whether this help is given in the form of the well-timed question during the oral hearing which indicates to counsel the points upon which the Bench still requires enlightenment, or of further exposition during the private deliberations of the tribunal."[24]

4–18   International commercial arbitrations (other than those involving issues or sums of money that are not significant) are usually most effective when an arbitral tribunal of three arbitrators is appointed. This is more expensive than an arbitration conducted by a sole arbitrator; and it will usually take longer to obtain an award. However, an arbitral tribunal of three arbitrators is likely to prove more satisfactory to the parties; and the "quality of justice" is likely to be less subject to the individual predispositions and particular characteristics of a sole arbitrator. It follows that the ultimate award is more likely to be acceptable to the parties.

Four or more arbitrators

4–19   It is difficult to envisage circumstances in which it would make sense to appoint four arbitrators—or, indeed (leaving aside trade tribunals), any even number. So far as the mainstream of international commercial arbitration is concerned, it is sensible to follow the lead of those countries that make it compulsory for an uneven number of arbitrators to be appointed. Nor is there usually any good reason for appointing an arbitral tribunal of more than three members. The practice of states in appointing arbitral tribunals of five, seven or more is usually dictated by political rather than by practical considerations.

However, there are some exceptions. In the case of the Iran–US Claims Tribunal, practical considerations led to the appointment of a tribunal of nine members, three appointed by each party and three from third countries.[25] Individual cases have generally been dealt with by "chambers" of three arbitrators, in

---

[24] Simpson & Fox, *International Arbitration* (Stevens, 1959), p.88; although written many years before the publication of this edition the advice is clearly articulated and still sound.

[25] Customarily referred to as "third-country" rather than "neutral" arbitrators, to emphasise the point that all nine members are required by the UNCITRAL Arbitration Rules to be independent and impartial.

order that the massive caseload could be processed as speedily as possible. The full tribunal of nine members meets periodically to determine disputes between the two governments and other cases that raise issues of special importance.[26]

The special considerations that apply to inter-state arbitrations do not apply to international commercial arbitrations, where there is generally no valid reason for appointing an arbitral tribunal of more than three arbitrators.[27] The greater the number of arbitrators appointed, the greater the delay and expense likely to be incurred in the proceedings. Even in a case of major importance, three carefully chosen and appropriately qualified arbitrators should be sufficient to dispose satisfactorily of the issues in dispute. **4–20**

2. APPOINTMENT OF ARBITRATORS

(a) Generally

There are several different methods of appointing an arbitral tribunal. The most usual are as follows: **4–21**

- agreement of the parties;
- arbitral institution;
- list system;
- existing arbitrators;
- professional institution;
- trade or other association;
- national court.

Each method is now considered in turn.

(b) Agreement of the parties

One of the most common methods of appointing arbitrators is by agreement of the parties. A major attraction of arbitration is that it allows parties to submit a dispute to judges of their own choice. Parties should exercise this choice directly, rather than allow it to be exercised by a third party on their behalf. **4–22**

There are two obvious requirements for the appointment of an arbitrator or arbitrators by agreement. First, that the parties agree upon their choice; and, secondly, that the person or persons chosen accept the appointment. In some forms of contract there is a provision that, if a dispute should arise between the parties, it should be referred to the arbitration by a person who is named in the

---

[26] See Ch.1, para.1–131.
[27] Exceptionally, it may be necessary to appoint an arbitral tribunal of five or even more arbitrators in a multi-party arbitration, if it is necessary or desirable to give each party the opportunity to nominate an arbitrator.

contract. If a dispute subsequently arises, this agreement operates as a choice of the named person as arbitrator. All that remains is to secure the acceptance of the person chosen.

This is a procedure that has little to commend it and it should not be followed. There is no guarantee that the person designated in the agreement to act as an arbitrator will be willing and able so to act at the time when a dispute eventually arises. An arbitrator nominated in an arbitration agreement intended to cover future disputes may be too busy, too ill, or even dead by the time a dispute arises.[28] Nor is there any guarantee that a person chosen in advance to act as an arbitrator will be suitable to decide the particular dispute that arises. For example, an arbitrator may have been designated in advance as a person with specialist knowledge of a particular trade or profession; but if a dispute arises it may turn on a question of law, on which the award of a lawyer would be preferable to that of a person with technical or business expertise.

4–23 Where a sole arbitrator is to be appointed by agreement of the parties, it is preferable for this agreement to be reached *after* the dispute has arisen. There is no rigid rule or practice as to how the parties should proceed in order to reach agreement on their choice.[29] It is a matter for discussion and negotiation between the parties and their advisers. A method often adopted is for each party to prepare a list of three or four persons considered suitable, perhaps with a brief note of the relevant experience and qualifications of each, and then to exchange lists. It sometimes happens that the same person is named on each list. Even if this does not happen, the process focuses the thinking of the parties and their advisers on the type of arbitrator required and may help to pave the way towards agreement.[30]

Not only must the parties agree upon whom they wish to appoint as an arbitrator. The person chosen must also consent to the appointment. Although this consent may be obtained informally (for instance, by telephone) a written and dated confirmation should be obtained, since the date of appointment may prove to be important (for example, in the calculation of time-limits); and indeed, in some states (such as the Netherlands) written acceptance is a statutory requirement.[31] It may also be necessary for the person chosen to complete a declaration of independence and impartiality.[32]

Where an arbitral tribunal is to consist of more than a single arbitrator, the parties may be able to reach agreement on all the arbitrators to be appointed, but in practice this is rare. It is usually difficult enough to reach agreement upon a

---

[28] In this event, the arbitration agreement will be inoperative unless it is "rescued" by some provision of the relevant law.

[29] It is essential to incorporate a provision to the effect that, if they cannot agree, one of the other methods set out below must be adopted, as appropriate.

[30] A variation of this approach is for a party not to nominate the person it wants on the first list, but to keep the name in reserve, so that it might emerge in subsequent negotiations. However, such gamesmanship may prove to be self-defeating if the other party agrees to a person named on the first list!

[31] Netherlands Arbitration Act 1986, Art.1029(1).

[32] As with the ICC, for example.

sole arbitrator, without trying to constitute a larger arbitral tribunal by agreement. Where the arbitral tribunal is to consist of three arbitrators, it is usual for each party to nominate one arbitrator, leaving the third arbitrator to be appointed by one of the methods discussed below.

Sometimes a party seeking to undermine an arbitration will refuse to appoint **4–24** an arbitrator; or a party-appointed arbitrator will refuse to agree on a third arbitrator. This situation can best be avoided by a provision in the arbitration agreement, or in the applicable arbitration rules, that allows an experienced institution to intervene and make the appointment.[33] In an ad hoc arbitration it is often necessary to fall back on the *lex arbitri,* which normally provides for the appointment to be made by the relevant court. Although most national courts will make an appointment in such a situation, relying on national courts inevitably leads to greater delay and relative uncertainty.[34] Furthermore, national courts may not have the appropriate level of international outlook required to make a suitable appointment.

(e) Arbitral institution

Arbitral institutions invariably have mechanisms for appointing arbitrators **4–25** under their own rules of arbitration. The ICC Rules, for example, provide that where there is to be a sole arbitrator, and the parties fail to nominate him one within 30 days from the communication of the Request for Arbitration to the other party, the arbitrator will be appointed by the ICC's Court. The Rules also provide that where there is to be an arbitral tribunal of three arbitrators, the third arbitrator will be appointed by the ICC's Court, unless appointed by agreement of the parties within a limited time.[35] The ICDR, LCIA and WIPO Rules contain similar provisions.[36]

Many arbitral institutions are willing to offer their services as appointing authority, even where the arbitration is not to be conducted under their own rules. The ICC is prepared to do so for a fee,[37] as are the ICDR, the LCIA and the PCA. The Secretary-General of ICSID is also prepared to act as "designating" or appointing authority in connection with ad hoc arbitration agreements that do not fall within the scope of the ICSID Convention.

The advantage that the arbitral institutions and international bodies have to offer, compared to professional societies and trade associations, is their day-to-day involvement in international arbitration. They know the qualities required in the persons they appoint and they usually know the potential candidates.

---

[33] See, *e.g.*, ICC Arbitration Rules, Art.8.4; LCIA Arbitration Rules, Art.7.2.
[34] This was among the subjects discussed in depth by a working group of the 1990 ICCA Congress in Stockholm; see "Preventing Delay or Disruption of Arbitration", ICCA Congress Series No.5 (Kluwer, 1991), pp.61 *et seq.*
[35] ICC Arbitration Rules, Arts 8.3 and 8.4.
[36] ICDR International Arbitration Rules, Art.6; LCIA Arbitration Rules, Art.5; WIPO Arbitration Rules, Art.19.
[37] In 2004, US$2,500 payable by the requesting party plus a maximum of US$10,000 for administrative expenses to be fixed at the ICC's discretion (see the ICC's Rules as Appointing Authority in UNCITRAL or Other Ad Hoc Arbitration Proceedings, Art.1 of the Appendix).

(f) List system

4–26   When a "list system" is used, each party compiles a list of three or four persons considered to be acceptable arbitrators. The lists are then exchanged in an attempt to reach agreement. The procedure has several advantages. The exchange of lists helps to indicate the kind of person each party is seeking; and so prepares the ground for possible agreement on the person to be appointed. However, a list system is very much a "hit and miss" system, since the odds are slight that the same name or names will appear on each list.

A variation on this system, sometimes used by arbitral institutions, particularly the ICDR and the Netherlands Arbitration Institute, and by appointing authorities under the UNCITRAL Rules, is that the institution sends out the *same* list of names to each party.

The UNCITRAL Rules procedure shows how this works. The appointing authority sends to each party to the dispute an identical list, with at least three names on it. Each party returns the list, deleting any name to which it objects and grading the remainder in order of preference. The appointing authority then chooses an arbitrator from the list, in accordance with the order of preference indicated by the parties. The system is slower than that of direct appointment by an arbitral institution, but has the advantage of offering the parties an element of choice (even though this choice is necessarily restricted to persons initially named by the institution on its list).

4–27   The same procedure may also used to choose the presiding arbitrator for an arbitral tribunal of three arbitrators.[38] The disadvantage is that the use of peremptory rejections by the parties may effectively disqualify a number of the most suitable candidates and may restrict the options available if the appointing authority is ultimately called upon to make the appointment.

(g) Existing arbitrators

4–28   Where an arbitral tribunal of three arbitrators is to be constituted, the arbitration clause or submission agreement often provides that each party is to appoint one arbitrator, and that the two arbitrators so appointed will choose the third, who acts as the presiding arbitrator. Of the various methods of appointing a third arbitrator, this is perhaps the most satisfactory. The party-nominated arbitrators are likely to have confidence in the skill and judgment of their chosen presiding arbitrator; otherwise they would not have chosen the person concerned. It is also permissible for them to refer back to the parties who nominated them, and by this means ensure that the appointee is acceptable to all concerned.

It sometimes happens that, try as they may, the party-nominated arbitrators are unable to agree upon the choice of the third arbitrator. The problem is then similar to that which arises where the parties themselves cannot agree upon the choice of a sole arbitrator. Where an arbitral institution is involved, either as administering authority under its rules or simply as appointing authority, this will

---

[38] UNCITRAL Arbitration Rules, Art.7.3.

provide a means of breaking the deadlock. But in ad hoc arbitration where the parties have not designated an appointing authority in their arbitration agreement, and are unable to designate one after the dispute arises, it is necessary to consider whether recourse to a competent court is possible. If not, the arbitration agreement is inoperable.

(d) Professional institution

The president or a senior officer of a professional institution is often named in arbitration clauses, and sometimes in submission agreements, as the person who is to appoint a sole arbitrator, or the presiding arbitrator of an arbitral tribunal, if the parties (or the two party-nominated arbitrators) fail to agree. The persons so named are usually ready to discharge this duty. Indeed, professional institutions often maintain lists of members ready to serve as arbitrators. However, the fact that a person is ready to serve as an arbitrator is not by itself any guarantee that he or she has the necessary experience or qualifications to do so. They may be ready to learn; but it is unfortunate if their learning has to take place at the expense of the parties in terms of money, and of their lawyers in terms of patience.

The task of a sole arbitrator or of the presiding arbitrator in an international commercial arbitration is not an easy one. The rights of the parties, and in particular the right to a fair hearing, must be scrupulously observed. The sole or presiding arbitrator may have to perform this function against a background of conflict between the rules of procedure agreed by the parties and the requirements of the law of the place of arbitration, as well as a conflict of culture and legal backgrounds of the parties' representatives. At the same time, the proceedings must maintain their momentum. They must not be allowed to sink in a quagmire of procedural problems. There may be language problems, both in relation to communications between members of the arbitral tribunal and in the reception of evidence. A timetable must be set for the various steps to be taken in the arbitration (production of documents, exchange of witness statements and so on) as well as dealing with travel and hotel arrangements, and other administrative matters. These are all tasks that call for skill and, above all experience, in the practice of international arbitration.

(e) Trade association

An arbitration clause may provide that the appointment of an arbitral tribunal is to be made by a trade association or some other marketplace "club". Even if the arbitration clause does not contain such a provision, the parties may agree that this is how the appointment should be made. Where the appointment of an arbitrator or arbitrators is to be made in this way, care should be taken to discover exactly what kind of arbitration is envisaged.

Many groups or associations of merchants and traders throughout the world, whether diamond merchants in New York or commodity traders in London, prefer to resolve disputes by arbitration amongst themselves rather than by recourse to national courts or arbitration in the classic mode. This ensures that disputes are dealt with by experienced practitioners in the relevant trade, who do not need to have the technicalities explained to them.[39] The procedure followed is often quick and informal, with lawyers excluded from the hearings unless the parties "expressly" agree otherwise.[40] Trade tribunals often consist of two arbitrators.[41] The two arbitrators, one appointed by each party, are usually experienced in the particular trade concerned; they are expected to reach their decision not merely on the basis of the evidence and arguments presented to them, but also on the basis of their own experience. If they cannot agree, the dispute is referred to an "umpire".

The English courts, respecting the autonomy of the parties, have traditionally been tolerant of this practice. However, it is by no means certain that courts in other countries would be prepared to take a similar view.[42]

4–31   Non-neutral arbitrators may be encountered occasionally in the practice of mainstream arbitration where the parties have so agreed; but neither trade tribunals nor arbitral tribunals with non-neutral arbitrators are representative of the arbitral tribunals that deal with international commercial disputes.[43] Such arbitral tribunals are, or should be, characterised by the independence and impartiality of the arbitrators appointed to serve on them. They are intended to act judicially and if they fail to do so, their awards may be refused recognition and enforcement under international conventions such as the New York Convention.[44]

(h) National courts

4–32   Where the parties are unable to reach agreement upon the appointment of an arbitrator, and where no one is expressly empowered to make the appointment for them, it is necessary to consider whether there is any national court that has:

- the jurisdiction; and

- the power to make the necessary appointment.

---

[39] *e.g.* many of the arbitration clauses used by the Grain and Feed Trade Association provide that an arbitrator must be a member or an employee of a member firm of GAFTA, "engaged or who has been engaged in the trade." It is estimated that there are approximately 80 standard forms of GAFTA contract in use, covering grain and feed products of many origins; indeed, half the world's trade in grain, and slightly more of the world's trade in proteins, is carried out on GAFTA contracts, or in accordance with their terms.

[40] The GAFTA Arbitration Rules 2003, Art.16, para.A34-24.

[41] Indeed, it would be contrary to the law in some countries, which insist upon an uneven number of arbitrators; see Ch.3, para.3–46.

[42] Practices such as that of the arbitrators discussing the merits of the case with a party without the other side being present, or making their decisions on the basis of evidence that is not put before them by the parties, are practices that are alien to the general concept of international commercial arbitration; see below, on impartiality and independence of arbitrators, paras 4–52 *et seq.*

[43] See Smith, "Impartiality of the Party-Appointed Arbitrator" (1990) 6 Arbitration International 320.

[44] See Ch.8.

If the court has both jurisdiction and power, the consent of the parties is not necessary. It is sufficient for the claimant (who is almost invariably the party anxious to constitute the arbitral tribunal) to apply to the court for the appointment of a sole arbitrator, or of a presiding arbitrator, as the case may be. In making such an appointment, the court will often ask the parties' lawyer, or the party-appointed arbitrator, to put forward possible candidates.

Jurisdiction

In principle, a national court will have *jurisdiction* where the arbitration is to **4–33** be conducted on its territory.[45] Accordingly, there should be no problem where the place of arbitration is specified in the arbitration clause or submission agreement. The party wishing to proceed with the arbitration simply applies to the appropriate national court for the appointment to be made. However, a problem arises if, as sometimes happens, the seat of arbitration has not been specified in the arbitration clause or submission agreement.

It may be possible to persuade a court to assume jurisdiction—for example, on the basis that the law governing the substantive issues in dispute is the law of the country of that court; or on the basis that the respondent is within the jurisdiction of the court (and so capable of being compelled to carry out its orders).[46] Failing this, the claimant may have to abandon hope of submitting the dispute to arbitration and may be forced to resort to litigation in a national court instead.

This situation offers a clear example of the dangers inherent in a defective arbitration clause. A clause that fails to provide either for an effective method of constituting the arbitral tribunal, or for the place of arbitration, may turn out to be inoperable. It is likely to lead to the claimant being unable to enforce the arbitration agreement. Yet if, recognising the defective nature of the clause, a claimant takes its claims to a national court, that claim may be met by an application for a stay of the proceedings on the grounds of the existence of an arbitration clause. At best there is considerable potential for delay. At worst, there is the possibility that the claimant may find that there is no effective remedy at all, since the courts will refuse to entertain an action and the arbitration clause is defective.

Powers

The powers of a national court to appoint an arbitrator are less likely to give **4–34** rise to problems. Countries with developed systems of arbitration law recognise the role that needs to be played by their law, and by their courts, in assisting the arbitral process. As part of this role, national courts are usually empowered to appoint arbitrators in circumstances in which it becomes necessary for one of the parties to a dispute to request them to do so.

---

[45] See the discussion concerning the *lex arbitri* in Ch.2, paras 2–08 *et seq.*
[46] *e.g.* the English court may appoint an arbitrator where the seat of arbitration has not been designated provided that the proceedings have sufficient connection with England. Arbitration Act 1996, ss.2(4) and 18.

Wide powers to appoint arbitrators and umpires are contained in most modern national codes of law governing arbitration.[47] However, it should not be assumed that the relevant court will necessarily have the requisite power. Nor should it be assumed that any powers that it does possess will necessarily apply to the particular situation which has arisen. The position under the relevant local law should be checked carefully at the time of selecting the place of arbitration, particularly if no specific method of establishing the arbitral tribunal has been agreed.

(i) Designating an appointing authority

4–35   An application to a national court to act as appointing authority, in order to "rescue" an arbitration agreement from inoperability, is unsatisfactory in a number of ways and should be regarded as a last resort. Parties should recognise that it is in their common interest to choose an appointing authority by agreement—or, at least, to choose a method of designating an appointing authority. One way of doing this, after the dispute has arisen, is to agree to adopt the UNCITRAL Rules, or simply the articles of those Rules that relate to the appointing authority and its functions.

An essential element in the establishment of the arbitral tribunal under the UNCITRAL Rules is the "appointing authority." In all arbitration systems, a method of appointing the arbitral tribunal should be available to break the deadlock that arises if the parties cannot agree on the composition of the arbitral tribunal. This may normally be left to the courts of the country in which the arbitration takes place, but since the modern trend is to minimise intervention by the courts at the place of arbitration, it is easy to understand why UNCITRAL considered it desirable to incorporate the concept of an appointing authority into the Rules.

The parties may designate a court as the appointing authority, but the intention of the Rules is that they should nominate a person or, more usually, an institution likely to maintain a list of names of suitable arbitrators. If the parties have not agreed upon an appointing authority then, after fulfilling certain preliminary requirements, a party may request the Secretary-General of the PCA to designate one.[48]

Designation by the Secretary-General of the PCA

4–36   As mentioned in Ch.1, the International Bureau of the Permanent Court of Arbitration is located at the Peace Palace in The Hague, a great centre of international law built in 1913 for arbitration between states. It is also the

---

[47] See, *e.g.*, Swiss Private International Law Act 1987, Ch.12, Art.179; and Art.1493 of the French New Code of Civil Procedure, Decree Law No.81-500 of May 12, 1981. Art.11 of the Model Law confers upon the appropriate national courts the power to appoint arbitrators where necessary. In England the Arbitration Act 1996, s.18, gives the court the power to make an appointment where the arbitration agreement provides for an appointing authority to perform the task and the authority refuses or fails to do so.
[48] UNCITRAL Arbitration Rules, Art.6.2.

headquarters of the International Court of Justice. The staff of the International Bureau is headed by the Secretary-General, who performs the functions allocated to him under the UNCITRAL Rules. These include the designation of an appointing authority if the parties have not agreed on one.[49]

The UNCITRAL Rules do not specify the information that must be supplied to the Secretary-General for the purposes of designating an appointing authority, but in practice the Bureau asks for the same documents that are to be provided to an appointing authority under Art.8.1 of the Rules for the purposes of appointing an arbitrator. These are: first, the notice of arbitration; secondly, the contract out of or in relation to which the dispute has arisen; and, thirdly (if it is not contained in that contract), the arbitration agreement. The Secretary-General will usually also request copies of correspondence indicating that the appointment of an appointing authority is needed because:

- a party has failed to appoint an arbitrator; or

- it has been impossible to reach agreement on a sole or presiding arbitrator; or

- there is a contested challenge of an arbitrator.

If the respondent does not participate in making a request, the Secretary-   **4–37**
General writes to the respondent to invite comments and specifies a reasonable time within which the respondent must reply.

Before designating an appointing authority, the Secretary-General may also ask for details of the names of potential arbitrators and appointing authorities that have been discussed between the parties and rejected. After reviewing the documents submitted and considering any comments received from the parties, the Secretary-General selects the organisation or individual best placed to perform the function of appointing authority.[50] The Secretary-General then enquires whether that organisation or individual is willing to accept the designation. If the answer is positive, the parties are informed of that decision and requested to approach the appointing authority direct for the next step to be taken in the

---

[49] In 2004, the party making the request was required to pay an administrative fee of €750 for the designation of an appointing authority. The fee for acting directly as an appointing authority in 2004 was €1,500.

[50] The views of the parties, as well as concerns of speed and cost, may influence the Secretary-General's choice of an individual rather than an organisation. The Secretary-General's designations of organisations include the American Arbitration Association, the Arbitral Centre of the Austrian Federal Economic Chamber, the Australian Centre for International Commercial Arbitration, the Bombay Incorporated Law Society, the Cairo Regional Centre for International Commercial Arbitration, the Chartered Institute of Arbitrators, the German Arbitration Institute, the Hong Kong International Arbitration Centre, the ICC, ICSID, the Kuala Lumpur Regional Centre for Arbitration, the LCIA, the Singapore International Arbitration Centre, and the Swiss Arbitration Association. Examples of designations of individuals include a former Chief Justice of New South Wales, Australia, in a dispute between a Korean company and an Asian state entity; an international arbitration practitioner based in the UK, in a dispute between a French company and the government of a Central European Republic; and an international arbitration practitioner based in the US, in a dispute between a Dutch company and an African state entity.

arbitration. The Secretary-General does not usually give reasons for the decision.

The first occasion on which the Secretary-General was called upon to designate an appointing authority under the UNCITRAL Rules was in 1983 in connection with the Iran–US Claims Tribunal. In the special circumstances of this tribunal, the Secretary-General chose the then President of the Supreme Court of the Netherlands. This choice appears to have been motivated by the fact that the state parties had expressed confidence in the Netherlands by locating the tribunal there, and the belief that it would be convenient to have an appointing authority in the same city as that in which each of the state parties had official representatives to conduct business related to the Claims Tribunal. The Chief Justice was appointed in his personal capacity, and his appointment continued after he retired from the judiciary.

4–38   By January 2004, the Secretary-General had dealt with over 200 requests to designate an appointing authority, or to act directly as the appointing authority. The UNCITRAL cases in which the Secretary-General has acted include disputes between parties of 95 nationalities, with approximately 51 per cent of these cases involving a state or state entity. The system appears to have operated satisfactorily, and indeed may be regarded as a strong point in favour of the UNCITRAL Rules; but most parties and their advisers are aware that it is better to nominate an appointing authority at the time of preparing their arbitration clause or submission agreement, since failure to do so may lead to delay[51] and unnecessary expense.

3. QUALITIES REQUIRED IN INTERNATIONAL ARBITRATORS

(a) Generally

4–39   Any natural person may be chosen to act as an arbitrator, the only general requirement being that the person chosen must have legal capacity. Some legal systems may not even insist upon legal capacity. Nevertheless, the general rule is a sensible one and should be followed in the practice of international commercial arbitration.

(b) Restrictions imposed by the parties

4–40   Some standard forms of international contracts, and particularly those used in the shipping and commodity trades and the insurance and reinsurance industries, identify the kind of arbitrator to be chosen in the event of a dispute. For example, the GAFTA Rules provide that an arbitrator must be "a GAFTA Qualified Arbitrator".[52] Or the restriction may be drawn rather more widely and provide that the arbitrators and umpire are to be "commercial men". While this phrase

---

[51] UNCITRAL Arbitration Rules, Arts 6.2 and 7.2; and commentary by Sanders (1977) II Yearbook Commercial Arbitration 178 at 186.
[52] 2003 GAFTA Arbitration Rules, Art.3.7, para.A34–08

appears too vague to be accorded recognition in any legal sense,[53] the English courts at least have been prepared to give effect to it.[54] It has been held that the wording indicates an intention by the parties to have their disputes resolved on what might be called "commercial lines", without close regard for legal formalities. Paradoxically, it does not mean that the arbitral tribunal may decide *ex aequo et bono* or as *amiables compositeurs*.

In practice, there is no point in incorporating a provision that the arbitrators should be "commercial men" into an agreement for conventional international commercial arbitration. In countries with experience of the arbitral process, it is well understood that arbitration is intended to be a flexible method of solving disputes, not a mere mirror image of proceedings in national courts. Furthermore, it is usually unwise to make an advance determination of any specific qualifications which should be possessed by an arbitrator. The choice of a suitable arbitrator is best made when it needs to be made; that is to say, when a dispute has arisen.

(c) Restrictions imposed by the applicable law

The number of countries that impose restrictions on the choice of an arbitrator **4–41** has become smaller since the previous edition of this work. In its latest arbitration legislation, Spain, for example, repealed its former rule that the arbitrator must be a qualified lawyer where the dispute involves issues of law.[55] However, it is understood that the rule in Saudi Arabia that foreigners may not serve as arbitrators still exists; and in Switzerland, although the appointment of lawyers is not obligatory, it is not possible to exclude lawyers from acting as arbitrators in domestic arbitrations.

(d) Professional qualifications

International trade disputes are too varied and too numerous for it to be **4–42** sensible to identify any general rule as to the kind of person who should or should not be chosen to act as an arbitrator. Parties must make up their own minds as to the qualifications they require in an arbitrator. The most that can be done is to indicate some of the more important considerations.

Sole arbitrator

In international commercial arbitrations (as distinct from domestic arbitra- **4–43** tions) before a sole arbitrator, it is usual to appoint a lawyer. Even where the

---

[53] It has been argued that the phrase was capable of at least eight different meanings; see *Rahcassi Shipping Co SA v Blue Star Line Ltd* [1969] 1 Q.B. 173 at 177.

[54] Whatever the parties may intend when using the expression "commercial men", the effect in English law is to exclude practising members of the legal profession from selection as arbitrators, see: *Pando Compania Naviera SA v Filmo SAS* [1975] 1 Q.B. 742, [1975] 1 Lloyds Rep. 560. It appears that the English 1996 Act did not resolve the position; parties should therefore resist the temptation to use the expression in their arbitration agreements.

[55] Spanish Arbitration Act 2003, Art.13, repealing the 1988 Act, s.12(2).

dispute is relatively simple, difficult problems of procedure and of conflict of laws frequently arise. These are problems a lawyer with suitable experience is generally better equipped to handle than a person whose expertise lies in another area. As it was expressed in an ICC publication:

"Because of the legal nature of international arbitration, most [ICC arbitrators] are lawyers or university professors."[56]

Three arbitrators

4–44   Where the arbitral tribunal is to consist of three arbitrators, at least one member of the arbitral tribunal (preferably the presiding arbitrator) should be a lawyer or at least a person specifically qualified as an arbitrator, having studied arbitration law.[57]

There is no reason why the other two members of the arbitral tribunal should also be lawyers, unless the dispute is one in which the issues involved are principally issues of law. Part of the attraction of arbitration is the way in which the expertise necessary for the understanding and resolution of the dispute may be found amongst the arbitrators themselves. For example, if a dispute arises out of an international construction contract, involving matters of a technical nature, it may be appropriate that one or more of the members of the arbitral tribunal should be a civil engineer or someone skilled in the particular technical matters that are in issue.

However, where the presiding arbitrator is likely to be a lawyer (as in ICC arbitrations) a party should consider his position carefully before being left in a situation in which, the other party having nominated a lawyer, the arbitral tribunal is composed of two lawyers "against" a technical expert arbitrator nominated by him. It may be better for the parties to agree that each of them will appoint, say, an engineer or an economist and that the presiding arbitrator will be a lawyer.

(e) Language

4–45   An arbitrator must have an adequate working knowledge of the language in which the arbitration is to take place. This is an obvious requirement, but one that is sometimes forgotten not only by parties but by appointing authorities as well. If an arbitrator is appointed who does not have a sufficient knowledge of the language of the arbitration, it becomes necessary to engage an interpreter to translate the evidence of the witnesses and the arguments of the lawyers into a language which *can* be understood by the arbitrator concerned.

Translating oral evidence accurately into another language is a difficult task, particularly where a witness is being examined in detail on his evidence of fact or opinion. It also adds considerably to the expense of the arbitral proceedings;

---

[56] ICC Arbitration: the International Solution to International Business Disputes, ICC Publication No.301 (1977), p.20.
[57] See below, para.4–47.

first, because of the interpreter's fees and, secondly, because of the extra time which is taken if everything of importance has to be translated from the working language of the arbitration into a language which the arbitrator himself can understand.[58]

(f) Experience and outlook

It has become increasingly important for international arbitrators to show their **4–46** awareness of the world of international trade relations and of the different traditions, aims and expectations of the people of that world. Arbitrators, like everyone else, are inevitably conditioned by their education and training, as well as the culture in which they have grown up. However, most experienced international arbitrators are adept at maintaining awareness of their own inbuilt preconceptions respect and are able to adopt an outlook free from national or cultural prejudice. This enables them to understand the conduct of the parties in the particular business and cultural environment in which they entered into and implemented their transaction. It does no service to the disputing parties, or indeed to international commercial arbitration in general, if personal or political background is allowed to influence an arbitrator's approach to resolving the issues in dispute.

This remains a real problem; and the world's major international arbitral institutions have become increasingly aware of it. Some less-developed nations lack confidence in international commercial arbitration. This is largely because of the fear that arbitral tribunals, established under the auspices of arbitral institutions based in the world's major trading nations, will have an inbuilt cultural and social bias against them, however impeccable the intellectual integrity of the individual arbitrators.

Nevertheless, it would be inappropriate to choose an arbitrator (and particularly a sole or presiding arbitrator) solely because the individual concerned comes from a less-developed country. Ability and qualifications should be the essential criteria, not nationality or political background. It is also important that arbitrators should be selected increasingly from outside the charmed circle of relatively wealthy nations; and the international arbitration community (particularly the international arbitral institutions) should recognise the need to assist in the development of a breed of experienced arbitrators from such countries.

(g) Education and training

Probably the most important qualification for an international arbitrator is **4–47** experience in the law and practice of arbitration. There is no sense in appointing as a sole or presiding arbitrator someone who is an experienced lawyer, if that experience does not include practical experience of arbitration. Nor, for that matter, is it sensible to appoint a civil engineer or a structural engineer or an

---

[58] The Supreme Court of Austria has held that an order made by the arbitrators specifying the language of the proceedings will not be interfered with by the court. See (1997) XXII Yearbook Commercial Arbitration 263.

expert in nuclear physics, however distinguished and however relevant the experience may be to the issues in dispute, unless the expert in question also has practical experience of international arbitration procedures. This may be less important when there is an arbitral tribunal of three arbitrators, but only if the presiding arbitrator at least has relevant experience of the practice of international arbitration.

This point cannot be overemphasised. The reputation and acceptability of international arbitration depends upon the quality of the arbitrators themselves. The task of presiding over the conduct of an international commercial arbitration is no less skilled than that of driving a car or flying an aircraft. It should not be entrusted to someone with no practical experience of it.

It follows that there should be some recognised and effective process by which potential international arbitration practitioners, who may eventually become arbitrators, can acquire the necessary skills. There must always be a new generation in prospect, otherwise there will only be a diminishing group of ever-more elderly people suitable for appointment. This has been recognised by arbitration institutions based in various countries. The ICC, the PCA and UNCITRAL operate internship schemes, under which young lawyers and postgraduate students work inside those institutions for a period of several months.

4–48   The need was also recognised during a discussion at the ICCA Congress in 1998, when various solutions were proposed. One practical proposal[59] that has gained popularity is that young practitioners and students from different parts of the world are invited—with the consent of the parties—to attend hearings as observers. They are also offered internships by leading international arbitrators who, again with the consent of the parties, arrange for them to serve as administrative secretaries to arbitral tribunals.

Relevant statistics are not easy to find, but by the end of the twentieth century there were encouraging signs that more arbitrators from the less-developed countries were being appointed. The ICC's statistics, for example, show that the tribunals in a growing number of cases include arbitrators from outside the developed countries.

The ICDR maintains a list of people experienced in arbitration from which arbitrators may be selected for individual cases.[60] The ICC does not maintain a formal panel of arbitrators in Paris, but relies on its national committees to propose names. Some are well equipped to perform this process. Others keep lists of prospective arbitrators and then nominate persons in strict rotation from it as cases are referred. Fortunately, the ICC's Court is aware of this practice, where it occurs, and sometimes rejects nominations from national committees where the nominee may be unsuitable for the particular assignment.

4–49   Training programmes for prospective arbitrators are run by a number of arbitral institutions. Such programmes are to be encouraged, although institutions

---

[59] Made by Jan Paulsson during the proceedings of Working Group III.
[60] The ICDR also runs education programmes for arbitrators, including seminars and "on-the-job" training: see Hoellering, "Training and Development of Commercial Arbitrators (USA)" (1985) X Yearbook Commercial Arbitration 551.

should be careful to avoid any perception that they offer these products purely for the purposes of generating profits.[61]

(h) Interviewing prospective arbitrators

In the early 1990s a practice of interviewing prospective arbitrators was **4–50** imported from the US into Europe. US law firms draw up a list of approximately five or six prospective party-nominated arbitrators who are invited to interviews by representatives of the prospective appointor. Caravans of external and internal US lawyers and assistants (sometimes accompanied by their clients) began to progress around the capital cities of the major arbitration centres in Europe comparing the merits of alternative candidates. A number of eminent European arbitrators declined to participate in such events on the grounds that they were at best demeaning, and at worst improper. However, it is hard to perceive the practice as being objectionable in principle, provided that it is not done in a secretive way and that the scope of the discussion is appropriately restricted.

An attorney from the US may feel at risk of a malpractice suit if a client was advised to nominate an arbitrator without first carrying out a "due diligence" enquiry; and it must surely be reasonable for a prospective arbitrator to be questioned in person on matters relating to experience, qualifications for the case in hand as well as availability. It is also reasonable for a party's representatives to have an opportunity of assessing the candidate's physical and mental health. Clearly there should be no probing of the prospective arbitrator's views on the merits of the case, nor should party representatives take the opportunity to test their forthcoming submissions of fact and law.

One distinguished US arbitrator has identified his own guidelines, having informed the interviewers of them in advance. First, other than in exceptional circumstances, the interviewers must travel to see him in his office (*i.e.* he will not respond to a "summons" to the premises of the party concerned or their representatives). Secondly, the interviewing delegation must be led by an *external* lawyer retained by the party in question (*i.e.* he will not see the party's employees on their own). Thirdly, the meeting should not be conducted over lunch or other event involving hospitality—regardless of who will pay the bill. Fourthly, the meeting should not last for more than half an hour. Fifthly, he will take a note of the discussion that he will regard as disclosable to interested parties if appropriate. Sixthly, if appointed, he will inform the arbitrator nominated by the other party of both the fact and the content of the discussion with his appointor. These are eminently sensible guidelines that should avoid any real risk of impropriety; and prospective arbitrators would be wise to adopt a similar

---

[61] The Chartered Institute of Arbitrators, headquartered in London, offers courses that include a two-part examination structure and a system of "pupillage" under which, with the consent of the parties, trainee arbitrators may attend at hearings. The Institute also provides special programmes for potential international arbitrators, which are held all over the world. The ICDR also conducts training programmes for arbitrators on its various panels, and offers courses in a number of different countries.

system, or to adapt them in a way that seems appropriate to the circumstances of individual cases.

4–51   More difficult is the question of interviewing prospective sole or presiding arbitrators in cases where the arbitration agreement calls for the appointment to be made by agreement between the parties. Again, there can be no objection in principle if both parties' representatives are present and the discussion is carefully controlled. There is indeed much to recommend the practice, since proceedings will at least start on a sound footing if the person who is to preside over the hearings commands the respect and confidence of both parties.

It occasionally happens that a suitable candidate has been proposed by one of the parties, who may know the candidate well, and that the other party knows little more about the person concerned other than the information that is in publicly available biographical details. This arises, for example, in disputes between US parties and English parties where the arbitration is to be held in London and the applicable law is English law. The parties may agree that a senior English barrister or solicitor should be appointed, and the English party may propose a list of three or four possible candidates. What are the prospective arbitrators to do if the US party wants to interview the listed candidates and the English party's lawyers say that they know them well and do not wish to attend any such interviews? It is suggested, with some misgivings, that the appropriate solution may be for the candidates to agree to the interviews but only on the basis that the party which does not wish to participate has a full opportunity to send an observer.

4. Impartiality and Independence of Arbitrators

(a) Generally

4–52   It is a fundamental principle in mainstream international commercial arbitration that an arbitrator must be and remain independent and impartial.

In some countries a party is entitled to challenge an arbitrator on the same grounds as those on which objection may be made to a judge in court proceedings. However, in this context, the analogy between a judge and an arbitrator should not be taken too far. A judge is a servant of the state and has responsibilities flowing from public policy which go beyond those of an arbitrator, whose duties may be terminated by the parties or by an arbitral institution under whose auspices the particular arbitration is being held.

In international disputes, the practice of appointing arbitrators who are overtly non-neutral arbitrators is usually seen only in fully ad hoc arbitrations, since the rules of most arbitral institutions (and the UNCITRAL Rules) expressly require arbitrators to be independent and/or impartial.[62] However, arbitrators who are appointed to represent the interests of their appointing parties is not a new

---

[62] Including the ICDR International Arbitration Rules (2003 ed.), Art.7; see also below, paras 4–54 *et seq.*

phenomenon. It was a common feature of arbitrations between states in which each state appoints one or more of its nationals to the arbitral tribunal, with the balance of power being held by one or more arbitrator(s) of neutral nationality. In the *Alabama* arbitration[63] one member of the arbitral tribunal was appointed by each of the parties and the remaining three members by three heads of state, namely the King of Italy, the President of Switzerland and the Emperor of Brazil.[64] Significantly, the award, which was favourable to the US, was not signed by the arbitrator appointed by the UK.

In the *Buraimi Oasis* arbitration there was an apparent misunderstanding between the parties as to the role of the arbitrators nominated by the parties (the governments of the UK and Saudi Arabia) which led to the abandonment of the proceedings.[65] In the Iran–US Claims Tribunal, three Iranian and three US arbitrators were joined by three arbitrators appointed from "third countries", to comprise the full Tribunal, as already described. The Tribunal operates under the UNCITRAL Rules which require all arbitrators to be impartial. Nevertheless, the reported proceedings of the Iran–US Claims Tribunal indicate that partisan elements have not been absent.[66]

Where an arbitral tribunal contains party-nominated arbitrators, it is important **4–53** that everyone concerned in the arbitration should know from the start whether they are expected to be impartial, or whether they are to be the advocates of the party who appointed them. The practice followed in the US of regarding party-nominated arbitrators as non-neutral, unless an indication to the contrary is given, is not applied in international commercial arbitration. Indeed, the reverse is the case. The presumption is that, even if nominated by one of the parties, the arbitrator will be independent and impartial unless the parties agree otherwise.[67]

Experienced practitioners recognise that the appointment of a partisan arbitrator is counterproductive, because the presiding arbitrator will very soon perceive what is happening and the influence of the partisan arbitrator during the tribunal's deliberations will be diminished. It is a far better policy to appoint a person who may, by reason of culture or background, be broadly in sympathy

---

[63] Which, as described in Ch.1, took place between the US and the UK in the aftermath of the American Civil War.

[64] Stuyt, *Survey of International Arbitrations, 1794–1970* (1976), Case No.94.

[65] Documented by Wetter, *The International Arbitral Process* (Oceana, 1979), Vol.III, p.357.

[66] Exchanges between arbitrators have sometimes become heated, but not usually to the point reached by one of the Iranian arbitrators who is reported to have said that if one of the other arbitrators "tries to enter this Tribunal again . . . either his body or mine will roll down the steps of the Court." *The Times*, September 8, 1984, p.5.

[67] The AAA's Supplementary Procedures for International Arbitrations (which are still in occasional use, where the arbitration clause expressly refers to the Commercial Arbitration Rules) contemplate that all arbitrators, including those appointed by a party, must be neutral. These procedures were replaced by the AAA's International Arbitration Rules in 1993. The edition current at the time of preparation of this text was the July 2003 edition of the ICDR International Arbitration Rules, which provide in Art.7 that all arbitrators appointed under those Rules shall be impartial and independent. The ICDR is the international division of the AAA, with offices in New York and Dublin.

with the case to be put forward, but who will be strictly impartial when it comes to assessing the facts and evaluating the arguments on fact and law.

(b) Independence and/or impartiality

4–54 It is useful to review the concepts of independence and impartiality in the light of the slightly different provisions of the ICC Rules, the ICDR Rules, the ICSID Rules, the LCIA Rules and the UNCITRAL Rules.

The ICDR Rules and the UNCITRAL Rules provide for the challenge of an arbitrator if circumstances exist that give rise to justifiable doubts as to that arbitrator's impartiality or independence.[68] The ICC Rules provide for the challenge of an arbitrator for lack of independence *or otherwise.*[69] The LCIA Rules specify that all members of the arbitral tribunal must remain impartial and may not act as advocates of the parties.[70] The requirement of the Model Law that an arbitrator must be independent and impartial is considered to be a mandatory provision from which the parties may not derogate,[71] although no doubt the parties are free to agree that a specific disclosed relationship between and arbitrator and a party is not to be considered as sufficiently substantial as to disqualify the person concerned.

In previous editions of this book, a distinction was drawn between "independence" and "impartiality". However, since the third edition was published, there has been a distinct trend towards viewing these two elements as the opposite side of the same coin. There has therefore been a move towards considering them as a "package", and to use them as parallel tools for assessing the potential for actual or apparent bias. They are rarely used on their own, individually, but are usually joined together as a term of art.

4–55 It is generally considered that "dependence" is concerned exclusively with questions arising out of the relationship between an arbitrator and one of the parties, whether financial or otherwise. This is considered to be susceptible to an *objective* test, because it has nothing to do with an arbitrator's (or prospective arbitrator's) state of mind. This is why, in revising its rules for the 1998 edition, the ICC's Court decided to stay with "independence" as the appropriate test.

By contrast the concept of "impartiality" is considered to be connected with actual or apparent bias of an arbitrator—either in favour of one of the parties or

---

[68] Art.10.

[69] Art.11(1); the ICC Rules do not use the term "impartiality", for reasons that are explained in Derains & Schwartz, *A Guide to the New ICC Rules of Arbitration* (Kluwer, 1998), Ch.4, p.109, as follows: "While the main purpose of Art.7(1) is to secure the appointment of impartial arbitrators, the drafters of the ICC Rules have preferred to express the relevant requirement in terms of independence because independence is a more objective notion. Independence is generally a function of prior or existing relationships that can be catalogued and verified, while impartiality is a state of mind, which it may be impossible for anyone but the arbitrator to check or to know when the arbitrator is being appointed. It is therefore easier for the Court to determine, when confirming or appointing an arbitrator, whether that person is independent rather than to assess the extent of his or her impartiality."

[70] Art.5.2.

[71] This requirement is implicit in Art.12(2) of the Model Law: see Holtzmann & Neuhaus, *A Guide to the UNCITRAL Model Law on International Commercial Arbitration* (1989), p.409.

in relation to the issues in dispute. Impartiality is thus a *subjective* and more abstract concept than independence, in that it involves primarily a state of mind. This presents special difficulties in terms of objective measurement, which was the basis on which the ICC's Court decided not to include it as an express part of the test for disqualification, although it could clearly be included in the "or otherwise" language of the relevant article of the Rules.

In the 1998 version of its Rules, the LCIA decided that impartiality rather than independence was the appropriate test, because an arbitrator who lacked "independence" in the most restrictive sense might still be impartial. Similarly, an arbitrator who would pass the independence test might lack the necessary quality of impartiality.[72]

Impartiality distinguished from neutrality

Another concept, used mainly in the USA, is "neutrality". At first sight it **4–56** might be thought that no valid distinction can be drawn between the concepts of "impartiality" and "neutrality". However, it has been suggested[73] that a party may nominate an arbitrator who is generally predisposed towards it personally, or as regards its position in the dispute, provided that the person concerned is at the same time capable of impartial and judicial application to the evidence and arguments submitted by both parties. This concept can apply only in the case of party-nominated arbitrators. The presiding arbitrator must both be, and be seen to be, entirely impartial as well as independent.

In practice it is sometimes difficult to distinguish the so-called "non-neutral" arbitrator from the "neutral" arbitrator.[74] This is hardly surprising. The terms "neutral" and "non-neutral" suggest a difference as marked as night and day. In reality, this is not so. Most "non-neutral" arbitrators do not allow the fact of their appointment by a party to dictate the outcome of the proceedings. They may be favourably disposed to the party who appointed them, but they do not allow this to override their conscience and professional judgment if they believe that the other party has made the better case.

Similarly, most so called "neutral" arbitrators are likely to start the proceedings with more sympathy for the party who appointed them than for the other party. This is because they are likely to share with that party the same background, tradition and culture. Once again, however, neutral arbitrators do not usually allow this shared outlook to override their conscience and professional judgment.

Some of the guidelines for non-neutral arbitrators laid down in the ABA/AAA **4–57** Code of Ethics, 2004 edition, are of particular interest—even though they are

---

[72] For a comprehensive review of the position in relation to party-appointed arbitrators see Bishop & Reed, "Practical Guidelines for Interviewing, Selecting and Challenging Party-Appointed Arbitrators in International Arbitration" 14 Arb. Int. No.4, pp.395 *et. seq.*

[73] See Craig, Park & Paulsson, *International Chamber of Commerce Arbitration* (3rd ed., 2000), p.196, para.12.04.

[74] This is one of the reasons why the English Arbitration Act 1996, s.24(1)(a) refers only to impartiality and not to independence.

intended for use in domestic arbitrations in the USA.[75] First, non-neutral arbitrators, whilst they may be predisposed towards the party who appointed them, are in all other respects obliged to act in good faith and with integrity and fairness. For example, non-neutral arbitrators should not engage in delaying tactics or the harassment of a party or a witness and should not knowingly make untrue or misleading statements to the other arbitrators. Secondly, in an arbitration in which the two party-nominated arbitrators are expected to appoint the third arbitrator, non-neutral arbitrators may consult with the party who appointed them concerning the acceptability of persons under consideration for appointment as a third arbitrator. Thirdly, non-neutral arbitrators may communicate with the party who appointed them concerning any other aspect of the case, provided that they first inform the other arbitrators and the parties of their intentions.

It occasionally happens that party-nominated arbitrators make little or no secret of their sympathy with the party who nominated them, both at hearings and in the private deliberations of the arbitral tribunal. There are two remedies if this occurs. The first, which is extreme and in any event rarely successful, is for the aggrieved party to make a formal challenge of the offending arbitrator.[76] The second, which is usually followed in practice and is generally more constructive, is to rely on the other members of the arbitral tribunal, and in particular on the presiding arbitrator, to deal with the situation in a diplomatic manner.

(b) Nationality

4–58   In an ideal world, the nationality of a sole arbitrator, or of the presiding arbitrator, should be irrelevant. The qualifications, experience and integrity of the arbitrator should be the essential criteria. The country in which the arbitrator was born, or the passport carried, should be irrelevant. It ought to be possible to proceed in the spirit of the Model Law which, addressing this question, provides simply: "No person shall be precluded by reason of his nationality from acting as an arbitrator, unless otherwise agreed by the parties."[77] Nevertheless, as stated above, the usual practice in international commercial arbitration is to appoint a sole arbitrator (or a presiding arbitrator) of a different nationality from that of the parties to the dispute.

This insistence on neutral nationality sometimes produces curious results. In particular, it may lead to a situation where the law applicable to the merits of the dispute is that of one or other of the parties (a situation that is by no means uncommon); but the sole or presiding arbitrator will not be qualified or experienced in that system of law. Consider, for instance, a dispute between a Swiss company and a French company, where the law applicable to the dispute is the law of Switzerland. It seems sensible that the person chosen as the sole or presiding arbitrator should be a Swiss lawyer, particularly if the seat of the arbitration is Switzerland. Yet the insistence on a so-called "neutral" nationality

---

[75] Distributed but not formally published at the date of preparation of the present edition.
[76] For further discussion of challenge of arbitrators see above, paras 4–67 *et seq.*
[77] Model Law, Art.11(1).

ensures that the one person who cannot be chosen (unless the parties agree otherwise) is a Swiss lawyer.

Nonetheless, the current practice under most sets of institutional rules is that the sole or presiding arbitrator will almost certainly be someone of a different nationality from that of the parties to the dispute. The UNCITRAL Rules, for example, provide that:

"In making the appointment, the appointing authority shall have regard to such considerations as are likely to secure the appointment of an independent and impartial arbitrator and shall take into account as well the *advisability* of appointing an arbitrator of a nationality other than the nationalities of the parties."[78]

The ICC Rules go further and provide that: **4–59**

"The sole arbitrator or the chairman of an arbitral tribunal *shall* be of a nationality other than those of the parties."[79]

A proviso allows an exception to this rule "in suitable circumstances and provided that neither of the parties objects", but nevertheless the general rule is clear. It is a rule of neutral nationality.

The LCIA Rules take a similar line in providing:

"Where the parties are of different nationalities, a sole arbitrator or chairman of the Arbitral Tribunal shall not have the same nationality as any party unless the parties who are not of the same nationality as the proposed nominee all agree in writing otherwise."[80]

The equivalent WIPO Rule states as follows: **4–60**

"(a) An agreement of the parties concerning the nationality of arbitrators shall be respected.

(b) If the parties have not agreed on the nationality of the sole or presiding arbitrator, such arbitrator shall, in the absence of special circumstances such as the need to appoint a person having particular qualifications, be a national of a countries other than the countries of the parties."[81]

The 2003 edition of the ICDR's International Arbitration Rules takes a slightly different approach, whilst broadly embracing the same principle:

---

[78] UNCITRAL Arbitration Rules, Art.6.4 (emphasis added).
[79] ICC Arbitration Rules, Art.9.5 (emphasis added).
[80] LCIA Arbitration Rules, Art.6.1.
[81] WIPO Arbitration Rules, Art.20.6. See Lalive, "On the Neutrality of the Arbitrator and of the Place of Arbitration" in *Swiss Essays on International Arbitration* (1984), pp.23, 25.

"In making such appointments, the administrator, after inviting consultation with the parties, shall endeavour to select suitable arbitrators. At the request of any party or on its own initiative, the administrator may appoint nationals of a country other than that of any of the parties."[82]

The fact that an arbitrator is of a neutral nationality is no guarantee of independence or impartiality. However, the *appearance* is better and thus it is a practice that is generally followed.[83]

(c) Disclosure

4–61   The most important element in the requirement of impartiality and independence is *disclosure*. If a prospective arbitrator, on being approached with a view to appointment, discloses all the facts that could reasonably be considered to be grounds for disqualification (and no objection is made), any subsequent challenge during or after the proceedings should be unsuccessful. The right to an independent and impartial arbitrator is deemed to have been waived in respect of objections founded upon facts contained in the disclosure statement.

The duty of impartiality, to maintain an open mind and to decide the case on the evidence presented free from any preconceptions or connection with the parties or witnesses, nevertheless remains. The requirement of disclosure is a continuing duty that continues throughout the arbitration. If new circumstances arise that might give rise to any doubt as to an arbitrator's independence and/or impartiality, they should be disclosed immediately to the parties and to the other arbitrators.

In practice, a person approached by a party to act as a party-nominated arbitrator usually discloses any relevant facts informally to the prospective appointing party in the first instance. If the circumstances disclosed do not give any cause for concern either to the prospective arbitrator or to the appointor, the prospective arbitrator accepts the nomination and writes formally to both parties setting out the relevant facts if they are of a nature that should be disclosed on the basis that they might be considered "in the eyes of" the other party to give rise to doubts as to the prospective arbitrator's independence or impartiality.

4–62   There is thus a subtle difference, in this context, between the *objective* test as to whether the relevant facts would cause doubt in the mind of a reasonable third party, and the *subjective* test as to whether they might cause doubt in the mind of the parties involved in the specific case in question. The explanatory notes to the IBA's 2004 Guidelines on Conflicts of Interest state as follows:

---

[82] ICDR International Arbitration Rules, Art.6.4.

[83] The British Columbia International Commercial Arbitration Act, s.11 was amended to add a subs.(9): "Unless the parties have previously agreed to the appointment of a sole or third arbitrator who is of the same nationality as any of the parties, the Chief Justice shall not appoint a sole or third arbitrator who is of the same nationality as that of any of the parties." The arbitration that led to this amendment was *Nippon Steel Corp v Quintette Coal Ltd*; see commentary by Smith in [1989/90] 4 O.G.L.T.R. 105.

" . . . because of varying considerations with respect to disclosure the proper standard for disclosure may be different. A purely objective test for disclosure exists in the majority of the jurisdictions analyzed and in the UNCITRAL Model Law. Nevertheless, the Working Group recognizes that the parties have an interest in being fully informed about any circumstances that may be relevant in their view. Because of the strongly held views of many arbitration institutions (as reflected in their rules and as stated to the Working Group) that the disclosure test should reflect the perspectives of the parties, the Working Group in principle accepted, after much debate, a subjective approach for disclosure. The Working Group has adapted the language of Article 7.2 of the ICC Rules for this standard."[84]

In the case of a third arbitrator, who is normally approached jointly by the parties or by the two party-nominated arbitrators, the two-stage process that generally operates in relation to a party-nominated arbitrator is not necessary; any circumstances that should be disclosed should be made known both parties simultaneously. In both instances it is highly desirable that any matters disclosed should be confirmed to the parties in writing. Some arbitral institutions have a specific declaration form that every arbitrator is required to sign before an appointment is confirmed.[85] Of the major institutions the ICC, the ICDR and the LCIA give no specific guidelines as to matters that ought to be disclosed. It is not an easy topic, because people from different cultures approach the problem from different viewpoints.

The IBA Guidelines on Conflicts of Interest project is clearly useful. The Working Group of the IBA charged with preparing the document was comprised of 19 experienced practitioners from different jurisdictions. One of the greatest strengths of the IBA is its ability to constitute such diverse groups, and to undertake wide consultation processes.

The Guidelines start with a general introduction; continue by setting out "General Standards Regarding Impartiality, Independence and Disclosure", which is the core of the document; and conclude with a section on the "Practical Application of the General Standards".

This last section, which appeared to generate most of the discussion during the consultation process, divides a non-exhaustive list of "circumstances" into four separate groups. These are: (1) a "Non-Waivable Red List"; (2) a "Waivable Red List"; (3) an "Orange List"; and (4) a "Green List". **4–63**

The Non-Waivable Red List contains examples of situations that illustrate the principle that no person should be a judge in his or her own cause.

The Waivable Red List contains examples of situations that, while potentially leading to disqualification, may be accepted by express agreement of the parties

---

[84] IBA Guidelines on Conflicts of Interest in International Arbitration, 2004, Explanation to General Standard 3. Text was approved by the Council of the International Bar Association on May 22, 2004.
[85] See ICC Arbitration Rules, Art.7.2; ICSID Arbitration Rules, r.6(2); LCIA Arbitration Rules, Art.5.3.

to the dispute as not requiring disqualification in the circumstances of the particular case.

4–64   The Orange List is a non-exhaustive enumeration of specific situations which (depending on the facts of a given case) in the eyes of the parties may give rise to justifiable doubts as to the arbitrator's impartiality or independence. This category is intended to deal with situations where a prospective arbitrator has be a duty to disclose such circumstances. It is contemplated that, once properly disclosed, the parties will be deemed to have waived their rights to object after a certain length of time has elapsed.

The Green List contains examples of situations where no appearance of (or actual) conflict of interest arises from an objective viewpoint. Thus, there is no duty on a prospective arbitrator to disclose such circumstances.

Whether the guidelines will command acceptance by the wider international arbitration community remains to be seen. To be effective, any such guidelines must achieve the general approval of arbitral institutions and of national courts when they consider challenges of arbitrators. It is also important that they should gain the respect of parties' counsel and arbitrators in ad hoc arbitrations.

The courts of the ICC and the LCIA, and the Administrators at the ICDR, will no doubt continue to use their own internal criteria in considering whether or not to confirm appointments of nominated arbitrators, and in connection with challenges; but may nevertheless consult the IBA Guidelines as a kind of checklist.

Governmental agencies

4–65   A special situation arises where a government or one of its agencies or corporations is involved in an arbitration. Like a private party, the state party often wishes to nominate an arbitrator of its own nationality; but in many countries the choice may effectively be limited to persons who have some connection with the government whether as employees, consultants, university professors or in some other way. The usual practice is for such persons to be nominated despite their governmental connection It is certain that there will be at least the suspicion that the arbitrator concerned is likely to be under pressure from the governmental agency that made the appointment; however, the practice is accepted by many arbitral institutions, which are prepared to accept declarations of independence from such arbitrators.[86]

(d) Communications with the parties

4–66   An independent and impartial arbitrator must not engage in any *ex parte* communications with the parties regarding the merits of the case during the course of the proceedings. Nevertheless, at the Iran–US Claim Tribunal hearings it has been alleged in one case that an arbitrator revealed the contents of a draft

---

[86] *e.g.* each arbitrator, whether nominated by the parties or otherwise, is required to sign a form of declaration relating to his independence: ICC Arbitration Rules, Art.7.2; ICSID Arbitration Rules, Art.6(2); LCIA Rules, Art.5.3.

award to his nominating party, leading to a last-minute settlement of the claim; and in another that an arbitrator solicited further evidence from his appointing party to satisfy questions that arose during the deliberations.[87] This type of conduct is in violation of the UNCITRAL Rules under which that Tribunal operated.

As discussed in Ch.8,[88] the secrecy of the tribunal's deliberations is fundamental to the arbitral process. This requirement is explicitly set out in some national laws and in the IBA's Ethics For International Arbitrators. A more difficult question arises in relation to communications before and during the hearings. In practice, it is generally accepted that there will be communications with a party-nominee before his appointment and also in respect of the choice of a third arbitrator. This makes good sense, as it is clearly appropriate to take steps to ensure that the presiding arbitrator is acceptable to both parties.

The IBA's Ethics for International Arbitrators permit communications prior to an appointment for the purpose of determining the suitability and availability of the potential third arbitrator. Notice to the other party of any unilateral communications that do occur is required.[89] In principle all communications with only one of the parties should be reduced to writing and furnished to the other party, and in no event should there ever be discussions regarding the merits of the case.

5. CHALLENGE AND REPLACEMENT OF ARBITRATORS

(a) Generally

Challenges of arbitrators were at one time a rare event. If a vacancy occurred, **4–67** it was usually because of the death or resignation of an arbitrator. However, modern commercial arbitrations often involve vast sums of money, and the parties have become more inclined to engage specialist lawyers, who are expert in manoeuvres designed to obtain a tactical advantage, or at least to minimise a potential disadvantage.[90]

This is not to say that all challenges are unmeritorious. On the contrary, in the past there was probably too great an acceptance by the parties of manifestly dependent or biased arbitrators nominated by their opponents. Furthermore, challenge is not merely a tactic employed by respondents to cause delay and

---

[87] Baker & Davis, "Establishment of an Arbitral Tribunal Under the UNCITRAL Arbitration Rules" (1989) 3 The International Lawyer 112.

[88] See paras 8–28 *et seq.*

[89] IBA Ethics for International Arbitrators, Art.5.

[90] Until the 1980s the ICC's Court ruled on no more than a handful of challenges each year under Art.2.7 of the ICC Arbitration Rules; during the 1990s the ICC's Court often considered several challenges at any one of its monthly plenary sessions. In 2003 the ICC's Court received 20 challenges; only one was accepted. The use of challenges to delay and disrupt an arbitration, and the measures that can be used to respond to and minimise the effectiveness of such tactics, was discussed at the 1990 ICCA Congress in Stockholm: see "Preventing Delay or Disruption of Arbitration" ICCA Congress Series No.5 (Kluwer, 1991), pp.131–159.

disruption for the claimant; it is a matter that must be considered seriously by claimants, notwithstanding the inevitable delay, where the arbitral tribunal may be constituted in a manifestly inappropriate form. Challenges of a presiding arbitrator are rare, but not unknown; they are usually based upon some prior connection with one of the parties that gives rise to doubts as to the appointee's independence.

(b) Grounds for challenge

4–68   In general, the parties to an arbitration may challenge an arbitrator only where they have reasonable doubts as to his impartiality or independence. The UNCI-TRAL Rules provide:

> "1. Any arbitrator may be challenged if circumstances exist that give rise to justifiable doubts as to the arbitrator's impartiality or independence.
>   2. A party may challenge the arbitrator appointed by him only for reasons of which he becomes aware after the appointment has been made."[91]

The rules of the international arbitral institutions contain similar provisions, as does the Model Law[92]; and equivalent provisions, under which a competent court may remove an arbitrator who is lacking in impartiality or independence, are to be found in most developed national arbitration laws. For example, Art.1033 of the Netherlands 1986 Act provides that an arbitrator may be challenged if circumstances exist that give rise to justifiable doubts as to his impartiality or independence. By contrast, the Swiss Private International Law Act 1987 refers to doubts as to independence but not impartiality. This is said to allow for bias by an arbitrator in favour of the nominating party,[93] but the better view is that strict impartiality remains a requirement of Swiss law.[94]

4–69   The 1996 English Act is more comprehensive:

> "(1) A party to arbitral proceedings may (upon notice to the other parties, to the arbitrator concerned and to any other arbitrator) apply to the court to remove an arbitrator on any of the following grounds:
>
> (a) that circumstances exist that give rise to justifiable doubts as to his impartiality;
> (b) that he does not possess the qualifications required by the arbitration agreement;
> (c) that he is physically or mentally incapable of conducting the proceedings or there are justifiable doubts as to his capacity to do so;
> (d) that he has refused or failed—

---

[91] UNCITRAL Arbitration Rules, Art.10.1.
[92] Model Law, Art.12.
[93] Blessing, "The New International Arbitration Law in Switzerland" (1988) 5 Journal of International Arbitration 9 at 39.
[94] Smith, "Impartiality of the Party-Appointed Arbitrator", p.328.

    (i) properly to conduct the proceedings, or

    (ii) to use all reasonable despatch in conducting the proceedings or making an award,

and that substantial injustice has been or will be caused to the applicant".[95]

In general, arbitrators may be trusted to resign if faced with a genuine conflict of interest. The position is expressed in the authoritative notes to the ICSID Rules as follows:

" . . . an arbitrator is to [resign] if, for instance, he may have an interest in the result of the dispute. In fact, in view of the qualities he is required to possess, a candidate is unlikely to accept an appointment as arbitrator where his personal interest is involved and, if he realises such involvement after the appointment, he may be trusted to resign. The experience of other international arbitration bodies has, in this respect, apparently been reassuring; it therefore seems unnecessary to particularise grounds for resignation."[96]

A prospective arbitrator should not accept an appointment if there is reason to believe that either party will genuinely feel that the person concerned is not independent, or not capable of approaching the issues impartially. The position is more difficult where a party objects *after* the arbitrator has been appointed. If both parties agree that the arbitrator should resign, then this is determinative. The arbitrator should also resign if it seems, on reflection, that the objection is or appears to be well founded, whether or not the parties agree.

However, if the objection appears to be without merit the arbitrator should not **4–70** resign, but should permit the matter to be dealt with by the relevant challenge procedure. Even though this course may create delay, it helps to discourage unmeritorious disruptive tactics. If a party nominates a perfectly acceptable arbitrator, the "judge of his choice", and wishes that arbitrator to remain even though an objection has been made, that arbitrator should in principle remain unless the appropriate authority, whether it is a national court or another body, issues a ruling to the contrary.

The same general principle applies in the case of a presiding arbitrator, although a presiding arbitrator is probably under a greater duty to examine carefully the grounds for objection before deciding whether or not to proceed with the case.

In the USA, the duty of avoiding evident partiality as required under s.10(a) of the Federal Arbitration Act has been interpreted as including a strict duty of disclosure. The US Supreme Court set a high standard in *Commonwealth Coatings* by requiring disclosure of any dealings which might create an impression of bias. In that case an arbitral award was set aside for failure to disclose business

[95] Arbitration Act 1996, s.24(1).
[96] ICSID Arbitration Rules, r.8, n.C.

connections with one of the parties, even though the award was unanimous and the court found that there was no *actual* bias.[97]

4–71   The Swiss Federal Tribunal has found that the failure to disclose that the wife of one of the arbitrators was the assistant of the lawyer of one of the parties was sufficient to warrant the disqualification of that arbitrator.[98]

The Supreme Court of Canada has ruled that the parties to an arbitration agreement are entitled to a sustained sense of confidence in the independence of mind of the arbitrators. Even a reasonable apprehension that an arbitrator was not acting impartially would lead to the award being set aside:

> "From its inception arbitration has been held to be of the nature of judicial determination and to entail incidents appropriate to that fact. The arbitrators are to exercise their function not as the advocates of the parties nominating them, and *a fortiori* of one party when they are agreed upon by all, but with as free, independent and impartial minds as the circumstances permit. In particular they must be untrammelled by such influences as to a fair minded person would raise a doubt of that impersonal attitude which each party is entitled to."[99]

(c) Procedure for challenge

4–72   The procedure for challenge of an arbitrator appears either in the law of the country where the arbitration takes place, or in any rules of arbitration that have been adopted by the parties. Where a challenge falls to be dealt with by the courts, the procedure to be followed is specified in the applicable law. Where the rules of an arbitral institution apply, the procedure is normally *either* that a complaint should be made in the first instance to the arbitral tribunal itself, with recourse to the courts, *or* that the complaint is made direct to the arbitral institution.

Most national laws provide for a challenge to an arbitrator to be made during the course of the arbitration as well as on an application to set aside the award.[1] Delays are often minimised by provisions that restrict challenges to objections founded on information which has recently come to the attention of the challenging party, prohibit any appeal from the initial ruling on the challenge, and permit the arbitration to proceed while the challenge is pending. Such provisions are to be found in the Model Law and, for example, in the English 1996 Act.[2]

---

[97] *Commonwealth Coatings Corp v Continental Casualty Co*, 393 US 145 (1968). For further examples of US cases, see: 141, A.L.R. Fed.1 (1998), Construction and Application of para.10(A)(1)–(3) of Federal Arbitration Act (9) US T.A. para.10(A)(1)–(3), Providing for vacating of Arbitration Awards where Award Procured by Fraud, Corruption, or Undue Means where Arbitrators Evidence, Partiality or Corruption and where Arbitrators engage in Particular acts of Misbehavior; and subsequent supplements.

[98] *Centrozap v Orbis* (1966) A.T.F. 92 I (Staatsrecht No.47) 271.

[99] *Szilard v Szasz* [1955] S.C.R. 3 at 4.

[1] English Arbitration Act 1996, s.24; Model Law, Art.13; Swiss Private International Law Act 1987, Ch.12, Art.180; Netherlands Arbitration Act 1986, Arts 1034 and 1035.

[2] Model Law, Art.13; English Arbitration Act 1996, s.24(3).

A curious gap in the US Federal Arbitration Act leaves the parties no avenue of judicial review of an appointment until after an award has been rendered, unless the rules of procedure adopted by the parties provide for earlier review.[3] This means that a party with a valid objection to the composition of the tribunal would have to make the objection "on the record" and then wait until the end of the case before challenging the award (with the attendant waste of time and money if the challenge is successful).

The ICC Rules provide that the ICC's Court decides on the merits of a **4–73** challenge after the Secretariat has afforded an opportunity to the arbitrator concerned, the other party and any other members of the arbitral tribunal, to comment in writing within a suitable period of time.[4]

The LCIA Rules contain a detailed challenge procedure. A party who intends to challenge an arbitrator must send a written statement of the reasons for challenge to the LCIA within 15 days of the establishment of the arbitral tribunal, or within 15 days of becoming aware of the circumstances justifying the challenge if this is later. Unless the challenged arbitrator withdraws (or the other party agrees to the challenge) within 15 days of receipt of the written statement of reasons, the LCIA decides whether or not the challenge should be upheld.[5]

Under the UNCITRAL Rules, any challenge must be notified to the other party and to the members of the arbitral tribunal, including the challenged arbitrator. A similar 15-day time-limit for submitting a challenge is adopted, and the merits of challenges are decided upon by the appointing authority.[6]

Challenges under the ICSID Rules

The Washington Convention, which governs ICSID arbitrations, recognises **4–74** that there may be circumstances in which an arbitrator should be removed:

"A party may propose to a Commission or Tribunal the disqualification of any of its members on account of any fact indicating a manifest lack of the qualities required by paragraph (1) of Article 14. A party to arbitration proceedings may, in addition, propose the disqualification of an arbitrator on the ground that he was ineligible for appointment to the Tribunal under Section 2 of Chapter IV."[7]

The qualities required by Art.14(1) include the ability to "exercise independent judgment"; the grounds on which an arbitrator is "ineligible for appointment" refer to the nationality provisions, which are designed to ensure that (unless the parties agree otherwise) the majority of arbitrators are not of the

[3] *Morelite Construction Corp v New York City District Carpenters Benefit Funds* 748 F.2d 79 (1984).
[4] ICC Arbitration Rules, Art.11.3.
[5] LCIA Arbitration Rules, Art.10.4.
[6] UNCITRAL Arbitration Rules, Art.11.
[7] Washington Convention, Art.57.

nationality of the state party or of the private party to the dispute.[8] Any challenge of an arbitrator made under the provisions of the Washington Convention must be made "promptly, and in any event before the proceeding is declared closed".[9]

The party making the challenge (or "proposing the disqualification of an arbitrator", as it is phrased in the ICSID Rules) must state the reasons in a document to be filed with the Secretary-General of ICSID. This proposal for disqualification is then transmitted to all the members of the arbitral tribunal and to the opposing party. If the challenge is directed at a sole arbitrator, or to a majority of the arbitrators, it is also transmitted to the Chairman of the Administrative Council of ICSID. The arbitrator whose position is challenged may then "without delay" furnish any appropriate explanations to the arbitral tribunal or the Chairman, as the case may be.[10]

4–75   If the challenge is directed against one arbitrator in an arbitral tribunal of three, the decision is taken by the other two arbitrators, who may accept or reject it. If they cannot agree, the decision will be made by the Chairman. The decision will also be made by the Chairman if the challenge is directed against a sole arbitrator, or against the majority of the arbitral tribunal.[11] So long as the constitution of the arbitral tribunal is in doubt because of a challenge to one or more of the arbitrators, the arbitral proceedings are suspended.[12] If the challenge is upheld a vacancy is created in the arbitral tribunal. It must be filled before the proceedings resume. If the challenge is rejected, the arbitration proceeds.

(d) Waiver

4–76   A question arises concerning the obligation of a party to raise promptly any objection concerning the independence or impartiality of an arbitrator (or any other ground of challenge), when the facts upon which the challenge is based come to the attention of the objecting party. As noted above, such a question may not arise in the US because there is no procedure available for challenges to a court until after the award has been rendered. Nevertheless, even there the objection should be made in a timely way to the arbitral tribunal "for the record".[13]

Under the Model Law, challenges related to impartiality or independence must be filed with the arbitral tribunal within 15 days of the party becoming aware of

---

[8] *ibid.*, Arts 38 and 39.

[9] ICSID Arbitration Rules, r.9(1). If the grounds for challenge only become known when the proceedings are closed, the remedy is a request for an annulment of the award under r.50.

[10] ICSID Arbitration Rules, r.9(3). If the grounds for challenge only become known when the proceedings are closed, the remedy is a request for an annulment of the award under r.50.

[11] *ibid.*, r.9(4).

[12] *ibid.*, r.9(6).

[13] A US court has held that failure to make an objection that an arbitrator was not impartial, when the grounds for the objection were known to the party early on in the proceedings, constituted a waiver of the objection and it could not be raised in court proceedings to confirm the award and enforce judgment thereon: *The Island Territory of Curaçao v Solitron Devices Inc* 356 F.Supp.1 (U.S.D.C., S.D.N.Y. 1973).

the circumstances giving rise to justifiable doubts as to those issues.[14] Is the objection to be deemed to be waived if the time-limit is not met or may the objection be raised in a challenge to the award or on enforcement proceedings? This question has not been resolved definitively. The better view is that on policy grounds a failure to comply with the time-limits should bar any attack of the award.

In common law jurisdictions, the concept of waiver is well established. A party may not "lie in ambush" with an objection to await the decision of the tribunal. The Supreme Court of Canada has stated that:

"There is no doubt that, generally speaking, an award will not be set aside if the circumstances alleged to disqualify an arbitrator were known to both parties before the arbitration commenced and they proceeded without objection."[15]

The concept of waiver is also known in civil law countries. A challenge to an **4–77** arbitrator under the Swiss 1987 Act must be brought "without delay".[16] An unreasonable delay in bringing a challenge amounts to a "forfeiture" which is a reflection of the bona fides principle in Swiss law.[17]

(e) Filling a vacancy

A replacement arbitrator must also be appointed where a member of a three- **4–78** person tribunal resigns and the other two members do not proceed as a truncated tribunal.[18] If the arbitration is being conducted under international or institutional rules, or under a properly drawn submission agreement, the procedure for replacing an arbitrator will be specified. In general, the new appointment is made in the same way as the original appointment.[19]

Problems are likely to arise in replacing an arbitrator only in ad hoc arbitrations. The parties themselves may be able to reach an agreement as to the method by which the arbitrator should be replaced, and this approach should certainly be attempted first. However, if the parties cannot agree, either on the choice of a replacement arbitrator or on the way of making that choice, an approach to the relevant national court must be considered. Since, by definition, an arbitral tribunal is already in existence and the place of arbitration will almost certainly have been decided, the request for the appointment of a replacement arbitrator is

---

[14] Model Law, Art.13(2).
[15] *Ghirardosi v Minister of Highways (BC)* (1996) 56 D.L.R. (2d) 469 at 473.
[16] Swiss Private International Law Act 1987, Ch.12, Art.180(2).
[17] See Blessing, "The New International Arbitration Law in Switzerland" (1988) 5 Journal of International Arbitration 9 at 40.
[18] Exceptionally, in the case of a three-member arbitral tribunal, the arbitration may proceed with the two remaining members. See the discussion of truncated tribunals below at para.4–79.
[19] A notable exception arises under the ICSID Arbitration Rules, r.11(2), where, in order to prevent abuse, a party-nominated arbitrator who resigns will be replaced by a person nominated by the Chairman of the Administrative Council of ICSID rather than by the relevant party, unless the remaining members of the arbitral tribunal have consented to his resignation, under r.8(2).

made to the courts at the seat of arbitration. It is necessary to ensure that the court has the power to make the necessary appointment but, as with the appointment of arbitrators *ab initio,* most developed national systems of law confer such powers upon their courts.[20]

Nevertheless, it is best not to rely upon recourse to national courts if it can be avoided. The following guidelines are suggested:

- where provision is to be made for an arbitration to be conducted according to the rules of one of the arbitral institutions, those rules should be checked to make sure that they contain adequate provision for the filling of a vacancy;

- where an arbitration is to be conducted ad hoc under the terms of a submission agreement, adequate provisions for the filling of any vacancy in the arbitral tribunal should be written into the submission agreement;

- where an arbitration is to be conducted ad hoc without any formal submission agreement, it should only be held in a country where the local law contains adequate provision for filling any vacancy that may arise.

(f) Truncated tribunals

4-79   Most party-appointed arbitrators act properly and in good faith. It occasionally happens, however, that a party-appointed arbitrator, despite having received adequate notice and sympathetic consideration of personal commitments, nevertheless refuses to participate in the arbitration or submits a resignation without sufficient reason. If this takes place early in the proceedings, or if the case is one in which the interests of justice do not require a quick decision, the recalcitrant arbitrator is usually removed and a replacement appointed.[21]

However, appointing a new arbitrator may be impractical when the resignation, or refusal to participate, occurs late in the arbitral proceedings. Finding and appointing a replacement, and allowing the new arbitrator to become familiar with the case, inevitably causes delay. The situation is particularly aggravated if the arbitrator chooses to resign, or refuses to participate when the stage of the tribunal's deliberations is reached. In such cases, and in cases where a quick conclusion to the arbitration is essential, the only sensible course may be for the two remaining arbitrators to continue with the proceedings and render an award.

---

[20] *e.g.* in English law, the court has wide powers to give directions as to the making of any appointments, and indeed to make any necessary appointments itself. See Arbitration Act 1996, s.18, and Goldman, "The Complementary Roles of Judges and Arbitrators in Ensuring that International Commercial Arbitration is Effective" *60 Years of ICC Arbitration—A Look at the Future* (ICC Publication No.412, 1984), pp.255, 275.

[21] In which case the procedures for filling vacancies would apply as described above.

A number of celebrated cases provide examples of situations in which arbitral tribunals have continued proceedings and rendered awards as truncated tribunals.[22] Most of these have been ad hoc arbitrations, but there have been cases under the UNCITRAL Rules[23] and the ICC Rules[24] in which proceedings have been continued and awards rendered by truncated tribunals. The AAA International Arbitration Rules (1991 edition) appears to have been the first set of rules to provide expressly for the two remaining arbitrators to continue where their colleague third arbitrator fails to participate,[25] and the provision remained unaltered in the ICDR's 2003 edition. If the parties have agreed that the arbitration may proceed with two arbitrators, national courts may be expected to enforce an otherwise valid award.[26] Careful parties who wish to avoid delays will choose rules, or prepare contract provisions, that provide for the possibility that one of the arbitrators may attempt to derail the arbitration for tactical reasons.

An eminent international arbitrator has written: **4–80**

"I find it very hard to imagine that, even in the absence of an express rule or agreement, a modern court in a state that otherwise has a public policy of supporting international commercial arbitration would invalidate an award issued by a majority of arbitrators because a party-appointed arbitrator, in an effort to frustrate the arbitration, chooses to absent himself at a late stage of the proceedings, or refuses to sign an award. National laws that refer to participation by three arbitrators should be interpreted to have been satisfied, as Professor Gaillard suggests, when all three have had a fair and equal *opportunity* to participate".[27]

Nevertheless, the majority of the world's most prominent international arbitral institutions followed the example of the AAA (as the ICDR was then known), including WIPO (in its 1994 Rules),[28] and both the ICC and the LCIA (in 1998). The LCIA and WIPO followed the philosophy of leaving the question of whether

---

[22] These cases were discussed at the 1990 ICCA Congress. See Reports of Schwebel & Böckstiegel, "Preventing Delay or Disruption of Arbitration" ICCA Congress Series No.5 (Kluwer, 1991), pp.241–247, 270–274. See also the French-Mexican Claims Commission Cases, discussed in Feller, *The Mexican Claims Commissions* (1935), pp.70–77. See also Schwebel, *International Arbitration: Three Salient Problems* (1987), pp.144–296.

[23] See, *e.g.*, Order of May 17, 1985, in *Sedco Inc v National Iranian Oil Co*, Case No.129, reprinted in 8 Iran-US C.T.R. 34 and concurring opinion of Judge Bower at p.40; *Uiterwiyk Corp v Islamic Republic of Iran,* Award No.375-381-1 (July 6, 1988), 19 Iran–US C.T.R. 107 at 116; also dissenting letter and supplemental opinion at 161, 169.

[24] See Böckstiegel, "Preventing Delay or Disruption of Arbitration" ICCA Congress Series No.5 (Kluwer, 1991), Topic 8, pp.271–274.

[25] AAA International Arbitration Rules, effective March 1, 1991, Art.11.

[26] See ICCA Congress Series No.5 (Kluwer, 1999), Gaillard & Veeder, Topic 7. Moreover, Veeder notes in his report that the UNCITRAL Model Law may be construed to authorise truncated tribunals.

[27] See Holtzmann, "Lessons of the Stockholm Congress" ICCA Congress Series No.5 (Kluwer, 1991), p.28.

[28] WIPO Arbitration Rules, Art.10.

or not to proceed on a truncated basis entirely to the discretion of the remaining arbitrators. However, the ICC adopted a more restrictive approach:

"(5) Subsequent to the closing of the proceedings, instead of replacing an arbitrator who has died or been removed by the Court pursuant to Articles 12(1) and 12(2), the Court may decide, when it considers it appropriate, that the remaining arbitrators shall continue the arbitration. In making such determination, the Court shall take into account the views of the remaining arbitrators and of the parties and such other matters that it considers appropriate in the circumstances."[29]

Thus, not only does it limit the possibility of a truncated tribunal to the deliberations phase, but it is the ICC's Court that takes the decision, rather than the remaining members of the tribunal.

4–81   Several cases in which arbitral tribunals have decided to proceed in "truncated" form have come into the public domain since the last edition of this work was published. The most sensational involved the government of a country in South-east Asia, which apparently exerted considerable pressure on the arbitrator it had appointed to withdraw. The final award contains a passage stating comprehensively the relevant facts and analysing the legal consequences. The conclusion of the two remaining arbitrators, relying on the published works of a well-known international jurist, was that it could—and should—proceed in truncated form to render a final award.[30]

So far as the UNCITRAL Rules are concerned, there is thus respectable authority supporting the legitimacy of a truncated tribunal's decision to proceed and render an award where appropriate. In institutional arbitration, the most modern sets of rules have created their own individual regimes—mostly leaving it to the governing bodies of the Institutions concerned to decide rather than the remaining arbitrators. In ad hoc arbitrations in which the parties have not chosen to arbitrate under the UNCITRAL Rules, it is wise for the remaining arbitrators to proceed with caution; at the very least, they should review any relevant provisions of the *lex arbitri* and (if they are aware of it) the law of the place of likely enforcement of the award.

It seems clear that the option of proceeding as a truncated tribunal, rather than as a reconstituted full tribunal, will remain as an exceptional measure to be adopted only where the arbitration is nearing its end and where there is clear evidence that the arbitrator concerned, voluntarily or involuntarily, has been associated with an abuse of the process.

---

[29] ICC Arbitration Rules, Art.12(5).
[30] *Himpurna California Energy Ltd v Republic of Indonesia* (2000) XXV Yearbook Commercial Arbitration 186, citing Schwebel's Cambridge Lauterpacht lectures in which he referred to *Republic of Colombia v Cauca Company*, the *French-Mexican Claims Commission* cases, the *Lena Goldfields* arbitration, the *Sabotage* cases, and the Advisory Opinion of the International Court of Justice in Interpretation of Peace Treaties with Bulgaria, Hungary and Romania.

(g) Procedure following the filling of a vacancy

A question of considerable practical importance arises when a vacancy does **4–82** occur in the arbitral tribunal and is filled to what extent must the arbitral tribunal retrace its steps?

If the oral hearings have not begun when the vacancy arises, it should not be necessary for either the newly constituted arbitral tribunal or the parties themselves to go back over old ground. It is sufficient for the replacement arbitrator to be given time to read the pleadings and other documents exchanged between the parties, to consider any procedural directions given by the former arbitral tribunal, and to signify his or her assent to them. This assent should as a matter of practice be recorded in writing, although no particular form is required.

However, if the vacancy arises *after* the oral proceedings have begun, it will necessarily bring them to a close for a period of time, unless the proceedings continue before a truncated tribunal. When the arbitral tribunal has been reconstituted, the question arises as to whether or not evidence that has already been heard and legal arguments that have already been advanced orally should be repeated for the benefit of the replacement arbitrator. Such repetition is both time-consuming and expensive. It is in the interests of both parties to the arbitration to try to avoid it if at all possible.

Transcripts

Where a transcript is available, it should be sufficient for the replacement **4–83** arbitrator to read the transcript and so come up to date with the proceedings. If, as a result of such reading, the replacement arbitrator wishes to have a particular witness recalled, or a particular argument explained in more detail, it is normally in the interests of both parties to agree that this should be done, rather than run the risk of having to start the oral proceedings again from the beginning.

Where there is no transcript of the oral hearing, the extent to which oral evidence and argument already presented needs to be repeated is a question which can only be resolved by discussion between the members of the arbitral tribunal (including the replacement member), the parties and their legal advisers.

The parties may generally be relied upon to co-operate in such matters. Once an arbitration has progressed so far, it is usually in the interests of all parties that the hearings should continue without the need for repetition because the costs are invariably substantial. Thus it is for the replacement arbitrator, in consultation with the remaining members of the tribunal, to decide the extent to which the previous steps in the proceedings should be retraced.

It is difficult to lay down any specific rule as to the attitude the replacement **4–84** arbitrator should adopt. It is not unreasonable (although it may be inconvenient) for a replacement arbitrator to insist upon hearing again at least some of the oral testimony heard by the previous arbitral tribunal. Nor would it be unreasonable (although again it may be inconvenient) for one of the parties to insist on it. The

UNCITRAL Rules lend support to this view. They provide that where a sole arbitrator or the presiding arbitrator is replaced "any hearings held previously *shall* be repeated".[31] But the same Rules also provide that if any other arbitrator is replaced, any hearing held previously "may be repeated at the discretion of the arbitral tribunal".[32]

The WIPO Rules provide that:

> "Whenever a substitute arbitrator is appointed, the Tribunal shall, having regard to any observations of the parties, determine in its sole discretion whether all or part of any prior hearings are to be repeated."[33]

The 2003 version of the ICDR International Arbitration Rules and the 1998 version of the ICC Rules contain broadly similar provisions,[34] but the 1998 version of the LCIA's Rules does not cover the position expressly.

(h) Insuring against a vacancy

4–85   At one time it was not unusual, in large and expensive international commercial arbitrations, for insurance to be taken out on the lives of the members of the arbitral tribunal. This was usually done when the oral hearings were about to begin; and in itself was a recognition of the fact that the oral hearings might have to be repeated if one of the members of the arbitral tribunal (and in particular the presiding arbitrator) were to die.

The advantage of taking out insurance is that, if an arbitrator were to die or become incapacitated, the proceeds of the insurance policy would be available to cover at least part of the considerable expenses involved in adjourning the hearing, reconstituting the arbitral tribunal, reconvening the hearing and, perhaps, going over again the ground already covered.

One problem, apart from that of the cost of such insurance, is that the members of the arbitral tribunal must be told that insurance on their lives is being taken out—if only because the insurance company will need medical information, and perhaps a medical examination, which only the arbitrators themselves can provide. It is a delicate, and sometimes invidious, task to suggest, or to appear to suggest, to members of the arbitral tribunal that they may not survive the proceedings! They may not like the message, or the messenger. If it is to be done, it is best done by both parties acting jointly, rather than by one party acting on its own.[35]

---

[31] UNCITRAL Arbitration Rules, Art.14 (emphasis added).
[32] *ibid.*
[33] WIPO Arbitration Rules, Art.34.
[34] ICDR Rules, Art.11.2; ICC Rules, Art.12.4.
[35] So far as the authors are aware, the practice of the parties insuring the lives or health of the arbitrators appears to have virtually disappeared.

6. The Organisation of the Arbitral Tribunal

(a) Generally

There is much work to be done "behind the scenes" to ensure that an **4–86**
international commercial arbitration runs smoothly. The arbitrators are generally
of different nationalities, as are the parties, their advisers and experts. Indeed, it
is not unusual to find that, at a meeting or hearing in an international commercial
arbitration, five or more different nationalities are represented. This mixture of
nationalities is one of the most intriguing challenges involved in the practice of
international commercial arbitration.

It needs more careful planning and organisation to bring together such a mixed
group of people, in what will be a foreign city for most of them, than it does to
arrange a domestic arbitration. Indeed, arranging a hearing in a large international commercial arbitration has much in common with arranging a series of
performances for a company of opera singers or actors embarking upon an
international tour.

There is a venue to be arranged; times and dates to be fixed; hotel rooms to be
booked; technicians (in the form of interpreters, transcription services and so
forth) to be engaged; and the whole performance has to be so organised that,
when the time comes, the assembled cast of parties, lawyers, experts and
witnesses are ready to present their offerings to their small but important
audience—the arbitral tribunal. The work involved in making the administrative
arrangements has led to it becoming an established practice in larger and more
complex international commercial arbitrations for the arbitral tribunal to appoint
an administrative secretary or registrar, whose function is to take care of the
arrangements.[36]

(b) Meetings and hearings

In arbitrations where the arbitral tribunal consists of more than a sole arbi- **4–87**
trator, it is usually necessary for the members of the arbitral tribunal to meet from
time to time for consultation amongst themselves. There is no reason why such
meetings should be held at the seat of the arbitration. If it is more convenient for
the members of the arbitral tribunal to meet elsewhere they may do so, subject
to any provisions to the contrary in the submission agreement or in the applicable
rules of arbitration.[37] The arbitrators may be required, however, to meet at the
seat of the arbitration for the purpose of drawing up or signing their award.[38]

---

[36] For a discussion of the role and functions of an administrative secretary or registrar see paras 4–108
et seq.
[37] The UNCITRAL Arbitration Rules give the arbitral tribunal complete freedom in this respect; see
Art.16. So also do the LCIA Arbitration Rules; see Art.7.2. The ICSID Arbitration Rules, however,
appear to contemplate that even meetings for consultation between the members of the arbitral
tribunal must take place "at the seat of the Centre or at such other place that may have been agreed
by the parties"; see r.13(3).
[38] See Ch.2, para.2–24.

Meetings and hearings at which the parties are present

4-88   In all but the simplest cases, it is likely that meetings will take place from time to time between the arbitral tribunal and the parties and their representatives so that procedural orders or directions may be considered. Unless the applicable law or rules forbid it, the arbitral tribunal may decide to hold meetings with the parties elsewhere if this is more convenient and, in particular, if savings of costs may be achieved. However, the arbitral tribunal should consult the parties before doing so. If the parties agree to hold all meetings and/or hearings at the place of arbitration, this would be binding on the arbitral tribunal.

Unless the case is to be decided on the basis of documents only, there is also a hearing, or a series of hearings, at which the parties and their representatives attend in order to put forward the evidence of their witnesses and their legal arguments. Witness hearings are generally but not always held at the seat of the arbitration; provision is sometimes made for the arbitral tribunal to meet elsewhere[39] when, for instance, the evidence of an important witness is required and it is more convenient for the arbitral tribunal and the parties to go to the witness, than for the witness to go to the arbitral tribunal.[40]

Fixing dates for hearings

4-89   Where the arbitral tribunal consists of more than a sole arbitrator, the date of the hearing will generally be fixed by the presiding arbitrator. The presiding arbitrator should, however, consult with the co-arbitrators so as to ensure that the date or dates proposed are convenient to them also. There should also be consultation with the parties and their advisers. The ICSID Rules deal with the question expressly:

> "(1) . . . The dates of such sessions shall be fixed by the President of the Tribunal after consultation with its members and the Secretary-General . . . and with the parties as far as possible.[41]
>
> (2) The dates of subsequent sessions shall be determined by the Tribunal, after consultation with the Secretary-General."

The arbitral proceedings should be conducted without undue delay, a consideration that may have to take precedence over the convenience of the parties' counsel, or one of them. If a reasonable agreement between the parties and the

---

[39] See, *e.g.*, the UNCITRAL Arbitration Rules, Art.16.2; and the LCIA Arbitration Rules, Art.7.2.
[40] This was so, *e.g.*, in *de Nora v The Government of Kuwait*. Evidence was required from an important member of the government. By the time his evidence came to be taken he had become prime minister and, since it was not convenient for him to leave his country at the relevant time, it was agreed that the arbitral tribunal, the parties and the lawyers involved in the case would go to see him. The Government provided a Kuwait Airways aircraft, specially fitted out with first class seating throughout, to convey the people involved from Geneva to Kuwait; to wait on the ground at the tribunal's disposal; and then to convey the party back to Geneva.
[41] ICSID Arbitration Rules, r.13(2). Consultation with the Secretary-General of ICSID is necessary, because it is he who makes the physical arrangements for the holding of the sessions.

arbitral tribunal on a date cannot be reached, the arbitral tribunal must fix a date without such agreement. There can be little objection to this, so long as the parties are given reasonable notice or, as it is put in the ICSID Rules, so long as the parties are notified "in good time".[42]

Avoiding local public holidays

In fixing a date for the hearing, the sole or presiding arbitrator should take **4–90** account of holiday periods in the countries of the arbitrators and the parties. The arbitrator would probably not wish to work during religious or family holidays in his or her own country and should not unreasonably insist that others must work during such periods in their countries. This is not a legal obligation. It is rather a matter of courtesy and of consideration for the other participants, and common sense. It may be difficult, or even impossible in some countries, to provide the necessary infrastructure for a hearing on a public holiday.

Length of hearings

In fixing a date for the start of the hearings, the sole or presiding arbitrator **4–91** must keep in mind the length of time the hearing is likely to take. Indeed, this is a question that will be asked repeatedly when making travel and hotel arrangements; when booking rooms in which the hearing is to take place; when making arrangements for the attendance of the parties and their witnesses; and so forth. It is extremely difficult to make an accurate estimate of how long a case is likely to last. Every lawyer experienced in litigation or arbitration knows of the supposedly "short" case which drags on through long summer days, as the witnesses fumble their evidence and the lawyers mumble their speeches. Similarly, every lawyer experienced in litigation or arbitration knows of the "big" case which was set to take weeks and instead is over in a few days.

The task of estimating how long a case is likely to take is not helped by lawyers whose technique of advocacy appears to be based, rather too literally, on the advice given by the King when asked by the White Rabbit where he should begin: "Begin at the beginning and go on until you come to the end; then stop."[43] This advice has considerable merit, as anyone who has tried to take a statement of evidence from a difficult witness will know. However, the task of a good lawyer in presenting his client's case to an arbitral tribunal is not to ramble through the case from beginning to end, but to focus attention on the facts and on the arguments of law that are important.

A structured and disciplined approach is likely to lead to a more effective and shorter presentation of the case. Indeed, lawyers would do well to learn from experts in other fields such as the construction industry, where targets are set with the aim of being met. A construction company invited to tender for a project cannot offer to start work and see how long it takes. The tenderer is required to

---

[42] ICSID Arbitration Rules, r.13(4).
[43] See Lewis Carroll, *Alice in Wonderland.*

give a completion date; and this means that the work must be organised so as to try to meet that date, rather than let things drift and see what happens.

4–92   Much time can be saved if the lawyers representing the parties remember that the arbitrators are familiar with the main arguments. They have read the documents, and they may well have put forward similar arguments themselves in previous cases. Mere repetition is nearly always counterproductive and irritating for the arbitral tribunal. Clients often like to hear their best points emphasised and repeated, but it is essential that "old" arguments should be presented in a fresh form, or given a new perspective.

Furthermore, an advocate should be prepared to react positively to the way in which the hearing develops. The shape of the case may change under the hammer of the opposition; or the arbitral tribunal may begin to approach the issue from a different angle. Here again, instead of merely repeating old arguments, a wise advocate shifts ground to follow a new approach initiated by the arbitrators, or to meet cogent arguments put forward by the other side. This is a much more effective use of the time set aside for the hearing than sticking to a preconceived line that almost invariably duplicates what has been stated in the written submissions.

What then should an arbitral tribunal do when it is trying to determine how much time to allow for a hearing? One effective way of proceeding is as follows:

- the arbitral tribunal gives directions to the parties as to the issues on which it particularly wishes to hear evidence and argument[44];

- the arbitral tribunal then asks the parties or their lawyers for an estimate of the time which each of them is likely to require for the presentation of its case;

- the arbitral tribunal considers these estimates and, if necessary, discusses them with the parties and their lawyers;

- the arbitral tribunal then makes its own assessment of the time likely to be required for the hearing and allocates this time between the parties, indicating to them that it has done so.[45]

4–93   If this, or some similar procedure is followed, the pre-hearing meetings are likely to take longer but the witness hearings will be much shorter, since proper preparation has been made.

(c) Administrative aspects

4–94   The place of the arbitration is chosen before any hearing is held; but it is necessary to fix a specific venue in appropriate premises offered by an arbitral institution, conference centre or other suitable building.

---

[44] See Ch.6.

[45] It is not always fair to divide the time equally; one party may have a heavier burden of proof than the other and may need to present more witnesses.

In deciding on a venue, the primary consideration must be to find accommodation that is fit for the purpose. Two particular requirements stand out. First, the room or rooms chosen must provide adequate space not only for the arbitral tribunal but also for the parties and their lawyers; for charts, drawings, plans and other documents, all of which may be voluminous; and for anyone else who is to assist in the conduct of the arbitration, including experts, stenographers and interpreters. In modern times, electronic aids of one kind or another are routinely deployed.[46]

Secondly, so far as possible, the rooms chosen must be available for the purposes of the arbitration throughout the whole period of the hearing. It is both irritating and inconvenient when the hearing room (at a hotel, for example) must be completely cleared at the end of the day's proceedings, to make way for a dinner or other function.

For a meeting between the arbitral tribunal and the parties, it is usually **4–95** sufficient if one room is available, provided that the room is big enough. For a witness hearing, and in particular a hearing that is likely to last for more than two or three days, it is useful (and in some cases, essential) if other rooms are available, so that each party can have its own room in which to store documents, check transcripts, prepare for the next day's hearings and generally engage in the often frantic activity that goes on behind the scenes in any international commercial arbitration.

The arbitral tribunal should also have a room available for its deliberations, because it is often inconvenient or impracticable to ask the parties to withdraw completely from the hearing room. Security can also present problems; the parties (and the arbitral tribunal) usually wish to be able to leave documents at the venue without fear of them being seen by others. Suitable accommodation, particularly for a lengthy hearing, is not easy to find. Specialist international arbitration groups within law firms often keep comprehensive lists of the facilities available in their localities, categorising them in terms of relative expense and convenience. Some of the commonly used alternatives are described below.

Arbitration centres

Most major arbitration institutions and centres are able to provide, or at least **4–96** recommend, accommodation that is suitable for almost every type of hearing. Where one of the parties is a government or other state enterprises, it is worth considering whether the arbitration can be brought within the aegis of either the PCA at the Peace Palace in The Hague or of ICSID in Washington. Even where an arbitration does not fall within the PCA Rules, the Secretary-General of the PCA is generally willing to accommodate arbitrations between private parties, as well as those under the PCA's Rules, provided that space is available. There are also good facilities in the major European international arbitration venues, such as Geneva, London, Paris, Stockholm, The Hague and Vienna.

---

[46] Such as Powerpoint displays on a screen.

Arbitral institutions

4–97   Some of the established international arbitral institutions, such as the ICC, ICDR and LCIA, can also provide accommodation for use both as hearing rooms and conference rooms. However, since the rooms tend to be much in demand, it is usually essential to reserve them well in advance. At the ICC in Paris, for example the rooms are not likely to be available for more than a few days at a time since they are also used for conferences, seminars and other meetings of the ICC itself.

Universities, clubs and other institutions

4–98   Universities, clubs, learned societies and other institutions often have rooms that are available for hire and suitable for use for meetings and hearings. Indeed, holding an arbitration in the venerable ambience of these institutions may add a touch of class to the proceedings!

Hotels

4–99   The most frequent solution to the problem of finding a suitable venue for an international commercial arbitration is to check with the leading hotels of the town or city in which the arbitration is to take place. Such hotels are mostly accustomed to looking after business visitors and will be able to offer, in addition to conference or other function rooms, photocopying, fax and other services.

The prices charged for the use of conference rooms in hotels are likely to be much higher than those charged by the professional organisations mentioned above. Experience dictates that if a meeting or a hearing is to be held in a hotel, it should be held in one of the function rooms rather than, say, the presiding arbitrator's own room. In theory it may seem both economical and convenient for the presiding arbitrator to take a suite and hold meetings in it. In practice it tends to mean that it is impossible to find adequate space for documents. Furthermore, a hearing taking place in someone's living accommodation may come to resemble a French farce, with the proceedings being continually interrupted by maids arriving to make up the bed, waiters arriving to check the mini-bar or to serve coffee, and personal telephone calls causing interruptions at critical points in the hearing.

Interpreters

4–100   Some witnesses may be unable to express themselves easily, if at all, in the language of the arbitration. It should be regarded as the fundamental right of a party or a witness to speak at a hearing in his mother tongue if he so wishes.[47] In such circumstances, it is necessary to arrange for skilled interpreters to be available, so that each of such witnesses may give testimony in the relevant

---

[47] It is not unreasonable, however, for an arbitral tribunal to require that a party who wishes to engage lawyers to present his case to be required to retain representatives who are able to perform their functions in the working language of the arbitration.

language. Arrangements for the engagement of interpreters are usually under-taken by the party who requires their services. If a witness is to give evidence through an interpreter, it is usual to notify both the arbitral tribunal and the other party of this fact well in advance of the hearing.

The use of an interpreter inevitably slows down the proceedings consider-ably.[48] This is something the arbitral tribunal must take into account in assessing the duration of the hearing. There is also the possibility that the opposing party may wish to engage its own interpreter, to check that questions and answers are being interpreted correctly, with the attendant risk that the arbitral tribunal itself may need to have its own interpreter to resolve differences. Arguments about the correct translation of what was said by a witness can become heated.

Some techniques are available to minimise the inevitable delays involved in the use of interpreters. One is to allow the witness to use the interpreter simply to help him understand the questions and formulate the answers, rather than proceed with the full formality of sequential translations. Another is to use videotaped depositions in the absence of the arbitral tribunal; the tapes are then edited to exclude the exchanges in the language that is "foreign" to the arbitra-tion. One method that is invariably unsatisfactory is to attempt the type of "simultaneous" translation that is used at international conferences and, for examples, UN agencies. However skilled the interpreters, simultaneous interpretation—by its very nature, cannot be sufficiently accurate for the purpose of recording the testimony of a witness in transcript form.

Verbatim records

A verbatim transcript, particularly of the evidence, can be of very great   **4–101** importance in international arbitrations where (as almost invariably occurs) the members of the arbitral tribunal have different levels of comprehension of the language of the proceedings. Furthermore, since arbitrators experienced in the civil law systems are more accustomed to rely on documentary rather than oral material, their instinct leads them to place greater reliance on the transcript of the hearing than on what is said during the hearing. Indeed, the experience of the authors is that international arbitrators rely heavily on transcripts of the proceed-ings when these are available.

There are several methods of obtaining transcripts. Most computer-aided transcription methods are less expensive than the old methods. The benefit of this technology to the parties' lawyers and the arbitrators is that relevant portions of testimony may be identified quickly by using a search programme. The savings to the parties may be substantial in terms of time saved by the arbitrators in writing their final award and by the lawyers in preparing closing arguments, since all references to a particular issue may be collected in seconds rather than hours or even days. One of the best systems is "Livenote", where the testimony of the

---

[48] Experience shows that it it is not unusual for the "productivity" of a hearing (measured in pages of transcript) to be reduced by up to 50 per cent where full sequential interpretation is required.

witness is shown almost instantaneously on laptop computer screens available to the participants in the arbitration room.

For most arbitrators, however, the value of the transcript lies in its availability during the deliberations and for drafting the award. For this purpose the proceedings are either recorded or taken down by a stenographer and then subsequently transcribed. This usually takes some days to achieve and the benefit for the arbitral tribunal may be lost if the deliberations start immediately after the close of the hearing.

4–102   Furthermore, the arbitrators often feel the need to make their own handwritten notes, which means that the speeches and evidence have to be delivered more slowly. However, the various "non-immediate" methods, whilst less speedy and efficient, at least provide a permanent record of the proceedings which may be beneficial later if, for example, a vacancy on the arbitral tribunal has to be filled, or if there are subsequent court proceedings for recourse against, or for enforcement of, the award.

For the lawyers engaged in an arbitration, the availability of a daily transcript is a mixed blessing. It means that there is yet another document (which may run to more than a hundred or more closely typed pages) that has to be read and analysed every day by one of the lawyers in the team, in order to keep abreast of the case. But equally it provides an authentic record of what has been said and so constitutes a valuable source of reference for the parties' closing submissions.[49]

Hearing hours

4–103   In most countries judges actually sit in their courts for a relatively short period each day, perhaps no more than five hours. This is sensible in that it gives them time to read through their notes of the evidence and argument and to reflect on what they have heard and what they would like to hear. Judges also have other duties to perform, and usually they did not accept their appointments—however honorific—to spend their weekends writing judgments or doing other paperwork. On a public employee's salary, many of them may justifiably feel that they are entitled to confine their working lives to ordinary office hours. It also allows the parties and their advisers essential time in which to produce any evidence, information or data the court may request; and it also gives them time to prepare for the next session.

This practice is not generally followed by arbitral tribunals engaged in international commercial arbitrations. People who are present at the hearing may have travelled a long way to be there; the cost of the proceedings is substantial and increases on a daily basis. However, such an approach is sometimes unfair to the parties, because it does not give them sufficient time (including time for reflection) in which to present their respective cases.

---

[49] It is usual to give such references by citing the day, page and paragraph number of the transcript; so, for instance, the arbitral tribunal might be referred to the evidence of a particular witness at "Day 10, page 70, paragraph B."

The witness hearings in an international commercial arbitration may be the culmination of many months, if not years, of work. It can be inappropriate for an arbitral tribunal, even with the best of intentions, to try to rush through the product of this work in a series of late night sessions. Any hearing or meeting that is likely to last for longer than a few days should be conducted on the basis that the hearing is not in session for more than six hours of actual hearing time per day (*i.e.* after taking account of breaks).

It should also be kept in mind that "comfort breaks" may be needed, partic- **4–104** ularly by elderly arbitrators who (unlike the parties and their representatives) cannot slip out for a few minutes while the hearing is in progress!

The arbitral tribunal should adopt a flexible approach, capable of adaptation to meet the circumstances of each particular hearing. It may actually save time, in the long run, if the parties are given time to consider their positions and to review the state of progress of their oral presentations. Shorter hours often make for shorter hearings. Lawyers can usually condense their speeches if they have additional time for preparation during the course of the hearing.

Conversely, if they have insufficient time their speeches will be longer, duller and more repetitive. An occasional half-day or even full-day adjournment may be worthwhile for this purpose. The arbitral tribunal may then put pressure on the parties to tailor their presentations to fit within an agreed timetable; but each party must be allowed a reasonable period of time in which to present its case.

If the arbitral tribunal proceeds firmly but fairly, each party must impose some **4–105** discipline upon itself as to the way in which its case is presented. This is as it should be. The arbitral tribunal should take charge of the hearings.[50] International commercial arbitration is an expensive way of resolving international trade disputes. It is unreasonable to allow the parties simply to begin at the beginning and go on until they reach the end.

Relations between the parties and the arbitral tribunal

It is important to remember that an arbitration, with its relatively informal **4–106** atmosphere, is regarded as being a more friendly method of resolving disputes than proceedings before judges in national courts. There are more opportunities in an arbitration for informal meetings between the parties and their lawyers and experts on the one hand and the members of the arbitral tribunal on the other. This is something to be encouraged so long as such contacts take place openly.

Functions of the presiding arbitrator

The presiding arbitrator acts as chairman of the arbitral tribunal, and will often **4–107** be referred to as "the president" or "the chairman", not only in established rules of arbitration but also by the parties and their lawyers during the course of the

---

[50] See ICC Arbitration Rules, Art.21.3: "The arbitrator shall be in full charge of the hearings."

proceedings. The task of the presiding arbitrator is to take charge of the deliberations of the arbitral tribunal and of the conduct of any meetings and hearings. It is the presiding arbitrator's responsibility to make sure that the proceedings move forward as smoothly and effectively as possible.

Depending on the rules under which the arbitration is being conducted, the presiding arbitrator may have no more than a voice equal to that of the co-arbitrators when it comes to making decisions, but the presiding arbitrator is nevertheless first amongst equals. A presiding arbitrator sometimes receives greater remuneration than the other members of the arbitral tribunal (usually described as the "co-arbitrators" because of the more pro-active role and the additional responsibilities involved).[51] This is frequently done where the fees are fixed on a lump sum basis. If the arbitrators' fees are based on an hourly rate, the presiding arbitrator is likely to be paid more than the others, because of the additional hours spent on the case compared with the co-arbitrators.

(d) The role of an administrative secretary or registrar

4–108   The conduct of an international commercial arbitration may involve the sole or presiding arbitrator in a considerable amount of administrative work. As mentioned above, arrangements must be made for meetings between the parties and the arbitral tribunal. In a three-member arbitral tribunal there is necessarily a certain amount of interchange between the arbitrators themselves, as well as between the arbitrators and the parties or their representatives.

When it comes to hearings, it may be necessary for the arbitral tribunal to arrange for the presence of interpreters and for a transcript of the proceedings to be made. It is essential for the smooth running of the arbitration that these arrangements should be made, and in good time. Since the arrangements fall to be made by or on behalf of the arbitral tribunal itself, rather than by the parties, it is an established practice in large and complex international commercial arbitrations for the arbitral tribunal to appoint an administrative secretary or registrar to take charge of all the administrative arrangements that would otherwise fall to be made by the arbitral tribunal and to act as a link between the parties and the arbitral tribunal.

The administrative secretary or registrar usually opens a bank account in the name of the presiding arbitrator and collects deposits from the parties, generally in equal shares. The sums deposited are usually paid into an interest-bearing bank account, from which fees and expenses of the arbitral tribunal are paid. The administrative secretary normally attends all meetings of the arbitral tribunal; and also usually attends the hearings, so as to ensure that the various administrative procedures are running smoothly. For example, the administrative secretary may organise the attendance of witnesses and verify that the transcript accurately

---

[51] For a comprehensive review of the functions of the presiding arbitrator, see Reymond, "Le Président du Tribunal Arbitral" in *Etudes offertes à Pierre Bellet* (Editions Litec, Paris, 1991), pp.467–482, subsequently translated into English and published under the title "The President of the Arbitral Tribunal" in Foreign Investment Law Journal (ICSID Review), 1994(a), No.1, pp.1–16.

records the evidence given. However, although even if present, the administrative does not take an active part in the private deliberations of the arbitral tribunal that lead to the award. The task is to assist the arbitral tribunal, not to usurp its function.

Institutional arbitrations

There is less need for the appointment of an administrative secretary or **4–109** registrar where the arbitration is administered by an arbitral institution, since such institutions discharge some of the more important administrative functions such as the collection and payment of fees and expenses. However, even in an administered arbitration, many detailed arrangements still fall to be made by the arbitral tribunal itself. In a particularly large or complex dispute, the arbitral tribunal often welcomes the appointment of an administrative secretary or registrar, although a special arrangement may need to be made to meet the related fees and expenses since these do not traditionally form part of the institution's administrative expenses. The ICC issues guidelines to arbitral tribunals explaining its policy.

Who to appoint

The obvious person to appoint as an administrative secretary or registrar is a **4–110** young lawyer with some experience of international commercial arbitration and of the administrative problems to which it can give rise. The usual procedure is for the arbitral tribunal to choose its own administrative secretary or registrar, who is generally (although not invariably) a junior practising lawyer, PhD or other postgraduate student based in the same city as the presiding arbitrator. A moderate fee, appropriate to the nature of the duties, is paid—but at a much lower rate than the fees of the arbitrators. Even if (unusually) the arbitral tribunal contemplates paying the fees and expenses of an administrative secretary or registrar out of its own remuneration, it is important to obtain the agreement of the parties before the appointment is made.

Where the arbitral tribunal expects the parties to pay the fees and expenses *in addition* to those of the arbitral tribunal, such agreement is essential. In order to persuade the parties to give their consent, the presiding arbitrator will often point out to the parties that such an appointment will be cost effective for them, since many of the administrative functions that would be remunerated at the arbitrators' higher rate will be carried out at lower cost to the parties by an administrative secretary.

Where an administrative secretary is appointed it is essential that both the **4–111** presiding arbitrator and the administrative secretary should have a clear understanding of the limits of his or her functions. An arbitral tribunal has no authority to delegate any of its functions, unless such authority is granted expressly either by the parties directly or indirectly through a set of rules that the parties have adopted. The UNCITRAL Notes on Organizing Arbitral Proceedings state as follows:

"Administrative services might be secured by engaging a secretary of the arbitral tribunal (also referred to as registrar, clerk, administrator or *rapporteur*), who carries out the tasks under the direction of the arbitral tribunal. Some arbitral institutions routinely assign such persons to the cases administered by them. In arbitrations not administered by an institution or where the arbitral institution does not appoint a secretary, some arbitrators frequently engage such persons, at least in certain types of cases, whereas many others normally conduct the proceedings without them.

To the extent the tasks of the secretary are purely organisational (*e.g.* obtaining meeting rooms and providing or coordinating secretarial services), this is usually not controversial. Differences in views, however, may arise if the tasks include legal research and other professional assistance to the arbitral tribunal (*e.g.* collecting case law or published commentaries on legal issues defined by the arbitral tribunal, preparing summaries from case law and publications, and sometimes also preparing drafts of procedural decisions or drafts of certain parts of the award, in particular those concerning the facts of the case).

Views or expectations may differ especially where a task of the secretary is similar to professional functions of the arbitrators. Such a role of the secretary is in the view of some commentators inappropriate or is appropriate only under certain conditions, such as the parties agree thereto. However, it is typically recognized that it is important to ensure that the secretary does not perform any decision-making function of the arbitral tribunal."

4–112 Most arbitral institutions discourage their arbitral tribunals from appointing administrative secretaries. This seems to have its origins in an instinctive feeling that the institution itself can offer all the administrative support that is needed. This may be so with some types of cases, and with arbitrators who spend most of their time in their offices in their home cities. However, for busy international arbitrators who spend a good deal of time travelling, the need is to have someone constantly at their desk managing the files and taking telephone calls. With the best will in the world, no arbitral institution is in a position to provide that kind of support service.[52]

7. Fees and Expenses of the Arbitral Tribunal

4–113 The cost of bringing or defending a claim before an international arbitral tribunal is likely to be considerably higher than that of bringing or defending the same claim before a national court. This is because, in addition to the usual expenses of litigation, it is necessary for the parties to pay the fees and expenses

---

[52] For a commentary on the use of administarative secretaries, see Partasides, "The Fourth Arbitrator? The Role of Secretaries to Tribunals in International Arbitration" (2002) 18 Arbitration International 147.

of the arbitral tribunal and the cost of hiring suitable accommodation for hearings.

In addition, where the arbitration is administered by an arbitral institution, the fees and expenses of that institution must be paid. This contrasts sharply with proceedings before a national court, where the court rooms, the attendants and the judges themselves are provided and paid for by the state. The parties often make no more than a nominal contribution to the state by way of a registration fee or other levy.[53]

The fact that arbitration before a private arbitral tribunal attracts these additional charges makes it more desirable that arbitrations should not be conducted with all the time-consuming formalities of proceedings in a national court. The aim should be to make use of the informality and flexibility of the arbitral process, so as to reduce both the time spent on the case and the cost of conducting it. In this way, the financial burden on the parties will be alleviated to some extent.

(a) Who fixes fees?

In some systems of domestic arbitration, it is customary for arbitrators to provide their services free of charge, on a *"pro bono"* principle. This is most unusual in an international commercial arbitration. Indeed, it would be wrong to expect an international arbitrator to serve on this basis. The work and travel involved is such as to make the commitment "professional" in the full sense of that word and so deserving of appropriate remuneration.   **4–114**

Where an arbitration is conducted under the auspices of an arbitral institution, it is not necessary for the parties to engage in any direct negotiations with the tribunal concerning the basis of its fees. These are generally fixed by the institution, sometimes acting independently, sometimes after consultation with the sole or presiding arbitrator. The parties have no say in the matter. In an ad hoc arbitration, however, it is necessary for the parties to make their own arrangements with the arbitrators as to their fees. This should be done at an early stage in the proceedings, in order to avoid misunderstandings later. To avoid any suggestion of impropriety, any discussions with arbitrators concerning the amount to be paid to them should only take place in the presence of all the parties to the dispute, or their representatives.

(b) Commitment or cancellation fees

A complex arbitration may involve protracted proceedings in several separate stages. Arbitrators are sometimes asked to reserve weeks or even months for hearings in complicated cases. Even though long sequential hearings are rare in arbitrations involving three arbitrators, because of the difficulty of assembling all the players for an extended period, substantial blocks of time are carved out of   **4–115**

---

[53] Although in some countries the court fees are calculated on an *ad valorem* basis, and may become substantial when large sums of money are in dispute.

the arbitrators' diaries and other remunerative work during the reserved periods must be refused.

Three factors may lead to this time being lost. The first is that the parties may settle their dispute, thus leading to the cancellation of witness hearings. The second is for the parties to terminate the mandate of an arbitrator. The third, and most common, is where the parties have agreed to a procedural schedule that turns out to have been too ambitious, with the result that witness hearings have to be postponed.

Courts in England have held that the right to a commitment fee is not an implied term of the contract created when an appointment is accepted,[54] and that it would be misconduct for an arbitrator to require a commitment fee as a condition of continuing to perform his services if the appointment had been accepted without such a reservation. Where the arbitrators were asked to hold available a 60-day period some two years in the future, it was not improper for the arbitrators to *request* a commitment fee, although "it did not accord happily with their status to become involved in negotiations about fees" after their appointment.[55] Further, it would be inappropriate for an arbitrator to conclude an agreement for a commitment fee with one of the parties when the other party refuses to participate in the negotiations. In any event, once the appointment is accepted the parties are under no obligation to agree to any commitment or cancellation fees.

4–116   It is therefore important for the arbitrators, if they wish to have a commitment or cancellation fee in place, to agree the arrangements with the parties at the time of accepting their appointments. Furthermore, it is important for international arbitrators to understand that commitment and/or cancellation fees are acceptable in some cultural environments, but so unusual as to be unacceptable in others.

(c) Methods of assessing fees

4–117   No universally established method exists for assessing the fees payable to an arbitrator for taking part in an international commercial arbitration. At least three methods are in current use. First, the *ad valorem* method, where the fee is calculated as a proportion of the amounts in dispute; secondly, the "time spent" method, which establishes an hourly or daily rate for work done by an arbitrator on the case; and, thirdly, the "fixed fee" method, where the sum payable to the arbitrator by way of remuneration is fixed at the outset without direct reference either to the amounts in dispute or to the time which the arbitrator spends on the case.

The ad valorem *method*

4–118   This method entails assessing the arbitrators' fees as a percentage of the total amount in dispute (including any counterclaim). It has the merit of being easy to

---

[54] *K/S Norjarl A/S v Hyundai Heavy Industries Co Ltd* [1991] 1 Lloyd's Rep. 260; an appeal was dismissed [1992] Q.B. 863; [1991] 1 Lloyd's Rep. 524.
[55] *ibid.*

use and capable of uniform application. It is only necessary to know (a) the total amount in dispute and (b) the percentage figure to be applied. With this information, the parties can work out for themselves what fees they are likely to have to pay, if they take their dispute to arbitration. The ICC is the most prominent of the institutions which adopt this method.[56] The ICC Rules contain a "scale of administrative costs and fees" which shows how the administrative charges of the ICC Secretariat are calculated by applying a different percentage to each successive slice of the sum in dispute. The fees payable to the arbitrator or arbitrators may be calculated on a similar basis, except that the percentages are different and that, for each successive slice of the sum in dispute, minimum and maximum percentages are given, to establish a "range".[57] In practice the ICC's Court fixes the fees of the arbitrators within the overall range, taking into account the diligence of the arbitrators, time spent, the rapidity of the proceedings and the complexity of the dispute.[58]

It was at one time common for fees in many professions to be assessed on an *ad valorem* basis. In effect, it means that the large cases subsidise the small ones. However, the modern tendency is for the amount involved in a particular case (whilst being of some significance as showing the degree of responsibility carried) to be regarded as only *one* of the factors to be taken into account in assessing professional fees; and the time spent on a particular case, reflecting as it does a more accurate measure of the cost of doing the work, is regarded as the dominant factor.

The "time spent" method

The usual method of assessing fees is to establish a rate at which the arbitrators **4–119** will be paid for the time spent working on the case. This rate covers not only work done at the hearing of the arbitration, but also any work done outside the hearing. It is usual to establish an hourly or daily rate, or sometimes a combination of both—generally a daily rate (or a "cap") for hearing days and hourly rates for work undertaken outside the hearings. A lower daily or hourly rate is sometimes fixed for travelling time, when the arbitrator is not available to undertake other work.

The successful operation of a method of payment based on a time-spent rate depends on the arbitrators keeping an accurate record of the time that they actually spend on the case. It also depends on the parties being prepared to trust this record, since (apart from time spent at meetings with the parties and at the hearing) it is not something that can easily be checked. It may be that the presiding arbitrator should consider it to be one of his functions to monitor the fee invoices submitted by the co-arbitrators. In an UNCITRAL arbitration this is

---

[56] See Craig, Park & Paulsson, *International Chamber of Commerce Arbitration* (3rd ed., Oceana Publications, 2000).

[57] Where the case is submitted to more than one arbitrator, the ICC's Court has discretion to increase the fee up to a maximum of three times the fee payable to a single arbitrator.

[58] ICC Arbitration Rules, Appendix III, Art.11(2), available on the ICC's website, *www.iccarbitration.org* (search under "arbitration costs calculator").

more or less inevitable, since the Rules[59] provide that the arbitrators' fees shall be "reasonable in amount" and shall be stated separately as to each arbitrator in the award.

The hourly and/or daily rate is likely to vary according to the status of the arbitrator and the size, importance and complexity of the arbitration. It is in this context that the amount in dispute will be taken into account, where the time spent method is used.[60] Most international arbitrators with recognised reputations are prepared to accept that smaller cases should be undertaken at a rate lower than their "normal" rate.

The "fixed fee" method

4–120   There are cases in which arbitrators ask to be paid on a fixed fee basis. These cases are usually cases of major importance, involving arbitrators of high international standing. Where remuneration is to be paid to the arbitrators on a fixed fee basis the sum agreed is intended to cover all the work done by the arbitrators on the case, including time spent at the hearing, however long it may last.

The problem is that it is difficult to know at the outset of a case what figure to agree as a fixed fee. It is difficult to know how the case will develop; whether or not it will settle before it reaches a hearing; and if it does not settle, how long the hearing itself is likely to take.

The best that can be done, in such circumstances, is to make an intelligent assessment of the total number of days likely to be spent by the arbitrators on the case, assuming that it runs its full course, and then to multiply this total by an appropriate daily rate, so as to arrive at a figure for the fixed fee. The arbitrators may have done a similar calculation; alternatively, they may have applied a percentage to the total amount in dispute, so as to calculate the fee to which they consider themselves entitled! It may then be necessary for a certain amount of bargaining to take place between the arbitrators on the one hand and the parties on the other, in order to arrive at an agreed figure.

(d) Negotiating arbitrators' fees

4–121   Parties and their legal advisers may find themselves obliged to negotiate with arbitrators over the question of their fees, if they think that the arbitrators are asking for too much. There is no reason why this should not be done. The problem is that each party is reluctant to upset the arbitrators by appearing to

---

[59] See UNCITRAL Arbitration Rules, Arts 38(a) and 39.1.

[60] In 2004, daily fees fell in the range US$2,000 to US$4,500 and hourly rates ranged from approximately US$300 to US$600 for ad hoc arbitrations. The LCIA's range as of June 2003 was £150 to £350 per hour, covering both hearings and preparatory work. In March 2004 the ICSID fee scale was raised to US$2,400 per day or eight-hour period of work. The ICDR simply asks individual arbitrators to propose rates in the biographical notes kept by the institution, on the basis that market forces will provide adequate checks and balances. The ICC operates a scale fee system, in which time spent is only one of several factors taken into account when fees are fixed by its Court. Most of the other major arbitral institutions operate a scale based on the amount in dispute.

criticise their fees, because each party has it well in mind that, at the end of the day, the arbitrators will be sitting in judgment on their case. It may seem foolish to bargain over a few hundred dollars per day if, by doing so, a claim worth thousands or even millions of dollars may be put in jeopardy.

However, it is wrong to think in this way. Arbitrators of the right calibre should not take offence if it is suggested to them that they are proposing to charge rather more than the "going rate" for the job, so long as the suggestion is made with proper courtesy. It is essential that, if such a suggestion is made to the arbitrators, it should be made by *all* the lawyers representing parties to the dispute. On this issue at least, the lawyers involved in the case should present a united front to the arbitrators. It is bad form to attempt to gain favour with the arbitrators by suggesting that, whilst you consider their proposed fees to be eminently reasonable, your opponents are seeking a reduction!

(e) Expenses of the arbitral tribunal

The question of the expenses incurred by the arbitrators will also have to be **4–122** settled, unless the arbitration is being conducted under the auspices of an arbitral institution (such institutions collect money from the parties and reimburse the arbitrators, as part of their routine administrative functions). This falls naturally to be dealt with at the same time as the question of the arbitrators' fees. The costs of air or train travel are invariably simply reimbursed on an "as incurred" basis. Two points must be clarified between the arbitral tribunal and the parties. The first concerns the class of travel[61] which, in order to avoid embarrassment later, should be established at the beginning. The second is to confirm that the arbitrators may claim immediate reimbursement of their expenses, rather than waiting for the end of the case or for the next stage payment date for fees. There is no justification for asking the arbitrators to fund the cash flow for the arbitral process.

This is all relatively straightforward. Less easy is the question of subsistence expenses. Broadly speaking, there are two methods of dealing with arbitrators' subsistence expenses. The first may be described as the "reimbursement method"; the second as the "*per diem* method".

The reimbursement method

If this method is adopted, the arbitrators must keep a detailed note of their **4–123** expenditure in connection with their work on the case, including air fares, hotel expenses and so on. Then, from time to time, they arrange to have these expenses reimbursed, by submitting details to the relevant arbitral institution, to a designated member or member of the arbitral tribunal (if there is one) or to the administrative secretary or registrar, or to the parties direct, as the case may be.

---

[61] The ICC's instructions to arbitrators enables them to be reimbursed for business class travel for flights of less than six hours' duration, and first class for longer flights. Thus flights between the US and Europe are generally mandated for first class travel; although in fact many ICC arbitrators make transatlantic flights in business class other than in exceptional circumstances.

Sometimes, a limit may be imposed on the amount for which an arbitrator is reimbursed (for example, in respect of hotel expenses) and any expenditure over this limit is then for the account of the arbitrator personally.

The per diem *method*

4–124   The alternative method is for the parties to pay an amount fixed at a daily rate to cover hotel and other subsistence expenses. This daily, or *per diem* rate, is fixed at a level sufficient to cover the cost of living away from home at a hotel of good standard at the place of arbitration. It will also cover incidental expenses such as meals, taxis, telephone calls and so on. It is paid to the arbitrator as a fixed amount of money, calculated on a *per diem* basis by reference to the number of days spent on the case, away from home. It is then for the arbitrator to meet the actual expenses out of this fixed allowance and to pay any excess personally. The ICC operates a *per diem* rate for reimbursement of subsistence expenses.[62]

There can be little doubt that, of the two methods discussed, the *per diem* method is better. It avoids the detailed clerical work of checking payments against receipts or other vouchers; and it also avoids prying into an arbitrator's style of living, so as to decide whether a particular expense was or was not necessary in the interests of the proper conduct of the arbitration. The *per diem* method should generally be adopted in any international commercial arbitration where payment of the arbitrators' expenses is the direct responsibility of the parties themselves or of the administrative secretary or registrar appointed by the arbitral tribunal.

The ICSID *system*

4–125   Although the methods discussed above are the methods most commonly encountered in practice for the payment of arbitrators' expenses, variations on these basic themes may be found. For instance, ICSID offer arbitrators some choice in the method of claiming their expenses. An arbitrator in an ICSID arbitration is entitled to the following allowances for attending meetings or hearings in connection with the case:

- the actual cost of air travel at "one class above coach", by air or other means of transport, "coach" being economy class;

- an "in-out" allowance of a fixed sum, to cover the costs of porterage, taxis, tips and other expenses of travelling;

- the actual cost of transport within the city in which the arbitration is taking place; and

---

[62] The standard ICC *per diem* allowance in 2004 was US$400; however, arbitrators could claim reimbursement of up to US$500 where supporting receipts are supplied.

- a *per diem* allowance, either at the full rate or at the so called "mixed rate".[63]

The last item on this list merits particular comment. Under the ICSID system, the full *per diem* rate varies from place to place, with different rates being established for different cities, according to whether or not they are "high-cost cities". As an alternative to claiming the full *per diem* rate, arbitrators may claim reimbursement under the "mixed rate". On this basis, reimbursement may be claimed for the actual cost of a hotel room (plus tax and service charge) together with an allowance of one-half of the applicable full *per diem* rate, to cover meals, tips and other expenses.

In practice, arbitrators taking part in an ICSID arbitration tend to choose reimbursement on the "mixed rate" basis unless otherwise agreed, since this comes nearest to covering the expenses likely to be incurred in staying, for instance, at a hotel in Washington, where arbitrations under the ICSID Rules usually take place.

(g) Securing payment of the fees and expenses of the arbitral tribunal

The question of establishing effective arrangements with regard to fees and **4–126** expenses is as important for the arbitrators as it is for the parties. The fact that arbitrators may become *functus officio* instantly at the joint will of the parties emphasises the importance for the arbitrators of obtaining adequate security for payment of their fees and expenses. The acceptance by the arbitrators of the functions bestowed upon them creates a legal relationship between the parties and the members of the arbitral tribunal. This relationship carries with it an implied undertaking by the parties to compensate the members of the arbitral tribunal fairly in respect of their work and expenses, whether or not an award is issued. However, even under those national systems of law where this is clear,[64] arbitrators do not usually wish to go to the trouble and cost of suing the parties for their fees and expenses.

Where the arbitration is being administered by an established arbitral institution, the arbitral tribunal need not concern itself with the collection of payments on account of its fees and expenses. This part of the administration of the case is handled by the arbitral institution concerned. In any other case, however, the arbitral tribunal should arrange for the parties to make sufficient deposits in respect of its fees and expenses.[65] There are two reasons for this: first, it helps the parties to keep a check on expenses as the case proceeds; and secondly, it is easier to collect payments from the parties whilst the arbitration is in progress than when the proceedings are over.

---

[63] The standard ICSID *per diem* allowance for subsistence expenses (*i.e.* meals, taxis, etc.) in 2004 was US$115; however, special *per diem* allowances of US$135, US$170 or US$185 applied for certain high-cost cities (*e.g.* US$170 for Washington, which is in the second highest category).

[64] See, *e.g.*, English Arbitration Act 1996, s.28.

[65] The UNCITRAL Rules make provision for this in Art.41.

A bank account should be opened for receipt of the deposits made by the parties. This account may then also be used for paying fees and expenses to the members of the arbitral tribunal as and when payments fall due. Any interest earned on the account should be credited to the account (and accordingly be accrued for the benefit of the parties). The account is usually opened in the name of the arbitral tribunal, with the sole arbitrator or the presiding arbitrator as signatory on the account. If an administrative secretary or registrar has been appointed, the maintenance and operation of the account should be one of that person's responsibilities.

CHAPTER 5

POWERS, DUTIES AND JURISDICTION OF AN ARBITRAL TRIBUNAL

1. BACKGROUND

(a) Generally

An arbitral tribunal established to determine an international commercial **5–01** dispute operates in an entirely different context from a judge sitting in a national court. Normally the judge sits in a legal environment that clearly defines the extent of his powers and duties. He is generally given full immunity in respect of any potential liability arising out of the conduct of his judicial function; and his jurisdiction, and the extent to which his decisions in relation to jurisdiction may be reviewed by an appellate court, are clearly established in the law governing the proceedings.

The position differs in arbitration, particularly in international arbitration, where the powers, duties and jurisdiction of an arbitral tribunal arise from a complex mixture of the will of the parties, the law governing the arbitration agreement, the law of the place of arbitration,[1] and the law of the place where recognition or enforcement of the award may be sought.

(b) Practical considerations

A balance must be struck between the sanctions that may be imposed on **5–02** arbitrators who carry out their functions in a careless or improper manner, and the equally necessary requirement that an arbitral tribunal should be able to perform its task without constantly "looking over its shoulder" in the fear of being challenged through legal process. On one view, it may be argued that arbitrators should be given virtually unlimited powers, in order to encourage speed and effectiveness in the arbitral process; but the requirements of public policy, whether national or international,[2] make some control necessary so as to ensure that the parties are not without recourse if there is wrongful conduct on the part of an arbitral tribunal. A single judge sitting in a court of first instance is usually subject to control by an appellate procedure. Although the modern trend is to

---

[1] Or, exceptionally, the law to which the parties have agreed to subject the arbitration; see Ch.2, paras 2–93 *et seq.*

[2] See Ch.10, paras 10–51 *et seq.*

allow decisions of arbitral tribunals to go unchallenged, so that they are effectively final and binding upon the parties, the need for some control over the way in which these decisions are reached is recognised by most, if not quite all, systems of law. In particular, it is considered important to ensure that an arbitral tribunal gives the parties a fair hearing and that it decides only matters within its competence, or jurisdiction.[3]

The normal, and generally effective, system for the protection of parties against excesses on the part of arbitral tribunals is contained in a framework for recourse against the award itself.[4] However, some national laws also permit another level of control imposed more directly upon individual arbitrators. Thus, arbitrators may be removed for certain types of wrongful conduct; this may be done under the rules of an arbitral institution, where applicable; or (in some circumstances) under the law governing the arbitration agreement; or, more usually, under the law governing the arbitration itself, by an application to the courts of the country in which the arbitration takes place.

The powers and duties of an arbitral tribunal are also closely aligned with the question of its jurisdiction (and in particular its jurisdiction to determine the extent of its own jurisdiction) and the difficult question of determining the validity of the arbitration agreement. These matters are reviewed in this chapter. First, the powers of the arbitral tribunal and the duties imposed upon it are considered; secondly the question of the jurisdiction of the arbitral tribunal to decide the particular dispute before it is reviewed.

2. POWERS OF ARBITRATORS

(a) Generally

5–03   The powers of an arbitral tribunal are those conferred upon it by the parties themselves within the limits allowed by the applicable law,[5] together with any additional powers that may be conferred by operation of law. In principle, these powers should be sufficient for the arbitral tribunal to carry out its task properly and effectively.

In a well-conducted international commercial arbitration, control of the proceedings moves smoothly from the parties to the arbitral tribunal. At first the parties are fully in charge. They alone know the issues in dispute, how they intend to set about proving the facts upon which they place reliance and the arguments of law they propose to put forward. The case which is to be put to the arbitral tribunal is "their" case. Indeed, the arbitral tribunal owes its very

---

[3] This was explicitly recognised in the English Arbitration Act 1996, s.33. For a discussion of the importance of this provision see the Departmental Advisory Committee on Arbitration Law Report on the Arbitration Bill 1996 (February 1996), paras 150–163. See also Ch.10.

[4] For further discussion of this subject, see Ch.9.

[5] So far as the tribunal's *powers* are concerned, the applicable law is usually the proper law of the arbitration agreement and the law of the place of arbitration; for discussion of applicable law generally, see Ch.2, paras 2–01 *et seq.*

existence to the parties; it is "their" arbitral tribunal. As the proceedings develop, however, the arbitral tribunal becomes increasingly familiar with the matters in dispute. It begins to decide for itself which facts it regards as relevant and which questions of law it regards as important. It is in a position to start making known its views as to how the case should be presented within the framework of the particular rules which govern the proceedings, whether these are ad hoc or the rules of an arbitral institution. The balance of power, in effect, shifts from the parties to the arbitral tribunal. It is right that this should be so. The arbitrators, not the parties, are the final judges of the matters in dispute. However, this shift in the balance of power only happens if the arbitrators themselves know when and how to take charge of the proceedings, and, in particular, if they understand the armoury of weapons their position puts at their command.

(b) Powers conferred by the parties

The parties may confer powers upon the arbitral tribunal directly or indirectly, **5–04** but only within the limits of the relevant law.[6] Any excess of power (that is to say, any power granted over and above that allowed by the relevant law) is invalid, even if it is contained in international or institutional rules of arbitration.

Directly

A "direct" conferment of powers takes place when the parties agree expressly **5–05** upon the powers they wish the arbitrators to exercise, possibly by setting them out in the terms of appointment, or some other special agreement to cover these matters. Such powers are likely to include the power to order production of documents, to appoint experts, to hold hearings and receive evidence, to inspect the subject matter of the dispute and so forth. The ways in which these powers may be expressly conferred upon the arbitral tribunal in submission agreements have been described in more detail earlier.[7]

Indirectly

An "indirect" conferment of powers takes place when the arbitration is **5–06** conducted according to rules of arbitration, whether institutional or ad hoc (such as UNCITRAL). Such rules confer certain express powers upon the arbitral tribunal. The UNCITRAL Rules, for instance, contain a general power for the arbitral tribunal to "conduct the arbitration in such manner as it considers appropriate, provided that the parties are treated with equality and that at any stage of the proceedings each party is given a full opportunity of presenting his case."[8] These Rules also confer specific powers, including:

- power to determine the place of arbitration, unless agreed by the parties[9];

---

[6] The "relevant law" is discussed below.
[7] See Ch.3, paras 3–01 *et seq.*
[8] UNCITRAL Arbitration Rules, Art.15.1.
[9] *ibid.*, Art.16.1.

- power to determine the language or languages of the proceedings, unless agreed by the parties[10];

- power to appoint experts[11]; and

- power to determine the law applicable to the substance of the dispute, unless agreed by the parties.[12]

The ICC Rules contain similar powers although, since the ICC's Court administers arbitrations, some of these powers may be conferred on the institution itself. For example, the place of arbitration is determined by the ICC's Court, unless it has been chosen by agreement of the parties.[13] Other institutional rules follow a similar pattern.[14]

(c) Powers conferred by operation of law

5–07   The powers conferred upon an arbitral tribunal by the parties, whether directly or indirectly, fall short of the powers which may be exercised by a national court. Such courts derive their authority from the state, and have formidable coercive powers at their disposal to ensure obedience to their orders. An arbitral tribunal does not possess such powers.[15] The parties cannot confer upon a private tribunal the coercive powers over property and persons that are conferred by the state on a national court. In recognition of this fact, many systems of law supplement the powers of arbitral tribunals. This may be done by:

- giving powers directly to arbitral tribunals;

- authorising national courts to exercise powers on behalf of arbitral tribunals or the parties themselves; or

- a combination of these two methods.

English law, for example, adopts a combination. The 1996 Act contains provisions expressly conferring procedural powers on arbitral tribunals. These include the power to:

- order a claimant to provide security for costs[16];

---

[10] *ibid.*, Art.17.1.
[11] *ibid.*, Art.27.1.
[12] *ibid.*, Art.33.1.
[13] ICC Rules, Art.14.1.
[14] *e.g.* LCIA Rules Art.16.1; ICDR Rules, Art.13.1.
[15] An interesting exception is Colombia, where the arbitrators are given a degree of *imperium* by the state and can enforce their orders directly as if they were a court of law. See Mantilla Serrano "Colombia" in *International Arbitration in Latin America*, eds. Blackaby, Lindsey, Spinillo (Kluwer, 2003) 122.
[16] English Arbitration Act 1996, s.38(3). The arbitral tribunal can enforce this order by dismissing the claim if it is not complied with: s.41(6).

- administer oaths to witnesses[17]; and

- generally determine procedural matters.[18]

The English 1996 Act also sets out the powers of the national *courts* in relation to arbitral proceedings. There are two types. First, the court acts as a "back-up" by ordering a party to comply with any peremptory order of the tribunal.[19] This effectively converts the breach of the tribunal's order into a contempt of court. Secondly, a court can assist a tribunal by making its own orders in relation to the proceedings.[20] These include orders freezing a party's assets (known as freezing injunctions)[21]; orders permitting the seizure of relevant evidence (known as search orders)[22]; and orders securing the attendance of witnesses.[23]

Other orders a court may make, such as an order requiring property to be **5–08** preserved, produced or photographed as an exhibit, are also clearly within the powers of an arbitral tribunal.[24] However the potential for overlapping jurisdiction is minimised by a requirement that English courts can only make orders in relation to an arbitration (as opposed to enforcing an order made by an arbitral tribunal) where the "tribunal has no power or is for the time being unable to act effectively".[25]

The English 1996 Act provides a good example, in theory at least, of how arbitral tribunals and national courts can work together to make the arbitration regime effective. An arbitral tribunal sitting in London may administer an oath to a witness who gives evidence before it. However, if the witness is not prepared to appear at the hearing voluntarily, the arbitral tribunal cannot compel attendance. This coercive power can only be exercised by the national courts. Accordingly, a party seeking to compel the attendance of a witness must apply to the court for an order that the witness should attend.[26]

This range of powers, whether exercised directly by the arbitral tribunal itself or indirectly by application to the courts, provides the support from *national* legal systems that *international* arbitration requires to achieve its purpose. Almost all developed systems of law assist in the conduct of arbitrations taking place within their territory. However, the interrelationship between the powers conferred on an arbitral tribunal by the parties to the dispute and those conferred by operation of law may pose problems.

---

[17] *ibid*, s.38(5).
[18] *ibid.*, s.34. This power is also granted by the Model Law, Art.19(1).
[19] *ibid.*, s.42. A court can only make such orders if it is satisfied that the person to whom the tribunal's order was directed has had sufficient time to comply.
[20] *ibid.*, ss.43 and 44.
[21] *ibid.*, s.44(3).
[22] *ibid.*, s.44(2)(c).
[23] *ibid.*, s.43(2).
[24] *ibid.*, s.38(4).
[25] *ibid.*, s.44(5). The UNCITRAL Model Law also avoid the risk of dual competence by stating in Art.5 that "in matters governed by this Law, no court shall intervene except where so provided in this Law".
[26] *ibid.*, s.43. A similar provision appears in most national arbitration laws. For another example see the German Arbitration Law 1998, s.1050.

5-09   It is not enough simply to refer to the arbitration agreement (including any institutional or international rules that may be incorporated in that agreement) in order to determine the powers of the arbitral tribunal; any relevant provisions of the law governing the arbitration agreement, and of the law governing the arbitration, must also be taken into account. These provisions usually extend the powers conferred by the parties; in some circumstances, however, they may restrict the powers which the parties have conferred, or have purported to confer, upon the arbitral tribunal. As already indicated, any such "excess" power is invalid, as are any orders or decisions made in reliance upon it.

In practice, the best approach when considering the powers of an arbitral tribunal is to look first at the arbitration agreement; then at the law governing the arbitration agreement; and finally at the law governing the arbitration.

The arbitration agreement should be considered to establish what powers the parties themselves have agreed to confer on the arbitral tribunal. In general, these powers are either set out in the submission agreement or in the rules to which the arbitration has been subjected.

5-10   The law governing the arbitration agreement should then be considered to identify the way in which it supplements or restricts the powers the parties have conferred, or have purported to confer, upon the arbitral tribunal. The law of the arbitration agreement, which governs its validity, effect and interpretation, may confer specific powers (or impose certain limitations) upon the arbitral tribunal.[27]

Finally, the law governing the arbitration itself, the *lex arbitri*, should be considered to see whether it supplements or restricts the powers the parties have conferred, or purported to confer, on the arbitral tribunal. An example of such a restriction is an arbitration agreement governed by English law, but which provides for the arbitration to take place in Zurich. The arbitration agreement might include an express provision that the arbitrator is entitled to administer oaths to any witnesses in the arbitration; if it did not, English law (if it were the *lex arbitri*) would imply such a provision.[28] The law of Switzerland, however, does not permit a private individual, such as an arbitrator, to administer oaths. This is a mandatory provision of Swiss law and, as the law governing the arbitration, would override the express or implied provisions of the arbitration agreement.

3. DUTIES OF ARBITRATORS

(a) Generally

5-11   Just as some directors of limited liability companies accept their appointments with only the vaguest notion of the legal duties they owe to the public at large,

---

[27] See, *e.g.*, New Zealand Arbitration Act 1998, s.2.12; Swiss Private International Law Act 1987, Art.183; Brazilian Arbitration Law 1996, Art.22.
[28] English Arbitration Act 1996, s.12.

and to the creditors and shareholders in particular, there are people prepared to accept appointment as an arbitrator without having an adequate knowledge of the duties and commitment involved. The blame for this rests primarily with the parties themselves, rather than with prospective arbitrators. The qualities required in an international arbitrator have been discussed above[29]; it is for the parties to ensure that a prospective appointee possesses those qualities.

The parties should also make specific enquiries to ensure that a prospective arbitrator is able and willing to give sufficient commitment to the case in terms of time and priority. The person approached must be given enough information in order to answer such questions. What volume of documents must be studied? Within what timescale? When and where will meetings or hearings be held? How long are they likely to take? The parties cannot expect a prospective arbitrator to make a realistic assessment of the commitment required without this information.

The duties of an arbitrator may be subdivided into three categories: duties imposed by the parties; duties imposed by law; and ethical duties. It is a useful discipline for an arbitral tribunal to draw up for itself a checklist of its specific duties, whatever their origin. Such a list will differ from case to case, since it must allow for the impact of different rules of arbitration and for the differing laws applicable to each case

(b) Duties imposed by the parties

Specific duties may be imposed upon an arbitral tribunal by the parties. This **5–12** may be done before the arbitrators are appointed, or during the course of the arbitration, or both. If it is done before the appointment of arbitrators (for example, in an ad hoc submission agreement) each arbitrator should check the agreement before accepting the appointment, in case it imposes unreasonable duties, or duties that are incapable of fulfilment. For example, there might be a provision that the award should be made within a limited time after the appointment of the arbitral tribunal; if the agreed timescale is unacceptable to the arbitrator, and cannot be changed, the appointment should be declined.

Duties may also be imposed on the arbitral tribunal during the course of the proceedings by the parties, but usually only after consultation with the arbitral tribunal. For example, in a dispute arising out of a construction project, the parties may decide that they wish the arbitral tribunal to inspect the construction site even though this is in some distant country. The proposal for such a site inspection would usually be discussed with, and agreed by, the arbitral tribunal; but if a particular arbitrator were unable to accept the proposal and the parties insisted upon it, the arbitrator concerned would have no option but to resign.

Where the arbitration is conducted under the auspices of rules of arbitration, the applicable rules impose specific duties on the arbitral tribunal, in addition to any imposed by the parties themselves. A review of the rules of two arbitral

---

[29] See Ch.4, paras 4–39 *et seq.*

institutions indicates what sort of duties these might be. Under the ICSID Rules an arbitrator must, before or at the first session, sign a declaration as to independence and readiness to judge fairly as between the parties, in default of which he or she is deemed to have resigned.[30] Under the same rules, the arbitral tribunal must meet for its first session within 60 days of its constitution or such other period as the parties to the arbitration may agree[31]; it must keep its deliberations secret[32]; it must take decisions by a majority vote[33]; and it must give reasons for its award.[34] The ICC Rules also impose their own obligations upon arbitral tribunals—to draw up terms of reference[35]; to make an award within a defined period of time[36]; to submit the award in draft form to the ICC's Court for scrutiny[37]; and so forth. In the same way, other rules of arbitration impose specific duties on arbitral tribunals operating under their rules.

5–13   The only safe way to ascertain the specific duties of an arbitral tribunal is to look at the terms of its appointment, including any particular rules that apply to that appointment. The duties of an arbitral tribunal may cover a varied range. Some may complement the specific powers conferred upon the arbitral tribunal by the parties. For example, where arbitrators are instructed to determine a dispute as *amiables compositeurs* then, subject to any contrary provisions of the applicable law, they are under a duty so to decide.

(c) Duties imposed by law

5–14   Other duties are imposed by law. For instance, the law may require an arbitral tribunal to decide all procedural and evidential matters,[38] to treat the parties fairly and impartially,[39] or make the award in a particular form.[40]

Duty to act with due care

5–15   It is generally recognised that members of a profession, such as lawyers, doctors, accountants, architects and engineers, are under a duty to carry out their professional work with proper skill and care and may be held liable in damages at the suit of an injured party if they fail to do so. In the course of their professional work, such professionals may well be required to formulate a

---

[30] ICSID Arbitration Rules, r.6(2).
[31] *ibid.*, r.13(1).
[32] *ibid.*, r.15.1.
[33] *ibid.*, r.16.1.
[34] *ibid.*, r.47.1(i).
[35] ICC Arbitration Rules, Art.18.1.
[36] *ibid.*, Art.24.1. Unless extended by the ICC's Court under Art.24.2, this time-limit is six months.
[37] *ibid.*, Art.27.
[38] English Arbitration Act 1996, s.34.
[39] *ibid.*, s.33(1)(a).
[40] Such as in writing or with reasons (see, *e.g.*, Art.1448 of the Mexican Commercial Code).

decision binding upon two or more parties. For example, an architect may be required, under a standard form of building contract, to certify the value of work as it is performed, by issuing interim certificates; if due care is not applied so that (for instance) the amount certified is too large and the employer loses money in consequence, the architect may be compelled by legal action to make good the loss caused by his or her negligence.[41] Equally, an accountant may be asked to determine the value of shares in a private company in a way that will be binding upon the parties to an agreement. In this case also, if the accountant acts without due care and a party suffers loss, he or she may be sued in respect of negligence.[42]

The distinction between a professional adviser who formulates a decision binding upon two or more parties in the course of a professional activity and an arbitrator who formulates a decision binding upon two or more parties in the course of an arbitration is not easy to identify. It seems appropriate to expect the same standard of professional care from a lawyer (or an accountant, architect or engineer) who is serving as an arbitrator as would be expected in the course of other professional work. The parties to an arbitration entrust an arbitral tribunal with an important task for which they are prepared to pay, often quite generously. They expect the arbitrator to perform the task with due care. There exists an obvious moral duty to do so. The question is whether there exists also a legal duty.

This question goes to the heart of the relationship between the arbitrator and the parties.[43] As the practice of international commercial arbitration becomes increasingly sophisticated, and as the sums at stake grow in size, a party who has suffered loss through manifest lack of care by an arbitrator may wish to seek to recover that loss from the arbitrator personally.

So how can a breach by the arbitrator of the obligation to act with due care be **5–16** sanctioned? This will depend on the nature of the relationship with the parties. There are two schools of thought. The first school considers that the relationship between the arbitrator and the parties is established by contract. The second school may be identified as the "status" school which considers that the judicial

---

[41] As in the English case *Sutcliffe v Thackrah* [1974] A.C. 727; [1974] 1 Lloyd's Rep. 312, HL.

[42] *Arenson v Arenson* [1977] A.C. 405; [1976] 1 Lloyd's Rep. 179, HL.

[43] The position in English law was discussed in Mustill & Boyd, *Commercial Arbitration* (2nd ed., 1989), p.220, where it was suggested that the position of an arbitrator might be governed by contract, quasi-contract or status. The authors suggested that it would be wrong to define the relationship between the parties and the arbitrator in contractual terms and that their preference was in favour of the "status" approach (pp.222–223): " . . . with a little ingenuity a contract between these two persons could undoubtedly be devised. We suggest, however, that this would be a mistake. To proceed by finding a contract and then applying to it the ordinary principles of the law of contract will not produce a reliable answer unless a contract really exists to be found. Even in the extreme case of a massive reference, employing a professional arbitrator for a substantial remuneration, we doubt whether a business man would, if he stopped to think, concede that he was making a contract when appointing the arbitrator. Such an appointment is not like appointing an accountant, architect or lawyer. Indeed it is not like anything else at all."

nature of an arbitrator's function should result in a treatment assimilated to that of a judge. In some jurisdictions, such assimilation may give rise to immunity; in others it simply results in the application of rules on judicial liability.[44]

The contractual school considers that an arbitrator is appointed by or on behalf of the parties to an arbitration to perform a service (that of resolving a dispute between them) for a fee. In these circumstances, a contractual relationship arises between the parties and the arbitrator. The terms of this contract may be set out in the submission to arbitration, the relevant rules of arbitration, the terms of reference or terms of appointment. Other terms may be imposed by operation of law and include the duty to act with due diligence and the duty to act judicially.

The contractual approach finds favour in most civil law jurisdictions. Austrian law, for instance, takes the position that there is a contract between the arbitrator and the parties. This contract (*Schiedsrichtervertrag*), although it resembles a contract for services, is considered to be *sui generis* by some authors.[45] Certain duties, as well as rights, are imposed upon an arbitrator under the contract. One of the rights is a right to remuneration; the duties include conducting the proceedings in an appropriate way and making an award. The Austrian Code of Civil Procedure provides that an arbitrator who does not fulfil the duties assumed by accepting an appointment, or who does not fulfil them in due time, may be liable to the parties for loss caused by wrongful behaviour.[46] Nevertheless liability in respect of procedural mistakes and wrong decisions is limited to damage caused by intent or gross negligence.[47]

5–17 A similar position is adopted by Dutch law. An arbitrator is held to be in contractual relationship with the parties and may be liable for damages in the event of committing "gross negligence".[48]

Other jurisdictions, such as Argentina, consider that the arbitral contract renders arbitrators liable for losses caused by any failure to perform duties: "acceptance by arbitrators of their appointment shall entitle the parties to compel them to carry out their duties and to hold them liable for costs and damages derived from the non-performance of arbitral duties."[49]

---

[44] For a detailed study on the sources of arbitral liability and the implications in connection with immunity, see Franck, "The Liability of International Arbitrators: A Comparative Analysis and Proposal for Qualified Immunity" (2000) 20 N.Y.L.Sch. J.Int'l & Comp.L. 1. For a discussion of the status of the arbitrator see Fouchard, "Relationships between the Arbitrator and the Parties and the Arbitral Institution" published in "The Status of the Arbitrator", ICC International Court of Arbitration Bulletin (December, 1995) p.12 at pp.22–23; and P. Jolidon *Commentaire Concordat Suisse sur l'Arbitrage* (Staempfli ed., Berne, 1984), p.231.

[45] See Melis in *The Immunity of Arbitrators* (Lew ed., Lloyd's, 1990), p.18.

[46] See Melis, *A Guide to Commercial Arbitration in Austria* (1983), pp.16 and 17.

[47] *ibid.*

[48] van den Berg in *The Immunity of Arbitrators* (Lew ed., Lloyd's, 1990), p.59. See also the Swiss Condordat, Art.14, which describes arbitrators as accepting a "commission" (*mandat*).

[49] National Code of Civil and Commercial Procedure, Art.745. A virtually identical provision is contained at Art.18 of the Peruvian General Arbitration Law.

The "status" school is based on the performance by arbitrators of a judicial or quasi-judicial function, which grants an element of "status" entitling them to treatment similar to that of a judge. In most common law jurisdictions, this leads to certain immunities. Their independence must therefore be protected.[50] Courts in common law countries are prepared to extend immunity to arbitrators on such grounds,[51] although they may qualify the immunity where the arbitrator has acted in bad faith.[52]

Specifically, arbitrators and arbitral institutions in the US enjoy the broadest **5–18** degree of immunity from suit for actions taken within their duties.[53] Arbitrators acting in England cannot be held liable for the performance of their arbitral functions unless bad faith can be proved.[54] Similarly, arbitrators in New Zealand and Australia cannot be held liable for negligence.[55] This common law approach has now been followed by institutions such as the ICC and the LCIA, which have adopted rules seeking to exclude liability both for arbitrators and for the institution. Nevertheless, some commentators from common law systems are questioning the appropriateness of almost absolute immunity for arbitrators and several have argued that arbitrators have professional duties of care, skill and diligence, and should be liable for breach of such duties.[56]

---

[50] See, *e.g.*, Gabriel M. Wilner, *Domke on Commercial Arbitration* (1992), para.23.01.

[51] See, *e.g.*, *Corey v New York Stock Exchange* 691 F.2d 1205 (6th Cir. 1982) at 1209; *Sutcliffe v Thackrah* [1974] A.C. 727 at 735D; *Pickens v Templeton* [1994] 2 N.Z.L.R. 718 at 727–728 (although a valuer was technically classified as an arbitrator by the Arbitration Act 1908, his actions were not sufficiently judicial to justify immunity, as they were based on his expertise and he did not make a final determination of the dispute); *Zittrer v Sport Maska Inc* (Quebec Court of Appeal) [1985] C.A. 386 at 392 (referred to in National Report on Canada, in *International Handbook*, above, Supp.16, October 1993, p.19).

[52] The laws of Australia, Canada, England and New Zealand all provide that arbitrators may be liable for fraud, bad faith or intentional actions. In the US, however, arbitrator immunity is only subject to rare exceptions: see, *e.g. Lundgren v Freeman* 307 F.2d 104 (9th Cir. 1962) at 118 and *Grane v Grane*, above, at 1119.

[53] Branson & Wallace in *The Immunity of Arbitrators* (Lew ed., Lloyd's, 1990), p.85. It is said that immunity of arbitrators in the US is absolute in contrast with the qualified immunity in Austria, Germany and Norway and no immunity in France, Spain and Sweden: see Introduction by Lew in *The Immunity of Arbitrators, op. cit.* For further information see "Arbitral Immunity" in *Lawyers' Arbitration Letter* (V. Young ed., AAA, 1990), Vol. 14, No.4; and M. Hoellering "The Role of the Arbitrator: an AAA Perspective" in "The Status of the Arbitrator", ICC International Court of Arbitration Bulletin (December 1995) p.59 at pp.65–66.

[54] English Arbitration Act 1996, s.29. See also s.74 which grants the same immunity to arbitral institutions, appointing authorities and their respective employees.

[55] New Zealand Arbitration Act 1996, s.13; Australian International Arbitration Act 1974, s.28 (this Act was amended in 1992 to incorporate the UNCITRAL Model Law), ICC Arbitration Rules, Art.34.

[56] David Bristow argues that the Canadian courts may soon move away from the concept of absolute immunity, allowing claims for professional negligence, and notes that in the case of *Cohen Highley Vogel Dawson v Bon Appétit Restaurant* (1999) 44 O.R. (3d) 731, in assessing the accounts of the arbitrator, the court applied the same standards as are applied to lawyers (see David I. Bristow Q.C., "The gathering storm of arbitrators' and mediators' liability" in (2000) 4 Alternative Dispute Resolution Journal 312 at 315; Manfred Arnold states that there is an actual duty on the arbitrator to exercise impartiality, skill, care and diligence (see Manfred W. Arnold, *What price immunity of arbitrators?* (Maritime Advocate, 1999)).

In many civil law countries, however, the conferring of a quasi-judicial status does not result in immunity. In Chile, for example, arbitrators are liable in the same way as judges for "deliberate actions which cause damage to the parties or to a third party".[57]

A rigid categorisation of the source of an arbitrator's obligation to act with due care risks obscuring the real debate. This is whether it is appropriate as a matter of policy to accord immunity or partial immunity to arbitrators. Public policy in this context is mainly concerned with the independence and integrity of the decision-making process, which could be jeopardised if, as a result of liability, arbitrators were subject to reprisals by disappointed parties.[58]

5–19 Other arguments in favour of immunity are that: it helps ensure the finality of arbitral awards, by preventing an unsuccessful party from suing the arbitrator[59]; fewer skilled persons would be prepared to act as arbitrators if they carried the risk of incurring substantial liability[60]; arbitrators have no interest in the outcome of the dispute and should not be compelled to become parties to it; and it ensures the protection of the public, in the cases where truly judicial functions are exercised (presumably by unburdening the courts of many disputes). Some commentators go so far as to base arbitral immunity entirely on public policy grounds, arguing that immunity can only satisfactorily be explained as a concession from the state, which weighs the potential wrongs caused by such immunity against the benefits of arbitration.[61]

But the arguments are not all one way. There are a number of policy arguments against immunity: immunity may encourage carelessness; the finality of the decision is given priority over individual justice; disciplinary remedies are generally unavailable against arbitrators; and alternative remedies such as *vacatur* of the award and withholding of fees are inadequate.

One substantial concern is the lack of uniformity in approach. The source of the arbitrator's duties and the public policy of the state in which the arbitrator is acting need to be examined on a case by case basis. It would be helpful if some overriding principles could be established at an international level to provide comfort to arbitrators in the exercise of their functions. Indeed, learned commentators have suggested that this issue might be addressed in any modifications

---

[57] See Blackaby, Lindsey & Spinillo (eds.) *International Arbitration In Latin America* (2003), p.100. Arbitrators in Colombia and Ecuador are also subject to the rules applicable to judicial liability.

[58] See, *e.g. Cort v AAA*, 795 F.Supp.970 (N.D.Ca. 1992) at 972, determining that in order to encourage independent judgments, the arbitration process is granted immunity.

[59] See Yat-Sen Li, "Arbitral Immunity: A Profession Comes of Age" (1998) 64 Arbitration 51 at 53.

[60] See, *e.g., Cort*, above, at 973. However, some comment that arbitration is now a fully developed profession, whose members should accept personal responsibility, including full legal liability for loss caused by any failure (see Yat-Sen Li, *op. cit.*, p.55). Note also the availability of professional liability insurance (see David I. Bristow Q.C., *op. cit.*, at 322).

[61] See Hong Lin Yu & Eric Sauzier, "From Arbitrator's Immunity to the Fifth Theory of International Commercial Arbitration" (2000) International Arbitration Law Review 114.

to the Model Law,[62] notwithstanding that it was left outside of the scope of the current text.[63]

The International Bar Association states its position in its rules on Ethics for **5–20** International Arbitrators of 1987. This is that "international arbitrators should in principle be granted immunity from suit under national laws, except in extreme cases of wilful or reckless disregard of their legal obligations." This appears to be a suitable middle ground but one it remains a wish rather than a reality in many jurisdictions. Pending the establishment of uniform or harmonised rules in this regard, potential arbitrators should ascertain the potential scope of their liability principally in accordance with the law of the seat.

Meanwhile, perhaps the practical answer is that where arbitrators are exposed to a risk of personal liability, by reason of the law under which the arbitration is to take place, they might refuse to accept appointment unless given an indemnity by the parties; in this way they would obtain immunity from liability by contract, even if they were not entitled to it by operation of law. Whether such an indemnity would be enforceable as a matter of public policy is uncertain. Professional liability insurance should also be available to cover the risks but the cost may be prohibitive and would have to be passed on to the parties by one means or another.

A separate issue which is the increasing subject of discussion is the eventual liability of the arbitral institution. Aggrieved parties who have lost an arbitration may look indiscriminately for defendants and arbitral institutions have not escaped this trend.

Like the relationship between the arbitrators and the parties, the relationship **5–21** between parties to the arbitration and the arbitral institution administering the arbitration is generally considered to be contractual. Whereas in common law jurisdictions arbitral institutions have more or less absolute immunity from liability,[64] in civil law jurisdictions they may be held liable for wrongful acts,[65] and such liability will usually be based on general principles of contractual liability.

---

[62] See Hermann, "Does the World Need Additional Uniform Legislation on Arbitration?" (1999) 15 Arbitration International 221.

[63] The current text contains no provision regarding the liabilities of arbitrators. The Secretariat suggested that the matter should not be dealt with in the Model Law "in view of the fact that the liability problem is not widely regulated and remains highly controversial"; and the Working Group entrusted with preparing a draft text expressly decided that this subject should not be covered. See UN Docs A/CN.9/207 and 9/216, and Holtzmann & Neuhaus, *A Guide to the UNCITRAL Model Law on International Commercial Arbitration* (Kluwer, 1989), pp.1119 and 1148–1150.

[64] In the US, institutions, like arbitrators, have absolute immunity. In *Austern v Chicago Board Options Exchange* 716 F.Supp.121 (S.D.N.Y. 1989), the plaintiffs sued an arbitral institution for damages for mental anguish, but were barred by the doctrine of immunity. In England, the Arbitration Act 1996, s.74 provides for immunity in relation to the discharge by the institution of its duties, unless it acts in bad faith.

[65] In France, institutions are required to follow the rules applicable to the arbitration and are potentially liable for any breach of the arbitration agreement (see *Société Cubic Défense Système v CCI* (1997) Revue de l'Arbitrage 417).

The basis for the immunity of arbitral institutions in common law jurisdictions is different from that relating to arbitrators: it is based on the fact that they operate as quasi-judicial organisations[66] in order to protect those functions that are closely related to the arbitral process and sufficiently related to the adjudicative phase of the arbitration, thereby ensuring that the policies behind immunity are fulfilled. Without this immunity, it is argued (mainly in the US) that immunity of arbitrators would be meaningless because liability would merely shift from the arbitrators to the arbitral organisation.[67]

In the US, breaches by an institution of its own rules and failure to abide by the arbitration agreement usually attract immunity. In France, however, arbitration institutions are required to adhere to their own rules, and are potentially liable for their failure to adhere to the arbitration agreement.[68]

5–22   Institutional rules usually provide for the institution's immunity in relation to any act or omission in connection with the arbitration,[69] but for some institutions this is subject to liability for conscious or deliberate wrongdoing.[70] The rules of the arbitral institution are usually incorporated in the contract between the parties and the institution, and as such may operate as an exclusion of liability. However, according to some commentators, it is unlikely that such provisions would be effective under the mandatory rules of the forum.[71]

Duty to act with due diligence

5–23   An arbitral tribunal has an obvious moral obligation to carry out its task with due diligence; justice delayed is justice denied.

Some systems of law endeavour to ensure that an arbitration is carried out with reasonable speed by setting a time-limit within which the arbitral tribunal must make its award.[72] The time-limit fixed is sometimes as short as six months (as indeed it is in the ICC Rules[73]), although generally it may be extended by consent of the parties or at the initiative of the institution[74] or the tribunal.[75] If an award is not made within the time allowed, the authority of the arbitral tribunal

---

[66] See *Rubenstein v Otterbourg* 357 N.Y.S. 2d 62 (N.Y. Misc. 1973) at 64 and *Boraks v AAA* 517 N.W.2d 771 (Mich. App. 1994) at 772.

[67] See *Corey v New York Stock Exchange*, above, at 1211.

[68] In *Société Cubic Défense Système v Chambre de Commerce Internationale* (above), a French court stated that an arbitral institution could be liable for a failure to adhere to the parties' agreement.

[69] See ICC Rules of Arbitration, Art.34; ICSID Convention Art.20; Netherlands Arbitration Institute, Art.66.

[70] AAA International (ICDR) Rules, Art.35; LCIA Rules, Art.31; Singapore International Arbitration Centre, r.32.

[71] See Philippe Fouchard, *Rapport final sur le statut de l'arbitre*, cited at para.16 of a case note by Lalive on *Société Cubic de Défense Système v CCI*, above.

[72] For examples, see: the Italian Code of Civil Procedure, Arts 813 and 820; Ecuadorean Law of Arbitration at Art.25 (150 days from the final hearing).

[73] ICC Arbitration Rules, Art.24.1.

[74] *ibid*, Art.24.2.

[75] Art.25 of the Ecuadorean Law permits the tribunal "where strictly necessary" to grant itself *ex officio* an extension of the time-limit by a further 150 days.

terminates and the award will be null and void.[76] Some systems of law provide that an arbitrator who fails to proceed with reasonable speed in conducting the arbitration, and making his award, may be removed by a competent court[77] and deprived of any entitlement to remuneration.[78] The Model Law provides that the mandate of an arbitrator terminates if he "fails to act without undue delay".[79]

Whilst these sanctions no doubt act as a spur to the indolent arbitrator, they do nothing to compensate a party who has suffered financial loss as a result of delay in proceeding with the arbitration. Delay in the conduct of an arbitration may have serious financial consequences; and an award of interest, even at a commercial rate, often fails to compensate the successful party for the financial loss suffered. The question accordingly arises as to whether or not an arbitrator may be made liable in damages for undue delay. No liability is imposed under the established international or institutional rules; and it would be most unusual to find a term imposing liability for delay in an ad hoc submission agreement. Liability might, however, be established on the basis of the contractual duty of care discussed earlier,[80] in those jurisdictions where the arbitrator does not benefit from immunity.

Duty to act judicially

It is important that an arbitral tribunal should act, and should be seen to act, **5–24** judicially (*i.e.* respect the rules of due process). It is suggested that this is more than a mere moral obligation. It is also one which, to some extent at least, may be enforced under international or institutional rules or under the applicable law. The duty to act judicially is a duty which extends to all aspects of the proceedings. Neither the arbitral tribunal as a whole nor any of its individual members should, for instance, discuss the case with one party in the absence of the other, unless the discussions concern purely procedural matters (of which the other party is then promptly informed), or unless the absent party has failed to attend a meeting or a hearing, having been given proper notice to do so. At the hearing the duty to act judicially means that each party must be accorded equality of treatment and given a fair opportunity to present its case. It would be wrong, for instance, to allow one party to call witnesses and to deny the other party a similar opportunity; similarly, it would be improper to allow one party to address the arbitral tribunal orally and to deny equivalence to the other party.

International and institutional rules, which are usually silent as to the duties of the arbitral tribunal, also exhibit common ground on this point. The UNCITRAL Rules provide that the arbitral tribunal may conduct the arbitration in such a

---

[76] See Arts 760 and 771 of the National Code of Civil Procedure of Argentina.

[77] As in England; Arbitration Act 1996, s.33(1)(b). An arbitrator has a duty to act fairly and without unnecessary delay. Breach of this duty may result in the removal of the arbitrator by the court (s.24(2)), and/or a challenge to the award (s.68).

[78] This is the position in Colombia (see Mantilla Serrano, "Colombia" in Blackaby, Lindsey & Spinillo (eds.) *International Arbitration in Latin America* (2003), p.121).

[79] Model Law, Art.14.

[80] See para.5–15.

manner as it considers appropriate: "provided that the parties are treated with equality and that at any stage of the proceedings each party is given a full opportunity of presenting his case".[81]

The ICSID Rules do not contain such a general statement, but detailed provisions ensure equality of treatment; and if any party fails to appear or present its case, a special default procedure must be followed.[82]

5–25 The law applicable to the arbitration proceedings often states explicitly that due process must be observed by the arbitral tribunal. For example, Art.21(2) of the Brazilian Arbitration Law states that "the principles of the presence of both parties to the dispute, equal treatment of the parties, impartiality of the arbitrator and freedom of decision, shall always be respected."[83] English law has gone even further. The 1996 Act provides that an arbitral tribunal shall:

"(a) act fairly and impartially between the parties giving each party a reasonable opportunity of putting his case and dealing with that of his opponent; and

(b) adopt procedures suitable to the circumstances of the particular case, avoiding unnecessary delay or expense, so as to provide a fair means for the resolution of the matters falling to be determined."

This is an extremely important provision.[84] It is a mandatory provision, which cannot be derogated from by either the parties or the tribunal.[85] An arbitrator acting in breach of this duty can be removed.[86] Perhaps more significantly, awards made in breach of it are open to challenge[87]; and would face enforcement difficulties.[88]

Where an arbitral tribunal fails in its duty to act judicially, the immediate sanction is for it to be removed. In some circumstances this can be done without waiting for the award, either under the rules of the relevant arbitral institution[89] or by a national court, where the applicable law permits the courts at the place of arbitration to intervene.[90] However, in some jurisdictions there is no opportunity for concurrent court control, and the aggrieved party must wait until the end of the proceedings before challenging the award.

---

[81] UNCITRAL Arbitration Rules, Art.15. The ICC Arbitration Rules contain provisions to a similar effect (see Arts 14.1 and 15).

[82] ICSID Arbitration Rules, r.42.

[83] See also Art.1434 of the Mexican Commercial Code: "The parties shall be treated with equality and each party shall be given a full opportunity to present its case."

[84] Departmental Advisory Committee on Arbitration Law Report (above, para.5–02), para.150. See also paras 151–165.

[85] English Arbitration Act 1996, s.4(1) and the First Schedule to the Act.

[86] *ibid.*, s.24.

[87] *ibid.*, s.68(2)(a).

[88] New York Convention, Art.V.1(d) and possibly also Art.V.3(b).

[89] *e.g.* ICC Arbitration Rules, Art.12.2.

[90] *e.g.* International Arbitration Act 1974, s.28 for Australia; and in England under the Arbitration Act 1996, s.24.

Once again, the sanctions mentioned earlier do not bring any financial com-   **5–26**
pensation to the aggrieved party. Clearly their existence is necessary as they may
serve to prevent, or at any rate correct, a miscarriage of justice. Nevertheless a
party who has suffered financial loss as a result of the failure of an arbitrator to
act judicially may wish to make the arbitrator personally liable for the loss he has
suffered. The term "failure to act judicially" may cover a variety of lapses, trivial
and serious alike. Where the lapse is serious (for example, the acceptance of a
bribe), it seems right that the party who has suffered loss should be entitled to
recover that loss from the offending arbitrator, even in countries that traditionally
confer immunity from liability on arbitrators. This is the position in Australia,
England, and New Zealand.[91]

(d) Ethical duties

In addition to specific duties imposed on arbitrators, either by the parties or by   **5–27**
law, it is generally considered that an arbitrator has certain moral or ethical
obligations. One obvious example, discussed earlier,[92] is the obligation to decline
to accept an appointment if, as a prospective arbitrator, sufficient time and
attention cannot be given to the case. There has been much discussion as to how
these ethical standards, sometimes described as the "deontology" of arbitrators,
might be defined or established in some form of internationally accepted "code
of conduct". This was achieved in the context of domestic arbitration in the US
where the ABA/AAA Code of Ethics was introduced in 1977 (with substantial
modifications in 2004).[93]

There is no code of conduct for ICC arbitrators, but a general guide to
acceptable international standards of conduct may be discerned from the attitudes
and behaviour of leading international arbitrators. The IBA established "Ethics
for International Arbitrators" in 1987. This is a set of principles designed to
assist international arbitrators as to how the required arbitrator qualities of
impartiality, competence, diligence and discretion might be applied in practice in
order to ensure a degree of harmonisation in the approach of arbitrators to these
ethical issues.

As discussed in Ch.4, the IBA has adopted guidelines on impartiality, independence and disclosure in international commercial arbitration. The 1987 Rules
of Ethics are replaced by the 2004 guidelines only to the extent they cover the

---

[91] See Arbitration Act 1996, s.29 for England; Arbitration Act 1996, s.13 for New Zealand; in
general, see para.5–18.
[92] See para.5–11. See also the comments on this point in Schwartz, "The Rights and Duties of ICC
Arbitrators" in "The Status of the Arbitrator", ICC International Court of Arbitration Bulletin
(December 1995) 67 at 77–79.
[93] One of the principal changes is the reversal of the presumption of non-neutrality of party-appointed
arbitrators. The 1977 Rules reflected a common practice in US domestic arbitration for party-
appointed arbitrators to be non-neutral. The increasing influence of international arbitration has led
to this idiosyncrasy being abandoned in favour of fully neutral tribunals. The new rules encourage
this change of approach to bring US domestic practice in line with domestic arbitration practice
elsewhere in the world.

same ground.[94] The IBA recognised the problems posed by conflicts of interest in international commercial arbitration and the ever-increasing recourse to arbitrator challenges as a means of delaying arbitrations or depriving a party of the arbitrator of its choice. This trend was fuelled by the lack of clear guidance on the standards to apply in making disclosures and how those standards apply to specific situations. The guidelines seek to inject a greater degree of objectivity and clarity into conflict and disclosure obligations.[95]

5–28   Other ethical responsibilities may arise where an arbitrator suspects that the arbitral process is being hijacked for a criminal purpose. The principal concern is the laundering of the proceeds of crime through a fraudulent dispute which is rapidly settled. The parties ask the tribunal to embody a settlement of their "dispute" in a consent award through which an unlawful payment is successfully hidden. A tribunal should be particularly cautious in agreeing to an early consent award which simply involves the payment of money. A consent award is only of real utility where there is an element of future performance which may need to be enforced. An obligation to pay money is usually sufficiently protected by mutual releases in a settlement agreement conditional upon the receipt of funds.

Other parties may be more sophisticated and put up a weak defence. There are often "tell-tale" signs—the entities involved are often recently incorporated; their activities are usually of a nature which does not require any real investment; the contract in question is rarely detailed or well drafted.

What is an arbitrator to do when he or she suspects there may be criminal activity involved in an arbitration? There is a balance to be struck. It is not the job of the arbitrator to seek to uncover criminal activity but rather to resolve the dispute which has been referred to it within the scope of the arbitration agreement. Nevertheless, an EU Directive now requires "auditors, external accounting experts and tax consultants" as well as "notaries and other members of the independent legal professions" to report on their own initiative " . . . any fact which might indicate money laundering and provide the authorities with any information requested." Particular reference is made to the legal profession in respect of assisting clients in the implementation of transactions.[96]

5–29   It is questionable whether the definition would include arbitrators or whether resolving a dispute could be said to be assisting a "client" in the implementation of a transaction. The position of mediators is clearly closer to this definition. Nevertheless, it would seem inappropriate for an arbitrator to take a narrow approach and wash his or her hands of any responsibility where there were clear signs of criminal activity. In any event, an arbitrator who is suspicious of criminal activity and is sitting in the EU would do well to see how the terms of the directive have been implemented locally.

---

[94] See para.4–57.
[95] See paras 4–62 *et seq.* for further discussion of the IBA Guidelines on Conflicts of Interest and Disclosure.
[96] Directive 2001/97/EC dated December 4, 2001 requiring implementation by June 15, 2003.

If an arbitrator has grounds for suspecting a criminal offence, each party should be given an opportunity to provide an explanation. Once the tribunal believes it has sufficient justification it can then evaluate the facts. In case of fraud or corruption, this is likely to have an impact on the outcome of the dispute. In cases of money laundering or other manipulation of the process by the parties, the tribunal should terminate the proceedings on the basis that there is no actual dispute. In case of a consent award, the tribunal may issue a ruling refusing to approve the settlement.

Opinions nevertheless appear to be split as to whether the arbitrators should inform the appropriate authorities (whoever they might be). A Working Group of the ICC concluded that "it appeared contrary to the nature of arbitration, contrary in particular to the trust that the parties place in the arbitrator, for an arbitral tribunal to report to the authorities the offences found . . . "[97] But if the parties' trust is simply that the arbitral tribunal act as a mute observer of a criminal offence, then it should not be respected. There needs to be more reflection in this area but it seems wrong that the confidential nature of arbitral proceedings and the ultimate enforceability of an award should be open to abuse by international crime. The arbitration community must therefore be vigilant to ensure that it does not unwittingly assist such crime.

4. JURISDICTION

(a) Generally

An arbitral tribunal may only validly determine those disputes that the parties **5–30** have agreed that it should determine. This rule is an inevitable and proper consequence of the voluntary nature of arbitration.[98] In consensual arbitration, the authority or competence of the arbitral tribunal comes from the agreement of the parties; indeed, there is no other source from which it can come. It is the parties who give to a private tribunal the authority to decide disputes between them; and the arbitral tribunal must take care to stay within the terms of its mandate. The rule to this effect is expressed in several different ways. Sometimes it is said that an arbitral tribunal must conform to the mission entrusted to it[99]; or that it must not exceed its mandate; or that it must stay within its terms of reference,[1] competence or authority. Another way of expressing the rule (which is followed in this book) is to state that an arbitral tribunal must not exceed its

---

[97] ICC Report of Working Group on Criminal Law and Arbitration (Doc.420/492).
[98] In some states, such as Chile, some matters must be referred to arbitration (see Jorquiera & Helmlinger, "Chile" in *International Arbitration in Latin America* (Blackaby, Lindsey & Spinillo eds), p.95. It is questionable whether such compulsory arbitration is in fact arbitration in the true sense of the word since it lacks the necessary element of consent. Such "arbitrations" are outside the scope of this book.
[99] See, *e.g.*, French Code of Civil Procedure 1981, Art.1502.3.
[1] Under the ICC Arbitration Rules, Art.18, an arbitral tribunal must draw up its own "Terms of Reference" for signature by the parties and the tribunal and for approval by the ICC's Court, before proceeding with the arbitration.

jurisdiction (this term being used in the sense of mandate, competence or authority).

(b) Challenges to jurisdiction

5–31   A challenge to the jurisdiction of an arbitral tribunal may be partial or total. A partial challenge raises the question of whether certain (but not all) of the claims or counterclaims which have been submitted to the arbitral tribunal are within its jurisdiction. A challenge of this kind does not amount to a fundamental attack on the jurisdiction of the arbitral tribunal; a total challenge, by contrast, questions the whole basis upon which the arbitral tribunal is acting or purporting to act. A partial challenge is usually dependent on whether the particular matters referred to arbitration fall within the scope of the arbitration agreement; a total challenge usually questions whether there is a valid arbitration agreement at all.

Partial challenge

5–32   A partial challenge exists where it is asserted that *some* of the claims (or counterclaims) that have been brought before the arbitral tribunal do not properly come within its jurisdiction. For instance, in a civil engineering arbitration the claim often consists of a long list of disputed items.

This was the position in an ICC arbitration in which one of the authors was involved. The contractor's Request for Arbitration comprised 23 individual claims, for varied or additional work, and a general claim for compensation based on delay. Some of the individual claims had been included by the contractor in the Request for Arbitration without asking or waiting for the engineer's decision.[2] The respondent government contended that this failure to follow the contractual procedures meant that the claims concerned had not been properly submitted to arbitration and so were not within the jurisdiction of the arbitral tribunal. Nor was the respondent prepared to consent to jurisdiction in respect of these items, since as the project owner it regarded the contractual provisions as existing for its protection against possibly unfounded claims. The arbitral tribunal upheld the challenge to jurisdiction in respect of three of the individual claims and a further two were withdrawn for an admitted lack of jurisdiction. Similar issues have been tested in ICSID arbitrations where there is usually a requirement to notify disputes for the purpose of seeking an amicable settlement before the right to submit to arbitration crystallises. Respondent states have often argued that certain claims fall outside of the originally notified dispute.[3]

Any lack of jurisdiction in this sense may be cured by agreement of the parties. Even if certain items of claim or counterclaim are outside the scope of the initial reference to arbitration, the parties may agree that new matters should for

[2] As required by the then applicable cl.67 of the FIDIC Conditions of Contract (International) for Works of Civil Engineering Construction (4th ed., 1987).
[3] See, *e.g.*, *CMS Gas Transmission Company v The Republic of Argentina* (ICSID Case No.ARB/ 01/8), Decision of the Tribunal on Objections to Jurisdiction, July 17, 2003, (2003) 42 I.L.M. 788.

convenience be brought within the arbitration. By signing a memorandum to this effect, they may effectively bring new claims within the jurisdiction of the arbitral tribunal. This is not always as straightforward as might appear. Under some arbitration rules, where the arbitral process has already begun, new claims may only be added with the permission of the arbitral tribunal.[4]

Nevertheless, there are many cases in which the other party objects to new **5–33** claims being brought into the arbitration and has good legal grounds for its objection. Such a party is unlikely to agree to extend the jurisdiction of the arbitral tribunal. In these cases (and indeed, in any case where it seems that it may be exceeding its jurisdiction) the arbitral tribunal should proceed with caution. If it does exceed its jurisdiction, its award will be imperilled and may be set aside or refused recognition and enforcement in whole or in part by a competent court.[5]

National laws and the international conventions on arbitration emphasise how important it is that an arbitral tribunal should not exceed its jurisdiction. In French law, for example, one of the few grounds on which it is possible to challenge an international award in the French courts is where "the arbitrator's decision does not conform to the terms of his reference".[6] Internationally, the New York Convention provides that recognition and enforcement of an award may be refused on proof that:

> "The award deals with a difference not contemplated by or not falling within the terms of the submission to arbitration, or it contains decisions on matters beyond the scope of the submission to arbitration."[7]

Partial challenges to the jurisdiction of an arbitral tribunal have become **5–34** relatively common in modern times; and they do not in themselves raise any fundamental problems. It is different, however, when there is a total challenge to the jurisdiction of the arbitral tribunal which raises the more fundamental question of whether there is a valid arbitration agreement at all.

Total challenge

An arbitral tribunal that derives its authority from a submission agreement is **5–35** unlikely to face a total challenge to its jurisdiction. The purpose of a submission agreement is to give the arbitral tribunal jurisdiction to determine specific

---

[4] See, for instance, ICC Arbitration Rules, Art.19, which allows claims made after the drafting of the Terms of Reference only in the discretion of the arbitral tribunal.

[5] This will generally be the courts of the country in which the arbitration is held; or the courts of the country or countries in which recognition and enforcement of the award is sought; see Ch.8.

[6] The New Code of Civil Procedure 1981, Art.1502.3.

[7] New York Convention, Art.V.1(c). It should be pointed out, however, that the possibility of the "good" parts of an award being separated from the "bad" is explicitly recognised, since this paragraph of the New York Convention goes on to state that if the decision on matters submitted to arbitration can be separated from those which were not submitted: "that part of the award which contains decisions on matters submitted to arbitration may be recognised and enforced".

disputes between specific parties. It would be perverse indeed if, having signed such an agreement, one of the parties then launched a total challenge to jurisdiction; the only issue of jurisdiction likely to arise in such circumstances will be as to whether or not a particular item of claim (or counterclaim) is within the scope of the submission agreement. Total challenges to jurisdiction are therefore only likely to arise in practice where the authority (or purported authority) of the arbitral tribunal is derived from an arbitration clause.

The grounds for a challenge to jurisdiction are often related to the basic elements of arbitration clauses, as discussed in Ch.3. One of the alleged parties to an arbitration agreement may argue that it is not bound by the agreement, because the arbitration clause was contained in a document which was assented to by the other party only; or it may claim that the legal entity signing the agreement was a different and distinct legal person. Or again, it may be argued that the arbitration agreement is not an agreement in writing[8]; or that the whole dispute in issue is outside the scope of the arbitration agreement or not arbitrable under the applicable law. As a final example, one of the parties (invariably the respondent) may say that the claim is time-barred or that for some other reason the arbitration clause is inoperative or incapable of being performed.

Challenges to the jurisdiction of the arbitral tribunal of this type raise questions as to who may decide the challenge—the arbitral tribunal or a national court—and whether a ruling on jurisdiction by the arbitral tribunal may be reviewed by a national court and at what stage.

(c) The autonomy (or separability) of the arbitration clause

5–36   Closely linked to the question of *who* decides a total jurisdiction challenge is another issue, namely, whether the arbitration clause can be regarded as having an independent existence of its own, or only as a part of the transactional contract in which it is contained.

The link may not seem to be immediately obvious, but where the body deciding the arbitral tribunal's jurisdiction is the arbitral tribunal itself, the first issue often depends on the second. This issue concerns a challenge to an arbitration clause based on an allegation that the contract in which it is contained is invalid. There are many possible reasons for this. Perhaps the contract was not signed by both parties; perhaps one of the parties did not have legal capacity to sign it; perhaps it was entered into in reliance on a false representation; or perhaps the contract was illegal in the country in which it was made. Moreover, the contract may have simply come to an end by performance or total repudiation. Whatever the reason, this situation creates a major conceptual problem for an arbitral tribunal ruling on the validity of an arbitration clause. If the contract (and hence the arbitration clause) is not valid or is non-existent, then the basis for the tribunal to convene to decide whether or not the clause is valid is not immediately apparent.

---

[8] See Ch.3, para.3–07.

The solution usually adopted is known as the doctrine of separability. As discussed earlier, this doctrine is shorthand for regarding an arbitration clause as constituting a separate and autonomous contract. It means that the validity of the arbitration clause does not depend on the validity of the contract as a whole.[9] By surviving termination of the main contract, the clause constitutes the necessary agreement of the parties that any disputes between them (even concerning the validity or termination of the contract in which it is contained) should be referred to arbitration. In this way it provides a legal basis for the appointment of an arbitral tribunal.

In short, if the tribunal is to decide on its own jurisdiction, it must first assume that jurisdiction. This is what the doctrine of separability allows it to do. It is apparent that the doctrine is in many ways a convenient and pragmatic fiction. If the arbitral tribunal decides that the clause is not a valid agreement to arbitrate then the basis for its authority disappears. In reality, if the clause is not an enforceable agreement to arbitrate, that authority was never there. Nevertheless, because of its obvious practical advantages, this doctrine is widely accepted both by arbitration rules and in national laws.[10]   **5–37**

But a decision that the arbitration clause is legally separate from the main contract does not answer the larger question. If a challenge to the jurisdiction of the arbitral tribunal is made, by whom is the challenge to be determined? Is it to be determined by the arbitral tribunal itself, by an arbitral institution, by an appointing authority or by a court of competent jurisdiction?

Who judges?

It is generally accepted that an arbitral tribunal has power to investigate its   **5–38** own jurisdiction. This is a power inherent in the appointment of an arbitral tribunal; indeed, it is an essential power if the arbitral tribunal is to carry out its task properly. An arbitral tribunal must be able to look at the arbitration agreement, the terms of its appointment and any relevant evidence in order to decide whether or not a particular claim or series of claims comes within its jurisdiction. The arbitral tribunal's decision on the issue may be overruled subsequently by a competent national court; but this does not prevent the tribunal making the decision in the first place:

> "It is not the law that arbitrators, if their jurisdiction is challenged or questioned, are bound immediately to refuse to act until their jurisdiction has been determined by some court which has power to determine it finally. Nor is it the law that they are bound to go on without investigating the merits of the challenge and to determine the matter in dispute, leaving the question of their

---

[9] See, *e.g.*, the UNCITRAL Arbitration Rules, Art.21; ICC Arbitration Rules, Art.6.4; LCIA Arbitration Rules 23.1; AAA Arbitration Rules, Art.15.2; Model Law, Art.16(1); English Arbitration Act 1996, s.7. This is the reason most authors refer to the "law governing the arbitration agreement", rather than "the law governing the contract". An arbitration clause may be valid even if the contract of which it forms a part is found under the same law to be invalid.

[10] See Ch.3, paras 3–60 *et seq.*

jurisdiction to be held over until it is determined by some Court which had power to determine it. They might then be merely wasting their time and everybody else's. They are not obliged to take either of those courses. They are entitled to inquire into the merits of the issue whether they have jurisdiction or not, not for the purpose of reaching any conclusion which will be binding upon the parties—because that they cannot do—but for the purpose of satisfying themselves as a preliminary matter about whether they ought to go on with the arbitration or not."[11]

It is thus open to an arbitral tribunal to decide its own jurisdiction, although that decision may be subject to review by the courts as discussed later in this chapter.

Competence/competence

5–39   The power of an arbitral tribunal to decide upon its own jurisdiction is referred to above as an "inherent" power. However, the usual practice under modern international and institutional rules of arbitration is to spell out in express terms the power of an arbitral tribunal to decide upon its own jurisdiction or, as it is often put, its competence to decide upon its own competence.[12]

Furthermore, this implicit power is not merely spelt out. It is often extended. For example, Art.21 of the UNCITRAL Rules provides:

"1. The arbitral tribunal shall have the power to rule on objections that it has no jurisdiction, including any objections with respect to the existence or validity of the arbitration clause or of the separate arbitration agreement.

2. The arbitral tribunal shall have the power to determine the existence or the validity of the contract of which an arbitration clause forms a part. For the purposes of [this article], an arbitration clause which forms part of a contract and which provides for arbitration under these Rules shall be treated as an agreement independent of the other terms of the contract. A decision by the arbitral tribunal that the contract is null and void shall not entail *ipso jure* the invalidity of the arbitration clause."

Under the ICC Rules, the position is slightly more complex. When any question is raised as to the jurisdiction of the arbitral tribunal a two-stage procedure is followed. At the first stage, if one of the parties raises "one or more pleas concerning the existence, validity or scope of the agreement to arbitrate," the ICC's Court must satisfy itself of the prima facie existence of such an agreement.[13] If it is satisfied that such an agreement may exist, the ICC's Court must allow the arbitration to proceed so that, at the second stage "any decision

---

[11] *per* Devlin J., *Christopher Brown Ltd v Genossenschaft Oesterreichischer Waldbesitzer Holzwirtschaftsbetriebe Registrierte GmbH* [1954] 1 Q.B. 8 at 12 and 13.
[12] This is sometimes described in a form of shorthand as "competence/competence"; it is expressed in German as "*Kompetenz/Kompetenz*" and in French as "*compétence de la compétence*".
[13] ICC Arbitration Rules, Art.6.2.

as to the jurisdiction of the Arbitral Tribunal shall be taken by the Arbitral Tribunal itself."[14]

In practice, a claimant delivers to the Secretariat a Request for Arbitration that **5–40** includes a brief statement of its claims; a copy of the purported agreement that contains the arbitration clause; and the fee required by the ICC. The Secretariat checks whether a clause providing for ICC arbitration appears in the documents submitted by the claimant. If it does, the ICC's Court will establish an arbitral tribunal and refer the case to it. For example, in a case in which one of the authors was involved,[15] the respondent claimed that the agreement submitted to the ICC with the Request for Arbitration had been assigned to another party. The ICC's Court merely indicated that the matter would be considered by the arbitral tribunal pursuant to the previous version of Art.6.2 of the ICC Rules.[16]

The ICC Rules then provide, in terms similar to those adopted in the UNCITRAL Rules, that:

"Unless otherwise provided, the Arbitral Tribunal shall not cease to have jurisdiction by reason of any claim that the contract is null and void or allegation that it is non-existent provided that the Arbitral Tribunal upholds the validity of the arbitration agreement. The Arbitral Tribunal shall continue to have jurisdiction to determine the respective rights of the parties and to adjudicate their claims and pleas even though the contract itself may be non-existent or null and void."[17]

The English Court of Appeal has considered the meaning and effect of an **5–41** earlier, but similar, version of this article of the ICC Rules and has held that it gives an arbitrator a wide discretion to decide upon his own jurisdiction:

"We have no doubt, from the words used in those paragraphs, and from the general purpose and intent shown by the rules as a whole in respect of international arbitration, that the correct intention to be attributed to these rules is that a very wide jurisdiction is to be given to the arbitrator to decide on his own jurisdiction when that jurisdiction is challenged. We see no reason why, as a matter of construction of the words used, the court should be alert to try to cut down the width of the intended meaning."[18]

---

[14] See above.

[15] ICC Case No.4357.

[16] This left the respondent in the position of having the issue heard before an arbitral tribunal which (if the respondent was correct) could have no valid existence, and no valid mandate as regards the two parties in question. Thus in certain circumstances the ICC Arbitration Rules have the effect of permitting an arbitral tribunal to be established, and purporting to confer on it the power to make rulings relating to jurisdiction, where the requirement of consensuality between the parties may not exist. This may also occur in arbitrations under rules other than those of the ICC.

[17] ICC Arbitration Rules, Art.6.4.

[18] Megaw L.J. in *Dalmia Dairy Industries Ltd v National Bank of Pakistan* [1978] 2 Lloyd's Rep. 223 at 283. The court went on to indicate, however, that such powers could not be conferred under the law of India as the law governing the arbitration agreement.

Most institutional arbitration rules and modern national laws governing international arbitration also spell out the power of an arbitral tribunal to rule on its
own jurisdiction. The Model Law provides that:

"The arbitral tribunal may rule on its own jurisdiction, including any objections with respect to the existence or validity of the arbitration agreement. For
that purpose, an arbitration clause which forms part of a contract shall be
treated as an agreement independent of the other terms of the contract. A
decision by the arbitral tribunal that the contract is null and void shall not
entail *ipso jure* the invalidity of the arbitration clause."[19]

5–42   As identified earlier, there are essentially two elements to this rule: first, that
an arbitral tribunal can rule upon its own jurisdiction; and secondly that, for this
purpose, the arbitration clause is separate and independent from the terms of the
contract containing the transaction between the parties. Most countries, including
those that have adopted the Model Law, embrace both propositions.[20] However,
the two are interrelated, not identical. To understand the real scope of an
arbitrator's power in any given country, it is always important to check whether
both propositions appear in its national law. In the English 1996 Act, for
example, the competence of an arbitral tribunal to rule on its own jurisdiction is
established in s.30; the separability of the arbitration clause is established in
s.7.

Competence

5–43   A good example of the principle of competence in action is the decision in the
SNE v Joc Oil case.[21] A Bermudian company (Joc Oil) entered into a contract
with a Soviet foreign trade organisation (SNE) for the purchase of billions of
tonnes of oil. SNE brought arbitration proceedings in the Soviet Union, in
accordance with the terms of the contract, for payment under the contract. Joc Oil
was ordered to pay SNE almost US$200 million. The defence of Joc Oil, both at
the time of the arbitration and during enforcement proceedings in Bermuda, was,
inter alia, that there was no valid agreement to arbitrate, because there was no
valid contract. The basis of the argument was that, under Soviet law, a contract
for the foreign sale of oil required the signature of two authorised officials and
this contract was signed by only one official.

The arbitral tribunal accepted that there was no valid contract, as did the Court
of Appeal of Bermuda. But this was not a "non-existent" contract as claimed by
Joc Oil. The court held that, even if the main agreement were void *ab initio*, the
arbitration agreement did come into existence; and it was open to the arbitrators

---

[19] Model Law, Art.16.
[20] See, *e.g.*, the Swiss Private International Law Act 1987, Ch.12, Art.178(3); the Brazilian Arbitration Law, Art.8; the English Arbitration Act 1996, ss.7 and 30.
[21] *Sojuznefteexport (SNE) v Joc Oil Ltd*, summary of decision of the Bermuda Court of Appeal
considering an enforcement application for a USSR arbitral award in (1990) XV Yearbook
Commercial Arbitration 31.

to award the sum otherwise payable under the contract on the basis of restitution or unjust enrichment. The distinction made is between the nullity of a contract and its non-existence. If the contract does not exist (for example because the signature of one of the parties was a forgery, or because the signature of the person who signed was procured under duress) it is difficult to see how such a document can give rise to a valid arbitration clause and hence to a valid arbitration. However, where there is a main contract, even if it were always a legal nullity, the arbitration clause that it contains constitutes a genuine juridical "platform" upon which the arbitral tribunal may stand, to judge the validity of the main body of the contract.

This is logically sound. Although many institutional rules and national laws draft their separability rules to preserve the validity of arbitration clauses that are part of "non-existent" contracts,[22] this non-existence cannot mean "never existed", but must mean "ceased to exist". If a contract has ceased to exist by the time of the arbitration, an arbitral tribunal still has the platform on which it may stand. If the contract never existed at all, then there was never an agreement. So the arbitral tribunal can have no valid existence, authority or jurisdiction.

Limitations on jurisdiction

Rules of procedure that set out the power of an arbitral tribunal to decide on **5–44** its own jurisdiction, such as those contained in the UNCITRAL Rules mentioned above, serve a useful purpose. They make it clear that the parties to the arbitration have agreed (by adopting such rules, either expressly or by incorporation) that the arbitral tribunal is to have the powers conferred by the rules. Some caution must be expressed, however, with regard to the views of commentators who see these rules as giving an arbitral tribunal power to decide upon its jurisdiction in almost any circumstance. One commentator has stated: " . . . the most commonly applied international conventions and rules of arbitration all support the autonomy of the arbitration agreement and the power of the arbitrator to rule on his own jurisdiction."[23] He went on to state:

> "It goes without saying that when the arbitration is governed by one of these conventions or rules, it is that international source which defines the jurisdiction of the arbitrators, even where this would be contrary to the law of the place or the country where the arbitration takes place, or the law which is applicable to the arbitration by virtue of the convention or rules."[24]

It is, however, doubtful that the parties to an arbitration agreement may validly agree on rules that are contrary to "the law of the place . . . where the arbitration takes place, or the law which is applicable to the arbitration."

---

[22] See, *e.g.*, the ICC Arbitration Rules, Art.6.4; LCIA Arbitration Rules Art.23.1; English Arbitration Act 1996, s.7.

[23] Goldman, "The Complementary Roles of Judges and Arbitrators in Ensuring that International Commercial Arbitration is Effective" in *60 Years of ICC Arbitration—A Look at the Future* (ICC, 1984), pp.255, 263.

[24] Goldman, *op. cit.*, pp.263 and 264.

Further, whilst the conventions and rules referred to may define "the jurisdiction of the arbitrators", that jurisdiction itself is derived not from any international source but from the arbitration agreement; and the arbitration agreement can only confer powers which are permissible under the law applicable to the arbitration agreement and under the *lex arbitri*.

Award made without jurisdiction

5–45   The nullity of an award made without jurisdiction when there was no arbitration agreement is recognised both in national laws and in the international conventions governing arbitration. In French law, for example, one of the limited cases in which it is possible to challenge an international award in the French courts is where "the arbitrator gave judgment in the absence of an arbitration agreement or on the basis of a void or expired agreement."[25]

Likewise, under the New York Convention, recognition and enforcement of an award may be refused if the arbitration agreement "is not valid under the law to which the parties have subjected it or, failing any indication thereon, under the law of the country where the award was made."[26]

An almost identical provision is contained in the Model Law.[27]

(d) Court control

5–46   Any decision given by an arbitral tribunal as to its jurisdiction is subject to control by the courts of law, which in this respect have the final word. The relevant procedure and burden of proof varies from country to country, and sometimes within countries. In practice, recourse to the courts on issues of jurisdiction is likely to take place at one of three stages. It may take place at the beginning of the arbitral process; or during the actual course of the process, or following the making of the award.

These different stages, and the options open both to the arbitral tribunal and to the challenging party, are considered later in this chapter. First, however, it is necessary to review the question of concurrent court control.

Concurrent control

5–47   Any challenge to jurisdiction during the course of the arbitral proceedings is usually made to the arbitral tribunal itself. The arbitral tribunal will then usually (but not invariably) issue an interim award. In many jurisdictions[28] this interim award may be challenged immediately in the local courts. In some jurisdictions, a reluctant respondent can challenge the arbitral tribunal's jurisdiction in the

---

[25] Art.1502.1 of the Code of Civil Procedure 1981; for an example of the application of this Article, see *The Arab Republic of Egypt v Southern Pacific Properties Ltd and SPP (Middle East) Ltd*, Cour d'Appel de Paris, July 5, 1984.

[26] New York Convention, Art.V.1(a).

[27] Model Law, Art.36(1)(iv).

[28] *e.g.* in England under the Arbitration Act 1996, ss.32 and 67. See also Switzerland under the Concordat.

courts *before* any award has been issued.[29] By these means a final decision on the issue of jurisdiction may be obtained at an early stage in the arbitral proceedings. One notable exception is the ICSID regime where no application to local courts to review a jurisdictional decision is possible and where the internal annulment process only applies in respect of final awards which must "deal with every question submitted to the tribunal".[30] The annulment process would consequently only be open in respect of negative jurisdictional decisions which finally disposed of the matter.[31]

The system under which a national court is involved in the question of jurisdiction before the arbitral tribunal has issued a final award on the merits is known as "concurrent control". The advantage of this system is that it enables the parties to know relatively quickly where they stand; and (unless the arbitral tribunal decides to continue with the proceedings pending a decision from the relevant court) they will save time and money if the arbitration proceedings prove to be groundless.

There are broadly two arguments against concurrent control. First, it is argued that recourse to the courts during the course of arbitral proceedings should not be encouraged, since arbitral proceedings should so far as possible be conducted without outside "interference". Secondly, and more pragmatically, it is argued that to allow recourse to the courts during the course of an arbitration is likely to encourage delaying tactics on the part of a reluctant respondent. This question was much debated during the preparation of the Model Law. Finally, however, the solution of concurrent control *was* adopted.[32]

The choices open to the arbitral tribunal

As the practice of international commercial arbitration becomes more sophisti-   **5–48**
cated, challenges to the jurisdiction of arbitral tribunals become more frequent. It is useful to consider the alternatives open to an arbitral tribunal faced with a challenge to its jurisdiction. In effect, the arbitral tribunal has three choices:

- to decide at the outset that it has no jurisdiction; or

- to issue an interim award on jurisdiction; or

- to join the issue of jurisdiction to the merits.

If the arbitral tribunal decides at the outset that it has no jurisdiction, its decision puts an end to the arbitral proceedings and, indeed, to the existence of

---

[29] *e.g.* English Arbitration Act 1996, s.32. This particular option for challenging jurisdiction is narrowly drawn, and may only be pursued with the permission of the other party (or parties) and the tribunal. It was intended for cases where it is clear that a challenge to the courts on jurisdiction would almost inevitably follow an arbitral award on this matter.

[30] Washington Convention, Art.48(3).

[31] In two cases in which one of the authors has been involved, attempts to register applications for annulment of positive jurisdictional decisions were refused by the ICSID Secretariat.

[32] Model Law, Art.16. See also Ch.9, paras 9–12 *et seq.*

the arbitral tribunal itself. It will then be for the claimant (or counterclaimant) to seek such remedies as may be open to it. This usually means recourse to national courts.[33] However, it is only in an "open and shut" case that an arbitral tribunal is likely to be able to make such an instant decision on its jurisdiction.

Usually, the arbitral tribunal needs to receive the submissions of the parties, both as to facts and law, and it will then issue a reasoned interim award on the issues of jurisdiction that have been raised. This interim award will be binding on the parties—subject to any right of recourse that may be available to the disappointed party in the relevant national court.[34]

5–49   There is a third class of cases in which the issue of jurisdiction depends on facts which are so closely connected with the merits of the dispute that it is almost impossible to determine the one without determining the other. In such cases, the arbitral tribunal usually joins the issue of jurisdiction to the merits.

5–50   These two options are clearly spelled out in the ICSID Rules, which provide:

> "(3) Upon the formal raising of an objection relating to the dispute, [and raising the issue of jurisdiction] the proceeding on the merits shall be suspended. The President of the Tribunal, after consultation with its other members, shall fix a time limit within which the parties may file observations on the objection.
>
> (4) The Tribunal shall decide whether or not the further procedures relating to the objection shall be oral. It may deal with the objection as a preliminary question or join it to the merits of the dispute. If the Tribunal overrules the objection or joins it to the merits, it shall once more fix time limits for further procedures.
>
> (5) If the Tribunal decides that the dispute is not within the jurisdiction of the Centre or not within its own competence, it shall render an award to that effect."[35]

Usually the appropriate course for an arbitral tribunal is to issue an interim award on jurisdiction, if asked to do so. This enables the parties to know where they stand at an early stage; and it will save them spending time and money on arbitral proceedings that prove to be invalid. However, it is not always possible or desirable for an arbitral tribunal to take this course. First, as already indicated, if the facts on which the challenge to jurisdiction are based are virtually inseparable from the merits, the arbitral tribunal should continue with the hearing and make a final award that deals with both issues at the same time. Secondly, if the respondent, having raised the issue of jurisdiction, fails or refuses to take part in

---

[33] There is a possibility that the court concerned may decide that the arbitral tribunal was wrong in declining jurisdiction, in which case fresh arbitral proceedings would have to be commenced.

[34] It is in this context that the issue of concurrent control, which has already been discussed, arises.

[35] ICSID Arbitration Rules, r.41(3), (4) and (5). The choice is also clearly indicated in the English Arbitration Act 1996, ss.31 and 32.

the arbitral proceedings, the arbitral tribunal may consider it appropriate in the interests of justice to proceed with the case and deal with the issue of jurisdiction at the same time as it deals with the merits:

> "There being nothing to contradict the plaintiff's evidence, the arbitrators are entitled, as it seems to me, to proceed and say: 'We will hear your case, as the defendant does not appear, and we will then give our decision upon the contract which is placed before us, and stated to be a contract.' That is what they did here. The plaintiff, of course, in that case proceeds, so to speak, *ex parte*, and runs the risk that when he seeks to enforce his award, he may be met with the answer: 'This award is a nullity, because there was never a submission, because there was never a contract' ".[36]

This course of action has been adopted in several important international commercial arbitrations; and most notably in the famous Libyan oil nationalisation cases, in which the Libyan Government challenged the jurisdiction of the arbitral tribunals but did not participate in the proceedings.[37] **5–51**

Any award on jurisdiction made by an arbitral tribunal, whether as an interim or final award, is binding on the parties to the arbitration. However, it may be set aside by a competent court and it may be refused recognition or enforcement. This is the principle adopted in the Model Law with regard to both setting aside and refusal of recognition or enforcement[38]; it is also the principle adopted in the New York Convention with regard to the recognition and enforcement of awards.[39]

(e) Procedural aspects of resolving issues of jurisdiction

Objections to the jurisdiction of the arbitral tribunal are usually raised by a respondent in the early stages of the arbitration.[40] A claimant is unlikely to challenge the jurisdiction of an arbitral tribunal to determine the very claims submitted to arbitration; but may wish to raise an objection to jurisdiction in relation to any counterclaims put forward by the respondent. **5–52**

The time at which issues of jurisdiction should be raised

The UNCITRAL Rules indicate that any objections to jurisdiction should be raised and dealt with by the arbitral tribunal at an early stage, as a preliminary **5–53**

---

[36] *per* Lord Goddard in *M. Golodetz v Schrier* [1947] 80 Lloyd's Rep. 647 at 650. This procedure is now explicitly permitted under the English Arbitration Act 1996, s.31.

[37] As happened in the *Texaco, British Petroleum* and *Liamco* arbitrations: see Ch.2, paras 2–50 *et seq.*

[38] Model Law, Art.16(3); see Ch.9, paras 9–15 *et seq.*

[39] See Ch.10, paras 10–70 *et seq.*

[40] Certain laws require pleas as to the lack of jurisdiction of the tribunal to be raised before the submission of the defence on the merits. See, *e.g.*, the Model Law, Art.16(2). See also the English Arbitration Act 1996, s.31(1), which requires this plea to be made not later than "the time [the objecting party] takes the first step in the proceedings to contest the merits of any matter in relation to which he challenges the tribunal's jurisdiction".

issue. This is a sensible and practical provision. It is undesirable that a party who feels that the case is beginning to go against it should be able to raise objections to jurisdiction at a late stage of the proceedings, since this leaves open a means of abusing the arbitral process. Under the English Act, an objection to jurisdiction cannot be raised later than "the time [the party raising the objection] takes the first step in the proceedings to contest the merits . . . "[41] In Venezuela, any objection to jurisdiction has to be raised within five business days of the procedural hearing.[42] However, the UNCITRAL Rules cannot prevent the losing party from raising issues of jurisdiction as a ground for resisting the recognition or enforcement of the award.[43] On the other hand, failure to raise the objection early enough in an arbitration with an English seat does mean that the award will not be enforced by English courts unless exceptional circumstances can be shown.[44]

(f) Options open to the respondent

5–54   A respondent has four methods of challenging the jurisdiction of an arbitral tribunal established contrary to its assertion that the tribunal has no jurisdiction:

- boycott the arbitration;

- raise the objections with the tribunal;

- apply to the national court to resolve the issue; or

- challenge the award, once it has been made.

Boycott the arbitration

5–55   The first, and most extreme course of action, is to boycott the arbitration altogether. In this event the arbitration will proceed on an *ex parte* basis, and the respondent will seek the setting aside of the award or resist enforcement on the grounds of lack of jurisdiction after the final award has been issued. The Libyan Government took this course in the oil nationalisation cases that have been mentioned after writing to the arbitrator in each case to contend that the arbitral proceedings were invalid. Liberia behaved in the same way in the *Letco v Liberia* case before an ICSID tribunal.[45] It is ill advised since, provided the party has been properly notified of the constitution of the tribunal and relevant procedural

---

[41] Arbitration Act 1996, s.31(1). For the purposes of this section, the "first step" does not include any participation in the appointment of an arbitrator. See also the Swiss International Arbitration Law, Art.186.2.

[42] Venezuelan Law on Commercial Arbitration 1998, Art.25.

[43] Although if the grounds for objection were then known, the losing party's failure to object at an early stage in accordance with the rules under which the arbitration was conducted would no doubt influence the court in considering the objection who may consider the issue to have been waived.

[44] English Arbitration Act 1996, s.73.

[45] See award dated March 31, 1986, 2 ICSID Reports 356 at 378.

deadlines and hearings, an ultimate award will be enforceable against it notwithstanding non-participation. Further, a costs award against the recalcitrant party is likely.[46]

Raise objections with the arbitral tribunal

The second course of action (which is the most conventional) is to raise 5–56 objections to jurisdiction with the arbitral tribunal itself as a preliminary issue, as envisaged in the UNCITRAL Rules and in other sets of institutional rules. If this is done, the tribunal will usually schedule an exchange of written briefs on the jurisdictional issue often followed by a preliminary hearing at which the representatives of the parties will have the opportunity of making their case orally.

The disadvantage for the respondent in employing this strategy is that, in practice, an arbitral tribunal rarely makes a ruling that has the effect of putting itself totally out of business (although it is not uncommon for the arbitral tribunal to steer a middle course under which it will deny itself the competence to examine some but not all of the claims put forward by the claimant). It is not suggested that this arises from any cynical or self-interested desire on the part of individual members of the arbitral tribunal to keep the arbitration alive; it is rather that arbitral tribunals tend to be reluctant to adopt a course that may have the effect of leaving the claimant with no adequate remedy in respect of its claims.[47]

Application to a national court

The third course of action is for the respondent to ignore the arbitral tribunal 5–57 and to go to court to resolve the issue of jurisdiction. There are various ways in which this may be done. The respondent may, for example, seek an injunction or similar remedy to restrain the arbitral tribunal from proceeding. Or the respondent may seek a declaration to the effect that the arbitral tribunal does not have jurisdiction in respect of the particular claim or claims put forward by the claimant—for instance, on the basis that there was no valid arbitration agreement.

Alternatively, the respondent may take the offensive and commence litigation in respect of the matters in dispute. The claimant in the arbitration would presumably defend such a challenge to the jurisdiction of the arbitral tribunal by seeking to have the arbitration agreement enforced. This would be a straightforward matter of reliance upon Art.II of the New York Convention or the relevant provision of domestic law implementing the New York Convention (such as s.9 of the English 1996 Act) or a similar provision of the law governing arbitration at the seat of the arbitration (as in Art.8 of the Model Law). The relevant national court must decide whether the arbitration agreement is null and void, inoperative

---

[46] In the *Letco v Liberia* case, the tribunal awarded full costs against Liberia on the basis of "Liberia's procedural bad faith" (above, at 378).
[47] Because, if the arbitral tribunal rules that it has no jurisdiction, the claimant is usually left only with the possibility of suing the respondent in his "home" courts.

or incapable of being performed; if it is not, the parties will be referred to arbitration.

Such challenges to the jurisdiction of an arbitral tribunal are usually addressed to the courts at the seat of arbitration, if these courts have power to intervene in an international arbitration during the course of the proceedings.[48] The main disadvantage for a respondent who adopts this course is that he risks an adverse decision. This will enhance the standing of the arbitration and make it more difficult to resist enforcement of any subsequent award against him on the grounds of lack of jurisdiction.

5–58   Instead of applying to the courts of the place of arbitration, a reluctant respondent may apply to another national court, if that court has jurisdiction to entertain the application and if there is thought to be some advantage in doing so. Thus, as happened in the *Hubco v WAPDA* case[49] one party to the dispute may be seeking to arbitrate in one country, whilst the other party is seeking to litigate in another.

Attacking the award

5–59   The fourth course of action is for the respondent to participate in the arbitration, and to remain passive until after the final award has been issued by the arbitral tribunal. It may then either challenge the award in the courts of the country in which the arbitration took place or, alternatively, refuse to implement the award and wait for the successful claimant to attempt to enforce it. When such an action for enforcement is taken, the losing party might then argue the objections to jurisdiction as a ground for refusal of enforcement.

The disadvantage of this tactic is that the court to which the successful party has applied for enforcement may be prejudiced against the respondent by its failure to raise the issue of jurisdiction at an earlier stage. In other words the judge may regard the exercise as an unmeritorious attempt on the part of the losing party to use a technicality as a means of avoiding its obligations. Furthermore, under some systems of law, failure to raise an objection to jurisdiction promptly may operate as a waiver of the objection.[50]

The combined approach

5–60   What, then, is the reluctant party to do, when requested to take part in an arbitration under an agreement it considers as non-existent or invalid? Should it

---

[48] *e.g.* it would be possible in such countries as England and Switzerland, where the policy is that issues of jurisdiction should be finally resolved at the earliest possible stage by means of concurrent court control.

[49] See (2000) 16 Arbitration International 439 and the discussion in Ch.7 on the issue of interference by courts in the arbitral process.

[50] This would be the position under the Model Law, Art.4. If a party has appeared and participated in the arbitration without raising any objections to the jurisdiction of the tribunal, it may be deemed to have impliedly submitted to the arbitration, and any challenge to jurisdiction thereafter might be viewed as a mere device. It is significant though that Art.4 refers to provisions from which the parties "may derogate" and thus a party is not capable of waiving a mandatory provision of the applicable law. See the discussion of waiver in Ch.4, paras 4–76 *et seq.*

boycott the arbitration? Or should it take part, whilst protesting the jurisdiction of the arbitral tribunal? There is no simple answer. Much will depend on the circumstances of each particular case. On balance, it is probably best to take part in the arbitral proceedings. It should be made clear from the outset, however, that this is done under protest as to the jurisdiction of the arbitral tribunal; otherwise, participation in the proceedings might be construed as a waiver of this issue.

It is possible to use a combination of the first, third and fourth courses of action. Indeed, the proper and most effective course where there are genuine grounds upon which to challenge the jurisdiction of the arbitral tribunal is to raise the matter with the arbitral tribunal itself at the earliest possible stage, to insist that all objections should be fully argued before the arbitral tribunal and that the determination of the objections should be the subject of an interim award.

If the arbitral tribunal upholds its own jurisdiction, as it frequently does, the respondent should continue to participate in the arbitration, having expressly reserved its position in relation to the issue of jurisdiction so that this issue may be considered again after the final award is issued, either by a challenge of the award in the courts of the place of arbitration, or by resisting attempts to obtain recognition or enforcement of the award.

Form of court intervention

Although a national court's role in reviewing the correctness of a tribunal's **5–61** award on jurisdiction is well established, the type of intervention the court is meant to undertake is not so clear. Is the court to have a *de novo* hearing, considering the jurisdiction question afresh; or is it merely to review the tribunal's decision applying a presumption that this decision is correct?

There is little settled law on this point. A 1995 US Supreme Court decision held that the type of intervention depends upon whether the parties agreed to submit the "arbitrability" of their dispute to arbitration.[51] If so, the arbitral tribunal is the primary judge, and the court must apply a cautious standard of review; if not, the court is the primary judge and is required to undertake a full *de novo* hearing.[52] The court held that a clear intent to "arbitrate arbitrability" was required to limit the court's form of intervention. Arguably, however, an arbitration clause which incorporated a set of rules which stated the competence-competence principle could be said to do just this.[53]

(g) International agreements on the jurisdiction of national courts

Where there are treaties in place between different countries establishing rules **5–62** as to which courts may take jurisdiction, the parties may be restricted as to where they may go to seek a judicial remedy. Within the EU, for example, a measure of uniformity as to which state courts may accept jurisdiction is established by

---

[51] *Kaplan v MK Investments Inc* (US) 115 Supreme Court 1920 (1995); 131 L.Ed.2d 985 (1995).
[52] *ibid.*, at 1923–1924.
[53] Most rules do. See for instance, AAA Arbitration Rules, Art.15.1; ICC Arbitration Rules, Art.6.2; LCIA Arbitration Rules, Art.23.1; UNCITRAL Arbitration Rules, Art.21.1.

Regulation 44/2001,[54] which supersedes the Brussels and Lugano Conventions.[55] Article 1(2)(d) of Regulation 44/2001 specifically excludes arbitrations from the application of the Convention. Article 2 establishes a basic rule (subject to limited exceptions) that persons shall be sued in the courts of the state in which they are domiciled. A potential conflict consequently arises when a legal action is brought in one of the Member States but there is a claim that the dispute is covered by an arbitration clause providing for arbitration in a different Member State.

The party seeking to avoid arbitration may claim that there was no binding arbitration agreement and that the court of his or her domicile has jurisdiction and not the courts at the seat of the arbitration. The other party may reply that a question as to the validity of an arbitration agreement is itself excluded from the application of the Convention, under Art.1(2), as being connected with an arbitration.

This precise situation occurred in the *Marc Rich* case, in which an English court was asked to rule on the validity of an arbitration agreement as part of the process of considering an application for support of the arbitral process (in the appointment of an arbitrator), while simultaneously an Italian court (which would have jurisdiction under the Convention were it not for the arbitration agreement) was asked to act as if no valid arbitration agreement existed.

5–63   In 1991, the European Court held that the arbitration exclusion of the Brussels Convention (Art.1(2)(d) of Regulation 44/2001) extended to litigation before a national court in respect of the arbitrator. As a consequence, it was admissible for the English courts to intervene in the appointment of an arbitrator notwithstanding the domicile of the defendant in Italy.[56] This appears to be sound. The exclusion exception of Art.1(2)(d) would be deprived of any real meaning if the Regulation were to apply to applications in support of arbitration.

Another area of tension between the EU jurisdiction regime and the arbitration exception was exposed in *Van Uden Maritime v Deco-Line*.[57] The claimant was a Dutch corporation that had started an arbitration against a German respondent in the Netherlands for monies due under a charterparty. The claimant also sought an interim payment from the national courts in the Netherlands pursuant to the Netherlands Arbitration Act. The Hoge Raad of the Netherlands referred the question to the European Court of Justice as to whether it had jurisdiction to make a provisional order pending determination of a dispute by an arbitral tribunal on the basis of Art.24 of the Brussels Convention (now Art.31 of Regulation 44/2001) which states:

---

[54] Official Journal of the European Union, No.L12/1, January 16, 2001.

[55] With the exception of Denmark, which opted out of its adoption in accordance with the terms of its Protocol to the EU Treaty. The old Brussels Convention therefore continues to apply in relation to jurisdictional issues between Denmark and the rest of the EU.

[56] *Marc Rich & Co AG v Societa Italiana Impianti PA (The Atlantic Emperor)* [1989] 1 Lloyd's Rep. 548 (CA); the appeal of this case was referred to the European Court of Justice and was heard on October 17, 1990; [1992] 1 Lloyd's Rep. 342 (ECJ). See also the discussion in Hascher, "Arbitration under the Brussels Convention" (1997) 13 Arbitration International 33.

[57] Case C-391/95 [1999] 2 W.L.R. 1181.

"Application may be made to the courts of a Contracting State for such provisional, including protective, measures as may be available under the law of that State, even if, under this Convention, the courts of another Contracting State have jurisdiction as to the substance of the matter."

The respondent argued that there was no such jurisdiction since the arbitration exception applied. The European Court disagreed and held that "provisional measures are not in principle ancillary to arbitration proceedings but are ordered in parallel to such proceedings and are intended as measures of support. They concern not arbitration as such *but the protection of a wide variety of rights*." The net result is that such applications benefit from the protection of the Regulation such that there can be no concurrent proceedings (Arts 21–23). Further, an application for interim measures from an EU national court in support of an arbitration can be enforced under Regulation 44/2001 in any other court in the EU. This is a strong incentive to seek such measures within the EU since interim measures from a national court may not be enforced automatically elsewhere pursuant to the New York Convention.

CHAPTER 6

THE CONDUCT OF THE PROCEEDINGS

1. BACKGROUND

(a) Generally

6–01   An international arbitration may be conducted in many different ways. There are no fixed rules of procedure. Rules of arbitration often provide an outline of the various steps to be taken; but the detailed regulations of the procedure to be followed are established either by agreement of the parties or by directions from the tribunal—or a combination of the two. The one thing that is certain is that counsel should not bring the rule books from their home courts with them.

The relationship between the arbitrator and the parties has been considered in Ch.5.[1] Whether the duties of an arbitrator are primarily a matter of contract (as held by modern opinion) or a matter of status, as has sometimes been suggested,[2] remains to be finally determined. What is clear is that an arbitral tribunal must conduct the arbitration in accordance with the reasonable requirements of the parties. If it fails to do so, the award may be set aside or refused recognition and enforcement.[3]

This freedom of the parties to dictate the procedure to be followed in an arbitration is not totally unrestricted. The procedure they establish must comply with any mandatory rules[4] and public policy requirements of the law of the place of arbitration.[5] It must also take into account those provisions of the international conventions on arbitration that aim to ensure that arbitral proceedings are conducted fairly.[6] If this is not done, then again the award may be set aside or refused recognition and enforcement.[7] Accordingly, there is a balance to be struck between the parties' views on the procedure to be followed and any overriding requirements of the applicable law.

---

[1] See Ch.5, paras 5–03 et seq.

[2] See, e.g., Mustill & Boyd, *Commercial Arbitration* (2nd ed., 1989), pp.186–189, 220–223.

[3] An award may be set aside under the Model Law if "the arbitral procedure was not in accordance with the agreement of the parties"; and this is also a ground for refusal of recognition or enforcement of an award under the New York Convention: Model Law, Arts 34(2)(a)(iv) and 36(1)(a)(iv), and New York Convention, Art.V.1(d).

[4] See the provisions of the Model Law and the New York Convention, above, n.3; and see Ch.2.

[5] See Ch.2.

[6] See Ch.1.

[7] See generally Ch.9.

In some respects an international arbitration is like a ship. An arbitration may **6–02** be said to be "owned" by the parties, just as a ship is owned by a shipowners or series of shipowners. But the ship is under the day-to-day command of the captain, to whom the owner hands control. The owner may dismiss the captain if he wishes and hire a replacement, but there will always be someone on board who is in command.[8]

At the beginning of an arbitration the parties are firmly in control. In ad hoc arbitration, where there is no institution involved, they may—and sometimes do—write a set of procedural rules to govern the way in which the proceedings are to be handled. When they subsequently appoint an arbitral tribunal, by whatever method they have agreed, that tribunal is constrained by the agreed procedural framework. In institutional arbitration the procedural framework is provided by the institution's rules, to which the parties have agreed when they referred the resolution of disputes between them to the rules of the institution concerned.

Once an arbitral tribunal is established, day-to-day control of the proceedings begins to pass to the tribunal. However, the transfer of control is not total and is not immediate. The tribunal usually engages in a dialogue with the parties on procedural matters, and often an agreed "Procedural Order No.1" is issued to determine the essential stages of the process and the time-limits within which each stage is to take place. From this point the tribunal is more firmly in control, to ensure that the procedural steps are completed and on time, and partly to decide procedural issues between the parties as the proceedings move forward. By the time the oral hearings are reached the tribunal is fully in command (in the "captain of the ship" sense) and, in any event, the parties usually find it easier to apply for directions on disputed procedural issues than attempt to reach agreement between themselves.

Where the arbitral tribunal itself cannot resolve problems (for instance, to compel the attendance of a reluctant witness) it may be necessary to seek the help of a national court. The role of national courts during the proceedings is considered in the next chapter. This chapter is primarily concerned with the many different ways an arbitral tribunal exercises control over the proceedings.

(b) Party autonomy

Party autonomy is the guiding principle in determining the procedure to be **6–03** followed in an international commercial arbitration. It is a principle that has been endorsed not only in national laws, but by international arbitral institutions and organisations. The legislative history of the Model Law shows that the principle was adopted without opposition[9]; and the text of the Model Law itself contains the following provision:

---

[8] See Veeder, "Whose arbitration is it anyway: the parties or the arbitration tribunal—an interesting question?" in *The Leading Arbitrators' Guide to Internatinal Arbitration* (Juris, 2004), p.351.

[9] See, *e.g.*, UN Doc.A/CN.9/207, para.17: " . . . probably the most important principle on which the Model Law should be based is the freedom of the parties in order to facilitate the proper functioning of international commercial arbitrations according to their expectations".

"Subject to the provisions of this Law, the parties are free to agree on the procedure to be followed by the arbitral tribunal in conducting the proceedings."[10]

This principle follows in the steps of the Geneva Protocol of 1923 which provides that "the arbitral procedure, including the constitution of the arbitral tribunal, shall be governed by the will of the parties . . . "[11]; and the New York Convention under which recognition and enforcement of a foreign arbitral award may be refused if "the arbitral procedure was not in accordance with the agreement of the parties".[12]

The ICC, historically a champion of the autonomy of the parties, provides:

"The proceedings before the Arbitral Tribunal shall be governed by these Rules and, where these Rules are silent, any rules which the parties or, failing them, the Arbitral Tribunal, may settle . . . "[13]

Adopting the same approach, the LCIA Rules state:

"The parties may agree on the conduct of their arbitral proceedings, and they are encouraged to do so . . . "[14]

6-04   ICSID adopts a similar approach. Detailed provisions are set out with regard to the conduct of the proceedings. For example, the ICSID Rules state:

"As early as possible after the constitution of a Tribunal, its President shall endeavour to ascertain the views of the parties regarding questions of procedure. For this purpose, he may request the parties to meet him. He shall, in particular, seek their views on the following matters:

  (a) the number of members of the Tribunal required to constitute a quorum at its sittings;
  (b) the language or languages to be used in the proceedings;
  (c) the number and sequence of the pleadings and the time limits within which they are to be filed;
  (d) the number of copies desired by each party of instruments filed by the other;
  (e) dispensing with the written or the oral procedure;
  (f) the manner in which the cost of the proceeding is to be apportioned; and
  (g) the manner in which the record of the hearings shall be kept.

---

[10] Model Law, Art.19(1).
[11] Geneva Protocol of 1923, Art.2.
[12] New York Convention, Art.V.1(d).
[13] ICC Arbitration Rules, Art.15(1).
[14] LCIA Arbitration Rules, Art.14(1).

In the conduct of the proceeding the Tribunal shall apply any agreement between the parties on procedural matters, except as otherwise provided in the Convention or the Administrative and Financial Regulations."[15]

Similarly, the ICDR Rules give wide latitude to the arbitral tribunal in determining procedure, subject to the agreement of the parties.[16]

Some rules of arbitration are drawn so as to transfer control of the proceedings from the parties to the arbitral tribunal at a comparatively early stage of the proceedings. This is particularly so with the UNCITRAL Rules which provide: "Subject to these Rules, the *arbitral tribunal* may conduct the arbitration in such manner as it considers appropriate . . . "[17] Nevertheless, considerable freedom is still conferred on the parties; for example, they may request hearings[18]; agree upon the place of arbitration[19]; agree upon the language or languages to be used in the arbitration[20]; and so forth. The WIPO Rules adopt a similar formula.[21]

(c) Restrictions on party autonomy

In the exercise of their autonomy, the parties may confer upon the arbitral tribunal such powers and duties as they consider appropriate to the specific case. They may choose formal or informal methods of conducting the arbitration; adversarial or inquisitorial procedures; documentary or oral methods of presenting evidence and so forth. The exercise of this autonomy is, however, restricted by various requirements that can be grouped in the following general categories.   **6–05**

Equality

If party autonomy is the first principle to be applied in relation to arbitral procedure, equality of treatment is the second—and it is of the same importance. This principle is given express recognition both in the New York Convention[22] and in the Model Law, which states: "The parties shall be treated with equality and each party shall be given a full opportunity of presenting his case."[23]   **6–06**

The concept of treating the parties with equality is basic to all systems of justice. It is expressed in the UNCITRAL Rules by means of a specific proviso to the rule that the arbitral tribunal may conduct the arbitration in such manner

---

[15] ICSID Arbitration Rules, r.20(1) and (2): the first of these provisions is somewhat oddly phrased, but is presumably intended to apply to procedural matters rather than to the full hearing, where normally the full tribunal should be present.

[16] ICDR International Arbitration Rules, Art.16.

[17] UNCITRAL Arbitration Rules, Art.15.1 (emphasis added).

[18] *ibid.*, Art.15.2.

[19] *ibid.*, Art.16.1.

[20] *ibid.*, Art.17.1.

[21] WIPO Arbitration Rules, Art.38(a).

[22] New York Convention, Art.V.1(b): "Recognition and enforcement of the award may be refused . . . if . . . the party against whom the award was made was . . . unable to present his case".

[23] Model Law, Art.18.

as it considers appropriate[24]; and serves as a reminder to the arbitral tribunal that, in doing this, it must not grant privileges to one party that it denies to another. It is also a concept that underlies other sets of arbitration rules.[25]

The requirement that the parties must be treated equally operates as a restriction on party autonomy. For instance, a provision in a submission agreement that only one party should be heard by the arbitral tribunal might well be treated as invalid (for instance, by the enforcement court) even if both parties had agreed to it. The UNCITRAL Secretariat recognised the dilemma in its report leading to the Model Law:

" . . . it will be one of the more delicate and complex problems of the preparation of a Model Law to strike a balance between the interests of the parties to freely determine the procedure to be followed and the interests of the legal system expressed to give recognition and effect thereto."[26]

Public policy

6–07   The parties may not confer powers upon an arbitral tribunal that would cause the arbitration to be conducted in a manner contrary to the mandatory rules or public policy of the state in which the arbitration is held. One important mandatory rule that has already been considered requires that each party should be given a fair hearing or, as the Model Law expresses it, "a full opportunity of presenting his case". This is a significant element of the requirement that the parties must be treated with equality. In general, if each party has had a full opportunity to present his case, the parties will have received equal treatment. In theory the word "full" is somewhat disconcerting and conjures up visions of a party demanding the opportunity to present duplicative testimony for days or even weeks. But in this context the word "full" must be given an objective, not a subjective meaning.

Any agreement by the parties conferring a power on the arbitral tribunal to perform an act in conducting the arbitration contrary to a mandatory rule (or to the public policy) of the country in which the arbitration is taking place would be unenforceable in that country, at least to the extent of the offending provision. So would any provision that purported to give the arbitral tribunal power to perform an act that is not capable of being performed by arbitrators under the law applicable to the arbitration agreement, or under the law of the place of arbitration.[27]

---

[24] UNCITRAL Arbitration Rules, Art.15.1.

[25] See, *e.g.*, WIPO Arbitration Rules, Art.38(a); the corresponding provisions of the ICC Arbitration Rules, Art.15(2), ICSID Arbitration Rules, r.42 and the LCIA Arbitration Rules Art.14.1(i) do not expresly mention "equality", but the phrase "fairly and impartially" must encompass it.

[26] UN Doc.A/CN.9/207, para.21.

[27] *e.g.* the administration of oaths by arbitrators in a country where the law only allows oaths to be administered by judicial officers.

Arbitration rules

Restrictions may also be introduced by the operation of arbitration rules **6–08** chosen by the parties. However, such rules usually contain few mandatory provisions in relation to the conduct of the proceedings. For example, the UNCITRAL Rules specify only four:

- under Art.15(1), the parties must be treated with equality, and each party must be given a full opportunity of presenting his case;

- also under Art.15(1), the arbitral tribunal must hold a hearing if either party requests one;

- under Arts 18 and 19, there must be one consecutive exchange of written submissions (a "statement of claim" and a "statement of defence") which must include certain features;

- under Art.27, if the arbitral tribunal appoints an expert, it must give the parties the opportunity to interrogate the expert at a hearing, and the parties must be given an opportunity to present their own expert witnesses on the points at issue.

Third parties

An arbitration agreement may not validly confer any powers on an arbitral **6–09** tribunal that directly affect persons who are not parties to that agreement unless a special provision of the applicable law enables them to do so; and this is rare.[28] The principle applies to matters of substance as well as of procedure. For example, the award of an arbitral tribunal cannot properly direct a person who is not a party to the arbitration agreement to pay a sum of money or to perform a particular act. As regards procedural matters, the most common examples arise in relation to the production of documents and evidence.

An arbitral tribunal may direct the *parties* (or others under their control) to produce documents, or to submit to examination; but it usually has no power to compel third parties to do so, even if the parties to the arbitration have purported to confer such a power. The participation of third parties in arbitration proceedings, whether by giving evidence or producing documents, may usually be compelled only by invoking the assistance of a court of competent jurisdiction. This is considered later.[29]

(d) Adversarial and inquisitorial processes

Procedures followed by national courts for the resolution of civil disputes have **6–10** for centuries been classified under these two broad headings. In the adversarial

---

[28] In the US, *e.g.*, the Federal Arbitration Act, s.7, allows an arbitrator to issue a summons to order the attendance of a third party as a witness at the arbitral proceedings; but court assistance is necessary to enforce the summons if the third party refuses to obey it.

[29] See Ch.7, paras 7–15 and 7–24 *et seq.*

procedure—which is used primarily in England,[30] the US, Scandinavia and the Commonwealth countries comprising the former British colonies—alternative versions of the facts and interpretations of the law are presented to the judge. Each party has the opportunity to test and respond to the material submitted by the other, and the judge must ultimately choose between them. In the inquisitorial procedure the judge conducts his own enquiries into the factual and legal issues, with the assistance of the parties and their lawyers.

The principle of party autonomy allows the parties to an arbitration to choose either approach or a blend of the two, irrespective of the procedure followed by the courts at the place of arbitration. The arbitration clause or submission agreement does not need to specify the procedure to be followed. By submitting to arbitration under rules that give the arbitral tribunal discretion to determine the procedure to be followed, the parties will have conferred power on the arbitral tribunal to adopt either adversarial or inquisitorial procedures, or a mixture,[31] as it thinks fit.

Experience shows that the procedure adopted in international commercial arbitrations depends not so much on the place where the arbitration is conducted, but more on the background and experience of the individual members of the arbitral tribunal and the parties' advisers.

6–11   Thus, in a major arbitration held in the Canton de Vaud, Switzerland, the hearings were held in Geneva, Lausanne and Kuwait.[32] Neither party had any connection with England, and the substantive law governing the issues was the law of Kuwait. Nevertheless, the leading advocates representing both parties were English, and the agreed procedure set out in the detailed submission agreement was substantially adversarial in character. Formal written pleadings were exchanged and the witnesses and experts were called, examined and cross-examined by the parties, not by the arbitral tribunal. The fact that the place of the arbitration was the Canton de Vaud did not influence the choice of procedure. Similarly, in another arbitration involving a governmental agency,[33] the place of arbitration was Paris; the hearings took place there and in the Lebanon, but the parties (who were represented by US and English lawyers respectively) agreed upon an adversarial procedure and applied common law style rules of evidence.

Equally, arbitrators and counsel from civil law countries had a natural tendency to assume that the procedure would follow the rules applied in their own

---

[30] In England the Civil Procedure Rules 1998 signalled a move away from the adversarial procedure to a more inquisitorial approach.

[31] The practice of the Iran–US Claims Tribunal illustrates a blend of inquisitorial and adversarial procedures. See Holtzmann, "Fact-finding by the Iran–United States Claims Tribunal" in *Fact-finding by International Tribunals* (Transnational Publishers Inc, 1991), pp.101 *et seq.* (hereafter referred to as Holtzmann, *Fact-finding*).

[32] *Orazio de Nora Impianti Elettrochimici v The Government of Kuwait*: the award was subsequently challenged, unsuccessfully, by de Nora in public proceedings in Switzerland (Tribunal Cantonal Vaudois, April 9, 1968, *de Nora v Kuwait*).

[33] ICC Case No.1776.

national courts. By the early years of the twenty-first century, however, experienced international arbitral tribunals became more willing to avoid the traditional procedures of their own home courts. For example, modern arbitrators routinely enforce strict limitations on the length of written submissions, the scope of production of documents, the number of witnesses, the time permitted for cross-examination and so forth. The *IBA Rules on the Taking of Evidence in International Commercial Arbitration* (1999 edition), created a useful international standard for evidence gathering, and are often adopted by agreement between the arbitral tribunal and the parties.[34]

2. CHOICE OF THE PLACE OF ARBITRATION

(a) Generally

Parties to an international commercial arbitration are generally free to choose **6–12** for themselves the juridical seat[35] of their arbitration.[36]

Failure to make a clear choice of the place of arbitration in the arbitration clause of a contract may lead to unexpected results. A court in the US ordered an arbitration to proceed in California under the ICDR Rules where the arbitration clause did not specify a place of arbitration, even though a separate clause in the contract specified that if an arbitration became necessary it was to be held in Beijing and to be subject to the FETAC Rules.[37]

Parties may make the choice of a place of arbitration at any time before the arbitration begins; or they may leave it to be made on their behalf by an arbitral institution (if the arbitration is to be conducted under institutional rules) or by the arbitral tribunal itself. At some stage, however, a choice must be made. The question then arises as to where the arbitration should be held. Should it, for example, be held in London or Washington, Paris or Geneva, Cairo or Kuala Lumpur?

There is no simple or universal answer to this question.[38] The nationality of the parties must be taken into account, since the general practice is to hold an

---

[34] See below, paras 6–78, 6–85, 6–93 and 6–116.

[35] The word "seat" is a translation of the French word "*siège*" and in some ways a more accurate word than "place". "Seat" means the juridical base of the arbitration, whereas "place" can mean the place (or places) where the meetings occur, which need not always be at the "seat". However, in general parlance the words are often used interchangeably, as indeed they are in this book. See Ch.2 for further discussion of the significance of the seat of arbitration.

[36] Arbitrations under the Washington Convention are an exception to this general rule. If parties to such an arbitration wish the hearing to take place elsewhere than at the International Centre in Washington (or at an institution with which the Secretary-General of the International Centre has made the necessary arrangements), they must consult the Secretary-General and obtain the approval of the arbitral tribunal: see ICSID Arbitration Rules, r.13(3).

[37] *Bauhinia Corp v China National Machinery & Equipment Import & Export Corp,* 819 F.2d 247 (9th Cir. 1987). FETAC has been succeeded by CIETAC.

[38] For further discussion of relevant factors to be taken into consideration see Iwasaki, "Selection of situs: criteria and priorities" (1986) 2 Arbitration International 57.

arbitration in a country that is "neutral", in the sense that it is not the country of any of the parties to the dispute. The usual residence (or place of business of) the parties will have to be taken into account too, because of the need to cut down as far as possible on the expense and inconvenience of travelling. There are political factors, such as the general acceptability to the parties of some countries and, in particular, the question of whether any restrictions are likely to be imposed on the entry of the parties, their advisers and witnesses.[39]

6–13   There are economic factors, such as freedom to transfer the necessary funds to and from the country concerned. There may well be a need for skilled local support—from lawyers competent to advise on matters relevant to the conduct of the arbitration, or from engineers, surveyors, accountants and other professionals to provide expert assistance and evidence. Such assistance is less expensive if it is available at (or at least near) the place of arbitration.

There are other practical considerations too, such as the availability of suitable rooms for hearings, and hotel accommodation for the parties, their advisers and witnesses: some major cities experience an acute shortage of hotel rooms at certain times of the year. Other relevant requirements include good transportation facilities, by rail or by air; good communications, by telephone, email and fax; and support facilities such as transcription services, interpreters and so forth. These facilities form part of the infrastructure of an arbitration.

The suitability of a particular place for an international arbitration depends in part on whether there is an adequate infrastructure to accommodate the parties. However, the most important consideration is usually the legal environment. This is relevant both to the conduct of the arbitration and to the enforceability of the award.

(b) The law governing the arbitration

6–14   Whether or not a particular legal environment is right for the conduct of an international arbitration is as much a matter of personal judgment as of legal analysis. There are certain minimum international standards on which most arbitrators and practitioners agree. For example, the local law must be prepared to enforce international arbitration agreements, in line with the New York Convention and the Model Law. It must be prepared, if necessary, to assist in the constitution of the arbitral tribunal; and to give that arbitral tribunal, either directly or through its courts, such powers as it may need to carry out its task efficiently and effectively. Furthermore, it must be prepared to recognise and enforce foreign arbitral awards, if it expects awards made on its own territory to be recognised and enforced in other countries.

Beyond such minimum international standards, however, there is room for different points of view as to what does and what does not constitute a suitable

---

[39] Many years ago the authors recall working with a lawyer from a less-developed country who insisted that the venue for a particular arbitration should be Paris, when almost everyone else concerned would have preferred Geneva. It turned out that the reason was that he did not need a visa for France, whereas he did need one for Switzerland; in addition, there were daily direct flights between Paris and the capital city of his country.

legal environment for the conduct of an international commercial arbitration. Moreover, views are likely to vary according to whether the interest represented is that of claimant, respondent or arbitrator.

Level of control

Having decided to embark on an arbitration to secure what it considers to be **6–15** its due, a claimant usually wants those proceedings to be carried out as quickly and as cheaply as possible. Any assistance that the local law is prepared to give to this end, either directly or through its courts, will no doubt be welcomed; but any intervention by these courts at the suit of the respondent is likely to be seen as judicial "interference", as it merely adds to the length (and cost) of the proceedings.[40]

The position looks different from the point of view of the respondent. Unless there is a substantial counterclaim, a respondent has little to gain and much to lose through the existence of the arbitration. At best, after spending perhaps considerable time and money, the respondent's defence to the proceedings will be upheld. At worst, the respondent may be faced with being ordered to pay damages, interest and costs. In these circumstances, the speed with which the proceedings are likely to be conducted will be of less interest to the respondent than the assurance that they will be conducted properly, including a fair opportunity to present its defence. If such an assurance is built into the local law, by means of some form of review procedure, the respondent is likely to be more satisfied than if the only option is to submit to a process that it regards as unfair and then eventually resist enforcement of the award on one of the grounds available under the New York Convention or in the applicable law.[41]

The arbitral tribunal is likely to adopt a position nearer to that of the claimant than of the respondent in its view of what constitutes a suitable legal environment. It usually wants to carry out the task for which it has been appointed as quickly as reasonably possible, with *assistance* (where needed) but not *interference* from the local courts.

No ideal legal environment exists for the conduct of an international commer- **6–16** cial arbitration; and no system of law satisfies the often conflicting requirements of the claimant and the respondent. Further, the interest of the state cannot be ignored, since from time to time the state is called upon to lend its authority to the recognition and enforcement of arbitral awards. The best that can be done is to find a reasonable balance between these different interests.

Parties to an arbitration agreement may be presumed to have intended to carry out the agreement if it becomes necessary to do so; and, further, to carry it out properly and in good faith, without seeking (except in exceptional circumstances) to replace the decision of the arbitral tribunal with that of a national court.

This approach is reflected in the Model Law, which does not contemplate any right of appeal from arbitral awards on questions of fact or law; and it has been

---

[40] Intervention by national courts during the proceedings is covered in Ch.7.
[41] *e.g.* under the Model Law, Art.36(1)(a)(ii).

followed by most jurisdictions that have introduced arbitration legislation since
the Model Law was adopted by UNCITRAL towards the end of 1985. As more
and more states have adopted the Model Law, or amend their own laws to
conform closely to it, more countries are providing a suitable legal environment
for hosting international arbitrations.

The lex arbitri

6–17   In an international commercial arbitration, the proceedings are under the
general supervision of the national law of the country in which the arbitration has
its seat (except for arbitrations under the ICSID Rules, which are governed by
international law and treaties).[42] Any mandatory provisions of the law that
governs the conduct of the proceedings must be taken into account. In theory, it
is open to the parties to specify a national law to govern the arbitration proceedings which is not the law of the seat of the arbitration, provided that the law and
public policy of the place of arbitration so permit.[43] In practice, it is difficult to
see why parties should wish to complicate their lives in this way, particularly as
it may have the result that they will have to consult two different procedural laws
when problems arise. If the parties prefer the law of a particular country (country
A) to the law of the place of arbitration (country B) they should either:

- move the arbitration to country A; or

- adopt expressly any provisions from the law of country A they admire into
  a procedural agreement for their arbitration.

To attempt to conduct an arbitration in country B according to the supervisory
arbitration law of country A merely adds another tier of rules of law to those to
which the parties (and the arbitral tribunal) must pay heed. International commercial arbitration is complicated enough without such flights of fancy; fortunately,
however, it appears that in practice such a choice is rarely if ever made.[44]

Local restrictions on arbitrators and party representatives

6–18   In most countries there are no restrictions in the local law limiting the choice
of arbitrators and representatives. There may still be some exceptions, however,
that must be taken into consideration when choosing a place of arbitration.[45] If
the parties find that they are not permitted to be represented by their own
advocates, whether or not they are lawyers and, if so, whether or not they are "in
house", then they may consider that they are being unfairly treated. The problem
becomes most acute when the arbitration is conducted in a foreign country and

---

[42] See Ch.2, paras 2–05 *et seq.*
[43] See Chs 2 and 5.
[44] See the comments of Kerr L.J. in the *Peruvian Insurance* case, Ch.2, para.2–21.
[45] By the end of the twentieth century, the main examples (Japan and Singapore) had changed their
rules, thus coming more closely into line with the policy expressed in the UNCITRAL Arbitration
Rules, Art.4: "The parties may be represented or assisted by persons of their choice".

in a foreign language, and the party is not permitted to have its usual lawyers or other representatives in attendance to present its case.

Some countries impose restrictions on who may be appointed as an arbitrator. Where a foreign party is involved in an arbitration, a sense of alienation may develop if that party is prevented from having someone on the arbitral tribunal who shares a common cultural, legal and linguistic background. A few countries require the arbitrators to have special qualifications or to have local nationality or residence. In Saudi Arabia, a foreigner may not be an arbitrator, which may cause difficulties when a non-Saudi law must be applied, or where one of the parties does not speak the local language thus requiring expensive translation. By contrast, the Model Law provides that no person shall be precluded from acting as an arbitrator by reason of nationality.[46] Parties should be careful when choosing a place of arbitration (or a set of institutional rules) to ensure that there are no unreasonable restrictions as to who may represent them or who may act as arbitrators.

Such types of local restriction create difficulties when, for example, they effectively preclude persons knowledgeable in the law governing the merits of the dispute from being arbitrators. Fortunately, problems of this kind occur only in a small and diminishing number of countries.

Ethical and other duties

Difficult and perhaps unanswerable problems arise in determining who (if **6–19** anyone) has the right or duty to discipline lawyers for breach of professional ethics in international arbitrations. Is it the local bar association at the place of arbitration or the home bar association of the lawyers involved? May a court in the place of arbitration restrain foreign lawyers from improper conduct before an arbitral tribunal? And, on the substantive aspect, do lawyers representing parties in arbitrations outside their own countries have a duty to act in good faith?[47]

Professional bodies impose obligations and ethical duties on advocates, and these may follow them wherever they choose to practise; but that may not be sufficient to assist an arbitral tribunal in controlling the conduct of a party's lawyers in a country that is "foreign" to the professional body concerned. Instead, the tribunal must probably rely on any unofficial sanctions that are available. For example, a party whose advocate acts improperly may be penalised by having to pay the costs incurred in remedying the improper act.[48]

Party representatives may be required to produce a power of attorney, depending upon the place of the arbitration. No such formality is necessary, for example,

---

[46] Model Law, Art.11.
[47] See, *e.g.*, Veeder, "The Lawyer's Duty to Arbitrate in Good Faith", 2001 Goff Lecture, (2002) 18 Arbitration International 440.
[48] As in a publishesd NAFTA case, *Pope & Talbot v Government of Canada*, reported in *www.nafta-law.org*, where the Tribunal made a costs order against a party whose lawyer "leaked" confidential documents that had been disclosed by the opposing party. An arbitral tribunal probably does not have the power to prevent a lawyer from continuing to appear in an arbitration, but a party who does not comply with the reasonable directions of the tribunal runs a risk of being penalised, or even being excluded from the hearing in an extreme case.

in the UK or the USA. It is customary in those countries to accept oral assurances from the parties' representatives that they have appropriate authority to act in the case. However, if the other party had reasonable grounds to question the authority of the representative to appear, the arbitral tribunal could reasonably require the production of written instructions from the party being represented. In other countries, such as Japan, it is the general practice to submit formal powers of attorney; and in most Arab countries a power of attorney is required by law. In civil law systems, powers of attorney are not required in most cases but it is advisable to be prepared to produce one on request of the arbitrators.[49]

6–20   Some countries require the arbitrators themselves to have special qualifications or to have local nationality or residence. In Saudi Arabia a foreigner may not be an arbitrator, which may cause difficulties when a non-Saudi law must be applied; further, where one of the parties does not speak the local language expensive translation will be required. By contrast, the Model Law provides that no person shall be precluded from acting as an arbitrator by reason of his nationality.[50] Parties should be careful when choosing a place of arbitration (or a set of institutional rules) to ensure that there are no unreasonable restrictions as to who may represent them or who may act as arbitrators.

(c) Enforceability

6–21   Choosing a country that is a signatory to the New York Convention is of fundamental importance in ensuring the enforceability of an award.[51]

Problems may also arise where these countries do not have sufficiently developed laws relating to arbitration. Occasionally, they may have no arbitration law at all. The Model Law has greatly assisted in remedying this situation; and over time it will help to create a climate in which companies trading in less-developed countries will become willing to accept arbitration clauses that provide for arbitration in the place in which they are doing business. The establishment of regional arbitration centres in Cairo, Hong Kong and Kuala Lumpur was a useful start in the right direction. The work goes on, but some initiatives have been unsuccessful. For example, the Euro-Arab Chambers of Commerce, based in 18 European countries,[52] established rules of conciliation, arbitration and expertise in the mid-1980s. The Rules were drawn up in French, Arabic and English and were intended to offer to Arabs, Europeans and others directly or indirectly involved with the Arab countries the prospect of disputes being resolved by persons familiar with the Arab world.[53]

---

[49] For a description of the practices observed in the various countries referred to in this paragraph, see *Comparative Arbitration Practice and Public Policies in Arbitration* (Sanders ed.), ICCA Congress Series No.3 (Kluwer, 1987), pp.41 *et seq.*

[50] Model Law, Art.11.

[51] See, *e.g.*, Ch.10, para.10–23.

[52] Austria, Belgium, Bulgaria, Czech Republic, France, Germany, Greece, Hungary, Ireland, Italy, Malta, Netherlands, Poland, Portugal, Romania, Russian Federation, Switzerland and the UK.

[53] See Beaumont, "The Rules of Conciliation, Arbitration and Expertise of the Euro–Arab Chambers of Commerce" (1985) 2 International Construction Law Review 392.

The creation of arbitration centres and arbitral institutions in different parts of the world is important. The reluctance of transnational corporations to accept arbitration in the third world is mirrored by attitudes in some of the less-developed countries themselves:

" . . . the notion that there is a system of international justice will not be shared by some countries, notably those of Africa, Asia and Latin America, who still see arbitration as a foreign judicial institution which is imposed upon them. This fact must, therefore, be taken into account if we wish to approach certain areas of developing countries, that are rarely used as the place of arbitration, and which even more rarely produce arbitrators. The African concept of law, essentially orientated towards dialogue and conciliation, is also favourable to arbitration. But it is a form of tribal arbitration, rendered by arbitrators known to and respected by the parties.

In Africa, the governmental authorities and, in consequence, the judges, are hostile to international arbitration and no distinction is made between that and foreign arbitration. In addition, as everybody knows, *in fact arbitration is seldom freely agreed to by developing countries.* It is often agreed to in contracts of adhesion the signature of which is essential to the survival of these countries. Rendered abroad by foreigners, what is more, imposed, arbitration will only gradually obtain total Third World recognition."[54]

The importance of the enforceability of the award in relation to the choice of the place of arbitration cannot be overstated.[55] As global trade expands and the number of international arbitrations increase so does the participation of multinational corporations. The assets of these multinationals may be located in a number of different countries and their presence in any one country may disappear "in the twinkling of a telex".[56] It is accordingly necessary to have an award that is transportable across national boundaries. **6–22**

(d) Meetings need not all be held at the seat of arbitration

A determination of the seat of the arbitration, whether made by the parties, by the arbitral tribunal or by an arbitral institution, does not necessarily mean that *all* meetings and hearings must be held at that place. As already indicated in **6–23**

---

[54] Extract from an intervention by Mbaye, Judge of the International Court of Justice, published in *60 Years of ICC Arbitration—A Look at the Future*, ICC Publication No.412, 1984, p.295 (emphasis added). By the early years of the twenty-first century, however, there were encouraging signs that governments and governmental authorities had to recognise that participation in the regime of international dispute resolution systems was an essential element of transnational commerce: and their hostility was diminishing.

[55] See also Holtzmann, "The Importance of Choosing the Right Place to Arbitrate an International Case" in *Private Investors Abroad—Problems and Solutions in International Business* (1988).

[56] This expression appears to have been first used by Donaldson in *Deutsche Schachtbau-und Tiefbohrgesellschaft mbH v Ras Al Khaimah National Oil Co* [1987] 3 W.L.R. 1023 at 1027; [1987] 2 Lloyd's Rep. 246 at 248. However, electronic transfers have largely replaced the telex.

Ch.2, and subject to any agreement of the parties to the contrary, the arbitral tribunal is not prohibited from holding hearings, or meetings, either privately or with the parties, in any other place or country to suit the convenience of the arbitrators or the convenience of witnesses or of the parties themselves.[57] Modern arbitration laws often expressly provide for the arbitral tribunal to hold hearings at any place that it deems appropriate.[58] However, it is preferable to hold *hearings* at the seat of the arbitration unless the parties expressly agree that they may be held elsewhere.

(e) Where should an award be "made"?

6–24   In the first edition of this book the importance of signing the award (or at least deeming it to have been "made") at the seat of arbitration was emphasised. The validity of this proposition was subsequently confirmed in a case where the award in an otherwise entirely English arbitration was held to have been "made" in Paris because it was signed there.[59]

Under the UNCITRAL Rules the award must be made at the seat.[60] The motivation for this appears to be that the place where the award is made is an element in determining the applicability of the New York Convention, and thus may have an important role in relation to recognition and enforcement of the award. It may also be a requirement of the law governing the arbitration proceedings. This is discussed in more detail in Ch.2.[61] As indicated there, and by way of example, the Netherlands 1986 Act provides that if the place of arbitration has not been determined, either by the parties or the arbitral tribunal, the place of making the award, as stated in the award, is deemed to be the place of arbitration.[62]

The English 1996 Act, reflecting Art.31(3) of the Model Law, reaches the same result by a more logical route:

" . . . Unless otherwise agreed by the parties, where the seat of arbitration is in England and Wales or Northern Ireland, any award in the proceedings shall be treated as made there, regardless of where it was signed, despatched or delivered to any of the parties . . . "[63]

---

[57] See, *e.g.*, UNCITRAL Arbitration Rules, Art.16.2 and 3.

[58] See, *e.g.*, UNCITRAL Arbitration Rules, Art.16.2 and 3.

[59] *Hiscox v Outhwaite* [1992] 1 A.C. 562 (HL); see also Ch.2. So far as England is concerned this anomaly was corrected by the Arbitration Act 1996, s.100(2)(b): "An award shall be treated as made at the seat of arbitration, regardless of when it was signed, despatched or delivered to any of the parties." But, in view of the apparent ambiguity in Art.I.1 of the New York Convention, it is a point that must be addressed by any arbitral tribunal contemplating making its award in a place other than at the seat.

[60] *e.g.* under the UNCITRAL Arbitration Rules, Art.16.4; the award must be made at the place of arbitration.

[61] See Ch.2, paras 2–22 *et seq.*

[62] Netherlands Arbitration Act 1986, Art.1037.

[63] English Arbitration Act 1996, s.54.

(f) Changing the seat of arbitration

Very occasionally it may be desirable to change the seat of the arbitration even **6–25** if one of the parties does not agree. The need for a change may occur if, for example, through some political cause, the country in which the arbitration is to take place becomes inaccessible. International sanctions may be imposed (as with Iraq or the former Yugoslavia in the 1990s) making access difficult, if not impossible; or the country itself may be involved in conflict, internally or externally. Whether or not the place of the arbitration may be changed without the agreement of the parties depends on the arbitration clause or submission agreement, coupled with any institutional rules which may have been incorporated.

In an ICC arbitration, where the ICC's Court has chosen the place of arbitration under Art.14.1 of the Rules, there does not appear to be any compelling reason why it should not designate a new seat if, in the opinion of the arbitral tribunal, it has become impossible to continue with the arbitration at that place. But the power of the ICC's Court to do so where the parties themselves have chosen the seat in their arbitration agreement is less clear, unless all parties give their consent.

In an ad hoc arbitration, where the parties have chosen a specific place for the arbitration in the submission agreement, the submission agreement is probably frustrated if the arbitration cannot be held there. It has been said that it is a well-established practice of international arbitral tribunals to reject a forum selection clause when radical changes have fundamentally altered the circumstances that existed when the clause was negotiated.[64] An even more difficult issue arises in relation to the jurisdiction of courts to ignore a forum selection clause in an arbitration agreement, on the basis that the chosen forum could lead to injustice. In most cases the courts will give effect to the choice of forum but there are cases in the US, Canada and India which suggest that, in exceptional cases, where strong reasons are shown, the courts may not give effect to the parties' agreement to arbitrate in a specified place.[65]

Agreement inoperative or incapable of being performed

There is little authority from around the world on the issue of an arbitration **6–26** agreement proving to be "incapable of being performed". The most obvious examples appear to be when an institution chosen by the parties ceased to exist; or where the chosen place of arbitration had become inaccessible by reason of war or natural calamity; or where one of the parties or their representatives could not obtain the necessary entry visas.

---

[64] Berglin, "The Iranian Forum Clause Decisions of the Iran–United States Claims Tribunal" (1987) 3 Arbitration International 46 at 48. Citing the opinions of Holtzmann and Mosk in "Interlocutory Awards on Jurisdiction in Nine Cases Containing Various Forum Selection Clauses" (1983) 1 Iran–US C.T.R. 284 at 289 and 308.

[65] See *Mitsubishi Motors Corporation v Soler Chrysler-Plymouth Inc*, 473 US 614; 105 S.Ct. 3346; 87 L.Ed. 2d 444 (1985) and other cases cited by Rogers, "Forum Non Conveniens in Arbitration" (1988) 4 Arbitration International 240.

This problem has been reviewed by an English court,[66] in a case where the agreement provided that the seat of arbitration was to be Tehran, "unless otherwise agreed by the parties". Gatoil did not wish to arbitrate in Tehran and produced evidence to the English court to the effect that it was having difficulty finding a suitably qualified arbitrator who was ready to sit there. The National Iranian Oil Company was unwilling to agree to a change of place of arbitration. Gatoil began court proceedings in England. The National Iranian Oil Company applied for a mandatory stay under the English 1975 Act which was, at the time, the implementing legislation for the New York Convention in the UK. The court granted the stay, on the basis that it was not persuaded that the arbitration agreement was inoperative or incapable of being performed. The judge considered that there were likely to be: "English-speaking people, lawyers, and/or oil company executives, all over the world, including of course the important areas of the Third World, who would not be deterred from sitting in Tehran".

3. Preliminary Steps

(a) Generally

6–27   In domestic arbitrations, particularly where the arbitral tribunal is composed of a single arbitrator, it is common for preliminary matters concerning procedure to be established without a meeting between the arbitral tribunal and the parties. This reduces the cost. In international commercial arbitration, whether there are three arbitrators or only one, a preliminary meeting is useful in order to establish a framework for the proceedings. However, even in international cases preliminary meetings are not customary in a number of countries, including the CIS/Russian Federation, Japan and—in general—the Arab countries.[67]

Nonetheless, especially where the parties and their representatives come from different cultural backgrounds, or from different legal systems, it is sensible for the arbitral tribunal to convene a meeting with the parties as early as possible in the proceedings. This ensures that the arbitral tribunal and the parties have a common understanding of how the arbitration is to be conducted and enables a carefully designed framework for the conduct of the arbitration to be established.[68] It is possible, indeed it is not uncommon, for preliminary meetings to be conducted by video or telephone conference. This saves the costs inevitably incurred when one or more of the arbitrators or parties has to travel across national boundaries in order to be present at a meeting. However, there is no real

---

[66] *Gatoil International Inc (Panama) v National Iranian Oil Company (Iran)* (1992) XVII Yearbook Commercial Arbitration 587.

[67] See *Comparative Arbitration Practice*, ICCA Congress Series No.3 (Kluwer, 1987), pp.64–65, where the discussion did not clarify this point adequately.

[68] It is necessary to distinguish between a preliminary meeting (or preliminary hearing) and a pre-hearing conference. A preliminary meeting takes place as early as possible in the proceedings, and certainly before the written stage. A pre-hearing conference takes place after the written stage and has as its primary objective the organisation and order of proceedings at the hearing.

substitute for all the players coming together in one room as soon as possible after the arbitration has started.

English lawyers frequently refer to such a meeting as a "preliminary hearing". There is no magic in the precise form of words, but the phrase "preliminary meeting" is probably more appropriate, so as to emphasise the informality and intended lack of adversarial character of the session. Indeed the word "hearing" should more properly be reserved to identify a session at which the objective is for the arbitral tribunal to receive oral evidence or submissions from the parties in relation to disputed issues. There may be preliminary hearings (for example, in relation to issues of jurisdiction or evidence gathering); and/or indeed a "preliminary meeting" at which the procedural structure is discussed may be converted into a "preliminary hearing" at which the parties are heard on a disputed issue—such as a request for interim measures. Apart from ICSID, none of the major sets of institutional arbitration rules mention the concept of a preliminary meeting, thus they neither impose an obligation to hold one nor prohibit it. A term that was gaining in usage during the early years of the twenty-first century was "case management meeting".

Conduct of preliminary meetings

In practice, a preliminary meeting proceeds through various stages. The **6–28** members of the arbitral tribunal usually arrange to meet privately, prior to meeting the parties. This is partly to effect introductions, and partly to discuss provisional views as to the organisation of the arbitration.

Similarly, a substantial benefit may be gained if the representatives of the parties meet with each other before attending the preliminary meeting with the arbitral tribunal. This is particularly important in ad hoc arbitrations, since matters such as the fees and expenses of the arbitrators are normally dealt with at this stage. To avoid embarrassment it is important that the representatives of the parties should be able to present an agreed position to the arbitral tribunal on the question of the arbitrators' fees and expenses.

Representation at preliminary meetings

To obtain the maximum benefit from a preliminary meeting with the arbitral **6–29** tribunal, each party should be represented by persons with sufficient authority and knowledge to take "on the spot" decisions, both in discussion with the other party's representatives and during the course of the meeting with the arbitral tribunal itself. This means that it is usually necessary for the leader of each party's team of lawyers, as well as a person with appropriate executive authority from the clients, to attend. It is common practice, particularly where a government is involved, for an "agent" to be nominated.[69] The agent is the person to whom both the arbitral tribunal and the other party are entitled to address communications and from whom they may seek an authoritative statement or

---

[69] As in the *Aminoil* arbitration; see (1982) 21 I.L.M. 976 at 983.

response on any particular matter. Where an agent is appointed, communications will invariably be addressed to the party's agent, usually with a copy to that party's counsel.

Adjournment of preliminary meetings

6–30   As mentioned earlier, a private meeting of the arbitral tribunal, and a private meeting between the parties themselves, may take place before the main meeting between the arbitral tribunal and the parties. It is not uncommon for this main meeting to be adjourned, or even for there to be several short adjournments, whilst the members of the arbitral tribunal confer in private (or "caucus", as US lawyers describe it). This also gives the parties' representatives an opportunity for further private discussions. In this way, and with the guidance of the tribunal, the parties are often able to agree on the basic framework and organisation of the proceedings.

Arbitral tribunals usually prefer to avoid making rulings on disputed procedural matters in the early stages of the arbitration. Where there is disagreement between the parties, arbitrators often suggest compromise solutions. This appears to derive from the complexities of "tribunal psychology",[70] as a result of which individual members of the arbitral tribunal (and particularly the presiding arbitrator) are reluctant to make rulings at the start of the arbitration that one of the parties may regard (however unjustifiably) as amounting to unfair treatment. Nevertheless, if at the end of the meeting there are still matters outstanding upon which the parties are unable to agree, the arbitral tribunal has no alternative but to make a decision. Sometimes this is done immediately. More often the decision is reserved and notified to the parties later. It is unusual for a preliminary meeting to extend beyond one day, as a maximum; and it may well be disposed of within half a day. This means that, with careful planning, it is often possible to hold a preliminary meeting without the need for any of the participants to make an overnight stay in an hotel unless intercontinental travel is involved.

Matters to be determined at preliminary meetings

6–31   The specific matters that need to be determined at a preliminary meeting depend partly on the law governing the arbitration (for example, in some jurisdictions it may be necessary to establish a submission agreement or *compromis*),[71] and partly on whether the parties have already subjected the arbitration to a set of international or institutional rules, either for administered or for non-administered arbitration. If the arbitration is subject to the rules of one of the major international arbitration institutions it will not be necessary, for example, for the parties to deal directly with the arbitrators in connection with their fees. This is handled by the institution concerned. In an ad hoc arbitration, however,

---

[70] See Ch.8, paras 8–37 *et seq.*
[71] By the twenty-first century this had become rare. See Ch.3, paras 3–02 and 3–57 *et seq.*

it is important to deal not only with fees, also to resolve the manner in which the arbitral tribunal is to receive:

- the parties' written submissions;

- any documents upon which the parties wish to rely (or other documents disclosed pursuant to a direction or order by the arbitral tribunal);

- written and oral evidence to be submitted by the parties; and

- the oral arguments to be presented on behalf of the parties.

UNCITRAL Notes on Organizing Arbitral Proceedings

It is also useful at this early stage in the proceedings for the arbitral tribunal **6–32** and the parties to consider the items contained in the "checklist" that accompanies the Notes on Organizing Arbitral Proceedings ("the Notes"), adopted by UNCITRAL in 1996.

Although the original intention of the Notes was to provide guidelines for matters to be taken into account at a later stage of the proceedings, in preparing for the substantive hearing, many of the points listed should be considered as early as possible and may be dealt with in the arbitral tribunal's first procedural order.

The Notes provide a list of matters that the arbitral tribunal may need to keep in mind when it organises the proceedings. This list is not intended to be exhaustive or definitive, but it gives a useful indication of points the arbitral tribunal may wish to consider.

- The adoption of a set of procedural rules, in the event that the parties have not already done so.[72]

- The language of the proceedings, the language that is to be used in the hearings; and the need (if any) for translation of oral presentations and documents, and the costs involved.[73]

- The seat of arbitration and all its implications, if a seat has not already been decided upon by the parties. The arbitral tribunal may also wish to consider whether it will hold hearings outside the seat of arbitration.[74]

- Administrative services: if the arbitration is not being administered by an institution the arbitral tribunal may determine who will be responsible for the organisation of the arbitration. The arbitral tribunal may also wish to consider the appointment of a secretary and his functions.[75]

---

[72] paras 14, 15 and 16.
[73] paras 17, 18, 19 and 20.
[74] paras 21, 22 and 23.
[75] paras 24, 25, 26 and 27.

- Deposit in respect of costs: unless an institution is charged with organising the financial aspects of the arbitral procedure the arbitral tribunal may determine the costs that are to be paid and provide for their management.[76]

- Confidentiality of information: the arbitral tribunal may need make arrangements to ensure confidentiality.[77]

- Routing of information: the arbitral tribunal may make arrangements for lines of communication between the participants. It must make arrangements for the exchange of written submissions. It may decide on the means of communication and it should establish the extent to which fax and other means of communication should be used.[78]

- Arrangements for the exchange of written submissions: the arbitral tribunal should establish the conditions for the submission of further written submissions. It may decide on the number, method and time-limits of any such submission.[79]

- Definition of points of issue: the arbitral tribunal may prepare a list of issues and the order in which they should be decided and determine precisely the relief that is sought.[80]

- Possibility of settlement negotiations: the arbitral tribunal should consider the extent (if at all) to which it should offer to facilitate settlement negotiations.[81]

- Documentary evidence: the arbitral tribunal may set time limits for the submission of documents and determine the consequences of late submission. It should also determine whether the parties are going to be compelled to produce documents.[82]

- Physical evidence: the arbitral tribunal may make arrangements for any physical evidence to be presented as well as any site inspections it may wish to undertake.[83]

- Witnesses: the arbitral tribunal may wish to determine:

    (a) the advance notice required concerning witnesses and the content of such notice and the nature of the statement of the witness[84];
    (b) the possibility of pre-hearing witness depositions[85];

---

[76] paras 28, 29 and 30.
[77] paras 31 and 32.
[78] paras 33, 34, 36 and 37.
[79] paras 38, 39, 40, 41 and 42.
[80] paras 43, 44, 45 and 46.
[81] para.47.
[82] paras 48 and 49.
[83] paras 55, 56, 57 and 58.
[84] para.60.
[85] para.61.

(c) the manner in which the hearing of witnesses will take place, and the degree of control the arbitral tribunal wishes to exercise.[86]

- Experts and expert witnesses: the arbitral tribunal may wish to consider appointing an expert to report to it and determine how such a person is to be chosen. It may also determine the terms of reference for the expert and decide how the parties are to comment on such terms of reference.[87]

- Hearings: the arbitral tribunal may wish to decide on some or all of the following matters as concerning hearings:

  (a) should hearings be held at all? And if they are to held, how are they to be structured?[88]
  (b) should there be a limit on the time that each of the parties has? And in what order will the parties present their arguments?[89]
  (c) the length of the hearings and whether a record should be kept of the proceedings and how they are to be kept?[90]
  (d) whether the parties should be allowed to submit a summary of their oral arguments.[91]

- Multi-party arbitration: if the arbitration involves more than two, it may become more complex. The arbitral tribunal should pay attention to the points in issue, their order and the manner in which parties will participate.[92]

- Filing of award: if an award needs to be filed with a national court, or elsewhere who will do it?[93]

(b) Other preliminary issues

Apart from jurisdiction issues,[94] other matters may arise that either should be taken as preliminary issues before the arbitral tribunal can consider the substance of the claims or, alternatively, may be dealt with more conveniently at an early stage as preliminary issues, in order to facilitate the efficient and economical conduct of the proceedings.   **6–33**

Applicable laws

The most common examples of preliminary issues (other than those relating to jurisdiction) are those which involve the determination of the law governing the arbitration and the law applicable to the substantive issues between the parties.   **6–34**

---

[86] paras 62, 63, 64, 65, 66, 67 and 68.
[87] paras 69, 70, 71 and 72.
[88] paras 74, 75, 76 and 77.
[89] paras 78, 79 and 80.
[90] paras 81, 82 and 83.
[91] paras 84 and 85.
[92] paras 86, 87 and 88.
[93] paras 89 and 90.
[94] See Ch.5, paras 5–30 *et seq.*

Both issues arose in the *Aminoil* arbitration, where they were dealt with as *separate* issues (as the first item during the main hearing) but not as *preliminary* issues (since there was no preliminary award in respect of them). It is preferable to decide on the applicable law before proceeding with the rest of the arbitration, but sometimes this is not practicable (because issues of fact are involved) and so the arbitration proceeds on the basis of alternative submissions as to which law is the applicable substantive law.

Separation of liability and quantum

6–35   Another question that often arises is whether or not issues of liability and quantum should be dealt with separately. In many modern disputes arising out of international trade, particularly in relation to construction projects, or intellectual property disputes, the quantification of claims is a major exercise. It may involve both the parties and the arbitral tribunal in considering large numbers of documents, as well as complex technical matters involving experts appointed by the parties, or by the arbitral tribunal, or both. In such cases, it may often be convenient for the arbitral tribunal to determine questions of liability first. In this way, the parties avoid the expense and time involved in submitting evidence and argument on detailed aspects of quantification that may turn out to be irrelevant following the arbitral tribunal's decision on liability.[95]

It is easy to see the arguments in favour of separating issues of liability from issues of quantum in a large and complex case. For example, the claimant may have suffered a substantial loss (including loss of profit) through the breakdown or failure of an important piece of plant or equipment. The claimant seeks to recover this loss by way of arbitration proceedings against the respondent, who was responsible for the installation of the equipment. In his defence, the respondent alleges, first, that it is the sub-supplier who is liable for any breakdown or failure in the plant or equipment supplied; secondly, that liability is limited under the terms of the contract to a sum much smaller than the amount claimed; and, thirdly, that in any event, some of the losses claimed (such as loss of profit) are irrecoverable (because of the conditions of contract) and others are not fully recoverable, because they have been quantified on the wrong basis. This is a common situation in international commercial disputes, with the respondent putting forward a succession of defences, any one of which, if successful, may limit—or even defeat—the claim. How should an arbitral tribunal deal with it?

There are various possibilities. In the first place, it might decide to hear legal argument as to the effect of the clause limiting liability—on the basis that, if the clause is found to be effective, the respondent will make good his offer to pay the limited amount stated in the clause and the case will then be over.

6–36   At first sight, this seems to be an attractive option for both parties. There is no point in spending time and money on a complicated factual investigation if the

---

[95] See also the discussion of partial and interim awards in relation to the separation of liability and *quantum* in Ch.8, para.8–44.

dispute may be resolved by the determination of a legal point as a preliminary issue. It may emerge, however, that the correct legal interpretation to be put upon the clause which limits, or purports to limit, liability depends upon the factual situation, and that to ascertain and understand this factual situation adequately it is necessary to enquire fully into all the circumstances of the case, with the assistance of expert witnesses on each side. In other words, the findings of the arbitral tribunal on the *legal* issue might be so dependent on its finding on the *facts* as to make it difficult (and indeed undesirable), to disentangle the two issues. In this event, it would be appropriate for the arbitral tribunal to investigate the relevant facts, rather than attempt to deal with the legal issue in isolation.

Even though in practice the issues of liability and quantum may from time to time prove to be inextricably interwoven, it is usually possible to see a broad division between them. It is also often possible to determine the *principles* on which damages should be awarded, while leaving over the pure *arithmetical* calculations to a second stage.

Separation of other issues

It is more rare for an arbitral tribunal to separate issues where there is no clear **6–37** dividing line; to say, in effect: "there are only a limited number of issues on which we wish to hear evidence and argument from the parties, and these are as follows." In making such a ruling, an arbitral tribunal isolates certain issues that appear to be of decisive importance to the outcome of a case, and asks the parties to concentrate on these issues.

Before an arbitral tribunal can safely take this position, it must be satisfied that it has been apprised of all the issues that are relevant or likely to be relevant to its decision; and this stage is not likely to be reached until the written proceedings have been concluded. Even then, it is not often that an arbitral tribunal takes the initiative in this way. Most arbitral tribunals, even when all its members are from countries that follow the so-called inquisitorial method of procedure, seem content to sit back and allow the parties to develop the case as they wish. However, where an arbitral tribunal is satisfied that it has been adequately briefed on all the issues, and that the time has come for it to take the initiative in this way, the effect can be dramatic in terms of saving both time and money.

The *Aminoil* arbitration provides a classic example.[96] Many hundreds of millions of dollars were at stake, depending upon whether the Kuwait Government's act of nationalisation was *unlawful* (as claimed by Aminoil) thereby giving rise to the possibility of an award of damages on a full indemnity basis, which would have a punitive effect; or *lawful* (as claimed by the Government) and so susceptible to resolution by the payment of fair compensation.

At the close of the written stage of the proceedings, the arbitral tribunal held **6–38** a meeting with the parties to consider various procedural matters relating to the forthcoming oral hearings. Following this meeting, the arbitral tribunal made an order fixing the date for the opening of the hearings in Paris and specifying, *inter*

---

[96] See *Aminoil* arbitration, above, para.6–29.

alia, the issues the parties were to address, the order in which they were to be taken and which side was to speak first on each issue. There were seven issues in total and although, by way of caution, it was indicated that the wording of the issues implied no taking of a position by the arbitral tribunal, it was clear to the parties that these were the issues which the arbitral tribunal regarded as decisive. It was to these issues that evidence and argument were primarily addressed at the hearing of the arbitration; in the result, a hearing which might in other circumstances have taken many months in fact lasted for less than six weeks. This represented a significant saving in time and money for both parties.

At that time it was relatively rare for an arbitral tribunal to take charge of a case in this way. However, as international arbitrations became more complex, and as both arbitral tribunals and practitioners search for quicker and more effective ways of getting through the workload imposed by such cases, it seems essential that, providing they know what they are doing, arbitral tribunals should seek to control and direct the conduct of the arbitration from an early stage; and in particular, that they should seek to cut through the surrounding foliage in order to reach the essential issues as soon as possible.

(c) Expedited remedies

6–39   As the international commercial arbitration system has developed new methods have been devised to enable arbitral tribunals to move swiftly when it is necessary.

Pre-arbitral referee

6–40   The ICC Rules for a Pre-arbitral Referee Procedure were introduced on January 1, 1990.[97] These Rules provide a procedure by which rapid action can be taken when a dispute arises between parties who are in a contractual relationship.

The Rules can be used only where there is a written agreement between the parties to adopt them, whether the agreement is part of the relevant contract or made later. The use of the Pre-arbitral Reference Procedure does not usurp the jurisdiction of any body (whether arbitral tribunal or national court) that is ultimately responsible for deciding the merits of any underlying dispute.

Under the procedure a referee is appointed either by agreement of the parties or by the Chairman of the ICC's Court, following a request by one of the parties for the appointment of a referee (under Art.4.1). Article 2 gives the referee power to:

- order conservatory measures or restoration measures that are urgently necessary to prevent either immediate damage or irreparable loss and so to safeguard any of the rights or property of one of the parties;

---

[97] See "Pre-Arbitral Referee" at *www.iccwbo.org/court/english/pre_arbitral/all_topics.asp*.

- order payment by one party to any other party or to another person any payment which ought to be made;

- order a party to take any step which ought to be taken according to the contract between the parties, including the signing or delivery of any document or the procuring by a party of the signature or delivery of a document;

- order any measures necessary to preserve or establish evidence.

The referee does not have the power to make any order other than that **6–41** requested by a party in its Request, or in the Answer to the Request (Art.2.2). The powers of the referee can be altered by express written agreement between the parties (Art.2.1.1).

The referee must make the order within 30 days from the date on which the file was received (Art.6.2). The referee's orders are binding and remain in force unless and until the referee or the competent body (either a court or an arbitral tribunal) decides otherwise (Art.6.3). In other words, the referee's orders are not intended to be permanent.

The Pre-arbitral Referee Procedure has been described as "an excellent idea which thus far has not worked".[98] It was designed as a remedy that could provide urgent measures necessary to preserve evidence or other provisional measures to avoid irreparable harm. It would be used where urgency of the remedy required is beyond the scope of the existing range of technical pre-arbitration processes (such as recourse to the Centre for Technical Expertise).

Expedited formation of the arbitral tribunal

Under Art.9 of the LCIA Rules, in cases of exceptional urgency a party may **6–42** apply to the LCIA Court for the expedited formation of an arbitral tribunal. The application must be made in writing to the LCIA Court, with copies to all other parties to the arbitration, and must set out the specific grounds for the exceptional urgency in the formation of the arbitral tribunal. In practice, it is usually the claimant who requests expedited formation.[99]

---

[98] Craig, Park & Paulsson, International Chamber of Commerce Arbitration (3rd ed., 2000), p.706. It is understood that the procedure has been used on only a handful of occasions since the Rules were introduced in 1990.

[99] Art.9 of the LCIA Rules provides as follows:

    9.1 In exceptional urgency, on or after the commencement of the arbitration, any party may apply to the LCIA Court for the expedited formation of the Arbitral Tribunal, including the appointment of any replacement arbitrator under Articles 10 and 11 of these Rules.

    9.2 Such an application shall be made in writing to the LCIA Court, copied to all other parties to the arbitration; and it shall set out the specific grounds for exceptional urgency in the formation of the Arbitral Tribunal.

    9.3 The LCIA Court may, in its complete discretion, abridge or curtail any time limit under these Rules for the formation of the Arbitral Tribunal, including service of the Response and of any matters or documents adjudged to be missing from the Request. The LCIA Court shall not be entitled to abridge or curtail any other time limit.

The LCIA Court has discretion to abridge or curtail any time-limit under the LCIA Rules for the formation of the arbitral tribunal. The LCIA Court usually shortens the 30-day time-limit within which the respondent must reply to the Request for Arbitration. There have been a few cases where the time-limit has been "significantly" abridged, and one case in which a sole arbitrator was appointed within 48 hours of receipt of the Request for Arbitration.

The LCIA Court provides no guidance as to what considerations it takes into account in deciding what amounts to "exceptional urgency", or indeed by how many days it may curtail any applicable time-limit. It makes the decisions on a case-by-case basis on the merits of each request. Applications for expedited formation have been made in a range of different cases, such as maritime and finance cases, but the common theme is the fear that the respondent might shift its assets. The LCIA Court has rejected only one application for expedited formation out of a total of over 25 applications since the Art.9 was introduced in the 1998 edition of the LCIA Rules.[1]

"Fast track" arbitrations

6–43 To the extent that the term "fast track" may imply a distinct *system* of arbitration it is a misnomer. In fact what is meant is merely an accelerated procedure. In the 1990s there was a growing sense of frustration among people involved in international commerce because of the time it generally took from commencement of an arbitration to the delivery of the arbitral tribunal's award. Cash flow considerations, always important, become critical during periods of recession. Furthermore, trading partners were not content to have disputes outstanding between them for long periods of time. International arbitration, particularly where the arbitral tribunal is composed of three busy arbitrators of different nationalities, has never been a speedy form of dispute resolution—except by comparison with litigation in many national court systems. But this feature was made worse by the ever-increasing complexity of the underlying transactions and the particular circumstances that gave rise to the disputes.

Conscious of criticism from the ultimate users, the world's major arbitral institutions, notably the ICC's Court, searched for solutions. This gave birth to the notion of "fast track" arbitrations. Unfortunately, it soon became clear that no system would work properly unless *all* the parties and the arbitral tribunal were ready to co-operate in achieving accelerated timetables. Establishing a tribunal with the will and the capacity, as well as the necessary experience, was difficult but not impossible. The insuperable hurdle, with a few notable exceptions, was that in most disputes one of the parties had a positive disincentive to co-operate willingly in an accelerated procedure.

One of the notable exceptions involved Formula One (F1) racing cars.[2] At the relevant time the first race of the season was traditionally held in Melbourne,

---

[1] Source: Registrar of the LCIA Court.
[2] ICC Case No.10211/AER. None of this is confidential, as the proceedings and the procedure were fully reported in various motor racing journals.

Australia, in March of each year. It was necessary for the cars to be shipped from Europe around mid-February. At the end of one season, in the mid-1990s, one F1 team fell into dispute with the Formula One Association (F1A), which runs and regulates the F1 championship in accordance with a comprehensive set of rules. The team in question, which was sponsored by a tobacco company, wanted to paint one of its cars in the livery of one of its brands of cigarettes, and the other in the livery of another of its brands. The F1A objected, on the grounds that the championship is a team event, and insisted that each of the two cars that make up a team must be painted in identical livery. The constitution of the F1A, to which every team must sign up when entering the championship, contained an ICC arbitration clause.

By Christmas of the year in question, it became apparent that a resolution of   **6–44** the dispute would not be achieved by negotiation. The team and the F1A agreed that they would hold an arbitration with a view to completing it by the end of January, so that the cars could be painted and shipped in time to reach Australia by the end of February.

The F1 team filed a Request for Arbitration with the ICC between Christmas Day and New Year's Eve. A three-member arbitral tribunal was appointed on New Year's Day. The tribunal circulated draft Terms of Reference on the same day, and the Terms of Reference were signed within a couple more days. A sequential exchange of "Memoranda", to which the parties attached the documents on which they relied, then took place at seven-day intervals, followed by a simultaneous exchange of written witness statements within a few more days. A couple of disputed document requests were resolved by prompt procedural orders from the tribunal, and an eight-hour hearing took place on the last Saturday of January. The tribunal deliberated on the Sunday and sent its Final Award to the ICC's Court for scrutiny by fax and courier at lunchtime the next day (Monday), together with separate signed signature pages. The award was approved at an emergency session of the ICC's Court the same afternoon, and was notified to the parties by fax and overnight courier.

The parties received the fully reasoned award on the last day of January, and the cars were painted and shipped on time.[3]

These procedures are not likely to become common practice, particularly in   **6–45** institutional arbitrations. In fact the only major international institution to take a specific step in this direction by the end of the twentieth century was WIPO, which in 1994 included in its rules booklet a section entitled "WIPO Expedited Arbitration Rules"; but even this initiative went no further than providing that the statement of claim and defence must accompany the Request for Arbitration and Answer; that time-limits would be shortened; and that hearings (which would always be before a sole arbitrator) would not exceed three days. It is significant

---

[3] As a postscript, one of the present authors, who was a member of the tribunal (which unanimously upheld the F1A's position), recalls one of the other arbitrators during the deliberation making the observation: "Of course, you know what they [the F1 team] will do . . . they'll paint each car the same, one side in the livery of one brand and the other car in the livery of the other brand". His instinct served him well. This is precisely what the F1 team did.

that neither the ICC nor the LCIA, both of which gave careful consideration to the question, decided not to include any rules specifically dedicated to "fast track" procedures in the revised version of their rules which in both cases came into effect on January 1, 1998.

(d) Avoiding delay and disruption

6–46   In the last two decades of the twentieth century delay and disruption became important issues in international commercial arbitration, and were discussed extensively by working groups at ICCA Congresses during the 1980s and 1990s.[4]

Arbitration relies on speed and cost-effectiveness for its survival. Very often what is quick is cost-effective. This has been recognised by legislators and institutions alike.[5] However, it is important that the procedure adopted by arbitral tribunals should be fair. A balance must be struck between speed and fairness. This balance varies from case to case and no absolute time-limits can be prescribed. The parties have their own role to play in this context, and the issue of delay should be kept in mind. Procedures that are adopted in an arbitral proceeding should depend on the nature of the dispute,[6] and the arbitral tribunal should be free to design the procedure according to its requirements; detailed procedures agreed by the parties needlessly tie the hands of the arbitral tribunal. Delay may be avoided more easily by wise choice of the composition of the arbitral tribunal rather than by inserting detailed procedural rules into the arbitration agreement.[7]

Special procedures in small cases

6–47   Not all international arbitrations are concerned with huge stakes, and it is desirable that streamlined procedures should be devised for cases where the comprehensive procedures described in this chapter are not justified by the amount in dispute. The problem is that streamlined procedures can only be adopted by (a) agreement of the parties; (b) directions of the arbitral tribunal; or (c) imposition by an arbitral institution. It is relatively rare for the parties to agree on anything after a dispute has arisen; they are engaged in strategic and tactical skirmishes with each other, and one party usually wishes to move ahead faster than the other. The arbitral tribunal's ability to employ radical streamlining techniques at the start of an arbitration is hampered by insufficient knowledge. Probably the best medium-term solution is for arbitral institutions to adopt

---

[4] In Stockholm (1988); Vienna (1994); and Paris (1998). See ICCA Congress Series Nos 5, 7 and 9.

[5] English Arbitration Act 1996, s.1(a); German Arbitration Law 1998, ss.1028, 1046 and 1048. See also ICC's Arbitration Rules 1998, Art.20(1) and LCIA Arbitration Rules, Art.14(1)(ii).

[6] The same could be said about laws and rules; see Marriott, "Pros and Cons of More Detailed Arbitration Laws and Rules" ICCA Congress Series No.7 (Kluwer, 1996).

[7] See Pierre A. Karrer, "Pros and Cons of Terms of Reference and Specific Procedural Agreements" in *Arbitration Clauses: Storm into a Calm Sea, ibid.*

procedural rules that are to apply to such cases.[8] These rules might contain some or all of the following provisions:

- a sole arbitrator should be appointed;

- the arbitrator should encourage the parties to seek a mediated solution;

- a speedy mechanism should be adopted for communicating notices, documents, pleadings and correspondence (*e.g.* fax, email);

- the arbitrator should identify the issues to be determined as soon as possible after his appointment, in appropriate cases by telephone conference between the parties;

- page limits should be put on written briefs and memorials, and in appropriate cases written pleadings should be dispensed with altogether;

- time-limits for exchange of written pleadings (if any) should be short;

- the arbitrator should determine, in consultation with the parties, the extent of the direct witness testimony (if any), which should be presented in written form prior to the hearing;

- the parties should be required to deliver to the arbitrator a single joint set of exhibits at least 10 days prior to the hearing;

- the arbitrator should determine the total time for oral examination of witnesses (*i.e.* cross-examination and re-examination) and should allocate the time between the parties in appropriate proportions before the hearing;

- the arbitrator should fix time-limits for opening and closing statements at the hearing;

- the arbitrator's award should not contain extensive reasoning. It should merely list the considerations that weighed with the arbitrator so that the parties may understand the basis of his decision;

- all mechanisms for appeals (other than recourse for lack of due process or excess of jurisdiction) should be excluded.

4. WRITTEN SUBMISSIONS

(a) Generally

When an arbitral tribunal has been appointed, and the procedure to be followed **6–48** has been established, the first step taken in almost all international arbitrations is an exchange between the parties of some form of written submissions.

[8] The definition of a "small" case would be for individual arbitral institutions to decide; for some parties any case in which less than US$1 million is at stake may seem "small"; for others, anything over US$100,000 may be "large". Further, in many cases issues of principle are more important to the parties than the money involved.

Exceptionally, an arbitration may proceed without any such documents; but this is only practicable where both the parties and the arbitrators are fully aware of the issues in dispute and are able to evaluate the rival contentions either by going straight to an oral hearing, or by inspection of the subject-matter of the dispute. In practice, these cases are limited to the so-called "look-sniff" arbitrations, which arise from trading in commodities on international markets and to other similar situations.

The Model Law contains a mandatory provision to the effect that each party *shall* state the facts supporting his claim or defence, as the case may be, and *may* submit documents or references to the evidence that will be relied upon.[9] It is not easy to see how commodity arbitrations fit into this scheme, although the article does not provide expressly that the statements shall be in writing.

The function of written submissions

6–49   It is important to understand the *function* of written submissions in an arbitration, which may not be precisely the same in every case. Unless the parties have themselves already drawn up a detailed submission agreement, containing a list of the issues to be determined, the most immediate function of the initial exchange of written submissions is to identify the scope of the arbitral tribunal's mandate.

Another reason why it is important for the arbitral tribunal to have an adequate definition of the issues to be determined is to enable it to devise an appropriate procedural structure. As the arbitration progresses and the evidence emerges, it is not unusual for the parties to adjust the way in which their arguments are presented. Some contentions may be abandoned and new ones may be put forward as a result of the evidence produced by the other party. This is a legitimate and indeed necessary process, provided that the issues before the arbitral tribunal do not become so distorted that they are in substance completely different from those defined at the start of the arbitration.

Yet another function of the written submissions is to identify the facts and arguments in support of the parties' positions. In fulfilling this function, the written material submitted by the parties may take a wide variety of forms. At one extreme, they may contain very full arguments as to the issues of law and fact and be accompanied by documentary evidence and the written testimony of witnesses upon which the parties rely, as well as copies of the relevant legal authorities. This form of written pleading is used primarily where it is envisaged that there will be no oral hearing, or only a short hearing at which the arbitral tribunal will ask the parties to clarify, quite briefly, certain aspects of their arguments, or to provide further information.

6–50   At the other extreme, the written submissions may be a mere prelude to a substantial hearing, at which the arbitral tribunal receives the oral testimony of witnesses and the arguments of the parties presented by advocates. In this event, the secondary function of the written submissions is effectively limited to that of

[9] Model Law, Art.23.

informing the members of the arbitral tribunal, and the other party, of the parties' respective cases so that there will be no surprises at the hearing.[10]

The need to avoid ambiguity

It is important that the arbitral tribunal should make absolutely clear to the **6–51** parties the form of written submissions it expects. The parties must understand what is intended. Otherwise the arbitration may be delayed by inadequate written submissions or, alternatively, time and money may be wasted in making a voluminous and exhaustive written presentation when the arbitral tribunal intends to hold a full oral inquiry into the evidence and arguments at later hearings in the proceedings.

(b) Written pleadings in institutional arbitration

Under the ICC Rules, the claimant has to submit a "description of the nature **6–52** and circumstances of the dispute giving rise to the claims" with the Request for Arbitration, and the defendant has to submit his "comments as to the nature and circumstances of the dispute giving rise to the claims" with the Answer.[11] In an ICC arbitration the next stage (assuming that there is no counterclaim) is for the arbitral tribunal to draw up its "Terms of Reference" for signature by the arbitrators and the parties. It is at this stage that any issues of jurisdiction are likely to be debated, since the respondent will no doubt object if the Terms of Reference contain a "definition of the issues to be determined" that includes matters that the respondent considers are not covered by the arbitration agreement.[12]

It is important, therefore, that all of the claims and counterclaims are spelt out at an early stage. If a claimant omits to refer to some claims in its initial written submission, or fails to identify a dispute with sufficient clarity, it risks a successful plea at a later stage that the arbitral tribunal has no jurisdiction to determine that particular claim or group of claims.

In institutional arbitration, the immediate purpose of the parties' initial statements is to facilitate the appointment of the arbitral tribunal and to enable the arbitral tribunal to identify the issues; to make appropriate procedural orders for the next steps; and (in ICC cases) to draw up its Terms of Reference. In nearly all cases of any substance, the arbitral tribunal orders the exchange of further written pleadings as well as the production of documentary evidence before the oral stage of proceedings is reached.

The UNCITRAL Rules[13] clearly envisage that the initial written pleadings **6–53** submitted by the parties are not to be considered as final and definitive statements of the parties' respective positions. Articles 18 and 19 of those Rules make

---

[10] It is often said that arbitral tribunals should not permit "trials by ambush".
[11] ICC Arbitration Rules, Arts 4 and 5.
[12] *ibid.*, Art.18. Under the 1998 edition of the Rules the arbitral tribunal may dispense with identifying the issues to be determined if it considers this appropriate.
[13] UNCITRAL Arbitration Rules, Arts 18 and 19.

reference to "documents or other evidence he *will* submit", presumably at a later stage in the proceedings. The UNCITRAL Rules do not impose any strict time-limits, although they do give guidelines:

> "The periods of time fixed by the arbitral tribunal for the communication of written statements (including the statement of claim and statement of defence) should not exceed forty-five days. However, the arbitral tribunal may extend the time limits if it concludes that an extension is justified."[14]

By contrast, the LCIA Rules provide that after the parties have delivered the Request for Arbitration and Answer written pleadings consisting of a "Statement of Case", "Statement of Defence", and "Statement of Reply" (and further equivalent written pleadings in the event of a counterclaim) follow each other within certain time-limits. It is clear from these Rules that (subject to any directions to the contrary from the arbitral tribunal) the written statements are intended, in principle, to be the *only* written submissions in the arbitration,[15] and they are to be accompanied by copies of "all essential documents on which the party concerned relies . . . and . . . by any relevant samples or exhibits".[16]

The ICDR Rules provide for the exchange of initial statements of claim and defence,[17] and state that the arbitral tribunal may "decide whether the parties shall present any written statements in addition . . . "[18]

6–54 The ICSID Rules characterise the documents that are to be filed by the parties as a "memorial" and a "counter-memorial", followed if necessary by a reply and a rejoinder. The Rules also allow for simultaneous exchange of pleadings, if the request for arbitration was made jointly.[19] The Rules provide that a memorial should contain a statement of the relevant facts, a statement of law, and a submission; and that the counter-memorial, reply or rejoinder should respond to these statements and submissions and add any additional facts, statements of law or submissions of its own.[20] The explanatory note states that the scope of these pleadings represents:

> " . . . an adaptation of common law practice to the procedure of the civil law. These provisions, tested by international arbitral practice, are designed to prevent procedural arguments concerning the scope of pleadings, even if the parties have differing legal backgrounds. Where, however, the parties share a common experience with an identical or similar system of procedure, they may agree on different contents and functions for the pleadings."[21]

---

[14] *ibid.*, Art.23.
[15] LCIA Arbitration Rules, Art.15.
[16] LCIA Arbitration Rules, Art.15.6.
[17] ICDR International Arbitration Rules, Art.2.
[18] *ibid.*, Art.17.1.
[19] ICSID Arbitration Rules, Art.31(1) and (2).
[20] *ibid.*, Art.31(3).
[21] *ibid.*

Definition of the issues

Written submissions are normally exchanged sequentially, so that the claimant   **6–55**
fires the first shot and the respondent answers. The respondent normally submits
any counterclaim at the same time as its answer to the claimant's claim; this
document is often known as an "answer and counterclaim", or "defence and
counterclaim". The claimant then submits its reply to the respondent's counterclaim; and may also be allowed to submit a "rejoinder" to the respondent's
answer.

Exceptionally, however, the arbitral tribunal may direct that the parties should
submit their written pleadings simultaneously, so that each party delivers a
written submission of its claims against the other on a set date, and then on a
subsequent date the parties exchange their written answers and so forth. This
usually happens where there is a disagreement about which party should be the
claimant, with neither wishing to be categorised as the respondent. In practice, it
is most likely to occur where a government is a party, and considers that its
dignity would be offended if it were to be cast in the role of respondent.[22]

Terminology

Many different expressions are used to describe these written submissions, or   **6–56**
written pleadings. Examples are "statement of claim", "statement of case",
"memorial", "points of claim". These lead to corresponding expressions such as
"statement of defence", "statement of reply", "counter-memorial", "points of
defence", "replique" and so forth, with "rejoinder", "duplique", "counter-
rejoinder", "second rejoinder", "rebuttal" and similar phrases being used for
additional rounds of written submissions—since each side may wish to reply to
fresh material produced by its opponent in subsequent written pleadings.

It sometimes happens that further written submissions are made after the main
oral hearing, in order to comply with a request from the arbitral tribunal for
clarification, or where the allotted time for the hearing has expired without the
parties having had an adequate opportunity to cover all items comprehensively.
Again, where a party has produced fresh evidence or a novel argument at the
hearing, and the other party has asked for an opportunity to respond, the arbitral
tribunal is usually reluctant to refuse. Rather than make an order that involves the
time and expense of a further hearing, the arbitral tribunal usually permits a
further rebuttal in writing.

The different expressions used to describe written submissions are not wholly
interchangeable, and none are capable of precise definition. In general, it may be

---

[22] As, *e.g.*, in the *Aminoil* arbitration where, although Aminoil was the natural claimant in relation to
the primary issues, the Government had claims against Aminoil and did not concede that its
participation in the arbitration should be in the role of defendant. In this case, the terms "claimant"
and "respondent" were not used at all. Memorials and counter-memorials were exchanged
simultaneously, containing respectively "Aminoil's claims" and "The Government's claims"; and
at the main hearing, an agenda of issues was drawn up so that Aminoil's representatives would
speak first when one of its claims was being debated, and the Government's representatives would
speak first on issues where it was the claimant.

said that the terms "statement of claim" and "points of claim" indicate a relatively short document, the primary purpose of which is to define the issues and state the facts upon which the claimant's claims are founded.

6–57   By contrast, the expressions "statement of case" and "memorial" imply a more comprehensive documentary submission, intended to include argument relating to the legal issues as well as incorporating (in annexes or appendices) the documentary evidence relied upon and the written testimony of witnesses, together with any experts' reports on matters of opinion. However, the practitioner should not regard these general indications as conclusive; if there is any doubt as to what is required, this should be clarified by consulting the relevant rules of arbitration; and, if they are not clear, by addressing an appropriate enquiry to the arbitral tribunal.

Time-limits

6–58   The practice of arbitral tribunals varies greatly. Sometimes, an arbitral tribunal will fix time-limits for the submission of written pleadings that are tacitly accepted from the beginning as being unrealistic, and serve merely as targets to make sure that the parties start their preparatory work without delay. Such arbitral tribunals expect applications for extensions of time to be made and will grant them readily. Other arbitral tribunals regard this approach as both artificial and inappropriate, and prefer to assess realistic time-limits at an early stage in the hope that they will be observed. In principle, the second approach is to be preferred. Unfortunately, this sometimes leads to the parties requesting extensions to what were intended to be realistic time-limits. This naturally leads to greater overall delay in the conduct of the arbitration.

In fairness, it should be said that, whilst a claimant should know how long it will take to prepare the initial written pleading, the respondent may not be able to make a realistic evaluation of how long it will take to prepare the answer until he has seen the written material to be submitted by the claimant. Furthermore, the claimant may have worked on the statement of claim for many months before delivering the request for (or notice of) arbitration. Similarly, a claimant cannot assess how much time will be needed to prepare any rejoinder and, if applicable, his reply to any counterclaim, until it sees the respondent's written material.[23]

Admissibility of counterclaims

6–59   Jurisdiction in relation to a counterclaim is occasionally contested by a claimant on the grounds that the respondent's claims do not fall within the contract that contains the arbitration clause. If this is so, the arbitral tribunal has no option but

---

[23] The practice developed under the UNCITRAL Arbitration Rules by the Iran–US Claims Tribunal is summarised, with case citations, in Holtzmann, *Fact-finding, loc. cit.*, Sec.III-I. In deciding upon the admissibility of late-filed submissions, the Tribunal considered, in the light of the circumstances of each case, the needs for equality and fairness, the possibility of prejudice to the other party and the requirements for orderly conduct of the proceeding.

to exclude it. The arbitral tribunal may not exercise jurisdiction over claims that do not come within the scope of the arbitration clause.

The position is similar for claims of set-off, under which a respondent may resist payment of a debt on the basis that the claimant is in arrears with respect to contractual payments owing to the respondent. However, if the set-off is in relation to the same contract, or a contract with a sufficiently close connection to the main contract, then the arbitral tribunal may well have jurisdiction to consider the claim. This is a question of interpretation of the arbitration clause.

A more frequent problem arises where a respondent seeks to introduce a counterclaim at a very late stage. This may place the arbitral tribunal in great difficulty, depending on the circumstances and the type of arbitration. In an ICC arbitration the problem is solved by the terms of reference. If the counterclaim does not fall within those terms of reference, it may be admitted only if the arbitral tribunal so authorises having regard to "the nature of such new claims or counterclaims, the stage of the arbitration and other relevant circumstances".[24] If the arbitral tribunal determines that such a claim should not be admitted, the respondent is forced to initiate separate proceedings.

In ad hoc arbitrations, the question is a practical matter for the arbitral tribunal to determine, assuming that there is no detailed submission agreement defining the issues. The arbitral tribunal must decide whether the introduction of new claims would be an abuse of process that will lead to unnecessary delay and expense, or whether (assuming the counterclaim falls within its jurisdiction) the legitimate interest of resolving all issues in dispute between the parties in the proceedings should prevail.[25] **6–60**

5. EVIDENCE

(a) Generally

The purpose of presenting evidence is to assist the arbitral tribunal in determining disputed issues of *fact* and disputed issues of *opinion* (presented by "experts"). The dividing line between "fact" and "opinion" is not entirely clear-cut. In some systems, disputed aspects of "foreign" law must be proved as matters of fact. This is the rule in the court procedures of common law countries where foreign law is usually proved by calling an expert witness to give evidence on the foreign law. In other countries, foreign law is a question of law. The judge or arbitrator is presumed to know the law, even it is "foreign". **6–61**

Even in countries where foreign law is a question of law, it is not uncommon for an expert in the foreign law to be brought in to give an opinion, or to make an oral submission at the hearing. The characterisation of this issue as either a

---

[24] ICC Arbitration Rules, Art.19.
[25] The Iran–US Claims Tribunal considered "the reasons for the delay, the prejudice to the other party, and the effect of admitting the late-filed counterclaim on the orderly progress of the case"; Holtzmann, "Some Lessons of the Iran–United States Claims Tribunal" *Private Investors Abroad*, pp.16–21, see above, para.6–22.

matter of law or of fact may have relevance in relation to appeals, since appeals on questions of fact are generally not permitted, while appeals on grounds of error in law are contemplated under some national laws.

The Netherlands Arbitration Act 1986 provides that the arbitral tribunal may request the court to intervene to request information on foreign law through the agency of the European Convention on Information on Foreign Law.[26] However, in the Netherlands and elsewhere the usual practice before international arbitral tribunals is that all questions of law, whether they are technically "foreign" to individual members of the arbitral tribunal or not, will be *argued* either by the presentation of written opinions or orally, or both.[27] This is both sensible and pragmatic. Certainly the court procedures of the country in which the arbitration is held should have little or no influence on the way in which the arbitral tribunal approaches the question of how to deal with issues of "foreign" law that may arise.

Common and civil law procedures

6–62   In court procedures in most common law countries, the initiative as regards evidence is almost wholly in the hands of the parties.[28] The judge acts as a kind of referee to administer the rules of evidence, and to give a decision at the end on who has "won" the argument in the combative sense. The judge listens to the evidence and may question the witness; on the whole, however, the judge leaves it to the parties to present their respective cases and forms a judgment on the basis of what the elect to present to the court. Thus, the function of the court system in the common law countries is, as it were, to provide for the resolution of civil disputes by combat, and to enforce the ultimate result.

By contrast, in the courts of the civil law countries the judge takes a far more active part in the conduct of the proceedings and in the presentation of evidence, including the examination of witnesses.[29] It follows that proceedings in the civil law countries do not need to be bound by the same technical rules of evidence as exist in an adversarial forum. For example, if a judge in Germany considered that it would assist the court to have a witness examined on a matter that would be inadmissible in an English court, it would not be open to either party to block the reception of such testimony by invoking a rule of evidence. A technique followed by arbitral tribunals coming from different systems and cultures is to take "adverse inferences" from the silence of a party or the failure to comply with a

---

[26] The Netherlands Arbitration Act 1986, Art.1044.

[27] See the commentary on Art.1044, in Sanders & van den Berg, *The Netherlands Arbitration Act 1986: Text and Notes* (1987), p.2.

[28] English civil procedure was changed radically in 1999, converting the judge into a "case manager".

[29] See the discussion of comparative arbitration practices in ICCA Congress Series No.3 (1987), p.98. The extent to which the Iran–US Claims Tribunal took an active role in requiring evidence is described by Holtzmann in *Fact-Finding, loc. cit.*, Sec.II-A, para.6–10.

reasonable request from the arbitral tribunal for the production of documentary or witness evidence.[30]

There is some risk of overgeneralising in drawing distinctions between the so-called "common law" and "civil law" systems. Each system has many variations. The rules of procedure in the US are different from those in England, just as the German and French rules of procedure are different.

A distinguished Swiss practitioner has stated: **6–63**

"My first remark is that there is no such thing as 'Civil Law Procedure' in civil and commercial litigation. In common law countries, there are undoubtedly certain common basic principles of procedure, which go back to the procedure practised in the English courts. In continental Europe, there is no such common origin. In each country, one finds a different blend of civil procedure, largely influenced by local custom, the legal education received by judges and by counsel, and, to a varied extent, by the influence of the procedure practised in the old ecclesiastical courts, although such courts were abolished, in Protestant countries, at the time of the Reformation . . .

The result of this is that there is possibly as much difference between the outlook and practice of a French avocat and of a German Rechtsanwalt as between those of an English and of an Italian lawyer. The same applies within my own country, Switzerland, where civil and criminal procedure remain in the realm of the 26 sovereign states of the Confederation, thus leading to the existence of 26 different codes of civil or criminal procedure, plus a Civil Procedure Act for the Federal Supreme Court. There is as much difference between the type of civil procedure practised in Geneva and that practised in Zurich as between those featured in Madrid and Stockholm.

These differences are experienced daily in international arbitration, where they are sometimes the source of great difficulties. Certainly these difficulties are due, to a large extent, to the different patterns of civil procedure law, but, in my experience, to a far greater extent to the undisclosed assumptions and prejudices of municipal lawyers faced for the first time in their lives with a system of which they are not aware. Just to take a simple example, a common lawyer expects the claimant as a matter of course to have the last word at the end of the day, whereas a continental lawyer considers it a requirement of natural justice that the defendant should be the last to address the Court."[31]

Nevertheless, it is suggested that there is sufficient uniformity in the general **6–64** approach to questions concerning the presentation of evidence to justify using the

---

[30] The Iran–US Claims Tribunal drew adverse inferences from the silence of a party in the face of alleged breach or non-performance of the contract when some complaint would have been expected and from failure of a party to mention a point in a contract or in contemporaneous correspondence consistent with their position in the arbitration. Holtzmann, *Fact-finding, loc. cit.*, Sec.III-E.

[31] Prof. Claude Reymond in (1989) 8 Arbitration 159. See also Sandifer, *Evidence Before International Tribunals* (revised ed., 1975), pp.2 and 3.

expression "civil law countries" by way of contrast to the "common law countries" when discussing the presentation of evidence.

Admissibility

6–65   How does this difference translate itself into a situation in which an arbitral tribunal of three arbitrators, coming from different systems, approaches the question of the reception of evidence? The answer is that international tribunals composed of experienced international arbitrators, whether they are from common law or civil law countries, tend to focus on establishing the facts necessary for the determination of the issues between the parties, and are reluctant to be limited by any rules of evidence that might prevent them from achieving this goal. It is essential for practitioners, particularly when they have been raised in the common law tradition, to appreciate this and to learn not to place reliance upon technical rules concerning the admissibility of evidence during the course of the proceedings, particularly at witness hearings.

Conversely, in the exceptional case where all three arbitrators come from a common law background (or if there is a sole arbitrator from a common law country), and especially if they are relatively inexperienced in the world of international arbitration, a practitioner from a civil law country must take care that his case does not depend on proving facts that can only be established by the presentation of evidence that may be technically inadmissible under the system with which the arbitral tribunal is familiar.

Where a "non-hybrid" arbitral tribunal is established, the team of lawyers retained to represent each party should usually include a member who is familiar with the approach to the reception of evidence that the arbitral tribunal is likely to apply. This precaution should not be necessary where the arbitral tribunal is composed of members from different systems since, as stated above, such arbitral tribunals nearly always adopt a flexible approach to procedure, particularly with regard to the presentation of evidence. It is unlikely that a party will be prevented from submitting evidence that may assist the arbitral tribunal in establishing the truth in relation to disputed issues of fact.[32] The Iran–US Claims Tribunal developed an interesting practice concerning the admissibility of testimony of individuals concerned with the outcome of the case, including employees of a corporation. Under the civil law system such testimony is not admissible, whereas in the common law system it can be received and weighed taking due account of the source. The Iran–US Claims Tribunal treats "interested persons" not as *witnesses* but as representatives of the parties who may be heard to provide "information" for the Tribunal.

6–66   A further step forward in the creation of an international standard on the admissibility of evidence was made by the International Bar Association in the

---

[32] Holtzmann, *Fact-finding*, *loc. cit.*, Sec.III-B. See also Strauss, "The Practice of the Iran–United States Claims Tribunal in Receiving Evidence from Parties and from Experts" (1986) 3 Journal of International Arbitration 57.

1999 edition of its Rules on the Taking of Evidence. Article 9.2 of those Rules provides:

"The Arbitral Tribunal shall, at the request of a Party or on its own motion, exclude from evidence or production any document, statement, oral testimony or inspection for any of the following reasons:

    (a) lack of sufficient relevance or materiality;

    (b) legal impediment or privilege under the legal or ethical rules determined by the Arbitral Tribunal to be applicable;

    (c) unreasonable burden to produce the requested evidence;

    (d) loss or destruction of the document that has been reasonably shown to have occurred;

    (e) grounds of commercial or technical confidentiality that the Arbitral Tribunal determines to be compelling;

    (f) rounds of special political or institutional sensitivity (including evidence that has been classified as secret by a government or a public international institution) that the Arbitral Tribunal determines to be compelling; or

    (g) considerations of fairness or equality of the Parties that the Arbitral Tribunal determines to be compelling."[33]

Burden of proof

Another aspect of the presentation of evidence is the question of the burden of proof. The practice of nearly all international arbitral tribunals is to require each party to prove the facts upon which it relies in support of its case. This practice is recognised in the UNCITRAL Rules.[34] The only exceptions relate to propositions that are so obvious, or notorious, that proof is not required. The degree of proof that must be achieved in practice before an international arbitral tribunal is not capable of precise definition, but it may be safely assumed that it is close to the "balance of probability". This standard is to be distinguished from the concept of "beyond all reasonable doubt" required, for example, in countries such as the US and England to prove guilt in a criminal trial before a jury.[35] **6–67**

Methods of presenting evidence

The methods of presenting evidence to an arbitral tribunal on disputed issues of fact derive from a synthesis of party autonomy, discretion of the arbitral tribunal and court control at the stage of enforcement. These methods may be divided into four categories: **6–68**

---

[33] IBA Rules on the Taking of Evidence in International Commercial Arbitration (2nd ed., 1999).

[34] UNCITRAL Arbitration Rules, Art.24.

[35] In *Parker* (1926) 4 Rep. International Arb. Awards 39, the Mexican–US Claims Commission held that: "When the claimant has established a prima facie case and the respondent has offered no evidence in rebuttal the latter may not insist that the former pile up evidence to establish its allegations beyond a reasonable doubt without pointing out some reason for doubting."

- production of contemporary documents;

- testimony of witnesses of fact (written or oral);

- opinions of expert witnesses (written or oral); and

- inspection of the subject-matter of the dispute.

These methods may be used, or combined, in many different ways for the purpose of discharging the burden of proof to the satisfaction of an arbitral tribunal. It is important to recognise that each different arbitral tribunal may adopt a different approach not only to the manner in which it wishes the evidence to be presented, but also to the weight that it is willing to give to any particular type of evidence.

In general, however, the more startling the proposition a party seeks to prove, the more rigorous the arbitral tribunal will be in requiring that proposition to be fully established. A classic example of this general rule is that an arbitral tribunal will be reluctant to find an executive of a company guilty of fraudulent activity in the exercise of his ordinary commercial activities, unless this is proved conclusively. In deciding what evidence to produce, and the means by which it should be presented, the practitioner should therefore make an evaluation of the *degree* of proof that the particular arbitral tribunal is likely to require, before being sufficiently satisfied to make a finding of fact that his client is seeking.

(b) Production of documents

6–69   In international commercial arbitrations, the best evidence that can be presented in relation to any issue of fact is almost invariably contained in the documents which came into existence at the time of the events giving rise to the dispute.[36] This contrasts with the presentation of evidence in national courts in common law systems where most facts are proved by direct oral testimony, and even documentary evidence must in principle be introduced by a witness.

It is not difficult to appreciate why reliance on documentary evidence is favoured by international arbitral tribunals. Its presentation is easier and less time consuming; and, in an environment in which cross-examination is not regarded as a reliable method of testing the evidence of a witness, the evidentiary weight of contemporary documentary evidence is clearly more substantial than that of oral evidence that is not tested by an effective challenge, either through lack of expertise on the part of the opposing party's advocate or lack of time during the course of the hearings.

However, the main reason for the practice of international arbitration tribunals in relying primarily upon evidence contained in contemporary documents is that

---

[36] In two cases before the Iran–US Claims Tribunal, fact-finding on jurisdictional issues was based entirely on documentary evidence consisting of official documents, corporate documents prepared in the ordinary course of business, publications of which the Tribunal took judicial notice, certificates by independent certified public accountants and affidavits of corporate officers: see Holtzmann, *Fact-finding, loc. cit.*, Sec.II-B, para.6–10.

the application of the so-called "best evidence rule"[37] applies primarily to the *weight* of the evidence rather than to its *admissibility*, and the evidence of contemporary documents will invariably be regarded as being of great weight. The authenticity of documents must be capable of proof if challenged by the other party; but it is not usually necessary to produce original documents, or certified copies, unless there is some special reason to call for the original.[38]

Favourable and unfavourable documents

Documents relevant to the issues between the parties can be divided into three **6–70** categories: those that are favourable to the party which has them in its possession; those that are unfavourable; and those that are neutral. No difficulty arises in relation to the first and the third category. The party concerned no doubt wishes to produce them to the arbitral tribunal as early as practicable. The only problems that may arise in due course are questions as to their authenticity, and their evidentiary weight in relation to the proposition in respect of which they are produced. However, the second category may sometimes give rise to a philosophical difference of view and practice between the common law and the civil law systems.

Common law practice

In many common law countries it is usual in litigation in the national courts for **6–71** there to be an automatic "discovery" of documents procedure, which generally means disclosing to each other the existence of *all* relevant documents, whether favourable or unfavourable, including internal notes and memoranda.[39]

This is not the practice in international commercial arbitration, as will be seen below. Indeed, it is better to avoid the use of the term "discovery" because it is an ambiguous term. To a civil lawyer it means nothing; to a US lawyer it encompasses production of documents and depositions of potential witnesses and experts as well as inspection of the subject-matter of the dispute; to an English lawyer it refers only to production of documents.

There is no practice of automatic discovery in international commercial arbitration. The usual practice is to limit document production as much as possible to those documents that are strictly *relevant* to the issues in dispute and *necessary* for the proper resolution of those issues. There is no tradition or practice of the wholesale (or "warehouse") production of documents. Furthermore, most arbitral tribunals apply the principle of "proportionality"—that is, they will limit the scope (and thus the expense) of document production to an extent that is reasonable in the context of the amount in dispute and the relative significance of the issues in respect of which document production has been requested.

---

[37] See Sandifer, *op. cit.*, p.202.
[38] See the discussion of proof of authenticity of documents in "Comparative Arbitration Practice", ICCA Congress Series No.3 (Kluwer, 1987), p.79.
[39] In the USA, "discovery" is much wider than it is in many other common law countries, in that it is not limited to production of documents but includes depositions of potential fact and expert witnesses as well as inspection of the subject-matter of the dispute.

6–72   It is sometimes argued that the position is different in international arbitrations that take place in the US, and that a party is *entitled* to wide-ranging production of documents. It is true that the Federal Arbitration Act and a number of state arbitration statutes grant broad discretionary powers to arbitral tribunals to require the production of documents, as well as the testimony of potential witnesses given on deposition.[40] It is, however, a misconception that arbitrations taking place in the US are subject to the automatic and extensive discovery procedures available in court litigation in that country. The reality is that in the US there is generally no *right* to any discovery in international arbitrations and the extent to which discovery is permitted is entirely in the hands of the arbitral tribunal if the parties do not agree.[41] The national courts will not interfere to expand any right of discovery ordered by the arbitral tribunal.[42]

Civil law practice

6–73   In countries that follow the civil law tradition, the usual practice—although it is unwise to generalise—is for each party to produce the documents upon which it relies to establish its case and, exceptionally, to ask for the production of specific documents which it believes to be (a) in the possession of the opposing party and (b) likely to assist its case.

This practice has considerably influenced institutional rules, such as those of the ICC, the LCIA and also rules that are applied in ad hoc arbitrations, notably the UNCITRAL Rules.

Practice in international arbitrations

6–74   The usual practice in international commercial arbitrations is for the parties, and the tribunal, to follow a blend of common law and civil law procedures, with the latter being predominant. In part, this is a matter of economics. Wholesale disclosure of documents is an expensive and time-consuming process for all concerned and rarely reveals the "smoking gun" that is being sought.

In part, it is a matter of cultural differences. A US businessman will know that in the event of litigation, all his internal correspondence, memoranda, computer disks and emails may have to be disclosed to an opposing party. As a result, he will either be careful about what he writes down (or creates in electronic form); or involve his lawyers in the "paper trail" in the hope of invoking privilege; or

---

[40] See, *e.g.*, the US Arbitration Act, s.7, New York C.P.L.R. 7505, California Civ. Proc. Code 1282–1283, Illinois Ann. Stats. Ch.10, s.107 and Massachusetts Gen. Laws, Ch.251, s.7; for a discussion of pre-hearing discovery in the US see Stein, "Pre-hearing Discovery in International Arbitrations in the US" (1985) Forum New York, Vol.2, No.1; Born, "Court Ordered Discovery in Aid of Foreign Arbitration: The US Perspective" 12 *ASA Bulletin* pp.476–480 (314, 1994); Born, *International Commercial Arbitration in the United States: Commentary and Materials* (Kluwer, 1994).

[41] See Morgan, "Discovery in Arbitration" (1986) 3(3) Journal of International Arbitration, 9 at 15–18.

[42] *Coastal States Trading v Zenith Navigation SA* 446 F.Supp.330 (S.D.N.Y. 1977) and *Commercial Solvents Corp v Louisiana Liquid Fertilizer Co* 20 F.R.D. 359 (1957), but a US court will intervene only in exceptional circumstances: *Recognition Equipment v NCR Corp*, 532 F.Supp.271 (1981).

accept possible disclosure of damaging documents as a fact of life. A French businessman, by contrast, will be appalled if he finds that the internal documentation he handed to his own lawyers for their information is being passed on by them to the opposing party's lawyers.

It is usual, in international commercial arbitration, for each party to start by producing to the other, and to the tribunal, only the documents on which it relies in support of its case.

This practice is reflected in the rules of the major arbitration institutions. In **6–75** ICC arbitrations, the parties are required to produce the documents on which they rely with their respective Request for Arbitration, Answer (and Counterclaim, if any).

The LCIA Rules contain a provision to the effect that, subject to any procedural rules agreed by the parties or determined by the arbitral tribunal, written statements shall be exchanged and:

"All statements referred to in this Article shall be accompanied by copies (or, if they are specially voluminous, lists) of all essential documents on which the party concerned relies and which have not previously been submitted by any party, and (where appropriate) by any samples and exhibits."[43]

The UNCITRAL Arbitration Rules provide:

"The claimant *may* annex to his statement of claim all documents he deems relevant or may add a reference to the documents or other evidence he will submit."[44]

Disputed document requests

Neither party is likely to be satisfied, however, with the totality of the **6–76** documents produced by the other. Each will believe, with or without good reason, that there are other documents—memoranda of internal meetings, reports to, or from, the board of directors and so forth—which will assist its own case or damage its opponent's case. This is likely to result in each party asking the other to produce other, specified documents or classes of documents, and in the event of a refusal, to refer the dispute to the tribunal.

In civil law arbitrations, such requests are likely to be more focused and less frequent than in common law arbitrations. In such cases, the tribunal often reviews the exchange of correspondence and issues a procedural order, without further consultation with the parties.

In large or complex disputes, such as those involving international construction projects, the parties' requests for production of documents are often lengthy. This in turn has the result that each party will dispute the other's request and ask the tribunal for a procedural order limiting the scope of the documents it should be obliged to produce.

[43] LCIA Arbitration Rules, Art.15.6.
[44] UNCITRAL Arbitration Rules, Art.18 (emphasis added).

6–77   Dealing with disputed document production requests can be a laborious and time-consuming process for all concerned, and different tribunals adopt various different techniques to cut through the detail involved in resolving such disputed requests. In many instances, where practicable, the tribunal convenes a management meeting with the parties' counsel with the objective of thrashing out a compromise agreement between the parties on most of the categories of documents requested. This usually involves side meetings between the parties, during which—with the encouragement of the tribunal—they attempt to limit the scope of their requests to manageable proportions. If successful, this usually leaves only a few categories of documents that remain disputed. The tribunal may then convert the case management meeting into a hearing at which the parties make their arguments in respect of the remaining categories. The tribunal then makes its determinations on those categories. Experience shows that a day spent in this manner by the tribunal and the parties often cuts through what can otherwise be a lengthy document production phase that has the potential to delay the overall procedural schedule the tribunal originally designed for the arbitration in consultation with the parties.

Another technique that often works well in practice, either as an alternative to the case management meeting or in combination with it, is the so-called "Redfern Schedule", named after one of the authors. This is useful for both the parties and the tribunal in crystallising the points at issue where there have been discussions or correspondence between the parties, but there are matters still in dispute. The Schedule takes the form of a spreadsheet. This is a spreadsheet in which the first column sets out a list and description of the documents requested; the second column sets out the requesting party's justification for the request (including relevance and importance); the third column sets out the requested party's reasons for refusing the request (for example, no such document exists, lack of relevance, proportionality, legal professional privilege, etc.). The final column is left blank, for the tribunal to record its decision. The main advantage of this technique is that it sometimes avoids the need for a case management meeting or a hearing, which in turn involves a saving in costs and the inevitable delays in finding dates that are convenient for the parties' counsel and the arbitrators

Almost always, the tribunal will wish to limit document production as far as possible in order to focus the categories of materials to be produced on those that are likely to be relevant and necessary; and to insist that the requests should, so to speak, be fired from a rifle rather than a shotgun.

6–78   This pattern of disclosure of documents, with insistence on carefully specified and limited requests, is seen in the IBA Rules of Evidence, which provide in Art.3:

> "1. Within the time ordered by the Arbitral Tribunal, each Party shall submit to the Arbitral Tribunal and to the other Parties all documents available to it on which it relies, including public documents and those in the public domain, except for any documents that have already been submitted by another Party.

2. Within the time ordered by the Arbitral Tribunal, any Party may submit to the Arbitral Tribunal a Request to Produce.

3. A Request to Produce shall contain:

   (a) (i) a description of a requested document sufficient to identify it, or (ii) a description in sufficient detail (including subject-matter) of a narrow and specific requested category of documents that are reasonably believed to exist;

   (b) a description of how the documents requested are relevant and material to the outcome of the case; and

   (c) a statement that the documents requested are not in the possession, custody or control of the requesting Party, and of the reason why that Party assumes the documents requested to be in the possession, custody or control of the other Party.

4. Within the time ordered by the Arbitral Tribunal, the Party to whom the Request to Produce is addressed shall produce to the Arbitral Tribunal and to the other Parties all the documents requested in its possession, custody or control as to which no objection is made.

5. If the Party to whom the Request to Produce is addressed has objections to some or all of the documents requested, it shall state them in writing to the Arbitral Tribunal within the time ordered by the Arbitral Tribunal. The reasons for such objections shall be any of those set forth in Article 9.2.

6. The Arbitral Tribunal shall, in consultation with the Parties and in timely fashion, consider the Request to Produce and the objections. The Arbitral Tribunal may order the Party to whom such Request is addressed to produce to the Arbitral Tribunal and to the other Parties those requested documents in its possession, custody or control as to which the Arbitral Tribunal determines that (i) the issues that the requesting Party wishes to prove are relevant and material to the outcome of the case, and (ii) none of the reasons for objection set forth in Article 9.2 apply."[45]

---

[45] Art.9.2 states:

   "2. The Arbitral Tribunal shall, at the request of a Party or on its own motion, exclude from evidence or production any document, statement, oral testimony or inspection for any of the following reasons:

   (a) lack of sufficient relevance or materiality;

   (b) legal impediment or privilege under the legal or ethical rules determined by the Arbitral Tribunal to be applicable;

   (c) unreasonable burden to produce the requested evidence;

   (d) loss or destruction of the document that has been reasonably shown to have occurred;

   (e) grounds of commercial or technical confidentiality that the Arbitral Tribunal determines to be compelling;

   (f) grounds of special political or institutional sensitivity (including evidence that has been classified as secret by a government or a public international institution) that the Arbitral Tribunal determines to be compelling; or

   (g) considerations of fairness or equality of the Parties that the Arbitral Tribunal determines to be compelling."

Documents in the possession of third parties

6–79   An arbitral tribunal lacks power to order production of documents in the possession of a third party, even where such documents may be relevant to the matters in issue. However, in some countries a third party may be compelled by *subpoena* to attend at the hearings to give evidence, and the courts can assist the arbitral tribunal in enforcing the attendance of such witnesses. In England, a party may apply to a court to compel the attendance of a witness and to bring with him any material documents in his possession.[46] In the US, the Federal Arbitration Act provides that the arbitrators may summon a person to attend before them and to produce any material documents.[47]

It sometimes happens in arbitration proceedings that a third party appears voluntarily at the request of one of the parties and gives testimony helpful to that party. Then, on questioning by the other party, the witness may object to the production of documents. The arbitral tribunal does not usually require such a witness to produce documents, but an adverse inference may be drawn in respect of the evidence of the witness in question if it appears to the tribunal that the witness is deliberately withholding documents without good reason.

Presentation of documents

6–80   It is of considerable assistance to the arbitral tribunal if the parties are able to present the documentary evidence in the form of a volume (or volumes) of documents, in chronological order with each page numbered like a book, for use at the hearing. In this way, each member of the arbitral tribunal, and each party, has a complete set of documents with identical numbering. If there is a huge number of documents, it may be a good idea to identify the most important documents and include them in a separate volume or volumes (sometimes known as "the core bundle"). This has the additional benefit of avoiding tiresome and unnecessary duplication of documents.

Much valuable time may also be saved at hearings by using techniques such as colour-coded volumes of documents in order to avoid the delay that takes place while each member of the arbitral tribunal, the witnesses, and the lawyers representing both parties find the volume and the page to which the speaker is referring at any given time. Assistance given to the arbitral tribunal in these simple ways enables the arbitration to be conducted more speedily and efficiently.

The use of the word "agreed" in the context of volumes of documents occasionally gives rise to misunderstanding. The word is not intended to indicate that the parties are agreed on the meaning of the contents of the document, or its evidentiary weight, or even its admissibility. It simply indicates that the authenticity of the document is "agreed", in the sense that each party agrees that it is an accurate copy of an existing document.

---

[46] English Arbitration Act 1996, s.43.
[47] US Federal Arbitration Act 1925, s.7.

When the authenticity of documents is disputed, the arbitral tribunal usually **6–81** orders that the originals must be produced for inspection. This may be carried out by forensic experts if necessary. If the originals are not produced, the arbitral tribunal may disregard the documents in question, as being unreliable.

Translations

It is usually necessary to provide translations of any documents that are not **6–82** already in the language of the arbitration. Such translations should, if possible, be submitted to the arbitral tribunal jointly by the parties as "agreed translations". The most convenient practice is to include the document in its original language first, immediately following it in the volume with the translation into the language of the arbitration. If the correctness of the translation is disputed, each party's version may be inserted following the original. Where there is no specific dispute as to the accuracy of a translation, but nevertheless there is no agreed translation (either for lack of time or lack of co-operation between the parties) it is advisable but not essential for the parties presenting the translation to have it notarially certified.

(c) Testimony of witnesses

The second method of presenting factual evidence to an arbitral tribunal is **6–83** through the testimony of witnesses. There are several methods of undertaking this exercise, which may be inclined towards the common law model or towards the methods adopted in the civil law countries. Frequently a mixture of the two systems is adopted. When this is done, it is partly through a desire to achieve a compromise between the wishes of the parties, or of individual members of the arbitral tribunal, but also mainly for pragmatic reasons.

The primary motivation of the arbitral tribunal, in relation to the procedural aspects of the taking of evidence of witnesses, is to shorten the oral stage of the proceedings so far as practicable. This objective cannot be achieved if the arbitral tribunal adopts a fully inquisitorial process in which it calls all the witnesses and examines them orally in the presence of the parties. Neither will it be achieved if each party calls all its witnesses before the arbitral tribunal and subjects them to a long "examination-in-chief" ("direct examination"), followed by cross-examination and re-examination ("redirect").

In international commercial arbitration, it is not generally considered essential that witnesses should be heard orally:

> "The dispute being essentially, and indeed exclusively, of a legal nature, I have reached the conclusion that it was completely unnecessary to collect testimonies and hear witnesses as the Defendant requested . . . "[48]

---

[48] Extract from the award of the Swiss arbitrator reported in *Dalmia Dairy Industries Ltd v National Bank of Pakistan* [1978] 2 Lloyd's Rep. 223 at 269.

6–84   When an enforcement action was subsequently brought in the English courts, the contention that the arbitrator should have heard witnesses was rejected:

> "Article 20 of the [then applicable edition of] ICC Rules merely provides that the arbitrator 'shall have the power to hear witnesses'. It gives him a discretion but imposes no obligation . . . Indeed, the procedure followed by the arbitrator in this case is in my experience the usual procedure in ICC and other Continental arbitrations. There can, therefore, be no question of any infringement of any rule of English public policy."[49]

It is not often, however, that a dispute is essentially, or indeed exclusively, of a legal nature. Where any investigation into the factual background of the dispute is necessary, it is usual for an arbitral tribunal to hear the evidence of witnesses at a hearing. Such evidence is useful; indeed it is sometimes invaluable. However, when given orally, in question and answer form, it may take a long time to cover very little ground. This is particularly so where the witness does not speak the language of the arbitration and an interpreter is required. It is also the position where the witness is an expert, dealing with complicated technical matters.[50] Occasionally, and especially when oral testimony at the witness hearings has to be given with the help of an interpreter, it may be useful for the parties to take the testimony in advance and submit a transcript to the arbitral tribunal.

Presentation of witness evidence

6–85   It is common practice for parties to submit written statements of the witnesses on whose evidence they intend to rely. Sometimes these written statements are submitted on oath in the form of affidavits. More frequently, the statements are simply signed by the witnesses. Each party then indicates to the arbitral tribunal which of the other party's witnesses should be required to attend the hearing for oral examination; and the arbitral tribunal itself indicates to the parties which, if any, of the other witnesses it wishes to hear in person. It is relatively rare for the arbitral tribunal to require a witness to be present if neither party requires that witness to attend. The IBA codified this practice in the 1999 edition of its Rules on the Taking of Evidence.[51] Article 4 of those Rules provides:

> "1. Within the time ordered by the Arbitral Tribunal, each Party shall identify the witnesses on whose testimony it relies and the subject-matter of that testimony.

---

[49] *ibid.*, at 270 *per* Kerr J.
[50] Where he is an expert witness *and* needs an interpreter, the situation becomes virtually impossible.
[51] IBA Rules on the Taking of Evidence in International Commercial Arbitration (2nd ed., 1999), Art.10.

2. Any person may present evidence as a witness, including a Party or a Party's officer, employee or other representative.
3. It shall not be improper for a Party, its officers, employees, legal advisors or other representatives to interview its witnesses or potential witnesses.
4. The Arbitral Tribunal may order each Party to submit within a specified time to the Arbitral Tribunal and to the other Parties a written statement by each witness on whose testimony it relies, except for those witnesses whose testimony is sought pursuant to Art.4.10 (the "Witness Statement"). If Evidentiary Hearings are organized on separate issues (such as liability and damages), the Arbitral Tribunal or the Parties by agreement may schedule the submission of Witness Statements separately for each Evidentiary Hearing.
5. Each Witness Statement shall contain:

   (a) the full name and address of the witness, his or her present and past relationship (if any) with any of the Parties, and a description of his or her background, qualifications, training and experience, if such a description may be relevant and material to the dispute or to the contents of the statement;
   (b) a full and detailed description of the facts, and the source of the witness's information as to those facts, sufficient to serve as that witness's evidence in the matter in dispute;
   (c) an affirmation of the truth of the statement; and
   (d) the signature of the witness and its date and place . . .

6. [omitted]
7. Each witness who has submitted a Witness Statement shall appear for testimony at an Evidentiary Hearing, unless the Parties agree otherwise.
8. If a witness who has submitted a Witness Statement does not appear without a valid reason for testimony at an Evidentiary Hearing, except by agreement of the Parties, the Arbitral Tribunal shall disregard that Witness Statement unless, in exceptional circumstances, the Arbitral Tribunal determines otherwise.
9., 10., 11. [omitted]"

Institutional rules for administered or non-administered arbitration do not usually contain any specific or detailed provisions governing the procedure for the reception of witness evidence by the arbitral tribunal. Accordingly, the procedure to be followed under such rules is dealt with by agreement of the parties or, failing agreement, at the discretion of the arbitral tribunal. The LCIA Rules provide for the testimony of a witness to be presented in the form of a signed statement or sworn affidavit. Either party may request that the witness attend, subject to the discretion of the arbitral tribunal. If the witness fails to attend to give oral testimony this will affect the weight to be given to the written evidence presented by the witness in question or, in an extreme case, may result in it being excluded.[52]

6–86   An important aspect of the presentation of witness evidence is the question of whether, and if so to what extent, it is permissible for a party, its employees or counsel to interview and prepare the witnesses whose testimony they intend to present to the arbitral tribunal. This is largely a cultural matter, although the rules of some national courts (or bar associations) forbid or make it unethical for witnesses to be contacted by the parties or their counsel before they give their testimony in person.

In international arbitration, however, it is well recognised that witnesses may be interviewed and prepared prior to giving their oral testimony. This is confirmed by at least two of the sets of rules in common use. The LCIA Rules expressly permit it, subject to any mandatory provisions of the law governing the arbitration,[53] and the IBA Rules on the Taking of Evidence provide:

> "It shall not be improper for a Party, its officers, employees, legal advisors or other representatives to interview its witnesses or potential witnesses."[54]

It is generally accepted that there are certain limits. For example, it would be gross misconduct for a lawyer to try to persuade a fact witness to tell a story that both the lawyer and the witness in question knew to be untrue, and to prepare the witness to make the story sound as credible as possible. It would also almost always be counterproductive. Experienced arbitral tribunals tend to have good "noses" for sniffing out the truth, and invariably cross-check oral testimony against the available corroborative documentary and other evidence.

6–87   Another cultural division arises between lawyers from jurisdictions where a party cannot be a "witness" as such. This stems from the rules of court in some civil law countries under which a person (or officers or employees in the case of corporate entities) cannot be treated a witnesses in their own cause.[55] However, even in the courts of these countries a party can be heard—the rule merely forbids them from being categorised as *witnesses*.

As in the case of many other rules of national court procedure, this rule does not apply in international arbitrations. It may be that an arbitral tribunal will tend to give greater weight to the testimony of a witness who has no financial or other interest in the outcome of the arbitration, but that is a different matter.[56]

The role of counsel should be to assist witnesses in developing the confidence and clarity of thought required to testify truthfully and effectively based upon their own knowledge or recollection of the facts. It should be borne in mind that being examined in the "witness box" is, for most witnesses, an unfamiliar and

---

[52] LCIA Arbitration Rules, Art.20.3.
[53] LCIA Rules, Art.20.6.
[54] IBA Rules on the Taking of Evidence, Art.4(3).
[55] Germany is a significant example, followed by countries where the code of civil procedure broadly follows the German tradition, such as Austria and the Czech Republic.
[56] IBA Rules on the Taking of Evidence, Art.4(2).

intimidating experience.[57] The interests of justice are not well served by the transcripts of the interrogation of frightened witnesses by skilled and manipulative cross-examiners. Fortunately, experience indicates that experienced arbitrators tend to discount severe or bullying cross-examinations on the basis that it demonstrates no more than the cleverness of the cross-examiner—rather than the credibility of the witness.[58]

Evidentiary weight of witness evidence

An arbitral tribunal has a discretion to determine the evidentiary weight to be **6–88** given to witness evidence.[59] This arises from the general principles applicable to arbitration proceedings, and is expressly affirmed, for example, in the UNCITRAL Rules.[60]

In general, arbitral tribunals tend to give less weight to uncorroborated witness testimony than to evidence contained in contemporary documents. Arbitral tribunals also give greater weight to the evidence of a witness that has been tested by cross-examination, or by an examination by the arbitral tribunal itself. Similarly, although in some legal systems[61] a party cannot give evidence, the evidence of a party is rarely excluded in international commercial arbitration. However, the untested evidence of a witness who has a clear interest in the result of the case may be given less evidentiary weight than the evidence of a witness who is truly independent.

As stated earlier, arbitral tribunals normally reject any submission that they should not hear the evidence of any particular witness, even if it is secondary evidence. However, an arbitral tribunal will give less weight to secondary evidence if, in its opinion, the party calling that evidence *could have* produced a witness who would have been able to give direct evidence on the factual issue in question.

Taking evidence overseas

The Hague Convention of 1970[62] does not apply to arbitrations. Accordingly, **6–89** there is no method of compelling a witness who is not within the jurisdiction of the court of the place of arbitration to give testimony. However, some countries have legislation that enables arbitral tribunals sitting in other countries to obtain evidence from witnesses within their jurisdiction, either at the request of the

---

[57] D. Roney, "Effective Witness Preparation for International Commercial Arbitration: A Practical Guide for Counsel" (2003) 20 Journal of International Arbitration 429, which provides a useful practical six-step guide for the preparation of witnesses.
[58] Veeder, "The Lawyer's Duty to Arbitrate in Good Faith", 2001 Goff Lecture (2002) 18 Arbitration International 445.
[59] The practice of the Iran–US Claims Tribunal concerning the weight to be given to affidavits is discussed by Holtzmann, *Fact-finding, loc. cit.*, Sec.II-B(5).
[60] UNCITRAL Arbitration Rules, Art.25.6.
[61] *e.g.* Austria and Germany.
[62] The Hague Convention on the Taking of Evidence Abroad in Civil or Commercial Matters was concluded on March 18, 1970.

arbitral tribunal itself, or on the application of a party. The Model Law also envisages this possibility.[63]

(d) Expert evidence

6–90   The third method of presenting evidence to an arbitral tribunal is by the use of expert witnesses. Some issues of fact can only be determined by the arbitral tribunal becoming involved in the evaluation of elements that are essentially matters of *opinion*. Thus, in a construction dispute, the contemporary documents, comprising correspondence, progress reports and other memoranda, and the evidence of witnesses who were present on the site may enable the arbitral tribunal to determine what actually happened. There may then be a further question to be determined; namely whether or not what actually happened was the result of, for example, a design error or defective construction practices. The determination of such an issue can only be made by the arbitral tribunal with the assistance of experts, unless it possesses the relevant expertise itself. Equally, in shipping arbitrations, the performance of a vessel or its equipment may need to be evaluated by experts, so that the arbitral tribunal may make the relevant findings of fact.

There are two basic methods of proceeding in a situation where the arbitral tribunal itself does not have the relevant expertise. The first is for the arbitral tribunal to appoint its own expert or experts. The second is for the parties to present expert evidence to the tribunal and, since this evidence will presumably be in conflict, for the arbitral tribunal to evaluate it, after it has been tested by cross-examination or by some other method (including the appointment by the arbitral tribunal of its own expert). As many cases are determined on the basis of expert evidence, it often falls to the arbitral tribunal to draw the lines of battle by limiting the number of experts each side may present. This is usually agreed by the parties at a pre-hearing conference so that a protracted battle of experts may be avoided.

Experts appointed by the arbitral tribunal

6–91   In international commercial arbitration, the arbitral tribunal is usually composed of lawyers.[64] Where matters of a specialist or technical nature arise, such an arbitral tribunal often needs expert assistance in reaching its conclusions, in order "to obtain any technical information that might guide it in the search for truth."[65] For example, expertise in cryogenics may be required to determine why a metal storage tank cracked; or civil engineering experience may be required to determine why an airport runway became unusable. Expert help may be needed

---

[63] Model Law, Art.27, which does not limit court assistance in relation to the taking of evidence to arbitrations held within the territory of a Model Law country.

[64] See Ch.4, paras 4–13 *et seq.*

[65] See *Starrett Housing Corp v The Government of the Islamic Republic of Iran* (1987) 16 Iran–US C.T.R. 112, Award No.314-21-1, para.264 (August 14, 1987), quoting (at 196) the ICJ in the *Corfu Channel* case.

to investigate the quantification of a claim.[66] The arbitral tribunal may, for example, need quantity surveyors to assist in evaluating claims for measured work under a civil engineering contract; or accountants, to assist in determining the value to be put on a company's balance sheet.

Power to appoint experts

It is usual for an arbitral tribunal to be given express power to appoint experts **6–92** if it considers this to be necessary or desirable. Such a power of appointment of experts is generally found in the arbitration agreement, either as an express term (as in a submission agreement) or through the incorporation of international or institutional rules of arbitration.[67] In the absence of any express power, a question may arise as to whether or not an arbitral tribunal has implied power to appoint an expert under the law governing the arbitration.[68]

It is a well-established principle of most national systems of law that, unless authorised to do so by the terms of his appointment, someone to whom a duty has been delegated must not delegate that duty to someone else. So long as it is plain, however, that the arbitral tribunal is merely taking advice from an expert (and not attempting to delegate its task to him) it is difficult to see any objection in principle to the appointment of an expert by an arbitral tribunal.[69] If an arbitral tribunal needs expert technical assistance in order to understand complex technical matters, and it needs to understand these matters in order to arrive at a proper decision, there is no good reason to prevent it from obtaining such assistance. It seems to follow that, in the absence of an express provision of the governing law to the contrary, or of an equivalent agreement of the parties, an international arbitral tribunal may generally assume that it has power to call upon expert assistance if needed.[70] As a corollary to this power, the arbitral tribunal must give

---

[66] *e.g.* the Iran–US Claims Tribunal in the *Starrett Housing* case, above, made an initial decision that the claimant's property had been taken by Iran, before appointing an expert to assist the tribunal on issues of valuation.

[67] See, *e.g.*, UNCITRAL Arbitration Rules, Art.27; ICC Arbitration Rules, Art.20(4); and LCIA Arbitration Rules, Art.21.

[68] It is unusual for the applicable law to contain an express power, although the English Arbitration Act 1996, s.37 contains such a provision.

[69] This principle was expressed by the Iran–US Claims Tribunal in the *Starrett Housing* case (above, para.6–91): "No matter how well qualified an expert may be, however, it is fundamental that an arbitral tribunal cannot delegate to him the duty of deciding the case." (p.197, para.266). In applying this principle the Tribunal cited earlier international tribunals and stated at p.199, para.273: " . . . the Tribunal adopts as its own the conclusions of the Expert within his area of expertise when it is satisfied that sufficient reasons have not been shown that the Expert's view is contrary to the evidence, the governing law, or common sense." See also comment and cases cited at paras 270–272.

[70] For a statement to this effect (admittedly in the context of disputes between states) see White, *Use of Experts by International Tribunals* (1965), p.73: "Such practice as does exist, however, would seem to point to the recognition of an implied power to order an expert inquiry or to call independent expert witnesses in appropriate cases. This implied power is a concomitant of the principle that the function of the international judge is to resolve the dispute before him on the basis of all the relevant factual data, and that he has a duty to satisfy himself that he is in possession of this evidence and that he is equipped to understand its legal significance." Where reliance has to be placed upon an implied power, it is advisable first to check the provisions of the law governing the arbitration.

the parties an opportunity to comment on any expertise upon which the arbitrators have relied, including their own, if any.

The selection of an expert, or experts, and the formulation of his assigned tasks are matters on which the arbitral tribunal may or may not wish to consult the parties. Involving the parties may lengthen the process; however, their involvement may have the effect of reducing later objections to the expert's report. The measures adopted by the Iran–US Claims Tribunal in certain of its cases are instructive. In naming an expert the Tribunal has first given the parties the opportunity to agree on an expert, then presented the parties with a list of individuals and institutions from which to choose, stating that if the parties are still unable to agree, the Tribunal would choose the expert itself. Similarly, the Tribunal has also sought input from the parties concerning the expert's terms of reference, and instructed the expert to submit a preliminary report, upon which the parties may then comment. The expert is expected to take these comments into account when preparing his final report.[71] In this way the parties can assist the expert in making the report complete, while being reassured that important aspects of the case are not being decided without their involvement.

6–93   Article 6 of the IBA Rules on the Taking of Evidence provides:

1. The Arbitral Tribunal, after having consulted with the Parties, may appoint one or more independent Tribunal-Appointed Experts to report to it on specific issues designated by the Arbitral Tribunal. The Arbitral Tribunal shall establish the terms of reference for any Tribunal-Appointed Expert report after having consulted with the Parties. A copy of the final terms of reference shall be sent by the Arbitral Tribunal to the Parties.

2. The Tribunal-Appointed Expert shall, before accepting appointment, submit to the Arbitral Tribunal and to the Parties a statement of his or her independence from the Parties and the Arbitral Tribunal, the Parties shall inform the Arbitral Tribunal whether they have any objections to the Tribunal-Appointed Expert's independence. The Arbitral Tribunal shall decide promptly whether to accept any such objection.

3. Subject to the provisions of Art.9.2, the Tribunal-Appointed Expert may request a Party to provide any relevant documents, goods, samples, property or site for inspection. The authority of a Tribunal-Appointed Expert to request such information or access shall be the same as the authority of the Arbitral tribunal. The Parties and their representatives shall have the right to receive any such information and to attend any such inspection. Any disagreement between a Tribunal-Appointed and a party with an appropriate request or decision by the Arbitral Tribunal and shall describe its effects on the determination of the specific issue.

---

[71] See *Starrett Housing* case, para.6, pp.117–118, para.6–91.

4. The Tribunal-Appointed Expert shall report in writing to the Arbitral Tribunal. The Tribunal-Appointed Expert shall describe in the report the method, evidence and information used in arriving at the conclusions.

5. The Arbitral Tribunal shall send a copy of such Expert report to the Parties. The Parties may examine any document that the Tribunal-Appointed Expert has examined and any correspondence between the Arbitral Tribunal and the Tribunal-Appointed Expert. Within the time ordered by the Arbitral Tribunal, any Party shall have the opportunity to respond to the report in a submission by the Party or through an Expert Report by a Party-Appointed Expert. The Arbitral Tribunal shall send the submission or Expert Report to the Tribunal-Appointed Expert and to the other Parties.

6. At the request of a Party or of the Arbitral Tribunal, the Tribunal-Appointed Expert shall be present at an Evidentiary Hearing. The Arbitral Tribunal may question the Tribunal-Appointed Expert, and he or she may be questioned by the Parties or by any Party-Appointed Expert on issues raised in the Parties' submissions or in the Expert Reports made by the Party-Appointed Experts pursuant to Art.6.5.

Similar procedures are reflected in Art.26(2) of the UNCITRAL Model Law, as well as in Art.27 of the UNCITRAL Arbitration Rules and Art.12(2) of the LCIA Rules. All of these provisions emphasise the philosophy that, if a technical issue is important enough that the arbitral tribunal decides to appoint an expert, it is important enough that the parties should have full opportunity to challenge the expert's opinion by reasonable methods.

In summary, these include the opportunity to:

- participate in the establishment of terms of reference for any such expert;

- object to the proposed expert if they have reasonable concerns as to the expert's independence or competence in the relevant field of expertise;

- review all the material upon which the expert's report was based; and

- require the expert to attend at a hearing for oral examination.

Presentation of expert evidence

One of the most unsatisfactory features of procedure in international commer-   **6–94**
cial arbitrations is the prevailing practice whereby the parties present conflicting expert evidence on matters of complex technical opinion. However well the advocates for the parties are able to test evidence of expert opinion presented by the other side by means of cross-examination, such a procedure is highly suspect:

" . . . how can the jury judge between two statements each founded upon an experience confessedly foreign in kind to their own? The truth of either combating proposition lies just in its validity as an inference from a vast mass of experience, not usually in any great degree that of the witness, certainly in no part that of the jury, as to the truth of which trained powers of observation are quite essential, the result themselves of a life of technical training."[72]

It is rare for members of an arbitral tribunal to have the ability to make a reasoned evaluation between two wholly opposed professional opinions on technical matters. Nevertheless, this is by far the most common method employed by agreement between the parties, or on the directions of the arbitral tribunal, in the conduct of arbitral proceedings, regardless of where the arbitration takes place.

Expert evidence is normally furnished in the form of written reports in the first instance, usually at the same time as any written statements of witnesses of fact, but in any event well in advance of the hearing. If each party presents conflicting evidence of technical opinion, the expert witnesses must be prepared to appear in person before the arbitral tribunal for examination. Otherwise, the arbitral tribunal will have no means of evaluating the weight that should be given to the opinions presented by one side or the other.[73] The IBA Rules on the Taking of Evidence provide that party-appointed experts shall appear for testimony at an evidentiary hearing unless the parties agree otherwise and the tribunal accepts this agreement.[74] Article 5 of the Rules also provides a useful summary of the contents of a party-appointed expert report.

6–95   "The Expert Report shall contain:

(a) the full name and address of the Party-Appointed Expert, his or her present and past relationship (if any) with any of the Parties, and a description of his or her background, qualifications, training and experience;

(b) a statement of the facts on which he or she is basing his or her expert opinions and conclusions;

(c) his or her expert opinions and conclusions, including a description of the method, evidence and information used in arriving at the conclusions;

(d) an affirmation of the truth of the Expert Report; and

(e) the signature of the Party-Appointed Expert and its date and place."

---

[72] Judge Learned Hand, "Historical and Practical Considerations Regarding Expert Testimony" (1901) 15 *Harv. L. Rev.*, 40 at 54.

[73] The best material for the cross-examination of experts is usually to be found in their previous published materials. It is worthwhile to allocate a member of a party's team to read everything the other side's expert witness has published, in order to identify inconsistencies with that expert in the current arbitration.

[74] IBA Rules on the Taking of Evidence in International Commercial Arbitration, (2nd ed., 1999), Art.5.10.

Alternative methods of presenting expert evidence

Arbitration offers the possibility of the presentation of expert evidence in **6–96** various different ways. One method, which has become accepted in the English commercial court in appropriate cases, is to hear the experts for each party after all the factual evidence has been submitted by each party. Another, more innovative, concept is for the experts for each party to be heard simultaneously. The experts are seated opposite or alongside each other in front of the arbitral tribunal at the same time and each is asked to comment and respond to the opinions of the others on an agenda basis. This enables individual members of the arbitral tribunal to obtain the opinions of the experts on specific issues with a degree of immediacy that is not possible where there may be an interval of several days between the particular topics being dealt with by the opposing experts.

In 1998 one of the authors participated in an arbitration under the AAA's International Arbitration Rules in which a variation of this method was adopted. The expert witnesses submitted written reports as part of the Tribunal's pre-hearing briefing; they were then cross-examined and re-examined by the parties' counsel at the hearing; at the end of all the oral testimony and before the closing arguments, the Tribunal drew up an agenda of disputed "expert" matters and sat across the table from the two experts discussing the agenda items one by one in a quite informal manner; and, finally, the parties' counsel were offered an opportunity to ask further questions for clarification purposes.[75] This technique is sometimes described as expert witnesses "conferencing".

There are many different ways in which an arbitral tribunal may seek to educate itself on "expert" issues, and it should not shrink from pursuing innovative solutions. One common, and useful, mechanism is to direct the parties' experts to meet in advance of the hearing and draw up two lists—one comprising the matters on which they agree, the other identifying the matters on which they disagree (and summarising why).

It would be unusual (if only because it would be very expensive) for the parties **6–97** to produce evidence from independent experts, and then for the arbitral tribunal to appoint one or more experts of its own, in order to assess this evidence. However, where the technical issues involved are sufficiently complex, or where the amounts at stake are sufficiently large, this possibility cannot be ruled out. Indeed, it is a possibility expressly contemplated by the UNCITRAL Rules. After providing that the arbitral tribunal may appoint one or more experts to report to it, in writing, on specific issues to be determined by the arbitral tribunal,[76] the Rules go on to provide that, at the request of either party and after delivery of the expert's report, the expert may be heard at a hearing at which the parties must be given the opportunity to be present and to interrogate the expert; and that, at this hearing, either party may present expert witnesses to testify on the points at

---

[75] AAA Case No.13T1810031097.
[76] UNCITRAL Arbitration Rules, Art.27.1.

issue.[77] The Iran–US Claims Tribunal has adopted this approach in at least one of its cases.[78]

Admissibility of expert evidence

6–98   Where expert evidence is introduced by the parties, the rules regarding the admissibility of expert evidence applied by arbitral tribunals are in general the same as those applied to other forms of evidence in the same arbitration. Additionally, an arbitral tribunal usually makes a direction which has the effect of ensuring that each party will know the substance of the evidence of expert opinion to be presented at the hearing with sufficient advance notice, so that neither party will be taken by surprise.

It follows that if, at the hearing, an expert witness gives oral evidence of matters of opinion beyond that contained in the written report submitted to the arbitral tribunal and to the other party, this additional evidence should strictly speaking be ruled inadmissible. However, in practice, arbitral tribunals tend to allow such additional evidence to be given, on terms that the other party will be allowed adequate time to prepare and present its own further expert evidence in reply.

Categories of expert evidence

6–99   The evidence of experts is presented in relation to all kinds of matters of opinion. Engineers and scientists are frequently called upon to present reports, and give evidence, in relation to disputes where the quality of building work or the performance of plant and equipment is in issue. Accountants are called upon to give evidence as to the *quantum* of claims; and lawyers may sometimes be required to give evidence where provisions of a "foreign" system of law have to be explained to the arbitral tribunal.

In addition, it is not unknown for handwriting experts, or other persons expert in the forensic examination of documents, to be called upon where the authenticity of a document is in question.

(e) Inspection of the subject-matter of the dispute

6–100   The fourth method of presenting evidence to an arbitral tribunal is for the arbitral tribunal itself to inspect the subject-matter of the case. This is usually a site inspection and mainly arises in connection with construction contracts and disputes arising out of the performance of process plant and so forth. However, it may also apply in other types of case. For example, it is common in commodity arbitrations for the arbitrator to inspect the cargo or consignment, if the dispute concerns the quality of the goods supplied.

Site visits in civil law procedure were:

---

[77] *ibid.*, Art.27.4.
[78] See *Starrett Housing* case, para.11, p.120, above, para.6–91.

" ... designed ... mainly for use in actions involving land, but it is now used in many other situations in which judicial inspection of an object may be of value. Thus, courts frequently view the site, and may even proceed to a fairly elaborate reconstruction of an accident ... in passing upon a request for a *descente sur les lieux,* the court is guided by the usual principles determining the admissibility of evidence."[79]

Nonetheless, arbitral tribunals do not often use this opportunity to supplement the information and evidence available to them, probably because the additional expense involved is likely to be substantial in relation to the benefit gained. It is more common, in modern practice, for models, photographs, drawings or even videotape films to be used to fulfil the purpose that would have been served by a site inspection. For example, in an ICC arbitration, it was proposed to charter a helicopter to make a video showing the terrain in which a road was constructed over a length of some 60km.[80] And in a public international law case between two states, involving a boundary dispute, videos were made to be shown at the hearings.

Power of the arbitral tribunal to inspect the subject-matter

Although there is little direct authority on the question, an arbitral tribunal may **6–101** generally assume that it has power to make a site inspection, or require the parties to produce the subject-matter of the dispute for examination, unless the parties have agreed to the contrary. Such an agreement, which would be rare, might be contained expressly in a detailed submission agreement. If it were so included, no doubt the motivation of the parties would be to prevent the arbitral tribunal from incurring the expense of an exercise that they themselves regard as being of little value.

Procedure for inspection

An arbitral tribunal has broad discretion as to the manner in which it proceeds **6–102** with an inspection of the subject-matter of the dispute. Unless the parties specifically agree otherwise, the arbitral tribunal will normally be careful to ensure that the principle of equality of treatment is strictly observed. In particular, the arbitral tribunal will not normally make a site inspection except in the presence of representatives of both parties; and the arbitrators will not normally put questions directly concerning the case to persons working on the site, unless the advocates for the parties also have the right to ask additional questions of those persons.

Occasionally, the parties may agree that the arbitral tribunal should inspect a site, or the subject-matter of the dispute, without being accompanied at all. However, it would be inappropriate, and potentially dangerous when the award

---

[79] Herzog, *Civil Procedure in France* (1967), pp.355–356.
[80] In fact, the dispute was settled before this was done.

comes to be enforced, if the arbitral tribunal were to make an inspection in the presence of one party alone. If a site inspection is to be made, it is good practice for the arbitral tribunal to issue a note or even a procedural direction.

Who is to be present? Who will make what arrangements? Will questions and answers or any discussion be transcribed and form part of the record? In general it is suggested that the best practice is to direct that there will be no transcript, and that what is said should not form part of the record. Otherwise much of the usefulness of the inspection may be lost as a result of the inevitable formality that accompanies the presence of a reporter to make a transcript.

Inspection under institutional rules of arbitration

6–103   The UNCITRAL Rules and the ICC Rules are silent on the question of inspection of the subject-matter of the dispute, although the UNCITRAL Rules refer to the obligation of the parties to make available to any experts appointed by the arbitral tribunal any relevant information for inspection.[81] The LCIA Rules,[82] the AAA Rules[83] and the WIPO Rules[84] make specific provision for any inspection or investigation that the arbitral tribunal may require.

Each of these sets of rules provides that the parties may be present at such inspection if they wish. The ICSID Rules contemplate that a site inspection may be necessary. They contain power for the arbitral tribunal to "visit any place connected with the dispute or conduct inquiries there" if the arbitral tribunal deems it necessary; and they call upon the parties to co-operate in this, with the expenses forming part of the expenses of the parties.[85] The WIPO Rules also provide for experiments to be conducted and for the provision by the parties of "primers" and "models".

6. HEARINGS

(a) Generally

6–104   It has been said many times that the only thing wrong with "documents only" arbitrations is that there are not enough of them. Such arbitrations are commonplace in certain categories of domestic arbitrations, notably in relation to small claims cases involving, for example, complaints by holidaymakers against tour operators and claims under insurance policies. In the international context, the main examples of "documents only" arbitrations are those conducted under the rules of the London Maritime Arbitrators Association in connection with disputes arising out of charterparties and related documents.

---

[81] UNCITRAL Arbitration Rules, Art.27.2.
[82] LCIA Arbitration Rules, Art.21.
[83] AAA Commercial Arbitration Rules, Art.33.
[84] WIPO Arbitration Rules, Art.50.
[85] ICSID Arbitration Rules, r.34(2)(3) and (4).

However, in the mainstream of international commercial arbitration, it is unusual for the arbitral proceedings to be concluded without at least a brief hearing at which the representatives of the parties have an opportunity to make oral submissions to the arbitral tribunal, and the arbitral tribunal itself is able to ask for clarification of matters contained in the written submissions.

All the rules of the major international arbitration institutions provide for a hearing or hearings to take place at the request of either party, or at the instigation of the arbitral tribunal itself. Whilst an arbitral tribunal must proceed to make its award without a hearing if the parties have expressly so agreed, such an agreement would be unlikely to be contained in a simple arbitration clause in a contract involving international trade; and it would be most unusual in a detailed submission agreement prepared after a dispute has arisen.

(b) Organisation of the hearings

Hearings are normally held on a date fixed by the arbitral tribunal, either at the request of one or both of the parties, or on its own initiative. The administrative arrangements may be made by one of the parties, normally the claimant, with the agreement of the other. Alternatively, they may be made by the sole or presiding arbitrator or, if there is one, by the administrative secretary or registrar appointed by the arbitral tribunal.   **6–105**

In fully administered arbitrations, in some cases the institution itself makes the arrangements, for example, the AAA and the LCIA, but in others (sometimes referred to as semi-administered arbitrations) these matters are left to the arbitral tribunal and the parties. The ICC Secretariat will usually be willing to make the necessary arrangements if requested to do so by the arbitral tribunal.

The task of organising hearings in a major international commercial arbitration should not be underestimated. Nor should the cost. A suitable hearing room must be provided, with ancillary rooms and facilities for the parties and the tribunal. Access to a photocopying machine, and to telephones and fax lines, is invariably essential and facilities are required for each party to have documents typed, checked and copied. A verbatim record of the proceedings may be required; but it is an expensive item, particularly if the transcript is to be provided on a day-to-day basis. Accommodation is also required for witnesses, experts and all the members of the parties' teams.[86]

The UNCITRAL Notes on Organizing Arbitral Proceedings contain useful advice, as follows: **6–106**

"Whether one period of hearings should be held or separate periods of hearings

76. Attitudes vary as to whether hearings should be held in a single period of hearings or in separate periods, especially when more than a few days are

---

[86] For further discussion of administrative arrangements of an arbitral tribunal see Ch.4, paras 4–94 *et seq.*

needed to complete the hearings. According to some arbitrators, the entire hearings should normally be held in a single period, even if the hearings are to last for more than a week. Other arbitrators in such cases tend to schedule separate periods of hearings. Advantages of one period of hearings are that it involves less travel costs, memory will not fade, and it is unlikely that people representing a party will change. On the other hand, the longer the hearings, the more difficult it may be to find early dates acceptable to all participants. Separate periods of hearings are easier to schedule and they leave time for analysing the records and for negotiations between the parties aimed at narrowing the points at issue by agreement."

and:

"Whether there should be a limit on the aggregate amount of time each party will have for oral arguments and questioning witnesses

78. Some arbitrators consider it useful to limit the aggregate amount of time each party has for any of the following: (a) making oral statements, (b) questioning its witnesses, and (c) questioning the witnesses of the other party. In general, the same aggregate amount of time is considered appropriate for each party, unless the arbitral tribunal considers that a different allocation is justified. Before deciding, the arbitral tribunal may wish to consult the parties as to how much time they think they will need.

79. Such planning of time, provided it is realistic, fair and subject to judiciously firm control by the arbitral tribunal, will make it easier for the parties to plan the presentation of the various items of evidence and arguments, reduce the likelihood of running out of time towards the end of the hearings, and avoid that one party would unfairly use up a disproportionate amount of time."

Representation

6–107   Arbitration is a private process between the parties and the members of the arbitral tribunal. Accordingly, hearings are held *in camera*, and outsiders may only be present if the parties agree.[87] In general, the arbitral tribunal has wide discretionary powers with regard to permitting representation of the parties. Unless the parties have expressly agreed that they will *not* be represented by lawyers, an arbitral tribunal always permits a party to be represented by a lawyer, or a team of lawyers. Indeed, it would be risky for an arbitral tribunal to proceed otherwise since, on an application for enforcement, such a course might lead to

---

[87] The Model Law as adopted in the Province of British Columbia was amended to provide that: "Unless otherwise agreed by the parties, all oral hearings and meetings in arbitral proceedings are to be held *in camera*", International Commercial Arbitration Act of British Columbia, s.24(5). The UNCITRAL Rules also provide that "Hearings shall be held *in camera* unless the parties agree otherwise . . . " UNCITRAL Arbitration Rules, Art.25.4

an argument that the losing party had not had a proper opportunity to present its case, even if the parties were treated with equality in this respect.

In general, the parties may also be represented by engineers, or commercial men, for the purpose of putting forward the oral submissions, and even for the examination of witnesses.

It is not uncommon, where a case involves technical issues, for an engineer or other professional man to be part of the team of advocates representing a party at a hearing, although it is more usual for such technical experts to be called as witnesses in order that their opinions and submissions may be tested by cross-examination. However, it may sometimes be convenient and save time if technical experts address the arbitral tribunal directly as party representatives.[88]

The Supreme Court of California held in 1998 that representing a party in an arbitration held in California was "engaging in the practice of law" in that state. It followed that a New York lawyer, not a member of the Californian Bar, was not qualified to represent his client in a Californian arbitration; and was thus unable to recover his fee when he sued for it.[89] Fortunately the court stated that their rule did not apply in international arbitration. In England there is not, and never has been, any danger of a similar situation arising.[90] A party to an arbitration may, in theory, be represented by his plumber, his dentist or anyone else of his choosing, although the choice usually falls on a lawyer or specialist claims consultant in the relevant industry.[91]   **6–108**

An arbitral tribunal may not exclude a party who wishes to be present from any session of the hearing. However, an exception to this general principle probably exists where a party so disrupts the course of the hearing as to make it impossible for the arbitral tribunal to conduct the proceedings in an orderly manner. In such a case, the proper course seems to be for the arbitral tribunal to treat that party as being unwilling to participate in the hearing, thus enabling the arbitration to proceed *ex parte*. In principle, however, a party may rely on the right to be present, and the right to be accompanied by a representative of his choice, throughout all hearings.

Pre-hearing conferences

In large and complex cases, a properly planned pre-hearing meeting or conference can pay substantial dividends in terms of saving time and money at the hearing itself. Such conferences should be organised efficiently, both as to timing and content. They are the responsibility of the sole or presiding arbitrator. The timing is extremely important. If a pre-hearing conference takes place too near to the hearing itself, it will be too late for the "shape" of the hearing to be   **6–109**

---

[88] Both the UNCITRAL Arbitration Rules (Art.4) and the LCIA Arbitration Rules (Art.18) make it clear that parties are entitled to be represented by non-lawyers.

[89] *Birbrower, Montabano, Condon & Frank v The Superior Court of Santa Clara County*, 1998 Cal. Lexis 2; 1998 W.L. 1346 (Cal. 1/5/98).

[90] *i.e.* that only a member of the local bar should be entitled to represent a party in a judicial or quasi-judicial proceeding.

[91] English Arbitration Act 1996, s.36. This reaffirms the previous common law position.

influenced. However, if it takes place too early, the arbitral tribunal is not sufficiently well informed about the issues, and the evidence needed to supplement the material submitted in writing, to enable useful decisions to be taken with regard to the structure of the hearing.

It is also essential that the parties should have comprehensive advance knowledge of the matters to be discussed at a pre-hearing conference; they need to consider the questions to be discussed, and possibly to discuss them with each other before meeting the arbitral tribunal.

Pre-hearing conferences have been used to considerable effect by the Iran–US Claims Tribunal. The relevant provision appears as part of the Tribunal Rules which state:

> "The arbitral tribunal may make an order directing the arbitrating parties to appear for a pre-hearing conference. The pre-hearing conference will normally be held only after the Statement of Defense in the case has been received. The order will state the matters to be considered at the pre-hearing conference."[92]

6–110   It may be noted that this provision deals expressly with the two important points mentioned above; namely, the timing of the pre-hearing conference and the "matters to be considered". The Internal Guidelines of the Tribunal set out what is described as an "illustrative" list of topics for pre-hearing conferences:

> "(a) clarification of the issues presented and the relief sought;
> (b) identification of any issues to be considered as preliminary questions;
> (c) status of any settlement discussions;
> (d) whether any further written statements, including any reply or rejoinder, is requested by the arbitrating parties or required by the arbitral tribunal (see Tribunal Rules, Art.22);
> (e) fixing a schedule for submission by each arbitrating party of a summary of the documents or lists of witnesses or other evidence it intends to present (see Tribunal Rules, Art.24, para.2);
> (f) fixing a schedule for submission of any documents, exhibits or other evidence which the arbitral tribunal may then require (see Tribunal Rules, Art.24, para.3);
> (g) whether voluminous and complicated data should be presented through summaries, tabulations, charts, graphs or extracts in order to save time and costs;
> (h) desirability of appointing an expert by the arbitral tribunal, and if so the expert's qualifications and term of reference; whether the arbitrating parties intend to present experts, and, if so, the qualification of and the areas of expertise to be covered by any such expert;
> (i) determining what documentary evidence will require translation;

---

[92] Final Tribunal Rules of Procedure, May 3, 1983, n.4 to Art.15.

(j) fixing a schedule of hearings;

(k) other appropriate matters."[93]

Revised ICSID Rules

The potential value of pre-hearing conferences has been accepted by ICSID, **6–111** which formulated a rule to provide for them:

> "(1) At the request of the Secretary-General or at the discretion of the President of the Tribunal, a pre-hearing conference between the Tribunal and the parties may be held to arrange for an exchange of information and the stipulation of uncontested facts in order to expedite the proceeding.
>
> (2) At the request of the parties, a pre-hearing conference between the Tribunal and the parties, duly represented by their authorised representatives, may be held to consider the issues in dispute with a view to reaching an amicable settlement."[94]

The first part of this rule envisages a conventional role for the pre-hearing conference, namely that of helping to ensure that time is saved at the hearing itself. The second part of the rule is less conventional. It seeks to take advantage of the fact that the claims and counterclaims of the opposing parties tend to change shape under the hammer of contested proceedings, as each side begins to understand its opponent's case better; and it envisages that, at the request of the parties, a pre-hearing conference may be held with a view to arriving at an amicable settlement of the dispute.

The practice of holding pre-hearing conferences was discussed at the groundbreaking ICCA Congress in New York in 1986. Interestingly, in a number of countries—notably the Soviet Union, Japan and in general the Arab countries—the practice was at that time virtually unknown.[95] The rules of the major international arbitral institutions are generally silent on the question of pre-hearing conferences—although it is clear that an arbitral tribunal has power to convene one (or more) such events, in the exercise of its discretion. One arbitral institution that does provide for such conferences is WIPO, whose rules provide:

> "The Tribunal may, in general following the submission of the Statement of Defense, conduct a preparatory conference with the parties for the purpose of organizing and scheduling the subsequent proceedings."[96]

---

[93] Iran–US Claims Tribunal Reports 18 at p.98; set out in (1983) VII Yearbook Commercial Arbitration 255. For further discussion of pre-hearing conferences, see Holtzmann, "What an Arbitrator can do to Overcome Delays in International Arbitration" in *Justice for a Generation* (ABA, 1985), p.335 at p.340.

[94] This Rule was added as r.21, displacing the former r.21 (Procedural Languages), which became r.22. This renumbering continues until former r.37 (Minutes) is reached. This Rule was dropped; thus, from r.38 onwards the Rules bear the same numbers as before.

[95] "Comparative Arbitration Practice", ICCA Congress Series No.3 (Kluwer, 1987), pp.64–67; the rapporteurs appear to confuse preliminary meetings with pre-hearing conferences.

[96] WIPO Arbitration Rules, Art.47.

(c) Procedure at hearings

6–112   Individual arbitral tribunals approach the determination of the procedure to be followed at the hearing in different ways. Most have the common aim of keeping the duration of the hearing to a minimum so far as practicable, in order to assist the busy schedules of the arbitrators and parties, and in order to reduce expense.

However, ideas as to what is a reasonable length of time for a hearing differ widely. Formerly,[97] in English court practice, hearings could last for many weeks, causing great inconvenience and expense (not to say annoyance) to all concerned.[98] By contrast, arbitrators from the civil law countries tend to regard any hearing that takes more than three days as a long one. Indeed, many arbitrators from civil law jurisdictions would be unwilling to allocate more than three (or at the most five) days consecutively to the hearing of any particular case. This means that the hearing will have to be adjourned if it cannot be completed during the time allocated. The Iran–US Claims Tribunal held hearings exceeding two days in only the most complex cases. The trend in international arbitration is toward shorter hearings with greater reliance upon documentary evidence. This is a necessary step in the interests of economy of time and costs in cases that often involve arbitrators, lawyers, experts, company executives and other arbitrators, operating away from their home base.

International practice

6–113   There is also a trend in international arbitrations for the tribunal to take a role that is more typical of proceedings in the civil law inquisitorial tradition than the common law adversarial approach. In the view of an experienced arbitrator:

" . . . in most cases it is wise for an arbitral tribunal to take an active role in augmenting the parties' presentation of the facts. This can be done by conducting pre-hearing conferences with the parties and, in appropriate cases, by issuing orders requiring parties to submit specifically described evidence. Arbitration is more effective and efficient when the arbitrators actively seek to elucidate the facts, rather than merely evaluating what the parties choose to present. This active approach is particularly useful in international cases, which typically bring together parties and arbitrators who have different legal backgrounds and approaches to presenting evidence. In such circumstances

---

[97] Under the English Civil Procedure Rules 1998, however, the length of the hearing is restricted according to the value or complexity of the case.

[98] The oral tradition in England owes its origin to the "man who is no longer there"; that is to say, the juror. Jury trials lead to two inescapable procedural features. First, once started, the oral proceedings had to be completed because, once assembled, there was no real practical possibility of reconvening the same jury many weeks, or even months, later. Secondly, although jurors had to be property owners, there was no guarantee that they were literate; hence the need for all the documents to be read aloud at the hearing.

parties can greatly benefit from the arbitral tribunal's guidance concerning what it expects."[99]

This trend is confirmed by the UNCITRAL Notes on Organizing Arbitral Proceedings, which state as follows:

"81. Arbitration rules and national laws on arbitral procedure typically give broad latitude to the arbitral tribunal to determine the order of presentations at the hearings. Procedural patterns differ, for example, as to whether opening or closing statements are heard and their level of detail; the sequence in which the claimant and the defendant are to present their opening statements, arguments, witnesses and other evidence; and whether the defendant or the claimant should have the last word. In view of such differences, it may foster efficiency of the proceedings if the arbitral tribunal clarifies to the parties, in advance of the hearings, the manner of conducting oral hearings, at least in broad lines."

The general practice in international commercial arbitration, given the strict time-limits allocated, is to permit each side only a brief opening statement, in which the advocates assume that the arbitrators have a full knowledge of the documents that have been submitted. This is followed by the oral testimony of the witnesses for each party, the claimant's witnesses being heard first. There is usually no examination-in-chief ("direct" examination) as the witness testimony will have been submitted in writing. However, it is usual for a witness to be given the opportunity to elaborate on the witness statement, or add any new points, so long as this is done briefly.

A leading English international arbitrator put it thus: **6–114**

"Finally, since the arbitrators are likely to be busy professional people and often from different countries, oral hearings will usually be remarkably short by English standards. Their main purpose is to hear the cross-examination of the witnesses, bracketed by short opening and closing remarks from both sides, which are often supplemented by written post-hearing submissions . . . "[1]

Examination of witnesses

The examination of witnesses is dictated mainly by the arbitral tribunal itself. **6–115** Individual arbitrators usually restrict their questions to those that they regard as essential to clarify or expand the information they need to reach their determination. It would be most unusual for arbitrators to adopt a long line of questioning with the objective of attacking the credibility of a witness. However, there may be cases where specific questions are designed to test credibility when a case

---

[99] Holtzmann, *Fact-finding*, *loc. cit.*, Sec.IV, para.6–10.
[1] Sir Michael Kerr, "Concord and Conflict in International Arbitration" (1997) 13 Arbitration International 121 at 126–127; see also para.1–157.

turns on whether or not the testimony of a witness is reliable. In many civil law jurisdictions, cross-examination of witnesses by the parties is not permitted. However, in proceedings before international arbitral tribunals, an opportunity for cross-examination is almost always given if a party requests it.

US and English advocates nearly always want to cross-examine witnesses who attend the oral hearing, and in many instances wish to attack their credibility or the quality of their recollections. However, arbitrators from civil law countries are not accustomed to this procedure. They regard it as embarrassing (if not barbaric) for a witness to be subjected to attack at an arbitration hearing. Advocates brought up in the common law tradition do well to bear this in mind, in deciding whether to cross-examine any particular witness and, if so, how this examination should be conducted. To cross-examine witnesses at great length before arbitral tribunals composed primarily of arbitrators from civil law jurisdictions is often counterproductive.

Witnesses are sometimes excluded until they have given their testimony, although this practice is often dispensed with by agreement of the parties, out of deference to witnesses who may have to wait in hotel rooms until their turn comes. Much depends on whether or not a party is likely to gain an unfair advantage by having a particular witness present while the corresponding witness presented by the opposing party gives evidence.

6–116 If a transcript is taken, the parties may often agree that the witness should be given an opportunity to correct the record, either in consultation with representatives from each party or in discussion with the administrative secretary of the arbitral tribunal. However, the transcript should only be corrected to reflect what the witness actually said—not what the witness intended to say.

Once again, the IBA Rules on the Taking of Evidence confirm the international standards adopted by many international arbitral tribunals. Article 8 of those Rules provides as follows:

"1. The Arbitral Tribunal shall at all times have complete control over the Evidentiary Hearing. The Arbitral Tribunal may limit or exclude any question to, answer by or appearance of a witness (which term includes, for the purposes of this Article, witnesses of fact and any Experts), if it considers such question, answer or appearance to be irrelevant, immaterial, burdensome, duplicative or covered by a reason for objection set forth in Article 9.2. Questions to a witness during direct and redirect testimony may not be unreasonably leading.

2. The Claimant shall ordinarily first present the testimony of its witnesses, followed by the Respondent presenting testimony of its witnesses, and then by the presentation by Claimant of rebuttal witnesses, if any. Following direct testimony, any other Party may question such witness, in an order to be determined by the Arbitral Tribunal. The Party who initially presented the witness shall subsequently have the opportunity to ask additional questions on the matters raised in the other Parties' questioning. The Arbitral Tribunal, upon request of a Party or on its own

motion, may vary this order of proceeding, including the arrangement of testimony by particular issues or in such a manner that witnesses presented by different Parties be questioned at the same time and in confrontation with each other. The Arbitral Tribunal may ask questions to a witness at any time.

3. Any witness providing testimony shall first affirm, in a manner determined appropriate by the Arbitral Tribunal, that he or she is telling the truth. If the witness has submitted a Witness Statement or an Expert Report, the witness shall confirm it. The Parties may agree or the Arbitral Tribunal may order that the Witness Statement or Expert Report shall serve as that witness's direct testimony.

4. Subject to the provisions of Article 9.2, the Arbitral Tribunal may request any person to give oral or written evidence on any issue that the Arbitral Tribunal considers to be relevant and material. Any witness called and questioned by the Arbitral Tribunal may also be questioned by the Parties."

Unlike the position in relation to expert witnesses,[2] the "conferencing" (or, in an unfortunate description, "confrontation") technique had not gained the status of a common practice, or even a trend, by the early years of the twenty-first century. It is a somewhat adventurous path for an arbitral tribunal to take, and should not, in general, be used as an *alternative* to cross-examination of individual witnesses by the parties' counsel. However, it sometimes provides an effective way of identifying areas of dispute between witnesses, and areas of agreement. It also offers the opportunity to make an immediate and direct comparison between the testimony they have given earlier, both in writing and orally at the hearing.[3]

Some trial lawyers do not like to lose control over the way in which their **6–117** client's case is presented. They say that deprivation of the supposed right to present their case as they see fit could amount to lack of due process. Nevertheless, used with caution in relation to specified areas of disputed fact, witness conferencing may be regarded as a potentially useful way for an arbitral tribunal to assess the truth as between two conflicting versions of factual events.

In the conduct of the hearings generally, it is important for the arbitral tribunal to bear in mind the two principles that are likely to give rise to problems when enforcement of the award is sought. These are, first, that each party should have a fair opportunity to present its case and, secondly, that the parties must be treated equally. It is sometimes difficult to operate these principles in a manner consistent with minimising the duration of the hearing. However, an experienced presiding arbitrator can normally find a way of combining firmness with fairness.

---

[2] See para.6–90.
[3] See, *e.g.*, Wolfgang Peter, "Witness Conferencing" (2002) 18 Arbitration International 47.

Who has the last word?

6–118   In common law practice, the claimant (or "plaintiff" in some jurisdictions) in a court case speaks last, on the basis that the claimant carries the burden of proof. This means that the claimant has two opportunities to make oral submissions, while the defendant has only one. In arbitrations this practice is not widely followed, since arbitrators tend to feel, instinctively, that due process is generally served only if the parties are permitted an equal number of opportunities to make oral submissions. Furthermore, the "burden of proof" point is not wholly valid, because in practice the burden may fall on each party to prove the factual propositions on which it relies.

(d) *Ex parte* hearings

6–119   An arbitral tribunal may, and indeed should, proceed *ex parte* if one of the parties (almost invariably the respondent) refuses or fails to appear. In such cases, the arbitral tribunal should proceed with the hearing and issue its award, making sure that the precise circumstances in which the proceedings have taken place are specified in the award itself.[4]

This is necessary because there is a general presumption that a party who boycotts an international commercial arbitration intends to resist enforcement of any award ultimately rendered. Since it is a legitimate ground for refusal of recognition or enforcement of an award, whether under the New York Convention or otherwise, that a party has not had a full opportunity to present its case, it is desirable that the award should itself show, on its face, the circumstances in which the respondent did not participate. Two main problems commonly arise in relation to *ex parte* hearings. The first is what constitutes a "refusal" to participate; the second is how the arbitral tribunal should proceed in such circumstances.

Refusal to participate

6–120   In some circumstances the situation is clear. This was so in the three Libyan oil nationalisation cases[5] in which the Libyan Government made it clear from the beginning that it refused to take any part in the proceedings on the grounds that the arbitral tribunals, in each case, had no jurisdiction. It will also be clear if a respondent expressly refuses to reply to correspondence from the arbitral tribunal, or to comply with any procedural directions as to the submission of written pleadings and so forth.

There are two other circumstances in which an arbitral tribunal should proceed *ex parte,* but these are more difficult to identify. The first is where a party does not notify its unwillingness to participate, but creates a delay so unreasonable

---

[4] For a discussion of practice under various arbitration rules and national laws, see "Preventing Delay and Disruption of Arbitration" (Holtzmann ed.) ICCA Congress Series No.5 (Stockholm, 1990).

[5] The *Texaco, BP* and *Liamco* arbitrations; see Ch.2, paras 2–50 *et seq.*

that the arbitral tribunal (on the application of the other party) would be justified in treating the party in default as having abandoned its right to present its case. It is impossible to specify precisely when this point arises in any given proceedings, and an arbitral tribunal must use its best judgment, balancing the various factors involved. However, the arbitral tribunal should bear in mind that it may not be doing the claimant any favours if it accedes too early to an application to proceed *ex parte,* because the award may become the subject of a successful challenge when the claimant seeks to enforce it.[6]

The second situation, which has been referred to above,[7] is where a party so disrupts the hearing that it becomes impossible to conduct it in an orderly manner. Experience of such a situation is hard to find, but theoretically it could happen; the arbitral tribunal would then need to treat the defaulting party's conduct as being equivalent to a refusal to participate.

Procedure in ex parte *hearings*

Unlike a court, an arbitral tribunal has no authority to issue an award akin to **6–121** a default judgment. Its task is to make a determination of the disputes submitted to it. Accordingly, even if a party fails to present its case, the arbitral tribunal must consider the merits and make a determination of the substance of the dispute. Where it is clear from the beginning that a party (usually the respondent) does not propose to take part, the arbitral tribunal usually ensures that all the participating party's submissions and evidence are placed before it in written form. Then it will be justified in holding only a brief hearing, on an *ex parte* basis, to review the claims and raise any questions.

The best guideline as to how such a proceeding should take place is that the party who is taking part must prove its case to the satisfaction of the arbitral tribunal. The arbitral tribunal has no duty to act as advocate for a party who has elected not to appear, but it must examine the merits of the arguments of law and fact put to it by the participating party, so as to satisfy itself that these are well founded. It must then make a reasoned determination of the issues.

The practice of arbitral tribunals varies as regards hearings in such situations. Much will depend on the form in which the written stages of the arbitration have taken place. If the written stages have been very comprehensive, the arbitral tribunal may feel justified in holding a brief and purely formal hearing prior to issuing its award. If, on the other hand, the written pleadings have been simple, formal, documents in which only the issues have been defined, and no documentary or witness evidence has been submitted in writing, the arbitral tribunal would probably consider it necessary to hear oral evidence before being satisfied that the participating party has discharged the burden of proof in relation to his claims (or defences).

---

[6] It is rare, but not unknown, for the respondent to want the proceedings to go ahead, when the claimant has failed to take them forward, in order to obtain an award that will put an end to the claim. In such a case, similar considerations will apply: the respondent will require a solid award, capable of being *recognised* by the courts, if this becomes necessary.

[7] See above, para.6–119.

6–122   The Model Law contains a provision empowering the arbitral tribunal to continue the proceedings and to make an award where a party fails to comply with the requirements of the procedure agreed by the parties or established by the arbitral tribunal[8]; and similar provisions are to be found in modern laws of arbitration, even if they are not directly based on the Model Law.

Where a respondent fails to defend the case, and in particular where it fails to communicate a statement of defence in accordance with Art.23 of the Model Law, the arbitral tribunal may continue the proceedings, but without treating any such failure as an admission of the claimant's allegations. Accordingly, the arbitral tribunal is not given equivalent powers to that of the court to issue a "default" judgment in favour of a claimant. It must make determinations on the claims presented in the arbitration, and incorporate those determinations into the award. The ICSID Rules, which set out default procedures in useful detail, are to a similar effect.

7. Proceedings after the Hearing

(a) Generally

6–123   In theory, the hearing should conclude the participation of the parties in the arbitration. Indeed, it is good practice for the arbitral tribunal to declare the evidentiary record closed. This will not prevent the parties, if so agreed by the tribunal, from submitting post-hearing briefs, but it will prevent them from submitting new unsolicited material after the hearing, which will require further procedural orders to enable the other party to reply.

(b) Post-hearing briefs

6–124   So far as post-hearing briefs are concerned, increasingly it appears to be the custom to allow the parties to submit such briefs, limited to 15 or 20 pages, summarising the main points that have emerged in evidence and argument; and the emergence of such a practice may be seen as a direct corollary of the practice of limiting the length of the hearing—and, indeed, of imposing time constraints on the parties at the hearing.

It sometimes happens that the time allocated for the hearing does not permit the parties to have the full opportunity of presenting their cases that they believe to be necessary. This may happen either where the hearing has simply taken longer than anticipated, or where new material has been produced during the course of the hearing by one party and the opposing party, justifiably, requires an opportunity to respond and cannot reasonably do so within the time frame imposed by the duration of the hearing. In these circumstances, the arbitral tribunal may either adjourn the hearing to a future date convenient to all parties,

---

[8] Model Law, Art.25.

or permit a further submission in writing by the party seeking to respond to the fresh material.

(c) New evidence

This may not always be the end of the affair. First, fresh evidence may come **6–125** to light after the hearing, but before the arbitral tribunal has issued its award. In these circumstances the arbitral tribunal has discretion to reopen the proceedings at the request of the party wishing to present the new evidence. Clearly it should refuse to do so where the fresh evidence is not needed for the deliberations, or if the new material appears to be a spurious attempt to delay the proceedings. But, in general, arbitral tribunals prefer to determine a dispute with the benefit of all the relevant evidence in their possession. If the fresh evidence turns out to be valueless, or without merit, the party producing it may be penalised by the arbitral tribunal in relation to the additional costs incurred, and by an award of interest where this is appropriate.

The course that should be adopted by the arbitral tribunal depends on the circumstances of each case and the nature of the material to which a response must be made. However, arbitral tribunals normally (and rightly) try to ensure that adjourned hearings do not take place unless they are really necessary; they generally permit one party to put in further written evidence and submissions if the other has presented fresh material at the hearing. The other party will sometimes object, but this objection is not justifiable if that party has created the situation himself by producing new materials at a late stage. Any further written submissions, or evidence, should be seen by the opposing party, as well as by the arbitral tribunal; and the arbitral tribunal must decide when to call a halt in terms of further replies, rejoinders and rebuttals.

Thus, the most frequently adopted form of proceedings after the closure of the hearings is an exchange of post-hearing briefs. These are commonplace in US litigation, and it is one of the elements of US litigation practice that European arbitrators have found useful to import from across the Atlantic. They are usually ordered when the parties' representatives have not had time to prepare or deliver oral closing statements. This happens typically where a verbatim transcript of the oral testimony is being taken, and the parties want to have time to study the record before making their final submissions.

Post-hearing briefs are also sometimes permitted where the arbitral tribunal **6–126** has raised questions during the closing arguments and the parties' counsel wish to have time to undertake research before giving their answers. One of the authors experienced such a situation at a hearing in 1998, when the question of whether or not the Vienna Sales Convention applied to the transaction in question was raised during the closing arguments. This was not a matter upon which the parties' counsel could reasonably be expected to respond "off-the-cuff"; and, accordingly, the parties were directed to submit post-hearing memoranda on the question.[9]

---

[9] AAA Case No.13T1810031097.

Chapter 7

THE ROLE OF NATIONAL COURTS DURING THE PROCEEDINGS

1. Introduction

7–01   The relationship between national courts and arbitral tribunals swings between forced cohabitation and true partnership. In spite of protestations of "party autonomy", arbitration is wholly dependent on the underlying support of the courts who alone have the power to rescue the system when one party seeks to sabotage it. As a former senior English judge has stated:

> "[T]here is plainly a tension here. On the one hand the concept of arbitration as a consensual process reinforced by the ideas of transnationalism leans against the involvement of the mechanisms of state through the medium of a municipal court. On the other side there is the plain fact, palatable or not, that it is only a Court possessing coercive powers which could rescue the arbitration if it is in danger of foundering."[1]

A party who agrees to refer disputes to arbitration chooses a private system of justice and this, in itself, raises issues of public policy. There are limits upon this freedom of choice. Some states, for example, insist that only matters that are regarded under its own law as "commercial" may be referred to arbitration.[2] Even states that do not impose such a limitation will nevertheless restrict arbitration in some way to disputes that the state itself regards as being legally capable of being settled by arbitration; that is to say, to disputes that are "arbitrable" in the sense already discussed.[3] However, as has been seen, the concept of what is and what is not "arbitrable" differs from one country to another and even from one period of time to another.[4]

The state prescribes the boundaries of arbitration and enforces these boundaries through its courts. The state also determines other limitations upon the arbitral process; whether, for instance, arbitrators have the power to compel the attendance of witnesses or the disclosure of documents and, more importantly,

---

[1] Lord Mustill in *Coppée Levalin NV v Ken-Ren Fertilisers and Chemicals* [1994] 2 Lloyd's Rep. 109 at 116 (HL).
[2] See the discussion as to the meaning of "commercial" in Ch.1, para.1–31.
[3] See Ch.2.
[4] See, *e.g.*, the changed attitude of the US courts towards the arbitration of antitrust issues.

whether or not any appeal to the national court is possible and if so, how and when and upon what terms.

Insofar as the relationship between national courts and arbitral tribunals is said to be one of "partnership",[5] it is not a partnership of equals. Arbitration may depend upon the agreement of the parties, but it is also a system built on law and which relies upon that law to make it effective both nationally and internationally. National courts could exist without arbitration, but arbitration could not exist without the courts. The real issue is to define the point where this reliance of arbitration on the national courts begins and where it ends.

7–02

(a) The increasing independence of arbitration

It can fairly be said that there is now a consensus in the international business community that arbitration is a sensible and generally effective method of resolving international commercial disputes. This consensus has led the arbitral process to distance itself where possible from the risk of domestic judicial parochialism—particularly where the interests concerned are those of international trade. Modern international commercial arbitration has consequently achieved a considerable degree of independence from national courts. For example, the arbitration clause in an international commercial contract is generally recognised as being an independent agreement, which survives any termination of the contract in which it is contained.[6] The parties themselves are generally free to determine how their disputes are to be resolved, subject only to such safeguards as may be considered necessary as a matter of public policy; and arbitrators are free to decide on their own jurisdiction, subject only to a final decision by the relevant national court. The parties are free to choose which system of law will govern the dispute between them; and indeed, may even elect general principles, such as those of equity and good conscience or the UNIDROIT Principles of International Commercial Contracts.[7] Finally, judicial control of errors of law in international commercial arbitration has been virtually abandoned, leaving courts the limited role of policing procedural due process, such as the obligation of the tribunal to give each party a fair hearing.

7–03

Nonetheless the process remains subject to the laws of the many different countries in which arbitrations take place and in which awards fall to be enforced. This in turn means that the involvement of national courts in the international arbitration process remains essential to its effectiveness. Indeed, some commentators have spoken of a turn in the tide against unbounded "party autonomy" in favour of an increasing role for the courts and the state in general. Some states, such as Belgium, which set out to attract international arbitrations

---

[5] See, *e.g.*, Goldman, "The Complementary Role of Judges and Arbitrators", ICC Publication No.412, p.259.

[6] See the discussion of separability in Ch.3.

[7] One of the largest arbitrated disputes in history was decided under the UNIDROIT Principles of International Commercial Contracts: see Bonell: "A 'Global' Arbitration Decided on the Basis of the UNIDROIT Principles" (2001) 17 Arbitration International 249.

by denying any role at all for the local courts found that their policy had the opposite effect.[8] They have felt compelled to reintroduce an element of judicial supervision. Equally, the ever-increasing trend to seek interim measures has placed a renewed focus on the respective roles of the arbitral tribunal and the courts in that domain.

(b) Limitations on independence

7–04   The Model Law, which has become one of the benchmarks of any modern arbitration law, seeks to exclude the involvement of the courts as far as possible. It states:

> "In matters governed by this Law, no court shall intervene except where so provided in this Law."[9]

At first sight, this is a striking declaration of independence. Yet the Model Law cannot exclude, and does not seek to exclude, the participation of what it calls the "competent court" in carrying out "certain functions of arbitration assistance and supervision".[10] On closer examination of the Model Law itself, it becomes apparent that out of the 36 articles that it contains, no less than 10 recognise a possible role for the "competent court". For example, Art.11 acknowledges that the help of the competent court may be necessary to constitute the arbitral tribunal; Art.13 acknowledges that this court may have to decide upon a challenge to an arbitrator, if there are justifiable doubts as to that arbitrator's impartiality or independence; Art.16 acknowledges that a party to an international arbitration may appeal to the competent court against the decision of the arbitral tribunal on the issue of jurisdiction—in which case it is the decision of that court (and not the decision of the arbitral tribunal) that is final and binding. The Model Law also acknowledges[11] that the assistance of the competent court may be necessary in the taking of evidence; and that in any challenge to the arbitral award, or to its recognition and enforcement, the judgment of the competent court will be decisive.[12]

---

[8] See Hanotiau & Block, "The Law of 19 May 1998 amending Belgian Arbitration Legislation" (1999) 15 Arbitration International 97. The 1985 Belgian law offered no possibilities to apply to set aside the award in Belgium unless a party had Belgian nationality or resided in Belgium (Art.1717.4 of the Belgian Judicial Code). This operated as a deterrent to selecting Belgium as a seat for arbitration. The law was subsequently changed in 1998 to permit an application for setting aside irrespective of nationality or residence, unless the parties expressly opted out.

[9] Model Law, Art.5.

[10] The competent court is defined in Art.6 of the Model Law as the court or other authority specified by each state as being competent to perform the functions entrusted to it by the Model Law.

[11] Model Law, Art.27.

[12] See Arts 34, 35 and 36 of the Model Law. For a general discussion on this topic, see Schlosser, "The Competence of Arbitrators and of Courts" (1992) 8 Arbitration International 189, and Kerr, "Arbitration and the Courts: The UNCITRAL Model Law" (1985) 34 I.C.L.Q. 1.

(c) A relay race

If there is a partnership between arbitrators and the national courts, it is one in **7–05** which each has a different role to play at different times. The relationship between courts and arbitrators has been compared to a relay race:

> "Ideally, the handling of arbitral disputes should resemble a relay race. In the initial stages, before the arbitrators are seized of the dispute, the baton is in the grasp of the court; for at that stage there is no other organisation which could take steps to prevent the arbitration agreement from being ineffectual. When the arbitrators take charge they take over the baton and retain it until they have made an award. At this point, having no longer a function to fulfil, the arbitrators hand back the baton so that the court can in case of need lend its coercive powers to the enforcement of the award".[13]

In principle, there should be no disputes as to where the frontier between the public world of the courts and the private world of arbitration lies. At the beginning of an arbitration, national courts (not the arbitrators) have the task of enforcing the agreement to arbitrate if one of the parties should seek to resile from it. At the end of the arbitral process, national courts (not the arbitrators) must also enforce the arbitral award, if the losing party is not prepared to carry it out voluntarily. During the arbitral process, the arbitrators (not the courts) must take charge of the proceedings, set time-limits, organise meetings and hearings, issue procedural directions, consider the arguments of fact and law put forward by or on behalf of the parties and make their award.

It would be simple if the respective domains of arbitral tribunals and national courts could be so clearly distinguished. However, as Lord Mustill goes on to state:

> "In real life the position is not so clear-cut. Very few commentators would now assert that the legitimate functions of the Court entirely cease when the arbitrators receive the file, and conversely very few would doubt that there is a point at which the Court takes on a purely subordinate role. But when does this happen? And what is the position at the further end of the process? Does the Court retake the baton only if and when invited to enforce the award, or does it have functions to be exercised at an earlier stage, if something has gone wrong with the arbitration, by setting aside the award or intervening in some other way?"[14]

---

[13] Lord Mustill, "Comments and Conclusions" in *Conservatory & Provisional Measures in International Arbitration*, 9th Joint Colloquium (ICC Publication, 1993) (hereinafter referred to as *Conservatory Measures*), at 118.

[14] *ibid.*

2. At the Beginning of the Arbitration

7–06   It is possible to identify at least three situations in which the intervention of the court may be necessary at the beginning of the arbitral process. These are:

- the enforcement of the arbitration agreement;
- the establishment of the tribunal; and
- challenges to jurisdiction.

(a) Enforcing the arbitration agreement

7–07   A party to an arbitration agreement might decide to issue proceedings in a court of law, rather than take the dispute to arbitration. If the respondent is content to agree to this, the court action will proceed. This is not likely to happen, however. Having entered into an arbitration agreement, the respondent usually wishes to insist on its right to have the dispute decided by arbitrators rather than by the national court. For their part, most courts are prepared to enforce the agreement to arbitrate, by refusing to accept any proceedings in court and by referring the parties instead to arbitration. Indeed this is an obligation imposed by Art.II of the New York Convention on the courts of signatory states[15] and is also reflected in the Model Law which provides, at Art.8:

> "(1) A court before which an action is brought in a matter which is the subject of an arbitration agreement shall, if a party so requests not later than when submitting his first statement on the substance of the dispute, refer the parties to arbitration unless it finds that the agreement is null and void, inoperative or incapable of being performed.
>
> (2) Where an action referred to in paragraph (1) of this article has been brought, arbitral proceedings may nevertheless be commenced or continued, and an award may be made, while the issue is pending before the court."

(b) Establishing the arbitral tribunal

7–08   If the parties have failed to make adequate provision for the constitution of an arbitral tribunal, and if there are no applicable institutional or other rules (such as the UNCITRAL Rules), the intervention of a national court is usually required. In the absence of any such rules, it is also required if there is any challenge to the independence or impartiality of an arbitrator.

(c) Challenges to jurisdiction

7–09   If any issue is raised as to the jurisdiction of the arbitral tribunal, it will generally (although not always) be made at the beginning of the arbitration. If

---

[15] The New York Convention, Art.II(3), states: "The court of a Contracting State, when seized of an action, in a matter in respect of which the parties have made an agreement within the meaning of this article shall, at the request of one of the parties refer the parties to arbitration, unless it finds that the said agreement is null and void, inoperative or incapable of being performed."

this is done successfully, the arbitration is stopped dead in its tracks. The issue of challenge to jurisdiction is one of growing importance and is dealt with in a later chapter. The only point that should be made here, in the context of the relationship between national courts and arbitral tribunals, is that it is recognised in the Model Law (and in most, if not all, national systems of law) that whilst any challenge to the jurisdiction of an arbitral tribunal may be dealt with *initially* by the tribunal itself, the final decision on jurisdiction rests with the relevant national court. This is either the court at the seat of the arbitration, or the court of the state or states in which recognition and enforcement of the arbitral award is sought.

3. During the Arbitral Proceedings

What happens in the most important phase of an arbitration, when the arbi- **7–10** trators begin their task? The baton has been passed to them. Is there any need for national courts to be involved in the arbitral process?

The answer in almost every case is "no". Once an arbitral tribunal has been constituted, most arbitrations are conducted without any need to refer to a national court, even if one of the parties fails or refuses to take part in the proceedings. There may be times, however, when the involvement of a national court is necessary in order to ensure the proper conduct of the arbitration. It may become necessary, for instance, to ask the competent court to assist in taking evidence, or to make an order for the preservation of property which is the subject of the dispute, or to take some other interim measure of protection. The question that then arises is whether a national court may (or indeed should) become involved in a dispute which is subject to arbitration, and if so how far should this involvement extend? To put it more directly, when does "involve-ment" by a court become "intervention" in the arbitral process; and when does "intervention" become "interference" with a process which is supposed to stand on its own feet? This is not simply a philosophical question. It is one with important practical consequences; and it is one to which there is no simple answer.

(a) Interim measures: powers of the arbitral tribunal

During the course of an arbitration, it may be necessary for the arbitral tribunal **7–11** or a national court to issue orders intended to preserve evidence, to protect assets, or in some other way to maintain the status quo pending the outcome of the arbitration proceedings themselves. Such orders take different forms and go under different names. In the Model Law and in the UNCITRAL Rules, they are known as "interim measures of protection". In the English version of the ICC Rules, they are known as "interim or conservatory measures"[16] in the French version, as *"mesures provisoires ou conservatoires"*, whilst in the Swiss law

---

[16] ICC Arbitration Rules, Art.23.

governing international arbitration they are referred to as "provisional or conservatory measures".[17] Whatever their designation, however, they are intended in principle to operate as holding orders, pending the outcome of the arbitral proceedings.

In many cases where interim measures of protection are required, the arbitral tribunal itself has the power to issue them. For example, there is a provision in the ICC Rules to the effect that, unless the parties have agreed otherwise, and as soon as the file has been transmitted to it:

> "the Arbitral Tribunal may, at the request of a party, order any interim or conservatory measure it deems appropriate".[18]

There are similar provisions under other rules of arbitration.[19] The ICSID Rules are somewhat particular in that they appear to limit the powers of the arbitral tribunal to that of "recommending" interim measures:

> "At any time during the proceeding a party may request that provisional measures for the preservation of its rights be recommended by the Tribunal. The request shall specify the rights to be preserved, the measures the recommendation of which is requested, and the circumstances that require such measures."[20]

7–12   The use of the word "recommend" in this context stems from the concern of the draftsmen of the ICSID Convention to be seen as respectful of national sovereignty by not granting powers to private tribunals to order a state to do or not do something on a purely provisional basis. Thus, as one author suggests, "a conscious decision was made not to grant the tribunal the power to order binding provisional measures."[21] Basing their analysis on the word "recommend", some authors came to the conclusion that because they were only recommendations, the measures adopted by an ICSID tribunal could only entail a moral obligation for the parties. Recent arbitral jurisprudence, however, indicates that these measures may nevertheless be taken to constitute binding obligations.[22]

There is also a provision in the Model Law itself that states:

> "Unless otherwise agreed by the parties, the arbitral tribunal may, at the request of a party, order any party to take such interim measures of protection

---

[17] Swiss Private International Law Act 1987, Ch.12, Art.183.

[18] ICC Arbitration Rules, Art.23(1).

[19] *e.g.* UNCITRAL Arbitration Rules, Art.26; LCIA Arbitration Rules, Art.25; ICDR International Arbitration Rules, Art.21; ICSID Arbitration Rules, r.39.

[20] ICSID Convention, Art.47 and ICSID Arbitration Rules, r.39.

[21] Schreuer, *The ICSID Convention: A Commentary* (Cambridge University Press, 2001), p.758.

[22] In this regard, in *Emilio Agustín Maffezini v Kingdom of Spain*, the ICSID Tribunal came to the following conclusion: "The Tribunal's authority to rule on provisional measures is not less binding than that of a final award. Accordingly, for the purposes of this order, the tribunal deems the word 'recommend' to be of equivalent value as the word 'order'." (ICSID Case No.ARB/97/7), Decision on Request for Provisional Measures (October 28, 1999), (2001) 16 ICSID Review—Foreign Investment Law Journal 212, at para.9.

as the arbitral tribunal may consider necessary in respect of the subject matter of the dispute. The arbitral tribunal may require any party to provide appropriate security in connection with such measure."[23]

In these circumstances it may be asked why, if the arbitral tribunal itself has the power to issue interim measures, might the help or intervention of a national court be necessary? There are five situations where the tribunal's powers may be insufficient and thus favour recourse to a national court.

(1) No powers

First, the arbitral tribunal may *not have* the necessary powers. This is usually   **7–13** a result of antique domestic legislation hearkening back to a time when the power to grant such measures was considered to be a prerogative of the national courts for public policy reasons. The Greek Code of Civil Procedure, for example, states:

"The arbitrator may not order, amend or revoke interim measures of protection."[24]

A similar provision is to be found in the Italian Code of Civil Procedure as follows:

"The arbitrator may not grant attachment or other interim measures of protection."[25]

(2) Inability to act prior to the formation of the tribunal

Secondly, the arbitral tribunal cannot issue interim measures until the tribunal   **7–14** itself has been established.[26] The point may seem so obvious as to be hardly worth mentioning. Yet it is important and frequently overlooked until a crisis arises. It takes time to establish an arbitral tribunal; and during that time, vital evidence or assets may disappear. National courts may be expected to deal with such urgent matters; an arbitral tribunal that is not yet in existence plainly cannot do so. Some rules have sought to address this lacuna. For example, the new rules of the Netherlands Arbitration Institute ("NAI") provide for the appointment of a single arbitrator promptly by the NAI for the purpose of resolving interim

---

[23] Model Law, Art.17.
[24] Greek Code of Civil Procedure, Art.889.
[25] Italian Code of Civil Procedure, Art.818. The same limitations apply in Argentina—see Art.753 of Argentina's National Code of Civil and Commercial Procedure. Notwithstanding this apparent limitation, Argentine authors have argued that arbitral tribunals may grant such measures and the rules of two reputable arbitration institutions in Buenos Aires expressly recognise this power. See Blackaby, Lindsey & Spinillo (eds) *International Arbitration in Latin America* (Kluwer, 2003), p.44.
[26] And indeed, in the case of ICC arbitrations, interim measures cannot be issued until the file has been transmitted to the tribunal.

measure issues prior to the constitution of the formal tribunal (summary arbitral proceedings).[27] Once the measures have been issued, the arbitrator may take no further role in the proceedings.[28]

The ICC Pre-arbitral Referee Procedure established in 1990 is also aimed at providing a means of "recourse at very short notice to a third person—the Referee—who is empowered to order provisional measures needed as a matter of urgency." Unlike the NAI Rules, the ICC procedure requires a separate agreement in writing; the adoption of the ICC Arbitration Rules is not sufficient. It is perhaps because of that limitation that experience has been limited. Nevertheless, after a period of 10 years, the provisions have begun to be used. In one case, for example, a claimant was able to obtain an order requiring a state party to continue performance of a contract pending a decision on the merits.[29]

(3) An order can only affect the parties to the arbitration

7-15   The third factor, which is again important in understanding why the assistance of a national court may be necessary, is that the powers of an arbitral tribunal are generally limited to the parties involved in the arbitration itself. The Model Law, in the text which has already been set out above, makes it plain that an arbitral tribunal may only "order *any party* to take such interim measures of protection as the arbitral tribunal may consider necessary... " A third party order, for example, addressed to a bank holding deposits of a party would not be enforceable against the bank. It also raises particular problems in multi-contract, multi-party disputes.[30]

(4) Enforcement difficulties

7-16   Fourthly, the interim measures ordered by an arbitral tribunal do not, by definition, finally resolve any point in dispute. Such an order is therefore unlikely to satisfy the requirement of finality imposed by the New York Convention for an award. French and Australian courts, for example, clearly adopt this reasoning.[31] Consequently, where there may be a need for international enforcement of the interim measure, parties may consider applying for such measures before the courts of the place of execution.

Notwithstanding this limitation, some states have sought to "label" interim measures ordered by tribunals as "awards", at least as far as their own legislation is concerned. This is the case of Scotland which requires that an interim measures

[27] Arbitration Rules of the Netherlands Arbitration Institute, Art.42.
[28] *ibid.*, Art.43(2).
[29] See Gaillard & Pinsolle, "The ICC Pre-Arbitral Referee: First Practical Experiences" (2004) 20 Arbitration International 13.
[30] See Hanotiau, "Problems Raised by Complex Arbitrations Involving Multiple Contracts, Parties, Issues" (2001) 18 Journal of International Arbitration 251.
[31] See, *e.g.*, Cour d'Appel de Paris (First Civil Chamber) *Société Sardisud*, March 25, 1994 in (1994) Revue de l'Arbitrage 391. The Supreme Court of Queensland refused to enforce an interlocutory injunction issued by an Indiana State Court on the basis that it was not an "arbitral award" within the meaning of the New York Convention; see *Resort Condominiums Inc v Bolwell*, (1995) XX Yearbook of Commercial Arbitration 628.

order "take the form of an award" or New Zealand,[32] which make the provisions on enforcement of awards applicable to such an order. Arbitral practice varies on this question although the recent tendency appears to be in favour of tribunals making orders rather than awards. In the context of an ICC arbitration that may add considerably to the speed of the process as an order, unlike an award, will not need to be scrutinised by the ICC's Court before issue.

(5) No ex parte application

Fifthly, a party may need to make an application *ex parte* (*i.e.* without notice **7–17** to the party against whom the measure is directed), for example to freeze a bank account of the other party to prevent the transfer of funds abroad. The laws of the most popular arbitration seats and the rules of the leading institutions do not currently expressly envisage such a power for arbitrators and some commentators have suggested that it is incompatible with the consensual nature of arbitration and the respect for due process.[33] The possibility of granting arbitrators authority to order interim measures has nevertheless been discussed since the 1980s,[34] but it was not seriously debated until it entered the agenda of the Working Group formed by UNCITRAL to update the Model Law in 2001. Whilst the US delegation to UNCITRAL has been actively supporting the inclusion of such a power in the revised Model Law (albeit subject to a series of strict requirements), there has been considerable scepticism from other delegations. In particular, the concerns over enforcement of *inter partes* interim measures discussed above apply *a fortiori* to a situation where one party has not had the possibility of being heard.[35] Further, there is a serious concern that a party should not be given the right to address argument to the arbitral tribunal in the absence of the other party. As one commentator has indicated: "How will the other party know precisely what the requesting party has been told?"[36] Whilst the same question might be raised in an application for *ex parte* interim measures before a court, the judge of the *ex parte* interim measure application is unlikely to be the judge of the merits in that situation.

Even if the right to apply to an arbitral tribunal *ex parte* were to find itself in the text of a revised Model Law it is unlikely to cause a sea change overnight. It would only take effect on adoption by a state and most leading arbitral venues have recently renewed their laws without including such a power.

---

[32] New Zealand Arbitration Act, First Schedule, Art.17(2).

[33] See van Houtte, "Ten Reasons Against a Proposal for Ex Parte Interim Measures of Protection in Arbitration" (2004) 20 Arbitration International 85 at 89.

[34] The possibility of *"mesures pré-provisionelles"* was the subject of debate in Switzerland in the 1980s; see Andreas Bucher, *Le Nouvel Arbitrage International en Suisse* (Basle, 1988), p.75.

[35] It is noteworthy that *ex parte* orders of national courts within the EU are not enforceable in other European courts pursuant to the Brussels Convention (now the Brussels Regulation). In such circumstances, commentators have suggested that there may be an even greater reticence to enforce *ex parte* orders of arbitral tribunals.

[36] van Houtte, *op. cit.*

(b) Interim measures: powers of the competent court

7–18   For all of the above reasons, it is important that the competent court should have the power to issue interim measures in support of the arbitral process. In situations of extreme urgency, where third parties need to be involved or where there is a strong possibility that a party will not voluntarily execute the tribunal's order, there may be little option but to identify the appropriate state court and make the application there. The measures requested may include the granting of injunctions to preserve the status quo or to prevent the disappearance of assets, the taking of evidence from witnesses or the preservation of property or evidence.

The practitioner who is asked to obtain interim measures of protection for a client in arbitration proceedings may be comforted to know that, in general, both the court and the arbitral tribunal itself may have the power to order such measures. In practice, however, this is likely to give rise to at least two problems. First, if a party to an arbitration agreement makes an application for interim measures to the court rather than to the arbitral tribunal, will this be regarded as a breach of the agreement to arbitrate? Secondly, if the choice between seeking interim measures from the courts or from the arbitral tribunal is truly an open choice, should application be made to the courts or to the arbitral tribunal?

Incompatibility with the arbitration agreement?

7–19   The risk that the resort to interim measures before a court might operate as a waiver of the arbitration agreement or that any order so obtained might be dissolved in the face of a valid arbitration clause appears to be consigned to history. The judgment of the US Third Circuit in *McCreary Tire & Rubber Co v Seat SpA*[37] held in favour of such incompatibility, but has been widely condemned and not recently followed.[38] Most arbitration rules are explicit in confirming that the application for interim relief from a court is not incompatible with an arbitration agreement. For example, the ICC Rules state clearly that:

> "The application of a party to a judicial authority for such [interim or conservatory] measures or for the implementation of any such measures ordered by an Arbitral Tribunal shall not be deemed to be an infringement or a waiver of the arbitration agreement . . . "[39]

A similar provision is to be found in the UNCITRAL Rules, which provide that:

---

[37] 501, F.2d 1032 (3d Cir. 1974).

[38] In *Carolina Power & Light Co v Uranex* (451, F.Supp.1044, 1051 (N.D.Cal. 1977) another US District Court declined to follow *McCreary*, holding that "nothing in the text of the Convention itself suggests that it precludes pre-judgment attachment".

[39] ICC Rules, Art.23(2).

"A request for interim measures addressed by any party to a judicial authority shall not be deemed incompatible with the agreement to arbitrate, or as a waiver of that agreement."[40]

The Model Law also states categorically:

"It is not incompatible with an arbitration agreement for a party to request, before or during arbitral proceedings, from a court an interim measure of protection and for a court to grant such measure."[41]

Nevertheless, where an application is made to a national court for interim **7–20** measures, a judge may be reluctant to make a decision that would risk prejudicing the outcome of the arbitration. As was stated in the *Channel Tunnel* case, which is considered later:

"There is always a tension when the court is asked to order, by way of interim relief in support of an arbitration, a remedy of the same kind as will ultimately be sought from the arbitrators: between, on the one hand, the need for the court to make a tentative assessment of the merits in order to decide whether the plaintiff's claim is strong enough to merit protection, and on the other the duty of the court to respect the choice of tribunal which both parties have made, and not to take out of the hands of the arbitrators (or other decision makers) a power of decision which the parties have entrusted to them alone. In the present instance I consider that the latter consideration must prevail . . . If the court now itself orders an interlocutory mandatory injunction, there will be very little left for the arbitrators to decide."[42]

Should application be made to a national court or to the arbitrators?

As to the second question, whether to seek interim relief from the relevant **7–21** court or from the arbitral tribunal, much depends on the relevant law and the nature of the relief sought. The relevant law may make it clear, for instance, that any application should be made first to the arbitral tribunal and only then to the court of the seat of arbitration. This is the position taken by Swiss law, which empowers the arbitral tribunal to take "provisional" or conservatory measures (unless the parties otherwise agree); and then states that, if the party against whom the order is made fails to comply, the arbitral tribunal may request assistance from the competent court.[43] Other states spell out the position even more clearly. The State of Ohio, for example, repeats Art.17 of the Model Law (which gives the arbitral tribunal power to order interim measures) but adds that

---

[40] UNCITRAL Arbitration Rules, Art.26.3. See also LCIA Rules, Art.25.3 and ICDR International Arbitration Rules, Art.21.3.

[41] Model Law, Art.9.

[42] *Channel Tunnel Group Ltd v Balfour Beatty Construction Ltd* [1993] A.C. 334 at 367–68. See also *Patel v Patel* (unreported judgment of the Court of Appeal, March 24, 1999).

[43] Swiss Private International Law Act 1987, Ch.12, Art.183(1) and (2).

whilst a party may also request interim measures directly from the court, the court should not grant this request:

"Unless the party shows that an application to the arbitral tribunal for the measure of protection would prejudice the party's rights and that an interim measure of protection from the court is necessary to protect their rights."[44]

7–22   English law is equally careful to spell out the position. It does so in three provisos to the section of the 1996 Act that confers upon the court "powers exercisable in support of arbitral proceedings", including the preservation of evidence, the inspection of property, the granting of an interim injunction and the appointment of a receiver. These three provisos are as follows:

(i) if the case is one of urgency, the court may on the application of a party or *proposed* party to the arbitral proceedings make such order as it thinks necessary for the purpose of preserving evidence or assets;

(ii) if the case is *not* one of urgency, the court will only act on the application of a party to the arbitral proceedings made with the permission of the tribunal or with the agreement in writing of the other parties; and

(iii) in any case, the court will only act if or to the extent that the arbitral tribunal has no power or is unable for the time being to act effectively.[45]

Where the position is not spelt out as clearly as this (for instance, in the Model Law) the answer to the question of whether to seek interim relief from the court or from the arbitral tribunal is likely to depend upon the particular circumstances of each case. If, for example, the arbitral tribunal is not yet in existence (or, in an ICC case, has not yet received the file), and the matter is one of urgency, the only possibility *is* to apply to the relevant national court for interim measures,[46] whilst at the same time taking steps to move the arbitration forward, so as to show that there is every intention of respecting the agreement to arbitrate. Where the arbitral tribunal *is* in existence, it is appropriate to apply first to that tribunal for interim measures, unless the measures sought are ones that the tribunal itself does not have the power to grant.[47]

This is not simply a question of division of labour. Although an arbitral tribunal lacks the coercive powers of a court of law and in spite of questions

---

[44] Ohio Code, International Commercial Arbitration, s.2712.36.

[45] English Arbitration Act 1996, s.44.

[46] Subject to the special mechanisms available before the Netherlands Arbitration Institute and the ICC Pre-arbitral Referee Procedure discussed above.

[47] This appears to be the thinking behind the ICC Arbitration Rules, which provide in Art.23(2) that the parties may apply to any competent judicial authority either "before the file is transmitted to the arbitral tribunal" (that is to say, before the arbitral tribunal is in a position to make an order) and "in appropriate circumstances even thereafter . . . " See also the way in which the position is dealt with by those states that spell it out in more detail than is done in the Model Law.

concerning the international enforceability of an order for interim measures, parties should not forget that any order is binding as between them. It is not writ in water. Furthermore, it is a brave (or foolish) party which deliberately chooses to ignore interim measures ordered by the tribunal which will judge the merits of its dispute. As one experienced commentator has stated:

> "Ultimately, of course, the arbitrators' greatest source of coercive power lies in their position as arbiters of the merits of the dispute between the parties. Parties seeking to appear before arbitrators as good citizens who have been wronged by their adversary would generally not wish to defy instructions given to them by those whom they wished to convince of the justice of their claims."[48]

There are other logistical problems inherent in applying to a court for interim measures. Often, the merits of the dispute will be under a foreign law which the local court will be ill-prepared to consider at an interim stage; likewise the language of the dispute and the contract may be different. Finally, the chosen court is likely to be at the place of execution of the order to avoid concerns as to enforceability. This may give rise to a less objective analysis of the request if the measures sought are either against a state entity or a local entity in favour of a foreign corporation.[49] **7–23**

The nature of the relief sought is also likely to have an important bearing on the question of whether to go to a national court or to the arbitral tribunal. Interim measures of relief take many forms and differ from state to state. Moreover, new and important forms of relief may be crafted by the courts or set out in legislation, so that it would be unwise to regard the categories of interim measures as being in any sense closed. However, the classification which follows may be helpful:

- measures relating to the preservation of evidence;

- measures aimed at preserving the *status quo*;

- measures intended to provide security for costs; and

- injunctions and other forms of interim relief.

(c) Measures relating to the attendance of witnesses and preservation of evidence

The first category of interim measures, directed to the taking and preservation of evidence, is one of obvious concern. Since an arbitral tribunal does not in **7–24**

---

[48] Schwartz, "Conservatory and Provisional Measures in International Arbitration", ICC Publication No.519 (1993).

[49] In a recent ICC arbitration in which one of the authors was involved (ICC Case No.11681), the parties had to consider whether to apply to the tribunal or to the local courts of the respondent for an interim measure. Given that the applicable law and language were foreign to the local court and that the measure sought to stop an important commercial transaction of an entity local to the court, a decision was taken to apply to the arbitral tribunal. The measure was awarded and the respondent complied voluntarily.

general possess the power to compel the attendance of relevant witnesses, it may be necessary to resort to the courts, particularly if the witness whose presence is required is not in any employed or other relationship to the parties to the arbitration, and so cannot be persuaded by them to attend voluntarily. This need for the assistance of the court is recognised by the Model Law:

> "The arbitral tribunal or a party with the approval of the arbitral tribunal may request from a competent court of this State assistance in taking evidence. The court may execute the request within its competence and according to its rules on taking evidence."[50]

Some national arbitration laws, including those of countries such as Switzerland, which have not adopted the Model Law *per se*, follow this form of wording very closely.[51] In other arbitration laws, the position may be set out more fully. For example, the English 1996 Act provides that:

> "(1) A party to arbitral proceedings may use the same court procedures as are available in relation to legal proceedings to secure the attendance before the tribunal of a witness in order to give oral testimony or to produce documents or other material evidence.
>
> (2) This may only be done with the permission of the tribunal or the agreement of the other parties.
>
> (3) The court procedures may only be used if—
>
>   (a) the witness is in the United Kingdom, and
>
>   (b) the arbitral proceedings are being conducted in England and Wales or, as the case may be, Northern Ireland.
>
> (4) A person shall not be compelled by virtue of this section to produce any document or other material evidence which he could not be compelled to produce in legal proceedings."[52]

In addition, the English courts have the same power in relation to arbitration proceedings as they have for their own purposes in relation, *inter alia*, to the taking of the evidence of witnesses and the preservation of evidence.[53]

7–25   In an arbitration with a seat in the US, s.7 of the Federal Arbitration Act (FAA) grants arbitrators the power to *subpoena* witnesses within the jurisdiction either to appear to give evidence or to disclose relevant evidence in their possession:

> "The arbitrators selected either as prescribed in this title or otherwise, or a majority of them, may summon in writing any person to attend before them or any of them as a witness and in a proper case to bring with him or them any

---

[50] Model Law, Art.27.

[51] Swiss Private International Law Act 1987, Art.184(2).

[52] English Arbitration Act 1996, s.43. Under s.2(3) of the Act, this section of the Act (and that concerning court powers exercisable in support of arbitral proceedings) applies even if (a) the seat of the arbitration is outside England, Wales or Northern Ireland or (b) no seat has been designated or determined.

[53] *ibid.*, s.44(1).

book, record, document, or paper which may be deemed material as evidence in the case. The fees for such attendance shall be the same as the fees of witnesses before masters of the United States courts. Said summons shall issue in the name of the arbitrator or arbitrators, or a majority of them, and shall be signed by the arbitrators, or a majority of them, and shall be directed to the said person and shall be served in the same manner as subpoenas to appear and testify before the court; if any person or persons so summoned to testify shall refuse or neglect to obey said summons, upon petition the United States district court for the district in which such arbitrators, or a majority of them, are sitting may compel the attendance of such person or persons before said arbitrator or arbitrators, or punish said person or persons for contempt in the same manner provided by law for securing the attendance of witnesses or their punishment for neglect or refusal to attend in the courts of the United States."

Practically, a *subpoena* can only be issued by tribunals in respect of witnesses present in the jurisdiction and there appear to be few cases of the power having been exercised in the context of international arbitrations. In one unreported ICC case, a tribunal refused to exercise its power to issue a *subpoena* to produce documents against a foreign national only present in the jurisdiction for the arbitration hearing. The tribunal considered that the parties would not have contemplated the exercise of such power when electing New York as a seat for a dispute which had no connection with the US.

Another apparent limitation arising out of the consensual nature of arbitration is that s.7 *subpoenas* can only be issued against witnesses under the control of the parties to the arbitration.[54] However, this limitation appears to be under attack and several courts have held that it does not apply to documents in the possession of third parties[55] and may not even apply to third party witnesses.[56]

So far as the preservation of evidence is concerned, it is obviously important **7–26** that evidence should *not* be destroyed before a proper record can be made of it. If, for example, the dispute is over the quality of a consignment of coffee or cocoa beans, then some measurement of that quality must be made before the consignment is either sold or perishes. If for example, the dispute is over the number or quality of reinforcing bars used in the concrete foundations of a road, bridge or a dam, some record must be preserved, preferably by independent experts, before those foundations are covered over. This is self-evident and, on

---

[54] See US District Court for the Southern District of New York, *Integrity Insurance Co v American Centennial Insurance Co*, 885 F.Supp.69 (1995) holding that third parties who are not party to the arbitration agreement are outside of the scope of the arbitrator's subpoena power.

[55] See *Stanton v Paine Webber Jackson & Curtis Inc*, 685 F.Supp.1241 (S.D. Fla. 1988) and *Meadows Indemnity Co Ltd v Nutmeg Insurance Co*, 157 FRD 42 (M.D. Tenn. 1994) both holding in favour of the arbitrators' power to order subpoenas of third party documents.

[56] See *National Broadcasting Co Inc v Bear Stearns & Co Inc*, 165 F.3d 184, 188 (2nd Cir. 1999) ("open questions remain as to whether section 7 may be invoked as authority for compelling pre-hearing depositions and pre-hearing document discovery, especially where such evidence is sought from non-parties"). For a general discussion of the use of subpoenas in arbitrations in the US, see Brecher, "Use of Subpoenas in Arbitration" N.Y.L.J. July 18, 1996, 1.

the whole, uncontroversial. Indeed, it sometimes seems as if many (but not all) of the relevant rules and arbitration laws on the subject of interim measures are directed principally, if not solely, to the taking of evidence and to the preservation of any property which is in dispute. The UNCITRAL Rules[57] provide that:

> "At the request of either party, the arbitral tribunal may take any interim measures it deems necessary in respect of the subject matter of the dispute, including measures for the conservation of the goods forming the subject matter in dispute, such as ordering their deposit with a third person or the sale of perishable goods."

The references to the "subject-matter" of the dispute and to "measures for the conservation of goods forming the subject matter in dispute" suggest that the measures contemplated relate to preserving or selling of goods rather than, for instance, preventing the flight of assets. In this sense, they fall short of the interim measures that are needed in the modern world of international commerce.

The Model Law is no more explicit as to the interim measures that may be taken by an arbitral tribunal. As already seen, Art.17 simply states:

> "Unless otherwise agreed by the parties, the arbitral tribunal may, at the request of a party, order any party to take such interim measure of protection as the arbitral tribunal may consider necessary in respect of the subject matter of the dispute. The arbitral tribunal may require a party to provide appropriate security in connection with such measure."

7–27   The phrase "necessary in respect of the subject matter of the dispute" is not amplified or explained in any way. However, it appears to limit those interim measures that an arbitral tribunal is empowered to grant under the Model Law to such matters as ensuring that physical evidence (for instance, of defective welding in a gas pipeline) is preserved; or towards ensuring that appropriate orders are made for the safekeeping of property (such as a valuable painting or a piece of Fabergé jewellery) whose ownership may be in dispute.

The ICDR International Arbitration Rules appear to show the same narrow concern for goods and property:

> "1. At the request of any party, the tribunal may take whatever interim measures it deems necessary, including injunctive relief and measures for the protection or conservation of property.
> 2. Such interim measures may take the form of an interim award and the tribunal may require security for the costs of such measures."[58]

The ICC Rules are wider in scope. "Conservatory and interim" measures are deemed sufficiently important to be given an article to themselves and the

---

[57] UNCITRAL Arbitration Rules, Art.26(1).
[58] ICDR Rules, Art.21.

tribunal has the power to order any interim or conservatory measures it deems appropriate.[59] As already discussed, however,[60] any such orders could only sensibly be directed to the parties to the arbitration and, conceivably, to any persons or entities within their control.

(d) Measures aimed at preserving the *status quo*

There are many cases in which an award of damages, however substantial, **7–28** does not fully compensate the injured party for the loss that has been sustained. This may include damage to reputation, loss of business opportunities and similar heads of claim, which are real enough but difficult to prove and to quantify, even if they are considered to be legally admissible. For example, a manufacturer may refuse to continue supplies under a distribution agreement, alleging breach of contract. If the distributor does not receive the supplies for which he has contracted, he may not be able to fulfil the contracts that he in turn has made. This may cause damage to his reputation and to the network of agents that he has established. In such a case, the distributor would no doubt wish to argue that the *status quo* should be maintained, and that the manufacturer should continue to supply him, pending resolution of their dispute by arbitration. Or again, by way of example, a pharmaceutical company may produce a particular drug under licence and then decide to manufacture and market a competing product under its own name, claiming that there is nothing in the licence agreement to prevent it doing so. In such a case, the licensor probably wishes to argue that until the dispute is resolved by arbitration, the licensee should be restrained from manu- facturing and marketing the competing product.

What should an arbitral tribunal do if it is asked, in effect, to make an interim order or award to preserve the *status quo*? First, the arbitral tribunal will need to consider whether it has the power to make any such award. It is doubtful whether it could do so if it is operating, for instance, under the UNCITRAL Rules, or under an arbitration law that simply repeats the relevant provision of the Model Law. As already discussed, the scope of an arbitral tribunal's authority in such cases appears to be restricted to "the subject matter of the dispute" and to "the conservation of the goods forming the subject matter in dispute." Probably the best that an arbitral tribunal can do, in such circumstances, is to make a "recommendation" to the parties.

Where the arbitral tribunal's authority in respect of interim measures is less limited,[61] the arbitral tribunal *may* have the power to issue the interim order or

---

[59] ICC Arbitration Rules, Art.23.

[60] Above, paras 7–18 *et seq.*

[61] As with the ICC Arbitration Rules, for example. Indeed, as the ICC case law suggests, the view taken by the ICC tribunals is that interim and conservatory measures are justified in order to "avoid the 'aggravation' of the dispute that is the subject of the arbitration" and to "ensure the maintenance of the status quo between the parties". See ICC Case No.3896 in Jarvin & Derains, *Collection of Arbitral Awards 1974–1985*, p.161; and see generally Derains & Schwartz, *A Guide to the new ICC Rules of Arbitration*, and Schwartz, "The Practices and Experience of the ICC Court" in *Conservatory and Provisional Measures in International Arbitration* (ICC Publica- tion).

award that is sought. The tribunal must then consider very carefully whether or not it should exercise this power.

7–29   The institutional rules only establish the power of the tribunal to order interim measures but do not set out any rules which should be applied to assessing whether such measures should be granted. The tribunal is consequently left with no test against which the request should be measured. As one learned commentator has observed in relation to the ICC Rules:

> "When asked to issue orders for interim relief, a tribunal must first determine whether the factors justifying the relief sought exist. Article 23(1) of the [ICC] Rules provides no real help; it merely confirms the power of the tribunal to give relief."[62]

Some arbitrators have considered that the rules applicable to the judicial grant of such measures at the courts of the seat of the arbitration should apply,[63] while others have applied the applicable substantive law. Nevertheless, a consensus may be emerging to divorce the test from the law of the place of arbitration in favour of a developing international arbitral practice. The overriding criteria of this practice appear to be: (i) an arguable case on the merits; (ii) no prejudging of the merits; and (iii) a risk of serious or irreparable harm if the measure is not taken (including the need for urgency). These criteria are not likely to shock the sensibility of most national legal systems whose courts issue interim measures on similar grounds.[64]

In applying these criteria, the tribunal has first to make an overall assessment of the merits of the case, possibly at a very early stage in the proceedings, in order to determine whether the claimant's case is sufficiently strong as to deserve protection, sometimes referred to as *fumus bonis juris*.

7–30   Secondly, the tribunal must consider whether, by granting the relief sought, it would in effect be prejudging the result of the arbitration and so be preventing one of the parties from pursuing a course of action that it was entitled to pursue. As Professor Lew observes:

> "In dealing with a request for an interim measure, an arbitral tribunal must refrain from prejudging the merits of the case. By way of illustration, an arbitral tribunal will generally refuse to grant such a measure, where the request essentially covers what is asked to be resolved in the substantial arbitration."[65]

---

[62] Lew, "Commentary on Interim and Conservatory Measures in ICC Arbitration Cases", ICC Bulletin 11 (2000), p.23 (hereinafter "Lew").

[63] See interim award in ICC Case No.8786, where an arbitral tribunal relied on the provisions of Art.183 of the Swiss Private International Law Act 1987 to decide the application for interim measures between Turkish and German parties.

[64] See, *e.g.*, Arts 872 and 873 of the French New Code of Civil Procedure or Art.1168 of the Mexican Civil Code.

[65] See Lew, above, para.7–29.

Thirdly, there must be a risk of serious and irreparable harm. As a former Secretary-General of the ICC's Court has expressed:

"In one recent arbitral award rendered by a tribunal in Paris, the tribunal set forth a classic formulation, defining 'urgency' as arising where there is . . . a risk of serious and irreparable harm, present or future . . . that would render indispensable the taking of an immediate decision such as to eliminate, avoid or reduce such harm."[66]

This view is echoed by Professor Lew:

"The demonstration of irreparable or perhaps substantial harm is also necessary for the grant of a measure. This is because it is not appropriate to grant a measure where no irreparable or substantial harm comes to the movant in the event the measure is not granted. The final award offers the means of remedying any harm, reparable or otherwise, once determined."[67]

If the application for interim measures is made to a national court, rather than to the arbitral tribunal itself, the court will find itself in much the same position. The court may well have the power to act, for example, by issuing an interim injunction, but it would still need to consider very carefully whether or not it *should* do so. This problem confronted the English courts in the *Channel Tunnel* case, which brought into sharp focus the twin questions of (i) whether the court had the power to issue the interim injunction which was sought and (ii) if so, whether it should do so in order to preserve the *status quo*. It was a case which went on appeal from the court of first instance to the Court of Appeal and then to the highest English court, the House of Lords. Each court gave a different answer to the two questions posed.

The contract for the construction of the Channel Tunnel was an international contract that contained a "two-stage" provision for the resolution of any disputes that might arise between Eurotunnel (the owners and intended operators of the tunnel) and Trans-Manche Link (TML), a consortium of five French and five British construction companies that had agreed to construct the land terminals, bore and equip the tunnels, and provide the necessary rolling stock. At the first stage, any dispute between Eurotunnel and TML was to go to a Panel of Experts, who had to give a decision within 90 days. If either party disagreed with the Panel's decision, the dispute was to be referred to arbitration in Brussels under the ICC Rules.

7–31

---

[66] Schwartz, "The practices and experiences of the ICC Court" in *Conservatory and Provisional Measures in International Arbitration*, ICC publication No.519.
[67] See Lew, above, para.7–29.

One particularly serious dispute that arose between the parties was about payment for the tunnel's cooling system. This was not part of the original specification, but was added by a variation order. TML claimed that the monthly payments it received for the cooling system were insufficient. By the end of September 1991, the gap between what Eurotunnel had paid and what TML claimed had grown to approximately £17 million. In October 1991, TML wrote to Eurotunnel threatening to suspend work on the cooling system unless its claim was met in full and pointing out the "very serious" consequences this would have for completion of the project, with sub-contractors and other workers having to be laid off, equipment orders being delayed or cancelled, and so forth. In reply, Eurotunnel applied to the English court for an interim injunction to restrain TML from carrying out its threat. TML argued that the English courts had no power to intervene by granting the injunction that was sought. Instead, the court should stay the litigation and refer the parties to arbitration, in accordance with the then governing Act.[68]

7–32 The case had a chequered history, reflecting the difficult issues which it raised in this "no-man's land" between the national courts and arbitral tribunals. The judge who heard the case at first instance decided that he *did* have the power to grant an injunction, and would have done so but for an undertaking by TML to continue working pending further court proceedings. The Court of Appeal considered that it was an appropriate case for an injunction, but that it had no power to grant one, because of the arbitration agreement. The House of Lords considered that it *did* have power to grant an injunction, but thought it inappropriate to do so. In giving the House of Lords judgment, Lord Mustill highlighted the problem to which this kind of application for interim relief may give rise. He stated:

> "It is true that mandatory interlocutory relief may be granted even where it substantially overlaps the final relief claimed in the action; and I also accept that it is possible for the court at the pre-trial stage of the dispute arising under a construction contract to order the defendant to continue with a performance of the works. But the court should approach the making of such an order with the utmost caution and should be prepared to act only when the balance of advantage plainly favours the grant of relief. In the combination of circumstances which we find in the present case, I would have hesitated long before proposing that such an order should be made, even if the action had been destined to remain in the High Court."[69]

The fact that, in the *Channel Tunnel* case, three different courts gave different answers to the questions of whether or not there was power to issue an injunction, and if so, whether it would be appropriate to do so, underlines the difficulties

---

[68] The English Arbitration Act 1975.
[69] *Channel Tunnel Group v Balfour Beatty Ltd* [1993] A.C. 334 at 367.

posed by such questions.[70] It is no comfort to the practitioner to say so, but there is no clear rule as to whether or not an injunction will be issued in particular circumstances. Each case has to be assessed individually.

(e) Interim relief in respect of parallel proceedings

Whilst an uneasy truce may have been signed between the courts and arbitral **7–33** tribunals in the developed arbitral jurisdictions, the old "turf war" continues to rage in other parts of the world, where there is an uncomfortable trend towards the issue of "anti-arbitration" injunctions, either by the courts of the seat or by the courts of the place of eventual enforcement. The fact pattern is often similar: it consists of a dispute between a foreign party and a state or state-owned entity which has signed a clear arbitration agreement. The state entity wishes to sabotage the arbitral proceedings and have the case remitted for judicial determination in its own courts. It therefore seeks an injunction before those courts seeking to challenge the jurisdiction of the tribunal and an order requiring the arbitrators and adverse party to suspend or abandon the arbitral proceedings on pain of daily fines (or worse). This problem has raised serious challenges to the modern arbitrator: should such orders be obeyed, even where patently the product of improper government intervention or should the arbitrator seek to ensure justice in the individual case, often at risk of monetary penalties (or worse)?

In one such case, a subsidiary of a US corporation, Himpurna, had entered into a contract with the Indonesian state electricity corporation, PLN, to explore and develop geothermal resources in Indonesia and subsequently sell the power to PLN. In the wake of the Asian economic crisis, PLN failed to purchase the electricity supplied. Himpurna relied on the arbitration clause in the contract to commence an arbitration under the UNCITRAL Rules against PLN. A final award was made in favour of Himpurna which PLN refused to pay. Himpurna subsequently commenced a second arbitration proceeding against Indonesia, based on Indonesia's pledge to secure PLN's performance. Shortly after serving the Statement of Claim, proceedings were commenced by both PLN and Indonesia in the Indonesian courts which resulted in interim injunctions ordering the suspension of the arbitral proceedings pending a court decision on the merits with an attached fine of US$1 million per day for breach of the order.

The tribunal considered that the injunction was a transparent attempt to avoid the consequences of a freely signed arbitration agreement and refused to abandon the arbitration. To avoid the risk of breaching the Indonesian court order, the

[70] The former English arbitration legislation was amended to take account, *inter alia*, of some of the difficulties that the court faced in the *Channel Tunnel* case. The Court of Appeal, which would have been prepared to grant an injunction, considered that it had no power to do so, because the arbitration agreement provided for arbitration in Brussels. The English Arbitration Act 1996 (in s.44 (2)(e)) provides that the powers of the court which are "exercisable in support of arbitral proceedings" include the granting of an interim injunction; and this section of the Act applies even if the seat of the arbitration is outside England (s.2(3)). There may be resort to the courts if, or to the extent that, the arbitral tribunal or any other person empowered by the parties to decide the case "has no power or is unable for the time being to act effectively" (s.44(5)).

tribunal moved the place of the hearing to The Hague and convened witness hearings. Indonesia tried to stop such hearings from proceeding by seeking an injunction from the Dutch courts. This attempt failed and the hearings were held (albeit in truncated form without the presence of the Indonesian arbitrator) and a final award issued.

7–34   The colourful facts of this case raise important questions as to how an arbitral tribunal can seek to avoid injunctions of national courts in extreme circumstances. First, the place of hearings in an UNCITRAL case can be held "at any place [the tribunal] deems appropriate" and so the physical transfer of the hearings to The Hague was permitted by the rules. In connection with the injunction itself, Art.28 of the UNCITRAL Rules allows a tribunal to proceed with the arbitration notwithstanding one party's default whenever the defaulting party has failed to show "sufficient cause" for its default. In this regard, the arbitral tribunal found that the Indonesian injunction did not constitute "sufficient cause" because: (1) it was sought and obtained by a state agency that was under the *de jure* control of the Government of Indonesia; and (2) the Government of Indonesia had *de facto* made no attempt to rein in those actions that were inconsistent with its obligations under the parties' arbitration agreement.

As a second ground, the arbitral tribunal held that the very existence of an arbitration agreement, and the involvement of a state party, entitled the tribunal to apply international law. As a matter of international law, the actions of the Indonesian courts were attributable to the Republic of Indonesia. In *Benteler v Belgium*[71] an international tribunal had held that "a state which has signed an arbitration clause or agreement would be acting contrary to international public policy if it subsequently relied on the incompatibility of such an obligation with its internal legal system". The arbitral tribunal held that no distinction should be drawn between a legislative enactment and a court injunction, and that it would constitute "a denial of justice for the courts of a State to prevent a foreign party from pursuing its remedies before a forum to the authority of which the State consented". Thirdly, the tribunal held that an international arbitral tribunal is not "unconditionally subject" to the jurisdiction of the courts at the seat of the arbitration. Specifically, the "adjudicatory authority" of an international tribunal "does not emanate from a discrete sovereign but rather from an international order".

Similar issues were addressed in another matter concerning an arbitration between a European construction company and an Ethiopian municipal authority. It related to an infrastructure project to be undertaken in Addis Ababa. It arose under a FIDIC contract that, in the normal way, comprised a number of the FIDIC "general conditions", which were supplemented by "special conditions" specifically negotiated by the parties.

7–35   Confusingly, one of the FIDIC general conditions that was adopted was a standard ICC arbitration clause providing for ICC arbitration in Addis Ababa,

[71] (1985) 8 European Commercial Cases 101.

410

while one of the parties' special conditions was a separate arbitration clause that provided for arbitration in Addis Ababa pursuant to the Civil Code of Ethiopia.

When a dispute arose between the parties, and the European contractor commenced ICC proceedings, the Ethiopian municipal authority raised jurisdictional objections. It argued that, in specifically negotiating an arbitration agreement that did not make reference to the ICC in their "special conditions", the parties had evinced a clear intention not to refer disputes to ICC arbitration.

A hearing on the merits was scheduled in Paris to include the appearance of a number of witnesses resident in Ethiopia, even though the seat of the arbitration was Addis Ababa. In holding the hearing on the merits in a place other than the seat of the arbitration, the tribunal relied on Art.14(2) of the ICC Rules that allowed it to conduct hearings at any location it considered "appropriate" (a provision that had been restated in the parties' Terms of Reference).

The Ethiopian party was outraged, and applied to the ICC's Court to remove **7–36** the arbitrators claiming that in having regard to its own convenience, and that of the claimant alone, the tribunal's decision to hold hearings outside of Ethiopia gave the respondent reason to doubt the tribunal's impartiality. This application was rejected by the ICC's Court. Following this, and pursuant to the Ethiopian Civil Code, the Ethiopian party applied to the Ethiopian courts to remove the arbitrators. Pending its decision on the challenge, the Ethiopian Supreme Court issued an injunction enjoining the proceedings.

In an interim award in which it found that it did have jurisdiction over the parties' dispute, the ICC Tribunal also held that it had the discretion—indeed the duty—not to comply with the Ethiopian Supreme Court's injunction. How was the tribunal able to reach this decision?

As a practical matter, the arbitrators were personally insulated from the effects of the injunction. As a result of the tribunal's procedural ruling, the hearing took place outside Ethiopia and none of the three arbitrators were Ethiopian nationals. How did the tribunal justify ignoring the orders of the courts that had supervisory jurisdiction over the arbitration? At least four grounds were given, many of which are similar to—if not the same as—the grounds relied on by the UNCITRAL Tribunal in the Republic of Indonesia arbitrations.

First, the tribunal noted that it was not an organ of state, but a creature of **7–37** contract. As a result, it held that its primary duty was to the parties to ensure that their agreement to arbitrate was not frustrated. Secondly, the tribunal found that an agreement to submit disputes to international arbitration "is not anchored exclusively in the legal order of the seat . . . [rather it is] validated by a range of international sources and norms extending beyond the domestic seat." As to what these international sources were, the tribunal referred in particular to the New York Convention, which it suggested "embodied principles of general [recognition]". Thirdly, the tribunal held that although Art.35 of the ICC Rules imposes a duty on tribunals to "ensure" that their awards are "enforceable at law", and that in this case the likely place of enforcement was Ethiopia, this did not mean that an arbitral tribunal:

"should simply abdicate to the courts of the seat the tribunal's own judgment about what is fair and right . . . In the event that the arbitral tribunal considers that to follow a decision of a court would conflict fundamentally with the tribunal's understanding of its duty to the parties, derived from the parties' arbitration agreement, the tribunal *must follow its own judgment*, even if that requires non-compliance with a court order".

Finally, the tribunal concluded that to comply with the injunction would lead to a denial of justice. Specifically, it held that, in the same way that a state cannot rely on changes in its own laws to justify breach of contract, a state entity cannot resort to the state's courts to frustrate an arbitration agreement.

These cases may be considered either as brave innovations or as dangerous precedents depending upon the observer's perspective. Both tribunals seemed to agree that the power of the tribunal emanates from the parties and international law rather than finding its basis in the domestic law of the seat. The same approach appears to pervade those cases where an award annulled at its seat is nevertheless raised, like Lazarus from the dead, to be enforced elsewhere.[72] These precedents all suggest that the arbitral tribunal may use the rules at its disposal to divorce itself from interference by the courts of the seat. The traditional role of the state, prescribing the boundaries of arbitration and the enforcement of those boundaries through its courts, seems distant. Nevertheless, the boundaries of this new-found liberty may create their own problems, not least when faced with the ultimate test of enforcement.

7–38   In 2000, the High Court of Bangladesh revoked the authority of an ICC arbitral tribunal sitting in Dhaka based on a judicial action brought by the claimant. The action alleged irregularities committed by the arbitral tribunal in the admissibility of documentary evidence, a task left to the entire discretion of the arbitral tribunal by the ICC Rules. One commentator on this case has indicated that, had the tribunal continued to hear the case elsewhere, the ultimate award would, in all likelihood, be recognised in jurisdictions with modern arbitration laws.[73]

There are also examples of national courts with no supervisory jurisdiction which have sought to stay foreign arbitral proceedings. In *SGS v Pakistan*, the Pakistan Supreme Court issued an order against SGS restraining it from taking any action to pursue arbitration proceedings it had commenced under the ICSID rules on the basis of a bilateral investment treaty.[74] This decision followed on the heels of *Hubco v WAPDA*, in which the same court had upheld a claim brought

---

[72] See *In the Matter of the Arbitration of Certain Controversies between Chromalloy Aeroservices and the Arab Republic of Egypt* (*"Chromalloy"*) 939 F.Supp. 907 (D.D.C. 1996); (1997) XXII Yearbook Commercial Arbitration 1001 (A.J. van den Berg ed.); *République Arabe d'Egypte v Société Chromalloy Aero Services* (1997) Revue de l'Arbitrage 395, Cour d'Appel de Paris (First Civil Chamber), January 14, 1997; see also *Omnium de Traitement et de Valorisation (OTV) (France) v Hilmarton (UK)* (1997) XXII Yearbook Commercial Arbitration 696 (A.J. van den Berg ed.), Cour de Cassation, June 10, 1997 (excerpts).

[73] See Gaillard, "Interference of Courts in the International Arbitral Process", *New York Law Journal*, February 1, 2001.

[74] For a detailed analysis of the case, see Lau, "Note on *Société Générale de Surveillance v Pakistan*" (2003) 19 Arbitration International 179.

before the courts of Pakistan notwithstanding a pending ICC arbitration in London.[75]

Such cases nevertheless remain rare. The vast majority of arbitrations are pursued without interference from domestic courts. Nevertheless, the evolution of an international law to which tribunals must respond, even if in conflict with the dictates of the courts of the seat, may cause such courts to curtail their partisan zeal and conform to accepted international norms.

(f) Security for costs

The costs of fighting an international commercial arbitration, like the costs of proceedings in court, can be very high. Legal fees and expenses, the fees and expenses of experts, witnesses, transcript writers, interpreters and translators and others, together with the cost of air travel and hotel accommodation may amount to a considerable sum of money. Costs in excess of US$1 million are common. During the arbitration proceedings themselves, each party will be expected to bear its own side's fees and expenses (including those of any arbitral institution, such as the ICC). These may be heavy, but the money has to be found if the claim or counterclaim is to be defended properly. **7–39**

The question that then arises is whether, when the arbitrators come to make their award, they will order the loser to pay (or at least to contribute towards) the other side's costs. The practice varies. Sometimes parties provide, in their arbitration agreement or elsewhere, that each party will bear its own costs in any event or that the costs will be shared in a particular way. If so, the relevant arbitration law will generally uphold this agreement.[76] Where there is no such agreement, reference must be made to the relevant arbitration law and to the relevant rules of arbitration.

The issue of "costs" in an international commercial arbitration is an important one. It is discussed in more detail in Ch.8. The purpose of the present discussion is to consider whether, whilst the arbitration is in progress, an arbitral tribunal may order that one of the parties should provide some form of security for costs, in order to ensure that if that party loses the arbitration and is ordered to pay the legal costs and expenses of the winning party, there will at least be a bank guarantee, or other source of funds, from which those costs can be paid. It may be some consolation to a reluctant party to an arbitration to be told that, if successful, he may recover some of his costs. It is no consolation at all if such costs prove to be irrecoverable because, for instance, the losing party is insolvent or the award proves to be unenforceable.

Despite this, it is not usual for an application for security for costs to be made in an international arbitration. There are two reasons why this should be so. First, the arbitral tribunal may simply lack the power to make such an order. Secondly, even if it has this power, the tribunal may be reluctant to exercise it. This may be **7–40**

---

[75] For a commentary, see (2000) 16 Arbitration International 439.

[76] Although, under English law, this is so only if the agreement is made after the dispute has arisen.

either because it is not satisfied that there is a very real prospect of non-payment by the losing party, or because it prefers to wait and hear the whole case, before coming to any conclusions that are adverse to one of the parties. The granting of security for costs would risk prejudging this issue.[77]

4. At the End of the Arbitration

Judicial control of the proceedings and the award

7–41   One final aspect of the relationship between national courts and arbitral tribunals remains to be considered. This is the extent to which, if at all, national courts should exercise judicial control over the conduct of international commercial arbitrations and the resulting award. There are two extreme positions. As one English judge recognised:

> "It can be said on the one side that if parties agree to resolve their disputes through the use of a private rather than a public tribunal, then the court system should play no part at all, save perhaps to enforce awards in the same way as they enforce any other rights and obligations to which the parties have agreed. To do otherwise is unwarrantably to interfere with the parties' right to conduct their affairs as they choose.
>
> The other extreme position reaches a very different conclusion. Arbitration has this in common with the court system; both are a form of dispute resolution which depends on the decision of a third party. Justice dictates that certain rules should apply to dispute resolution of this kind. Since the state is in overall charge of justice, and since justice is an integral part of any civilised democratic society, the courts should not hesitate to intervene as and when necessary, so as to ensure that justice is done in private as well as public tribunals."[78]

The extent to which there should be judicial control at the seat of the arbitration over both the conduct of the arbitration and the resulting award is a matter on which different commentators, and more importantly, different states have taken different views. It is an important matter and is considered in more detail in Chs 9 and 10.

5. Conclusion

7–42   Powers that have been conferred on national courts by legislation, or that have been developed by the courts themselves, such as the power to attach bank

---

[77] See Rubins, "In God We Trust: All Others Pay Cash: Security for Costs in International Commercial Arbitration" (2000) 11 Am. Rev of Int'l Arb. 307.
[78] Lord Saville, Denning Lecture, 1995, "Arbitration and the Courts", p.157.

accounts, to appoint liquidators, or to issue injunctions, are there to serve the interests of justice. They are there to ensure that the ultimate purpose of legal proceedings is not frustrated by evidence or assets disappearing, or by people taking the law into their own hands. As international commercial transactions become more commonplace and as means of communication improve at startling speed, recourse to the courts, even where there is an arbitration agreement, may be more rather than less essential, if the aims of justice are to be properly served. As an experienced Swiss arbitrator expressed it:

"Over the last twenty years or so the development of law and international arbitration has been marked by an obvious tendency to limit the possibilities of court intervention in the course of an arbitration. Thus England abolished the special case and curtailed the powers of the courts even in support of an arbitration.

. . . It may be that the tide is now turning: it is increasingly realised in international arbitration circles that the intervention of the courts is not *necessarily* disruptive of the arbitration. It may equally be definitely *supportive* . . . "[79]

This view has been echoed by Lord Mustill who considers that "party autonomy is looking a little frayed round the edges".[80]

As in all relationships, the trick lies in establishing the appropriate balance between the rights of the courts to supervise arbitrations and the rights of parties to solicit their assistance in times of need. An increased "internationalisation" of international arbitration to permit arbitrators to take a "second look" at domestic court control and assess whether it conforms to international norms is all well and good, but those international norms may need to be rendered sufficiently transparent to enable the courts to understand the acceptable limits of their intervention.

---

[79] Claude Reymond, "The Channel Tunnel Case and the Law of International Arbitration" (1993) 109 L.Q.R. 337 at 341 (emphasis added).
[80] Lord Mustill at the LCIA conference entitled "International Economic Disputes: A Wider Perspective", St John's College, Cambridge, April 1–3, 2004.

CHAPTER 8

THE AWARD

1. BACKGROUND

(a) Generally

8–01   Parties who go to the trouble and expense of taking their disputes to international arbitration do so in the expectation that, unless a settlement is reached along the way, the proceedings will end with an award.

They also expect that, subject to any right of appeal or recourse,[1] the award will be final and binding upon them. This expectation is reflected in both international and institutional rules of arbitration. The UNCITRAL Arbitration Rules state simply:

> "The award shall be made in writing and shall be final and binding on the parties. The parties undertake to carry out the award without delay."[2]

The ICC Rules, recognising the possibility of some form of challenge to an award at the place of arbitration, under the *lex arbitri*, are more circumspect:

> "Every award shall be binding on the parties. By submitting the dispute to arbitration under these Rules, the parties undertake to carry out any Award without delay and shall be deemed to have waived their right to any form of recourse insofar as any waiver can validly be made."[3]

8–02   In both sets of rules the references are to *an* award in the singular; and the reader could be forgiven for assuming that the purpose and object of an arbitration is to arrive at a single award, just as, for most couples, a marriage might be said to be the purpose and object of an engagement.

However, in arbitrations (as in engagements) there may be diversions along the way. For example, the arbitral tribunal may be called upon to issue procedural orders and directions (sometimes misleadingly referred to as "interim *awards*"). Or the arbitral tribunal may be called upon to make awards (properly so called)

---

[1] See Ch.9, paras 9–03 *et seq.*
[2] UNCITRAL Arbitration Rules, Art.32(2).
[3] ICC Arbitration Rules, Art.28(6).

that determine certain issues between the parties, but leave other issues out-standing. The arbitral tribunal may, for example, make an interim award on jurisdiction, where one party has challenged the tribunal's jurisdiction in respect of some or all of the matters in dispute, rather than risk hearing the case through to the end and then deciding, perhaps, that it did indeed have no jurisdiction. Or it may make a partial award, for instance, of a sum of money that it considers to be indisputably due and payable by one party to the other.[4]

The distinction between a "final" award and the other types of award that may be made by an arbitral tribunal is that a final award will dispose of all (or all of the remaining) issues that have been raised in the arbitration. Thus, in this sense it means "last" award. It will usually result from proceedings that have been contested throughout. However, it may embody an agreed settlement between the parties, in which case it is generally known as a consent award or an award on agreed terms. Alternatively, it may result from proceedings in which the respondent has failed or refused to participate, in which case it is sometimes known as a default award.

These different categories of award are considered in this chapter. For the **8–03** present, the point to be made is that all awards are "final" in the sense that they dispose finally of the issues they decide (subject to any challenge or procedure for correction or interpretation) and are binding on the parties[5]; but a "final" award in the sense used in the various sets of international and institutional rules is literally the last award, the award that concludes the mandate of the arbitral tribunal. Since all awards are dispositive of the issues they determine, it is important that the arbitral tribunal does its best to ensure not merely that the award is correct, but also that it is enforceable across international frontiers.[6]

No arbitral tribunal can be expected to *guarantee* that its award will be enforceable in whatever country the winner chooses to enforce it. This is too much to expect, whether as a matter of law or of moral obligation. However, every arbitral tribunal must do its best. As it is expressed in the ICC Rules:

---

[4] Some modern arbitration statutes make a specific distinction between interim, partial and final awards. The Netherlands Arbitration Act 1986 in Art.1049 provides that: "The arbitral tribunal may render a final award, a partial award, or an interim award." The commentary on this article by Sanders & van den Berg, *The Netherlands Arbitration Act 1986* (Kluwer, 1987) suggests that partial awards are given in respect of substantive issues which are separated, such as liability and *quantum*; interim awards are given on jurisdictional issues; and simple orders are made in respect of procedural issues. The Swiss Private International Law Act 1987, Ch.12 provides for "preliminary awards" in relation to jurisdictional issues in Art.186(2). "Partial awards" that finally determine the issue they decide are provided for in Art.188. See Blessing, "The New International Arbitration Law in Switzerland" (1988) 5 Journal of International Arbitration 9 at 65.

[5] The English Arbitration Act 1996, s.39, is an exception to this general rule in granting a power to make "provisional awards", when the parties agree that the arbitral tribunal shall have the power. Interestingly s.39 only mentions the word "award" in the marginal note, and the body of the section refers to "orders". See Hunter & Landau, *The English Arbitration Act; Text and Notes* (1998, Kluwer), p.35; whether such orders are enforceable under the New York Convention is questionable, and would be a matter for the courts of the country concerned.

[6] See, *e.g.* ICC Arbitration Rules, Art.35.

"In all matters not expressly provided for in these Rules, the Court and the Arbitral Tribunal shall act in the spirit of these Rules and shall make every effort to make sure that the Award is enforceable at law."[7]

Expressions such as "make every effort" denote an obligation to perform, rather than an obligation to achieve a defined result. Nonetheless, the message is clear. In principle, the eventual result of every arbitration should be a final award that is enforceable.

Achieving the intended result

8–04   For an arbitral tribunal to achieve the standard of performance required to make an internationally enforceable award, it must first satisfy itself that it has jurisdiction to determine the matters it is called upon to determine. In the same spirit it must ensure that it deals with all of these matters. It must steer a course between the twin perils of Scylla and Charybdis: it must not do too little (so rendering an award *infra petita*) or too much (so rendering an award *ultra petita*).

Next, the arbitral tribunal must comply with any procedural rules governing the arbitration. If reference has to be made to the legal costs of the proceedings,[8] or to the seat of the arbitration, this must be done; and again, if the award needs to be formally approved by an arbitral institution (as with an ICC award) this must also be done.[9] Finally, the arbitral tribunal must sign and date the award and arrange for it to be communicated to the parties, in the manner laid down in the relevant law or in the rules that apply to the arbitration. If the arbitral tribunal has done its work well, it will not be called upon to interpret or correct its award.[10] On the contrary, it may consider its duties to be at an end and itself to be *functus officio*.

The task facing an arbitral tribunal must not be underestimated; and the need for arbitrators to be both trained and experienced is plain.[11] The difficulty that faces any court or arbitral tribunal in deciding between conflicting versions of events and conflicting legal opinions is complicated by the international dimension necessarily present in any international commercial arbitration. However, there are limits to what may reasonably be expected. For example, an award may comply meticulously with the agreed rules of procedure and with the law governing the arbitration, but may fail to comply with some special requirement of the law of the place of enforcement, so that the award is unenforceable in that place. Is the arbitral tribunal to be held responsible for this? The parties themselves—and perhaps, in particular, the claimant—are more likely than the

---

[7] See, *e.g.* ICC Arbitration Rules, Art.26; ICDR Arbitration Rules, Art.31; LCIA Arbitration Rules, Art.32.2.

[8] *e.g.* ICC Arbitration Rules, Art.31.3; UNCITRAL Arbitration Rules, Art.38.

[9] ICC Arbitration Rules, Art.27.

[10] For further discussion of interpretation, correction and revision of awards see below, paras 8–100 *et seq.*

[11] See Ch.4, paras 4–42 and 4–46.

arbitral tribunal to know where recognition and enforcement of an award is likely to be sought. It is in their interests to ensure, wherever possible, that a requirement that is peculiar to the law of a country that is likely to be the country of enforcement is taken into account.

Definition of award

There is no internationally accepted definition of the term "award". Indeed, **8–05** none is to be found in the international conventions dealing with arbitration, including the Geneva treaties, the New York Convention or the Model Law. Even though the New York Convention is directed to the recognition and enforcement of awards,[12] the nearest it comes to a definition is:

> "The term 'arbitral awards' shall include not only awards made by arbitrators appointed for each case but also those made by permanent arbitral bodies to which the parties have submitted."[13]

This is helpful, but incomplete. At one stage it was proposed that there should be a definition of the term "award" in the Model Law, but ultimately none was adopted. One suggested solution illustrates the difficulty of finding a definition which encompasses not only final awards but also partial and interim awards that dispose of some issues only and leave others until later. The proposed definition was as follows:

> "'Award' means a final award which disposes of all issues submitted to the arbitral tribunal and any other decision of the arbitral tribunal which finally determines any question of substance or the question of its competence or any other question of procedure but, in the latter case, only if the arbitral tribunal terms its decision an award."[14]

As this proposed definition shows, the need to distinguish between awards that are final, and those that are not, is a complicating factor. The possible solution of defining each separately was not adopted. The Model Law also plainly contemplates that there may be more than one award in the course of an arbitration. For example, a plea that the arbitral tribunal does not have jurisdiction may be dealt with either in the final award or as a "preliminary question".[15]

If the tribunal takes the second course, then its award, which will presumably **8–06** be known as a "partial award" or "interim award" (or possibly as a "preliminary

---

[12] And of arbitration agreements: see Ch.3.
[13] New York Convention, Art.I.2.
[14] Broches, "Recourse Against the Award; Enforcement of the Award", UNCITRAL's Project for a Model Law on International Commercial Arbitration, ICCA Congress Series No.2 (1984), p.208.
[15] Model Law, Art.16(3).

award"), may be challenged in the competent court within 30 days of its notification.[16]

As may be seen from this example, important consequences flow from a ruling or decision of the arbitral tribunal that has the status of an award. The time limit for challenge of the award will begin to run; and, once the final award has been made, it may be impossible for a party to challenge some element of that award if it follows from an earlier interim or partial award which was *not* challenged. Moreover, only an *award* will qualify for recognition and enforcement under the relevant international conventions. It is thus important to know whether or not a particular ruling or decision of the arbitral tribunal has the status of an award.

In practice, the term "award" should be reserved for decisions that finally determine the substantive issues with which they deal.[17] This involves distinguishing between awards (which are concerned with issues) and procedural orders and directions (which are concerned with the conduct of the arbitration). Procedural orders and directions help to move the arbitration forward; they deal with such matters as the exchange of written evidence, the production of documents and the arrangements for the conduct of the hearing. They do not have the status of awards; and they may perhaps be called into question after the final award has been made (for instance, as evidence of bias on the part of the arbitral tribunal).[18]

"Order" or "award"

8–07   Distinguishing between an "award" and a procedural "order" may not be as easy as simply reading the title that an arbitral tribunal chooses to give to its ruling. In recent years, both the Paris Cour d'Appel and a US Federal Court of Appeals have classified certain arbitral decisions as "awards", and therefore susceptible to amendment and/or recognition and enforcement proceedings in national courts, even though they were entitled "orders".

The Paris Cour d'Appel decision in *Brasoil*[19] arose from an ICC arbitration under a contract by which Brasoil agreed to drill a number of wells in the Libyan desert for the Management and Implementation Authority of the Great Man-Made River Project. Brasoil commenced ICC proceedings following the Authority's termination of the contract in 1990. In 1995, the arbitral tribunal rendered a partial award finding Brasoil liable for the malfunctioning of the wells it had constructed. In 1997, during the damages phase of the proceedings, the Authority

---

[16] *ibid.*

[17] Some commentators have suggested that a preliminary award may be treated as "provisional". However, this concept seems to be fraught with perils; the authors suggest that any decision that is not finally determinative of the issues with which it deals should not be called an "award".

[18] If a party is aggrieved by a procedural order or direction it is sensible for that party to make a formal protest. In this way he will reserve his position in case it emerges, at a later stage, that the procedural ruling in question has, *e.g.*, denied him a proper opportunity to present his case or to respond to the case submitted by the opposing party.

[19] *Braspetro Oil Services Company v The Management and Implementation Authority of the Great Man-Made River Project*, Paris Cour d'Appel (July 1, 1999) *Mealey's International Arbitration Report* (1999) Vol.14, No.8, pp.G-1–G-7.

submitted certain documents that Brasoil alleged had been fraudulently withheld during the liability phase. Brasoil requested the tribunal to review its partial award on liability. In May 1998, the tribunal denied Brasoil's request in what it described as an "order". Brasoil sought to have the "order" set aside, and the Paris Cour d'Appel granted its request on the grounds that, although described as an "order", the tribunal's decision was in fact an award because it purported finally to settle a dispute between the parties.

> "The qualification of [a decision as an] award does not depend on the terms used by the arbitrators or by the parties . . . after a five-month deliberation, the arbitral tribunal rendered the 'order' of 14 May 1998, by which, after a lengthy examination of the parties' positions, it declared that the request could not be granted because Brasoil had not proven that there had been fraud as alleged. This reasoned decision—by which the arbitrators considered the contradictory theories of the parties and examined in detail whether they were founded, and solved, in a final manner, the dispute between the parties concerning the admissibility of Brasoil's request for a review, by denying it and thereby ending the dispute submitted to them—appears to be an exercise of its jurisdictional power by the arbitral tribunal . . . Notwithstanding its qualification as an 'order', the decision of 14 May 1998 . . . is thus indeed an award."

The Seventh Circuit Federal Court of Appeal's decision in *True North*[20]   **8–08** addressed similar issues. True North, a US advertising company, and Publicis Communications, an affiliate of the Publicis global communications group, entered into a joint venture in 1989 which eventually led the parties to arbitration in London. As one of its requests for relief in the arbitration, True North requested that Publicis disclose tax records filed with the US Internal Revenue Service and the Securities and Exchange Commission. In October 1998, the chairman of the arbitral tribunal, "for and on behalf of the arbitrators", signed an unreasoned "order" directing Publicis to disclose the requested tax records to True North. Publicis failed to comply, and True North applied to the court to confirm the arbitral decision. Publicis argued that the Tribunal's decision constituted no more than an interim order and that only finally determinative "awards" are subject to confirmation or enforcement. The matter ultimately came before the Seventh Circuit Federal Court of Appeals, which disagreed, reasoning that the finality of a decision was the key to its recognition or enforcement under the New York Convention. In so doing, it described Publicis's approach as "extreme and untenable formalism", and observed:

> "Although Publicis suggests that our ruling will cause the international arbitration earth to quake and mountains to crumble, resolving this case actually

---

[20] *Publicis Communications and Publicis SA v True North Communications Inc* (2000) XXV Yearbook Commercial Arbitration 1152.

requires determining only whether or not this particular order by this particular arbitration tribunal regarding these particular tax records was final. If the arbitration tribunal's 30 October 1998 decision was final, then [the district court judge] had the authority to confirm it. If the arbitrators' decision was not final, then the district court jumped the gun."

Referring to an earlier edition of this book, the Federal Court of Appeals noted that the arbitral tribunal's decision on the tax records was intended to be final, and stated that the fact that the "order" was issued prior to the conclusion of the arbitration was no bar to its enforceability or finality.

"The tribunal's order resolved the dispute, or was supposed to, at any rate. Producing the documents was not just some procedural matter—it was the very issue True North wanted arbitrated . . . the tribunal explicitly carved out the tax records issue for immediate action from the bulk of the matter still pending, stating that 'the delivery of the documents should not await final confirmation in the Final Award'. Requiring the unrelated issues to be arbitrated to finality before allowing True North to enforce a decision the tribunal called urgent would defeat the purpose of the tribunal's order. A ruling on a discreet, time-sensitive issue may be final and ripe for confirmation even though other claims remain to be addressed by arbitrators."[21]

(b) Remedies

8–09   Arbitration awards may cover a range of remedies, including:

- monetary compensation;
- punitive damages and other penalties;
- specific performance and restitution;
- injunctions;
- declaratory relief;
- rectification;
- adaptation of contracts and filling gaps;
- interest; and
- costs.

---

[21] *ibid.* For a commentary on this decision, see Reichert & Murphy, "Enforceability of Foreign Arbitral Decisions" (2001) 67(4) Arbitration 369, in which they conclude that: "this decision has clearly announced that all orders or awards made in the arbitral process are capable of recognition and enforcement abroad by means of the New York Convention, so long as the finality test is satisfied . . . when rendering any decision, it may be prudent to determine whether or not the issue is being dealt with finally, to recite that in the decision and, despite the approach of the Seventh Circuit, to label the decision or order as an award to ensure that no argument of form over substance can take place."

Monetary compensation

The type of award most often made by an international arbitral tribunal is one **8–10**
that directs the payment of a sum of money by one party to the other. This
payment may represent money due under a contract (debt) or compensation
(damages) for loss suffered, or both. The sum of money awarded is usually
expressed in the currency of the contract or the currency of the loss. In large
international projects, however, it is not unusual for reference to be made to
several different currencies; so that, for example, plant and equipment manu-
factured or purchased overseas may be paid for in US dollars, whilst labour plant
and equipment made or purchased locally may be paid for in the local currency.
In such cases, unless the parties agree, the arbitral tribunal must hear argument
as to the currency or currencies in which the award is to be made.

Punitive damages and other penalties

It is tempting to think that an arbitral tribunal has precisely parallel jurisdiction **8–11**
to a national court to award damages in accordance with the law applicable to the
substantive merits of the dispute. However, the powers of an arbitral tribunal are
not necessarily the same as those of a court.

Although arbitrators in New York, for example, may issue *subpoenas*, it is
difficult to see what punitive sanctions they may impose if they are not obeyed.
An arbitral tribunal has no power to imprison anyone, nor does it have power to
impose penalties in the form of payment of fines to the state. These are sovereign
powers constitutionally reserved to judges appointed by, and operating under, the
authority of the state itself.

By contrast, an arbitral tribunal may in certain respects have *wider* powers
than those of a judge, because the tribunal's powers flow from, *inter alia*, the
arbitration agreement. Thus, in England a court applying US law has no power
to order the payment of triple damages, a power provided under US antitrust
legislation.[22] But an arbitral tribunal sitting in England *would* have the power to
award triple damages provided the parties' arbitration agreement was sufficiently
wide to encompass the determination of US antitrust law claims.[23] It is necessary
to look at the law applicable to the substance of the dispute as well as the law of
the seat of the arbitration. Most arbitrations are concerned with breaches of
contract. In civil law countries, the concept of punitive damages is scarcely
known, whether in breach of contract cases or otherwise, with a limited exception
in some countries where there has been a wilful intention to harm the claimant,

---

[22] *British Airways Board v Laker Airways Ltd* [1985] A.C. 58 (HL).
[23] It would lead to an absurd result if an arbitral tribunal applying US antitrust law could determine
the liability under that law but not award the mandatory remedy provided for in that law. The point
was considered by a US court in *PPG Inc v Pilkington Plc* (1995) XX Yearbook Commercial
Arbitration 885.

amounting in effect to fraud.[24] Under French and German law, punitive damages are not recoverable. Under English law, punitive damages may be awarded only in actions in tort, and even then only in three categories of cases. Punitive damages may not be awarded in an action for breach of contract.[25] However, such claims are permissible in the US, where statutes may provide expressly for the payment of multiple damages by one party to the other.[26]

8–12   Thus, there may be occasional circumstances in which claims for damages in civil suits go beyond the concept of compensating the winning party for his losses. But two other matters arise in the context of claims for punitive damages in arbitrations. The first concerns the threshold question of the power of the arbitral tribunal to impose penal sanctions. The second relates to enforceability.

The question of whether an arbitral tribunal has the power to impose penal sanctions depends:

- on the law of the place of arbitration (the *lex arbitri*); and

- on the terms of the arbitration agreement.

The *lex arbitri* may be unsympathetic. In one case in the US, the court stated that "the prohibition against an arbitrator awarding punitive damages is based on strong public policy indeed."[27] There are also cases in the US in which the arbitration clause was held to be wide enough to confer an express or implied power to award punitive damages: for example, where the context of the underlying transaction manifestly implied that any dispute would be likely to incorporate a claim for multiple damages.[28]

8–13   The same principles apply in the context of an ad hoc submission agreement. Little has been disclosed publicly about the *Greenpeace* arbitration. This case

---

[24] In an ICC arbitration held in Geneva a claim was made for exemplary damages, but this claim was refused on the basis that: "damages that go beyond compensatory damages to constitute a punishment of the wrongdoer... [punitive or exemplary damages] are considered contrary to Swiss public policy, which must be respected by an arbitral tribunal sitting in Switzerland even if the arbitral tribunal must decide a dispute according to a law that may allow punitive or exemplary damages as such: see Art.135(2) Swiss Private International Law Statute, which refuses to allow enforcement of a judgment awarding damages that cannot be awarded in Switzerland... " ICC Case No.5946, (1991) XVI Yearbook Commercial Arbitration 97.

[25] For contract cases see *Addis v Gramphone Co Ltd* [1909] A.C. 488, with exceptions to the general rule at 495. For actions in tort see *Rookes v Barnard* [1964] A.C. 1129; [1967] 1 Lloyd's Rep. 28 (HL).

[26] Examples of statutes which provide for multiple damages in the US are the Racketeer Influenced and Corrupt Organizations Act (18 U.S.C.S.) ("RICO") and antitrust laws which provide for treble damages.

[27] *Garrity v Lyle Stuar Inc*, 40 N.Y. 2d 354; 353 N.E. 2d 793 (1976).

[28] *Willoughby Roofing & Supply Co v Kajima International Inc*, 776 F.2d 269 (11th Cir. 1985), in which an arbitral award of punitive damages for wilful fraud in the inducement of a contract was upheld and *Mitsubishi v Soler Chrysler-Plymouth Inc*, 473 US 614 (1985), in which arbitral awards of statutory treble damages were approved for antitrust violations.

arose from the sinking of the *Rainbow Warrior* by agents apparently working for the French Government. It is widely assumed that the damages awarded to Greenpeace were not restricted to the cost of refloating and repairing the vessel and other direct damages, and that the submission agreement was drawn widely enough to justify an award of punitive damages. But this case, even if published, would be of limited general interest in the present context since it was not a case arising out of a breach of contract.

With regard to enforcement, the key question is whether an award of punitive damages would be enforceable under the New York Convention in a country that does not itself recognise such a remedy. The ground for refusal of enforcement would be Art.V.2 of the Convention, which allows refusal of recognition or enforcement of an award if recognition or enforcement would be contrary to public policy. For example, in a leading judgment rendered in Germany in 1992, the Federal Supreme Court (*Bundesgerichtshof*) refused to enforce that part of a US court decision that provided for the recovery of punitive damages on the grounds that such recovery was contrary to German public policy.[29] The authors are not aware of any German court decisions relating to attempts to enforce a foreign arbitral award providing for the recovery of punitive damages, but the same result is likely.[30]

In summary, it is suggested that arbitral tribunals should treat claims for punitive damages and other penalties with considerable caution. They should examine the question of whether or not such damages may be awarded under the law applicable to the substance of the dispute. They should also address themselves to the threshold question as to whether or not they have power to make such an award, even if a claim for punitive damages is admissible under the law applicable to the substance of the dispute, by examining both the *lex arbitri* and the scope of the arbitration agreement.[31]

Problems concerning enforceability should be left for the courts at the place of enforcement. However, it would be wise for arbitral tribunals to treat any award in respect of punitive damages or any other penalties as an entirely separate claim, in order to ensure that the punitive portion of the award is severable in the event of a successful challenge in the courts at the place of enforcement.

Specific performance

An arbitral tribunal may be authorised by the parties or by the applicable law **8–14** (either the substantive law or the *lex arbitri*, depending on the conflict of laws rule applicable) to order specific performance of a contract. An international

---

[29] *Bundesgerichtshof* (Neue Juristische Wochenschrift, 1992), pp.3096 *et seq.*

[30] Similarly, Dutch courts have held that a judgment to pay punitive damages cannot be recognised and enforced in the Netherlands without further enquiry. See the decision of the District Court of Rotterdam, February 17, 1995, N.I.P.R. 1996, pp.205 *et seq.* (207).

[31] For a comprehensive review of the powers of arbitrators to award punitive damages see Gotanda, *Supplemental Damages in Private International Law* (Kluwer, 1998), pp.226–229.

arbitral tribunal sitting in the US will have the power to award specific perform-ance[32]; and English law empowers an arbitral tribunal sitting in England to "order specific performance of a contract (other than a contract relating to land)" unless a contrary intention is expressed in the arbitration agreement.[33] In civil law jurisdictions, specific performance (rather than contractual damages) is the principal remedy for breach of contract. The question of whether an arbitral tribunal is empowered to order specific performance is thus rarely an issue in international arbitration. However, the question of whether it is an appropriate remedy, and whether it can be effectively granted in the circumstances of the particular case, may prove less straightforward.

Restitution

8–15   Restitution represents an attempt to put the clock back; that is to say, it seeks to put the aggrieved party in the same position as that party would have occupied if the wrongful act had not taken place. In common law terminology it is a form of specific performance. In the field of commercial arbitration it is a remedy that is hardly ever used in practice—perhaps because international tribunals quite rightly tend to avoid making awards that are difficult to enforce. There have also been doubts as to whether an arbitral tribunal has power to award restitution. In England, at least, the question was resolved by the 1996 legislation: unless the parties otherwise agree, an arbitral tribunal has the same powers as an English court to "order a party to do or refrain from doing anything".[34]

A good example of the use of this remedy in public international law is provided by the *Temple of Preha-Vihaer* case, in which the ICJ ordered the government of Thailand to restore to Cambodia certain sculptures and other objects that it had removed from the temple on the border between the two countries.[35] Even in the field of public international law, however, the remedy is little used. It seems rather to set a standard for the assessment of monetary compensation:

"The essential principle contained in the actual notion of an illegal act—a principle which seems to be established by international practice and in particular by the decisions of arbitral tribunals—is that reparation must, as far as possible, wipe out all the consequences of the illegal act and re-establish the situation which would, in all probability, have existed if that act had not been committed. Restitution in kind, or, if this is not possible, *payment of a sum corresponding to the value which a restitution in kind would bear*; the award,

---

[32] While neither the Federal Arbitration Act nor the Uniform Arbitration Act expressly specifies the remedies available in international arbitrations taking place in the US (*e.g.* the UAA empowers arbitrators to "order such remedies as the arbitrator considers just and appropriate under the circumstances of the arbitration proceeding" (s.21)), courts have held that arbitrators have the power to award specific performance even if the arbitration agreement does not specify this remedy. See, *e.g.*, *Brandon v MedPartners Inc* 203 F.R.D. 677 at 686 (S.D.Fla 2001).

[33] English Arbitration Act 1996, s.48(5)(b).

[34] *ibid.*, s.48(5)(a).

[35] [1962] 6 I.C.J. 36.

if need be, of damages for loss sustained which would not be covered by restitution in kind or payment in place of it—such are the principles which should serve to determine the amount of compensation due for an act contrary to international law."[36]

In practice restitution is rarely ordered, since it is usually impracticable to restore the *status quo ante*. An award of monetary compensation is generally the best available remedy, particularly in commercial disputes. An apparent exception is the award of the sole arbitrator in the *Texaco* arbitration.[37] On examination, however, it is difficult to accept this award as a precedent for the effective granting of restitution in international commercial arbitration. The sole arbitrator found that the Libyan Government had acted in breach of its obligations by nationalising the company's property and other assets in Libya. He held that *restitutio in integrum* was: "both under the principles of Libyan law and under the principles of international law, the normal sanction for non-performance of contractual obligations ... "[38] Although this award reads well at a scholarly level, it has been severely criticised and, on the same facts, a different conclusion was reached in the *BP* arbitration.[39] The arbitrator's decision in the *Texaco* arbitration in favour of restitution is indeed hard to accept. First, whilst it may be practicable for a state to hand back objects taken from a temple, it seems wholly impracticable for a state to hand back to a foreign company oil fields and installations which have been taken over by the state and which are in that state's own territory.[40] Secondly, it must be doubted whether the award was intended to be enforceable. At a preliminary meeting with the sole arbitrator at which only the agents and counsel of the company appeared,[41] and in a subsequent memorial, the claimants stated (according to the arbitrator) that: "they intended that the present arbitration should be an arbitration on matters of principle, a fact which the Sole Arbitrator did not fail to note on the occasion of the oral hearings."[42]

It seems that the claimants themselves were seeking an authoritative legal **8–16** opinion on the merits of the case, rather than an enforceable award. There is no objection in principle to the use of the arbitral process in this way; indeed this was done, by agreement of the parties, in the *Aramco* arbitration. However, such cases cannot serve as a reliable precedent for most commercial arbitrations, where what is sought is not a legal opinion but an award capable of enforcement.

---

[36] The *Chorzow Factory* case [1928] P.C.I.J., Series A, No.17.1, 47 (emphasis added).
[37] *Texas Overseas Petroleum Company and California Asiatic Oil Company (Texaco) v The Government of the Libyan Arab Republic* (1978) 17 I.L.M. 3.
[38] *ibid.*, at 36.
[39] *British Petroleum Company (Libya) Ltd v The Government of the Libyan Arab Republic* (1979) 53 I.L.R. 297.
[40] This impracticability was recognised by the parties in the *Aminoil* arbitration (1982) 21 I.L.M. 976; to avoid any doubt it was specifically agreed that restitution was not sought.
[41] The Libyan Government boycotted the proceedings throughout, after claiming that the dispute was not arbitrable because the acts of nationalisation were acts of sovereignty.
[42] The *Texaco* arbitration (1978) 17 I.L.M. 8.

The relief sought and granted in the growing number of investor-state arbitrations confirms that monetary compensation, rather than restitution, is the principal remedy in international arbitration. By way of example, Art.1135 of Chapter 11 of the NAFTA provides that although a tribunal may award "restitution of property", such awards "shall provide that the disputing party may pay monetary damages and any applicable interest in lieu of restitution". Thus, the host state of an investment that is condemned under a Chapter 11 arbitral award will always have the right to pay damages in place of restitution. And so it has proved more generally in practice. A review of the ICSID Reports over the last decade confirms that restitution has only been sought in a handful of ICSID arbitrations, and has not once been awarded. Indeed, of growing relevance in investor-state arbitration is the very opposite question of whether a victorious investor must relinquish title to property that it has claimed—successfully—has been expropriated.[43]

Injunctions

8–17   There is no objection in principle to an arbitral tribunal granting relief by way of injunction, if requested to do so, either on an interim basis or as final relief.

Injunctive relief is addressed in detail in Ch.7. For present purposes, suffice it to say that an arbitral tribunal is not usually empowered to make effective orders against third parties; and if injunctive relief is required, it is generally quicker and more effective to seek it direct from the court. Most sets of international and institutional rules make it clear that the arbitration clause is not to be taken as excluding the jurisdiction of the relevant national court or courts to make orders for interim measures of protection.[44]

Declaratory relief

8–18   An arbitral tribunal may be asked to make an award which is simply declaratory of the rights of the parties. Modern arbitration legislation,[45] often makes express provision for the granting of declaratory relief. Even when there is no such provision, however, there is no reason in principle why an arbitral tribunal should not grant such relief. Indeed, declaratory relief has become a common remedy in international arbitration, with requests for contractual damages often coupled with a request for a declaration that there has been a breach of contract.

The *Aramco* arbitration provides an example of an arbitration in which the parties only claimed declaratory relief.[46] Aramco claimed that its exclusive right

---

[43] In this regard, see Rubins, "Must the victorious investor-claimant relinquish title to expropriated property?", *Journal of World Investment*, Vol.4, No.3 (June 2003), p.481.

[44] See, *e.g.*, ICC Arbitration Rules, Art.23; UNCITRAL Arbitration Rules, Art.26; see also the discussion of this topic in Ch.7.

[45] See, for instance, the English Arbitration Act 1996, s.48(3).

[46] For further discussion of this arbitration see Ch.2.

to transport oil from its concession area in Saudi Arabia had been infringed by the agreement made between the Saudi Arabian Government and the late Aristotle Onassis, the Greek shipowner, and his company. The dispute between Aramco and the Government was a serious one; but neither party wished it to jeopardise their trading relationship, which was a continuing relationship dating back over many years.[47] Accordingly, it was agreed that the dispute should be referred to an ad hoc tribunal of three arbitrators sitting in Geneva. It was further agreed that the award should be of declaratory effect only, with neither of the parties claiming damages for any alleged injury. The arbitral tribunal said:

"There is no objection whatsoever to Parties limiting the scope of the arbitration agreement to the question of what exactly is their legal position. When the competence of the arbitrators is limited to such a statement of the law and does not allow them to impose the execution of an obligation on either of the Parties, the Arbitration Tribunal can only give a declaratory award."[48]

A declaratory award establishes the legal position definitively and has binding effect as between the parties. It is a useful device, particularly where the parties have a continuing relationship and want to resolve a dispute between them without the risk of damaging that relationship by a demand for monetary compensation. It is capable of recognition, but it is not itself capable of enforcement; for the purposes of enforcement an award must also involve an obligation to pay compensation or to take, or refrain from taking, a particular course of action.

Rectification

Rectification of a contract is a remedy virtually unknown in civil law coun- **8–19** tries, where it tends to be treated in the same sense as adaptation of contracts and "filling gaps". In common law countries these concepts are considered separately. However, in general, an arbitral tribunal may make an order for rectification of a contract if empowered to do so by the parties.

If no express power is conferred by the arbitration agreement, the question of the arbitral tribunal's jurisdiction to order rectification requires closer examination. For example, a standard form arbitration clause that refers to "disputes arising under the contract" is probably not wide enough to include a claim for rectification, since what is sought by rectification is a rewriting of the contract to reflect what one party claims to have been the agreement actually made. The phrase "in connection with" in the arbitration clause may, however, be considered to give the arbitral tribunal a wider power. In England any doubt about the position was resolved by the 1996 legislation. An arbitral tribunal has the power to "order" the rectification, setting aside or cancellation of a deed or other

[47] The original concession was granted by King Saud of Saudi Arabia in 1933, for a period of 60 years.
[48] *Saudi Arabia v Arabian American Oil Company (Aramco)* (1963) 27 I.L.R. 117 at 145.

document unless the parties agree otherwise.[49] This express power to rectify is also reflected in the LCIA Rules, Art.22.1(g) of which gives arbitral tribunals the "additional" power:

> "to order the correction of any contract between the parties or the arbitration agreement, but only to the extent required to rectify any mistake which the Arbitral Tribunal determines to be common to the parties and then only if and to the extent to which the law(s) or rules of law applicable to the contract or arbitration agreement permit such correction."

Adaptation of contracts and filling gaps

8–20   The adaptation of a contract, or the "filling of gaps" in it, raises a different issue from that of rectification.[50] When parties have a continuing business relationship, but have failed to provide in their contract for a particular contingency that arises, it may be useful if they are able to refer to a helpful outsider, such as an arbitral tribunal, for a decision on how the contingency should be dealt with. In the same way, where the parties have entered into a long-term agreement (perhaps for as long as 20 years or more) but circumstances change, it may be helpful if they are able to refer to an arbitral tribunal for a decision as to what is to happen in the changed circumstances. The problems are different. In the first situation, there is simply a "gap" in the contract to be filled; in the second the contract may need to be amended, in whole or in part, to meet changed circumstances.[51] Nevertheless, in both cases the "helpful outsider" is required to perform an innovative role; that is, either to complete or to rewrite the contract for the parties.

In legal theory, the filling of gaps in a contract poses fewer problems than its adaptation. It may only be a matter of degree, but adding an additional term to the contract, on the basis that it meets the presumed intention of the parties, is a less speculative undertaking than actually *changing* the contract to meet new circumstances. In practice, it is thus a smaller step for an arbitral tribunal to *imply* a power to fill a gap in the agreement than to imply a power to change it. Most tribunals shrink from changing the terms of a contract unless the arbitration agreement contained an express power. In an English case, for example, a contract for the sale of chickens over a five-year period left the quantity "to be

---

[49] English Arbitration Act 1996, s.48(5)(c). See also the discussion of the scope of the arbitration clause and adaptation and filling gaps, Ch.3, paras 3–37 *et seq.*

[50] See Bernini, "Adaptation of Contracts" in "New Trends in the development of International Commercial Arbitration and the role of arbitral and other institutions", ICCA Congress Series, No.1, p.193; Klaus Peter Berger, "Renegotiation and Adaptation of International Investment Contracts: the role of contract drafters and arbitrators", *Vanderbilt Journal of Transnational law*, Vol.36, No.4 (October 2003), pp.1347–1380.

[51] In this context so-called "hardship clauses" must be distinguished as they deal with the situation deliberately left open by the parties for consideration at a later date. For further consideration of hardship clauses see Strohbach, "*Force Majeure* and Hardship clauses in International Commercial Contracts and Arbitration: the East German approach" (1984) 1 Journal of International Arbitration 40.

agreed" in subsequent years. The parties could not agree, and the court treated the failure to agree as a "dispute or difference" within the arbitration clause and thus capable of determination by arbitration.[52] However, the ability to adapt contracts effectively expands the competence of the arbitral tribunal into the area of varying or substituting the legal instrument that is the source of the tribunal's own jurisdiction.

An arbitral tribunal's ability to adapt a contract may derive from the law applicable to the substance of the dispute. In some civil codes, the doctrine of *rebus sic stantibus* is implied. It is said that the contract is binding "so long as things stand as they are". The express terms may be absolute, but if a vital change of circumstances has occurred, those terms may need to be adapted to meet the changed circumstances. The doctrine is well developed in public international law,[53] and stands as a qualification, so to speak, of the doctrine of *pacta sunt servanda*—that is to say, the doctrine that the express words of the contract must be obeyed.

By way of example, this was one of the legal bases upon which Indonesian **8–21** state parties sought to change their payment obligations under various independent power project contracts in the wake of the South-east Asian economic crisis of the late 1990s. Similarly, the concept of hardship, which is again common to some civil codes, also accommodates the judicial adaptation of contracts in certain circumstances. Article 6.2 of the UNIDROIT Principles defines hardship and its legal consequences as follows:

"Article 6.2.2—Definition of Hardship

There is hardship where the occurrence of events fundamentally alters the equilibrium of the contract either because the cost of a party's performance has increased or because the value of the performance a party receives has diminished, and

(a) the events occur or become known to the disadvantaged party after the conclusion of the contract;

(b) the events could not reasonably have been taken into account by the disadvantaged party at the time of the conclusion of the contract;

(c) the events are beyond the control of the disadvantaged party; and

(d) the risk of the events was not assumed by the disadvantaged party.

Article 6.2.3—Effects of Hardship

(1) In case of hardship the disadvantaged party is entitled to request renegotiations. The request shall be made without undue delay and shall indicate the grounds on which it is based.

---

[52] *F. & G. Sykes (Wessex) Ltd v Fine Fare Ltd* [1967] 1 Lloyd's Rep. 53. See also Veeder, "England" in *ICCA International Handbook on Commercial Arbitration*.

[53] See, for instance, Bin Cheng, *General Principles of Law as Applied by International Courts and Tribunals* (Grotius Publications Ltd, 1987), pp.118, 119.

(2) The request for renegotiation does not in itself entitle the disadvantaged party to withhold performance.

(3) Upon failure to reach agreement within a reasonable time either party may resort to the court.

(4) If the court finds hardship it may, if reasonable,

    (a) terminate the contract at a date and on terms to be fixed; or

    (b) adapt the contract with a view to restoring its equilibrium."[54]

In some long-term contracts, particularly agreements for the exploitation of hydrocarbon reserves, parties have included express adjustment or renegotiation mechanisms. Thus, by way of example, the Model Exploration and Production Sharing Agreement of Qatar of 1994 contains the following provision:

"Article 34.12 Equilibrium of the Agreement—Whereas the financial position of the Contractor has been based, under the Agreement, on the laws and regulations in force at the Effective Date, it is agreed that, if any future law, decree or regulation affects Contractor's financial position, and in particular if the customs duties exceed [ ] per cent during the term of the Agreement, both parties shall enter into negotiations, in good faith, in order to reach an equitable solution that maintains the economic equilibrium of this Agreement. Failing to reach agreement on such equitable solution, the matter may be referred by either Party to arbitration pursuant to Article 31."[55]

8–22   Whatever the legal basis may be for adapting a contract, however, in practice arbitral tribunals have proved very reluctant to substitute their own views of a fair allocation of contractual risk for that of the parties at the time the contract was originally concluded. One of the arbitral tribunals appointed to determine the Indonesian independent power project disputes that followed the South-east Asian financial crisis, put it thus:

"It is not for the Arbitral Tribunal to question the motives or judgement of the parties, but to assess their rights and obligations in light of their legally significant acts or omissions. *That is all; that is enough.* To go beyond this role would be to betray the legitimate expectations reflected in the Parties' agreement to arbitrate, and indeed to impair the international usefulness of the arbitral mechanism . . .

The arbitrators cannot usurp the role of government officials or business leaders. They have no political authority, and no right to presume to impose their personal view of what might be an appropriate negotiated solution. Whatever the purity of their intent, arbitrators who acted in such a fashion

---

[54] International Institute for the Unification of Private Law (UNIDROIT), Principles of International Commercial Contracts 146-51, (1994) 34 I.L.M. 1067.

[55] See Bernardini, *ICSID Review* (1998) 411. More generally, for a survey of examples of express contractual adjustment and renegotiation clauses, see Berger, above, para.8–20.

would be derelict in their duties, and would create more mischief than good. The focus of the Arbitral Tribunal's inquiry has been to ascertain the rights and obligations of the Parties to the particular contractual arrangements from which its authority is derived."[56]

The ICC has drawn up special rules for the adaptation of contracts, but also **8–23** takes the view that the role is not one best fulfilled by a conventional arbitral tribunal:

"One could simply envisage giving to a regular arbitrator the task here assigned to a third person when the parties have agreed to confer on him a power of decision and not of mere recommendation. But the arbitral solution in such a case has dangers because the uncertainty as to the category into which the task falls could raise questions as to the validity of the decision of the 'arbitrator'. Under some national laws, unlike those that have a broader economic and jurisdictional concept of arbitration, we find that a distinction, arising from Roman Law, is made between contractual arbitration and jurisdictional arbitration. Pursuant to the case law of these countries, only the latter would be considered 'arbitration' within the strict meaning of that term and within the legal consequences related thereto whereas the former would retain a purely contractual character and thus fall outside the scope of the rules applicable to arbitration."[57]

The ICC thus bases the power of a third party to adapt the existing terms of a contract, or to insert new terms therein, on an *express* power given by the parties; and it indicates that an arbitrator appointed, for example under the ICC model arbitration clause, may not have such a power because the applicable law may not permit it.

Interest and costs

An award for the payment of a monetary sum generally includes an award of **8–24** interest; and an award in respect of the other forms of relief discussed above may carry with it an award of costs.[58] Interest and costs are discussed later in this chapter.[59]

(c) **How an arbitral tribunal reaches its decision**

The purpose of an arbitration is to arrive at a decision. When an award is **8–25** issued, the first step that the parties and their lawyers usually take is to turn to the dispositive section at the end of the document, to find out whether they have won

---

[56] UNCITRAL Award of May 4, 1999, (2000) XXV Yearbook Commercial Arbitration 13 at 61.
[57] "Rules for Adaptation of Contracts" (1978) ICC Publication No.326.
[58] Although in proceedings for a declaratory award each side often pays its own costs and shares equally those of the arbitral tribunal.
[59] See paras 8–84 *et seq.* and paras 8–91 *et seq.* respectively.

or lost. For the parties and their lawyers, it is the decision that is important. Yet, in all that is written and said about arbitration—and nowadays a great deal is written or said—there is very little about how a tribunal of arbitrators goes about reaching its decision.

The task which faces them is not easy. A leading English judge has described the special features of judicial decision making as follows:

> "The judge's role in determining what happened at some time in the past is not of course peculiar to him. Historians, auditors, accident investigators of all kinds, loss adjusters and doctors are among those who, to a greater or lesser extent, may be called upon to perform a similar function. But there are three features of the judge's role which will not apply to all these other investigations. First, he is always presented with conflicting versions of the events in question: if there is no effective dispute, there is nothing for him to decide. Secondly, his determination necessarily takes place subject to formality and restraints (evidential or otherwise) attendant upon proceedings in court. Thirdly, his determination has a direct practical effect upon people's lives in terms of their pockets, activities or reputations."[60]

The same task faces an arbitral tribunal—but with this difference. In a tribunal of judges—a court of appeal, for instance—the judges are likely to have a shared legal background and for the most part to be of the same nationality. This is not usually so in major international commercial disputes, which usually involve a tribunal of three arbitrators (rather than a sole arbitrator).

8–26   First, such an arbitral tribunal is not a permanent court or tribunal—except in special cases such as the Iran–US Claims Tribunal. Secondly, the tribunal may be composed of arbitrators of different professions—accountants, engineers or whatever the case may require. Thirdly, even if all the members of the tribunal are lawyers, they will often be of different nationalities, with different languages and different legal backgrounds—the common law, the civil law, the Shari'ah and so forth. They may know each other personally or professionally—or they may, as often happens, meet for the first time when they come together as a tribunal, chosen to resolve a dispute which the parties themselves have tried but failed to resolve.

How will this disparate, ad hoc group of people set about trying to reach their decision? They will read—patiently or impatiently—the parties' submissions, the witness statements and the lever-arch files full of photocopied documents. They will listen to evidence and argument and after this, although—as the saying goes—they may not be any wiser, they should certainly be better informed.

As the case proceeds, each arbitrator will no doubt begin to form his or her own view as to how the various issues that have arisen ought to be determined; but this should not be a solitary process. The tribunal consists of three arbitrators. There must obviously be some exchange of views, some dialogue between them,

---

[60] Lord Bingham, *The Business of Judging* (Oxford University Press, 2000), p.4.

if they are to try to arrive at a unanimous decision. In this situation, no man—or woman—is an island. It would seem to be a matter of plain common sense that there has to be an interchange of views between the arbitrators, however it takes place, until—like a jigsaw puzzle—the pieces of the award are put together.

In French law, such an interchange of views is formalised as a "deliberation". **8–27** The Civil Code which governs French internal (or domestic) arbitrations requires the arbitrators to fix the date at which their deliberations will start (*"le mise en délibéré"*).[61] After that, no further submissions by the parties are allowed. Under French law too—as in other civil law countries—the deliberations of the arbitrators are "secret".[62]

For Professor Bredin, the distinguished French academician and author, the rule that there must be a "deliberation", before there is any award by the tribunal, is a rule of international public order.[63] For Maître Matthieu de Boisséson, the rule that such a "deliberation" should be, and should remain, secret is a "fundamental principle, which constitutes one of the mainsprings of arbitration, as it does of all judicial decisions".[64]

In adopting this approach, these distinguished French lawyers have the support of the rules of the International Centre for the Settlement of Investment Dispute (ICSID) which stipulates, in Rule 15, that:

"(1) The deliberations of the Tribunal shall take place in private and remain secret.

(2) Only members of the Tribunal shall take part in its deliberations. No other person shall be admitted unless the Tribunal decides otherwise."

In a well-known case before the Swedish Court of Appeal to which the Czech **8–28** Republic was a party, an attempt was made to set aside an arbitral award. One of the grounds put forward was that the arbitrator nominated by the Czech Republic had, as he alleged in his dissenting opinion, been deliberately excluded by his fellow arbitrators from the deliberations of the tribunal. In considering this argument, the Swedish Court of Appeal considered what was necessary for a proper deliberation. The court referred to two principles which might appear to come into conflict—the principle of equality amongst the arbitrators; but also the need for the tribunal to reach a conclusion without undue delay. The court said, in summary, that the arbitrators should be treated equally, but that the procedures adopted should also be cost-effective and flexible. There were no formal rules

---

[61] Art.1468 of the French Civil Code states: "L'arbitre fixe la date à laquelle l'affaire sera mise en délibéré."

[62] Art.1469 of the French Civil Code states: "Les délibérations des arbitres seront secrètes."

[63] Professor J.D. Bredin, "Le Secret du Délibéré Arbitral" in *Études Offertes à Pierre Bellet* (Litec).

[64] de Boisséson, *Le Droit Français de l'Arbitrage National et International* (1990), p.296. See also the comment in Robert, "L'Arbitrage: Droit Interne, Droit International Privé (5th ed., Dalloz), para.360: "Although it is practised according to a certain number of foreign laws, notably Anglo-Saxon, the dissenting opinion is prohibited in French domestic law since it violates the secrecy of the tribunal's deliberation . . . " (authors' translation).

and so the deliberations might be oral or written, or both; deadlines could be set, but could also be changed as required and so forth.

The Swedish Court of Appeal added that whilst due process must be guaranteed:

" . . . when two arbitrators are agreed upon the outcome of the dispute, the third arbitrator cannot prolong the deliberations by demanding continued discussions in an attempt to persuade the others as to the correctness of his opinion. The dissenting arbitrator is thus not afforded any opportunity to delay the writing of the award."[65]

The rule as to the secrecy, or confidentiality, of the tribunal's discussions is important.[66] It was considered by Sir Robert Jennings, a former judge of the International Court of Justice, in considering a challenge to one of the members of the Iran–US Claims Tribunal, whose impartiality had been questioned on the basis of a dissenting opinion he had issued. In the course of his decision on the challenge, Sir Robert held that:

"A rule of the confidentiality of the deliberations must, if it is to be effective, apply generally to the deliberation stage of tribunal's proceedings and cannot realistically be confined to what is said in a formal meeting of all the members in the deliberation room. The form or forms the deliberation takes varies greatly from one tribunal to another. Anybody who has had experience of courts and tribunals knows perfectly well that much of the deliberation work, even in courts like the ICJ which have formal rules governing the deliberation, is done less formally. In particular, the task of drafting is better done in small groups rather than by the whole court attempting to draft round the table. Revelations of such informal discussion and of suggestions made, could be very damaging and seriously threaten the whole deliberation process."[67]

8–29 As previously stated, there must obviously be some interchange of views between the members of the tribunal as they try to arrive at a decision which can be expressed in their award. This interchange of views may be characterised, as it is in the ICSID Rules and in the French Civil Code, as a "deliberation"; but this does not mean that the members of the tribunal have to sit together in solemn conclave, like Cardinals electing a Pope, until a decision is reached.

---

[65] *Czech Republic v CME Czech Republic BV*, Svea Court of Appeal, Case No.T 8735-01 (2003). An English translation of the judgment can be found at *www.sccinstitute.com/_upload/shared_files/ svea_court_8735–01.pdf* (see p.86), and a case summary is provided in the Stockholm Arbitration Report Vol.2003, at pp.167–195 (see p.180).

[66] See *Fouchard Gaillard Goldman on International Commercial Arbitration* (E. Gaillard & J. Savage eds, Kluwer Law International, 1999), para.1374.

[67] Decision of May 7, 2001, at p.7. A summary of the decision was published in *Mealey's International Arbitration Report* (May 2001). The full text is available for purchase from Mealey's electronic database.

What is likely to happen in practice is that the arbitrators exchange views informally, as the case progresses—and particularly in the course of the hearing—and then decide how to proceed with the formulation of their award. The chairman of the tribunal often prepares a list of the issues that he or she considers critical and asks the co-arbitrators to amend, or add to, this list and perhaps express a preliminary view on the issues raised—either orally or, more commonly in writing, with each arbitrator being given the opportunity to see and comment upon what the other has written.

There are no set rules as to how a decision should be arrived at. Each **8–30** arbitration is different; and each arbitral tribunal is different too. What works well with one tribunal may not work at all with another. However, what a former President of the LCIA has written may serve as a useful guideline:

"Once the evidence is heard, and counsel and the parties take their leave, the case is taken under advisement and deliberations begin. Indeed, deliberations must begin immediately—ideally, within the first hours of the close of the final hearing. While it is important for the chairman not to rush his fellow arbitrators into reaching a definitive decision on all outstanding issues—indeed, it is incumbent on the chairman to remind the members of the tribunal that their work is only just beginning and that any opinions expressed will be considered to be provisional—it is, however, crucial to ascertain whether or not a consensus seems likely to emerge on one or more of the issues to be decided. If there is disagreement between the two party-appointed arbitrators, the chairman will begin to earn his extra stipend. In the event a consensus on certain issues is clear, the chairman will generally offer to prepare a first draft of an eventual award, for discussion at a later date.

No member of the tribunal must exert any pressure on his colleagues during this first session. This initial session should provide an opportunity for all arbitrators to engage in a relaxed dialogue with one another.

Each arbitrator must feel that he is allowed to 'think out loud' in this informal setting. Personally, whether I serve as chairman or party-designated arbitrator, I tend to listen at least as much as to speak during such a first encounter. I wish my colleagues to know what my initial views are, but I also want to know how my colleagues believe they can inform the decision-making process which has begun.

Before this all-important session ends, the chairman, if he has not already done so, will undertake to draw up a list of the issues to be resolved by the tribunal. He may also ask his colleagues to prepare and exchange short papers setting out their preliminary views on one or more of the issues which have been discussed. He will also undertake to prepare a first draft of those chapters on the award which are non-contentious, for example, summarising the facts and the parties' positions drawn from their written and oral pleadings."[68]

---

[68] Yves Fortier, "The Tribunal's Deliberations" in *The Leading Arbitrators' Guide to International Arbitration* (Juris Publishing Inc, New York, 2004), pp.393 and 394.

8–31   Of course, where the arbitral tribunal consists of a sole arbitrator, the need to consult with other members of the tribunal and to try to reconcile possibly differing opinions does not arise. However, the sole arbitrator will still need to consider the evidence and arguments of the parties, work through a list of the significant issues and generally come to a conclusion on the matters in dispute as part of the process of drafting an award.

For a sole arbitrator, it is his or her decision that counts. But what happens when there is a tribunal of three arbitrators and, despite their best efforts, they find themselves unable to agree?

Majority voting

8–32   Ideally, decisions are made unanimously; but there must be a "fall-back" position and, on this, the international and institutional rules of arbitration differ. Some favour majority voting; others give the presiding arbitrator a decisive role. As an example of majority voting, the UNCITRAL Arbitration Rules provide: "When there are three arbitrators, any award or other decision of the arbitral tribunal shall be made by a majority of the arbitrators."[69] However, Art.31(2) makes an exception to this rule, in relation to questions of procedure and allows the presiding arbitrator to decide such questions on his own, subject to revision by the tribunal. This provision gives rise to two potential problems.

The first is that of identifying matters of procedure. For example, is a determination of the place of arbitration under Art.16 of the Rules a question of procedure or not? If it is, then, in the absence of a majority, the presiding arbitrator may decide. However, Dr Sanders, who, as the special consultant to the UNCITRAL Secretariat, had a major role in drafting the UNCITRAL Arbitration Rules, has expressed the view that the determination of the place of arbitration should *not* be considered a procedural question, and is therefore not within the competence of the presiding arbitrator alone.[70]

The second, and more substantial problem under the UNCITRAL Arbitration Rules, is the possibility that there will be no award at all, if a majority cannot be achieved because there is no fall-back position. Dr Sanders states that "the arbitrators are forced to continue their deliberations until a majority, and probably a compromise solution has been reached."[71]

8–33   This is a potentially serious defect in the UNCITRAL Rules, since there may be cases in which it is genuinely impossible to achieve a majority. In construction industry arbitrations, for example, there are often many different issues in relation to separate claims. It is possible for each individual arbitrator to have a different view on these different issues. Furthermore, the arbitrators could have widely differing views on questions of *quantum* in such cases, with no real possibility of any compromise solution being achieved in order to obtain a

---

[69] UNCITRAL Arbitration Rules, Art.31.
[70] (1977) II Yearbook Commercial Arbitration 172 at 194.
[71] *ibid.*, at 172, 208.

majority award.[72] The Model Law, which in Art.29 adopts the same position as the UNCITRAL Arbitration Rules, is open to the same criticism.

The approach in the ICC Rules is different. These rules provide that where three arbitrators have been appointed the award, if not unanimous, may be made by a majority of the tribunal and that if there is no majority, the chairman of the arbitral tribunal makes the decision alone.[73] The same approach is adopted in the Swiss 1987 Act, the English 1996 Act and the LCIA Rules.[74]

Under the ICC Rules and the LCIA Rules, the pressure is not on the presiding arbitrator but on the other arbitrators, to join the presiding arbitrator in forming a majority. This is because, if no majority is formed, the presiding arbitrator may make an award alone. However, if this happens, the arbitrators of the parties' choice will not be parties to the award. Instead the award will have been made by a person who has often been imposed on the parties by an arbitral institution or by some other appointing authority.

In ICSID arbitrations, majority rule also prevails. The Washington Convention **8–34** provides that: "The Tribunal shall decide questions by a majority of the votes of all its members",[75] and this provision is carried into effect by the ICSID Rules, which state: "Decisions of the Tribunal shall be taken by a majority of the votes of all its members. Abstention shall count as a negative vote."[76]

In the ICSID context, majority rule means that at least two of the three members of the arbitral tribunal must be prepared to agree with each other, whatever element of bargaining or compromise this might involve. An arbitral tribunal is bound to render a decision. It is not permitted to say that it is undecided and unable to make an award. It may not bring in a finding of *non liquet*.[77]

It may well be difficult for individual members of an arbitral tribunal to alter their respective positions so as to achieve the necessary majority. The notes to the ICSID Rules record that when the Rules were originally formulated, consideration was given to providing for the possibility of the arbitral tribunal being unable to reach a majority decision. It was concluded, however, that no problem would arise with questions which admitted of only a positive or a negative answer. If a positive proposition (such as a submission) failed to achieve a majority, it would automatically fail (since under the ICSID Rules, an abstention is counted as a negative vote). Where the question was not capable of being answered by a simple "yes" or "no" (as in the determination of the amount of compensation to

---

[72] An arbitral tribunal has no mandate to return a verdict of *non licet*; therefore, if it is not possible to form a majority, the proper course is for the arbitrators to resign and for a replacement tribunal to be appointed.

[73] ICC Arbitration Rules, Art.25(1). In such a case the presiding arbitrator's role is very similar, but not identical to that of an umpire. The difference is that an umpire is not required to make a decision unless and until the arbitrators appointed by the parties disagree. If they disagree, they take no further part in the proceedings and the umpire proceeds as if he was sole arbitrator.

[74] LCIA Arbitration Rules, Art.26.3; Swiss Private International Law Act 1987, Ch.12, Art.189; English Arbitration Act 1996, s.20(4).

[75] Washington Convention, Art.48(1).

[76] ICSID Arbitration Rules, r.16(1).

[77] Washington Convention, Art.42(2).

be awarded) it was concluded that "a decision can normally be reached by a proper sequence of votes by which alternatives are successively eliminated."[78]

The bargaining process

8–35   An award of monetary compensation arrived at by a majority vote is usually the result of a bargaining process, more common in a marketplace or *soukh* than in a judicial or quasi-judicial proceeding. To describe it as a process of eliminating alternatives by "a proper sequence of votes" is an attractive euphemism. However, it is a sensible way in which to proceed. Indeed, a similar procedure is envisaged in the Strasbourg Uniform Law, which provides that:

> "Except where otherwise stipulated, if the arbitrators are to award a sum of money, and a majority cannot be obtained for any particular sum, the votes for the highest sum shall be counted as votes for the next highest sum until a majority is obtained."[79]

The international and institutional rules mentioned above proceed on the basis that "two heads are better than one." Under these rules, and in the absence of unanimity, two of the three arbitrators must reconcile their views sufficiently to produce a majority award.

Thus, there are various ways in which the awards of three-member arbitral tribunals may be made. They may be made unanimously; or by a majority; or by the presiding arbitrator alone because he or she is empowered to decide alone, if necessary, under the rules governing the proceedings.

8–36   Where there are a number of different issues, it is theoretically possible for the members of the arbitral tribunal to be split on some issues and unanimous on others. In such cases, the question arises as to whether all the issues should be decided by the presiding arbitrator alone (if this is permitted under the relevant rules of arbitration) or whether the award may be divided into various parts. In general it is unusual for an arbitral tribunal to split its award into a number of different parts, in which the operative directions in the award have been reached by different processes. If there is lack of unanimity in relation to one of many issues, the award as a whole will usually be issued by a majority. If there is no majority in relation to a number of issues, the award as a whole should be that of the presiding arbitrator if the relevant rules permit; otherwise, the arbitrators will have to continue, in one way or another, to try to reach a majority decision.

(d) Tribunal psychology

8–37   Most international commercial arbitrations are determined by an arbitral tribunal composed of three arbitrators. The process followed by a three-member

[78] ICSID Arbitration Rules, notes to r.47.
[79] Strasbourg Uniform Law, Art.22.3.

arbitral tribunal in reaching a decision has already been described. The aim must be to achieve a unanimous award since this will be seen as both authoritative and conclusive. If unanimity cannot be achieved, however, the next best thing is to have a majority award, rather than an award by the chairman alone—or no award at all. In one of the Iran–US arbitrations, Judge Holtzmann concurred in a majority award, although he thought the damages awarded were half what they should have been. "Why then do I concur in this inadequate award?" he asked rhetorically; "because", he answered, "there are circumstances in which 'something is better than nothing'."[80]

The role of party-nominated arbitrators

Parties rarely abuse the arbitral process to the extent of nominating an arbitrator whose specific function is to vote for the party who nominated him. But **8–38** parties do appoint arbitrators whom they believe are likely to be sympathetic to the case they wish to advance during the proceedings. As has been said: "It should not be surprising if party appointed arbitrators tend to view the facts and law in a light similar to their appointing parties. After all, the parties are careful to select arbitrators with views similar to theirs. But this does not mean that arbitrators will violate their duty of impartiality and independence."[81]

As already explained, in an international commercial arbitration each arbitrator, however appointed, is generally under a duty to act impartially and to reach his determination of the issues in a fair and unbiased manner.[82] It follows that it would be improper for a party-nominated arbitrator to hold private discussions with the party who nominated him about the substance of the dispute. However, it is not improper for a party-nominated arbitrator to ensure that the arbitral tribunal properly understands the case being advanced by that party[83]; and a party-nominated arbitrator who is convinced of the merits of the case being put forward by the party who nominated him can have a significant impact on the private deliberations of the arbitral tribunal when the award is discussed. If he is genuinely convinced, he is more persuasive than one who is merely (and perhaps in a half-hearted way) doing what he sees as his duty towards the party who nominated him.

---

[80] *Economy Forms Corporation v The Islamic Republic of Iran*, which is referred to in Schwebel, "The Majority Vote of an Arbitral Tribunal", *The American Review of International Arbitration*, Vol.62, No.6 at p.923.

[81] Judge Richard Mosk & Tom Ginsberg in *Dissenting Opinions in International Arbitration* (Liber Amicorum, Bengt Broms, Helsinki, 1999), p.275.

[82] See Ch.5, paras 5–14 *et seq.*

[83] Indeed this is a material part of the duties of party-nominated arbitrators. A party nominated arbitrator should do his best to ensure that he himself understands the case being put forward by the party which nominated him, and should seek to make sure that the arbitral tribunal as a whole is in the same position. It is of course necessary for party-nominated arbitrators to consider carefully the merits of the arguments on both sides and not to be seen as favouring appointing parties. For further discussion of this subject see Smith, "Impartiality of the Party-Appointed Arbitrator" (1990) 6 Arbitration International 320.

The presiding arbitrator will form his own view of the case and will reach his own conclusions. However, if it is difficult to achieve a majority award, inevitably the presiding arbitrator leans towards a compromise with a party-nominated arbitrator who follows the proceedings intelligently, asks good questions of each party and puts forward well-reasoned arguments, rather than with someone who shows little interest in the proceedings and gives the impression of being there simply as the nominee of the party who appointed him.

2. CATEGORIES OF AWARDS

(a) Generally

8–39   Reference has already been made to the difficulty of defining an "award", and to the various different kinds of award that may be made during the course of an arbitration; and the point has already been made that, in a sense, all awards may be said to be "final" in that (subject to the possibility of challenge in the courts) they dispose of one or more of the issues in dispute between the parties.

(b) Final awards

8–40   However, the term "final award" is customarily reserved for an award that completes the mission of the arbitral tribunal. Subject to certain exceptions, the delivery of a final award renders the arbitral tribunal *functus officio*. It ceases to have any further jurisdiction over the dispute, and the special relationship that exists between the arbitral tribunal and the parties during the currency of the arbitration ends. This has significant consequences. An arbitral tribunal should not issue a final award until it is satisfied that its mission has actually been completed. If there are outstanding matters to be determined, such as questions relating to costs (including the arbitral tribunal's own costs) or interest, or further directions to be given relating to the disposal of property, the arbitral tribunal should issue an award that is expressly designated as a partial or interim award.

(c) Partial and interim awards

8–41   The power to issue a partial or interim award is a useful weapon in the armoury of an arbitral tribunal. A partial award is an effective way of determining matters that are susceptible to determination during the course of the proceedings and which, once determined, may save considerable time and money for all involved.[84] One obvious example that has already been given is where an issue of jurisdiction is involved; an interim award on such an issue may shorten or at least simplify the proceedings considerably. An arbitral tribunal that spent

---

[84] See the discussion of enforceability of interim awards in the US in von Mehren, "The Enforcement of Arbitral Awards under Conventions and United States Law" (1985) 9 The Yale Journal of World Public Order 343 at 362.

months hearing a dispute only to rule in its final award that it had no jurisdiction would, to put it mildly, look foolish (unless the issue of jurisdiction was inseparably bound up with the merits of the case).

The power of an arbitral tribunal to issue partial or interim awards may derive from the arbitration agreement or from the applicable law. Where the arbitration agreement incorporates international or institutional rules of arbitration, these rules generally contain provisions for the making of such awards. The UNCITRAL Rules, for instance, state that:

"In addition to making a final award, the arbitral tribunal shall be entitled to make interim, interlocutory, or partial awards."[85]

The ICC Rules adopt a similar formula, defining the term "award" to include "an interim, partial, or final award". In practice, partial and interim awards are frequently made in ICC arbitrations, particularly where jurisdiction is challenged or the proper law has to be determined by the arbitral tribunal.[86] The LCIA Rules follow the same approach:

"The Arbitral Tribunal may make separate awards at different times. Such awards shall have the same status and effect as any other award made by the Arbitral Tribunal".[87]

In an ad hoc arbitration it is usual to make express provision in the submission **8–42** agreement for the arbitral tribunal to issue partial or interim awards, if it sees fit to do so. Where the power is not conferred expressly upon the arbitral tribunal by the agreement of the parties, it may nevertheless be conferred by operation of law. For example, the English 1996 Act provides:

"(1) Unless otherwise agreed by the parties, the tribunal may make more than one award at different times on different aspects of the matters to be determined.

(2) The tribunal may, in particular, make an award relating—

(a) to an issue affecting the whole claim; or

(b) to a part only of the claims or cross-claims submitted to it for decision.

---

[85] UNCITRAL Arbitration Rules, Art.32.1.
[86] For further discussion of partial and interim awards in ICC arbitrations, see Final Report on Interim and Partial Awards of a Working Party of the ICC's Commission on International Arbitration (1990) 2 ICC International Court of Arbitration Bulletin 26. In particular, see the discussion about terminology. The term "interlocutory award" should never be used as it leads to confusion with procedural directions, which are not given in the form of an award. The terms "interim award" and "partial award" tend to be used interchangeably. If a valid distinction can be made, "partial award" may be used when the issue determined is one of, or part of, a party's substantive claims; "interim award" may be used to describe an award that determines an issue such as jurisdiction or applicable law. (All awards in ICC cases must be submitted to the court for scrutiny.)
[87] LCIA Arbitration Rules, Art.26(7).

(3) If the tribunal does so, it shall specify in its award the issue, or the claim or part of a claim, which is the subject matter of the award."[88]

Other modern arbitration laws contain similar provisions; and although the Model Law itself does not otherwise expressly refer to partial or interim awards, it is clear from the context in which the expression "final award" is used and from the *travaux préparatoires* that the draftsmen intended that the arbitral tribunal should have such a power.[89] However, if there is no express or implied provision for an arbitral tribunal to make a partial or interim award, either in the arbitration agreement, the applicable arbitration rules or the applicable law, it is doubtful that the tribunal has the power to do so.[90]

Issues concerning the applicable law

8–43   Another example of a situation in which the device of an interim award is likely to prove useful is where there is a dispute between the parties as to the law or laws applicable to the merits of the case. If this is not resolved at an early stage, the parties must argue their respective cases by reference to different systems of law. They may even need to introduce evidence from lawyers experienced in each of these different systems. In such circumstances, it is often sensible for the arbitral tribunal to issue a preliminary decision on the question of the applicable law.

Separation of liability and quantum

8–44   A further example of the type of case in which it may be convenient to issue a preliminary award is where issues of liability may be separated from those of *quantum*. For example, the determination of a particular issue of liability in favour of the respondent may make it unnecessary for the arbitral tribunal to investigate questions of *quantum*.[91]

If it is possible to disentangle issues of principle from issues of *quantum*, it is often worth doing. A decision by an arbitral tribunal on certain issues of principle in a dispute may well encourage the parties to reach a settlement on *quantum*. They are usually well aware of the costs likely to be involved if the arbitral tribunal itself has to go into the detailed quantification of a claim, a process that often involves taking evidence from accountants, technical experts and others.

However, there are very real dangers in attempting to isolate determinative issues at an early stage of the proceedings. The nature of the dispute, and the way in which the parties present their cases may change during the course of the

---

[88] English Arbitration Act 1996, s.47.

[89] Model Law, Art.32(1); see Holtzmann & Neuhaus, *A Guide to the UNCITRAL Model Law on International Commercial Arbitration* (Kluwer, 1989), p.868.

[90] It was perhaps to avoid uncertainty in this respect that some jurisdictions have amended the Model Law to provide specifically that the arbitral tribunal may make an interim award on any matter on which it may make a final award. See, *e.g.*, the British Columbia International Commercial Arbitration Act, s.31(6).

[91] See Ch.6, paras 6–35 *et seq.*

proceedings; and it is not unknown for parties to alter their case fairly radically, in order to take advantage of a preliminary award on liability. Where this happens, savings of time and cost will not be achieved and the result will be the opposite of that intended. Moreover, the process of rendering a preliminary award can itself be a time-consuming and expensive one. It is suggested that an arbitral tribunal should not normally decide to issue a partial or interim award on its own initiative,[92] but should only do so following a request by one of the parties. Where both parties agree that an interim award should be made, the arbitral tribunal must follow the agreement of the parties. Where only one party requests an interim award (and the tribunal has the power to make such an award), it should reach its decision as to whether or not to comply with the request only after receiving the submissions of both parties and giving each party a reasonable opportunity to explain its position.

Limitation clauses in a contract

Major commercial contracts—for instance, for the supply of a process plant or **8–45** for a construction project—often contain a clause that limits, or purports to limit, the type or amount of damages payable in the event of breach. A typical example would be a clause providing that in no event would loss of profits be payable. There may be occasions when a partial award on the meaning and effect of such clauses will help to limit the amount of the claim, and make the prospect of settlement more likely.

It is usually apparent from its content that a partial or interim award is only that; but nevertheless, the award should state clearly that it is such an award. As mentioned earlier, the issue of a final award normally renders the arbitral tribunal *functus officio*, except for the purpose of correcting minor or clerical errors. It is important not to allow either party an opportunity to claim that the arbitral tribunal has no further jurisdiction in the matter because it has issued a final award, when it intended to issue only a partial or interim award.

The main disadvantage of a partial or interim award, whether it is on an issue of jurisdiction, applicable law or other matter in dispute is that a further avenue for judicial review (and consequent delay) is created. Judicial intervention during the course of the arbitration may occur on an application by one of the parties to nullify (or set aside) the interim or partial award or on an application to confirm it.[93]

---

[92] Except in relation to issues of jurisdiction, where the respondent has not raised them, or has elected not to participate. *E.g.* in *Liberian Eastern Timber Corporation v The Government of the Republic of Liberia* where the Government nominated one of the authors as an arbitrator but then refused to take part in the proceedings, the arbitral tribunal examined its jurisdiction (as required by the ICSID Arbitration Rules, Art.42(4)) and issued an interim award.

[93] In the US a partial award for the payment of freight was "confirmed" by a court while there were still outstanding matters in dispute in the arbitration: *Metallgesellschaft AG v M/V Capitan Constante and Yacimientos Petroliferos Fiscales* 790 F.2d 280 (2nd Cir. 1986). The majority judgment lists cases endorsing the "proposition that an award which finally and definitely disposes of a separate independent claim may be confirmed although it does not dispose of all the claims that were submitted to arbitration." However, the dissent of Feinberg C.J. notes the dangers of piecemeal review of arbitral awards.

The Model Law limits the potential for delay by specifying that an application to review an interim award on jurisdiction must be lodged within 30 days of the ruling, with no appeal beyond the first level of court in which the decision is made.[94]

(d) Default awards

8–46   Occasionally, international commercial arbitrations are held in which one party (usually the respondent) fails or refuses to take part. This failure or refusal may be complete; that is to say, it occurs from the outset of the proceedings. Or it may happen during the proceedings, as a result of a change of mind or policy. Often the sums at stake in such arbitrations are large. Whether this is so or not, however, the task of an arbitral tribunal is made more difficult by the failure of one of the parties to take part in the proceedings. The arbitral tribunal is compelled to take a more positive role. In effect, the tribunal takes on itself the burden of testing the assertions made by the active party; and it must call for such evidence and legal argument as it may require to this end. The task of an arbitral tribunal is not to "rubber stamp" claims that are presented to it. It must make a *determination* of these claims. If one of the parties is not there to help, the arbitral tribunal must make this determination on its own.

The procedure to be followed where one party fails or refuses to participate in an arbitration has been considered earlier.[95] The importance of ensuring that the defaulting party is given, and is seen to have been given, a full and proper opportunity of presenting its case to the arbitral tribunal is clear. If the arbitral tribunal makes an award in favour of the active party in the proceedings, it will want to do its best to ensure that the award is effective. To this end, it should ensure, in particular, that the award recites in considerable detail the procedure followed by the arbitral tribunal and the efforts made by the arbitral tribunal to communicate the active party's case to the defaulting party, so as to give that party every opportunity to present its own arguments and evidence. Further, the motivation, or reasons, given in the award should (without necessarily being lengthy) reflect the fact that the arbitral tribunal has genuinely addressed itself to the merits of the case, in order to show that a reasoned determination has been made of the claims before the arbitral tribunal.

The award should also deal with any questions of jurisdiction that appear to the arbitral tribunal to be relevant, whether or not such issues have been raised by one or other of the parties. In this context, the ICSID Rules, which contain detailed provisions for default proceedings, expressly stipulate that:

"The Tribunal shall examine the jurisdiction of the Centre and its own competence in the dispute and, if it is satisfied, decide whether the submissions made are well founded in fact and in law."[96]

---

[94] Model Law, Art.16(3).
[95] See Ch.6.
[96] ICSID Arbitration Rules, r.42(4).

If these guidelines are followed by the arbitral tribunal, there is less risk of the **8–47** money spent by the active party in obtaining the award being wasted, as a result of a subsequent decision by national courts that the award is unenforceable.

(e) Consent awards

As in litigation, parties to an international commercial arbitration often arrive **8–48** at a settlement of their dispute during the proceedings. If this occurs the parties may simply implement the settlement agreement and in effect revoke the mandate of the arbitral tribunal. This means that the jurisdiction and powers previously given to the arbitral tribunal by the parties are terminated.[97]

In many cases, however, the parties will find it desirable or convenient for the terms of settlement to be embodied in an award. There are many reasons for this. The most important is where the terms of settlement incorporate an element of future performance by one or both of the parties, either in relation to the payment of sums of money or in some other respect. It is usually easier for a party to enforce performance by the other party of a future obligation if that obligation is contained in an award (in respect of which the assistance of the New York Convention may be available) rather than in a simple agreement. Other reasons for obtaining a consent award include the desirability (particularly where a state or state agency is involved) of having a definite and identifiable "result" of the arbitral proceedings, in the form of an award which may be passed to the appropriate paying authority for implementation. In this context, the signatures of the arbitrators on the consent award indicate a measure of approval by the arbitral tribunal to the agreement reached by the parties. This may help to meet politically motivated criticism of those responsible for taking the decision to reach a compromise settlement.

There should be little or no problem so far as capacity to compromise is concerned. Many countries adopt as their definition of matters which are arbitrable (that is to say, capable of resolution by arbitration) the concept that parties may refer to arbitration any disputes in respect of which they are entitled to reach a compromise. The reverse holds good. If parties are entitled to refer a dispute to arbitration, they are usually entitled to reach a compromise in respect of that dispute.

No restrictions are imposed by national law or international or institutional **8–49** rules of arbitration to the effect that, once arbitral proceedings have been commenced, the parties cannot terminate them by agreement. On the contrary, a settlement is invariably welcomed; and the possibility of having it recorded in an agreed award is offered to the protagonists. The Model Law provides for such an agreed award[98]; and the UNCITRAL Rules provide for a settlement to be recorded by an order or by an award if so requested by the parties:

---

[97] This follows from the consensual nature of arbitration, see Ch.5, para.5–30; and see below, para.8–49.
[98] Model Law, Art.30.

"If, before the award is made, the parties agree on a settlement of the dispute, the arbitral tribunal shall either issue an order for the termination of the arbitral proceedings or, if requested by both parties and accepted by the tribunal, record the settlement in the form of an arbitral award on agreed terms. The arbitral tribunal is not obliged to give reasons for such an award."[99]

8–50   The ICC Rules contain a similar provision: if the parties reach a settlement, after the file has been transmitted to the arbitral tribunal in accordance with Art.13:

"the settlement *shall* be recorded in the form of an Award made by consent of the parties if so requested by the parties and if the Arbitral Tribunal agrees to do so."[1]

The word "shall" is mandatory and suggests an obligation to record any settlement in a consent award. However, it is qualified by the words "if so requested by the parties" and "if the arbitral tribunal agrees to do so". This indicates that under the ICC Rules there is no obligation on either the parties or the tribunal to make a consent award. Under whatever rules the parties are proceeding, however, it would be a normal act of courtesy to inform the arbitral tribunal (and the appropriate arbitral institution, if one is involved) of any settlement agreement reached between the parties, particularly if meetings or hearings have already been held. There may also be sound financial reasons for doing what normal courtesy demands. First, notifying the arbitral tribunal of a settlement will ensure that it does not incur further fees and expenses (apart from any cancellation fees that may have been agreed). Secondly, such notification might lead to a refund of advance payments made to cover fees and expenses, since the actual costs incurred may well be less than expected if the case has been settled without a hearing. Thirdly, as already indicated, it is desirable to put the terms of settlement into an enforceable form when there is an element of future performance. Although most settlements involve immediate implementation of the agreed terms, it is nevertheless not unusual for there to be provision for payment by instalments or for some future transaction between the parties to be carried out.

8–51   A question occasionally arises as to the role of an arbitral tribunal that is requested by the parties to make a consent award ordering the performance of an unlawful act. Examples might be the manufacture of an internationally banned drug, or the smuggling of contraband or—perhaps more realistically—an agreement that manifestly contravenes relevant competition or antitrust laws. At one time various sets of rules (including the ICC Rules prior to 1998) seemed to leave the tribunal with no discretion, but modern rules and legislation allow the arbitral tribunal to refuse to make a consent award.[2]

---

[99] UNCITRAL Arbitration Rules, Art.34.1.
[1] ICC Arbitration Rules, Art.26 (emphasis added).
[2] *ibid.*

3. VALIDITY OF AWARDS

(a) Generally

An arbitral tribunal should do its best to ensure that its award is not only **8–52** correct, but also valid and enforceable. It may have to do so as a matter of legal duty to the parties, under some systems of law.[3] Or it may have to do so under rules of arbitration, such as those of the ICC, which (as already indicated) state that an arbitral tribunal "shall make every effort to make sure that the award is enforceable at law."[4] Whether or not there is a legal obligation the arbitral tribunal will want to do its best, as a matter of professional pride, to ensure that the award is enforceable; having been entrusted with the duty of determining a dispute for the parties, it will naturally wish to ensure that its duty is properly and effectively discharged.

As one senior arbitrator has suggested:

> "A valid yardstick for assessing the diligence shown by the arbitrators in drawing up an arbitral award that is enforceable and likely to be recognised, is to apply the criteria established under the New York Convention, since compliance therewith will enable recognition and enforcement of the arbitral award in all the signatory countries. Consequently, no arbitral tribunal could be held responsible in a case where its decision was not recognised in a given country for failing to fulfil some mandatory requirement imposed by that country's domestic law, unless the parties had expressly advised the tribunal of this circumstance, which should rightly have been taken into account when the arbitral award was drawn up."[5]

In certain circumstances, the award of an arbitral tribunal may be challenged in the courts of the place of arbitration.[6] In other circumstances, recognition and enforcement of the award may be refused by a competent court in the place or places in which such recognition or enforcement is sought. This subject is discussed in detail later.[7] The point to be made here is that an arbitral tribunal should bear the possibilities of challenge and recourse in mind when drawing up its award. Against this background, the validity of an award must be considered under two headings: form and content.

(b) Form of the award

In general the requirements of form are dictated by: **8–53**

- the arbitration agreement; and

---

[3] See Ch.5.
[4] ICC Arbitration Rules, Art.35.
[5] Cremades, "The Arbitral Award" in *The Leading Arbitrators' Guide to International Arbitration* (Juris Publishing Inc, New York, 2004), p.414.
[6] Or, exceptionally, if the parties have agreed to subject the arbitration to the law of a "foreign" country, in the courts of that country.
[7] See Ch.10, para.10–33.

- the law governing the arbitration (the *lex arbitri*).

The arbitration agreement

8–54   It is necessary to check whether the arbitration agreement specifies any particular formalities for the award. In practice this means examining any set of rules that the parties have adopted. The UNCITRAL Rules, for example, lay down the following requirements:

- the award shall be made in writing;
- the reasons upon which the award is based shall be stated;
- the award shall be signed by the arbitrators and shall contain the date on which and the place where it was made;
- where there are three arbitrators and one of them fails to sign, the award shall state the reason for the absence of the signature.[8]

These requirements are sparse by comparison with the requirements of the ICSID Rules which state:

"(1) The award shall be in writing and shall contain:

    (a) a precise designation of each party;

    (b) a statement that the Tribunal was established under the Convention, and a description of the method of its constitution;

    (c) the name of each member of the Tribunal, and an identification of the appointing authority of each;

    (d) the names of the agents, counsel and advocates of the parties;

    (e) the dates and place of the sittings of the Tribunal;

    (f) a summary of the proceedings;

    (g) a statement of the facts as found by the Tribunal;

    (h) the submissions of the parties;

    (i) the decision of the Tribunal on every question submitted to it, together with the reasons upon which the decision is based; and

    (j) any decision of the Tribunal regarding the cost of the proceeding.

(2) The award shall be signed by the members of the Tribunal who voted for it; the date of each signature shall be indicated.

(3) Any member of the Tribunal may attach his individual opinion to the award, whether he dissents from the majority or not, or a statement of his dissent."[9]

These two examples, drawn from institutional rules of arbitration, indicate the importance for the arbitral tribunal of checking the form (and contents) of its award against the relevant rules.

[8] UNCITRAL Arbitration Rules, Art.32.
[9] ICSID Arbitration Rules, r.47.

The law governing the arbitration

The requirements of form imposed by national systems of law vary from the **8–55** comprehensive to the virtually non-existent. The Swiss Concordat, which may still govern domestic arbitrations in Switzerland, lays down detailed requirements,[10] but for international cases these are narrowed to just four, namely that the award be in writing, reasoned, dated and signed.[11]

The English 1996 Act follows the same line[12]:

"(1) The parties are free to agree on the form of the award.
(2) If or to the extent that there is no such agreement, the following provisions apply.
(3) The award shall be in writing signed by all the arbitrators or all those assenting to the award.
(4) The award shall contain the reasons for the award unless it is an agreed award or the parties have agreed to dispense with reasons.
(5) The award shall state the seat of the arbitration and the date when the award is made."

The introductory section of an award

Awards usually contain a brief narrative setting out a number of facts relating **8–56** to the arbitration. These may include an identification of the arbitration agreement or document containing the arbitration clause, a brief description of the disputes that have arisen between the parties, the way in which the arbitral tribunal was established, with dates, and any specific procedural agreement of the parties or rulings of the arbitral tribunal.[13] The requirement that the parties should be identified is often fulfilled by giving the award a formal title on a separate title page.

Signatures

Some national systems of law require that all arbitrators should sign the award **8–57** in order for it to be valid.[14] This is highly unsatisfactory, since in such cases a dissenting arbitrator may frustrate an arbitration simply by refusing to sign the award. Any country whose law contains such a mandatory rule without any means of "rescue" is unsuitable for international arbitration.[15]

The rules of arbitration of the major international arbitral institutions all deal expressly or impliedly with signature of the award. The ICC Rules make it clear that the award must be signed, but that the award of a majority of the arbitrators

---

[10] Swiss Concordat, Art.33.
[11] The Swiss Private International Law Act 1987, Ch.12, Art.189.
[12] English Arbitration Act 1996, s.52.
[13] *ibid.*
[14] See *ICCA International Handbook on Commercial Arbitration.*
[15] This situation does not apply to countries such as Switzerland, which require an award to be signed but allow for the signature of the majority or the presiding arbitrator as the case may be: Swiss Private International Law Act 1987, Ch.12, Art.189.

or, if there is no majority, the award of the presiding arbitrator alone, is effective.[16] A similar provision is found in the LCIA Rules.[17]

Language of the award

8–58   The award will normally be rendered in the language of the arbitration, although occasionally it may be made either in the language which is the *de facto* working language of the arbitral tribunal or in the language that is most convenient for the parties.[18] Any mandatory rule of law of the place of arbitration concerning the language of the award must be respected. It is a condition of recognition and enforcement under the New York Convention that a foreign arbitral award must be accompanied by an officially certified translation into the language of the place in which recognition or enforcement of the award is sought, when this is not the language of the award.[19]

(c) Contents of the award

8–59   The contents of an award, like its form, are dictated primarily by:

* the arbitration agreement; and

* the law governing the arbitration (the *lex arbitri*).

The arbitration agreement

8–60   Arbitration agreements usually provide that the award is to be final and binding upon the parties. It follows that the award should deal with all matters referred to arbitration, in so far as they have not been dealt with by any interim or partial awards. However, arbitration agreements rarely go on to describe the content of the award. The nearest they get is to incorporate a set of arbitration rules. Such rules invariably also provide that the award should deal with such matters as the costs of the arbitration,[20] and the payment of interest. The rules may also provide that the award shall state the reasons upon which it is based.[21] Even if not specifically required, the giving of reasons is a practice that should be followed unless there is some very good reason why it should not be.[22]

Unambiguous

8–61   So far as national systems of law are concerned, the laws of most states require an award to be both unambiguous and dispositive. Ambiguity is frequently

---

[16] ICC Arbitration Rules, Art.25(1).
[17] LCIA Arbitration Rules, Art.26.
[18] See, *e.g.*, the UN/ECE Arbitration Rules for Certain Categories of Perishable Agricultural Products, Art.29.
[19] New York Convention, Art.IV.
[20] See, *e.g.*, UNCITRAL Arbitration Rules, Art.38; ICC Arbitration Rules, Art.31; LCIA Arbitration Rules, Art.28(2).
[21] See, *e.g.*, UNCITRAL Arbitration Rules, Art.32.3; ICSID Arbitration Rules, r.47(1)(i).
[22] For further discussion on this topic, see below, paras 8–63 *et seq.*

capable of being cured, either by the arbitral tribunal interpreting the award at the request of the parties (or occasionally at the request of only one of them)[23] or, alternatively, by an application to the relevant national court for an order that the award should be remitted to the arbitral tribunal for clarification. The position is similar where the award contains provisions that are inconsistent.

Effective determination of the issues

An award must also be *dispositive*, in that it must constitute an effective   **8–62** determination of the issues in dispute. It is not sufficient for the arbitral tribunal to issue a vague expression of opinion. The award must be formulated in an imperative tone: "we award", "we direct", "we order" or the equivalent.[24]

Equally, if there is more than one respondent and a monetary award is made in favour of the claimant, it is essential for the arbitral tribunal to make it clear whether one of the respondents, and if so which one, has the obligation to make the payment; or, alternatively, whether the obligation is joint and several.

An award should not direct the parties to perform an illegal act, or require the parties to do anything which may be considered contrary to public policy.[25] Nor may the award contain any directions that are outside the scope of authority of the arbitral tribunal.

Reasons

Years ago, when many national laws were simpler and less sophisticated than   **8–63** they are today, Lord Mansfield gave some excellent advice to his fellow English judges, which might equally have been given to arbitrators:

"Consider what you consider justice requires and decide accordingly. But never give your reasons; for your judgment will probably be right, but your reasons will certainly be wrong."[26]

Even today, there are arbitrations where the giving of reasons is likely to seem superfluous. An arbitrator in a quality arbitration, for example, who is asked to decide whether goods that have been supplied do or do not correspond to sample, can hardly do more than answer "yes" or "no":

"There are some arbitrations, those of the 'look-sniff' variety in particular, where there is really no room for the giving of reasons: tapioca pellets either

---

[23] See para.8–100.

[24] This is less important with a declaratory award, which by its nature is not enforceable *per se*; nevertheless a declaratory award should be clear as to its findings if it is to be of real assistance to the parties.

[25] However, since public policy considerations vary from country to country, it may be difficult to avoid this in all cases; an award of interest, *e.g.*, may be acceptable in the country in which the award is made, but not in the country of enforcement.

[26] Cited in Bingham, "Reasons and Reasons for Reasons: Differences Between a Court Judgment and an Arbitral Award" (1988) 4 Arbitration International 141.

are, in the experienced judgment of a trade arbitrator, of fair average quality or they are not; whichever way his opinion goes there is probably not much that he can usefully add by way of exegesis."[27]

Although he may not formulate them expressly, the quality arbitrator will have good and valid reasons for his decision based both upon his inspection of the goods in dispute and his years of experience in the trade; and this is the same, wherever the arbitration is conducted.[28] But this hallowed practice will not do in the world of international commercial arbitration. Internationally, the requirement is on giving reasons (unless the parties agree otherwise, which rarely happens). For example, the Model Law provides:

"The award shall state the reasons upon which it is based, unless the parties have agreed that no reasons are to be given or the award is an award on agreed terms under Article 30."[29]

8–64   The Washington Convention calls for a reasoned award, without any exception[30]; and in practice, the ICC's Court deems awards that are insufficiently reasoned to be defective as to form. They are therefore remitted to the arbitral tribunal for amendment before they are approved in accordance with Art.27 of the ICC Rules. The UNCITRAL Rules take the same approach as the Model Law: reasons should be given, unless the parties agree otherwise.[31]

The pattern is the same in national laws. Switzerland requires a reasoned award, as do the Netherlands and England, unless the parties agree to dispense with them.[32] In the US, however, the highest court has ruled that: "Arbitrators have no obligation to the court to give their reasons for an award."[33] An exception to this rule is where the parties have provided for reasons to be given in their arbitration agreement or in any arbitration rules they have chosen. The ICDR Rules require reasons to be given unless the parties agree otherwise[34] (although the AAA's domestic rules maintain the tradition in the US that reasons are not given).

The general consensus in favour of a reasoned (or "motivated") award is reflected in the European Convention of 1961, which states:

"The parties shall be presumed to have agreed that reasons shall be given for the award unless they

---

[27] *ibid.*, at 145.

[28] To this effect, see Delvolvé, "Essai sur la motivation des sentences arbitrales" (1989) 2 Revue de l'Arbitrage 149.

[29] Model Law, Art.31(2).

[30] Washington Convention, Art.48.3.

[31] UNCITRAL Rules, Art.32(3).

[32] English Arbitration Act 1996, s.52(4).

[33] *United Steelworkers of America v Enterprise Wheel & Car Corp*, 363 US 593, 598 (1960). US federal courts appear to have continued to rule consistently that arbitrators are "not required to justify, explain, or otherwise give reasons for the ... award"; see, *e.g.*, *Michael M. Pfeifle v Chemoil Corporation* 73 Fed. Appx 720 at 722 (2003).

[34] ICDR International Arbitration Rules, Art.27(2).

(a) either expressly declare that reasons shall not be given; or

(b) have assented to an arbitral procedure under which it is not customary to give reasons for awards, provided that in this case neither party requests before the end of the hearing, or if there has not been a hearing then before the making of the award, that reasons be given."[35]

Different ways of giving reasons

The way in which reasons are given in arbitral awards varies considerably. **8–65** Sometimes the reasoning (or "motivation") is set out with extreme brevity. However, a mere statement that the arbitral tribunal accepted the evidence of one party and rejected the evidence of the other, which was a common practice in some circles, had rightly fallen into disrepute by the end of the twentieth century. Certainly such a practice would be regarded as being defective as a matter of form by the ICC's Court. In other cases, awards may run into hundreds of pages, including a detailed review of the evidence and arguments put forward by the parties, followed by a closely reasoned conclusion.

The general practice of arbitral tribunals in international cases is to devote more time and space in the award to giving the reasons for its determination of the legal arguments than it devotes to a review of the factual issues. This is not surprising, since most arbitral tribunals in international cases are composed of lawyers.[36] However, it should be borne in mind by such tribunals that what is needed is an intelligible decision, rather than a legal dissertation. The object should be to keep the reasons for a decision as concise as possible and limited to what is necessary, according to the nature of the dispute. The parties want the essential *reasoning* underlying the decision, not a lesson in the law.[37]

(d) Time-limits

A limit may be imposed as to the time within which the arbitral tribunal must **8–66** make its award. When this limit is reached, the authority or mandate of the arbitral tribunal is at an end and it no longer has jurisdiction to make a valid award. This means that where a time-limit exists, care must be taken to see that either:

- the time-limit is observed; or

- the time-limit is extended before it expires.

The purpose of time-limits is to ensure that the case is dealt with speedily; such limits may be imposed on the arbitral tribunal by the rules of an arbitral institution, by the relevant law, or by the agreement of the parties.

---

[35] European Convention 1961, Art.VIII.

[36] Even where the party-nominated arbitrators are technical specialists, expert in the subject matter of the project or transaction, it is usual for the presiding arbitrator to be a lawyer.

[37] To this effect, see Delvolvé, *loc. cit.*; see also Bingham, *loc. cit.*; and for the risks that the alleged absence of reasons may lead to an arbitral award being overturned, see Redfern, "ICSID—Losing its Appeal?" (1987) 3 Arbitration International 98.

The laws of a number of countries provide for time-limits within which an award must be made, sometimes starting from the date upon which the arbitration itself commenced. In India, the 1996 Arbitration Act has dispensed with a time-limit that was imposed by the old law. In the US the position varies from state to state. In some states the limit is 30 days from the date on which the hearings are closed. However, time-limits in the US may also be extended by mutual agreement of the parties or by court order.

8–67 It is important that a fixed time-limit for rendering the award should not enable one of the parties to frustrate the arbitration. This might happen if a fixed limit were to run from the appointment of the arbitral tribunal rather than, for example, the end of the hearings. If a court has no power to intervene on the application of one party alone, and the time-limit can be extended only by agreement of the parties, a party might frustrate the proceedings simply by refusing to agree to any extension of time. However, the courts of many countries would be reluctant to invalidate a late award in such a case. For example, in New York it was held that an untimely award was not a nullity, even though the issue of timeliness was properly raised. The court stated that, without a finding of prejudice, there was no justification for denying confirmation of the award.[38]

Time-limits may also be imposed by the rules of arbitral institutions. The ICDR's Arbitration Rules and the WIPO Rules do not impose any time-limits for delivery of the award. However, the ICC Rules provide:

> "1. The time limit within which the Arbitral Tribunal must render its final award is six months. Such time limit shall start to run from the date of the last signature by the Arbitral Tribunal or of the parties of the Terms of Reference, or, in the case of application of Article 18(3), the date of the notification to the Arbitral Tribunal by the Secretariat of the approval of the Terms of Reference by the Court.
>
> 2. The Court may extend this time limit pursuant to a reasoned request from the Arbitral Tribunal or on its own initiative if it decides it is necessary to do so."[39]

The disadvantages of mandatory time-limits

8–68 It is rare to find time-limits for delivery of the award in non-institutional rules. Where such limits are imposed, it is usually by an express agreement between the parties, contained in the arbitration clause or the submission agreement. No doubt such a provision is inserted with the intention of putting pressure on the arbitral tribunal to complete its work with due despatch and in order to minimise the opportunities for delaying the resolution of disputes by the parties themselves. However, it is a strategy that may well prove to be counterproductive. In most substantial international cases before an arbitral tribunal consisting of three arbitrators, it is wholly impracticable to complete the arbitration within such a

---

[38] *State of New York Department of Taxation and Finance v Valenti* 57 A.D. 2d 174 and 393 N.Y.S. 2d 797.
[39] ICC Arbitration Rules, Art.24.

short period of time as three or six months. The result is that the arbitral tribunal may be forced into a situation in which in order to comply with the time-limit, it must issue its award without giving the respondent a proper opportunity to present its case. Such an award is vulnerable to an action for nullity or to a successful defence to enforcement proceedings. Thus the successful party finds that, far from the time-limit having assisted in a speedy resolution of the dispute, it contributes to overall delay and ineffectiveness in the arbitral process.[40]

In general it is preferable that no time-limit should be prescribed for the making of the award in an arbitration clause or submission agreement. However, if the parties consider it desirable to set a limit, or if it is necessary to do so under the applicable law, the time-limit should if possible be related to the closure of the hearings and not to the appointment of the arbitral tribunal or to some other stage in the arbitration at which the respondent will have opportunities to create delay. A provision that the award must be issued within a certain time after the closure of the hearings helps to ensure that the arbitral tribunal proceeds diligently with its task. It is frustrating for the parties if the arbitral tribunal takes many months to deliberate and to issue its award. However, any time-limit should be realistic and not merely one that incites the arbitral tribunal to make the award in too great a hurry, thus potentially exposing the award to successful challenge.

Non-mandatory provisions

Perhaps the best way for the parties to put time pressure on an arbitral tribunal, **8–69** without placing the effectiveness of the proceedings at risk, is to insert some form of non-mandatory provision. In one ICC case the arbitration clause contained a provision to the effect that " . . . the parties wish that the award shall be issued within five months of the date of the appointment of the third arbitrator."

The arbitral tribunal considered it necessary to clarify the position and, at its request, the parties confirmed that this provision:

- superseded the provision of Art.18.1 of the then applicable ICC Rules, which provided that the award was to be made within six months of the signing of the Terms of Reference; and

- did not affect the power of the Court of Arbitration to extend the time-limit provided for by the parties, in accordance with Art.18.2 of the then applicable ICC Rules.

In effect, therefore, the parties set a *target* for the arbitral tribunal in their arbitration agreement, without imposing any mandatory provision which might have placed at risk the effectiveness of that agreement.[41]

---

[40] For a potential horror story (which, fortunately for the winning party, turned out not to be so), see the commentary on *Kreindler v Kravitz*, "Agreed deadlines and the setting aside of arbitral awards", *ASA Bulletin*, Vol.4, 1997.
[41] ICC Case No.5051.

(e) Notification of awards

8–70   International and institutional rules of arbitration generally make provision for the notification of the award to the parties. The UNCITRAL Rules provide that: "Copies of the award signed by the arbitrators shall be communicated to the parties by the arbitral tribunal."[42] However, no time-limit is imposed within which this must be done. The position is similar under the ICSID Rules, which merely state that a certified copy of the award (including individual opinions and statements of dissent) will be sent to the parties "promptly" when the last arbitrator has signed it. The ICC Rules provide that the Secretariat will notify the parties once an award has been made, provided that the costs have been fully paid.[43]

The party which expects to have won the case will invariably make it its business to obtain a copy of the award as soon as practicable, either directly from the arbitral tribunal or from the relevant arbitral institution.[44] If that party has won, it will immediately communicate the award to the unsuccessful party. The time-limit within which a party may apply to the appropriate court for recourse against the award often runs from the date of communication of the award and not from the making of the award itself.[45] If this were not so, the possibility of injustice arises. The arbitral tribunal might make its award and then fail to communicate it to the unsuccessful party until after the time-limit for recourse had expired. However, the position should be checked under the law of the place where recourse may be sought, which is normally the place of arbitration.

(f) Registration or deposit of awards

8–71   In some countries, it may be necessary to register or deposit the award with the national court, generally on payment of an appropriate fee.[46] In other countries, registration for the purposes of recognition by the courts is optional. It may be a necessary prelude to enforcement of a foreign award. In such cases there may be an element of "double *exequatur*", which has been strongly criticised by the ICC and by the draftsmen of the New York Convention, amongst others.[47] The principle on which the New York Convention is based is that the award needs only to be binding on the parties in order for it to be enforceable. This binding force is generally considered to be acquired as soon as the award is no longer open to an appeal on the merits, to an appellate arbitral tribunal or to a court. Nonetheless, registration is a matter that may affect the validity of the award if the mandatory provisions of the place in which the arbitration is held require it.[48]

---

[42] UNCITRAL Arbitration Rules, Art.32.6.
[43] ICSID Arbitration Rules, r.48(1).
[44] ICC Arbitration Rules, Art.28(1).
[45] In England, *e.g.*, communication of the award to the parties is an essential ingredient, since the time-limits for challenging an award run from its delivery to the parties; see Arbitration Act 1996, ss.55(2) and 70(3).
[46] *e.g.* Germany, India, Indonesia; see *ICCA International Handbook of Commercial Arbitration.*
[47] See Ch.9.
[48] This must be considered separately from any requirement for the deposit of the award with an arbitral institution.

Where the requirement is mandatory, it *must* be deposited in order to protect the validity of the award.

Even when it is not mandatory, registration or deposit of an award may be desirable in order to put pressure on the unsuccessful party. In some cases, registration of the award is relevant for the purposes of the time-limit within which any application for nullification of the award must be made. Although registration will not necessarily assist the successful party in relation to enforcement actions in other countries, it may protect the award from any further challenge in the country in which the arbitration took place.

4. Other Considerations

(a) *Res judicata* effect of award

There are three different aspects of *res judicata*. First, the effect of an award 8–72 on existing disputes between the parties; secondly, its effect on subsequent disputes between the parties; and, thirdly, its effect on third parties.

Existing disputes

So far as the parties themselves are concerned, it is clear that (subject to 8–73 challenge before a competent court) the award disposes of those disputes between the parties that were submitted to arbitration.[49] If one party were to bring a court action against the other in relation to the subject matter of the arbitration, based on the same cause of action, the court would dismiss the action on the ground that the issues had been disposed of and were *res judicata*.[50] However, if the award is invalid and is set aside by a court of competent jurisdiction, the nullified award does not operate as *res judicata* in any subsequent proceedings. An example of this is the *Pyramids* arbitration, where the claimant started an ICSID arbitration after the award in the ICC arbitration was nullified in the French courts.[51]

Subsequent disputes

Where there are subsequent disputes between the same parties, more difficult 8–74 questions arise. Since there is no doctrine of *stare decisis* in arbitration, the previous decision of an arbitral tribunal will not be binding on any subsequent disputes that arise between the same parties. However, this does not mean that a

---

[49] See the commentary on the award in ICC Case No.3383, S. Jarvin & Y. Derains, *Collection of ICC Arbitral Awards 1974–1985*, p.394 at p.397.
[50] In France, Arts 1476 and 1500 of the Nouveau Code de Procédure Civile provide that an arbitral award has a *res judicata* effect with respect to the dispute that it determines. Similar provisions also exist in Belgium, Germany, Austria and Switzerland. See Hanotiau, "The *Res Judicata* effect of Arbitral Awards", ICC International court of Arbitration Bulletin: Complex Arbitrations, Special Supplement 2003, pp.43–51.
[51] For further discussion of the *Pyramids* arbitration, see Ch.9.

previous decision will necessarily be irrelevant to the resolution of a subsequent dispute between the same parties, particularly for the purposes of establishing an issue estoppel. Thus, the Privy Council of the UK decided that, notwithstanding a confidentiality agreement concluded by the parties to an arbitration not to disclose material generated therein to third parties, an award rendered in that arbitration could be relied upon by one of the parties in a subsequent arbitration to found a plea of issue estoppel. The second arbitration took place between the same parties and concerned the same clause under the same reinsurance agreement as the first arbitration. In so finding, the Privy Council reasoned that relying on an issue estoppel in a subsequent arbitration was "a species of the enforcement of the rights given by the [previous] award" and that this legitimate use of the earlier award was not a breach of the confidentiality agreement.[52]

In the US, courts have often applied *res judicata* (also referred to as "claim preclusion") to bar claims that could have been, but were not, asserted in a prior arbitral proceeding. Some US courts have also invoked principles of collateral estoppel (or "issue preclusion") to exclude issues raised in litigation that were previously adjudicated fully and fairly during an arbitration, thus rejecting the argument that procedural differences between arbitration and litigation prevent the application of general collateral estoppel principles to arbitral awards. A few exceptions apply to this practice, notably where the award is considered unreasoned[53] or fails to dispose clearly of the disputed issues. Nevertheless, even where an award is not entitled to preclusive effect, it may be admissible in evidence.[54]

Effect of award on third parties

8–75   An arbitral tribunal has no power to make orders or to give directions against someone who is not a party to the arbitration agreement, unless that party has in some way acquiesced in a manner which, without actually making him a party to the arbitration agreement, indicates an intention on his part to be bound by the award.[55]

It follows that an award can neither directly confer rights nor impose obligations upon a person who is not a party to the arbitration agreement. For example, the award of an arbitral tribunal in the main arbitration between an employer and a contractor under a building contract does not have the effect of *res judicata* in respect of a claim for an indemnity by the contractor against its sub-contractor in a subsequent arbitration. Although the facts in both arbitrations may be substantially the same, the second arbitral tribunal may come to a different conclusion from the first; and there is very little that the sub-contractor can do apart

---

[52] *Associated Electric and Gas Insurance Services Ltd v European Reinsurance Co of Zurich* [2003] 1 W.L.R. 1041.
[53] As indicated earlier, US courts have frequently held that there is no obligation to provide reasons in arbitral awards. See para.8–63.
[54] For a more detailed discussion of the preclusive effects of arbitral awards in the US, see Born, *International Commercial Arbitration, Commentary and Materials* (2000), pp.914–918.
[55] See Mustill & Boyd, *Commercial Arbitration* (2nd ed., 1989), pp.414–415.

from agreeing (with the consent of both parties to the main arbitration) to be joined as an additional party in the main arbitration. (This gives the sub-contractor the right to present evidence and argument in relation to any claims which affected it.[56])

Nonetheless, an award may often have a significant *indirect* effect on persons who were not parties to the arbitration. For example, a third party may be affected by an award where one person is jointly liable with another who is a party to the arbitration. The award would not be *res judicata* in any subsequent claim against the third party, but it should be of persuasive significance. Conversely, it is possible that an award (even if unsatisfied) against one of the persons who was jointly liable would have the effect of discharging the third party's liability. Finally, where an award orders performance (for example in relation to the delivery of property by one of the parties) it is doubtful whether it is effective if the property concerned is temporarily in the hands of a third party under a licence.

(b) Separate, concurring and dissenting opinions

A "separate" or "concurring" opinion is one that is given by an arbitrator who **8–76** agrees with the result of the arbitration, and so is willing to signify his or her agreement with the dispositive part of the award, but who either does not agree with the reasoning or with the way in which the award is formulated. Separate opinions are rarely given in commercial arbitrations.[57] They are more frequently found in public law arbitrations, where the practice of the ICJ tends to be followed.[58]

Dissenting opinions

Dissenting opinions pose greater problems. There is a broad division of **8–77** philosophy and practice as to whether or not the giving of dissenting opinions should be permitted. In arbitrations between states, the right to submit a dissenting opinion was asserted as long ago as the middle of the nineteenth century, in the *Alabama Claims* arbitration between the UK and the US. The Statute of the ICJ[59] expressly entitles judges in the minority to deliver dissenting opinions; and this right has been exercised frequently, not only in judgments but also in connection with procedural orders, advisory opinions and interim proceedings.

In international commercial arbitrations, arbitrators sometimes indicate dissent simply by refusing to sign the award. Dissenting opinions are less frequently delivered. Where this is done, the dissenting opinion may generally be annexed to the award if the other arbitrators agree; or it may be delivered to the parties

---

[56] For further discussion of consolidation of arbitrations see Ch.3, paras 3–84 *et seq.*

[57] Separate opinions frequently occurred in proceedings before the Iran–US Claims Tribunal; but the hybrid nature of this tribunal has already been noted at Ch.1, paras 1–131.

[58] The ICJ's Statute, Art.57, is generally interpreted as permitting the practice of giving separate opinions. See Simpson & Fox, *International Arbitration* (1959), p.227.

[59] ICJ Statute, Art.57.

separately. In either case, the dissenting opinion does not form part of the award itself. It is not an "award"; it is an *opinion*.

The position in national laws

8–78   The point has already been made that, in a tribunal of three arbitrators, there must be some "deliberation" between them, even if this takes the form of an exchange of notes or emails or telephone conference calls; and that the views exchanged during this deliberation should not be disclosed to the parties.[60] In France, it is sometimes said that the principle of the secrecy of the deliberations is such that even to disclose that the decision was unanimous is a breach of the secrecy of the deliberation.[61] This is not an approach that is favourable to the concept of a dissenting opinion; yet such opinions are given in international commercial arbitrations—even in France.

Modern arbitration legislation tends not to refer expressly to dissenting opinions. For example, there is no mention of dissenting opinions in the 1987 Swiss Act,[62] although a commentator states that an arbitrator has the right to give reasons for his dissent.[63] The Netherlands Arbitration Act 1986 similarly contains no express provision, but the authoritative commentary notes state that, whilst dissenting opinions are not customary in the Netherlands, they are not excluded.[64] No prohibition against dissenting opinions is known in the common law countries. Indeed it is not unusual for common law arbitrators to consider themselves under a duty to inform the parties of their reasons for any dissent.

The position under institutional rules

8–79   Of the world's arbitral institutions, ICSID is alone in expressly recognising the right of an arbitrator to issue an individual opinion and, in particular, a dissenting opinion:

> "any member of the tribunal may attach his individual opinion to the award, whether he dissents from the majority or not, or a statement of his dissent."[65]

The LCIA Rules do not mention dissenting opinions although, as the right of an arbitrator to issue a dissenting opinion is recognised in England, it may be assumed that the draftsmen considered that no express provision was necessary;

---

[60] See Art.1468 of the French Civil Code, which states *"L'arbitre fixe la date à laquelle l'affaire sera mise en délibéré"*; Art.1469 of the French Civil Code, which states *"Les délibérations des arbitres seront secrètes"*; and Professor J.D. Bredin, "Le Secret du Délibéré Arbitral" in *Etudes Offertes à Pierre Bellet* (Litec).

[61] Cass. Soc. November 9, 1945, Gaz. Pal. 1946 1.22. Note, however, Professor Bredin's comment that legal opinion on this point seems divided, "Le Secret du Délibéré Arbitral", *op. cit.*

[62] Swiss Private International Law Act 1987.

[63] Blessing, "The New International Arbitration Law in Switzerland" (1985) 5 Journal of International Arbitration 9 at 67.

[64] Sanders & van den Berg, *The Netherlands Arbitration Act 1986* (Kluwer, 1987), p.33.

[65] ICSID Arbitration Rules, r.47(3); Washington Convention; Art.48(4).

nor do the ICDR or ICC Rules contain any provision relating to dissenting opinions.

The practice in ICC arbitrations

The question of how dissenting opinions should be handled in ICC arbitrations **8–80** requires special consideration, in view of the provisions of the ICC Rules relating to scrutiny of awards.[66] Should the ICC's Court "scrutinise" the dissenting opinion, or indeed take any notice of it at all? At one time, the ICC discouraged the submission of dissenting opinions; but in 1985 a Working Party was set up to consider dissenting opinions and its Final Report was adopted in 1988.[67] As might be expected, the Report made a series of sensible suggestions. It did not attempt to rule out dissenting opinions; and it suggested that the only circumstances in which a dissenting opinion should not be sent to the parties with the award was where such opinions were prohibited by law or where the validity of the award might be imperilled, either in the place of arbitration or—to the extent that this could be foreseen—in the country of enforcement. The ICC has issued guidelines to its staff which reflect the conclusions of the Working Group, and in practice dissenting opinions are sent out by the ICC with the majority award.

Practice at the Iran–United States Claims Tribunal

Separate and dissenting opinions were submitted by both the Iranian and US **8–81** arbitrators in many reported cases. In some of these, the dissenting arbitrator went too far, as shown by the decision of Sir Robert Jennings referred to earlier in this chapter.[68] In at least one case, problems were also caused when the dissenting opinion was issued after the majority decision and contained allegations of procedural misconduct on the part of the majority arbitrators. The majority arbitrators felt compelled to file an additional opinion, whereupon the dissenting arbitrator continued the process by issuing yet another opinion! This was in turn followed by a second additional opinion by the chairman who, whilst stating that he would make no further response, indicated that he considered this exceptional procedure to be necessary to vindicate the integrity of the tribunal and its staff, and to answer allegations which were factually incorrect.[69] Acrimonious trading of allegations and insults could go on indefinitely, and it is clearly desirable that the arbitrators should disclose their concerns to each other in an exchange of draft opinions *before* the formal issue of the majority award and the dissenting opinion.

---

[66] The ICC Arbitration Rules, Art.27, provides that no award shall be rendered by the arbitral tribunal until it has been approved by the ICC's Court.
[67] Final Report of the Working Party on Dissenting Opinions (1991) ICC International Court of Arbitration Bulletin, Vol.2, No.1 at p.32.
[68] See para.8–28.
[69] *Grainger Associates v The Islamic Republic of Iran* (1987) 16 Iran–US C.T.R. 317.

When and how should dissenting opinions be given in international arbitrations?

8–82   As already indicated, there is no tradition of dissenting opinions in the civil law.[70] Dissenting opinions have come to international commercial arbitration as a gift of the common law. Has this gift added value to the arbitral process?[71] The traditional justification for dissenting opinions in common law judicial systems is that they may contribute to the development of the law. Although rare, there are examples of higher courts adopting dissenting opinions rather than the judgment of the majority. It might well be said—particularly by common lawyers—that if dissenting opinions can contribute in this way to a national judicial system of justice, why might they not also contribute to the system of international arbitration? To this there are at least three responses.

First, in most cases there is no appeal from the award of an arbitral tribunal and, moreover, there exists no system of *stare decisis* in international arbitration. A dissenting opinion cannot therefore inform an appellate arbitral jurisdiction, nor will it guide future arbitral tribunals searching for the wisdom of precedent. Dissenting opinions, thus, have far less to contribute to the arbitral process than to a common law judicial system.

Secondly, rather than contribute to the arbitral process, dissenting opinions may endanger the efficacy of the process by threatening the validity and enforceability of the award. One might imagine an argument in response to this concern along the following lines: if an award is flawed, then a dissenting arbitrator has a right—indeed perhaps even a duty—to provide ammunition that may assist the losing party in challenging the award. However, such an argument ignores the very purpose of an arbitration, which is to arrive at a determinative decision. Depending on the rules of arbitration agreed by the parties, that decision can be a majority decision, or the decision of the presiding arbitrator alone. It is that *decision* which matters; and it matters not as a guide to the opinions of a particular arbitrator, or as an indication of the future development of the law, but because it resolves the particular dispute that divides the parties, in the manner chosen by the parties, even if one of the arbitrators believes that decision to be wrong.

8–83   The third and final reason is more sensitive, and follows from the different way in which arbitrators—as opposed to judges—are appointed. Judges are appointed by the state. They do not depend in any way on the parties who appear before them. In an international commercial arbitration, by contrast, two of the three members of the tribunal will usually have been appointed (or nominated) by the parties, and it is those parties who will pay the fees and expenses of the arbitrators. When a dissenting arbitrator disagrees with the majority, and does so in terms which favour the party which appointed him or her, it may cause some

---

[70] Levy "Dissenting Opinions in International Arbitration in Switzerland" (1989) 5 Arbitration International 35.

[71] This question was asked and answered in Alan Redfern's 2003 Queen Mary College/Freshfields Lecture entitled "Dissenting Opinions in International Commercial Arbitration: The Good, The Bad and The Ugly".

concern: does the dissent arises from an honest difference of opinion or is it influenced by a desire to keep favour with the party which appointed the dissenting arbitrator? As Maître Matthieu de Boisséson has said:

"Certain arbitrators, so as not to lose the confidence of the company or the state which appointed them, will be tempted, if they have not put their point of view successfully in the course of the tribunal's deliberation, systematically to draw up a dissenting opinion and to insist that it be communicated to the parties."[72]

Other authors concur:

"Although party-appointed arbitrators are supposed to be impartial and independent in international arbitrations, some believe that with the availability of dissent, arbitrators may feel pressure to support the party that appointed them and to disclose that support."[73]

The efficacy (and some would argue the integrity) of the arbitral process militates against the giving of dissenting opinions other than in exceptional circumstances. For the same reasons, any dissent that is made should not take the form of an alternative award. On the contrary, it should ideally be short, polite and restrained, so as to permit an arbitrator to express his or her disagreement without imperilling the authority of the award arrived at by the majority.

(c) Interest

The payment of interest on a loan, or in respect of money that is paid later than **8–84** it should have been, is a common feature of modern business relationships; and the award of interest in international arbitration has likewise become routine.[74] Indeed it has become rare for interest not to be awarded where an award provides for the payment of monies due. As one leading international arbitrator has said:

"In all international commercial arbitrations where a claim for the payment of money is advanced, whether debt or damages, it is highly probable that the

---

[72] de Boisséson, *Le Droit Français de l'Arbitrage National et International* (1998), p.802 (translation by the authors).

[73] Judge Richard Mosk & Tom Ginsberg *Dissenting Opinions in International Arbitration* (Liber Amicorum Bengt Broms, Finnish Branch of the International Law Association, Helsinki, 1999), p.275. See also de Boisséson *Le Droit Français de l'Arbitrage National et International* (1998), p.802.

[74] The exceptions to this are arbitrations in which Islamic law may be applicable, and in respect of which the law against usury ("riba") may prevent the levying of interest. See Samir Saleh, "The recognition and enforcement of foreign arbitral awards in the States of the Arab Middle East" in *Contemporary Problems in International Arbitration* (1986), pp.348, 349. See, however, the decision of the English courts in *Sanghi Polyesters Ltd (India) v The International Investor KCFC (Kuwait)* [2000] 1 Lloyd's Rep. 480, which suggests that, even in some Islamic jurisdictions, interest may be awarded under another name.

claimant has also suffered a financial loss resulting from late payment of the principal amount. That loss can amount to a significant proportion of the total claim; and in certain cases, it can exceed the principal amount. In a modern arbitration regime, it is unthinkable that a claimant should not have the right to recover that loss in the form of interest."[75]

The basis upon which interest can be awarded

8–85   The basis upon which interest is awarded in international arbitration does, however, vary. Most institutional rules of arbitration do not contain express provisions for the payment of interest, largely because their draftsmen assumed that an arbitral tribunal has the power to make an award in respect of interest in just the same way as it has the power to make an award in respect of any other claims submitted to it.[76] The right to interest will therefore flow from the parties' underlying contract (*i.e.* from a contractual provision for the levying of late payment interest), or by virtue of applicable law. The law which governs the power of a tribunal to award interest will itself vary. In some jurisdictions, for example Bermuda, Hong Kong, England and Scotland, the power to award interest is governed by the law of the place of arbitration.[77] In others, for example under German conflict of law rules, the liability to pay interest is a question of substantive law, and thus governed by the law of the contract.[78]

How much interest to award

8–86   More problematic in practice than the question of whether an arbitral tribunal can award interest in principle, are the more practical questions of what rate of interest to award, from what start date and in which currency. Most applicable laws will leave these questions to the tribunal's discretion. Thus, the English Arbitration Act 1996 empowers a tribunal seated in England to award interest "from such dates, at such rates and with such rests as it considers meets the justice of the case".[79] Similarly, the law of Australia permits a tribunal to award interest "at such reasonable rate as the tribunal determine for the whole or any part of the money, for the whole or any part of the period between the date on which the cause of action arose and the date on which the award is made" and

---

[75] Veeder, "Whose Arbitration is it Anyway: The Parties or the Arbitration Tribunal—an Interesting Question?" in *The Leading Arbitrators' Guide to International Arbitration* (Juris Publishing, 2004), p.354.

[76] Exceptionally, the LCIA Arbitration Rules provide at Art.26.6 that the arbitral tribunal may award compound interest, not limited to the period up to the date of the award. For a discussion of compound interest, see paras 8–87 *et seq.*

[77] See, *e.g.*, the English Arbitration Act 1996, s.49.

[78] Accordingly, under German conflict of laws rules, if an arbitral tribunal sitting in Germany concluded that the substantive law of the contract was English, it would apply not only those rules of English law governing interest which English law classifies as substantive, but also those rules which English law classifies as procedural, because a court of arbitral tribunal sitting in Germany would classify such *procedural* rules as being of a *substantive* nature for this purpose.

[79] English Arbitration Act 1996, s.49(3). Almost identical provisions are found in the Irish Arbitration (International) Commercial Act 1998, s.10(2).

thereafter "from the day of the making of the award or such later day as the tribunal specifies, on so much of the money as is from time to time unpaid".[80] Other jurisdictions such as Hong Kong, India and Singapore have also enacted laws that give arbitrators similar discretion in the award of interest.[81]

In exercising this discretion, the tribunal will typically invite submissions and evidence from the parties on these issues in the same way as it would in respect of any other request for relief. Thus, parties will typically have an opportunity to set out their respective positions on the rate of interest to be applied, the period for which it should be applied and whether a different rate (for example a statutory legal interest rate) should be applied for the period following the rendering of an award up until payment. In making such submissions, parties would do well to make an award of interest as easy for a tribunal as possible by providing the calculations upon which such an award would be based (complete, if appropriate, with the calculation of an amount of interest that would accrue daily until satisfaction of an award).[82]

Compound interest

Most systems of national law expressly permit arbitral tribunals to award some **8–87** form of interest on an amount awarded in respect of a claim or counterclaim, whether the principal amount awarded is due under a contract or as compensation or as restitution. However, the award of compound—as opposed to simple—interest remains less clear.[83] Although the UNCITRAL Model Law does not contain any express provisions concerning interest, recent arbitration legislation in common law jurisdictions such as England, Ireland, Hong Kong and Bermuda give arbitral tribunals express power to award compound interest. Thus, s.49 of the English Arbitration Act 1996 provides that "unless otherwise agreed by the parties . . . the tribunal may award simple or compound interest from such dates, at such rates and with such rests as it considers meets the justice of the case". This is, however, by no means a feature of all common law jurisdictions. In Canada and the US, the power to award compound interest varies from state to state and province to province; and in Australia and New Zealand the power to award compound interest (if any) is very limited indeed. In civil law jurisdictions, arbitral tribunals typically have the power to award a statutory (or legal) rate of interest, which is simple interest at a rate defined by statute. Like the

---

[80] Australian International Arbitration Acts 1974–1989, ss.25(1) and 26; equivalent provisions are also found in the Maltese Arbitration Act 1996, ss.63(1) and 64.

[81] Hong Kong Arbitration Ordinance 1997, Ch.341, ss.2GH and 2GI; Indian Arbitration and Conciliation Act 1996, s.31(7)(a) and (b); Singapore International Arbitration Act (Ch.143A) 2002, ss.12(5)(b) and 20.

[82] As Professor Park observed in his 2002 Freshfields Lecture, there are in theory three kinds of arbitrators: those who can count, and those who cannot. See Park "Arbitration's Protean Nature: The Value of Rules and the Risks of Discretion" (2003) 19 Arbitration International 279.

[83] For the avoidance of doubt, compounding interest involves capitalising interest, and accruing further interest on such capitalised interest. The difference between simple and compound interest can be significant where the amount in dispute is large and the time periods involved are lengthy.

common law, however, there are once again exceptions to the rule: the Dutch and Japanese civil codes provide, for example, that statutory interest is automatically capitalised at the end of each year. Moreover, an ICC arbitral tribunal in Geneva awarded compound interest in a dispute between a state party and a French entity on the application of trade usage under Art.13 of the ICC Rules.[84] Sources of international law are no clearer. Article 38 of the International Law Commission's *Draft Articles on Responsibility of States for Internationally Wrongful Acts*, provides simply that: "interest shall be payable on any principal sum when necessary in order to ensure full reparation".[85]

Although the law on this issue varies from jurisdiction to jurisdiction, awards of compound interest are becoming less rare. In the *Santa Elena* arbitration, an international tribunal found that, although simple interest seems to be awarded more frequently than compound: "no uniform rule of law has emerged from the practice in international arbitration as regards the determination of whether compound or simple interest is appropriate in any given case."[86] In *Wena Hotels*, an ICSID Tribunal went further and found that an award of compound interest is generally appropriate in modern commercial arbitration.[87] Furthermore, in recent years two NAFTA tribunals have also awarded compound interest.[88]

8–88   While awarding compound interest still remains the exception, where the applicable law allows, an increasing number of international arbitral tribunals appear to be reaching the same view as that reached over 20 years ago by Judge Howard Holtzmann in his dissenting opinion in *Starrett Housing Corporation v Iran*,[89] namely that simple interest may not always—in the language of Art.38 of the *Draft Articles on Responsibility of States*—"ensure *full* reparation of loss suffered."

Enforcing awards that carry interest

8–89   It has already been seen that an award of interest (whether simple or compound) may be prohibited by a relevant national law. If this is the law of the arbitration agreement, or of the contract under which the dispute arises, it seems that an arbitral tribunal has no option but to apply it. Where parties to a contract have chosen (or are deemed to have chosen) as the substantive law of their agreement a law that prohibits the payment of interest, they can scarcely complain if interest is not payable.

---

[84] Arnaldez, Derains & Hascher, *Collection of ICC Arbitral Awards 1991–1995* (1997), p.459.
[85] Official Records of the General Assembly, F50, 6th Session, Supplement No.10 (AR/56/10), Ch.IV, E.1).
[86] *Compañia del Desarollo de Santa Elena SA v Republic of Costa Rica* (2000) 39 I.L.M. 1317, para.103.
[87] *Wena Hotels Ltd v Egypt* ICSID Case No.ARB/98/4.
[88] *Pope & Talbot v Government of Canada* (Damages Award of May 31, 2002); *SD Myers Inc v Government of Canada* (Second Partial Award of October 21, 2002). Both awards are in the public domain, and can be found online at *www.appletonlaw.com*, *www.dfait-maeci.gc.ca* or *www.naftalaw.org*.
[89] *Starrett Housing Corporation v Iran* Iran–US C.T.R. 122, 269 (1983).

Other Considerations

If the law of the place of arbitration (the *lex arbitri*) forbids the payment of interest, it may theoretically be possible for the arbitral tribunal to disregard this local law and apply the substantive law of the contract. But if the provisions of the local law are mandatory, there is a risk that the award could be attacked and rendered invalid under the law of the place where it was made. It follows that an arbitral tribunal, sitting in Saudi Arabia but applying French law as the substantive law of the contract, should be cautious when considering an award in respect of interest, even though this is permitted by the substantive law of the contract; and certainly any award of interest should be clearly separated from the other parts of the award.

What of the law of the place of enforcement? If an award cannot be enforced, it is worth no more than a bargaining tool. However, at the time of the arbitration, it is hardly possible for an arbitral tribunal to do more than make an informed guess as to the likely place of enforcement of its eventual award; and even this will be difficult until the arbitral tribunal has formed a view as to which party is likely to win the arbitration. It is suggested that, in deciding whether or not to award interest, an arbitral tribunal cannot be expected to take into account the likely consequences of such an award in a potential place of enforcement, unless the point is expressly brought to its attention by one or both of the parties—in which case, the point would no doubt have to be considered.

Post-award interest

In general, it is also open to arbitrators to set a rate of post-award interest in any amount they deem appropriate.[90] This is often the rate that would apply to a judgment in the country where the award is made. But in modern practice arbitral tribunals usually award interest to run from a certain date (either the date of the breach, or the date on which the loss was suffered, or the date of the request for arbitration depending on the applicable law and on the way the arbitral tribunal decides to exercise any discretion available to it) up to the date of payment of the award.[91]   **8–90**

Once an arbitral award is enforced in a particular country as a judgment of a court, the post-award interest rate may be replaced by the rate applicable to civil judgments. In England, however, as already stated, the 1996 Act permits the arbitral tribunal to exercise its discretion to award interest up to the date of payment.[92]

(d) Costs

The term "costs" in the context of arbitration may be divided into two broad categories; the costs of the arbitration and the costs of the parties.   **8–91**

---

[90] See para.8–86.
[91] For a comprehensive review of the power of arbitrators to award post-award interest see Gotanda, *Supplemental Damages in Private International Law* (Kluwer, 1998), pp.85–93.
[92] English Arbitration Act 1996, s.49(3)(b).

Costs of the arbitration

8–92   The costs of the arbitration usually include not only the fees, travelling and other expenses payable to the individual members of the arbitral tribunal itself, but also related expenses including (for instance) the fees and expenses of any administering institution or of experts appointed by the arbitral tribunal. Also included in the costs of the arbitration are the fees and expenses of any administrative secretary or registrar and any other incidental expenses incurred by the arbitral tribunal for the account of the case.

The costs involved in hiring rooms for meetings and hearings, as well as the fees and expenses of any translators, interpreters, and the reporters who prepare the transcript are usually paid directly by the parties. They generally have a "budget" for what they may have to spend on the arbitration; and it is also generally easier for them to make the necessary arrangements. These costs are usually paid by the parties in equal shares pending the tribunal's final award. Occasionally, where the arrangements are made by the chairman of the tribunal, or by an administering institution, such costs are paid from the deposits held by the arbitral tribunal or the institution; in general, however, the parties usually prefer to control these costs themselves rather than give the tribunal what may amount to a "blank cheque" to buy in such services.

Costs of the parties

8–93   The costs of the parties include not only the fees and expenses of the lawyers engaged to represent the parties in the arbitral proceedings, but also money spent in the preparation and presentation of the case. There will also be other professional fees and expenses, such as those of accountants or expert witnesses, as well as the hotel and travelling expenses of the lawyers, witnesses and others concerned; copying charges and the expenses of telephone, fax, email and so on will also form part of the parties' so-called "legal costs and expenses".

Anyone who has been involved in international arbitration proceedings knows that these direct costs are likely to be substantial. Even so, they rarely include any allowance for the time spent on the case by senior officials, directors or employees of the parties themselves and the indirect costs of disruption of their ordinary business. The hidden cost of such "executive" or "management" time may be very high. Indeed, it may occasionally exceed the direct costs. In general, the larger the case the more the executive time that must be spent on it. If it is possible to recover the legal costs and expenses of bringing or defending a claim in arbitration, why is it unusual to recover the cost of executive time, particularly if this includes—as it frequently does—the cost of "in-house" counsel or of an internal legal department?

The answer, which rather begs the question, seems to be that traditionally such costs have been regarded as part of the normal cost of running a government department or a business enterprise.[93] The UNCITRAL Rules, for example, do

---

[93] See Gotanda, *Supplemental Damages in Private International Law* (Kluwer, 1998), p.191.

not include such costs in the definition of what constitutes "the costs of the arbitration", although, for instance, the "travel and other expenses of witnesses" and "the costs for legal representation and assistance" *are* included.[94] More promisingly, the ICC Rules refer simply to "the reasonable legal and other costs incurred by the parties" as part of the costs of the arbitration.[95] As businesses become more accustomed to putting a value on time, through their internal accounting systems, it is to be expected that claims for "executive" or "management" time will be made more regularly, whether as part of the parties' legal costs or as part of a claim for damages.[96]

In some countries, such as the US, the usual practice is for each party to bear **8–94** its own costs, including the cost of calling witnesses, and to share the administrative costs equally.[97] In general, however, the procedure in international commercial arbitration is for the arbitral tribunal to have power to require the losing party to pay or contribute towards the legal costs of the winning party. The UNCITRAL Rules, the ICDR Rules, the ICC Rules, the LCIA Rules, the SCC Rules and the WIPO Rules each make it clear that the arbitral tribunal has such power. But on what basis should the tribunal proceed?

Assessing the costs of the parties

An arbitral tribunal in an international commercial arbitration is generally **8–95** reluctant to order the unsuccessful party to pay the whole of the winning party's legal costs. There are many reasons why this should be so. First, as already noted, the practice under which the unsuccessful party is expected to pay or contribute towards the other party's legal costs is by no means a universal practice, either in international arbitrations or, indeed, in national systems of law. Secondly, it is rare indeed for the winner to have been wholly successful on all the issues in dispute in the arbitration. Thirdly, even where a tribunal decides that some contribution towards the winning party's costs should be ordered, there is the problem of deciding upon what basis, and when, this contribution should be assessed.

Would it be "normal" or "reasonable", for example, to award costs on a contingency basis; or to assess them on an *ad valorem* basis related to the amount claimed (rather than the amount awarded), in the same way as the ICC's own administrative charges are assessed?[98] In many countries, this would be unacceptable or even improper; in others, it might be acceptable. The modern

---

[94] UNCITRAL Arbitration Rules, Art.38.

[95] ICC Arbitration Rules, Art.31(1). The 1988 version of the rules only referred to "the *normal legal* costs" (emphasis added).

[96] This possibility was considered, although no firm conclusion was reached, at an ICC Colloquium on controlling costs in arbitration proceedings held in London in December 1998.

[97] See the AAA's Commercial Arbitration Rules, Arts 50 and 51. In British Columbia, where only limited costs are recoverable in respect of lawyers' fees in litigation, the Model Law has been adopted and amended to provide that the arbitral tribunal may award costs including legal fees and expenses and any expenses incurred in connection with the arbitration: International Commercial Arbitration Act, s.31(8).

[98] ICC Arbitration Rules, Art.31(1).

practice, in lawyers' offices, is to calculate costs on a time basis, with each lawyer recording, usually in units of six minutes or more, the time spent on a particular case. However, there is no necessary correlation between the time spent on a particular line of research or argument and the value of that time, in terms of the end result. Even if it is assumed that every minute spent on the case was of value—a somewhat brave assumption—the relevant hourly charging rate may vary from one country to another, and even from place to place within the same country.[99] And what of the position where the parties come from different legal backgrounds, with one party represented by a team of lawyers and paralegals and the other party relying on one, or at most two, outside counsel? One party may claim, with justification, that its legal costs exceed $US1 million, whilst the other party protests that its own legal costs are barely a tenth of that amount.

One final problem is that of knowing when the assessment of costs should be made. Arbitration rules, such as those of the ICC and UNCITRAL, provide for the costs of the arbitration to be fixed in the award. The arbitral tribunal then has a choice. It can either ask each of the parties for details of their costs and expenses before making its award, so as to deal with them in that award; or it can deal with costs in a separate final award, which will then reduce what was intended to be a final award on the merits of the case to the status of a partial award.

8–96   Practical problems of this kind led many international arbitral tribunals to refrain from ordering the unsuccessful party to pay the legal costs of the winning party, or simply to order the losing party to pay an arbitrarily chosen fixed sum towards the winner's legal costs. This practice may well change, as more attention is directed by lawyers and their clients to the costs of the arbitration, including the cost of executive time. For the present, however, most international arbitral tribunals that decide to make an award of costs in favour of the winning party tend to adopt a "broad-brush" approach in assessing the amount to be paid, if any. In doing so, they no doubt adopt, whether consciously or not, the approach adopted by one of the arbitrators in a case before the Iran–US Claims Tribunal. In a separate opinion, this arbitrator laid down the following criteria to be applied in determining the costs of the parties and by whom they should be borne.

- Were costs claimed in the arbitration?

- Was it necessary to employ lawyers in the case in question?

- Is the amount of the costs reasonable?

- Are the circumstances of the particular case such as to make it reasonable to apportion such costs?

After stating that the first two tests are normally satisfied in complex arbitrations, the reasonableness of the *amount* of costs was reviewed as follows:

---

[99] In an UNCITRAL case in the late 1990s the hourly rate claimed for a senior partner in a New York law firm was more than double the hourly rate of a senior partner of a New Orleans firm.

"A test of reasonableness is not, however, an invitation to mere subjectivity. Objective tests of reasonableness of lawyers' fees are well known. Such tests typically assign weight primarily to the time spent and complexity of the case. In modern practice, the amount of time required to be spent is often a gauge of the extent of the complexities involved. Where the Tribunal is presented with copies of bills for services, or other appropriate evidence, indicating the time spent, the hourly billing rate, and a general description of the professional services rendered, its task need be neither onerous nor mysterious. The range of typical hourly billing rates is generally known and, as evidence before the Tribunal in various cases including this one indicates, it does not greatly differ between the United States and countries of Western Europe, where both claimants and respondents before the Tribunal typically hire their outside counsel. Just how much time any lawyer reasonably needs to accomplish a task can be measured by the number of issues involved in a case and the amount of evidence requiring analysis and presentation. While legal fees are not to be calculated on the basis of the pounds of paper involved, the Tribunal by the end of a case is able to have a fair idea, on the basis of the submissions made by both sides, of the approximate extent of the effort that was reasonably required.

Nor should the Tribunal neglect to consider the reality that legal bills are usually first submitted to businessmen. The pragmatic fact that a businessman has agreed to pay a bill, not knowing whether or not the Tribunal would reimburse the expenses, is a strong indication that the amount billed was considered reasonable by a reasonable man spending his own money, or the money of the corporation he serves. That is a classic test of reasonableness."[1]

A number of subsequent Iran–US Claims Tribunal awards have referred to this judgment.[2] It is suggested that it is an approach which provides a useful, common-sense guide to the practice that international tribunals should adopt when they are required to exercise their discretion in relation to an award of costs.

Requirements imposed by national law

As with interest, and indeed all other matters touching upon the powers of the **8–97** arbitral tribunal, any specific provisions of the *lex arbitri* concerning costs must be taken into account. Most systems of law in developed countries give arbitral tribunals a wide discretion; that part of the award which deals with costs will not be set aside merely because the arbitral tribunal has exercised its discretion in a particular way. However, the practice varies from place to place. In Austria and

---

[1] Separate opinion of Judge Holtzmann; reported in *Iranian Assets Litigation Reporter* 10860 at 10863; 8 Iran–US C.T.R. 329 at 332–333.
[2] For a detailed review of the practices of the Iran–US Claims Tribunal, see van Hof *Commentary on the UNCITRAL Arbitration Rules* (Kluwer, 1991), pp.293–311.

Germany, for example, it is normal for the reasonable costs of legal representation to be ordered against the losing party. In the US, by contrast, each party usually pays the fees of its own lawyer and, unless otherwise provided in the arbitration agreement (or in any relevant arbitration rules), lawyers' fees are not considered as part of the expenses of the arbitration.[3] In England, the 1996 Act gives the arbitral tribunal a wide discretion in relation to how the parties' costs may be awarded.[4]

The practice of national courts in following their own rules in relation to awarding costs hardly seems to provide compelling guidelines for the way in which an international tribunal should exercise the discretion granted to it either by the relevant set of rules or by the *lex arbitri*[5]; and it is suggested that international tribunals, wherever the seat of arbitration, should be guided by the *lex arbitri* and the substantive law as to the scope of its discretion, and by the applicable arbitration rules (if any) as to the exercise of that discretion.

(e) Proceedings after the award

8–98   Exceptions to the general rule that an arbitral tribunal becomes *functus officio* on the issue of a final award arise from specific provisions of the national system of law governing the arbitration; from the parties' arbitration agreement; or from any rules of arbitration adopted by them.[6]

Under national law

8–99   Many developed systems of national law permit the correction of minor clerical or typographical errors in awards, either at the request of one or both of the parties or by the arbitral tribunal on its own initiative. In England this power is conferred expressly by statute. The 1996 Act provides:

> "(1) The parties are free to agree on the powers of the tribunal to correct an award or make an additional award.
>
> (2) If or to the extent there is no such agreement, the following provisions apply.
>
> (3) The tribunal may on its own initiative or on the application of a party—
>
> > (a) correct an award so as to remove any clerical mistake or error arising from an accidental slip or omission or clarify or remove any ambiguity in the award, or
> >
> > (b) make an additional award in respect of any claim (including a claim for interest or costs) which was presented to the tribunal but was not dealt with in the award.

---

[3] See Holtzmann, "USA" *ICCA International Handbook on Commercial Arbitration*, p.26.

[4] Arbitration Act 1996, s.61.

[5] For a comprehensive review of the practices of international tribunals concerning the award of costs see Gotanda, *Supplemental Damages in Private International Law* (Kluwer, 1998), pp.173–192.

[6] See Ch.9.

These powers shall not be exercised without first affording the other parties a reasonable opportunity to make representations to the tribunal."[7]

The US Federal Arbitration Act provides that the relevant District Court may make an order modifying or correcting errors.[8] Similar provisions are contained in the arbitration statutes of many individual states in the US, some of which also permit corrections and modifications on the initiative of the arbitral tribunal. Additionally, in some countries the arbitral tribunal may complete the award where a determination of a claim, or ruling as to costs, has been omitted.[9]

The *interpretation* or *clarification* of a final award is a different matter. The Model Law provides for interpretation of a specific point or a part of the award *only* when the parties agree that such a request should be made to the tribunal.[10] The problem with *interpretation*, as opposed to *correction* of an award, as will be seen later, is that it risks giving the aggrieved party an opportunity to reopen the case.

Under rules of arbitration

The position under different sets of arbitration rules varies considerably. The **8–100** LCIA Rules contain an express power for the arbitral tribunal to correct accidental mistakes or omissions, but not to make interpretations of awards.[11] Prior to 1998 the ICC Rules did not mention either correction or interpretation. This was presumably on the basis that the process of scrutiny, under Art.21 of the previous version of the Rules, should be sufficient to ensure that all mistakes would be identified. However, the 1998 Rules contain the following provision:

"On its own initiative, the Arbitral Tribunal may correct a clerical, computational or typographical error, or any errors of a similar nature contained in an Award, provided such correction is submitted for approval to the Court within 30 days of the date of such Award."[12]

Similarly, the SCC Rules contain a provision granting the arbitral tribunal power to give a written interpretation of its award at the request of a party, in addition to the power to correct clerical errors:

"If a party so requests within 60 days after receiving the award, the arbitral tribunal shall give a written interpretation thereof. Any obvious miscalculation

---

[7] English Arbitration Act 1996, s.57.
[8] US Federal Arbitration Act 1925, s.11 (as amended 1970).
[9] For the powers of an arbitral tribunal to correct or complete an award in various national states, see the National Reports in *ICCA International Handbook on Commercial Arbitration*.
[10] Model Law, Art.33(1)(b); see also the English Arbitration Act 1996, s.57(3).
[11] LCIA Arbitration Rules, Art.27.
[12] ICC Arbitration Rules, Art.29. For a comprehensive survey of applications for correction and/or interpretation of awards under the ICC Rules that have been made since the introduction of Art.29, see Brooks Daly "Correction and Interpretation of Arbitral Awards under the ICC Rules of Arbitration", *ICC International Court of Arbitration Bulletin* Vol.13, No.1, Spring 2002.

or clerical error shall also be corrected by the tribunal. Each party shall be given an opportunity to state its views. Unless the arbitral tribunal otherwise decides, the award already rendered shall be enforceable."[13]

The UNCITRAL Rules contain powers for the arbitral tribunal to interpret its award (if so requested) and to issue additional awards to correct its award within narrow time-limits. The arbitral tribunal may only issue an interpretation at the request of a party, not on its own initiative.[14] Similarly, the arbitral tribunal may only issue an additional award at the request of a party.[15] The purpose of the provision relating to additional awards is to ensure that the arbitrators may complete their mission, if they have omitted from their award decisions in relation to any of the claims presented in the proceedings. By contrast, the *correction* of an award (normally in relation to clerical or typographical errors) may take place either at the request of the party or on the initiative of the arbitral tribunal itself.

8–101   Time-limits for complying with each of these provisions are set out in the relevant articles. In each case, the provisions of Art.32 (referred to above) relating to the formalities required in making an award must be observed.

Where the arbitral tribunal is asked to issue an interpretation of its award,[16] whether under the UNCITRAL Rules or otherwise,[17] this may pose difficulties for the tribunal. Its members will have to recapitulate their thinking as best they can and clarify what is unclear—unless they take the view, as well they might, that the request is without substance and may be dealt with in a summary manner.

8–102   The ICSID Rules go further than those of other arbitral institutions. They permit applications for the award to be interpreted and revised not only by the original arbitral tribunal but also, if that arbitral tribunal cannot be reconstituted, by a new one specially appointed for the purpose.[18] This is a cumbersome procedure; but it appears to be part of the price to be paid for the self-contained and totally autonomous nature of ICSID arbitrations, which means that even obvious errors may only be corrected within the system and not by an outside authority such as a national court.

---

[13] SCC Rules, r.20.
[14] Curiously Art.35(2) does not contain the express safeguard for the arbitral tribunal that appears in Art.37(2): " . . . if the arbitral tribunal considers the request for an additional award to be justified . . . " But common sense dictates that the literal language meaning of Art.35(2) could not be used to force the arbitral tribunal to give an interpretation, at least when it considers the request to be spurious.
[15] UNCITRAL Arbitration Rules, Arts 35(1) and 37(1).
[16] In a case where one of the authors was an arbitrator the losing respondent requested an interpretation; but the arbitral tribunal determined that this was a manifest attempt by that party to cause the arbitral tribunal to review its decision on the merits of the case.
[17] The ICDR Arbitration Rules, Art.30, contain similar provisions to those of the UNCITRAL Arbitration Rules.
[18] ICSID Arbitration Rules, r.51(1).

Review procedures other than by national courts

Challenging awards in national courts is considered in Ch.9. However, in a **8–103** limited number of cases, there may be a prior review of awards by some other authority. The main instances in which this arises are as follows. First, in certain specialised types of arbitration, particularly in the commodity trades, there is usually provision for either party to appeal to a specially constituted arbitral appeals tribunal.[19] Secondly, in a small number of countries, it is possible to make an objection to an award to a body other than a national court. One example is Saudi Arabia, where a party can submit an objection to the Committee for the Settlement of Commercial Disputes. Thirdly, in the ICC system the award may not be signed by the arbitral tribunal until it has been scrutinised by the ICC's Court. This provision, which has provoked some controversy, states:

> "Before signing any Award, the Arbitral Tribunal shall submit it in draft form to the Court. The Court may lay down modifications as to the form of the Award and, without affecting the Arbitral Tribunal's liberty of decision, may also draw his attention to points of substance. No Award shall be rendered by the Arbitral Tribunal until it has been approved by the Court as to its form."[20]

This provision calls for two different standards of review. The first is as to *form*, and the ICC's Court may "lay down" modifications in this respect. The second is as to points of *substance*, which the ICC's Court may only "draw to the attention" of the arbitrator.

The review of awards by the ICC's Court causes concern to some arbitrators, who consider it unnecessary and time consuming. It also arouses suspicion on the part of some parties, who fear that the case may be reviewed by a "court" before which they have had no opportunity of presenting their cases. However, the Swiss Federal Court has ruled that this particular provision of the ICC Rules does *not* contravene Swiss law because, by adopting the Rules, the parties have agreed that the ICC's Court should act as the auxiliary of the arbitral tribunal in relation to the form of the award and as advisor to the tribunal in relation to the substance of the award.[21]

The advantages and disadvantages of the ICC's scrutiny process were subject **8–104** to extensive consultation and debate in the period running up to the formulation of the ICC's 1998 Rules. Overall, it was found that a substantial majority of arbitrators and other arbitral practitioners considered the scrutiny process to be valuable, and that the advantages outweighed the disadvantages. It is important that, with such a wide range of arbitrators being called on to act in ICC cases, there should be a degree of control over the form of awards, and over their

---

[19] See Ch.9, para.9–08.
[20] ICC Arbitration Rules, Art.27.
[21] *Syrian Petroleum Company v GTM-Entrepose SA*, Swiss Federal Court decision of July 16, 1990, Proc. No.58/1990 (unpublished).

enforceability.[22] The ICC prides itself on the overall quality of ICC awards; and the scrutiny process acts as a measure of quality control, ensuring amongst other things, that the arbitrators deal with all the claims, including interest and costs, with which they are called upon to deal.

Review procedure under the ICSID Rules

8–105   Under the ICSID Rules, an application may be made for the interpretation, revision or amendment of an ICSID award.[23] This topic is dealt with later.

Publication of awards

8–106   A conflict emerged during the 1990s between the "inherent confidentiality" of the arbitral process and the desire for publication of awards in the interests of establishing a body of precedent that might guide—if not bind—other arbitrators. The prevailing trend appears to favour publication. Awards of the Iran–US Claims Tribunal have been comprehensively reported and have been of guidance in other arbitrations. As already described in Ch.1,[24] the ICDR Rules provide that, unless otherwise agreed by the parties, selected awards may be made publicly available, with the names of the parties and other identifying features removed. The ICC may similarly publish sanitised versions of ICC awards unless any of the parties expressly objects. Less officially, it is becoming increasingly common for complete versions of awards rendered in investment treaty arbitration to be circulated via email and the internet between practitioners active in the field. Finally, there are other circumstances in which, even without the consent of the parties, an award may more legitimately find its way into the public domain. This may occur, for example, during court proceedings to challenge or enforce an award; or when a publicly quoted corporation is obliged to disclose in its published accounts material information relating to its liability.[25]

---

[22] For a description of the procedures followed by the ICC Court of Arbitration in scrutinising awards, see Craig, Park & Paulsson, *International Chamber of Commerce Arbitration* (3rd ed., Oceana, 2000), Pt. III, Ch.20.

[23] ICSID Arbitration Rules, Arts 50–52.

[24] See Ch.1.

[25] Ch.1; and see Paulsson & Rawding "The Trouble with Confidentiality" (1995) 11 Arbitration International 303.

CHAPTER 9

CHALLENGE OF ARBITRAL AWARDS

1. BACKGROUND

No one likes losing. So it is not surprising that when a client is disappointed **9–01**
with an arbitral award, the first question he asks his lawyer is: "How can I
appeal?"[1] As so often happens when a lawyer is asked a question, the answer is:
"It depends".

First, it depends on whether the relevant rules of arbitration establish an
internal appeal procedure, as is the case in many maritime and commodity
arbitration systems. Secondly, it depends on whether the law of the seat of the
arbitration[2] contains any provisions for challenging an arbitral award; and, if so,
what provisions. Even where the relevant rules of arbitration provide that an
award is to be final and binding on the parties and that the parties agree to carry
it out without delay,[3] the law of the seat of arbitration usually provides some way
of challenging an arbitral award.[4]

(a) The purpose of challenge

The purpose of challenging an award before a national court at the seat, or **9–02**
place, of arbitration is to have it modified in some way by the relevant court, or
more usually to have that court declare that the award is to be disregarded (*i.e.*
"annulled" or "set aside") in whole or in part. If an award *is* set aside or annulled
by the relevant court, it will usually[5] be treated as invalid and accordingly
unenforceable, not only by the courts of the seat of arbitration but also by
national courts elsewhere. This is because, under both the New York Convention

---

[1] Craig, "Uses and Abuses of Appeal from Awards" (1988) 4 Arbitration International 174 at
177.
[2] Or, if the parties have chosen a different procedural law to govern the arbitration, under that law:
New York Convention, Art.V.1(e); Model Law, Art.36(1)(a)(v). On the inadvisability of choosing
a procedural law other than that of the place of arbitration, see Ch.2.
[3] See, for instance, the UNCITRAL Arbitration Rules, Art.32(2); the ICC Arbitration Rules,
Art.28(6); the LCIA Arbitration Rules, Art.26(9).
[4] Including a partial, or interim, award that is final as to the issue or issues with which it deals.
[5] There are some celebrated cases in which an award that has been set aside by the court of the place
of arbitration has nevertheless been granted recognition and enforcement. Thus in *Hilmarton I*, an
award that had been set aside by the Swiss court was nevertheless granted recognition in France;
and in *Chromalloy*, an award that had been set aside by the Egyptian court was nevertheless
granted enforcement in the USA and in France: for further discussion of these cases, see
Ch.10.

and the Model Law, the competent court may refuse to grant recognition and enforcement of an award that has been "set aside" by a court of the seat of arbitration.[6]

(b) The meaning of challenge

9–03   The concept of a "challenge" to an arbitral award is well established, but the term itself is relatively new. In common law jurisdictions, it is customary to speak of an "appeal" against an award. This means either an appeal to a different tribunal (where this is possible under the internal rules of the arbitration) or an appeal to the relevant court which may be asked to vary the award, or to send it back to the arbitrators for reconsideration; or to order that it should be set aside in whole or in part. In civil law countries, the customary language is that of "recourse" to a court of law against an award (*le recours en nullité* of French law, for example). This is the terminology used in the Model Law, in establishing the grounds on which an application may be made to the relevant court to set aside an arbitral award.[7]

The problem is to find a word that is adequate to encompass both "appeal" and "recourse". It seemed to the authors (in the first edition of this book) that "challenge" would serve this purpose and it is a term that has gained acceptance. As one leading practitioner has expressed it:

> "Challenge captures the idea of an offensive effort to overturn an award, as distinct from mere resistance to enforcement. It covers recourse to a court for the setting aside or the revision of an award; it also covers an appeal on a point of law which might lead to the setting aside or revision of an award."[8]

(c) Introductory remarks

9–04   Some further introductory remarks are necessary before looking in more detail at the ways in which an arbitral award may be challenged.

First, before challenging an award before the relevant court, it will usually be necessary[9] to exhaust other available remedies, which may include:

(a) any available process of appeal or review; and

(b) any available provision for the correction of the award or for an additional award.

As to the first requirement, certain rules of arbitration (which are examined later) provide for appeals to "second-tier" tribunals. It is the award of that

---

[6] New York Convention, Art.V.1(e); Model Law, Art.36(1)(v).

[7] Model Law, Art.34.

[8] Craig, *op. cit.* (although he preferred to speak of "appeal" and "judicial review" on the basis that this was the language a client would use). The English Arbitration Act 1996 has now made use of this terminology and speaks of the "challenge" of an award (mainly on procedural grounds).

[9] See, for instance, to this effect, the English Arbitration Act 1996, s.70(2).

superior tribunal, and not any earlier award, that is final and binding upon the parties.

As to the second requirement, it is usual for standard rules of arbitration, as well as national legislation, to provide some mechanism for the correction of awards by the arbitral tribunal itself. For example, the ICC Rules provide that the arbitral tribunal, on its own initiative or at the request of a party, may correct "a clerical, computational or typographical error, or any errors of similar nature, contained in an Award".[10] A "slip rule" of this kind is useful, but it does not go very far. The Rules also provide that, at the request of a party, the arbitral tribunal may issue an "interpretation" of the award.[11] The UNCITRAL Rules contain not only an interpretation rule and a "slip rule",[12] but also a rule that permits either party to ask the arbitral tribunal to make an additional award "as to claims presented in the arbitral proceedings but omitted from the award".[13] The rule goes on to state that the arbitral tribunal may do this if it considers the request to be justified and "considers that the omission can be rectified without any further hearings or evidence".[14] At a time when the pleadings and the debates in international commercial arbitrations are becoming more and more complex, such a rule is likely to prove useful.[15]

The second introductory remark is a general warning that time-limits for **9–05** making an application for the correction or amendment of an arbitral award, or for challenging the award by an application to the relevant national court, are likely to be extremely short. The position in each case will depend upon the relevant rules or legislation, but by way of example:

(a) under the UNCITRAL Arbitration Rules, requests for interpretation or correction of an award, or for an additional award, must be made within 30 days after receipt of the Award[16];

(b) under the Model Law, an application for setting aside an award must be made within three months of receiving the award or, if a request for an interpretation, correction or additional award has been made, within three months of that request being disposed of by the arbitral tribunal.

---

[10] ICC Arbitration Rules, Art.29(1).
[11] Art.29(2). For a comprehensive analysis of Art.29 of the ICC Rules, by which an ICC arbitral tribunal may correct and interpret its awards, see Brooks W. Daly, "Correction and Interpretation of Arbitral Awards under the ICC Rules of Arbitration", *ICC International Court of Arbitration Bulletin*, Vol.13, No.1, Spring 2002, pp.61–91.
[12] UNCITRAL Arbitration Rules, Arts 35 and 36.
[13] UNCITRAL Arbitration Rules, Art.37.
[14] *ibid.* The Model Law also permits the arbitral tribunal, at the request of either party, to issue an additional award; see Model Law, Art.33.
[15] It has been adopted in the English Arbitration Act 1996 under s.57, and s.70(2) is one of the means of recourse which must be exhausted before any application or appeal to the court against an arbitral award may be made.
[16] UNCITRAL Arbitration Rules, Arts 35, 36 and 37.

9–06   The final, and perhaps the most important, introductory remark concerns the intended finality of arbitral awards. Arbitration rules, such as those of UNCITRAL, the LCIA, and the ICC, provide unequivocally that an arbitral award is final and binding.[17] These are not intended to be mere empty words. One of the advantages of arbitration is that it is meant to result in the final determination of the dispute between the parties. If the parties want a compromise solution to be proposed, they should opt for mediation. If they are prepared to fight the case to the highest court in the land, they should opt for litigation. By choosing arbitration, the parties choose a system of dispute resolution that results in a decision that is, in principle, final and binding. It is not intended to be a mere proposal as to how the dispute might be resolved; nor is it intended to be the first step on a ladder of appeals through national courts.

To the losing party this "advantage" of arbitration may seem in retrospect to be the very opposite. However, the laws of many countries, reflecting the policy of the New York Convention and the Model Law, have what has been described in another context as "a pro-enforcement bias".[18] This means that whilst it may be possible to challenge an arbitral award, the available options are likely to be limited.

2. METHODS OF CHALLENGE

9–07   The relevant arbitration rules sometimes provide for "internal" challenges to an award. This form of challenge is considered first. Then correction and interpretation of awards is considered; and, finally, the challenge of awards by application to national courts is reviewed.

(a) Internal challenge

9–08   As already indicated, the rules under which an arbitration was conducted may contain provision for review of the procedure that was followed, or of the award itself. This is frequently the case with maritime and commodity arbitrations, and other forms of arbitration established by trade associations.[19]

The arbitration rules of the Grain and Feed Trade Association ("GAFTA") provide a useful example of "internal" appeal procedures. GAFTA has long experience of the international trade in grain and feedstock, where buyers and sellers come from many different parts of the world, and has its own set of arbitration rules for dealing with the different types of disputes to which these international transactions may give rise. The Rules themselves,[20] which provide for arbitration to take place either in London or elsewhere (if agreed in writing by the parties) are detailed and well thought out. An arbitrator appointed under

---

[17] See para.9–09.
[18] *Parsons Whittemore Overseas Co Inc v Société Générale de l'Industrie du Papier*, 508 F.2d 969 (2nd Cir. 1974).
[19] It is also the case with ICSID, as to which see para.9–09 below.
[20] GAFTA Form 125, Arbitration Rules, effective January 1, 2003.

the Rules is required to be a qualified arbitrator member of GAFTA, who has no financial or other interest in the transaction.[21]

A party who is dissatisfied with the award of the arbitrators has the right[22] to appeal to a Board of Appeal. A time-limit requires that notice must be given no later than 12 noon on the thirtieth consecutive day after the date on which the award was made. The Board of Appeal consists of three members of the Association where the first tier award was made by a sole arbitrator, and five members where it was made by three arbitrators.[23] After submission of written statements and evidence (which may include new evidence) a date is set for the hearing of the appeal.[24]

An appeal involves a new hearing of the dispute. The Board of Appeal may confirm, vary, amend or set aside the award of the first-tier tribunal.[25] The award of the Board of Appeal replaces that of the first tribunal and is expressed to be "final, conclusive and binding".[26] Accordingly, any further challenge to the award would have to be by recourse to a national court at the place of arbitration.[27] **9–09**

A similar appeal procedure exists under the Rules of the Chambre Arbitrale Maritime de Paris, which deals with most of the maritime arbitrations in France. Under the 2003 Rules of the Chambre a list is kept of persons of French and other nationalities who are considered to have the necessary experience to act as maritime arbitrators. A dispute is first referred to a tribunal of one or more arbitrators,[28] which makes a decision upon it. If either party is dissatisfied with this decision, and the amount in dispute exceeds €30,000, that party may ask for the case to be reconsidered (*"examen au second degré"*) by a new tribunal.[29]

As a final example of the challenge of arbitral awards by internal review procedures, mention must again[30] be made of ICSID. A party who is dissatisfied with the award of an ICSID arbitral tribunal may apply for the interpretation, revision or amendment of the award. The grounds for so doing include excess of powers on the part of the tribunal, serious departures from a fundamental rule of procedure and failure to state the reasons on which the award is based.[31] If the

---

[21] GAFTA Arbitration Rules, Art.3.5. For a commentary on commodity trade arbitrations, see Perry in *Bernstein's Handbook of Arbitration Practice* (4th ed., Sweet & Maxwell, London, 2003), Pt 16.

[22] Except in certain cases, including cases where the obligations of the parties are defined by reference to the condition of the goods on arrival (the so-called "Rye Terms" clause), where the parties have agreed in writing to dispense with the two-tier arbitration system: GAFTA Arbitration Rules, Art.10.1.

[23] GAFTA Arbitration Rules, Art.11.1.

[24] *ibid.*, Art.12.1–3.

[25] *ibid.*, Art.12.4.

[26] *ibid.*, Art.12.6.

[27] See the discussion below.

[28] The parties are free to agree on a sole arbitrator, for confirmation by the Chambre, but if they cannot agree the Chambre appoints an arbitrator from its list; similarly, it will appoint the presiding arbitrator of a tribunal of three.

[29] Chambre Arbitrale Maritime de Paris, Art.XV(3).

[30] See Ch.1, para.1–123 *et seq.*

[31] ICSID Arbitration Rules, r.50.

application is for annulment of the award, then an ad hoc committee of three members (in effect, a new arbitral tribunal) is constituted to determine the application.[32] If the award is annulled, in whole or in part, either party may ask for the dispute to be submitted to a new tribunal, which then delivers a new (and final) award.[33]

9–10　　This is a cumbersome procedure and has been much criticised. Because of the lengthy nature of the annulment mechanism, ICSID proceedings in the *Klöckner*[34] and *Amco*[35] arbitrations lasted nine years and eleven years respectively, and led one of the authors of this book to describe it as an expensive version of the childhood game of snakes and ladders.[36] It is, however, the only method of challenging ICSID awards since, as part of the special status they enjoy under the Washington Convention, such awards cannot be challenged in national courts.[37] Moreover, more recent experience suggests that the ICSID annulment mechanism is becoming more efficient. For example, in *Wena Hotels* both the merits and annulment phases were disposed of in under four years.[38]

(b) Correction and interpretation of awards; additional awards

9–11　　There is little more to say under this heading.[39] It is usual for there to be some provision either in the relevant arbitration rules, or in the law governing the arbitration, for an arbitral tribunal to correct any clerical or other errors in the award. Similarly, it has already been noted that an arbitral tribunal may be asked to issue an "interpretation" of its award.

Of more interest is the power that is sometimes given to an arbitral tribunal to deal with any claims that were presented in the arbitral proceedings, but with which the tribunal omitted to deal.[40] One of the grounds on which an arbitral award may be challenged under some systems of law is failure by the arbitral

---

[32] *ibid.*, r.52.

[33] ICSID Arbitration Rules, r.55. If the original award has only been annulled in part, the new tribunal will not reconsider any portion of the award that has *not* been annulled: r.55(3).

[34] *Klöckner Industrie-Anlagen GmbH v United Republic of Cameroon and Société Camerounaise des Engrais* (Case No.ARB/81/2). The claim was registered on April 14, 1981. The first award was rendered on October 21, 1983; see (1984) 111 Journal du Droit International 409 (excerpts). The decision on the first annulment proceeding was issued on May 3, 1985; see ad hoc committee Decision of May 3, 1985 (1987) 114 Journal du Droit International 163 (excerpts). Requests for resubmission of the dispute to a new tribunal were registered with ICSID on June 7, 1985 and July 3, 1985 and the final award was issued on January 26, 1988. A second annulment proceeding was registered on July 1, 1988 but was dismissed by the ad hoc committee on May 17, 1990.

[35] *Amco Asia Corp v Republic of Indonesia* (1985) 24 I.L.M. 1022, ICSID Award of November 21, 1984.

[36] Redfern, "ICSID—Losing its Appeal?" (1987) 3 Arbitration International 98.

[37] Washington Convention, Art.54(2); and see Carrias-Borjas, "Recognition and Enforcement of ICSID Awards" (1991) 2 Am. Rev. Int'l Arb. 354; S. Choi, "Judicial Enforcement of Arbitration Awards under ICSID and New York Conventions" (1993) 28 N.Y.Un. J. Int'l Law Pol. 175.

[38] *Wena Hotels Ltd v Arab Republic of Egypt*, ICSID Case No.ARB/98/4. The Request for Arbitration commencing proceedings was submitted in July 1998, and the decision of the ad hoc committee rejecting Egypt's annulment application was rendered on February 5, 2002.

[39] See Ch.6.

[40] See, *e.g.*, Model Law, Art.33; UNCITRAL Arbitration Rules, Art.37; English Arbitration Act 1996, s.57.

tribunal to deal with all the issues that were put to it.[41] If the defect can be put right by the arbitral tribunal itself, without recourse to the courts, this is a sensible solution.

(c) Recourse to the courts

What is a losing party to do if its grievance is not something that can be put   **9–12** right by interpretation or correction of the award and there is no provision for internal review of the award? There are grounds on which an arbitral award may be challenged before a national court at the place of arbitration (the "competent" court as it is described in the Model Law).[42] These grounds are considered in turn, beginning with the one that is most frequently met; namely, a plea that the arbitral tribunal lacks jurisdiction.[43]

3. GROUNDS FOR CHALLENGE

(a) Lack of jurisdiction

It is a requirement of a valid arbitration that there should be an enforceable   **9–13** arbitration agreement. If there is no valid arbitration agreement, or if the matters submitted to arbitration do not fall within that agreement, whether for reasons of public policy or otherwise,[44] there can be no valid arbitration. If there is no valid arbitration, there can be no valid arbitral award.

As international commercial arbitration becomes increasingly established as the usual method of resolving disputes in international business, it is becoming more common for one party or another to object to the jurisdiction of the arbitral tribunal.[45]

Jurisdictional issues may include:

- whether there is a valid arbitration agreement;

- whether the tribunal is properly constituted;

- what matters have been submitted to arbitration in accordance with the arbitration agreement; and

---

[41] See, *e.g.*, English Arbitration Act 1996, s.68(2)(d).

[42] The Model Law, Art.6 provides for each state to designate the court, courts or other authority competent to perform the functions laid down by the Model Law, which include the setting aside of awards under Art.34.

[43] For a comparative survey of the way in which courts in a selection of major European jurisdictions have interpreted and applied the grounds for challenging an award, see Christoph Liebscher *The Healthy Award: Challenge in International Commercial Arbitration* (Kluwer, 2003), Ch.V.

[44] See the discussion of "arbitrability" in Ch.3.

[45] In most cases, no doubt, the objection is seriously intended. In some cases, however, it is used as a procedural tactic, in an attempt to defeat the arbitration agreement, so that the claimant will have to pursue its claim (if it is not too late) by litigation before the national court in the respondent's country.

- whether these matters are arbitrable.

9–14   Two possibilities are open to a party wishing to challenge the jurisdiction of the arbitral tribunal. The first is to challenge jurisdiction at the outset of an arbitration (or at the latest, as soon as the reasons for objection are known) and ask the tribunal to deal with this challenge, either by means of an interim award or as part of its award on the merits. The second is to wait until the award is made and then challenge it, or attempt to resist enforcement,[46] on the basis that the tribunal had no jurisdiction and so its award has no validity.

The second course is usually adopted by a party that has decided to boycott the arbitration—that is, to take no part in the proceedings. The risk is that it may be held that the tribunal *did* have jurisdiction. In such a case, the non-participating party will be faced with a valid award, which may be enforced against it.

Parties that take part in an arbitration but fail to raise a jurisdiction issue when they may have been entitled to do so, risk losing the right to object. For example, consider an international commercial arbitration in London, where the respondent is in doubt as to the validity of the arbitration agreement but nevertheless takes part in the arbitration without raising the issue, in the hope that the arbitral award will be in its favour. Suppose this does not happen. The tribunal makes an award against the respondent, who then seeks to challenge the award on the ground that the tribunal lacked jurisdiction. Such a respondent will find that it is too late to challenge the award, since English law requires an objection to jurisdiction to be raised at the earliest possible opportunity[47]; and provides that if this is not done the right to object is lost.[48] Accordingly, the award would be a valid award under the law of England (as the law of the seat of arbitration) and enforceable under the New York Convention. The risk of losing the right to object in this way does not only exist in England, and is not limited to jurisdictional objections alone. The Cour d'Appel de Paris has also rejected challenges based on objections that the challenging party failed to raise—and was therefore deemed to have waived—during the arbitration itself.[49] Indeed, most developed arbitral jurisdictions uphold awards in these circumstances, and most state parties to the New York Convention are ready to enforce such awards.

9–15   If an objection to jurisdiction is to be taken, it should be taken without delay. Similar provisions to those of English law, to the effect that a plea as to lack of jurisdiction should be raised at an early stage, are to be found in the UNCITRAL Rules and the Model Law.[50] The implication is that if this is not done the right to object is lost unless the delay is considered to be justified.

---

[46] See Ch.10.
[47] English Arbitration Act 1996, s.31.
[48] *ibid.*, s.73.
[49] See, *e.g.*, the Cour d'Appel de Paris decision in *SA Caisse Fédérale de Crédit Mutuel du Nord de la France v Banque Delubac et Compagnie* (2001) Revue de l'Arbitrage 918.
[50] UNCITRAL Arbitration Rules, Art.21(3): "not later than in the statement of defence or, with respect to a counterclaim, in the reply to the counterclaim"; Model Law, Art.16(2): "not later than the submission of the statement of defence".

Under the doctrine of *competence/competence*,[51] the present practice is generally to regard an arbitral tribunal as being empowered to decide for itself whether or not it has jurisdiction over a particular dispute. If its jurisdiction is challenged, the arbitral tribunal may decide the point as a preliminary issue in an interim award,[52] or as part of its award on the merits. In either case, however, the decision of the arbitral tribunal is not necessarily the last word on the subject. That rests with the national court. The Model Law, for instance, states that if the arbitral tribunal rules as a preliminary question that it has jurisdiction, this ruling may be referred to the competent court (within 30 days) for the court's decision, which *is* final.[53] If the ruling on jurisdiction is made in an award on the merits, this may likewise be challenged under the Model Law; and the award may be set aside, on the basis that the arbitration agreement was not valid (if that is the reason for which jurisdiction is opposed) or that it dealt with a dispute that was not within the arbitration agreement, or that it went beyond the scope of that agreement.[54]

When a national court is called upon to decide on the issue of jurisdiction, it generally needs to review both the facts and the law in order to arrive at its decision. This is less likely to be so with the other grounds of challenge: for instance, the argument that the composition of the arbitral tribunal was not in accordance with the agreement of the parties[55] should not require a complete review of the dispute. It can and should be treated as a discrete issue.

(b) Other grounds for challenge

Each state that has a law governing arbitration has its own concept of what **9–16** measure of control it wishes to exercise over the arbitral process and, in particular, whether it wishes in this respect to distinguish between "domestic" and "international" arbitration. The extent of this control varies from state to state. In any given case, it is necessary to consult the law (or the lawyers) of the state concerned in order to determine the grounds (if any) on which a particular award may be challenged.

It is beyond the scope of this book to review all these different systems of law. Even those publications which attempt to do so need to be treated with caution, since the pace of change is rapid. What can be done, however, is to try to discern the areas in which judicial control, or review, is likely to occur and then to consider each of these areas in turn. Leaving aside the issue of jurisdiction, which has already been considered, there are perhaps two broad grounds on which an arbitral award is likely to be challenged before a national court at the seat of the arbitration. These grounds may exist alone, or in one or more combinations, depending on the law of the seat of arbitration.

---

[51] Discussed in Ch.5.

[52] The term "partial award" is usually reserved for decisions on the substantive claims of the parties.

[53] Model Law, Art.16(3).

[54] Model Law, Arts 16(3) and 34(2)(i), (iii).

[55] Model Law, Art.34(2)(iv).

First, an award may be challenged on what may broadly be described as "procedural" grounds, such as failure to give proper notice of the appointment of an arbitrator.[56] Secondly, an award may be challenged on substantive grounds, on the basis that the arbitral tribunal made a mistake of law or on the grounds of a mistake of fact (although in practice such a challenge is not generally permitted).

9–17   The "procedural" grounds for challenge are those that are most likely to be encountered in the international practice of arbitration. They are reviewed here by reference to the Model Law, which was designed for international arbitration[57] and which regards these grounds as the *only* grounds for challenge of an award in an international arbitration.

4. Grounds for Challenge under the Model Law

9–18   Under the Model Law an action for setting aside may only be brought in respect of an award made within the territory of the state concerned. It *must* be brought before the designated court in that state[58] and it may *only* be brought on the grounds set out in the Model Law. These grounds are taken from Art.V of the New York Convention. There is a pleasing symmetry here. The New York Convention, in Art.V, sets out the grounds on which recognition and enforcement of an international award may be refused. Article 34 of the Model Law sets out the same grounds (with slight differences of language) as the grounds on which such an award may be set aside. In summary, these grounds are as follows:

- lack of capacity to conclude an arbitration agreement, or lack of a valid arbitration agreement;

- where the aggrieved party was not given proper notice of the appointment of the arbitral tribunal or the arbitral proceedings or was otherwise unable to present its case;

- where the award deals with matters not contemplated by, or falling within, the arbitration clause or submission agreement, or goes beyond the scope of what was submitted;

- where the composition of the arbitral tribunal or the arbitral procedure was not in accordance with the agreement of the parties, or with the mandatory provisions of the Model Law itself;

- where the subject matter of the dispute is not capable of settlement by arbitration under the law of the state where the arbitration takes place;

---

[56] Model Law, Art.34(2)(ii).

[57] The full title of the Model Law as has been seen, is the "Model Law on *International* Commercial Arbitration" (emphasis added). Some states, however, do not distinguish between "international" and "domestic" arbitrations and have either adopted or adapted the Model Law for both types of arbitration.

[58] *ibid.,* Art.1(2). Under Art.6, a state that enacts the Model Law must designate the court or courts within its territory that will fulfil the various functions entrusted to the courts.

- where the award (or any decision in it) is in conflict with the public policy of the state where the arbitration takes place.[59]

The *travaux préparatoires* of the Model Law make it clear that the public **9–19** policy provision is intended to cover, *inter alia*, the possibility of setting aside an award if the arbitral tribunal has been corrupted in some way, or if it has been misled by corrupt evidence. This was considered necessary because doubts were raised as to whether the other provisions adequately covered all the circumstances in which awards might be set aside.[60]

An application under the Model Law for setting aside an award must be made within three months from the date on which the aggrieved party receives the award (subject to any extended time-limit that may be appropriate where corrections, interpretations or additional awards have been issued under Art.33).[61] The procedure to be followed by the court designated in Art.6 for this purpose is the procedure laid down by that court.

Article 34(4) mitigates to some extent the "all or nothing" approach of the Model Law, under which an award is either set aside or left to stand. Where appropriate, and where requested by a party to do so, the court may suspend for a given period of time the proceedings for setting aside the award. This allows the arbitral tribunal an opportunity to resume the arbitral proceedings, or to take such other action as, in the arbitral tribunal's opinion, will eliminate the grounds for setting aside.[62] In effect this is an equivalent provision to that of remitting the award to the tribunal for reconsideration.

(a) Incapacity: invalid agreement to arbitrate

The first ground for recourse against an arbitral award under the Model Law **9–20** is where:

"(i) a party to the arbitration agreement . . . was under some incapacity; or the said agreement is not valid under the law to which the parties have subjected it or, failing any indication thereon, under the law of this State."[63]

The issue of *capacity* has been discussed earlier in this book, as have the requirements for an enforceable arbitration agreement.[64] It is useful to note again, however, that if the parties have *not* subjected the arbitration agreement to a particular law, expressly or by implication,[65] its validity may be judged according

---

[59] *ibid.*, Art.34(2).
[60] The doubts were expressed by the UK delegation; see UN Doc.A/CN.9/263, Add.2, paras 29–35. The clarification of the Commission is found in UN Doc.A/40/17, para.297. The UN documents are reproduced in Holtzmann & Neuhaus, *A Guide to the UNCITRAL Model Law on International Commercial Arbitration: Legislative History and Commentary* (Kluwer, 1989).
[61] Art.34(3).
[62] For a detailed commentary on Art.34(4), see Holtzmann & Neuhaus, *op. cit.*, p.967.
[63] Model Law, Art.34(2)(a)(i).
[64] See Ch.3.
[65] The words "failing any indication" of the relevant law, in Art.34(2)(a)(i) of the Model Law, suggest that an implied choice of law would be sufficient.

to the law of the place of arbitration. This may turn out to be a purely accidental choice.[66]

(b) Lack of due process

9–21   The second and probably the most important ground for recourse against an arbitral award under the Model Law is as follows:

> "(ii) the party making the application was not given proper notice of the appointment of an arbitrator or of the arbitral proceedings or was otherwise unable to present his case."[67]

Certain minimum procedural standards must be observed if international commercial arbitrations are to be conducted fairly and properly. These procedural standards are designed to ensure that the arbitral tribunal is properly constituted; that the arbitral procedure is in accordance with the agreement of the parties (subject to any mandatory provisions of the applicable law); and that the parties are given proper notice of the proceedings, hearings and so forth. In short, the aim is to ensure that the parties are treated with equality and are given a fair hearing, with a full and proper opportunity to present their respective cases.[68]

Most lawyers with experience of litigation or arbitration, whether domestic or international, should find it relatively easy to agree upon these basic principles. The same body of lawyers, however, might find it more difficult to agree upon a specific set of rules designed to implement them. Some national systems of law, whilst rightly insisting upon the need for each of the parties to an arbitration to be given a fair hearing, have little or no legislation to guide the parties or the arbitral tribunal. The approach (as in France) is minimalist. In practice, it is left to national courts to determine, from case to case, exactly what is required to constitute a "fair hearing". Other systems of law try, in their legislation, to indicate what is meant by this concept. Their laws provide, for example, that the selected rules of arbitral procedure must permit the parties to exercise their right to be heard; to attend any sittings for the taking of evidence or any oral hearings which the arbitral tribunal may order; to be represented or assisted by a representative of their choice; and so forth. Failure to observe these rules of procedure may be a ground for the challenge of an award.[69]

9–22   Each national system usually works well according to its own concepts.[70] US Federal Courts, for example, have regarded the failure to give the parties an oral hearing as a violation of due process and it recognises this as a ground for setting aside an award or for refusing recognition and enforcement under the New York

---

[66] If it is made, *e.g.*, by an arbitral institution rather than by the parties themselves.

[67] Model Law, Art.34(2)(a)(ii).

[68] The requirement of equality is a specific requirement of some laws. See, *e.g.*, the Swiss Private International Law Act 1987, Ch.12, Art.190.

[69] See, *e.g.*, the kinds of "serious irregularity" referred to in the English Arbitration Act 1996, s.68(1), (2) and (3).

[70] See Liebscher, *op. cit.*, Ch.V(3).

Convention.[71] In the civil law systems, the right of the parties to have a full opportunity to present their case, the classic *droit de la defense*, often incorporates the *principe du contradictoire*, which requires that no evidence or argument serve as a basis for a decision unless it has been subject to the possibility of comment and contradiction by the parties.[72]

When a question arises as to whether or not an arbitration was conducted properly, each national court approaches the question from its own particular national standpoint. This is understandable, and indeed inevitable, but it may lead to difficulties. The arbitration proceedings may have been conducted by lawyers from different legal backgrounds, accustomed to different procedures and even perhaps a different legal etiquette.[73] The rules of the leading arbitral institutions are themselves vague on the question of what procedure should be followed. This is deliberate policy, since the rules are intended to be suitable for use in many different countries of the world, with many different systems of trial. However, international commercial arbitration has become sufficiently established and sufficiently wide spread for it to have become necessary to develop some common procedures. Experience shows that this is the case.[74]

Three examples may help to illustrate the approach of courts in different countries to the concept of "proper notice" of the appointment of an arbitrator and to the wider concept of a "fair hearing".[75]

The first case involved an arbitration between a Danish buyer and a German   **9–23** seller before the Copenhagen Arbitration Committee for Grain and Feedstuff Trade. In accordance with the Rules of the Arbitration Committee, only the name of the chairman (but not that of the other arbitrators) was made known to the parties. An award was made against the German seller, who resisted enforcement before the national court in Cologne. The defence was successful. The court held, *inter alia*, that, since the German seller was not told the name of *all* the members of the arbitral tribunal, he was not given proper notice of the appointment of the arbitrators.[76]

The second case involved a dispute between four Mexican companies, on the one hand, and an Italian company and its Dutch subsidiary, on the other, in respect of a share subscription agreement by which one of the four Mexican companies agreed to sell shares in a company to the Italian and Dutch companies.

---

[71] See *Parsons & Whittemore Overseas Co Inc v Société Générale de l'Industrie du Papier (RAKTA)* 508 F.2d 969 (2nd Cir. 1974).

[72] See, *e.g.*, the decision of the Cour d'Appel de Paris in *Burkinabe des Ciments et Matérieux (CIMAT) v Société des Ciments d'Abidjan (SCA)* (2001) Revue de l'Arbitrage 165, n. Cohen. See also *Guignier v HRA Europe* (2001) Revue de l'Arbitrage 199, n. Pinsolle.

[73] In the common law systems, for instance, it is usual for lawyers to interview witnesses and take statements from them before the hearing—a practice which may be frowned upon (and indeed regarded as a breach of professional etiquette) in other countries.

[74] The UNCITRAL Notes on Organizing Arbitration Proceedings (1996) have been discussed in Ch.6 and should assist in establishing common and acceptable procedures.

[75] Although two of the cases arose on applications for enforcement under the New York Convention, the grounds of objection were identical to those set out in the Model Law, Art.34(2)(a)(ii).

[76] As required by Art.V.1(b) of the New York Convention, as well as by the Model Law, Art.34-(2)(a)(ii). The case is reported in (1982) VII Yearbook Commercial Arbitration 345 at 346.

Following the parties' conclusion of the agreement, the Italian and Dutch companies commenced ICC arbitration in Ontario against their Mexican contractual counterparty, as well as three of its affiliates, seeking rescission of the share subscription agreement. After the arbitral tribunal found that it had jurisdiction over all of the Mexican respondents (including the non-signatories to the share subscription agreement), the respondents boycotted the arbitration. Following an award against them, the Mexican parties applied to the Ontario court to set aside the award; *inter alia*, on the grounds that they had been denied a full opportunity to present their case. Considering the grounds for challenging an award under the Model Law, which was enacted in Ontario by way of the International Commercial Arbitration Act 1990, the Ontario Superior Court of Justice held that in order to justify setting aside an award, the conduct of the arbitral tribunal must be sufficiently serious to offend the basic notions of morality and justice. In boycotting the arbitration, the court determined that the Mexican parties had deliberately forfeited the opportunity to be heard. In so doing, they were deemed to have deprived themselves of the right to be heard. In other words, the "due process" safeguard was not intended to protect a party from its own failures or strategic choices.[77]

The third case arose out of a dispute between an Iranian helicopter company and a US corporation that came before the Iran–US Claims tribunal. The tribunal made an award against the US corporation. However, in the course of the arbitration, there was discussion at a procedural meeting as to whether or not the tribunal required the US corporation to produce the actual supporting invoices, or whether it would be more convenient to have a summary of them prepared by independent accountants. The chairman of the tribunal indicated (and it is not difficult to sympathise with him) that the tribunal would not be "very much enthusiastic getting kilos and kilos of invoices". Accordingly, it was agreed that the US corporation would retain an international firm of accountants to verify that the accounts submitted to the tribunal accurately summarised the invoices in the records. This was done. However, before the case came to a hearing, the chairman of the tribunal who conducted the procedural review resigned and was replaced. At the hearing itself, the question was raised as to why the actual invoices were not produced. This question was answered by the US corporation's counsel. Nevertheless in its award, the tribunal disallowed the claims that had been documented by the accountants, stating:

"The Tribunal cannot grant [the claimant's] claims solely on the basis of an affidavit and a list of invoices, even if the existence of the invoices was certified by an independent audit."[78]

---

[77] *Corporacion Transnacional de Inversiones SA de CV v STET International SpA and STET International Neterlands NV* (1999) 45 O.R. (3d) 183 (Ont. S.C.J.).

[78] *Iran Aircraft Ind. v Avco Corp*, majority opinion, reported in (1993) XVIII Yearbook Commercial Arbitration 599. The case is also reported in 980 F.2d 141 (2nd Cir. 1992).

The US Court of Appeals held that by "misleading [the US corporation], **9–24** however unwittingly, the tribunal denied [it] the opportunity to present its claim in a meaningful manner."[79]

In Europe, the concept of "due process" has found expression in the European Convention of Human Rights (the "ECHR"),[80] Art.6(1) of which provides that:

"In the determination of his civil rights and obligations or of any criminal charge against him, everyone is entitled to a fair and public hearing within a reasonable time by an independent and impartial tribunal established by law."

An agreement to arbitrate constitutes a valid waiver of Art.6 in that arbitration provides no entitlement to a public hearing and an arbitral tribunal is not, within the meaning of Art.6, considered a "tribunal established by law".[81] For these reasons, the Swiss Federal Supreme Court held that Art.6 does not apply in arbitration proceedings.[82] In so doing, however, it also held that the arbitral tribunal must nevertheless respect fundamental rules of due process. This finding was echoed in England following the coming into force of the Human Rights Act 1998, which enacted the ECHR into English law. Thus, in *Mousaka v Golden Seagull Maritime*,[83] the court held that:

"The tentacles of the Human Rights Act 1998 reach into some unexpected places. The Commercial Court, even, when exercising its supervisory rule as regards arbitration, is not immune."

It would be difficult to reach a contrary conclusion. An arbitration agreement **9–25** may constitute a waiver of the right of access to the courts, but it surely is not intended to be a blanket waiver of the guarantees to a "fair hearing" contained in Art.6.[84] When considering a challenge to an award on grounds of a violation

---

[79] (1993) XVIII Yearbook Commercial Arbitration 602. Accordingly, enforcement of the award was denied (with Cardamone C.J. dissenting) on the basis that the US corporation had been "unable to present its case" as required by Art.V.1(h) of the New York Convention, as well as by the Model Law Art.34(2)(a)(ii).

[80] Convention for the Protection of Human Rights and Fundamental Freedoms (Rome, November 4, 1950) (as amended), (1955) 213 United Nations Treaty Series 221.

[81] For a comprehensive survey of case law on the relationship between Art.6 and arbitration, see Liebscher, *op cit.*, pp.61 *et seq.*

[82] Swiss Federal Supreme Court, June 11, 2001 [2001] Bull. A.S.A. 566. See also the Cour d'Appel de Paris decision of September 15, 1998 in *Cubic Defence Systems v Chambre de Commerce International* (1999) Revue de l'Arbitrage 103, n. Lalive, and the Cour de Cassation decision in the same case two years later (2001) Revue de l'Arbitrage 511, n. Clay, in which the French courts found that, as an arbitral institution, the ICC International Court of Arbitration was not a "judicial body" within the meaning of Art.6.

[83] [2001] 2 Lloyd's Rep. 657.

[84] See Georgios Petrochilos, *Procedural Law in International Arbitration* (Oxford Private International Law Series, 2004), para.4.51.

of "due process", courts in Europe may well therefore have regard to the safeguards contained in Art.6.

(c) Issues of jurisdiction

9–26   The third ground for recourse against an arbitral award under the Model Law turns on issues of jurisdiction. The wording of the ground of challenge is as follows:

> "(iii) the award deals with a dispute not contemplated by or not falling within the terms of the submission to arbitration, or contains decisions on matters beyond the scope of the submission to arbitration, provided that, if the decisions on matters submitted to arbitration can be separated from those not so submitted, only that part of the award which contains decisions on matters not submitted to arbitration may be set aside."[85]

The jurisdiction of an arbitral tribunal has already been discussed.[86] This third ground of challenge under the Model Law contemplates a situation in which an award has been made by a tribunal that *did* have jurisdiction to deal with the dispute, but which exceeded its powers by dealing with matters that had *not* been submitted to it.[87] By way of example, the Cour d'Appel de Paris has found that a tribunal exceeded its mission by awarding a party damages in an amount that significantly exceeded the damages claimed.[88]

As to the broader issue of jurisdiction, where it is denied (for instance) that the arbitral tribunal has *any* jurisdiction at all, the application to set aside the award is likely to arise under the first of the grounds set out in the Model Law. For example, it may be argued that one of the parties to the arbitration was not a party to the agreement providing for the submission of disputes to arbitration[89]; or that such an agreement was made but was void (for instance, because of illegality).[90] A common example of a provision for an award to be set aside for lack of jurisdiction is found in the French law governing international arbitrations. This provides that an international award may be set aside if it is made "in the absence of an arbitration agreement, or on the basis of a void or expired agreement".[91]

9–27   Where the arbitral tribunal fails to deal with *all* the issues referred to it for determination, it is usually said that the award should at least be held valid in

---

[85] Model Law, Art.34(2)(a)(iii).
[86] See Ch.5.
[87] See Liebscher, *op. cit.*, Ch.V(6).
[88] *Paris Lapeyre v Sauvage* (2001) Revue de l'Arbitrage 806, n. Derains.
[89] As in the *Pyramids* case (1984) 23 I.L.M. 1048.
[90] As in *Dalmia Dairy Industries Ltd v Pakistan* [1978] 2 Lloyd's Rep. 223.
[91] By a combination of Arts 1502 and 1504 of Decree Law No.81–500 of May 12, 1981; this is similar to the provision in the Model Law, which states that an award may be set aside if the party making the application furnishes proof that "the said agreement is not valid under the law to which the parties have subjected it or, failing any indication therein, under the law of this State"; Model Law, Art.34(2)(a)(i).

respect of the issues with which it *does* deal.[92] However, this is perhaps too simplistic. The significance of the issues that were not dealt with has to be considered in relation to the award as a whole. For example, it is not difficult to envisage a situation in which the issues that were overlooked were of such importance that, if they had been dealt with, the whole balance of the award would have been altered and its effect would have been different. In such circumstances, it seems fair that the aggrieved party should have a right of recourse against the award. Such a right of recourse is found in many national systems of law,[93] but not in the Model Law; and whilst it appeared as a ground for refusal of recognition and enforcement of an award under the Geneva Convention of 1927, it is not found in the New York Convention.[94]

(d) Further procedural issues

The fourth ground for recourse against an arbitral award under the Model Law **9–28** is as follows:

"(iv) the composition of the arbitral tribunal or the arbitral procedure was not in accordance with the agreement of the parties, unless such agreement was in conflict with provision of this Law from which the parties cannot derogate, or, failing such agreement was not in accordance with this Law."[95]

The effect of this provision is to state that both the composition of the arbitral tribunal and the procedure adopted in the arbitration must be in conformity with the agreement of the parties or, failing such agreement, with the law.[96] By way of example, a failure to comply with the agreement of the parties as to the appointment of the tribunal could include cases in which an arbitrator does not meet the particular qualifications specified in the arbitration agreement; failure to comply with the required procedure could include the rendering of an award without reasons where such a requirement is imposed by law.

Presumably, if there is no particular agreement between the parties as to the composition of the tribunal, there can be no complaint under this head of the Model Law if the arbitrators are selected according to the method prescribed by

[92] To this effect, see van den Berg, *The New York Arbitration Convention* (1981), p.318, who points out that the making of an award *infra petita* is no longer a ground for refusal of recognition and enforcement under the New York Convention, as it was under the Geneva Convention of 1927.
[93] See the Netherlands Arbitration Act 1986, Art.1065, for an example of a national system containing such a provision. But note that where the parties have discovered that the arbitral tribunal omitted to decide an issue before it, an additional award must first have been applied for and rejected before there is an admissible ground for setting aside (Art.1065(6)). As regards the Model Law, Art.33(3) may provide the answer to this problem in that, at the request of a party, the arbitral tribunal may make an additional award where claims have not been dealt with in the award.
[94] However, it has been suggested that the same result can be achieved by applying to set aside the award in its country of origin and then by relying on Art.V.1(e) of the New York Convention, which provides that recognition and enforcement of the award may be refused if it has been set aside in the country in which it was made; see van den Berg, *op. cit.*, p.321.
[95] Model Law, Art.34(2)(a)(iv).
[96] See Liebscher, *op. cit.*, Ch.V(5).

the relevant law. Similarly, if there is no agreement between the parties as to the arbitral procedure, there can be no complaint if the procedure that is followed is imposed by the arbitral tribunal—provided that there is compliance with the other relevant requirements of the Model Law (as to a fair hearing and so on). Moreover, if there is an agreement between the parties as to the composition of the arbitral tribunal or as to the procedure to be followed or both, this agreement may be safely disregarded if it is in conflict with a mandatory provision of the law of the place of arbitration.

Summary

9–29   These then are the four grounds for recourse against an arbitral award that, under the Model Law, must be proved by the applicant. There are two further grounds, however, which may be raised by a national court of its own initiative, namely arbitrability and public policy. These grounds are now considered separately.

(e) Arbitrability

9–30   The Model Law states that an arbitral award may be set aside if the court of the place of arbitration finds that "the subject matter of the dispute is not capable of settlement by arbitration" under its own law.

The concept of "arbitrability" has already been discussed[97] and there is no need to repeat the discussion here. What should be noted, however, is that for the purposes of this section of the Model Law, it is expressly the law of the place of arbitration which decides whether or not the dispute is "capable of settlement by arbitration" or whether it belongs to the domain of disputes that must be decided by a national court.

In many jurisdictions, a challenge to an award based on grounds of arbitrability will often be linked to the concept of public policy.[98] For example, one area in which "public policy" was in the past used as a reason for limiting the domain of arbitration was that of antitrust. In *American Safety*, the reaction of the court was that:

> "A claim under the antitrust laws is not merely a private matter . . . Antitrust violation can affect hundreds of thousands, perhaps millions, of people and inflict staggering economic damage. We do not believe Congress intended such claims to be resolved elsewhere than the courts."[99]

9–31   Subsequently, in *Mitsubishi*, the US Supreme Court allowed an arbitration involving antitrust claims to continue; but added this word of warning:

---

[97] See Ch.3.

[98] In France, *e.g.*, limits to arbitrability are set by French concepts of international public policy. See, *e.g.*, the decision of the Cour d'Appel de Paris in *Ganz v Nationale des Chemins de Fer Tunisiens* (SNCFT) (1991) Revue de l'Arbitrage 478, n. Ilot.

[99] *American Safety Equipment Corp v J.P. Maguire & Co*, 391 F.2d 821, 826 (2nd Cir. 1968).

"Having permitted the arbitration to go forward, the national courts of the United States will have the opportunity at the award enforcement stage to ensure that the legitimate interest in the enforcement of the antitrust laws has been addressed."[1]

In invoking the "legitimate interest" in ensuring proper enforcement of US antitrust laws, the Supreme Court was referring to the opportunity to ensure that an award does not conflict with US public policy. Moreover, although the court referred to the opportunity of a "second look" at the enforcement stage, the same opportunity would arise in the event of a challenge of the award. Understanding the concept of public policy is therefore critical to understanding the scope that exists for setting aside an award, and it is this concept that is considered next.

(f) Public policy

Lastly, the Model Law states that an arbitral award may be set aside if a national court of the place of arbitration finds that the award is in conflict with the public policy of its own country.   **9–32**

Each state has its own concept of what is required by its "public policy" (or *ordre public*, in the civil law terminology). It is possible to envisage, for example, a dispute over the division of gaming profits from a casino. The dispute is taken to arbitration and an award is made. In many states, the underlying transaction that led to the award would be regarded as a normal commercial transaction and the award would be regarded as valid. However, in states that do not tolerate gambling, the award might well be set aside on the basis that it offends public policy and is illegal. Similarly, it is possible to envisage a dispute between a wine producer and a distributor being regarded as arbitrable in many countries except perhaps in a strict Islamic country in which the production, sale or consumption of alcohol is prohibited.

Most developed arbitral jurisdictions have similar conceptions of public policy. According to the Swiss Federal Supreme Court, public policy denotes fundamental legal principles, a departure from which would be incompatible with the Swiss legal and economic system.[2] Similarly, German courts have held that an award will violate public policy if it conflicts with fundamental notions of justice, *bonos mores* or conflicts with principles which are fundamental national or economic values.[3] Again in similar terms, the Superior Court of Justice of Ontario refused to set aside an award rendered by a NAFTA tribunal, holding that for an award to offend public policy:

"[it] 'must fundamentally offend the most basic and explicit principles of justice and fairness in Ontario, or evidence intolerable ignorance or corruption

---

[1] *Mitsubishi Motors Corp v Soler Chrysler-Plymouth Inc* 473 US 614, 628 (1985).
[2] See, *e.g.*, the decision of the Swiss Federal Supreme Court of September 18, 2001 (2002) Bull. A.S.A. 311.
[3] See the decision of the Karlsruhe Court of Appeal of September 14, 2001.

on the part of the arbitral Tribunal' . . . The Applicant must establish that the awards are contrary to the essential morality of Ontario."[4]

9–33   Notwithstanding these similarities, the fact that different states have different concepts of their own public policy means that there is a risk that one state may set aside an award that other states would regard as valid. More generally, the nebulous nature of the concept has on occasion also been used by courts in some jurisdictions as licence to review—inappropriately—the merits of a dispute. With this in mind, the concept of "international public policy" (*"ordre public inter-national"*) has been developed by some jurists and is embodied in the New French Code of Civil Procedure. This Code allows an international arbitral award to be set aside "if the recognition or execution is contrary to *international* public policy".[5] In this way, French law recognises the existence of two levels of public policy, the national level, which may be affected by purely domestic considerations, and the international level, which is less restrictive in its approach.

There is nothing new, so far as arbitration is concerned, in differentiating between national and international public policy. Indeed, it is a consistent theme to be found in the legislation and judicial decisions of many countries.[6] On this basis, an international award would not be set aside simply because it failed to conform to a domestic requirement. For example, the absence of reasons, which might lead to an award being annulled in a domestic arbitration, has been held not to vitiate an international award.[7]

If a workable definition of "international public policy" could be found, it would provide an effective way of preventing an award in an international arbitration from being set aside for purely domestic policy considerations. International public policy would not concern itself with matters of form, or of a purely domestic nature. It would look to the broader public interest of honesty and fair dealing. In its interim report on public policy as a bar to the enforcement of international arbitration awards, the Committee on International Commercial Arbitration of the International Law Association (the "ILA") reviewed the development of the concept of public policy during the latter part of the twentieth century.[8] In so doing, it observed that beyond purely domestic public policy (*"ordre public interne"*), there exists a narrower category of international public policy (*"ordre public externe"* or *"international"*), which is confined to the violation of really fundamental conceptions of the legal order in the country

---

[4] *United Mexican States v Marvin Roy Feldman Karpa*, File No.03-CV-23500, Ontario Superior Court of Justice, December 3, 2003, at para.87 (available online at: *www.naftalaw.org*).

[5] French Decree Law No.81-500 of May 12, 1981, Art.1502.5 (emphasis added).

[6] Portugal, *e.g.*, has a similar provision at Art.1096(f) of the Code of Civil Procedure (1986), which refers to the principles of "Portuguese international public policy". See also the German Federal Supreme Court Decision of February 1, 2001, (2001) No.1 R.P.S. 14, in which it held that the notion of public policy is more restricted when applied to foreign awards, and in which it distinguished between domestic and international public policy.

[7] French Decree Law No.81-500 of May 12, 1981, Arts 1471 and 1495. See also Delvolvé, "Essai sur la motivation des sentences arbitrales" (1989) 2 Revue de l'Arbitrage 149.

[8] ILA Committee on International Commercial Arbitration's Interim Report on Public Policy as a Bar to Enforcement of International Arbitral Awards (London Conference, 2000).

concerned. Narrower still, the ILA identified a further category, namely "truly international" or "transnational" public policy, which it found to be of "universal application—comprising fundamental rules of natural law, principles of universal justice, *jus cogens* in public international law, and the general principles of morality accepted by what are referred to as 'civilised nations'".[9] Such definitions are undoubtedly helpful, yet for now remain to be widely accepted. At the beginning of the twenty-first century, the warning note sounded by an English judge almost two hundred years ago thus still resonates:

> "[public policy is] a very unruly horse, and when once you get astride it you never know where it will carry you. It may lead you from sound law. It is never argued at all, but when other points fail".[10]

(g) Conclusion

As already indicated, the Model Law grounds for challenge of an arbitral **9–34** award are strictly limited. Indeed, the four grounds on which the party making the application is entitled to rely are concerned with largely procedural irregularities, either in the course of the arbitration or in the award itself. Nor is there much subtlety in the Model Law. If a challenge is successful, the award will generally be set aside, in whole or in part—although, as has been seen, there is a possibility of "rescue" by remission to the tribunal for reconsideration.

When there is an appeal against a judgment in a national court, the successful party may have the opportunity to make a cross-appeal; that is to say, to bring before the court aspects of the judgment to which it may object. There is no such provision in the Model Law. Accordingly, only the losing party is likely to challenge an award. In this way, the Model Law reflects the modern movement towards finality of arbitration awards. There is a belief that, so far as international arbitrations are concerned, the parties should be prepared to accept the decision of the arbitral tribunal even if they consider it to be wrong, so long as the correct procedures are observed. If a court is allowed to review this decision on the law or on the merits, the speed and, above all, the finality of the arbitral process is lost. Indeed, arbitration then becomes merely the first stage in a process that may lead, by way of successive appeals, to the highest appellate court at the place of arbitration.

The Model Law has proved influential in the world of international commercial arbitration. Some countries have enacted it entirely without amendment (indeed Cyprus did not even translate UNCITRAL's English text into Greek when it adopted the Model Law). Even countries such as Spain, Germany and England, which have a long tradition of arbitration and have worked out a reasonably effective partnership between arbitration and the national courts, have to varying degrees taken the Model Law as a guide in the modernisation of their own arbitration laws.

---

[9] *ibid.*, at pp.6 and 7.
[10] *Richardson v Mellish* (1824) 2 Bing. 229 at 252, [1824–34] All E.R. 258, *per* Burrough J.

5. SUBSTANTIVE GROUNDS FOR CHALLENGE

(a) Mistake of law

9–35   When an arbitral award is challenged on a particular issue under the Model Law, the national court at the place of arbitration must review the relevant facts and law in order to reach its decision. However, the court is only concerned with that particular issue, so that—for example—a court that has to determine a claim that the composition of the arbitral tribunal was not in accordance with the agreement of the parties,[11] needs only to deal with that claim.[12] The court is not called on to review the award as a whole. Indeed, and this is an important point, there is no provision in the Model Law for any form of appeal from an arbitral award, on the law or on the facts, or for any judicial review of the award on its merits. If the tribunal has jurisdiction, the correct procedures are followed and the correct formalities are observed, the award—good, bad or indifferent—is final and binding on the parties.

This is the critical point. In most of the major trading nations of the world,[13] the award of an arbitral tribunal, irrespective of whether it is a partial, interim[14] or final award, disposes of the matters in dispute, is binding on the parties (unless set aside) and in principle is enforceable against the losing party not only at the seat of arbitration, but also in other jurisdictions under such international treaties as the New York Convention. For the purpose of these treaties, the award carries with it in effect the *imprimatur* of the state where it was made (or deemed to have been made). If the award was made in Geneva, it is a Swiss award; if in Paris, a French award.

The question then arises as to the extent to which the law of the seat of the arbitration provides for the review of awards that are made in its territory and that go out into the world, so to speak, as Swiss awards, or French awards. In particular, is it enough to ensure that the correct procedures have been observed, as the Model Law requires, or is something more needed—ranging from correction of any mistakes of law to a complete review of the dispute—so as to ensure that the arbitral tribunal has reached the correct decision?

9–36   The argument in favour of reviewing arbitral decisions in order to guard against mistakes of law is not difficult to make. There are obvious risks in having a legal system that leaves arbitral awards free from appeal or judicial review.

---

[11] Under the Model Law, Art.34(2)(a)(iv).

[12] Such an issue came before a Hong Kong court, where it was raised as a defence to a request for enforcement of an award under the New York Convention. The judge held that the composition of the arbitral tribunal was *not* in accordance with the agreement of the parties; but he nevertheless allowed enforcement on the basis that this had been known to the parties and they had nevertheless proceeded with the arbitration: see Ch.10.

[13] For recognition and enforcement of awards, see Ch.10.

[14] If a partial or interim award is final, in the sense of being dispositive of an issue with which it deals, it should be enforceable under the New York Convention. The problem arises where the interim award deals with interim measures of relief: see, for instance, *Resort Condominiums International Inc v Bolwell* (a judgment of an Australian court) (1995) XX Yearbook Commercial Arbitration 628; and see the discussion of interim measures in Ch.7.

First, there is the risk of inconsistent decisions as the same or similar points come before different tribunals, each one of which is independent of the other. Such tribunals are generally unaware that the same point of law may already have been decided in a different way by another tribunal. This is likely to be of particular importance where the decision turns upon the correct interpretation of a standard form clause in a widely used contract—such as the FIDIC Suite of Model Conditions that are widely used for international construction projects or the standard form contracts used throughout the worldwide commodity, shipping, insurance or reinsurance markets. Secondly, there is the risk that the arbitral tribunal may not do its work as competently or as professionally as it should if its awards are not subject to scrutiny, either by an arbitral institution[15] or by a competent court.

Experience shows, however, that there are serious disadvantages in having a system of arbitration that gives an unrestricted right of appeal from arbitral awards. First, the decisions of national judges may be substituted for the decisions of an arbitral tribunal specifically selected by or on behalf of the parties. Secondly, a party that agreed to arbitration as a private method of resolving disputes may find itself brought unwillingly before national courts that hold their hearings in public. Thirdly, the appeal process may be used simply to postpone the day on which payment is due, so that one of the main purposes of international commercial arbitration—the speedy resolution of disputes—is defeated. One commentator on the ICSID appeal procedures wrote:

"[T]he final disheartening moral is that as long as the motivation to review and overturn awards exists, no carefully limited set of grounds for appeal will necessarily protect an arbitration award from being nullified."[16]

It is not easy to strike a balance between the need for finality in the arbitral **9–37** process and the wider public interest in some measure of judicial control, if only to ensure consistency of decisions and predictability of the operation of the law. Internationally, however, the balance has come down strongly in favour of finality, and against judicial review, except in very limited circumstances. The Model Law sets the tone, as has been seen, when it proclaims that:

"In matters governed by this Law, no court shall intervene except where so provided in this Law."[17]

The extent of court intervention permitted by different states may be viewed as a spectrum. At one end of the spectrum are states such as France, which

---

[15] The ICC Arbitration Rules, Art.27, *e.g.*, provides for the scrutiny of an award by the ICC's Court before the award is finalised and issued to the parties. This helps to ensure a measure of "quality control"; but the scrutiny is principally as to form and in any event does not affect the tribunal's liberty of decision.

[16] Craig, "Uses and Abuses of Appeal from Awards" (1988) 4 Arbitration International 174 at 214.

[17] Model Law, Art.5.

exercise a minimum control over international arbitral awards, and Switzerland, which allows non-Swiss parties to "contract out" of controls altogether. In the middle of the scale, are grouped a considerable number of states that have adopted (either in full or with some modifications) the grounds of recourse laid down in the Model Law. At the other end of the spectrum are countries such as England, which operate a range of controls, including mandatory procedural controls, as well as a limited right of appeal on questions of law that the parties may agree to waive. The examples that follow illustrate the various different approaches.

The admonition in the Model Law *against* intervention by national courts in the process of international commercial arbitration, has been taken to extremes by some states where the court may not intervene at all in an international commercial arbitration. A similar attitude was adopted by Belgium, which in 1985 "delocalised" international commercial arbitration by eliminating the possibility of setting aside an award made in Belgium when none of the parties was a natural person having Belgian nationality or residence; or a legal person having its main office or a seat of operations in Belgium. However, the position has since changed. Parties were apparently discouraged from choosing Belgium as a place of arbitration[18]; thus, since 1998 recourse to the Belgian courts to set aside an award made in Belgium is possible, even for foreign nationals or corporations, unless they expressly exclude any such application either in the arbitration agreement itself or in any subsequent agreement.[19]

9–38 France distinguishes between "domestic" and "international" arbitrations, and does not permit appeals to its courts from an international award. Under French legislation of 1981,[20] the grounds for recourse against an international award made in France are more limited than those set out in the Model Law.[21] They are:

- if the arbitrator decided in the absence of an arbitration agreement or on the basis of a void or expired agreement;

- if the arbitral tribunal was irregularly composed or the sole arbitrator irregularly appointed;

- if the arbitrator decided in a manner incompatible with the mission conferred upon him;

---

[18] In the second edition of this book, the authors predicted that this lack of recourse might discourage participants, particularly if they were likely to be respondents in any arbitral proceedings, from choosing Belgium as a suitable place for arbitration.

[19] Art.1717.4, of the Law of May 19, 1998, amending the Belgian law on arbitration, reads as follows: "The parties may, by an express statement in the arbitration agreement or by a subsequent agreement exclude any application to set aside the arbitral award when none of the parties is either an individual of Belgian nationality or residing in Belgium or a legal person having its head office or a branch there". (Translation by Bernard Hanotiau and Joanne Riches.)

[20] New Code of Civil Procedure, Art.1502, introduced by the Decree Law of May 12, 1981.

[21] Model Law, Art.34.

- when due process has not been respected[22];

- if the recognition or enforcement is contrary to international public policy (*ordre public international*).

These grounds may be viewed as somewhat minimalistic. The Model Law, which goes further, sets the internationally accepted standard for judicial control of international arbitration—at least, so far as observance of the correct procedures is concerned; many states have been content to accept this level of control.

However, as has been seen, there is *no* provision in the Model Law for **9–39** challenging an award on the basis of mistake of fact or law. Some states with a long tradition of arbitration have taken the view that it should be open to the parties to appeal against an arbitration award if it contains a serious mistake of law. This view is reflected in the English 1996 Act. The right of appeal is preserved by s.69 of the Act, but it is not unrestricted. First, the parties may "contract out" of any right of appeal to the national court. Although their agreement to do so must be in writing, the provision contained in standard form rules of arbitration to the effect that the award shall be final and binding has been held to constitute a valid agreement to give up this right.[23]

Secondly, even if the right of appeal has been retained—and it is consistent with the autonomy of parties to an arbitration that they should be allowed to decide this for themselves—it is in effect a right of appeal *only* on questions of *English* law.[24] This is important, because in many of the international arbitrations held in England, the law governing the substance of the dispute is that of another state—of India, or New York, or Kuwait, or as the case may be.[25] Thirdly, the right of appeal is only available with leave of the court and then only if the decision of the tribunal on the question of law is "obviously wrong" or the question is one of "general public importance" and the decision "is at least open to serious doubt", so that it would be "just and proper in all the circumstances for the court to determine the question".[26] On an appeal, the court has power to confirm the award, to vary it, to remit it to the arbitral tribunal or to set it aside[27]; but the court should not set aside the award, in whole or in part, unless satisfied that it would be inappropriate to submit the matters in question to the tribunal for reconsideration.[28] No further appeal is possible, unless the court considers the

---

[22] This equates to the right of each party to be heard.
[23] *Sanghi Polyesters Ltd v The International Investor (KCFC)* [2001] 1 Lloyd's Rep. 480.
[24] English Arbitration Act 1996, ss.69(1) and 82(1). The underlying policy of the English legislators was related to the long-established tradition of arbitration by non-lawyers in certain commercial sectors, *e.g.* the construction industry, trading in commodities and so forth.
[25] See, *e.g.*, *AEK v National Basket Association* [2002] 1 All E.R. (Comm) 70, in which permission to appeal on a point of law under s.69 was rejected as it related to the arbitrator's application of Greek law.
[26] English Arbitration Act 1996, s.69(2) and (3).
[27] *ibid.*, s.69 (7).
[28] *ibid.*

question to be one of general importance or one that for some special reason should be considered by the Court of Appeal.

Parties to an international arbitration in Switzerland have three options open to them. The first is to conduct the arbitration under the Swiss Private International Law Act 1987, Ch.12 of which applies to international arbitrations.[29] Under this statute, proceedings for setting aside an award may only be initiated where there was some defect in the appointment of the arbitral tribunal; lack of jurisdiction; failure to decide a claim; deciding claims not submitted to arbitration; failure to treat the parties equally; or, finally, incompatibility with public policy.[30] Setting aside proceedings may only be brought before the Federal Supreme Court.[31]

9–40 The second option is available where none of the parties has its domicile, habitual residence or business establishment in Switzerland. It permits parties to agree (either in the arbitration agreement or subsequently) to exclude all setting aside proceedings or to limit such proceedings to one or more of the grounds listed in the Act.[32]

The third option is for the parties to take a step back into the past[33] and agree to the application of the law of one of the Swiss cantons, which for all cantons is the Intercantonal Convention on Arbitration of 1969 (generally known as the "Concordat"). Under the Concordat, the grounds for setting aside an award are more extensive than under the Swiss Arbitration Act and they include a provision[34] for setting aside an award on the basis that it is "arbitrary". Under Swiss case law, "arbitrary" awards have been held to include awards which are "manifestly unsupportable" or "made without any objective reasons and in violation of a right certain" or " . . . seriously violating a clear and undisputed legal norm or principle".[35]

Under the US Federal Arbitration Act,[36] a court may set aside (or, in the language of the statute, "vacate") an award in the following circumstances:

(1) where it was procured by corruption, fraud, or undue means;

(2) where there was evident partiality or corruption in the arbitrators, or any of them;

(3) where the arbitrators were guilty of misconduct in refusing to postpone the hearing, upon sufficient cause shown, or in refusing to hear evidence

---

[29] An English translation of the Swiss Private International Law Act 1987 was published by the Swiss Arbitration Association in (1998) 6 ASA Bulletin. The Act applies where the seat of arbitration is in Switzerland and where at least one of the parties had neither its domicile nor its habitual residence in Switzerland: Art.176(1).

[30] This is a précis of the full text of Art.190.

[31] Swiss Private International Law Act 1987, Art.191.

[32] *ibid.*, Art.192(1).

[33] This is known by Swiss lawyers as the "nostalgia" clause; and parties to an international commercial agreement are unlikely to adopt it.

[34] Concordat, Art.36(f).

[35] See Bucher & Tschanz, *International Arbitration in Switzerland* (Helbing & Lichtenhahn, Basle, 1989), p.141.

[36] Title 9, US Code, ss.1 *et seq.* The statute was first enacted in February 1925, but has been amended since.

pertinent and material to the controversy; or any other misbehaviour by which the rights of any party have been prejudiced; or

(4) where the arbitrators exceeded their powers, or so imperfectly executed them that a mutual, final, and definite award upon the subject matter submitted was not made.[37]

The statute does not provide expressly for any judicial review of an arbitral **9–41** award on the basis of a mistake of law, and US courts have held that an award may not be set aside on such grounds.[38]

(b) Mistake of fact

The principal justification for allowing an appeal from the award of an arbitral **9–42** tribunal on questions of law is that it is in the public interest—and especially in the interest of commercial men—that the law should be certain and that, in particular, there should not be different findings by different tribunals as to the meaning and effect of the same words in different contracts.[39] There can be no such general interest in the findings of fact of a particular tribunal in a particular case. They may be wrong, even badly wrong, but that is likely to be of interest only to the parties. Accordingly, almost all states with developed laws of arbitration refuse to allow appeals from arbitral tribunals on issues of fact. It is possible that parties to an international arbitration in Switzerland could "contract in" to the Concordat, as previously described, and then be able to challenge the award as "arbitrary" if it was "manifestly unsupportable" on the facts, but the chances of this happening must be small.[40]

A potentially more disturbing example of parties "contracting in" to judicial review comes from the US. As has been seen,[41] under the 1925 Federal Act, the grounds for challenge of an arbitral award are limited. However, in *LaPine Technology Corporation v Kyocera Corporation*[42] (hereinafter "*LaPine*") the arbitration clause, after providing for arbitration in accordance with the ICC Rules and the Federal Arbitration Act, went on to say:

"The United States District Court for the Northern District of California may enter judgment upon any award, either by confirming the award or by vacating, modifying or correcting the award. The Court shall vacate, modify or correct any award: (i) based upon any of the grounds referred to in the Federal Arbitration Act, (ii) where the arbitrators' findings of fact are not supported by

---

[37] Federal Arbitration Act, s.10. There is a possibility of the award being remitted to the arbitrators, where the time within which the award was to be made has not expired: s.10(5).

[38] See, *e.g.*, *Baxter Int'l Inc v Abbott Labs*, 315 F.3d 829 (US App., 2003).

[39] Compare the English Arbitration Act 1996, s.69(3)(c)(ii), which provides that one of the requirements for leave to appeal is that the question of law is "one of general public importance".

[40] See para.9–40.

[41] See para.9–40.

[42] 130 F.3d 884 (9th Cir. 1997).

substantial evidence or (iii) where the arbitrators' conclusions of law are erroneous."

In the District Court, Kyocera applied to modify and vacate the award on the grounds that there were findings of fact that the evidence did not support, and that there were wrong conclusions of law. The US court held that its jurisdiction was determined by the 1925 Federal Act and could not be expanded by a private contract.[43] However, the Court of Appeals overturned this decision and allowed the appeal. The court took the view that "the parties indisputably contracted for heightened judicial scrutiny of the arbitrators' award when they agreed that review would be for errors of fact or law" and the court held that this agreement should be upheld. Accordingly, the District Court was required to review the award, on issues both of fact and of law.

9–43   Yet this proved not to be the end of the *LaPine* saga. Applying the broader standards of review laid down by the Ninth Circuit Court of Appeals, the District Court nonetheless confirmed the award. This led Kyocera to appeal again. In an *en banc* ruling that has been referred to as *LaPine II*, the Ninth Circuit then chose to revisit the issue of whether expanded review clauses are enforceable, and in so doing overturned its earlier decision, holding that:

> "a Federal Court may only review an arbitral decision on the grounds set forth in the [Federal Arbitration Act]. Private parties have no power to alter or expand those grounds, and any contractual provision purporting to do so is accordingly legally unenforceable."[44]

At the time of writing, there remains a difference of opinion between US courts as to whether or not parties may expand the scope of review.[45] Freedom of contract is a well-established and well-honoured concept; it is nevertheless somewhat surprising that, without express statutory authority, parties to an arbitration may be allowed to pick and choose in this way. As Professor Lowenfeld has said, the US legislature could authorise parties to consent to judicial review of arbitral awards; but he then added:

> "Without some such legislative authorisation, however, I do not think that the courts can assert jurisdiction to review awards of arbitrators on the basis of an implied grant and I do not think the parties have it within their power to confer such jurisdiction on the courts."[46]

---

[43] *LaPine*, 909 F.Supp.697 (1995).

[44] *Kyocera Corp v Prudential-Bache Trade Services Inc*, 341 F.3d 987 (9th Cir. 2003).

[45] See, *e.g.*, *Gateway Tech. Inc v MCI Telecomms Corp*, 64 F.3d 993 (5th Cir. 1995), enforcing a provision requiring the review of arbitral awards for errors of law, and *Bowen v Amoco Pipeline Co*, 254 F.3d 925 (10th Cir. 2001), declining to enforce a provision providing for expanded review. See also John Fellas, "The Scope of Judicial Review of Arbitration Awards", *New York Law Journal*, Vol.230, No.92 (November 7, 2003).

[46] Lowenfeld, "Can arbitration co-exist with Judicial Review?" *Currents*, September 1998, p.11 (published by the AAA).

Summary

This brief review demonstrates that most states are broadly content to restrict **9–44**
the challenge of arbitral awards to excess of jurisdiction and lack of due process.
These grounds for challenge are either adopted direct from the Model Law, or at
any rate reflect the policy behind those grounds. In general the parties are
expected to abide by the decision of the tribunal, however disappointed they may
be by the outcome. Other states are prepared to offer a limited measure of judicial
review on questions of law, if this is what the parties wish; but the possibility of
the review of an award on issues of fact is rare.

6. PLACE, TIME AND EFFECTS OF CHALLENGE

(a) Place of challenge

Where a challenge to the validity or effect of an award is possible, it must be **9–45**
addressed to a national court of competent jurisdiction. In general, this is a court
of the seat of the arbitration. If the arbitration was held in Switzerland, for
example, the competent court is the Federal Supreme Court (although the parties
may agree to the court of the canton in which the arbitration took place).[47] In
France, it is the Cour d'Appel de Paris. In England, it is the Commercial
Court.

There is one notable exception to this general rule, although it is probably
more theoretical than real. The freedom of the parties to an international arbitration to decide how it should be conducted is generally taken to include freedom
to subject the arbitration to the procedural law of a country *other than* that in
which the arbitration is held. It seems to be both unnecessary and unhelpful for
parties to use their freedom in this way.[48] Nevertheless, the existence of such
freedom is accepted, even by commentators who do not accept the concept of
delocalised arbitration.[49] Indeed, the New York Convention itself acknowledges
that recognition and enforcement of an award may be refused on the basis that the
award has been "set aside or suspended by a competent authority of the country
in which, *or under the law of which*, that award was made".[50]

---

[47] The Swiss Private International Law Act 1987, Ch.12, Art.191.
[48] "Unnecessary", because if the law of a particular country contains procedures which the parties
prefer, the parties would do better to adopt those specific procedures, rather than try to adopt a law
of procedure which is alien to the *lex arbitri* and might indeed be in conflict with it. "Unhelpful"
because it means adding another set of legal rules to which the arbitration will be subject, in
addition to those agreed by the parties or imposed by the *lex arbitri*. This topic is more fully
discussed in Ch.2.
[49] *per* Kerr L.J. in *Bank Mellat v Helliniki Techniki SA* [1984] Q.B. 291 at 301 (CA).
[50] New York Convention, Art.V.1(e) (emphasis added). See also *International Electric Corp v Bridas
Sociedad Anonima Petrolera, Industrial Y Commercial*, 745 F.Supp. 172, 178 (S.D. N.Y. 1990),
when the New York Court held that the italicised words referred to the procedural law governing
the arbitration, and not to the substantive law governing the agreement between the parties: "since
the *situs* of the arbitration is Mexico, and the governing procedural law that of Mexico, only
Mexico courts have jurisdiction under the Convention to vacate the award."

Accordingly, the possibility exists, in theory at least, that an award might be challenged under the law of a country other than that in which the award was made. It seems that in practice the point has never arisen.[51]

(b) Time-limits

9–46   When a challenge to an award is being considered, this should be done as a matter of urgency. Many countries that permit the challenge of arbitral awards do so only on the basis that the challenge is launched within a very short space of time following publication, or in some cases deposit, of the award. As has been seen, the Model Law requires that an action for the annulment or review of a partial award on jurisdiction must be brought within 30 days of notification of it to the party wishing to make the challenge.[52]

By way of example, English law provides that any challenge to an award (including any appeal from it) must be made within 28 days of the date of the award (or of the completion of any internal review of it).[53] However, not only do time-limits vary from country to country, they may also vary from state to state within a given country. In the US, the Federal Arbitration Act lays down a time-limit of three years for the confirmation and enforcement of awards under the New York Convention.[54] Every state has its own law governing arbitrations, but where time-limits are specified three months is the period most commonly chosen:

> "Prudence thus indicates that a party intending to oppose confirmation of an award should file a motion to vacate within three months of the award."[55]

In these circumstances, where challenge of an award is being considered, it is usually essential to consult a lawyer at the seat of the arbitration and to lose no time in doing so.

(c) The effects of a successful challenge

9–47   The effects of a successful challenge differ depending upon the grounds of the challenge, the relevant law and the decision of the court that dealt with it. This decision in itself may take several forms. The court may decide to:

- confirm the award;

---

[51] van den Berg (*op. cit.*, p.328) states that in none of the cases reported under the New York Convention have the parties designated a law of procedure foreign to that of the place of the arbitration; and he suggests, sensibly, that this provision of the Convention should be regarded as a "dead letter".

[52] Model Law, Art.16(3).

[53] English Arbitration Act 1996, s.70(1), (2) and (3).

[54] Title 9, US Code, s.12.

[55] Brenner, "Enforcement of Awards in Arbitration: a viable alternative to litigation", ABA Annual Meeting, 1984, Chicago. See also Gary Born, *International Commercial Arbitration— Commentary and Materials* (2nd ed., 2000), Ch.13, Pts A5–6.

- refer it back to the arbitral tribunal for reconsideration;

- vary the award; or

- set it aside, in whole or in part.

When an award is set aside, it is unenforceable in the country in which it was made and it will usually be unenforceable elsewhere.[56] In this situation, the party who won the arbitration but lost the challenge is in an unenviable position. If, for example, the award has been set aside completely on the basis that the arbitration agreement was null and void, a further resort to arbitration (on the basis of the void agreement) would be out of the question. Resort to litigation might be considered, but there could well be problems of time-limits—to say nothing of more substantive difficulties, such as (for example) the absence of a valid contract.

If the award has been set aside for procedural defects (for example, lack of due **9–48** process) the party who won the arbitration but lost the challenge is still in an unenviable position. The arbitration agreement will usually (but not always) still be effective. Providing the claim is not time-barred, the dispute must be submitted to arbitration and the process started over again. This is a daunting prospect for even the bravest claimant.

A successful party does not wish to be deprived of victory because of a procedural failure on the part of the arbitral tribunal. As the practice of international commercial arbitration becomes increasingly litigious, a party who expects to be on the losing side may seek, during the course of the proceedings, to lay the basis for a claim that the hearing was not conducted fairly. The losing party has the most to gain from having an award set aside for lack of a fair hearing. This point should be kept well in mind by parties to an arbitration (usually the claimants) who consider that the arbitral tribunal is being too generous to their opponents in allowing extensions of time and giving them a full opportunity to state their case.

---

[56] But see the discussion in Ch.10 relating to cases where an award has been set aside at the seat of the arbitration but has nevertheless been enforced in another country.

CHAPTER 10

RECOGNITION AND ENFORCEMENT OF ARBITRAL AWARDS

1. BACKGROUND

(a) Generally

10–01   The successful party in an international commercial arbitration expects the award to be performed without delay. This is a reasonable expectation. The purpose of arbitration, unlike mediation and most other methods of alternative dispute resolution, is to arrive at a binding decision on the dispute. Once this decision has been made in the form of an award, it is an implied term of every arbitration agreement that the parties will carry it out.[1] To put the point beyond doubt, an express provision to this effect is generally set out in arbitration clauses and submission agreements, as well as in international and institutional rules of arbitration. Indeed the model arbitration clauses recommended by arbitral institutions often contain words to emphasise the binding nature of the award, and their rules underline the commitment of the parties to carry it out.[2] For example, the UNCITRAL Rules state that the award "shall be final and binding on the parties" and that "the parties undertake to carry out the award without delay".[3]

Such statistics as are available suggest that most arbitral awards are in fact carried out voluntarily, that is to say, without the need for enforcement proceedings in national courts.[4] However, reliable statistics about arbitration are not readily available for two main reasons. First, arbitration is a private process. Secondly, and in any event, there is no particular reason why an arbitral tribunal (or indeed an arbitral institution) should know whether or not an award has been carried out. Unlike a national court, an arbitral tribunal has no role to play in the enforcement of its decision. Once the award has been rendered, the arbitral tribunal usually has nothing more to do with the dispute, unless it is required to make an additional award, or to correct or interpret its award.[5] When an arbitral

---

[1] See: Mustill & Boyd, *Commercial Arbitration* (2nd ed.), p.47; Expert report of Dr Lewis, *Esso/BHP v Plowman* (1995) 11 Arbitration International 282.

[2] UNCITRAL Arbitration Rules, Art.32(2); see also ICC Arbitration Rules, Art.28(6); LCIA Arbitration Rules, Art.26(8).

[3] UNCITRAL Arbitration Rules, Art.32(2).

[4] See Lalive, "Enforcing Awards" in *60 years of ICC Arbitration—A Look at the Future*, (1984), p.315 at p.318.

[5] See Ch.9, para.9–11.

tribunal has made a final award, its work is usually done and the tribunal is *functus officio.*

It is sometimes said that the test of a good arbitral award is that it leaves both parties feeling disappointed! Whether or not this is so, it is often true that in practice at least one party to an arbitration is dissatisfied with the result. Arbitration is not like conciliation or mediation, where the process has failed if it does not produce a result acceptable to both parties. In arbitration there is almost always a "winner" and a "loser". What happens if the winner is in fact dissatisfied with an award, considering that there were other claims too which should have succeeded?

In a national court, an appeal on some aspects of the judgment might be possible. In certain circumstances, and on limited conditions as already indicated,[6] an appeal may be possible in arbitration; but the trend is towards the acceptance of arbitral awards, good or bad, unless they can be attacked on grounds of excess jurisdiction, lack of due process or breach of public policy. A winning party who challenges an award because of dissatisfaction with certain aspects of it risks winning a pyrrhic victory. The usual result of a successful challenge is for the award to be set aside. If this happens, the winner then faces the prospect of being obliged to start or face fresh proceedings. This will involve either a new arbitration or (if, for example, the reason for setting aside was lack of jurisdiction on the part of the arbitral tribunal) a court action.   **10–02**

The losing party generally has more room for manoeuvre. First, such a party may simply carry out the award voluntarily, in accordance with its undertaking so to do—however unwelcome this may prove to be. Secondly, the losing party may use the award as a basis for negotiating a settlement. It is perhaps surprising that the successful party to an arbitration might settle for less than the amount awarded, but it might be considered better to accept a lesser payment forthwith, rather than face further challenge or enforcement proceedings to recover the full amount. Thirdly, the losing party may challenge the award, if this is possible under the rules of arbitration or the relevant law.[7] Finally, it may resist any attempt by the winning party to obtain recognition or enforcement of the award, in whatever jurisdiction this is sought.

The purpose of this chapter is to examine the recognition and enforcement of awards. However, it is appropriate to start by discussing the carrying out, or performance of awards from a wider perspective, so as to place recognition and enforcement in their proper contexts.

(b) Performance of awards

As already stated, the majority of awards are performed voluntarily. However, if the losing party fails to carry out an award, the winning party needs to take steps to enforce performance of it. Effectively, only two steps may be taken. The   **10–03**

---

[6] See Ch.9, para.9–12.
[7] As to which, see Ch.9, paras 9–07 *et seq.*

first is to exert some form of pressure, commercial or otherwise, in order to show the losing party that it is in its interests to perform the award. The second is to invoke the powers of the state, exercised through its national courts, in order to obtain a hold on the losing party's assets or in some other way to compel performance of the award.[8]

Commercial and other pressures

10–04   Sometimes a successful party can exert commercial pressure on a party who fails or refuses to perform an award. For example, if a continuing trade relationship exists between the parties, it may well be in the interests of the loser to perform the award, since a failure to do so may entail the loss of further profitable business. In such a case the successful party quickly makes this clear to the other party. In other cases, such as where a government or state agency is concerned, other pressures may be brought to bear by the diplomatic services of the successful party. It may be pointed out, for instance, that further development loans depend upon the carrying out of existing awards; or that foreign companies may be discouraged from making further investments, if outstanding obligations are not honoured.[9]

Pressure may also be exerted by the threat of adverse publicity. This method is one that is sometimes adopted by trade associations and has the effect of discouraging other traders in the market from dealing with the defaulting party. The GAFTA Rules for example, contain the following provision:

"22. Defaulters

22.1   In the event of any party to an arbitration or an appeal held under these Rules neglecting or refusing to carry out or abide by a final award of the tribunal or Board of appeal made under these Rules, the Council of the Association may post on the Association's Notice Board and/or circulate amongst Members in any way thought fit notification to that effect. The parties to any such arbitration or appeal shall be deemed to have consented to the Council taking such action as aforesaid."[10]

Before "posting", GAFTA communicates with the defaulter and asks whether there is anything to be said—for instance, whether there is an outstanding balance due to him from the successful party. However, where GAFTA is satisfied that there is a default, its members are informed. This will naturally

---

[8] For instance, by the winding-up of a company.
[9] The setting up of the Iran–US Claims Tribunal, discussed in Ch.1, is an example of state action to protect private investors.
[10] GAFTA Form 125, Arbitration Rules (effective for contracts dated from January 1, 2003 onwards), Art.22.1.

make them reluctant to deal with the defaulter, unless and until the award has been carried out.[11]

Similarly, but less explicitly, debtor states that end up as losing parties in **10–05** ICSID arbitrations may feel (rightly or wrongly) that refusal to perform an award voluntarily may adversely affect their creditworthiness at the World Bank. It may be no coincidence, therefore, that to date all ICSID awards have been voluntarily performed.

Arbitrator's duty to render an enforceable award

Some rules of arbitration contain an express provision that the arbitrator shall **10–06** "make every effort" to ensure that the award is enforceable.[12] This is an obligation to use best endeavours, rather than an obligation to secure a result. Indeed, it is difficult to see how it could be otherwise. The most conscientious arbitrator in the world cannot guarantee that his or her award is enforceable in whatever country enforcement may be sought. The most that can be expected is that the arbitrator will do his best to ensure that the appropriate procedure is followed and, above all, that each party is given a fair hearing.

Enforcement by court proceedings

The ultimate sanction for non-performance of an award is enforcement by **10–07** proceedings in a national court. This is something that should be borne in mind from the outset of an arbitration. Sometimes one of the parties (usually the claimant) urges the arbitral tribunal to run through the proceedings as quickly as possible, so as to obtain a speedy decision. This is understandable; but it is in the interests of the party that stands to gain most from the arbitration (whether by way of claim or counterclaim) to *ensure* that the proper procedures are followed, in case it should become necessary to apply to a national court for enforcement of the award.

Similar considerations apply when it comes to setting time-limits for the filing of submissions during the course of an arbitration. For instance, in a Swiss arbitration, one of the parties missed by two days an agreed deadline for the submission of certain new claims. The chairman of the arbitral tribunal extended time, but the agreed procedures for doing so were not followed and the losing party challenged the award, on the basis that there had been a violation of due process or of public policy, contrary to Swiss law. The Swiss Supreme Federal Tribunal refused to set aside the award, considering that the agreed deadline was a matter of procedure rather than of jurisdiction. However, the risk is clear. As stated by counsel, who represented the claimant before the tribunal:

---

[11] See Art.22 of the GAFTA Rules, reproduced *Bernstein's Handbook on Arbitration Practice* (4th ed., Sweet & Maxwell, London, 2003), paras A34–001 *et seq.*
[12] See, *e.g.*, ICC Arbitration Rules, Art.35.

"What parties fail to realise is that by setting themselves deadlines, the arbitration may end up with the worst possible result: a lack of finality."[13]

Enforcement usually takes place against assets.[14] This means that, as a first step, it is necessary to trace the assets of the losing party—money in a bank account, an aircraft or a ship, a cargo of oil in transit, or whatever it may be—before applying to the relevant national court for an order against those assets or, less constructively, for an order that the trade or business of the losing party should be wound up or liquidated, if payment of the award continues to be refused.[15]

10–08   There are four principal methods of enforcing an arbitral award against a recalcitrant party. The first is where the award is deposited, or registered, with a court or other authority,[16] following which it may be enforced as if it is a judgment of that court. The second is where the laws of the country of enforcement provide that, with the leave of the court, the award of an arbitral tribunal may be enforced *directly* without any need for deposit or registration.[17] The third is where it is necessary to apply to the court for some form of recognition (or *exequatur*) as a preliminary step to enforcement.[18] The fourth is to sue on the award as evidence of a debt, on the basis that the arbitration agreement constitutes a contractual obligation to perform the award. This last method is cumbersome, and frequently leaves it open to the losing party to reopen by way of defence the issues already determined by the arbitral tribunal. It is therefore to be avoided, unless no other method is available.

The procedures to be followed in any given case vary from country to country and from court to court. It is not possible to lay down detailed procedural guidelines here; nor would it be particularly helpful to do so, since if action has to be taken to enforce an award in a particular jurisdiction, it is necessary to obtain competent advice from experienced lawyers who practise in that jurisdiction.

What follows, therefore, is a review of the general principles underlying recognition and enforcement; the choice of the appropriate forum (including "forum shopping"); the role of the international conventions (in particular the

---

[13] See Kreindler & Kautz, "Agreed Deadlines and the Setting Aside of Arbitral Awards" (1997) 4 ASA Bulletin 576.

[14] Although there might, for instance, be an award ordering the return of a specific object, such as a valuable painting or, as in *The Temple of Preha-Vihear* case ((1962) I.C.J. 6 at 36–37), the return of artefacts and national treasures. It has been said that arbitral tribunals should not, in general, grant orders for specific performance. See Elder, "The case against arbitral awards of specific performance in transnational commercial disputes" (1997) 13 Arbitration International 1. But, as always, this depends on the scope of the arbitration agreement and the relevant applicable law(s). See Ch.8 above.

[15] The successful party may sometimes seek recognition and enforcement of an award in a country where the losing party may have no assets in order (so to speak) to obtain the *imprimatur* of a respected court upon the award.

[16] As, *e.g.*, under the Swiss Private International Law Act 1987, Ch.12, Art.193.

[17] As, *e.g.*, in England under the English Arbitration Act 1996, s.66.

[18] As, *e.g.*, in France under the Code of Civil Procedure 1981, Art.1498.

New York Convention) in assisting recognition and enforcement; and the defences that may be raised, including that of state immunity.

(c) The general principles governing recognition and enforcement

The challenge of an arbitral award, discussed in the previous chapter, is **10–09** concerned with attacking an award at its source, in the hope of having it modified or set aside in whole or in part. Recognition and enforcement, by contrast, are concerned with giving effect to the award, either in the state in which it was made or in some other state or states.

A distinction may be drawn at the outset between: (i) the enforcement of an award in the state that is the "seat" of the arbitration; and (ii) the enforcement of an award which is regarded as a "foreign" or "international" award because it was made *outside* the territory of the state in which recognition or enforcement is sought. Enforcement of an award in the country that is the seat of the arbitration is usually a relatively easy process. It generally involves the same processes as are required for the enforcement of an award in a domestic arbitration.[19] Enforcement of an award that is regarded by the place of enforcement as a "foreign" or "international" award is a more complex matter. This section is mainly concerned with the recognition and enforcement of such "foreign awards".[20]

The difference between recognition and enforcement

It is necessary to distinguish recognition from enforcement. The terms are **10–10** sometimes used as if they are always inextricably linked. For example, the New York Convention[21] itself speaks of "recognition *and* enforcement" of foreign arbitral awards. The terms are, however, distinct. On this point, the Geneva Convention of 1927 is more precise, when it speaks of "recognition *or* enforcement".[22] An award may be recognised without being enforced.[23] However, if it is enforced then it is necessarily recognised by the court which orders its enforcement. The precise distinction, in other words, is between "recognition" and "recognition and enforcement".

[19] France being a notable exception.
[20] The New York Convention, which is in fact entitled the Convention on the Recognition and Enforcement of *Foreign* Arbitral Awards (emphasis added), also applies to arbitral awards "which are not considered as domestic awards in the State where their recognition and enforcement is sought". This may lead to an award made in one state being enforced in that same state under the New York Convention, on the basis that it is not regarded as a domestic award.
[21] In Arts IV and V; but Art.IV also speaks of "recognition *or* enforcement" (emphasis added).
[22] The usage is followed in the English Arbitration Act 1996, which distinguishes between the "recognition" of a New York Convention Award (s.101(1)) and its "enforcement" (s.101(2)). The statute also makes this distinction in other relevant sections.
[23] As happened, *e.g.*, in *Dallal v Bank Mellat* [1986] Q.B. 441, where the English judge held that an award of the Iran–US Claims Tribunal was not enforceable under the New York Convention, but should nevertheless be *recognised* as the valid judgment of a competent tribunal. The case is also reported in (1986) XI Yearbook Commercial Arbitration 547 at 553.

Recognition

10–11 Recognition on its own is generally a defensive process.[24] It will usually arise when a court is asked to grant a remedy in respect of a dispute that has been the subject of previous arbitral proceedings. The party in whose favour the award was made will object that the dispute has already been determined. To prove this, he will seek to produce the award to the court and ask the court to recognise it as valid and binding upon the parties in respect of the issues with which it dealt. The award may have disposed of *all* the issues raised in the new court proceedings, and so put an end to those new proceedings as *res judicata*, that is to say, as matters in issue between the parties which in fact have already been decided. If the award does not dispose of all the issues raised in the new proceedings, but only some of them, it will need to be recognised for the purposes of issue estoppel, so as to prevent the issues with which it does deal from being raised again.

The use of recognition on its own may be illustrated by taking the example of a company that is made a defendant in legal proceedings by a foreign supplier for goods sold and delivered, but allegedly not paid for. Suppose that the dispute between the company and the foreign supplier has already been submitted to arbitration; and that an award has been made, in which the foreign supplier's claim was dismissed. In these circumstances, the company would ask the court to *recognise* the award as a valid defence to the foreign supplier's new claim. If the court is prepared to do this, the claim is dismissed. The legal force and effect of the foreign award will have been recognised, but the award itself has not been enforced.

Enforcement

10–12 By contrast, where a court is asked to enforce an award, it is asked not merely to recognise the legal force and effect of the award, but also to ensure that it is carried out, by using such legal sanctions as are available. Enforcement goes a step further than recognition. A court that is prepared to grant enforcement of an award will do so because it recognises the award as validly made and binding upon the parties to it and, therefore, suitable for enforcement. In this context, the terms recognition and enforcement do run together. One is a necessary part of the other.

Purpose

10–13 As the example shows, the purpose of recognition on its own is generally to act as a shield. Recognition is used to block any attempt to raise in fresh proceedings issues that have already been decided in the arbitration that gave rise

---

[24] Although in some countries it may be a necessary step along the way to enforcement.

to the award whose recognition is sought.[25] By contrast, the purpose of enforce-ment is to act as a sword. Enforcement of an award means applying legal sanctions to compel the party against whom the award was made to carry it out. Such legal sanctions may take many forms. When the defaulting party is an individual, sanctions may include seizure of property and other assets, forfeiture of bank accounts, and even, in extreme cases, imprisonment. Where the default-ing party is a corporate body, enforcement is usually directed primarily against the property and other assets of the corporation, such as its stock-in-trade, bank accounts, trading accounts and so on. In certain situations, however, the directors of the company may be held personally liable (for instance, on a guarantee). In such cases, the sanctions may be directed against them personally.

(d) Place of recognition and enforcement

A party who simply seeks *recognition* of an award will generally do so because **10–14** he needs to rely on the award by way of defence or set-off, or in some other way in court proceedings. For this purpose, he asks the court concerned to recognise the award as binding on the parties between whom it was made. But the choice of court is not his; it is wherever the proceedings against him are brought; and this fact of itself emphasises how important it is that international awards should be accepted as truly "international" in their validity and effect.

Where, however, the successful party in an arbitration is seeking to *enforce* an award, the position is different. The first step is to determine in which country or countries enforcement is to be sought. To reach this decision, it is necessary to locate the state or states in which the losing party has (or is likely to have) assets available to meet the award. This usually calls for careful (and possibly difficult) investigative work. If enquiries suggest that assets are only likely to be available in one state, the party seeking enforcement of the award has no choice: for better or worse, he must seek enforcement in that state. Where there is a choice, the party seeking enforcement is able to proceed in one or more places as seems appropriate.

Court proceedings are generally necessary to obtain title to a defaulting party's assets or their proceeds of sale; and these proceedings are usually[26] taken in the state or states in which the property or other assets of the losing party are located. For example, an order by the French courts, for seizure and sale of the defaulting party's goods and chattels in France, would not produce any real money if these assets proved to be non-existent; nor would an order for the attachment of the

[25] As expressed in the English Arbitration Act 1996, s.101(1), the award is recognised "as binding on the persons as between whom it was made" so that it may accordingly be used by these persons "by way of defence, set-off or otherwise" in any legal proceedings in England and Wales or Northern Ireland.
[26] "Usually" because it may perhaps be thought worthwhile to obtain a court order in a state in which the defendant has no assets, simply to obtain that court's *imprimatur* on the award: see para.10–07.

defaulting party's bank accounts in England if these accounts turned out to be overdrawn.[27]

10–15   One of the factors to be taken into account in selecting a forum for the enforcement of an award is whether the prospective forum recognises and enforces awards rendered at the place of arbitration—by the New York Convention or by some other relevant international convention. Another factor is the attitude of the local courts to requests for recognition and enforcement of foreign awards, and notably, whether their outlook is likely to be internationalist or parochial. The attitude that the prospective forum adopts on the question of state immunity[28] is an additional relevant factor if enforcement is being sought against a state or a governmental agency.

Forum shopping

10–16   The need to locate the place or places in which a defaulting party has assets is not confined to international commercial arbitration. In domestic proceedings, it may also be necessary to locate the defaulting party's assets in order to enforce a court's judgment or an arbitral tribunal's award. However, in a domestic dispute, the assets of the losing party are usually situated within the country in which the proceedings take place, since this is normally the country of that party's residence or place of business. In international commercial arbitration, the contrary is likely to be the case. The place of arbitration[29] will usually have been chosen, by or on behalf of the parties, precisely because (*inter alia*) it is a place with which they have *no* connection. In other words, the place of arbitration has been chosen as a neutral forum. It would be purely fortuitous if the parties happened to have assets situated within this neutral country. If the award has to be enforced, it must generally be enforced in a country other than that in which it was made. Again, this is why it is important that international awards should be recognised and enforced *internationally,* and not merely in the country in which they are made.

If, as often happens in international commerce, assets are located in different parts of the world, the party seeking enforcement of the award has a choice of country in which to proceed—a chance to go "forum shopping", as it is sometimes expressed. In looking for the appropriate forum, not merely the location of assets but also the other factors already mentioned (such as the attitude of the local courts, the adherence of the target country to the New York Convention and so on) must be taken into account.

---

[27] Unfortunately, in practice all that is generally known is that the defaulting party is a holder of bank accounts in the country concerned. The state of those accounts is not usually known until an order is issued against the bank.

[28] For a discussion of state immunity, see below, paras 10–62 *et seq.*

[29] The chosen place of arbitration is a geographical location, in a given country or, more usually, in a given town or city. The arbitration agreement generally states, *e.g.*, that any arbitration is to take place in Paris, or that it is to take place in New York, or wherever it may be. But (as has been seen in Ch.2) once chosen, the physical "place" of arbitration becomes the juridical "seat" of the arbitration—an event which may have important legal consequences, depending on the *lex arbitri*.

(e) **Methods of recognition and enforcement**

Internationally, it is generally much easier to obtain recognition and enforce- **10–17** ment of an international award than of a foreign court judgment. This is because the network of international and regional treaties providing for the recognition and enforcement of international awards is more widespread and better developed than corresponding provisions for the recognition and enforcement of foreign judgments.[30] Indeed, this is one of the principal advantages of arbitration as a method of resolving international commercial disputes.[31]

The method of recognition and enforcement to be adopted in any particular case depends on the place where the award was made (that is to say, whether it qualifies, for example, as a New York Convention award). It also depends on the relevant provisions of the law at the place of intended enforcement ("the forum state"). On this aspect, it is usually essential to obtain advice from experienced lawyers in the forum state.[32]

Local formalities are bound to be involved, whether or not one of the international conventions is applicable. For example, the original or certified copies of the arbitration agreement and award is usually required. The language of the award may well be different from the language of the court of the forum state, so that a translation is required—and it may be necessary for this to be undertaken with considerable formality (for example, by consular attestation in the country of origin).

(f) **Time-limits**

Time-limits for the commencement of proceedings for the recognition and **10–18** enforcement of an arbitral award are usually laid down in national legislation. Careful attention must be paid to such time-limits (and to any other time-limits contained in the rules of court of the forum state). In this respect, it would be foolhardy not to consult an experienced local practitioner; and this applies as much to the party seeking recognition or enforcement of an award as it does to the party wishing to challenge an award. In the US, for instance, as already mentioned,[33] time-limits vary from state to state: and when it comes to enforcement of an award, the relevant period may be anything from one year to three years.[34]

---

[30] Other than European Council Regulation 44/2001, which has replaced the Brussels Convention of 1968, and which provides for the enforcement of European national court judgments solely within Europe, there is no treaty for the international recognition and enforcement of court judgments. The Hague Conference on Private International Law has been struggling in recent years to produce an "interim" draft of a "Convention on jurisdiction and the recognition and enforcement of foreign judgments in civil and commercial matters", but the finalisation of that convention appears still to be out of sight.

[31] See Ch.1, paras 1–41 and 1–101.

[32] Recognition and enforcement is likely to be easiest to obtain under an international convention where the forum state is bound by such a convention; but other methods of recognition and enforcement may be available, as discussed below.

[33] Ch.9, para.9–46.

[34] The period for enforcement of an award under the New York Convention in the US is three years, whereas for domestic awards it is one year.

(g) Consequences of refusal of recognition or enforcement

10–19   The immediate consequence of a refusal to enforce an award is that the winning party fails to get what he wants; namely, seizure of the loser's assets in the place in which enforcement was sought. Although this is a disheartening result for the party seeking enforcement, it should be borne in mind that he may still have an award that can be enforced in another state in which the losing party *has* assets. Much depends upon the reason for which enforcement was refused. If, for example, enforcement was refused for local public policy considerations, it may be possible to find another country in which the same considerations do not apply. However, if enforcement was refused because of failure by the arbitral tribunal to give the losing party an opportunity to present his case, it may not be possible to enforce the award elsewhere, since other courts may take the same view.[35] In such an event, the party seeking enforcement will probably have no option but to recommence arbitral proceedings, assuming that the right to do so has not been lost by lapse of time.

2. THE ROLE OF THE INTERNATIONAL CONVENTIONS

(a) Generally

10–20   The dependence of the international arbitral process upon national systems of law is most clearly seen in the context of the recognition and enforcement of international awards. An arbitral tribunal is limited in the powers it can exercise; and these powers, although usually adequate for resolving a particular dispute, fall short of the coercive powers possessed by national courts. Indeed, a state is generally reluctant to confer on a private arbitral tribunal the frequently draconian powers it confers on the judges in its own courts. The power to enforce an award against a reluctant party, by such summary methods as the attachment of bank accounts or the sequestration of assets, is a power that forms part of the prerogative of the state. It is not a power that is possessed by an arbitrator; and it is not a power the state is likely to delegate. In consequence, the enforcement of awards must take place through the national court at the place of enforcement, operating under its own procedural rules. The detailed procedures adopted in these courts will vary from country to country. However, the effect of the international conventions, culminating in the New York Convention, has been to secure a considerable degree of uniformity in the recognition and enforcement of awards in most of the important trading countries of the world.

This serves to emphasise that one of the most important features of an award in an international commercial arbitration is that it should be readily transportable. It must be capable of being taken from the state in which it was made, under one system of law, to other states in which it is able to qualify for recognition and enforcement, under different systems of law. To render an award effective, means

---

[35] See New York Convention, Art.V.1(b); Model Law, Art.36(1)(a)(ii).

must be available for enforcing it and these means must be available *internationally* and not simply in the country in which the award was made.

The main international treaties that apply to the recognition and enforcement of international awards are reviewed in the section that follows, beginning with the Geneva Protocol of 1923 and the Geneva Convention of 1927. Although these conventions have been largely superseded by the New York Convention, they marked the first step in recognising the importance of international commercial arbitration to the development of international trade. Both were promulgated under the auspices of the League of Nations, the predecessor of the United Nations. Both contain features that are retained in the New York Convention, in the conventions that are based on it and in the Model Law.

(b) The Geneva treaties

The Geneva Protocol of 1923

The Geneva Protocol of 1923 was limited in its range and effect.[36] Nevertheless, it made an important contribution to the international recognition and enforcement of international arbitration agreements and awards.[37] The Geneva Protocol had two objectives. First, it sought to make arbitration agreements (and, in particular, arbitration clauses) enforceable internationally; secondly, it sought to ensure that awards made pursuant to such arbitration agreements would be enforced in the territory of the state in which they were made. In other words, the Geneva Protocol of 1923 was concerned to ensure that states that became parties to the Protocol would support international commercial arbitration at the beginning and at the end of the arbitral process. At the beginning of the process, contracting states would ensure that parties to an arbitration agreement resolved their disputes by arbitration, rather than by resorting to national courts.[38] At the end of the arbitral process, they would at least grant recognition and enforcement to awards made in their own territory.[39]

10–21

The Geneva Convention of 1927

Like the Geneva Protocol of 1923, the Geneva Convention of 1927 is now mostly of only historic interest. However, it represents an early attempt to address

10–22

---

[36] It only applied to arbitration agreements made "between parties subject respectively to the jurisdiction of different Contracting States": Geneva Protocol of 1923, Art.(1). The interpretation of this phrase caused difficulty, with some national courts taking it to be a requirement of nationality, whilst others took it to be a requirement of residence, domicile or usual place of business. It could be further limited by states availing themselves of the "commercial reservation". Moreover, so far as the enforcement of awards was concerned, each contracting state undertook only to execute awards *made in its own territory* pursuant to an arbitration agreement which was covered by the Protocol, a provision that did nothing for the international enforceability of awards.

[37] The states that became parties to the Protocol were mostly European, including Czechoslovakia, Denmark, Finland, France, Germany, Greece, Ireland, Norway, Poland, Portugal, Spain and the UK; but one Latin American country, Brazil, became a party to the Protocol; as did India, Japan, New Zealand and Thailand.

[38] Geneva Protocol of 1923, Art.(4).

[39] *ibid.*, Art.(3).

the kind of problem that still arises in seeking the international enforcement of arbitration awards. The Geneva Protocol only provided for the *domestic* enforcement of Protocol awards: that is to say, enforcement of awards in the territory of the state in which they were made. The Geneva Convention of 1927 went further. It provided that an award would be recognised as binding and would be enforced internationally, in the territory of *any* of the contracting states, subject to certain conditions.[40] If an award satisfied these relevant conditions, it satisfied the preliminary requirements of the Geneva Convention. It then had to satisfy certain additional requirements, which had to be proved by the party seeking enforcement. Since the Geneva Convention of 1927 is no longer of great practical importance,[41] it is only necessary to mention two of these requirements:

> "(d) That the award has become final in the country in which it has been made;"

and:

> "(e) That the recognition or enforcement of the award is not contrary to the public policy or to the principles of the law of the country in which it is sought to be relied upon."[42]

The provision that the award should be "final in the country in which it has been made" seems simple enough; but it led to what became known as the problem of the "double *exequatur*". In some countries, an award was only recognised as final if the local court had granted leave to enforce it, whether by way of *exequatur* or otherwise. This meant that in such countries an *exequatur* had to be obtained first from the court of the place in which the award was made in order to show that the award was final. Another *exequatur* then had to be obtained from the court in the forum state, in order to enforce the award.

The Geneva Convention's requirement that the award should not be contrary to "the principles of the law of the country in which it is sought to be relied upon" also posed problems. It meant that an award would be open to attack not merely on the grounds of public policy, but also on the grounds that it offended the legal principles of the forum state. It is understandable that a state should not recognise and enforce an award that runs contrary to its public policy: and indeed, this ground for refusal of recognition and enforcement is maintained both in the New York Convention and in the Model Law. It is less understandable that the principles of law of the *forum* state should be taken into account, when an award has been made in another state in accordance with other, no doubt equally

---

[40] They were: (1) that the award was made pursuant to an agreement to which the Geneva Protocol of 1923 applied; (2) that the award was made in the territory of one of the contracting states; and (3) that the parties to the award were subject to the jurisdiction of one of the contracting states.
[41] Because almost all of the contracting states have become bound by the New York Convention.
[42] Geneva Convention of 1927, Art.1(d) and (e).

valid, legal principles. This requirement was not carried through to the New York Convention and does not appear in the Model Law.[43]

(c) The New York Convention

The origins of the New York Convention have already been described in Ch.1. **10–23** The New York Convention replaces the Geneva Convention of 1927 as between states which are parties to both Conventions,[44] and was a substantial improvement thereon since it provides for a more simple and effective method of obtaining recognition and enforcement of foreign awards. The Convention also replaces the Protocol as between states that are bound by both,[45] and again constitutes a substantial improvement as it gives much wider effect to the validity of arbitration agreements than that given under the Protocol. As a result, and deservedly, the New York Convention has been praised in glowing terms. It has been described as "the single most important pillar on which the edifice of international arbitration rests"[46] and as a convention which "perhaps could lay claim to be the most effective instance of international legislation in the entire history of commercial law".[47]

Enforcing the agreement to arbitrate

Although the title of the New York Convention refers to the recognition and **10–24** enforcement of "foreign arbitral awards", the Convention also deals with the recognition and enforcement of arbitration agreements. This has already been discussed in Ch.1.

Enforcing foreign awards

In its opening statement, the Convention adopts a strikingly international **10–25** attitude:

> "This Convention shall apply to the recognition and enforcement of arbitral awards made in the territory of a State other than the State where the recognition and enforcement of such awards are sought, and arising out of differences between persons, whether physical or legal. It shall also apply to arbitral awards not considered as domestic awards in the State where their recognition and enforcement are sought."[48]

---

[43] The States that adhered to the Geneva Convention of 1927 were substantially those that adhered to the Geneva Protocol of 1923 (with some omissions, such as Brazil, Norway and Poland; and with some additions, such as Burma, Kenya and Zambia).

[44] New York Convention, Art.VII.2.

[45] *ibid.*, Art.VII.2.

[46] Wetter, "The Present Status of the International Court of Arbitration of the ICC: An Appraisal" (1990) 1 American Review of International Arbitration 91.

[47] Mustill, "Arbitration: History and Background" (1989) 6 Journal of International Arbitration 43; see also Schwebel, "A celebration of the United Nations' New York Convention" (1996) 12 Arbitration International 823.

[48] New York Convention, Art.I.1.

If this opening article stood without qualification, it would mean that an award made in any state (even if that state was not a party to the New York Convention) would be recognised and enforced by any other state that was a party, so long as the award satisfied the basic conditions set down in the Convention. There is, however, a qualification to this welcome internationalist approach. Article I.3 of the Convention allows states that adhere to the Convention to make two reservations. The first of these is the reciprocity reservation; the second is the commercial reservation, which was also in the Geneva Protocol of 1923.

The first reservation: reciprocity

10–26   The New York Convention provides that:

> "When signing, ratifying or acceding to this Convention, or notifying extension under Article X hereof, any State may on the basis of reciprocity declare that it will apply the Convention to the recognition and enforcement of awards *made only* in the territory of another Contracting State."[49]

To the extent that states take advantage of it, the reciprocity reservation has the effect of narrowing the scope of application of the New York Convention. Instead of applying to *all* foreign awards wherever they are made, the scope of the New York Convention may be limited to "Convention awards", that is, awards made in a state which is a party to the New York Convention.[50]

States that have entered into the New York Convention on the basis of reciprocity have agreed, in effect, that they will only recognise and enforce Convention awards. Accordingly, when seeking a suitable state in which to hold an international commercial arbitration, it is advisable to select a state that *has* adopted the New York Convention, so as to improve the chances of securing recognition and enforcement of the award in other Convention countries.

10–27   Nevertheless, the limiting effect of the first reservation should not be exaggerated. The number of states that make up the international network for the recognition and enforcement of arbitral awards established by the New York Convention grows year by year. The Convention now links the world's major trading nations—Arab, African, Asian and Latin American as well as European and North American. As more countries become Convention countries, the reciprocity reservation becomes less significant. Indeed, it is becoming a relic. The Model Law, for example, in Articles 35 and 36, requires the recognition and enforcement of an arbitral award "*irrespective* of the country in which it was made."

---

[49] New York Convention, Art.I.3 (emphasis added).
[50] As at April 2004, 134 states had adhered to the New York Convention. Of these, 68 had done so on the basis of the reciprocity reservation. Some countries that had adopted the reciprocity reservation (such as Germany and Switzerland) have subsequently withdrawn it. See UNCITRAL's Status of Conventions and Model Laws at *www.uncitral.org/en-index.htm*.

The second reservation: commercial relationships

The New York Convention contains a further reservation.[51] This entitles a **10–28** contracting state to declare that it will only apply the Convention to differences arising out of legal relationships, whether contractual or not, "which are considered as commercial under the national law of the state making such declaration".[52]

The effect of this reservation, like the reservation as to reciprocity, is to narrow the scope of application of the New York Convention[53]; and the fact that each contracting state may determine for itself what relationships it considers to be "commercial" has created problems in the application of the New York Convention. Relationships which are regarded as "commercial" by one state are not necessarily so regarded by others; and this does not assist in obtaining a uniform interpretation of the Convention. Indeed, the commercial reservation has led to difficulties of interpretation within the same state, as is shown by two cases that arose in India. In the first,[54] the High Court of Bombay (Mumbai) was asked to stay legal proceedings that had been commenced despite the existence of an arbitration agreement. Under the relevant Indian legislation enacting the New York Convention, the court was obliged to grant such a stay, so long as the arbitration agreement came within the Convention. In ratifying the New York Convention, India had entered the commercial reservation. The court held that, whilst the agreement under which the dispute arose was commercial in nature, it could not be considered as commercial "under the law in force in India". The judge said:

> "In my opinion, in order to invoke the provisions of [the Convention], it is not enough to establish that an agreement is commercial. It must also be established that it is commercial by virtue of a provision of law or an operative legal principle in force in India."[55]

This decision has since been disapproved by the High Court of Gujarat. In this **10–29** second case, the plaintiffs moved for a stay of legal proceedings that, again, had been commenced despite the existence of an arbitration agreement. The court granted this motion. On the argument as to whether or not the contract was commercial in nature, the judge said the term "commerce":

> " . . . is a word of the largest import and takes in its sweep all the business and trade transactions in any of their forms, including the transportation, purchase,

---

[51] New York Convention, Art.I.3.
[52] A similar commercial reservation was permitted in the Geneva Protocol of 1923.
[53] Of the 134 states which were parties to the Convention by April 2004, 44 had taken advantage of the commercial reservation. On March 12, 2001, Serbia and Montenegro confirmed Yugoslavia's declaration of 1982 restricting the application of the Convention to "economic" disputes. Norway's reservation stated that it would not apply the Convention in any disputes if the subject matter was immovable property in Norway, or rights in such property.
[54] *Indian Organic Chemical Ltd v Subsidiary 1 (US) Subsidiary 2 (US) and Chemtex Fibres Inc (Parent Company) (US)* (1979) IV Yearbook Commercial Arbitration 271.
[55] *ibid.*, at 273.

sale and exchange of commodities between the citizens of different countries."[56]

The judge added:

"It should be noted that the view of the learned single Judge of the Bombay High Court in *Indian Organic Chemical Ltd's* case has not been approved by the Division Bench of the Bombay High Court. The Division Bench after setting out the view of [the judge] in the aforesaid decision, ultimately disagreed with it . . . "[57]

This position was confirmed by the Indian Supreme Court in its decision in *RM Investment & Trading Co Pvt Ltd (India) v Boeing Company*,[58] in which it held that:

"[in] construing the expression 'commercial' in Section 2 of the Act it has to be borne in mind that the 'Act is calculated and designed to subserve the cause of facilitating international trade and promotion thereof by providing for speedy settlement of disputes arising in such trade through arbitration and any expression or phrase occurring [therein] should receive, consistent with its literal and grammatical sense, a liberal construction' . . . The expression 'commercial' should, therefore, be construed broadly having regard to the manifold activities which are integral part of international trade today."

10–30   Nevertheless, the point remains that each national state may decide for itself, under the provisions of the New York Convention, what relationships it considers to be "commercial" for the purposes of the commercial reservation.[59]

Recognition and enforcement under the New York Convention

10–31   The New York Convention provides for both recognition and enforcement of awards to which the Convention applies. So far as *recognition* is concerned, a state bound by the Convention undertakes to respect the binding effect of awards to which the Convention applies; and accordingly, as has been seen, such awards may be relied upon by way of defence or set-off in any legal proceedings. So far as *enforcement* is concerned, a state that is a party to the Convention undertakes to enforce awards to which the Convention applies, in accordance with its local procedural rules. It also undertakes not to impose substantially more onerous

---

[56] *Union of India and Ors v Lief Hoegh & Co (Norway)* (1984) IX Yearbook Commercial Arbitration 405 at 407.
[57] *ibid.*, at 408.
[58] Reported in (1997) XXII Yearbook Commercial Arbitration 711.
[59] The Tunisian courts, *e.g.*, have construed the commercial reservation so broadly as to exclude enforcement of an award relating to obligations arising under a contract for professional services. See *Société d'Investissement Kal (Tunisia) v Taieb Haddad (Tunisia) and Hans Barrett* (1998) XXIII Yearbook Commercial Arbitration 770.

conditions or higher fees or charges for such enforcement than are imposed in the enforcement of its own domestic awards.[60]

Formalities

The formalities required for obtaining recognition and enforcement of awards to which the New York Convention applies are simple.[61] The party seeking such recognition and enforcement is merely required to produce to the relevant court: **10–32**

- the duly authenticated original award or a duly certified copy thereof; and

- the original agreement referred to in Art.II or a duly certified copy thereof.[62]

If the award and the arbitration agreement are not in the official language of the country in which recognition and enforcement is sought, certified translations are needed.[63] Once the necessary documents have been supplied, the court will grant recognition and enforcement unless one or more of the grounds for refusal, listed in the Convention, are present.

3. Refusal of Recognition and Enforcement

(a) Generally

The various grounds for refusal of recognition and enforcement of an arbitration award that are set out in the New York Convention must be reviewed. This is not only because of the importance of the Convention itself but also, and equally crucially, because the provisions of the Model Law governing recognition and enforcement of awards (in Arts 35 and 36) are almost identical to those set out in the Convention. **10–33**

---

[60] New York Convention, Art.III.

[61] Nevertheless, cases are from time to time reported in the *Yearbook of Commercial Arbitration* in which the application for enforcement fails, because a party has failed to comply with these "simple" requirements: see, *e.g.*, the decisions of the Italian Court of Cassation in *Lampart Vegypary Gepgyar (Hungary) v srl Campomarzio Impianti (Italy)* reported in (1999) XXIVa Yearbook Commercial Arbitration 699; and the Bulgarian Supreme Court's decision in *National Electricity Company AD (Bulgaria) v ECONBERG Ltd (Croatia)* in (2000) XXV Yearbook Commercial Arbitration 678. Equally, some jurisdictions take a liberal and pragmatic approach to the fulfilment of formal requirements. By way of example, a Geneva court recognised a Chinese award that had not been translated into French, noting that the spirit of the Convention was to reduce the obligations for the party seeking recognition and enforcement, and that the burden of proof in respect of any questions relating to the authenticity of the arbitration agreement or the award lay on the party opposing recognition. See *R. SA v A. Ltd* (2001) XXVI Yearbook Commercial Arbitration 863.

[62] New York Convention, Art.IV.

[63] *ibid.*, Art.IV.2.

First, the New York Convention does not permit any review[64] on the merits of an award to which the Convention applies. Nor does the Model Law.

Secondly, the grounds for refusal of recognition and enforcement set out in the New York Convention (and in the Model Law) are exhaustive. They are the *only* grounds on which recognition and enforcement may be refused.

10–34 Thirdly, the New York Convention sets out five separate grounds on which recognition and enforcement of a Convention award may be refused at the request of the party against whom it is invoked.[65] It is significant that under both the Convention and the Model Law (which follows the Convention in this respect) the burden of proof is *not* upon the party seeking recognition and enforcement.[66] (The remaining two grounds on which recognition and enforcement may be refused, which relate to the public policy of the place of enforcement, are grounds which may be invoked by the court of that place on its own motion.)[67]

Fourthly, even if grounds for refusal of recognition and enforcement of an award are proved to exist, the enforcing court is *not obliged* to refuse enforcement. The opening lines of paras (1) and (2) of Art.V say that enforcement "may" be refused. They do not say that it "must" be refused. The language is permissive, not mandatory.[68] The same is true of the Model Law.

Fifthly, the intention of the New York Convention and of the Model Law is that the grounds for refusing recognition and enforcement of arbitral awards should be applied restrictively. As a leading commentator on the Convention has stated:

---

[64] This statement, which was made in an earlier edition of this book, has since been cited with approval by the Supreme Court of India in *Renusagar Power Co Ltd v General Electric Co*. The court added that in its opinion "the scope of enquiry before the court in which the award is sought to be enforced is limited [to the grounds mentioned in the Act] and does not enable a party to the said proceedings to impeach the Award on merits", (1995) XX Yearbook Commercial Arbitration 681 at 691.

[65] These grounds are set out in Art.V of the New York Convention. Some courts have, however, refused enforcement on grounds derived from other articles of the Convention. Thus, in *Monegasque de Reassurance SAM (Monde Re) v NAK Naftogart of Ukraine and State of Ukraine* 311 F.3d 488 (2002), the US Second Circuit refused enforcement of a Moscow award on grounds of *forum non conveniens*. In so doing, it rejected the contention that Art.V of the Convention sets forth the only grounds for refusing to enforce a foreign arbitral award, and held that Art.III made the enforcement of foreign arbitral awards subject to the rules of procedure of the courts where enforcement is sought which, so it held, included the rule of *forum non conveniens*.

[66] This represents a major change from the Geneva Convention of 1927.

[67] New York Convention, Art.V.2.

[68] This interpretation of the relevant provision of the Convention seems to be generally accepted, both in court decisions and by experienced commentators: see, for instance, van den Berg, *The New York Convention of 1958* (Kluwer), p.265; Dicey & Morris *The Conflict of Laws* (12th ed., Sweet & Maxwell, 1993), p.624; Delaume, "Enforcement against a foreign state of an arbitral award annulled in the foreign state" (1997) Revue du Droit International des Affaires 254; and for a US decision to this effect see *Chromalloy Aeroservices Inc v Arab Republic of Egypt* 939 F.Supp.907 at 909 (D.D.C. 1996); and for an English decision see *China Agribusiness Development Corp v Balli Trading* [1998] 2 Lloyd's Rep. 76. The suggestion that the French text of the Convention (in contrast to the equally authentic Chinese, English, Spanish and Russian texts) is mandatory, rather than permissive, is demolished by Paulsson in "May or Must under the New York Convention: An exercise in Syntax and Linguistics" (1998) 14 Arbitration International 227.

"As far as the grounds for refusal for enforcement of the Award as enumerated in Article V are concerned, it means *that they have to be construed narrowly.*"[69]

Most national courts have recognised this. There has been approval in the US, **10–35** for example, of the "pro-enforcement bias" of the Convention.[70] However, not all courts follow this internationalist approach. Practitioners of international commercial arbitration are aware, either from their own experience or from the experience of others, of the difficulties that may arise in seeking enforcement of an award under the New York Convention. In particular, the "public policy" exception, discussed below, enables some states to play the game less fairly than others. Nor is this the only problem.[71] There are states that have ratified the Convention, but have either not brought it into effect or have brought it into effect inadequately. There are states in which the local courts or the local bureaucracy are unfamiliar with international arbitration—and perhaps even suspicious of it. There are also oddities of legislation, such as those provisions of the law in India (now repealed) and in Pakistan,[72] which stated that where the governing law was that of India (or Pakistan, as the case may be), the ensuing award was deemed to be a domestic award, even though the seat of the arbitration was in a foreign state.[73]

Problems of this kind cannot be ignored, but they should not be exaggerated. The New York Convention *has* proved to be a highly effective international instrument for the enforcement of arbitration agreements and, more importantly in the present context, arbitration awards.[74] The Convention is now somewhat dated[75]; and it is by no means applied consistently by all the states that have adopted it (or which claim to have done so).[76] Nevertheless, it has made the greatest single contribution to the internationalisation of international commercial arbitration. Even though the Model Law may eventually take its place, decisions under the Convention will still be important, since the Model Law's

---

[69] van den Berg, *The New York Arbitration Convention of 1958* (Kluwer, 1981) pp.267 and 268 (emphasis added).

[70] *Parsons Whittemore Overseas Co v Société Générale de L'Industrie de Papier (RAKTA),* 508 F.2d 969 (1974); also reported in (1976) I Yearbook Commercial Arbitration 205.

[71] For further discussion of these problems, see, for instance, Kerr, *Concord and Conflict in International Arbitration,* para.1–157, pp.129 *et. seq.*; *ASA Bulletin* (1996); and the proceedings of the 14th ICCA Congress, Paris, May 1998.

[72] This is sometimes somewhat cryptically referred to as "the s.9(b) problem": see Kerr, *op. cit.,* p.131.

[73] Such an award is normally regarded as a foreign (or international) award under the New York Convention.

[74] Indeed, it has been estimated (although statistics about arbitration are notoriously difficult to collect) that 98 per cent of awards in international arbitrations are honoured or successfully enforced and that enforcement by national courts has been refused in less than 5 per cent of cases: see van den Berg, *ASA Bulletin* (1996), p.25.

[75] For instance, in its definition of an "agreement in writing" as discussed in Chs 1 and 3.

[76] See, for instance, Paulsson, "The New York Convention in International Practice—Problems of Assimilation", Swiss Arbitration Association Conference, Zurich, February 1996, collected papers, pp.100 *et seq.*

provisions governing recognition and enforcement of arbitral awards are taken directly from the New York Convention.

(b) Grounds for refusal

10–36 Under the New York Convention, recognition and enforcement of an arbitral award *may* be refused if the opposing party proves that:

- the parties to the arbitration agreement were, under the law applicable to them, under some incapacity, or the said agreement is not valid under the law to which the parties have subjected it or, failing any indication thereon, under the law of the country where the award was made; or

- the party against whom the award is invoked was not given proper notice of the appointment of the arbitrator or of the arbitration proceedings or was otherwise unable to present his case; or

- the award deals with a difference not contemplated by or not falling within the terms of the submission to arbitration, or it contains decisions on matters beyond the scope of the submission to arbitration, provided that, if the decisions on matters submitted to arbitration can be separated from those not so submitted, that part of the award which contains decisions on matters submitted to arbitration may be recognised and enforced; or

- the composition of the arbitral authority or the arbitral procedure was not in accordance with the agreement of the parties, or, failing such agreement, was not in accordance with the law of the country where the arbitration took place; or

- the award has not yet become binding on the parties, or has been set aside or suspended by a competent authority of the country in which, or under the law of which, the award was made.

Recognition and enforcement may also be refused if the competent authority of the country in which enforcement is sought finds that:

- the subject-matter of the difference is not capable of settlement by arbitration under the law of that country; or

- the recognition or enforcement of the award would be contrary to the public policy of that country.[77]

These grounds for refusal of recognition and enforcement of foreign arbitral awards are of considerable importance. They represent an internationally accepted standard: not only because of the widespread acceptance of the New York Convention throughout the world, but also because the Model Law adopts

---

[77] New York Convention, Art.V.2.

the same grounds (although not in precisely the same words) for refusal of recognition and enforcement of an arbitral award, irrespective of the country in which that award was made.[78] In addition, six of these seven grounds for refusal are also set out in the Model Law as grounds for the *setting aside* of an arbitral award by the national court of the place of arbitration.[79] Finally, the first four of these grounds also appear in the European Convention of 1961.[80] A commentator on that Convention has described them as grounds for setting aside an award that "are common to most systems of judicial review of awards at the seat of the arbitration."[81]

In an ideal world, the provisions of the New York Convention and of the **10–37** Model Law would be interpreted in the same way by courts everywhere. Sadly, this does not happen. There are inconsistent decisions under the New York Convention, just as there may be inconsistent decisions within a national system of law (although the latter may be corrected on appeal). Nevertheless, it is useful to consider how national courts in different parts of the world have applied the different grounds for refusal set out in the New York Convention. Whilst these decisions have no binding authority on national courts in other jurisdictions, they may provide useful guidelines for the interpretation of a particular ground for refusal in a particular case.

(c) First ground for refusal: incapacity; invalid arbitration agreement

The first ground for refusal of recognition and enforcement under the New **10–38** York Convention[82] is as follows:

"(a) The parties to the agreement . . . were, under the law applicable to them, under some incapacity, or the said agreement is not valid under the law to which the parties have subjected it or, failing any indication thereon, under the law of the country where the award was made . . . "

The issue of capacity to enter into an arbitration agreement, which may raise particular difficulties in relation to states and state agencies, has already been discussed in Ch.3; as have issues as to the validity of the arbitration agreement.

An example of a successful defence to enforcement based on invalidity is provided by the decision of the Administrative Tribunal of Damascus in *Fougerolle SA (France) v Ministry of Defence of the Syrian Arab Republic.*[83] The

---

[78] Model Law, Art.36.
[79] Model Law, Art.34. The ground that is omitted, naturally, is that of the award being set aside by a national court of the place of arbitration.
[80] Art.IX(1).
[81] Hascher, "European Convention on International Commercial Arbitration of 1961—Commentary" (1995) XX Yearbook Commercial Arbitration 1006 at 1036.
[82] New York Convention, Art.V.1(a). As already noted, this ground for refusal, and the others that follow, also appear in virtually the same terms in the Model Law, Art.36 as a ground for refusing enforcement of arbitral awards wherever made.
[83] (1990) XV Yearbook Commercial Arbitration, 515.

Administrative Tribunal of Damascus (in its decision of March 31, 1988) refused enforcement of two ICC awards holding that they were "non-existent" because they were rendered "without the preliminary advice on the referral of the dispute to arbitration, which must be given by the competent Committee of the Council of State."

As an example of an unsuccessful attempt to use the defence of an invalid arbitration agreement, an Italian company argued that the agreement to arbitrate printed on the reverse side of a purchase order was not valid under the law to which the parties had subjected it. The Court of Appeal in Florence, Italy, rejected this defence. It also rejected the argument that lack of reasons in an award violated Italian public policy and accordingly it ordered enforcement of the award.[84]

(d) Second ground: no proper notice of appointment of arbitrator or of the proceedings; lack of due process

10–39   The second ground for refusal of recognition and enforcement of an award under the New York Convention is as follows[85]:

> "(b) The party against whom the award is invoked was not given proper notice of the appointment of the arbitrator or of the arbitration proceedings or was otherwise unable to present his case . . . "

This is the most important ground for refusal under the New York Convention (and the Model Law). It is directed at ensuring that the arbitration itself is properly conducted, with proper notice to the parties and procedural fairness.

The point as to notice is a matter of formality, but it is important nonetheless. However, the main thrust of this provision of the Convention is directed at ensuring that the requirements of "due process" are observed and that the parties are given a fair hearing. If parties from different countries are to have confidence in arbitration as a method of dispute resolution it is essential that the proceedings should be conducted in a manner that is fair, and that is seen to be fair. This is something that should be borne in mind, by parties and arbitrators alike, from the very outset of the arbitration.

10–40   The court of the forum state will naturally have its own concept of what constitutes "a fair hearing". In this sense, as was said in a leading case in the US, the New York Convention "essentially sanctions the application of the forum state's standards of due process".[86] This does not mean, however, that the hearing must be conducted as if it were a hearing before a national court in the

---

[84] *Bobbie Brooks Inc (USA) v Lanificio Walter Banci SaS (Italy)* (1979) IV Yearbook Commercial Arbitration 289. In the same vein, see the decision of the Paris Cour d'Appel in *Inter-Arab Investment Guarantee v Banque Arabe et Internationale d'Investissement* (1998) XXIII Yearbook Commercial Arbitration 645.

[85] New York Convention, Art.V.1(b).

[86] *Parsons & Whittemore Overseas Co Inc v Société Générale de l'Industrie du Papier (RAKTA)* 508 F.2d 969 (2nd Cir. 1974) 975.

forum state. It is generally enough if the court is satisfied that the hearing was conducted with due regard to any agreement between the parties and in accordance with the principles of equality of treatment and the right of each party to have a proper opportunity to present its case.

The national court at the place of enforcement thus has a limited role. Its function is *not* to decide whether or not the award is correct, as a matter of fact and law. Its function is simply to decide whether there has been a fair hearing. One mistake in the course of the proceedings may be sufficient to lead the court to conclude that there was a denial of justice. For example, in a case to which reference has already been made,[87] a US corporation, which had been told that there *was* no need to submit detailed invoices, had its claim rejected by the Iran-US Claims Tribunal, for failure to submit detailed invoices! The US court, rightly it is suggested, refused to enforce the award against the US company. In different circumstances, a German court held that an award that was motivated by arguments that had not been raised by the parties nor the tribunal during the arbitral proceedings, and thus on which the parties had not had an opportunity to comment, violated due process and the right to be heard.[88]

Examples of unsuccessful "due process" defences to enforcement are, however, more numerous.[89] In *Minmetals Germany v Ferco Steel*,[90] the losing respondent in an arbitration in China opposed enforcement in England on the grounds that the award was founded on evidence that the arbitral tribunal had obtained through its own investigations. An English court rejected this defence on the basis that the respondent was eventually given an opportunity to ask for the disclosure of evidence at issue and comment on it, but declined to do so. The court held that the due process defence to enforcement was not intended to accommodate circumstances in which a party had failed to take advantage of an opportunity duly accorded to it.[91]

(e) Third ground: jurisdictional issues

The third ground for refusal of recognition and enforcement of an award under the New York Convention is as follows[92]:   **10–41**

"(c) The award deals with a difference not contemplated by or not falling within the terms of the submission to arbitration, or it contains decisions on matters beyond the scope of the submission to arbitration, provided that, if the decision on matters submitted to arbitration can be separated

---

[87] *Iran Aircraft Ind. v Avco Corp* 980 F.2d 141 (2nd Cir. 1992). See Ch.9.
[88] See, *e.g.*, the decision of the Stuttgart Court of Appeal dated October 6, 2001 referred to in Liebscher, *The Healthy Award, op. cit.*, p.406.
[89] See Liebscher, *The Healthy Award, op. cit.*, Ch.VIII paras 2.2 and 2.3.
[90] *Minmetals Germany v Ferco Steel* (1999) XXIV Yearbook Commercial Arbitration 739.
[91] Many jurisdictions have taken a similarly restrictive interpretation of the due process defence to enforcement. *E.g.* German courts have held that a tribunal's refusal to hear evidence can only breach the right to be heard if such evidence is relevant; see the Bremen Court of Appeal's decision of September 30, 1999 in [2001] 4 Int.A.L.R. N-26.
[92] New York Convention, Art.V.1(c).

from those not so submitted, that part of the award which contains decisions on matters submitted to arbitration may be recognised and enforced . . . "

It is becoming increasingly common for the issue of jurisdiction to be raised as the first line of defence in a reference to arbitration. The issue may be raised as part of a plea that there was no valid agreement to arbitrate,[93] in which case it would fall under Art.V.1(a) of the New York Convention; or it may be raised under the present heading.

Jurisdictional issues as a ground for challenging an award have already been discussed[94]; and it has been noted that the right to raise such an issue may have been lost because of failure to do so at the appropriate time.[95]

10–42 The first part of this ground for refusal of enforcement under the Convention (and under the Model Law) envisages a situation in which the arbitral tribunal is alleged to have acted in excess of its authority, *i.e. ultra petita*, and to have dealt with a dispute that was not submitted to it. According to a leading authority on the Convention, the courts almost invariably reject this defence.[96] By way of example, the German courts have rejected *ultra petita* defences raised in complaint of an arbitral tribunal's application of *lex mercatoria*,[97] and an arbitral tribunal's award of more interest than was claimed.[98] A Further robust rejection of such a defence comes from the US Court of Appeals for the District of Columbia, in a case in which it was pleaded that the arbitral tribunal had awarded a considerable sum of damages for consequential loss, when the contract between the parties clearly excluded this head of damage.[99] The court stated that, without an in-depth review of the law of contract, the court could not state whether a breach of contract would abrogate a clause which excluded consequential damages. However, "the standard of review of an arbitration award by an American

---

[93] As in the *Pyramids* arbitration. The award of the ICC Tribunal in this case was challenged by the Egyptian Government, on the basis that it was not a party to the relevant agreement and so not bound by the arbitration clause. The Cour de'Appel de Paris agreed and the award was set aside. *The Arab Republic of Egypt v Southern Pacific Properties*, Cour d'Appel de Paris, July 12, 1984, published in English at (1984) 23 I.L.M. 1048; for a discussion of the case see Redfern, "Jurisdiction Denied: The Pyramid Collapses" (1986) Journal of Business Law 15. See also (1984) IX Yearbook Commercial Arbitration 113 and (1985) X Yearbook Commercial Arbitration 487. The claimants then started fresh arbitration proceedings, under the Washington Convention. For the rest of the story, see Delaume, *ICSID Review*, Vol.8 (1993), p.231; Craig "The Final Chapter in the Pyramids Case: Discounting an ISCID Award for Annulment Risk", *ICSID Review*, *op. cit.*, p.264; and Paulsson "Arbitration without Privity", *ISCID Review*, Vol.10 (1995), p.232.

[94] See Ch.9, para.9–13.

[95] See Ch.9, para.9–14.

[96] van den Berg, "Court Decisions on the New York Convention", Swiss Arbitration Association Conference, February 1996, Collected Reports, p.86.

[97] See the decision of the regional court of Hamburg of September 18, 1997, (2000) XXV Yearbook Commercial Arbitration 710.

[98] See the decision of the Court of Appeal of Hamburg of July 30, 1998, (2000) XXV Yearbook Commercial Arbitration 714.

[99] *Libyan American Oil Company (Liamco) v Socialist Peoples Libyan Arab Yamahirya, formerly Libyan Arab Republic* (1982) VII Yearbook Commercial Arbitration 382.

Court is extremely narrow",[1] and (adopting the words of the US Court of Appeals in the well-known case of *Parsons Whittemore*[2]) the Convention did not sanction "second-guessing the arbitrators' construction of the parties' agreement". Nor would it be proper for the court to "usurp the arbitrators' role".[3] Accordingly, enforcement was ordered.

The second part of this ground for refusal is concerned with the situation where it is alleged that the tribunal exceeded its jurisdiction in some respects, but not in others. In such a situation, even if the partial excess of authority is proved, that part of the award that concerns matters submitted to arbitration *may* be saved and enforcement ordered. For example, in a case that came before the Italian courts, the court examined the award to determine whether or not the arbitral tribunal had exceeded the limits of its jurisdiction. Having done so, the Italian court granted partial enforcement of the award, to the extent that it dealt with matters within the jurisdiction of the arbitral tribunal.[4]

(f) Fourth ground: composition of tribunal or procedure not in accordance with arbitration agreement or the relevant law

The fourth ground for refusal of recognition and enforcement of an award **10–43** under the New York Convention is as follows:

> "(d) The composition of the arbitral authority or the arbitral procedure was not in accordance with the agreement of the parties, or, failing such agreement, was not in accordance with the law of the country where the arbitration took place . . . "[5]

The Geneva Convention of 1927, mentioned above, provided that enforcement of an award could be refused if the composition of the arbitral tribunal, or the arbitral procedure, was not in accordance both with the agreement of the parties *and* the law of the place of arbitration. This double requirement meant that if an arbitration was not held in strict accordance with the procedural law of the place of arbitration, the consequent award would not be enforced. In the New York Convention, the double requirement has been dropped. The agreement of the parties comes first. Only if there is no agreement are the arbitration laws of the place of arbitration to be taken into account.

In a case that came before the Supreme Court of Hong Kong in 1994, it was argued that enforcement of an award made in China should be refused because the composition of the arbitral tribunal was not in accordance with the agreement of the parties. The arbitrators who had been appointed were on the Shenzhen list

---

[1] *ibid.*, at 388.
[2] *Parsons Whittemore Overseas Co Inc v Société Générale de l'Industrie du Papier (RAKTA)* 508 F.2d 969 (2nd Cir. 1974).
[3] (1982) VII Yearbook Commercial Arbitration 382 at 388.
[4] (1983) VIII Yearbook Commercial Arbitration 386.
[5] New York Convention, Art.V.1(d).

of arbitrators but not (as specified in the arbitration agreement) on the Beijing list.[6]

10–44 Giving judgment, Kaplan J. said:

"It is clear therefore that the only grounds upon which enforcement can be refused are those specified . . . and that the burden of proving a ground is upon the defendant. Further, it is clear that even though a ground has been proved, the Court retains a residual discretion."[7]

After considering the facts, the judge said:

"I conclude therefore, somewhat reluctantly, that technically the arbitrators did not have jurisdiction to decide this dispute and that in all the circumstances of this case, the ground specified in the section has been made out. I say technically because the parties did agree to have a CIETAC Arbitration and that is what they got, even though it was held at a place within China not specified in the contract and by arbitrators who apparently were not on the Beijing list."[8]

Although the ground for refusal of enforcement had been made out, the judge allowed enforcement of the award to go ahead on the basis that the party objecting to enforcement had taken part in the arbitration knowing that technically the arbitrators were not selected from the correct list. Having done so they could not now seek to profit from this error. The learned judge considered the application of the doctrine of estoppel to other aspects of the New York Convention and said:

"If the doctrine of estoppel can apply to arguments over the written form of the arbitration agreement under Article II(2), then I fail to see why it cannot also apply to the grounds of opposition set out in Article V. It strikes me as quite unfair for a party to appreciate that there might be something wrong with the composition of the tribunal yet not make any formal submission whatsoever to the tribunal about its own jurisdiction, or to the arbitration commission which constituted the tribunal and then to proceed to fight the case on the merits and then two years after the award, attempt to nullify the whole proceedings on the grounds that the arbitrators were chosen from the wrong CIETAC list."[9]

He went on to say:

---

[6] See *China Nanhai Oil Joint Service Cpn v Gee Tai Holdings Co Ltd* (1995) XX Yearbook Commercial Arbitration 671. Similarly, see *Tongyuan International Trading Group v Uni-Clan* [2001] 4 Int.A.L.R. N-31.

[7] *ibid.*, at 672.

[8] *ibid.*, at 673.

[9] *ibid.*, at 677.

" . . . even if a ground of opposition is proved, there is still a residual discretion left in the enforcing court to enforce nonetheless. This shows that the grounds of opposition are not to be inflexibly applied. The residual discretion enables the enforcing court to achieve a just result in all the circumstances . . . "

(g) Fifth ground: award not binding; suspended or set aside

The fifth ground for refusal of recognition and enforcement under the New **10–45**
York Convention is as follows:

"(e) The award has not yet become binding on the parties, or has been set aside or suspended by a competent authority of the country in which, or under the law of which, that award was made . . . "[10]

This fifth ground for refusal of recognition and enforcement of an arbitral award (which, like the others, also appears in the Model Law) has given rise to more controversy than any of the previous grounds. First, there is the reference to an award being "not binding". In the Geneva Convention of 1927, the word "final" was used. This was taken by many to mean that the award had to be declared as "final" by the court of the place of arbitration; and this gave rise to the problem of the double *exequatur*, which has already been discussed.[11] It was intended that the word "binding" would avoid this problem, particularly since many international and institutional rules of arbitration state in terms that the award of the arbitral tribunal is to be accepted by the parties as final and "binding" upon them.[12] However, some national courts still consider it necessary to investigate the law applicable to the award to see if it is "binding" under that law[13]—although the better position appears to be that an award is "binding" if it is no longer open to an appeal on the merits, either internally (that is to say, within the relevant rules of arbitration) or by an application to the court.[14]

There are other problems too, with this fifth ground for refusal that have led to considerable controversy. At first sight, the proposition that an award *may* be refused recognition and enforcement if it has been set aside or suspended by a court at the place (or seat) of the arbitration seems reasonable enough. If, for example, an award has been set aside in Switzerland, it will be unenforceable in that country; and it might be expected that, if only as a matter of international comity, the courts of other states would regard the award as unenforceable also.

---

[10] New York Convention, Art.V.1(e).
[11] See para.10–22.
[12] See, for instance, the UNCITRAL Arbitration Rules, Art.32(2).
[13] van den Berg, *op. cit.*, pp.87 and 88.
[14] van den Berg, *op.cit.*, p.88. If an appeal is pending, the enforcement court may, if it considers it proper, adjourn the decision on enforcement. It may also order the party against whom enforcement is sought to give security: New York Convention, Art.VI.

10–46   This is not necessarily so, however. Courts in other countries may take the view (and indeed, as will be described, in some countries they *have* taken the view) that they will enforce an arbitral award even if it has been set aside by the courts of the seat of the arbitration. This leads to a situation in which an award that has been set aside and so is unenforceable in its country of origin, may be refused enforcement under the New York Convention in one country, but granted enforcement in another.

The problem arises because the New York Convention does not in any way restrict the grounds on which an award may be set aside or suspended by the court of the country in which, or under the law of which, that award was made.[15] This is a matter that is left to the domestic law of the country concerned; and this domestic law may impose local requirements (such as the need to initial each page of the award) that judges and lawyers elsewhere would not regard as sufficient to impeach the validity of an *international* arbitral award.

The allowance for local requirements that is made in the New York Convention has been described by a former Secretary-General of the ICC Court of Arbitration as:

> "a hitherto rock-solid rampart against the true internationalisation of arbitration, because in the award's country of origin all means of recourse and all grounds of nullity applicable to purely domestic awards may be used to oppose recognition abroad . . . "[16]

10–47   Another experienced commentator has referred to the "anathema of local particularities" which are capable of leading to the setting aside of international awards; and has suggested that "such local standard annulments" should only be given local effect and should be disregarded internationally.[17]

The argument in favour of the fifth ground is a familiar one. It is the classic argument that the courts of the place of arbitration should have some control over arbitral proceedings conducted on their territory, if only to guard against lack of due process, fraud, corruption or other improper conduct on the part of the arbitral tribunal. Perhaps the real argument is: how far should this control go? Should it be limited to the first four grounds of the New York Convention[18] or

---

[15] Unlike the Model Law which, in Art.34, sets out the limited grounds on which an award may be set aside.

[16] Derains, Foreword in *Hommage à Frédéric Eisemann* 5, 13 (1978) (translated by Paulsson in (1996) 7 American Review of International Arbitration 99). This is not true of states that have different laws to govern international arbitrations from those that govern domestic arbitrations, but nevertheless the point is a valid one.

[17] Paulsson, "The case for disregarding local standard annulments under the New York Convention" (1996) 7 American Review of International Arbitration (Columbia University) 99. In a sense, this comes back to the "delocalisation" debate, which was a source of lively controversy at the time: see, for instance, Paulsson, "Arbitration Unbound: Award detached from the law of its country of origin" (1981) 30 I.C.L.Q 358 and "Delocalisation of International Commercial Arbitration, When and Why it Matters" (1983) 32 I.C.L.Q. 53. See also the discussion in Ch.2.

[18] As with the European Convention of 1961.

should it go further? And if so, how much further? The problem is to strike the correct balance between control and *laissez-faire*.

Whilst the argument continues, courts in France, Belgium, Austria and the US have shown themselves prepared to recognise and enforce arbitral awards, even though they have been set aside by the courts at the seat of arbitration.[19] The justification for this is twofold. First, the language of Art.V of the New York Convention (as already discussed) is permissive, not mandatory. Specifically, the English language version of the Convention says that the enforcing court *may* refuse recognition and enforcement—not that it *must* do so. Secondly, the New York Convention recognises that there may be more favourable provisions under which an award may be recognised and enforced. The Convention contains the following provision, in Art.VII.1:

"The provisions of the present Convention shall not affect the validity of multilateral or bilateral agreements concerning the recognition and enforcement of arbitral awards entered into by the Contracting States nor deprive any interested party of any right he may have to avail himself of the arbitral award in the manner and to the extent allowed by the law or the treaties of the country where such award is sought to be relied upon."

In this way, the New York Convention recognises explicitly that in any given **10–48** country there may be a local law that, whether by treaty or otherwise, is more favourable to the recognition and enforcement of arbitral awards than the Convention itself. The Convention gives its blessing, so to speak, to any party who wishes to take advantage of this more favourable local law.

The New York Convention has long been regarded as being of fundamental importance to the recognition and enforcement of international arbitral awards. It remains so. However, the possibility of obtaining recognition and enforcement under a more favourable local law, which does not reflect or rely upon the Convention, should not be overlooked. It is a possibility which is illustrated by such well-known cases as *Hilmarton*,[20] where the French court enforced an award that had been set aside in Switzerland, and *Chromalloy*,[21] where the US Federal Court for the District of Columbia enforced an award that had been set aside in Egypt.[22] In *Chromalloy*, the court explicitly contrasted the permissive nature of Art.V of the Convention with the mandatory nature of Art.VII:

"While Article V provides a discretionary standard, Article VII of the Convention requires that, 'The provisions of the present Convention *shall not . . .* deprive any interested party of any right he may have to avail himself of an

---

[19] For a comprehensive survey of instances in which national courts have recognised or enforced awards set aside by the courts of the place of arbitration, see Hamid G. Gharavi, *The International Effectiveness of the Annulment of an Arbitral Award* (Kluwer, 2002).

[20] *Hilmarton Ltd v Omnium de Traitement et de Valorisation (OTV)* (1994) Revue de l'Arbitrage 327 ; English excerpts in (1995) XX Yearbook Commercial Arbitration 663.

[21] *Chromalloy Aeroservices Inc v Arab Republic of Egypt*, 939 F.Supp. 907 (D.D.C. 1996).

[22] See paras 10–72 *et seq.*

arbitral award in the manner and to the extent allowed by the law . . . of the country where such award is sought to be relied on."'[23]

Notwithstanding decisions such as *Hilmarton* and *Chromalloy*, enforcing awards that have been set aside by the courts of the place of arbitration remains controversial. With some notable exceptions, courts around the world are still more than likely to decline to enforce annulled awards.[24]

10–49 Finally, it should be noted that the only national court that is competent to suspend or set aside an award is the court of the country "in which, or under the law of which, that award was made."[25] This court will almost invariably be the national court at the seat of the arbitration. The impracticability of holding an arbitration in country X but subjecting it to the procedural law of country Y has already been discussed,[26] and so the prospect of an award being set aside under the procedural law of a state other than that at the seat of arbitration is unlikely. However, an ingenious (but unsuccessful) attempt was made to persuade the US District Court to set aside an award made in Mexico, on the basis that the reference to the law under which that award was made was a reference to the law governing the dispute and not to the procedural law.[27] The court firmly rejected this argument, stating:

"Decisions of foreign courts under the Convention uniformly support the view that the clause in question means procedural and not substantive (that is, in most cases, contract law) . . .

Accordingly, we hold that the contested language in Article V(1)(e) of the Convention . . . refers exclusively to procedural and not substantive law, and more precisely to the regimen or scheme of arbitral procedural law under which the arbitration was conducted."[28]

The court went on to hold that since the forum of the arbitration was Mexico, only the Mexican court had jurisdiction to set aside the award.[29]

This completes this review of the five grounds for refusal of recognition and enforcement of an arbitral award laid down in the New York Convention, and the Model Law, and which it is for the party resisting enforcement to prove. As already mentioned, however, there are two other grounds that may be invoked by the enforcement court itself. These concern, first, arbitrability, and secondly, public policy.

---

[23] *Chromalloy*, at 909–910.
[24] See, *e.g.*, *Baker Marine (Nig.) Ltd v Chevron (Nig.) Ltd* 191 F.3d 194 (2nd Cir. 1999), in which, notwithstanding *Chromalloy*, the US Second Circuit refused to enforce an award that had been set aside by the court of the place of arbitration (in this case Nigeria). See also *Spier v Tecnica* 71 F.Supp.2d 279 (S.D.N.Y. 1999).
[25] New York Convention Art.V.1(e).
[26] Ch.2.
[27] *International Standard Electric Corp (US) v Bridas Sociedad Anonima Petrolera (Argentina)* (1992) VII Yearbook Commercial Arbitration 639.
[28] *ibid.*, at 644 and 645.
[29] *ibid.*, at 645.

(h) Arbitrability

The New York Convention provides, as does the Model Law, that recognition **10–50** and enforcement of an arbitral award may be refused "if the competent authority in the country where recognition and enforcement is sought finds that: (a) the subject matter of the difference is not capable of settlement by arbitration under the law of that country . . . "[30]

Arbitrability has already been discussed in Chs 1 and 3. As indicated, each state has its own concept of what disputes should be reserved for the courts of law and what disputes may be resolved by arbitration. This question may arise at the beginning of an arbitration (is this dispute capable of being referred to arbitration?) and at the end (would this dispute have been capable of settlement by arbitration under the law of the enforcement state?). The issue of "arbitrability" under this provision of the New York Convention is, of course, an issue for the law of the enforcement state and, being governed largely by questions of public policy, varies from state to state.

One somewhat surprising concept of a dispute that was not arbitrable came from the Belgian court, in a case involving the German car manufacturer, Audi. The German company terminated the distributorship of their Belgian distributor and commenced arbitration proceedings in Zurich, pursuant to the arbitration clause in the distribution agreement. The arbitral tribunal held that the agreement was duly terminated and the distributor was not entitled to recover any damages from Audi. However, the Belgian Cour de Cassation held that the dispute was not capable of settlement by arbitration, since the Belgian law concerning the "Unilateral Termination of Concessions for Exclusive Distributorships for an Indefinite Time" gave exclusive jurisdiction to the Belgian courts.[31] The importance of the decision is not confined to Belgium, since many Arab states have similar laws designed to protect agency agreements in their countries and to render any disputes non-arbitrable.

(i) Public policy

Recognition and enforcement of an arbitral award may also be refused if it is **10–51** contrary to the public policy of the enforcement state.[32] It is understandable that a state may wish to have the right to refuse to recognise and enforce an arbitration award that offends that state's own notions of public policy, and in some jurisdictions an enforcing court is required to examine the possibility of a public policy violation *ex officio*.[33] Yet when reference is made to "public policy" it is

---

[30] New York Convention, Art.V.2(a). See also "public policy" as a ground to challenge an award, paras 9–19 and 9–32.

[31] *Audi-NSU Auto-Union AG (Germany) v Adelin Petit & Cie (Belgium)* (1980) V Yearbook Commercial Arbitration 257.

[32] New York Convention, Art.V.2(b).

[33] See the decision of the Cour de Justice of Geneva dated December 11, 1997 (1998) XXIII Yearbook Commercial Arbitration 764.

difficult not to recall the sceptical comment of the English judge who said, almost two centuries ago, "It is never argued at all but where other points fail."[34]

Certainly, the national courts in England are reluctant to excuse an award from enforcement on grounds of public policy. At one time it was said that: "there is no case in which this exception has been applied by an English court."[35] Inevitably, of course, the exception was then applied in *Soleimany v Soleimany*.[36] In this case, an English court refused to enforce an award giving effect to a contract between a father and son that involved the smuggling of carpets out of Iran in breach of Iranian revenue laws and export controls. The father and son had agreed to submit their dispute to arbitration by the Beth Din, the Court of the Chief Rabbi in London, which applied Jewish law. As a matter of the applicable Jewish law, the illegal purpose of the contract had no effect on the rights of the parties and the Beth Din proceeded to make an award enforcing the contract. In declining to enforce the award, however, the court held that:

> "The Court is in our view concerned to preserve the integrity of its process, and to see that it is not abused. The parties cannot override that concern by private agreement. They cannot by procuring an arbitration conceal that they, or rather one of them, is seeking to enforce an illegal contract. Public policy will not allow it."[37]

Rare exceptions such as this aside, in most countries the "pro-enforcement bias" of the New York Convention has been faithfully observed.[38] Indeed, this pro-enforcement bias is itself considered a matter of public policy, as the English courts confirmed in *Westacre Investments Inc v Jugoimport-SPDR Holding Co Ltd*.[39] This dispute arose from a "consultancy" agreement for the procurement of contracts for the sale of military equipment in Kuwait. Westacre commenced arbitration claiming payment of its "consulting fee". Jugoimport defended the claim on the grounds that, in violation of Kuwaiti law and public policy, the contract involved Westacre bribing various Kuwaitis to exert their influence in

---

[34] *per* Burrough J. in *Richardson v Mellish* (1824) 2 Bing. 229 at 252, [1824–34] All E.R. 258.

[35] Kerr, "Concord and Conflict in International Arbitration" (1997) 13 Arbitration International 140.

[36] [1999] Q.B. 785.

[37] *ibid.*, at 800.

[38] *Parsons v Whittemore op. cit.*, para.10–42. More recently, see the Second Circuit decision in *MGM Productions Group Inc v Aeroflot Russian Airlines* 2004 W.L. 234871 (2nd Circ. (NY)), in which Aeroflot sought to challenge a Stockholm award because it compensated the claimant for Aeroflot's non-performance of an agreement whose provisions allegedly violated the US Iranian Transactions Regulations adopted pursuant to Executive Orders issued by the President of the United States under the International Emergency Economic Powers Act. The Second Circuit rejected the challenge, holding that "Courts construe the public policy limitation in the Convention very narrowly and apply it only when enforcement would violate the forum state's 'most basic notions of morality and justice'." In this case, even if the agreement in operation did violate the Iranian Transactions Regulations, which the arbitral tribunal itself had found was not the case, the award would not contravene public policy because "a violation of United States foreign policy does not contravene public policy as contemplated in Art.V of the Convention."

[39] [1999] 2 Lloyd's Rep. 65 (CA).

favour of entering sales contracts with Jugoimport. The agreement between Westacre and Jugoimport was governed by Swiss law and provided for arbitration in Switzerland. The arbitral tribunal found that there was no evidence of corruption, and that lobbying by private enterprises to obtain public contracts was not illegal under Swiss law. The award was first challenged in the Swiss Federal Court, which rejected the challenge on the basis that allegations of corruption had already been dealt with and rejected by the arbitral tribunal. Attempts to enforce the award were subsequently challenged in the English courts, where Jugoimport filed new affidavit evidence in support of its allegation of corruption.

In decisions that have attracted some critical commentary,[40] the English courts **10–52** rejected the challenge to enforcement, both at first instance and in the Court of Appeal, on the basis that: the arbitral tribunal itself had considered the allegations of bribery and found that they had not been substantiated; "lobbying" was not, as such, an illegal activity under the governing law chosen by the parties; and the court was faced with international arbitration awards that had been upheld by with Swiss Federal Tribunal, and therefore, had to balance the public policy of discouraging international commercial corruption with the public policy of sustaining international arbitration awards.

It is clear that the "public policy" referred to in the New York Convention is the public policy of the enforcement state.[41] The real question is whether that public policy differentiates between international awards and purely domestic awards.

The approach of the US courts was summarised by the Federal District Court of Massachusetts in *Sonatrach*.[42] The court stated:

"The line of decisions which conclusively tip the judicial scale in favour of arbitration [are] a line of United States Supreme Court opinions which enthusiastically endorse an internationalist approach towards commercial disputes involving foreign entities. These decisions, the *Bremen v Zapata Offshore Co* (forum selection clauses in international commercial contract enforced) *Scherk v Alberto-Culver Co* (international arbitration clause held enforceable when in conflict with federal securities laws); and most recently *Mitsubishi* (international arbitration clause held enforceable when in conflict with Federal Antitrust laws) eschew the parochial tendencies of domestic tribunals in retaining jurisdiction over international commercial disputes. The Supreme

---

[40] See Rogers and Kaley, "The Impact of Public Policy in International Commercial Arbitration", *Journal of the Chartered Institute of Arbitrators*, Vol.65, No.4.

[41] This is clear from the text of Art.V(2) itself; and, accordingly, the Supreme Court of India was right to reject the argument that the references (in the Indian statute which enacted the Convention) to "public policy" rather than to the "public policy of India" meant that the words were not restricted to India, but would extend to the laws governing the contract and the place of arbitration: see *Renusagar Power Co Ltd (India) v General Electric Co (US)* (1995) XX Yearbook Commercial Arbitration 681.

[42] *Sonatrach (Algeria) v Distrigas Corp (United States District Court) Massachusetts,* reported in (1995) XX Yearbook Commercial Arbitration at 795.

Court powerfully advocates the need for international comity in an increasingly interdependent world. Such respect is especially important, in this Court's view, when parties mutually agree to be bound by freely negotiated contracts."[43]

10–53   A similar line of reasoning is found in the decision of the New York District Court in the well-known case of *Parsons & Whittemore Overseas Co Inc v Société Générale de l'Industrie du Papier (RAKTA)*.[44] The court was confronted by an argument that recognition and enforcement of an award should be refused on the grounds that diplomatic relations between Egypt (the respondent's state) and the US had been severed. The court rejected this argument and referred to "the general pro-enforcement bias" of the New York Convention.[45] It held that the Convention's "public policy" defence should be construed narrowly; and that enforcement of foreign arbitral awards should only be denied on this basis "where enforcement would violate the forum state's most basic notions of morality and justice".

Courts in other countries have also recognised that, in applying their own public policy to Convention awards, they should give it an international and not a domestic dimension. In India, in the case to which reference has already been made,[46] the Supreme Court said:

"This raises the question of whether the narrower concept of public policy as applicable in the field of public international law should be applied or the wider concept of public policy as applicable in the field of municipal law. The Court held that the narrower view should prevail and that enforcement would be refused on the public policy ground if such enforcement would be contrary to (i) fundamental policy of Indian law; or (ii) the interests of India; or (iii) justice or morality".[47]

The decision of a Swiss court in *K.S. AG v C.C. SA*[48] was to a similar effect:

"The Swiss public policy defence has a more limited scope in the context of proceedings for the recognition and enforcement of foreign arbitral awards than [the one allowed] in proceedings before a Swiss court deciding on the merits . . . From a formal point of view, we find that a procedural defect in the

---

[43] The citation for *Zapata* has already been given above. The other citations are: *Scherk v Alberto Culver Co*, 417 US 506 1974; and *Mitsubishi Motor Corporation v Soler Chrysler-Plymouth Inc* 473 US 614; 105 S.Ct. 3346; 87 L.Ed.2d. 444 (1985).

[44] *Parsons & Whittemore Overseas Co Inc v Société Générale de l'Industrie du Papier (RAKTA)*, op. cit., para.10–42.

[45] *ibid.*, at 973.

[46] *Renusagar Power Co Ltd v General Electric Co*, above, para.10–52.

[47] *ibid.*, at 702.

[48] (1995) XX Yearbook Commercial Arbitration 762.

course of the foreign arbitration does not lead necessarily to refusing enforcement even if the same defect would have resulted in the annulment of a Swiss
award (with the obvious exception of the violation of fundamental principles
of our legal system, which would contrast in an unbearable manner with our
feeling of justice) . . . "[49]

The German Federal Supreme Court has expressed a similar concept in   **10–54**
different terms[50]:

"From the viewpoint of German procedural public policy, the recognition of a
foreign arbitral award can therefore only be denied if the arbitral procedure
suffers from a grave defect that touches the foundation of the State and
economic functions."[51]

These decisions, from courts in different parts of the world, show a readiness
to limit (and sometimes to limit severely) the public policy defence to enforcement. However, the boundaries of national public policy are not fixed. There are
cases, for instance, in which the Turkish courts have allowed the public policy
defence in circumstances in which, to an outside observer, it seems to be
unjustified.[52] Japanese legislation applies the test of "public policy or good
morals" in the enforcement process[53]; and Vietnamese legislation requires that
the award should not be contrary to the basic principles of Vietnamese law.[54] In
China, too, it seems that the public policy defence may be used to protect what
some might regard as purely local interests.[55]

(j) The Washington Convention

ICSID was established by the Washington Convention of 1965[56] to facilitate   **10–55**
the resolution of international investment disputes and thereby promote foreign
investment.[57] This Convention is considered in some detail in Chs 1 and 11. The
only point which needs to be emphasised in the present context is that, unless an
ICSID award is revised or annulled under ICSID's own internal procedures, each

---

[49] *ibid.*, at 763 and 764.
[50] (1987) XII Yearbook Commercial Arbitration at 489.
[51] *ibid.*, at 496. This was a case in which the arbitrator appointed by one party became the sole
   arbitrator, through the other party's failure to appoint an arbitrator. The German court held that it
   had not been shown that the arbitrator was not impartial.
[52] See Kerr, *Concord and Conflict in International Arbitration, op. cit.*, pp.140 and 141.
[53] *ibid.*, p.141, para.10–35.
[54] Paulsson, "The New York Convention in International Practice: Problems of Assimilation", *ASA
   Bulletin* (1996) pp.101–102.
[55] Rather than refer to "public policy", Chinese law refers to the "social and public interest", which
   is an even vaguer concept. Whilst local courts may refuse enforcement on this ground, it seems
   that the Supreme People's Court is less likely to do so: for a discussion of this topic see, for
   instance, Wang Sheng Chang, "Enforcement of Awards in the P.R. China", 14th ICCA Congress,
   Paris, 1998.
[56] For the text of the Convention, see *UN Treaty Series* (1966) Vol.575, p.160, No.8359.
[57] For the meaning of this term, see Ch.1, paras 1–125 *et seq.*

contracting state must recognise and enforce an ICSID award as if it were a final judgment of its own national courts.

By the end of 2003, the Washington Convention was in force in 140 countries. These include states from Latin America such as Paraguay, El Salvador and Costa Rica. They also include capital-exporting countries of the Arab world, such as Kuwait, Saudi Arabia and the United Arab Emirates.[58]

There are a number of regional conventions that may also have a significant bearing on the recognition and enforcement of foreign arbitral awards. The principal conventions are discussed briefly in turn.

(k) Refusal of recognition and enforcement under regional conventions

The European Convention of 1961

10–56   The European Convention on International Commercial Arbitration was signed in Geneva on April 21, 1961.[59] This Convention is designed primarily to deal with the problems of establishing and operating procedures for disputes arising out of trading agreements between European countries (in particular, those between East and West Europe).[60] As already mentioned, the European Convention contains limitations upon the grounds on which an award covered by the Convention may be set aside. It provides that the setting aside of an award in a contracting state will only constitutes a ground for the refusal of recognition or enforcement of that award in another contracting state if the award has been set aside for reasons specified in the Convention.[61]

These reasons, which correspond closely to the first four grounds for refusal of recognition and enforcement of awards under the New York Convention,[62] are the only reasons which the European Convention recognises as valid reasons for setting aside an award. This means that an award that has been set aside in its state of origin for a reason recognised as valid by that state, such as a mistake of law, may still qualify for recognition and enforcement because mistake of law is not recognised by the Convention as a valid ground for setting aside an award. In this respect, the European Convention goes further than the New York Convention and so avoids the problem of local annulments.[63]

The European Convention does not deal with the recognition and enforcement of awards. It leaves this to be dealt with by other treaties, including the New York Convention, to which the European Convention is a supplement.[64]

---

[58] For a list of contracting states and signatories to the Washington Convention see *www.worldbank. org/icsid/constate/c-states-en.htm.*

[59] For discussion of the background and objectives of the Convention, see Benjamin, "The European Convention on International Commercial Arbitration" (1961) B.Y.I.L. 478.

[60] However, it is open for accession by non-European countries; European Convention of 1961, Art.X(1) and (2). The Convention has been either signed, ratified, or acceded to by 27 countries. For a list see Smit & Pechota, *International Arbitration Treaties* (1998); *International Commercial Arbitration*, Bergsten ed. (Oceana).

[61] European Convention of 1961, Art.IX.1.

[62] New York Convention, Art.V.1.

[63] Referred to in connection with Art.V.1(e) of the New York Convention. See para.10–23.

[64] van den Berg, *op. cit.*, p.95; (1986) XI Yearbook Commercial Arbitration 473.

The Moscow Convention

The Moscow Convention was signed on May 26, 1972, the original signatories **10–57**
being the Eastern European states that were grouped together in the Council for
Mutual Economic Assistance. Now that the German Democratic Republic has
ceased to exist and Poland, the Czech Republic and Hungary have withdrawn, it
only applies to Bulgaria, Cuba, Mongolia, Romania and Russia.

The Convention regulates the settlement by arbitration of disputes arising from
economic, scientific and technical co-operation within the member countries of
CMEA.

The Convention provides that arbitration awards "shall be final and binding"[65]
and they are to be "voluntarily" enforced by the parties; failing which they may
be enforced in the same way as final decisions made in the courts of the country
of enforcement.[66] Enforcement proceedings must be brought within two years of
the date of the award, and the three grounds of refusal of enforcement closely
parallel those in the New York Convention, namely, lack of jurisdiction, denial
of a fair hearing and when the award has been set aside.[67]

The Panama Convention

In January 1975, following the Inter-American Conference on Private Inter- **10–58**
national Law in Panama, a new Inter-American Convention on International
Commercial Arbitration ("the Panama Convention") was signed by 12 South
American states.[68] The Convention represents a significant shift away from a
former hostility toward international arbitration, as reflected in the Calvo Doctrine.[69]

The Panama Convention recognises an agreement to submit existing or future
disputes to arbitration[70] and it also provides for the reciprocal enforcement of
arbitral awards in member states. This takes place as if the award were a
judgment of a court:

"An arbitral decision or award that is not appealable under the applicable law
or procedural rules shall have the force of a final judicial judgment. Its
execution or recognition may be ordered in the same manner as that of
decisions handed down by national or foreign ordinary courts, in accordance

---

[65] Moscow Convention, Art.IV.1.
[66] *ibid.*, Art.IV.2.
[67] *ibid.*, Art.V.1.
[68] The text of the Convention appears in (1978) III Yearbook Commercial Arbitration 15 and in
(1975) 14 I.L.M. 336. See also Blackaby, Lindsey & Spinillo eds, *International Arbitration in
Latin America* (Kluwer, 2002), pp.3–6. The Convention came into effect in the US on October 27,
1990.
[69] As at the beginning of 2004, 17 states had ratified this Convention, including the US. For a
commentary on US participation see Lowry, "The United States Joins the Inter-American Arbitration Convention" (1990) 7 Journal of International Arbitration 83.
[70] Panama Convention, Art.1. Unlike the New York Convention, however, it does not deal with the
problem of enforcing an arbitration agreement if one of the parties takes court proceedings
notwithstanding the agreement to arbitrate.

with the procedural laws of the country where it is to be executed and the provisions of international treaties."[71]

The Convention speaks of "execution" of an award rather than "enforcement", but in practice there is no difference. Recognition and execution of an award may be refused, at the request of the party against which it is made, only if that party is able to prove to the competent authority of the state in which recognition and execution is sought, that one of the five grounds for refusal laid down in Art.5 of the Panama Convention applies.[72] By Art.5.2 of the Panama Convention, recognition and execution of an award may also be refused if the competent authority of the state in which recognition and execution is sought, finds:

"(a) That the subject matter of the dispute cannot be settled by arbitration under the law of that State; or

(b) That recognition or execution of the decision would be contrary to the public policy (*"ordre public"*) of that State."[73]

10–59   Where an application has been made to annul or suspend the award, the authority before which recognition and execution is sought may,[74] under the Panama Convention, postpone its decision; at the request of the party seeking execution, it may also instruct the other party to provide appropriate guarantees.[75]

It is clear that the Panama Convention was strongly influenced by the provisions of the New York Convention. Indeed, many of the provisions of the former have been copied more or less word for word from the latter. According to one informed commentator, the Panama Convention "has a tremendous and vital significance".[76] Certainly, whether because of the Convention or because of other influences—such as the Model Law—arbitration is becoming a more acceptable way of settling disputes in Latin America. In Venezuela, for example, the Colon Project Law of 1993[77] *requires* ICC arbitration of joint venture agreements between the state-owned oil company and foreign companies for the exploration and extraction of oil.

The Amman Convention

10–60   This regional agreement is open to membership by the Arab states. It was signed in 1987 by Algeria, Djibouti, Iraq, Jordan, Lebanon, Libya, Mauritania, Morocco, Palestine, Sudan, Syria, Tunisia, North Yemen and South Yemen.

[71] Panama Convention, Art.4.
[72] These five grounds of refusal closely follow the five grounds set out in the New York Convention Art.V.1.
[73] This provision follows the New York Convention, Art.V.2.
[74] Panama Convention, Art.6.
[75] This provision follows the New York Convention, Art.V.I.
[76] Norberg, "General Introduction to Inter-American Commercial Arbitration" (1978) III Yearbook Commercial Arbitration 1 at 13.
[77] Published in the *Venezuelan Official Gazette*, September 9 and 30, 1993.

Whilst the Amman Convention is modelled on the Washington Convention, it is of limited international interest in that it restricts submissions and pleadings to the Arabic language and the proceedings it contemplates are thus not accessible to most parties to international commercial agreements.[78]

Other regional conventions

This review of various regional conventions is not intended to be exhaustive. **10–61** Parties or lawyers who are concerned with the recognition and enforcement of arbitration agreements or arbitral awards would be well advised to consider whether there are any regional conventions that may be both relevant and helpful.

(l) The defence of state immunity

The defences to recognition and enforcement of an international arbitral **10–62** award, which are laid down in the New York Convention and the Model Law, have been considered.[79] There is one standard form of defence, however, that is not mentioned in the Convention or the Model Law but which may be encountered in practice. This is where the unsuccessful party is either a sovereign state or a state agency. This is the defence of state immunity, or sovereign immunity as it is sometimes known; and, in essence, it means that a sovereign state cannot be compelled to submit to the jurisdiction of another state:

"The sovereign was a definable person, to whom allegiance was due. As an integral part of this mystique, the sovereign could not be made subject to the judicial processes of his country. Accordingly, it was only fitting that he could not be sued in foreign courts. The idea of the personal sovereign would undoubtedly have been undermined had courts been able to exercise jurisdiction over foreign sovereigns. This personalisation was gradually replaced by the abstract concept of state sovereignty, but the basic mystique remained. In addition, the independence and equality of states made it philosophically as well as practically difficult to permit municipal courts of one country to manifest their power over foreign sovereign states, without their consent."[80]

State immunity does not prevent a state or state agency from agreeing to submit to the authority of an arbitral tribunal. It is a well-established principle of

---

[78] For further information see Jalili, "Amman Arab Convention on Commercial Arbitration" (1990) 7 Journal of International Arbitration 139.
[79] See paras 10–36 *et seq.*
[80] Shaw, *International Law* (2nd ed., 1988), p.373; see also Lauterpacht, "The Problem of Jurisdictional Immunities of Foreign States" (1951) 28 B.Y.I.L. 220; and Higgins, "Certain Unresolved Aspects of the Law of State Immunity" (1982) 29 Netherlands International Law Review 265.

international law that a sovereign is bound by an agreement to arbitrate contractual disputes[81]; and the ability so to submit may itself be seen as an incident or attribute of sovereignty.

State immunity exists at two levels: first, at the level of jurisdiction, and secondly, at the level of execution. Accordingly, there may be both immunity from jurisdiction and immunity from execution; and in considering state immunity, a distinction may need to be made between acts of a state taking place in its capacity as a state (acts *jure imperii*) and those taking place in its commercial capacity (acts *jure gestionis*). As a distinguished Swiss commentator has written, this distinction is clear in theory, but difficult to apply in practice.[82] The distinction is important because some states claim absolute immunity—that is, immunity for all acts carried out by or on behalf of the state—whilst others claim restricted immunity, that is, immunity only for acts *jure imperii*.

Jurisdictional immunity

10–63   During the course of arbitration proceedings to which a state is a party, the distinction between absolute and restricted immunity should be of no relevance. The arbitration can only proceed validly on the basis that the state concerned has agreed to arbitrate; and such an agreement is generally held to be a waiver of immunity. This is also taken to extend to the jurisdiction of the relevant court at the seat of the arbitration to supervise the arbitration taking place in its territory.

The restricted theory of sovereign immunity has been adopted by national courts in many Western countries[83] and indeed, in some countries the position has been established by legislation. In the UK, for example, the State Immunity Act 1978 provides that where a state has agreed in writing to submit existing or future disputes to arbitration, the state is not immune in respect of proceedings in the courts of the UK that relate to the arbitration.[84] Once again, however, the precise position adopted by a given country can only be established by reference to the law and practice of that country. In the US, for example, it was not clear under the original Foreign Sovereign Immunities Act[85] whether a foreign state's agreement to arbitrate could be regarded as a waiver of immunity from the

---

[81] This principle of international law is highlighted in the award of April 12, 1977 of Mahmassani, sole arbitrator in *Libyan American Oil Company (Liamco) v Government of the Libyan Arab Republic* (1982) 62 I.L.R. 140 at 178. It was noted that even UN General Assembly Resolution No.1803, dated December 21, 1962, which proclaims permanent sovereignty over natural resources, confirms the obligation of states to respect arbitration agreements.

[82] J.-F. Lalive, "Quelques observations sur l'immunité d'exécution des Etats et l'arbitrage international" in *International Law at a Time of Perplexity* (1989), p.370.

[83] Whilst this position has evolved from case law in some countries, reference must be had also to those countries which have given effect to the European Convention on State Immunity (Basle, May 16, 1972, Cmnd 54081).

[84] English State Immunity Act 1978, s.9.

[85] Foreign Sovereign Immunities Act 1976, Title 28, US Code, s.1605(a)(1). See Kahale, "New Legislation Facilitates Enforcement of Arbitral Agreements and Awards" (1989) Journal of International Arbitration 57.

jurisdiction of a US court. Following the *Liamco* case,[86] in which an award made against the Libyan state was recognised, an amendment to the Foreign Sovereign Immunity Act[87] made it clear that the US courts have jurisdiction, *inter alia*, to confirm an arbitration award made under an agreement to arbitrate where the arbitration takes place, or is authorised to take place, in the US or where the award is governed by a treaty to which the US is a party.

Immunity from execution

Problems are most likely to arise when a winning party attempts to enforce and **10–64** execute its award against a state or state entity. If the state concerned wishes to evade its obligations[88] it may do so by claiming immunity from execution.[89] It may be thought inappropriate that a state or state entity can escape its legal obligations in this way, but this is the logical result of conferring immunity upon states. Moreover, whilst the existence of an arbitration agreement is usually held to be a waiver of immunity from jurisdiction, such a waiver is generally not held to extend to immunity from execution.

Thus, under the Washington Convention, an ICSID award must be treated by a contracting state as if it were a final judgment of a court of that state. However, this provision for the automatic recognition of such an award does *not* mean that it will be treated as overriding any immunity from *execution* that exists in the contracting state. It is surprising that in a Convention that was intended to encourage investment, the state parties did not agree to waive their immunity from execution. It seems, however, that "abandonment of immunity of execution was mentioned by only one representative and his statement found no echo whatsoever".[90]

However, courts in some jurisdictions have found ways of circumventing this obstacle to the efficacy of the arbitral process. The decision of the French Cour de Cassation in *Creighton v Qatar* is a notable example.[91] In 1982, Creighton Ltd, a Cayman Islands corporation with offices in the US, contracted with the government of Qatar to build a women's hospital in Doha. After obtaining the

---

[86] *Libyan American Oil Company (Liamco) v Libyan Arab Republic,* 20 I.L.M. 1 (1981). For the full title see para.10–62, above.
[87] s.1605(a)(6), as amended November 16, 1988; for commentary see Delaume, "Recognition and Enforcement of State Contract Awards in the United States: A Restatement" (1997) 91 American Journal of International Law 476.
[88] If it did not, presumably the question of enforcement would not arise since it would carry out the award voluntarily.
[89] For further discussion of this topic, see Bernini & van den Berg "The Enforcement of Arbitral Awards against a State—the Problem of Immunity from Execution", in *Contemporary Problems in International Arbitration* (Lew ed., 1986), p.359.
[90] See Broches, *loc. cit.*, p.332. For a view that the problem of immunity from execution of an ICSID award is more theoretical than real, by reason, *inter alia*, of the obligation in Art.53 of the Convention to comply with the award, see Delaume, "Sovereign immunity and transnational arbitration" (1987) 3 Arbitration International 28 at 43.
[91] *Creighton Ltd (Cayman Islands) v Minister of Finance and Minister of Internal Affairs and Agriculture of the Government of the State of Qatar* (2000) XXV Yearbook Commercial Arbitration 458, decision of the Cour de Cassation of July 6, 2000. See also (2001) 1 Revue de l'Arbitrage 114.

necessary authorisations, Creighton entered into a contract with the Ministry of Municipal Affairs and Agriculture of Qatar on June 19, 1982. In November 1986, Creighton was expelled from the project by the Qatari government, and in 1987, pursuant to the arbitration clause in the agreement, commenced ICC arbitration in Paris. In October 1993, final awards were rendered against Qatar.

10–65 After a failed Qatari attempt to challenge the award in France, Creighton sought to enforce the awards against, *inter alia*, bank accounts held in France by the Qatari Ministry of Agriculture and Domestic Affairs. Following Creighton's seizure of those accounts, Qatar initiated proceedings before the Tribunal de Grande Instance de Paris to have those seizures lifted on the grounds of Qatar's immunity from execution. In January 1997, the Tribunal de Grande Instance de Paris ordered the lifting of the seizures, and concluded that the subject-matter of the agreement prevented any waiver of Qatar's immunity from execution. Specifically, it held that the construction of a hospital was an activity of a public nature and, therefore, subject to state immunity.

In June 1998, the Paris Cour d'Appel confirmed that there was no waiver of immunity from execution. Creighton appealed again, and on July 6, 2000 the Cour de Cassation overturned the Paris Cour d'Appel's decision. Relying on Art.24 of the then applicable ICC Rules of Arbitration (now reflected in Art.28(6) of the ICC Arbitration Rules that came into force as from January 1, 1998), by which the parties are "deemed to have undertaken to carry out the resulting award without delay and to have waived their right to any form of appeal insofar as such waiver can validly be made", the Cour de Cassation found that in agreeing to ICC arbitration, a state waives not only its immunity from jurisdiction but also its immunity from execution.[92]

As to the assets over which the immunity from execution can be waived, the position varies. The successful party to an arbitration against a state or state entity is in a better position where the forum state allows execution against the *commercial* assets of a foreign sovereign. This is the position, for example, in countries such as Austria, England, France, Germany and the US, amongst others. Execution is allowed against funds held by the defaulting state or state entity *for commercial purposes*. Care must be taken to ascertain whether all commercial property of the foreign state is subject to execution (such as in England) or merely that property which is (or was) used for the commercial activity upon which the claim is based.[93]

---

[92] See Nathalie Meyer-Fabre, "Enforcement of Arbitral Awards against Sovereign States—A New Milestone: Signing ICC Arbitration Clause Entails Waiver of Immunity from Execution held French Court of Cassation in *Creighton v Qatar*, July 6, 2000", *Mealey's International Arbitration Report*, Vol.15, No.9, September 2000, pp.48–52. See also R. Carrier, "France: Shrinking of Immunity from Execution and Discovery of Diplomatic Immunity from Execution", *Mealey's International Arbitration Report*, Vol.18, No.1, January 2003, pp.46–50, in which Carrier suggests that the wording of Art.24 of the ICC Arbitration Rules is not clear enough to deduce such a waiver.

[93] See Paulsson, "Sovereign Immunity From Jurisdiction: French Case Law Revisited" (1985) 19 *International Lawyer* 277.

However, even where execution against state assets is allowed, national courts **10–66** have tended to show considerable (and perhaps unwarranted) respect for foreign states. For example, in 1984 the highest appellate court in England decided that a declaration by the ambassador of a foreign state that its account with a London bank was *not* held for commercial purposes, should be accepted as sufficient evidence of this fact, unless the contrary could be proved by showing that the account *was* used almost exclusively for commercial purposes.[94] In reaching this decision, the court was strongly influenced by a decision of the Constitutional Court of the Federal Republic of Germany in the *Philippines Republic* case of 1977,[95] where a similar dispute was decided according to principles of public international law.

In the US, the Liberian Eastern Timber Company ("LETCO"), a company registered in France, failed in its attempt to enforce an ICSID award[96] by an arbitral tribunal against those assets of the Government of Liberia that were in the US. There were a series of proceedings in the courts, and LETCO was permitted to enter judgment against the Liberian Government. However, because of state immunity, LETCO was refused leave to execute this judgment, first against shipping fees due to the Liberian Government and, secondly, (and more predictably) against Liberian embassy bank accounts.[97]

More recently in France, the Compagnie NOGA d'Importation et d'Exportation SA, a Swiss company, was frustrated in its attempt to enforce an ICC award rendered in Stockholm against assets of the Russian Federation. In March 2000, the Tribunal de Grande Instance de Paris granted *exequatur* of the award, and in May 2000 NOGA proceeded, *inter alia*, to seize bank accounts opened in the names of the embassy of the Russian Federation in France, the commercial delegation of the Russian Federation, and the permanent delegation of the Russian Federation at the UNESCO. Following Russia's failed attempt to have the seizures lifted by the Tribunal de Grande Instance, Russia appealed to the Paris Cour d'Appel. Notwithstanding explicit contractual waivers of immunity from execution in the underlying agreements, the Cour d'Appel held that Russia had not waived its diplomatic immunity, which is governed by the distinct regime of the Vienna Convention on Diplomatic Relations of April 18, 1961. A general waiver of immunity from execution did not, thus, extend to diplomatic assets.[98] The Paris Cour d'Appel based its decision on Arts 22.3 and 25 of the Vienna

---

[94] *Alcom Ltd v Republic of Columbia* [1984] A.C. 580.

[95] *Philippine Republic* (1977) B.Verf.G.E. 342.

[96] One of the authors was a member of the tribunal.

[97] *Liberian Eastern Timber Company v Government of the Republic of Liberian*, 650 F.Supp.73 (S.D.N.Y. 1986). For a commentary, see Broches, "Awards Rendered Pursuant to the ICSID Convention: Binding Force, Finality, Recognition, Enforcement, Execution" (1987) 2 ICSID Review-FILJ 1987.

[98] *Ambassade de la Féderation de Russie en France v Compagnie NOGA d'Importation et d'Exportation SA*, Cour d'Appel de Paris (1 Ch.A) August 10, 2000, (2001) 1 Revue de l'Arbitrage 114. For excerpts in English, see also (2001) XXVI Yearbook Commercial Arbitration 273. Although the Cour de Cassation subsequently overturned the Cour d'Appel's decision in its decision of May 12, 2004, it did not impugn the Cour d'Appel's reasoning on the relationship between a waiver of immunity from execution and diplomatic immunity.

Convention, and concluded that all the accounts that had been seized by NOGA were held by Russian diplomatic bodies, and as such could not be part of Russia's waiver of immunity from execution.[99]

10–67   The effect of these decisions is to render meaningless the distinctions between "sovereign" and "commercial" activities, so far as embassy accounts are concerned. As one experienced commentator has written:

> "By making it nearly impossible for private claimants to prove that embassy accounts may be used for commercial activities, these decisions restore, for all practical purposes and for the benefit of foreign states, the doctrine of absolute immunity that modern immunity rules were meant to supersede."[1]

The sensible way forward appears to be to establish, by international convention if need be, that a state's waiver of immunity from jurisdiction necessarily carries with it a waiver of immunity from execution; also to put upon the state party, rather than the private claimant, the burden of proving the use to which embassy accounts are put. Until then, it remains advisable for a party negotiating an arbitration agreement with a state or state entity to ask for an *express* waiver of immunity from the jurisdiction of national courts in relation to *both* the recognition and the enforcement of any arbitral award. It can do no harm; and it may do some good.[2]

4. PRACTICAL CONSIDERATIONS

(a) An "entry of judgment" clause

10–68   In the US, many arbitration agreements contain an express provision to the effect that judgment may be entered upon the award in any court of competent jurisdiction. Thus, for example, the standard arbitration clause recommended by the AAA for domestic commercial dispute resolution procedures concludes "and judgment upon the award rendered by the arbitrator(s) may be entered in any court having jurisdiction thereof." An alternative and older provision, still to be found in some common law maritime arbitration agreements, states that for the purpose of enforcing awards the arbitration agreement may be made a "rule of court".[3] These provisions seek to facilitate arbitration, by making it clear that a national court may enforce the arbitration agreement, and any award resulting from it. Although the court may well have this power irrespective of the

---

[99] Separately, in February 2000, the Brussels Cour d'Appel followed the decision of the Paris Cour d'Appel in *NOGA* (whilst basing its reasoning soley on Art.25 of the Vienna Convention) and found the Embassy of Iraq's bank accounts to be immune from execution.

[1] Delaume, *op. cit.,* at 487.

[2] For a more detailed discussion of this suggestion, see Delaume, "Contractual Waivers of Immunity: Some Practical Considerations" (1990) 5 ICSID Review 232.

[3] The "entry of judgment" clause is similar to the old common law provision that an arbitration award could be made a "rule of court", so that it could be enforced as if it were a judgment of the court. In English law this provision, despite its distinguished ancestry, is now obsolete.

agreement of the parties, the use of an "entry of judgment" clause is recommended where the arbitration is likely to take place in the US. It is advisable to incorporate the entry of judgment provision in the arbitration agreement in order to avoid the challenge that its omission indicated the parties' intent to exclude any court procedure on the award.[4]

It seems, however, that in practice an agreement that a dispute will be "finally **10–69** settled" by arbitration will be taken as consent by the parties to "entry of judgment" in respect of the arbitrators' award. This was one of the issues which came before the US Court of Appeals (in the Seventh Circuit) in *Daihatsu Motor Co Ltd (Japan) v Terrain Vehicles Inc (United States)*.[5] The US statute that enacts the provisions of the New York Convention contains a provision[6] to the effect that, within three years after an arbitral award falling under the Convention is made, a party may apply to any court having jurisdiction under the statute for an order confirming the award. In addition, all the provisions of the Federal Arbitration Act apply to the Convention, unless they conflict with its enabling statute. The question that arose in *Daihatsu* was whether the Federal Arbitration Act (which requires a "consent to judgment" clause and establishes a one-year, rather than three-year, period for confirmation of an award) was in conflict with the provisions of the enabling statute.

The court reviewed the authorities and concluded:

"The language in the arbitration clause and the parties' conduct, when assessed in its totality, make clear that the parties contemplated judicial confirmation of an arbitral award regardless of which party chose the forum.

In short, Daihatsu and Terrain agreed that any given dispute that arose between them would be 'finally settled' by arbitration. Under our precedent, this language is sufficient to satisfy the 'consent-to-confirmation' of section 9 (assuming *arguendo* that it is applicable in a case under the Convention) . . . Under these circumstances, we must conclude that the language of the agreement and the conduct of the parties evidences the parties' intent that any arbitral award be subject to judicial confirmation."[7]

(b) Enforcing under the New York Convention or a more favourable treaty or local law

In considering recognition and enforcement of international arbitral awards, it **10–70** is usual to think first of enforcement under the New York Convention, or possibly the Washington Convention, because of the significant number of states that are parties to these conventions. However, it may be that in a particular case, simpler and more effective measures of enforcement are available. For example, it may

---

[4] See: Holtzmann, *ICCA Handbook*, Suppl.13, September 1997, pp.1–40.
[5] US Court of Appeals, Seventh Circuit, December 17,1993: see Vol.XX (1995) Yearbook Commercial Arbitration 925.
[6] 9 USC., s.207.
[7] *ibid.*, p.931.

be possible to take advantage of a more favourable local law, as in *Chromalloy*[8]; or there may be a multilateral or bilateral treaty which itself sets out a more favourable enforcement regime and of which, in a given case, it is possible to take advantage.

As previously mentioned, this possibility is explicitly recognised in the New York Convention, which states:

> "The provisions of the present Convention shall not affect the validity of multilateral or bilateral agreements concerning the recognition and enforcement of arbitral awards entered into by the Contracting States nor deprive any interested party of any right he may have to avail himself of the arbitral award in the manner and to the extent allowed by the law or the treaties of the country where such award is sought to be relied upon."[9]

This means in practice that, when it becomes necessary to enforce an arbitral award in one or more states in which the losing party has (or is thought to have) assets, it is wise to consider:

- whether, apart from the New York Convention, there exist any bilateral treaties under which recognition and enforcement of the award may be sought, on more favourable terms; and

- whether, irrespective of any treaties or conventions, the provisions of the local law are themselves more favourable to the recognition and enforcement of international arbitral awards.[10]

10–71 A series of cases in France, Belgium, the US and elsewhere has shown how, in practice, local law may be more favourable to the recognition and enforcement of such awards than the provisions of the New York Convention.

As stated earlier, the fifth ground for refusal of recognition and enforcement of an award under the New York Convention is that the award has been "set aside or suspended" under the law of the place of arbitration.[11] An award that has been "set aside" or "vacated" by a national court at the place of arbitration would at first glance appear to be obviously invalidated—not only in the state in which it has been set aside, but other states also. However, in *SEEE v Yugoslavia*, a decision made in 1956 by a two-member tribunal in Lausanne, declared by a Swiss court in 1957 *not* to be an arbitral award, was nevertheless enforced almost 30 years later by a French court.[12] It may have been possible to treat the decision

---

[8] para.10–72.
[9] New York Convention, Art.VII.1.
[10] In his survey entitled "Recent Swiss Case Law on the New York Convention—an Update" published in (2003) 21 ASA Bulletin, Roland Müller refers to an unpublished decision of February 14, 2003 in which a court in Zurich rejected the inverse submission that, by virtue of Art.VII, a party opposing enforcement could rely on the terms of an applicable bilateral treaty on enforcement that was less favourable for the recognition of awards than the New York Convention.
[11] New York Convention, Art.V.1(e); discussed above at paras 10–45 and 10–56.
[12] (1985) Revue de l'Arbitrage 115; (1985) 24 I.L.M. 345.

of the French court as a mere curiosity, except for the fact that the highest French court came to a similar decision in *Norsolor* in 1984.

In this case an ICC Tribunal with a seat in Vienna found itself unable to choose an appropriate national system of law to govern the merits of the dispute. It chose instead international *lex mercatoria*, relying in particular on the requirement of good faith in the making and performance of contracts. The defendant, who was ordered to pay damages, sought an annulment of the award in the Court of Appeal in Vienna (the court of the country in which the award was made). The Viennese court considered that the arbitral tribunal had not carried out its task correctly in disregarding national systems of law. It described international *lex mercatoria* as "world law of doubtful validity" and set aside parts of the award.[13] The claimants nevertheless sought enforcement in France of those parts of the award that had been set aside by the Court of Appeal in Vienna.[14] Under the New York Convention recognition and enforcement of an award might have been refused where:

"The award has been set aside or suspended by a competent authority of the country in which . . . that award was made."[15]

However, the New York Convention recognises the right of a party to avail **10–72** itself of any more favourable law or treaty that might exist in the country where the award is sought to be relied upon.[16] Unlike the New York Convention, French law does *not* in principle refuse recognition and enforcement to a foreign award that has been "set aside or suspended" by a court at the place of arbitration. Accordingly, enforcement of the award was allowed. A distinguished French commentator stated:

" . . . the outlook for the execution of transnational awards in France has changed profoundly. And thereby, precisely because of its liberal character which no longer needs emphasising, the importance of the French law of arbitration in international disputes has greatly increased."[17]

France was not alone in taking this path. An ICC award made in Algiers in favour of a US corporation was declared enforceable in Belgium, despite having been declared invalid by the Court of Appeal in Algiers.[18] In the celebrated *Hilmarton* case (where the claim had been dismissed on the basis that the contract was obtained by corruption and was unenforceable) the French court again recognised the Swiss award, despite the fact that it had been set aside by the Swiss court and that a new tribunal (which reached a different conclusion)

---

[13] See (1984) IX Yearbook Commercial Arbitration 159.
[14] The Austrian Supreme Court subsequently reversed the decision of the Court of Appeal in Vienna, but the French proceedings were conducted whilst that decision still stood.
[15] New York Convention, Art.V.1(e).
[16] *ibid.*, Art.VII.1.
[17] *Norsolar* case ((1985) Dalloz 103, with note by J. Robert (translated by the authors)).
[18] *Sonatrach v Ford Bacon & Davis Inc* (1990) XV Yearbook Commercial Arbitration 370.

had been established.[19] In *Chromalloy*,[20] a District Court in the US granted enforcement of an award made in Cairo, even though it had been set aside by the Court of Appeal in Cairo on the grounds that the arbitral tribunal had failed to apply the law agreed by the parties to the subject-matter of the dispute.[21] The court pointed out that, while Art.V gave it a discretion to decline to enforce an award that had been set aside by the courts of the place of arbitration, Art.VII required it not to deprive Chromalloy of more favourable provisions in the law of the enforcement state.[22] The French court also granted enforcement of the same award in 1997,[23] following which it appears that payment was made.

The ability to enforce, in some states, an award that is likely to prove unenforceable in others, is plainly a matter to be taken into account in seeking a suitable forum for the enforcement of international arbitral awards. Indeed, it highlights the importance of considering methods of enforcing awards other than those established by the international conventions. Even within a given area, where the countries concerned share the same language and the same (or a similar) legal background, the method of enforcing international arbitral awards may differ from country to country. For example, within the Arab countries there are some states that have acceded to the New York Convention,[24] others whose laws are less advanced than the Convention and others still whose law might be said to be more advanced, in that "local particularities" of the place of arbitration are disregarded.[25]

Enforcement as a "domestic" award

10–73   The law of the country in which enforcement is sought may allow a foreign award to be treated as if it were a domestic award and enforced in the same manner. This is, for example, the position under English law, where the successful party may apply to the court[26] for leave to enforce the award as if it were a judgment or order of the court; and the court has power to order direct enforcement of the award against the losing party's assets.[27]

---

[19] (1995) XX Yearbook Commercial Arbitration 663; also (1994) Revue de l'Arbitrage 328 at 332; see also the continuation of the *Hilmarton* saga in (1997) XXII Yearbook Commercial Arbitration 696—decision of the Cour de Cassation concerning the second arbitral tribunal.

[20] *Chromalloy Aeroservices v Arab Republic of Egypt* 939 F.Supp.907 (D.D.C. 1996); for commentary on this case see Paulsson, *The Case for disregarding local standard annulments under the New York Convention, op. cit.*; and Delaume, "Recognition and Enforcement of State Contract Awards in the US: A Restatement", (1997) 91 A.J.I.L. 476.

[21] An authoratative Egyptian commentator has since referred to the Egyption Court of Appeal abandoning the position it took in *Chromalloy* "on a number of occasions". See Atallah, "The 1994 Egyption Arbitration Law Ten Years On", *ICC Bulletin*, Vol.14, No.2 (Autumn 2003).

[22] *Chromalloy* at 909–910. See para.10–48.

[23] Decision of January 14, 1997, (1997) 12(4) Int'l Arb. Rep. B-1.

[24] Including Jordan, Bahrain, Tunisia, Algeria, Syria, Kuwait, Egypt, Morocco and Saudi Arabia.

[25] See Abdul Hamid El-Ahdab, "Enforcement of Arbitral Awards in the Arab Countries" (1995) 11 Arbitration International 169.

[26] English Arbitration Act 1996, ss.66 and 104.

[27] *Dalmia Cement Ltd v National Bank of Pakistan* [1975] Q.B. 9 at 22; [1974] 2 Lloyd's Rep. 98.

Enforcement as an obligation

If the law of the country in which enforcement is sought does not allow a   **10–74**
foreign award to be treated in this way, the party seeking enforcement may need
to start a court action in that country, on the basis that an award gives rise to an
obligation which the court should enforce. However, the plaintiff in such an
action must prove that the award was duly made under a valid arbitration
agreement; and this gives the losing party the opportunity to challenge the
validity of the award. If the application for enforcement is successful, the
national court will give judgment in the terms of the award; the successful party
may then enforce this judgment against the losing party.

(c) Options open to the successful party: a checklist

The options open to a party who succeeds in obtaining a favourable award and   **10–75**
seeks recognition and enforcement of it, have already been discussed.[28] In
summary, it is usually necessary to:

* take steps to locate the country or countries in which the losing party has
  assets upon which to levy execution;

* consider "forum shopping", in order to attain the quickest and most effective result, if these assets are located in different countries; and then

* take advice, from experienced lawyers in the relevant country or countries,
  as to whether it is preferable (if the option is open) to proceed under the
  New York Convention (or any other relevant treaty) or to seek enforcement
  under a more favourable local law.

(d) Options open to the unsuccessful party: a checklist

The loser, disappointed though he may be at the outcome of the arbitration, has   **10–76**
a far wider range of choices. Apart from the possibility of simply carrying out the
award, he may:

* take the initiative by challenging the award in the courts at the place where
  it was made[29];

* do nothing until the winning party makes the first move;

* use the award as the starting point for a negotiating process.

The disadvantage for the losing party is that he cannot go "forum shopping".
If he decides to challenge the award, he must usually do so in the competent court
at the place of arbitration.[30] If he decides to resist enforcement, he must do so in
the national court of the enforcement forum.

---

[28] Above at paras 10–03 *et seq.*
[29] See Ch.9.
[30] See discussion in Ch.9, paras 9–12 and 9–45.

To challenge or not?

10–77   The choice is plain: to act or not to act? The answer is important, since the financial consequences of a wrong decision may be serious.

In general, and subject to any local advice to the contrary, a party who is aggrieved by an award will do better to take the initiative and to mount an attack upon it, if legally possible, rather than adopt a passive attitude in order to resist recognition and enforcement later. First, there is a risk that by doing nothing the opportunity to challenge the award will be lost, either by lapse of time, by estoppel or in some other way. Secondly, to take the initiative in such circumstances is generally a sound tactic, because a party who is genuinely aggrieved by an award naturally wishes to challenge it at the earliest possible opportunity. Such an attitude is more likely to impress the relevant national court (and the other party) than an attitude of passive resistance. It may also be a sensible course as a matter of law, since the grounds upon which an award may be challenged are usually wider than those upon which recognition and enforcement of an award may be resisted.[31]

As to the possibility of using the award as a basis for negotiating a settlement, this is a course that is far more commonly adopted than is realised. The losing party is not without bargaining power. First, he may be able to point out to the winning party that there is a risk of the award being set aside by a national court, or of recognition and enforcement being refused. He can also point to the time, trouble and expense involved in enforcement proceedings in what, for the winning party, is likely to be a foreign jurisdiction. He can also argue that immediate payment of a sum of money, even though it is less than the amount awarded, may be more attractive than payment of the full amount of the award at a much later date (even if interest is taken into account).

10–78   Faced with such arguments, the successful party may well take the view that "a bird in the hand is worth two in the bush". Thus the losing party may find that, despite appearances, all is not lost. Even after an award has been made, a compromise settlement may be reached. Failing such a settlement, the possibilities that remain for the losing party are to challenge the award, if this is legally possible, or to attempt to resist recognition and enforcement of it.

(e) The need for local advice

10–79   A major attraction of international commercial arbitration is that, although the proceedings will generally be held in a country that is "foreign" to both parties, their usual legal advisers will be permitted to represent them before the arbitral tribunal. It is not essential to call upon a local or national bar or group of lawyers for this purpose. This is a considerable advantage, particularly for a company or governmental agency that has developed a special relationship of trust and understanding with its own legal advisers over a period of years.

---

[31] Although this is not always so. In France, *e.g.*, the grounds are the same.

Once the transition is made from the private world of arbitration to the more public world of national courts, it becomes necessary to consult local lawyers with "hands-on" experience of the local law and practice of arbitration. This is so for two reasons. First, the lawyers who acted in the arbitration are unlikely to have any right of audience before a foreign court; and, secondly, the grounds upon which international awards may be challenged vary considerably from place to place, so that good and experienced local advice is essential. It is also essential that this advice be taken as quickly as possible, following receipt or publication of the award. The time-limits for challenging an award may be short[32] and it may be necessary to act quickly. Indeed, if it is considered likely that the arbitral tribunal will bring in a "perverse" award, it may be sensible to brief a local lawyer before the award is issued. In this way, he will have more time to grasp the complexities of the case and so be better placed to advise on any action that should be taken to challenge the award.

The same considerations apply to the successful party who wishes to take action to enforce an award. When national courts are asked to recognise and enforce a foreign award they are usually being asked, in effect, to apply the provisions of international conventions. Nevertheless, they will do so in their own way. This is well established. For instance, the New York Convention, which lays down the conditions under which awards are to be recognised and enforced by contracting states,[33] leaves the rules of procedure to the determination of each contracting state. Nor is it only procedural matters that are left to the forum state. The New York Convention, the other conventions that are modelled upon it as well as the Model Law leave such important matters as "arbitrability" and "public policy" for determination under the law of the forum state. This is so, also, when it comes to determining whether or not there was a fair hearing. This provision of the New York Convention "essentially sanctions the application of the *forum state's* standards of due process".[34] In consequence, and before embarking upon proceedings for recognition and enforcement of an international award, it is essential to consult lawyers experienced in the arbitration law of the state in which enforcement is sought.

---

[32] See para.9–46.

[33] New York Convention, Art.III.

[34] *Parsons Whittemore Overseas Co Inc v Société Générale de l'Industrie du Papier (RAKTA)* 508 F.2d 969 (2nd Cir. 1974) 975 (emphasis added).

CHAPTER 11

ARBITRATION UNDER INVESTMENT TREATIES

1. INTRODUCTION

11–01   Historically, an individual or a corporation who wished to assert a claim against a foreign state for breach of customary international law could not do so directly. Instead, the individual or corporation concerned had to rely upon its government taking up the claim on its behalf. In the course of the nineteenth century, influential individuals or corporations would convince their government to send a small contingent of warships to moor off the coast of the offending state until reparation was forthcoming. This form of "gunboat diplomacy" was exercised frequently by European powers on behalf of their subjects in the not-so-distant past. For example, when faced with Venezuela's default on its sovereign debt in 1902, the governments of Great Britain, Germany and Italy sent warships to the Venezuelan coast to demand reparation for the losses incurred by their nationals.

The Argentine jurist and diplomat, Carlos Calvo, fought for the right of newly independent states to be free of such intervention by foreign powers and promoted the so-called Calvo doctrine, whereby foreign investors should be in no better position than local investors with their rights and obligations to be determined through the exclusive jurisdiction of the courts of that state.[1] His thesis was adopted by the First International Conference of American States in 1889, whose ad hoc Commission on International Law (without the support of the US) concluded:

> "Foreigners are entitled to enjoy all the civil rights enjoyed by natives and they shall be accorded all the benefits of said rights in all that is essential as well as in the form or procedure, and the legal remedies incident thereto, absolutely in like manner as said natives. A nation has not, nor recognizes in favour to foreigners, any other obligations or responsibilities than those which in favour of the natives are established in like cases by the constitution and the laws."[2]

---

[1] Calvo first published this thesis in 1868 in his seminal work "Derecho internacional teórico y práctico de Europa y América" (Paris, 1868).

[2] *The International Conferences of American States (1889–1928)* (James Brown Scott ed., New York, Carnegie Endowment, 1931).

The doctrine was incorporated into the forerunner of the modern investment treaty, the "treaty of friendship, commerce and navigation" (FCN treaty). For example, Art.21 of the FCN treaty between Italy and Colombia of 1894 stated as follows:

"The Contracting Parties express their desire to avoid all types of dispute which might affect their cordial relations and agree that, in connection with disputes which involve individuals arising out of criminal, civil or administrative matters, their diplomatic agents will abstain from intervening except in cases of denial of justice or extraordinary or unlawful delay in the administration of justice."[3]

Gunboat diplomacy was finally laid to rest at the Second International Peace **11–02** Conference of The Hague in 1907 when the Convention on the Peaceful Resolution of International Disputes was signed. This convention provided the framework for the conclusion of bilateral arbitration treaties. In accordance with these treaties, in the event of a dispute between two states arising out of the particular interests of a national of the other state, an independent arbitral tribunal would be formed. In effect, a state could espouse the claim of its national (the so-called right of diplomatic protection) through a horizontal inter-state procedure. There was no direct cause of action by the foreign national whose interests had been harmed.

The legal basis of the right of "diplomatic protection", in the words of the Permanent Court of International Justice in the *Panevezys-Saldutsikis Railway* case,[4] was that:

"in taking up the case of one of its nationals, by resorting to diplomatic action or international judicial proceedings on his behalf, a state is in reality asserting its own right, the right to ensure in the person of its nationals respect for the rules of international law. This right is necessarily limited to the intervention on behalf of its own nationals because, in the absence of a special agreement, it is the bond of nationality between the state and the individual which alone confers upon the state the right of diplomatic protection, and it is as a part of the function of diplomatic protection that the right to take up a claim and to ensure respect for the rules of international law must be envisaged."

As Professor Brierley stated,[5] the procedure was unsatisfactory from the individual claimant's point of view:

"He has no remedy of his own, and the state to which he belongs may be unwilling to take up his case for reasons which have nothing to do with its merits; and even if it is willing to do so, there may be interminable delays

---

[3] Free translation from the Italian.
[4] Series A/B 76, p.16.
[5] J.L. Brierley, *The Law of Nations* (6th ed., Oxford University Press, 1963), p.277.

before, if ever, the defendant state can be induced to let the matter go to arbitration. Delay, besides being unjust to the Claimant, creates difficulties in securing satisfactory evidence, and also often leads to the original claim being exaggerated beyond all recognition. It has been suggested that a solution might be found by allowing individuals access in their own right to some form of international tribunal for the purpose, and if proper safeguards against merely frivolous or vexatious claims could be devised, that is a possible reform which deserves to be considered. For the time being, however, the prospect of states accepting such a change is not very great."

11–03   This was written some 40 years ago. Since then, the situation has changed dramatically and what Professor Brierley thought unlikely has become a commonplace reality. The validity of his concerns and the inevitable "politicisation" of disputes "leaving investors, particularly small and medium-sized enterprises, with little recourse save what their government cares to give them after weighing the diplomatic pros and cons of bringing any particular claim"[6] led to a radical reform in the dispute settlement provisions of many bilateral investment treaties.

This reform was made possible by the creation of the ICSID mechanism through the conclusion of the ICSID Convention of 1965.[7] This Convention was aimed primarily at creating a new arbitral forum for the resolution of disputes between investors and states through the inclusion of arbitration clauses in state contracts. Nevertheless, the *travaux préparatoires* of the ICSID Convention also made clear that the consent of the state to arbitration could be established through the provisions of an investment law.[8] Following the 1959 Abs-Shawcross Draft Convention on Investments Abroad and the 1967 OECD Draft Convention on the Protection of Foreign Property,[9] many states had begun a programme of bilateral treaties for the promotion and protection of investments (so-called "Bilateral Investment Treaties" or "BITs") which set out explicit protections in favour of foreign investment. They were a natural successor to the FCN treaties of the early part of the twentieth century but still suffered from the limitations imposed by diplomatic protection. Once the ICSID Convention was in place, treaty drafters from signatory states quickly seized on the possibility of using this specialist

---

[6] Testimony of Dan Price, one of the NAFTA Treaty negotiators, addressing investment protection issues before a Senate Ways and Means Committee Hearing on the Free Trade Area of the Americas.

[7] ICSID was established by the 1965 Convention on the Settlement of Investment Disputes between States and Nationals of Other States ("ICSID Convention"). It has been ratified by 135 states. For a detailed analysis of the ICSID Convention, see Schreuer, *The ICSID Convention: A Commentary* (Cambridge University Press, Cambridge, UK, 2001). The process of ICSID arbitrations is described in Reed, Paulsson & Blackberry, *Guide to ICSID Arbitration* (Kluwer, 2004).

[8] See para.24 of the Report of the Executive Directors on the ICSID Convention: " . . . Nor does the Convention require that the consent of both parties be expressed in a single instrument. Thus, a Host State might in its investment protection legislation offer to submit disputes arising out of certain classes of investments to the jurisdiction of the Centre, and the investor might give his consent by accepting the offer in writing."

[9] See(1968) 7 I.L.M. 117; and earlier draft at (1963) 2 I.L.M. 241.

forum for the resolution of treaty disputes between states and investors and did so by incorporating a clause establishing the consent of the state to arbitrate with covered investors. Professor Brierley's vision of a diagonal clause, permitting investors to claim directly under a treaty against the state where the investment was made (the "host state"), thus became a reality. Switzerland, for example, inserted a diagonal clause for the first time in its 1981 BIT with Sri Lanka and has done so systematically ever since.[10]

This right of direct recourse ensures that the investor's claim is not subject to the political considerations inherent in diplomatic protection. Whether or not a contract or agreement has been concluded with the host state, after an initial "cooling off" period for amicable negotiation, the investor may usually commence arbitration directly against the host state of the investment.[11] Foreign investors were nevertheless slow to take up their new-found rights—the first case brought by an investor under the investment protections of a BIT was not decided until 1990.[12]

In light of the dramatic increase in the number of BITs[13] and the emergence of **11–04** clearer legal principles through case law, the number of investor-state arbitrations has mushroomed. Whilst in 1998 ICSID registered 8 cases with 19 cases pending, in 2003 it registered 30 new cases with 63 cases pending.

The wholesale acceptance of arbitration and the protective standards of treatment of foreign investment in BITs, evidenced by the dramatic growth of BITs since the mid-1980s, has led to the adoption of similar provisions in the "investment chapters" or collateral agreements to multilateral economic co-operation treaties and free trade agreements.[14] Among these are the 1987 ASEAN Agreement for the Promotion and Protection of Investments,[15] Ch.11 of the 1994

---

[10] See Liebeskind, "State-Investor Dispute Settlement Clauses in Swiss Bilateral Investment Treaties" (2002) 20 ASA Bulletin 1 at 27.

[11] Obviously, the investor could have access to litigation before the courts of the host state. However, this would clearly be a last resort since it raises serious questions of neutrality of forum and ultimate enforceability of the judgment elsewhere. Further, international law protections are less likely to be applied in domestic court proceedings than in international arbitration. On the advantages of international arbitration to resolve investment disputes, see Parra, "Provisions on the Settlement of Investment Disputes in Modern Investment Laws, Bilateral Investment Treaties and Multilateral Instruments on Investment" (1997) 12 ICSID Review—Foreign Investment Law Journal 287 at 288–289.

[12] *Asian Agricultural Products Ltd (AAPL) v Republic of Sri Lanka*, ICSID Case No.ARB/87/3, Final Award, June 27, 1990, (1991) 6 ICSID Review—Foreign Investment Law Journal 526.

[13] According to UNCTAD, the number of BITs increased from 385 at the end of the 1980s to a total of 2,099 by the end of 2001. See *Trends in International Investment Agreements: An Overview*, UNCTAD Series, United Nations, New York and Geneva.

[14] In spite of this, the negotiations on a proposed global Multilateral Agreement on Investment, commenced in May 1995 under the auspices of the OECD, were abandoned in December 1998, due to the states' clear inclination towards a more selective BIT approach. A very ambitious multilateral investment protection chapter is being negotiated as part of the Free Trade Area of the Americas project that aims to integrate all American states into a single hemispheric free trade area.

[15] This agreement covers investment from investors of Brunei Darussalam, Indonesia, Malaysia, Philippines, Singapore and Thailand in the territory of these states.

NAFTA,[16] Pt 3 and Art.26 of the 1994 Energy Charter Treaty (the "ECT"),[17] the 1994 Colonia and Buenos Aires Investment Protocols of Mercosur,[18] and Ch.17 of the 1990 Group of Three Agreement.[19] Similar provisions have found their way into bilateral free trade agreements such as Ch.10 of the 2003 USA–Chile Free Trade Agreement ("FTA") and Ch.15 of the 2003 USA–Singapore FTA. With the exception of NAFTA (which, through its Ch.11 arbitrations has provided a fertile ground for debate and reflection in international arbitration) and a handful of ECT cases, there are no reports of arbitrations under any of the other multilateral agreements.[20]

Many foreign investments are therefore protected by investment treaties. The question is whether an investor can rely on one or more of these investment treaties to vindicate its legal rights in a particular case. This raises fundamental issues relating to the scope and application of those treaties. It is to these issues that we now turn.

2. JURISDICTIONAL ISSUES

(a) Existence of an applicable treaty

11–05   To determine whether an investor enjoys investment treaty protection, an applicable treaty between the state where the investment was made and the home state of the investor must be identified. It is easy to identify multilateral investment treaties as they are sufficiently notorious. It is, however, more difficult to detect applicable BITs, considering their number and the absence of a comprehensive list.[21] In practice, the only accurate means of verifying the existence of a BIT, and/or whether it is in force,[22] is by contacting the treaty section of the relevant government or embassy.

Most BITs contain provisions with respect to their effective date and the duration of the treaty. An issue may arise as to whether investments prior to the date on which the BIT came into effect are eligible for protection under the BIT. Earlier practice inclined towards granting protection only to investments made

---

[16] This agreement covers investment from investors of Canada, Mexico and the USA in the territory of these states.

[17] The ECT covers investments in the energy sector for investors of the 47 state parties (which include all the states of Europe and the former Soviet Union) within the territory of those states.

[18] The Colonia Protocol covers investment from investors of the Member States of Mercosur (Argentina, Brazil, Paraguay and Uruguay) in the territory of these states. The Buenos Aires Protocol covers investment from investors of third states in the territory of Mercosur states.

[19] This agreement covers investments from investors of Colombia, Mexico and Venezuela in the territory of these states.

[20] *AES Summit Generation Ltd v Republic of Hungary* (ICSID Case No.ARB/01/4), was the first case brought under the ECT and it is now settled.

[21] The ICSID website (*www.icsid.org*) contains a list up to 1996 but it has not been updated since. The UNCTAD website (*www.unctad.org*) provides a list updated as of 2000.

[22] Treaties signed may not necessarily be in force. A treaty enters into force in accordance with the procedure provided for in the treaty itself. This usually involves the exchange of instruments of ratification between the contracting states.

after the BIT had come into effect. This reasoning underlined the basic purpose of a BIT, which was to promote new investment. However, recent BITs have taken the position that prior investments are also afforded protection. The Argentina–US BIT, for example, provides that it shall apply to investments existing at the time of entry into force as well as to investments made or acquired thereafter.[23] However, in *Tecnicas Medioambientales Tecmed SA v The United Mexican States*,[24] the tribunal made a distinction between application of a BIT to investments made prior to the BIT coming into effect and its application to alleged breaches which occurred prior to such date. The arbitral tribunal held that whilst the concerned investment was eligible for protection under the BIT, the BIT could not have retrospective application to host state actions prior to the effective date of the BIT.

BITs also commonly include provisions regarding the legal status of investments after the termination or expiry of the particular BIT. Generally, such provisions indicate that investments which were otherwise covered by the treaty whilst in force would continue to be under similar protection for a specified period, usually of between 10 and 15 years after termination or expiry.

(b) Protected investors

Once a potentially applicable treaty has been identified, the relevant treaty provisions defining the eligible "investors" or "nationals" should be reviewed. In some cases, the eligibility requirements for investors may be linked to the definition of "investment". Although treaties may vary substantially in this respect, the following provision of the Switzerland–Pakistan BIT is representative:

11–06

"For the purposes of this Agreement:

(1) The term "investor" refers with regard to either Contracting Party to:

(a) natural persons who, according to the law of that Contracting Party, are considered to be its nationals;

(b) legal entities, including companies, corporations, business associations and other organisations, which are constituted or otherwise duly organised under the law of that Contracting Party and have their seat, together with real economic activities, in the territory of that same Contracting Party;

(c) legal entities established under the law of any country which are, directly or indirectly, controlled by nationals of that Contracting Party or by legal entities having their seat, together with real

---

[23] Art.XIV(1) of the Argentina–US BIT.
[24] ICSID Case No.ARB(AF)/00/02, Award, May 29, 2003, (2004) 43 I.L.M. 133. The tribunal noted, however, that the pre-BIT acts of the host state would be relevant to consider continuing or aggravating breach of the BIT.

economic activities, in the territory of that same Contracting Party."

Investors covered by protection of investment treaties can thus be divided into natural persons and legal entities.

Natural persons

11–07   Most BIT provisions establish the nationality of a natural person by reference to the domestic laws of the respective contracting states. This is consistent with the concept of absolute state sovereignty in deciding the criteria for identifying its nationals. Certain BITs may contain an additional requirement of residence[25] or domicile.[26]

A difficulty may arise in a situation of dual nationality where a national of one contracting state is also the national of another contracting state. Whilst most BITs do not address such an issue,[27] the solution may lie in determining the effective nationality of the person in accordance with the relevant rules of the contracting states (if they are similar) or by reference to the general principles of international law.[28] There may also be an issue in a case where a person changes his nationality after making an investment which was protected under a particular investment treaty on the basis of his former nationality.

Legal entities

11–08   All investment treaties extend the benefit of their protection to legal entities such as companies. Many BITs may be content with the basic requirement that the entity be incorporated or constituted under the laws of the contracting parties. Some treaties add the requirement that entities also have their seat[29] and/or actually carry out business in the relevant state.[30]

Some treaties extend protection to entities incorporated in the host state of the investment provided that they are controlled by entities incorporated in the other

---

[25] *e.g.* Art.1(3)(b) of the Germany–Israel BIT.
[26] *e.g.* Art.1 of the Denmark–Indonesia BIT.
[27] An exception to this is the Canada–Venezuela BIT which excludes persons holding citizenship of both the contracting states from the definition of "investors" (Art.I(g)) for the purposes of the agreement.
[28] See *Marvin Roy Feldman Karpa v United Mexican States* (ICSID Case No.ARB(AF)/99/1), Interim Decision on Preliminary Jurisdictional Issues, December 6, 2000, where an ICSID Tribunal was faced with a case under NAFTA involving a US citizen with a permanent residence in Mexico. Mexico challenged the jurisdiction based on dual nationality. The Tribunal rejected the objection relying on general international law and held that residence fulfils only a subsidiary function to that of citizenship, see (2001) 40 I.L.M. 615.
[29] This is particularly true of German BIT practice. See, for instance, Art.1(4)(a) of the Germany–Guyana BIT.
[30] *e.g.* Art.1(b) of the Netherlands–Argentina BIT: "the term 'investor' shall comprise with regard to either Contracting Party: . . . (ii) . . . legal persons constituted under the law of that Contracting Party and actually doing business under the laws in force in any part of the territory of that Contracting Party in which a place of effective management is situated; and (iii) legal persons, wherever located, controlled, directly or indirectly, by nationals of that Contracting Party."

contracting state. This extension is expressly permitted by Art.25(1)(b) of the ICSID Convention.[31] For example, Art.1(2)(c) of the Argentina–France BIT extends protection to "legal persons effectively controlled directly or indirectly by nationals of one of the Contracting Parties or by legal persons having their registered office in the territory of one of the Contracting Parties and constituted in accordance with legislation of the latter".[32] Thus, a locally incorporated entity may claim against its state of incorporation if controlled by a national or company of the other contracting state. This enables minority shareholders in the local entity (many of whom may be local investors) to obtain indirect relief through treaty arbitration.

Another issue arises where the claimant is an intermediate entity incorporated for structuring purposes. Can such an entity be said to "control" the entity in which it holds its shares? No decision has yet been rendered on this point. However, the decision in *Banro American Resources Inc v Democratic Republic of the Congo* suggests that forum shopping at different levels of the corporate chain may be frowned upon. In this case, an ICSID Tribunal declined jurisdiction as it was of the opinion that the claimants were attempting to use their corporate structure to benefit both from diplomatic protection and direct treaty protection.[33]

(c) Protected investments

In order to rely on an investment treaty, the investor must establish that it has **11–09** made a protected investment. Interestingly, the ICSID Convention does not have a definition of "investment". This has provided treaty draftsmen with a great degree of flexibility.

Most investment treaties contain a definition of what constitutes such an "investment". Many of the earlier treaties used a general definition such as "the term 'investment' shall comprise all categories of assets including all categories of rights and interests".[34] Subsequent BITs tend to provide a more elaborate definition which commence with a broad statement, often referring to "investments comprises every kind of asset"[35] or "every kind of investment in the

---

[31] Art.25(1)(b) states: "National of another Contracting state means: . . . any juridical person which had the nationality of the Contracting state party to the dispute . . . and which, because of foreign control, the parties have agreed should be treated as a national of another Contracting state for the purposes of this Convention."

[32] Free translation from the French original.

[33] ICSID Case No.ARB/98/7, Award, September 1, 2000, (2002) 17 ICSID Review—Foreign Investment Law Journal 382 at para.24. The Tribunal noted that the investors were attempting to "avail themselves, depending on their own interests at a given point in time, simultaneously or successively, of both diplomatic protection and ICSID arbitration, by playing on the fact that one of the companies of the group does not have the nationality of a Contracting State party to the Convention, and can therefore benefit from diplomatic protection by its home State, whilst another subsidiary of the group possesses the nationality of a Contracting State to the Convention and therefore has standing before an ICSID tribunal."

[34] Germany–Sri Lanka BIT (1963).

[35] Art.1(a) of the UK–USSR (now UK–Russia) BIT and Art.1(6) of the ECT.

territory"[36] and then adding a non-exhaustive list of examples. Typical in this respect is the UK–Russia BIT, which provides at Art.1(a) that:

> "the term 'investment' means every kind of asset and in particular, though not exclusively, includes:
>
> (i) movable and immovable property and any other related property rights such as mortgages;
> (ii) shares in, and stock, bonds and debentures of, and any other form of participation in, a company or business enterprise;
> (iii) claims to money, and claims to performance under contract having a financial value;
> (iv) intellectual property rights, technical processes, know-how and any other benefit or advantage attached to a business;
> (v) rights, conferred by law or under contract, to undertake any commercial activity, including the search for, or the cultivation, extraction or exploitation of natural resources."

Similar broad definitions are found in most treaties. The open-ended definition is an acknowledgment that the concept of "investment" is dynamic and may evolve over time. The "investment" for the purposes of the treaty may also be linked to the conditions under which the investment is to be admitted into the host state.[37] In some treaties, there may be a stricter condition requiring that the investment should be specifically approved or "classified" as approved by the host state.[38]

11–10 The definition of "investment" has evolved and now covers direct and indirect investments and modern contractual and other transactions having economic value.[39] This is confirmed by numerous decisions of arbitral tribunals in BIT arbitrations. For example, in *Fedax NV v The Republic of Venezuela*, the arbitral tribunal held that promissory notes issued by Venezuela, and acquired by the claimant from the original holder in the secondary market by way of endorsement, were an investment under the Netherlands–Venezuela BIT.[40] The relevant BIT included "titles to money" as a category of investment and the tribunal

---

[36] Art.I(1)(a) of the US–Argentina BIT.
[37] *e.g.* Art.I(a) of the Argentina–Canada BIT requiring that the investment be "made in accordance with the laws" of the host state.
[38] See *Gruslin v Malaysia*, Award, November 27, 2000, 5 ICSID Reports 492, where the Tribunal examined the Intergovernmental Agreement between Malaysia and Belgo–Luxemburg Economic Union, 1979. The Tribunal declined jurisdiction on the ground that the concerned investment was not made in a project *approved* by Malaysia which was a precondition to accessing the protection of the agreement.
[39] See, *e.g.*, Parra, "The Scope of New Investment Laws and International Instruments," in *Economic Development, Foreign Investment and the Law* (R. Pritchard ed., 1996), p.35. See also *UNCTAD, Series on issues in international investment agreements, Scope and Definition* (1999).
[40] *Fedax NV v The Republic of Venezuela*, ICSID Case No.ARB/96/3, Decision on Objections to Jurisdiction, July 11, 1997, 5 ICSID Reports 186. The definition contained in the applicable BIT was substantially the same as the one quoted above.

rejected the contention of the Republic of Venezuela that this item was restricted to classic forms of direct foreign investment or portfolio investment, *i.e.* "the laying out of money or property in business ventures, so that it may produce a revenue or income". The tribunal also held that "it is a standard feature of many international finance transactions that the funds involved are not physically transferred to the territory of the host country but are put at its disposal else-where".[41] This indicates a clear movement from the conventional notion of "foreign investment" which involves an inflow of funds into the host state.

In *Ceskoslovenska Obchodni Banka AS v The Slovak Republic*,[42] the ICSID Tribunal held that a loan may constitute an investment if it contributes sub-stantially to the economic development of a state. Whilst it was held that certain financial transactions taken in isolation might not qualify as investments, they may nevertheless be so considered if the overall operation of which they are part, or to which they are connected, constitutes an investment.

A shareholding in a local company in the host country is sufficient to constitute investment for the purposes of treaty protection.[43] In the case of *CMS v Republic of Argentina*, the tribunal held that as a result of the *lex specialis* of the ICSID Convention and the applicable BIT, the claimant shareholder could claim in respect of the losses caused to the value of its shares in the entity to whom the adverse measures were addressed.[44] This is important for effective investor protection as host states often impose an obligation that the ultimate investment vehicle be a locally incorporated entity.

In *AMT v Zaire*,[45] the jurisdiction of the ICSID Tribunal was challenged by the **11–11** Republic of Zaire on the ground that AMT, a US company, had not made any direct investment in Zaire and could not rely on the US–Zaire BIT. According to Zaire, AMT had merely participated in the share capital of a Zairian company (whose assets had been allegedly destroyed in breach of investment treaty protections). The arbitral tribunal examined the relevant provisions of the BIT

---

[41] *ibid.*, at 198.
[42] *Ceskoslovenska Obchodni Banka AS v The Slovak Republic*, ICSID Case No.ARB/97/4, Decision on Objections to Jurisdiction, May 24, 1999, (1999) 14 ICSID Review—Foreign Investment Law Journal. In this case, no funds were actually transferred to the Slovak Republic pursuant to the loan. However, due to the close connection of the loan facility to the development of banking facilities in the Slovak Republic, the same was held to be an investment.
[43] See *Lanco International Inc v Argentina*, Preliminary Decision on Jurisdiction, December 8, 1998, (2001) 40 I.L.M. 457. The tribunal made a finding that the definition of the term "investment" in the BIT was "*very broad and allowed for many meanings*". It was held that the treaty did not require a foreign shareholder to have control over the administration of the company and mere ownership of 18.3 per cent share capital was considered sufficient to avail of the protection of the BIT. A similar decision was reached by the tribunal in *Emilio Agustín Maffezini v Kingdom of Spain*, ICSID Case No.ARB/97/7, Award on Jurisdiction, January 25, 2000, (2001) 16 ICSID Review—Foreign Investment Law Journal 212.
[44] *CMS Gas Transmission Company v The Republic of Argentina*, ICSID Case No.ARB/01/8, Decision of the Tribunal on Objections to Jurisdiction, July 17, 2003, (2003) 42 I.L.M. 788 at paras 36–65.
[45] *American Manufacturing & Trading Inc v Republic of Zaire*, Award, February 21, 1997, 5 ICSID Reports 10.

and rejected this objection, holding that investments through share capital of a local entity was eligible for protection under the BIT.[46]

Whilst the notion of investment has been expanding, it has its limitations. In 1985, for example, the ICSID Secretary-General refused to register a case because the dispute related to a mere commercial sale and could not be qualified as an investment.[47] In the case of *Mihaly International Corporation v Republic of Sri Lanka*, the arbitral tribunal held that expenses incurred in bidding for a public contract were not an investment under the applicable BIT. The tribunal considered the fact that the respondent state had expressly disclaimed any rights and obligations between the parties of material significance.[48]

In addition to interpretative issues, the kind of "investments" from which disputes may be referred to investment treaty arbitration may be specifically curtailed by host countries. For instance, Jamaica has excluded legal disputes arising directly out of an investment relating to minerals or other natural resources.[49]

(d) Other jurisdictional issues

11–12   If the investor opts for ICSID arbitration, it will have to fulfil the jurisdictional requirements provided under Art.25 of the ICSID Convention. The relevant part of this provision reads as follows:

> "The jurisdiction of the Centre shall extend to any legal dispute arising directly out of an investment, between a Contracting State (or any constituent subdivision or agency of a Contracting State designated to the Centre by that State) and a national of another Contracting State, which the parties to the dispute consent in writing to submit to the Centre . . . "

Under this provision, therefore, the investor will have to demonstrate that:

(i) there is a legal dispute arising directly out of an investment;

(ii) both contracting states are parties to the ICSID Convention; and

(iii) both the host state and the investor have consented to arbitration.

---

[46] *ibid.*, at para.24. It is significant that the tribunal noted the fact that the AMT itself was majority owned and controlled by Americans and *therefore* was a US company. It is a matter of speculation whether the tribunal would have reached the same conclusion if AMT had merely been an intermediate entity owned and controlled by the national of a third country with whom Zaire had no investment treaty.

[47] (1985) ICSID Annual Report 6.

[48] *Mihaly International Corporation v Democratic Socialist Republic of Sri Lanka*, ICSID Case No.ARB/00/2, March 15, 2002, (2002) 17 ICSID Review—Foreign Investment Law Journal.

[49] On May 8, 1974, Jamaica notified ICSID that: "In accordance with Art.25 of the Convention establishing the International Centre for the Settlement of Investment Disputes, the Government of Jamaica hereby notifies the Centre that the following class of dispute at any time arising shall not be subject to the jurisdiction of the Centre: Class of Dispute: Legal dispute arising directly out of an investment relating to minerals or other natural resources."

The ICSID Convention provides no definition of "legal dispute" or "investment". This requirement is satisfied if the investor's assets qualify as investments under the BIT, and the investor claims are prima facie plausible BIT claims arising directly out of its investments.

Host states set out their (usually conditional) consent in the text of the BITs as **11–13** open offers which can be accepted by a covered investor. Classically, the conditions include the completion of a notification period within which the investor must engage the host state in amicable negotiations. Other treaties require the investor to pursue remedies before the courts of the host state for a minimum period prior to commencing arbitration. Does the failure to abide by such conditions vitiate the consent of the host state?

Some recent arbitral decisions suggest that the consultation period is a procedural rather than a jurisdictional obligation and that failure to comply does not vitiate consent. In the recent case of *Ronald S. Lauder v The Czech Republic*,[50] the tribunal waived the waiting period in the following terms:

> "However, the Arbitral Tribunal considers that this requirement of a six-month waiting period of Art.VI(3)(a) of the Treaty is not a jurisdictional provision, *i.e.* a limit set to the authority of the Arbitral Tribunal to decide on the merits of the dispute, but a procedural rule that must be satisfied by the Claimant (*Ethyl Corp v Canada*, UNCITRAL June 24, 1998, 38 I.L.M. 708 (1999), paras 74–88). As stated above, the purpose of this rule is to allow the parties to engage in good-faith negotiations before initiating arbitration."[51]

Moreover, in the tribunal's view, "[t]o insist that the arbitration proceedings cannot be commenced until six months after the 19 August 1999 Notice of Arbitration would, in the circumstances of this case, amount to an unnecessary, overly formalistic approach which would not serve to protect any legitimate interests of the Parties".[52]

This approach was not followed in the ICSID case of *Enron v Argentina* where **11–14** the tribunal concluded in *obiter dicta* that[53]:

> "The Tribunal wishes to note in this matter, however, that the conclusion reached is not because the six-month negotiation period could be a procedural and not a jurisdictional requirement as has been argued by the Claimants and affirmed by other tribunals. Such requirement is in the view of the Tribunal very much a jurisdictional one. A failure to comply with that requirement would result in a determination of lack of jurisdiction."

[50] *Ronald S. Lauder v The Czech Republic*, Final Award, September 3, 2001. Text available on the CME website at: *www.cetv-net.com/arbitration.asp*.

[51] *ibid.*, at para.187.

[52] *ibid.*, at para.190.

[53] *Enron Corporation v Argentine Republic*, Decision on Jurisdiction dated January 14, 2004, at para.88. A copy of the decision is available on the website of the American Society of International Law. See the *International Law in Brief* Newsletter of March 15, 2004 at *www.asil.org*.

Further, a failure to fulfil such preconditions might result in a rejection of registration by the ICSID Secretariat.

Separately from the issue of whether preconditions are procedural or jurisdictional is the question of whether the preconditions can be avoided (or replaced) by relying on the "most favoured nation clause" ("MFN clause") of the applicable treaty in order to access more favourable preconditions in other treaties concluded by the host state of the investment.

11–15   This possibility was upheld by an ICSID Tribunal in the *Maffezini* case.[54] Mr Maffezini was an Argentine investor who had a dispute with the Government of Spain arising out of an investment he had made in Spain. He submitted his dispute to ICSID arbitration under the Spain–Argentina BIT, despite the fact that the treaty had a dispute settlement clause requiring prior recourse to local courts for a period of 18 months. Mr Maffezini pointed out that the MFN clause of the Spanish treaty obliged Spain to treat investors of Argentina no less favourably than third party investors. Consequently, rather than taking his dispute to local courts, he invoked the MFN clause of the Spanish treaty in order to rely on the more favourable dispute settlement clause of another BIT concluded by Spain with Chile. This treaty provided for access to international arbitration after just a six-month negotiation period.

On the facts of the case, the ICSID Tribunal held that the MFN clause of the Spanish treaty embraced the dispute settlement provisions of that treaty. Therefore, relying on the more favourable arrangements contained in the Chile–Spain BIT and, *inter alia*, the legal policy adopted by Spain with regard to the treatment of its own investors abroad (whereby it generally tried to secure for them the right to access international remedies without prior recourse to local remedies), Mr Maffezini had the right to submit the dispute to international arbitration without first accessing the Spanish courts.

A second issue is whether a state's consent to arbitration in a BIT is overridden by a contractual arbitration clause in a related investment contract. Tribunals have generally held that, as long as the arbitration claims allege a cause of action under the BIT, they are not subject to the contractually elected jurisdiction. In *Lanco v Argentina*, for example, the contract contained an exclusive jurisdiction clause in favour of the Argentine courts. Argentina argued that this clause applied and that the dispute was not within the jurisdiction of the ICSID Tribunal. The Tribunal rejected this argument, holding that the exclusive jurisdiction clause in the contract could not exclude the jurisdiction of the ICSID Tribunal in relation to the BIT claim.[55]

11–16   The case of *Salini v Morocco* was an arbitration instituted on the basis of an investment treaty relating to a dispute around the amount payable under a construction contract. The contract contained a local jurisdiction clause. The ICSID Tribunal held that, notwithstanding the clause, it "remain[ed] competent

---

[54] *Emilio Agustín Maffezini v Kingdom of Spain*, ICSID Case No.ARB/97/7, Award on Jurisdiction, January 25, 2000, (2001) 16 ICSID Review—Foreign Investment Law Journal 212.
[55] *Lanco International Inc v The Argentine Republic*, ICSID Case No.ARB/97/6, Preliminary Decision, December 8, 1998, 40 I.L.M. 457 at paras 39–40.

for the breaches of contract which would, at the same time, constitute a breach of the treaty by the state."[56]

In the *Vivendi* case, the relevant investment was a concession contract concluded by the claimant with Tucumán, a province of Argentina. The claims concerned mainly acts by Tucumán authorities interfering with the claimant's rights under the concession contract. Argentina argued that the dispute resolution clause of the contract, Art.16.4, establishing the jurisdiction of the local courts for the purpose of interpretation and application of the contract, precluded jurisdiction under the French treaty. Rejecting this argument, an ICSID Annulment Committee held:

" . . . where 'the fundamental basis of a claim' is a treaty laying down an *independent standard* by which the conduct of the parties is to be judged, the existence of an exclusive jurisdiction clause in the contract between the Claimant and the respondent state or one of its subdivisions cannot operate as a bar to the application of the treaty standard."[57]

The Committee went on to clarify that BIT claims often involve taking into account the terms of a contract in determining whether there has been a breach of the BIT. This does not prevent the claims being BIT claims for which treaty arbitration is available.

On the basis of this case law, in the *CMS* case the Tribunal rejected an **11–17** objection raised by Argentina on the basis of the existence of contract dispute resolution clauses. The Tribunal held:

"This Tribunal shares the views expressed in those precedents. It therefore holds that the clauses in the License or its Terms referring certain kinds of disputes to the local courts of the Republic of Argentina are not a bar to the assertion of jurisdiction by an ICSID tribunal under the Treaty, as the functions of these various instruments are different."[58]

The case law also suggests, however, that there may be cases in which the claims are, in reality, only linked to the underlying contract such that the contract is the "fundamental basis" of the claims rather than the BIT. In this case, the contract clause may apply, even if the claims are formally presented as BIT claims. This protective phrase may be used by tribunals to dismiss purely contractual claims at the jurisdictional stage. However, no tribunal has yet made that finding, even where an apparent simple breach of contract is alleged (without more) to constitute a breach of a substantive treaty protection. It is apparently for

---

[56] *Salini Costruttori SpA v Kingdom of Morocco*, ICSID Case No.ARB/00/4, Jurisdictional Decision, July 23, 2001, (2002) 1 Journal du Droit International 196 at para.62.

[57] *Compañía de Aguas del Aconquija SA and Vivendi Universal (formerly Compagnie Générale des Eaux) v Argentine Republic*, ICSID Case No.ARB/97/3, Decision on Annulment, July 3, 2002, (2002) 41 I.L.M. 1135 at para.101 (emphasis added).

[58] *Emilio Agustín Maffezini v Kingdom of Spain*, ICSID Case No.ARB/97/7, Award on Jurisdiction, January 25, 2000, (2001) 16 ICSID Review—Foreign Investment Law Journal 212.

the claimant to characterise its claims as it sees fit, and whether that character-isation is made out will only be determined at the merits phase.[59]

In sum, the most fundamental characteristic separating treaty rights from contract rights is the source of the right. The foundation of a treaty claim is a right established in an investment treaty, while the basis of a contract claim is a right established in a contract.

11–18   A third issue of consent to arbitration under investment treaties is whether it may be vitiated by the pursuit of remedies before a local court through the operation of a so-called "fork in the road". Many dispute settlement clauses of BITs provide that investors may choose to submit a dispute either to the local courts of the host state or to arbitration and, once made, the choice is final. Thus, if the investor has already submitted the dispute to the local courts it may no longer consent to arbitration. This is the so-called "fork in the road" provision.

To date no ICSID Tribunal has ever found that an investor has actually triggered the "fork in the road" provision of the applicable BIT. This is usually because disputes submitted to local courts relate to contractual or regulatory issues which are distinct from the BIT breach issues submitted to arbitration, and thus cannot trigger the "fork in the road" provision. As stated by the *CMS* tribunal in its recent decision on jurisdiction:

> "As contractual claims are different from treaty claims, even if there had been or there currently was a recourse to local courts for breach of contract, this would not have prevented submission of the treaty claims to arbitration."[60]

3. LAW APPLICABLE TO THE SUBSTANCE OF THE DISPUTE

11–19   BITs provide specific provisions on the law to be applied by the arbitral tribunals appointed to resolve disputes under the treaties.[61] The tenor of these clauses is very similar. By way of example, Art.8 of the UK–Argentina treaty provides that:

> "The arbitral tribunal shall decide the dispute in accordance with the provi-sions of this Agreement, the laws of the Contracting Party involved in the

---

[59] See para.145 of the decision on jurisdiction in the case of *SGS Société Générale de Surveillance SA v Islamic Republic of Pakistan*, ICSID Case No.ARB/01/13, August 6, 2003, (2003) 42 I.L.M. 1290.

[60] *Emilio Agustín Maffezini v Kingdom of Spain*, ICSID Case No.ARB/97/7, Award on Jurisdiction, January 25, 2000, (201) 16 ICSID Review—Foreign Investment Law Journal 212.

[61] See Art.8 of the UK–Argentina BIT. The ICSID Convention also contains a rule on the law applicable to ICSID arbitrations, Art.42(1), which provides as follows:
"The Tribunal shall decide a dispute in accordance with such rules of law as may be agreed by the parties. In the absence of such agreement, the Tribunal shall apply the law of the Contracting State party to the dispute (including its rules on the conflict of laws) and such rules of international law as may be applicable."

dispute, including its rules on conflicts of laws, the terms of any specific agreement concluded in relation to such an investment and the applicable principles of international law."[62]

Thus, BITs often provide for the application of up to four different sources of law, without any indication as to how they are to be combined. Recent BIT arbitration practice accords a controlling role for international law, by providing the standard by reference to which the legality of the conduct of the host state is to be assessed. Arbitral tribunals in BIT cases have relied on the substantive provisions of the BITs and general international law rather than domestic law in deciding their cases.[63] In *Maffezini v The Kingdom of Spain*, a case based on the Spanish–Argentina BIT, and the *Vivendi* case, based on the French–Argentina BIT, tribunals had no hesitation to sidestep the domestic law of the respondent's state, even in the face of the applicable law clauses contained in those BITs. The Annulment Committee in the *Vivendi* case, for example, held:

" . . . in respect of a claim based upon a substantive provision of that BIT . . . the inquiry which the ICSID tribunal is required to undertake is one governed by the ICSID Convention, by the BIT and by applicable international law. Such an inquiry is neither in principle determined, nor precluded, by any issue of municipal law . . . "[64]

Antonio Parra, Deputy Secretary-General of ICSID, writing about the rules of law applicable to the substance of disputes brought under BITs, states:

"These mainly have been the rules set out in the substantive provisions of the treaties themselves. In most instances, this follows simply from the investor's invocation of those rules in bringing the claim, such reliance on the rules being explicitly or implicitly authorized by the investor-to-State dispute settlement provisions of the treaty. The treaty being an instrument of international law, it is I think also implicit in such cases that the arbitrators should have recourse

---

[62] Agreement between the Government of the UK of Great Britain and Northern Ireland and the Government of the Republic of Argentina for the Promotion and Protection of Investments, signed on December 11, 1990 and entered into force on February 19, 1993.

[63] *Emilio Agustín Maffezini v Kingdom of Spain*, ICSID Case No.ARB/97/7, Award on Jurisdiction, January 25, 2000, (2001) 16 ICSID Review—Foreign Investment Law Journal 212. *Compañía de Aguas del Aconquija SA & Compagnie Générale des Eaux v Argentine Republic*, ICSID Case No.ARB/97/3, Award, November 21, 2000, (2001) 40 I.L.M. 426. See also *American Manufacturing & Trading Inc v Republic of Zaire*, ICSID Case No.ARB/93/1, Award, February 21, 1997, 5 ICSID Reports 10; and *Wena Hotels Ltd v Arab Republic of Egypt*, ICSID Case No.ARB/98/4, Final Award, December 8, 2000, (2002) 41 I.L.M. 896.

[64] *Compañía de Aguas del Aconquija SA & Vivendi Universal SA (formerly Compagnie Générale des Eaux) v Argentine Republic*, ICSID Case No.ARB/97/3, Decision on Annulment, July 3, 2002, (2002) 41 I.L.M. 1135 at para.102.

to the rules of general international law to supplement those of the treaty."[65]

11–20   This position also finds support in other ICSID awards. For instance, in *AAPL v Sri Lanka*, jurisdiction was based on the Sri Lanka–UK BIT. The tribunal held the BIT to be the "primary source of the applicable legal rules," and added that the BIT was not a "closed legal system" but had to be seen in the "wider juridical context" of international law. This led the tribunal to apply general international law to complement the provisions of the BIT.[66]

As BITs are international law instruments, international law is applicable by virtue of the Vienna Convention on the Law of Treaties, which provides that treaties are "governed by international law" and must be interpreted in the light of "any relevant rules of international law applicable."[67] The point is also made clear in Art.3 of the International Law Commission's Articles on State Responsibility, which provides that the "characterisation of an act of a State as internationally wrongful is governed by international law . . . "[68]

The applicable law provisions in investment contracts or other agreements forming part of the background of the dispute do not alter this conclusion. In *Wena v Egypt*, the Annulment Committee rejected the argument that the applicable law clauses of the lease agreements between *Wena* and an Egyptian state authority, which named Egyptian law, applied to the BIT dispute:

"The leases deal with questions that are by definition of a commercial nature. The IPPA [the BIT] deals with questions that are essentially of a governmental nature, namely the standards of treatment accorded by the State to foreign investors. It is therefore apparent that Wena and EHC agreed to a particular contract, the applicable law and the dispute settlement arrangement in respect

---

[65] A. Parra, "Applicable Substantive Law in ICSID Arbitrations Initiated Under Investment Treaties," (2001) 16 ICSID Review—Foreign Investment Law Journal 20. The overriding importance of international law is also upheld by Professor Weil, "The State, the Foreign Investor, and International Law: The No Longer Stormy Relationship of a Ménage à Trois," (2000) 15 ICSID Review—Foreign Investment Law Journal 401.

[66] *Asian Agricultural Products Ltd (AAPL) v Republic of Sri Lanka*, ICSID Case No.ARB/87/3, Final Award, June 27, 1990, (1991) 6 ICSID Review—Foreign Investment Law Journal 526 at paras 20–21.

[67] Arts 2(1)(a) and 31(3)(c), Vienna Convention on the Law of Treaties, opened for signature May 23, 1969, 1155 United Nations Treaty Series 331, reprinted in (1969) 8 I.L.M. 679.

[68] Art.3, Articles on Responsibility of States for Internationally Wrongful Acts, adopted by the International Law Commission (2001). See the ICSID Annulment Committee's reliance on this provision in *Compañía de Aguas del Aconquija SA & Vivendi Universal SA (formerly Compagnie Générale des Eaux) v Argentine Republic*, ICSID Case No.ARB/97/3, Decision on Annulment, July 3, 2002, (2002) 41 I.L.M. 1135, paras 95–96. All this is in conformity with Art.42(1) of the ICSID Convention. Indeed, ICSID practice under this rule clearly indicates that in ICSID cases international law is fully applicable and prevails over municipal law. In *Compañía del Desarrollo de Santa Elena SA v The Republic of Costa Rica*, e.g., the tribunal held that under Art.42(1), international law would prevail over municipal law, was "controlling" and governed the arbitration. *Compañía del Desarrollo de Santa Elena SA v The Republic of Costa Rica*, ICSID Case No.ARB/96/1, Final Award, February 17, 2000, (2000) 15 ICSID Review—Foreign Investment Law Journal 167 at paras 64–65.

of one kind of subject, that relating to commercial problems under the leases. It is also apparent that Wena as a national of a contracting state could invoke the IPPA for the purpose of a different kind of dispute, that concerning the treatment of foreign investors by Egypt. This other mechanism has a different and separate dispute settlement arrangement and might include a different choice of law provision or make no choice at all.

. . .

This Committee accordingly concludes that the subject matter of the lease agreements submitted to Egyptian law was different from the subject matter brought before ICSID arbitration under the IPPA."[69]

This approach does not ignore domestic law. Rather, it should be remembered **11–21** that the ICSID Convention was itself drafted principally with investor-state contracts in mind where domestic law would play the critical (if not exclusive) role. Treaty interpretation, however, calls for a different approach. If a domestic legal system were to provide rules of decision then a state could simply legislate itself out of a breach of treaty. As the tribunal held in the *Santa Elena* case[70]:

"To the extent that there may be any inconsistency between the two bodies of law, the rules of public international law must prevail. Were this not so in relation to takings of property, the protection of international law would be denied to the foreign investor and the purpose of the ICSID Convention would, in this respect, be frustrated."

Further, many treaties include a provision that investments not be accorded treatment less favourable than that required by international law. Kenneth Vandevelde states that such a clause:

" . . . serves in effect as an explicit choice of law provision for all dispute settlement mechanisms. Because treatment of investment must never be less that required by international law, international law provides the governing rules of decision, except where national law is more favourable."[71]

Professor Michael Reisman favours a more limited application of international law based on Art.42 of the ICSID Convention.[72] He comes to the conclusion that international law should only be applied: "(i) where the parties have so agreed; (ii) where the law of the contracting state party to the dispute calls for the application of international law, including customary international law; (iii)

---

[69] *Wena Hotels Ltd v Arab Republic of Egypt*, ICSID Case No.ARB/98/4, Decision on Annulment, February 5, 2002, (2002) 41 I.L.M. 933 at paras 31 and 36.
[70] *Compania del Desarrollo de Santa Elena SA v Republic of Costa Rica*, (2000) 15 ICSID Review—Foreign Investment Law Journal 167 at para.64.
[71] K. Vandevelde, *United States Investment Treaties: Policy and Practice* (Aspen Publishing, 1992), p.106.
[72] See M. Reisman, "The Regime for *Lacunae* in the ICSID Choice of Law Provision and the Question of Its Threshold" (2000) 15 ICSID Review—Foreign Investment Law Journal.

where the subject matter or issue is directly regulated by international law, such as a treaty between the states party to the dispute; and, finally; (iv) where the law of the contracting state party to the dispute, or action taken under that law, violates international law. In this last situation, international law operates as a corrective to national law".

11–22   In a BIT context, it appears that the interplay between domestic law and international law will result in the application of the rule more favourable to the foreign investor. The domestic law of the host state, together with any applicable contracts, will nevertheless play an important role in respect of the facts of the dispute, since the misconduct of the state will usually manifest itself through internal legal acts which may not be consistent with international law protections. A typical example would be an analysis of the facts surrounding a tender process, subsequent grant of concession and later interference with the concession. At all three stages, the state may have issued decrees, regulations and laws which will provide the framework against which the international law protections must be viewed.

4. THE MERITS OF THE DISPUTE

11–23   If jurisdictional hurdles are overcome, the question arises whether the host state has breached its substantive obligations. There is a surprising degree of uniformity between substantive protections in the treaties, aided by model treaties established as negotiating models by the main capital-exporting nations. We set out here the core protections and seek to give an idea of their potential scope through the recent decisions of investment tribunals. This chapter should nevertheless bear a triangular warning sign "Building site: please enter with care". The law is in full development and many cases remain of first impression. There is no doctrine of precedent and subsequent tribunals have reached different conclusions based on the same facts and law.[73] Commenting on this issue, the tribunal in the recent case of *SGS Société Générale de Surveillance SA v Republic of the Philippines* noted[74]:

> "In the Tribunal's view, although different tribunals constituted under the ICSID system should in general seek to act consistently with each other, in the

---

[73] *e.g.* see the recent decisions in *CME Czech Republic BV (The Netherlands) v The Czech Republic*, Final Award, March 14, 2003 and *Ronald S. Lauder v The Czech Republic*, Final Award, September 3, 2001, where claims were brought under two different treaties based on identical facts. In the case of *Lauder v Czech Republic*, the case was dismissed. In the case of *CME v Czech Republic*, the Czech state was condemned to pay over US$300 million. Both texts are available online on the CME website: *www.cetv-net.com/arbitration.asp*. On legal issues, there was a recent clear split on the scope of so-called "umbrella clause" in the cases of *SGS Société Générale de Surveillance SA v Islamic Republic of Pakistan*, ICSID Case No.ARB/01/13, August 6, 2003, (2003) 42 I.L.M. 1290 and *SGS Société Générale de Surveillance SA v Republic of the Philippines*, Case No.ARB/02/6, text available on the ICSID website: *www.icsid.org*.

[74] *SGS Société Générale de Surveillance SA v Republic of the Philippines*, Case No.ARB/02/6, Decision on Jurisdiction, January 29, 2004, *ibid.*

end it must be for each tribunal to exercise its competence in accordance with the applicable law, which will by definition be different for each BIT and each Respondent State. Moreover there is no doctrine of precedent in international law, if by precedent is meant a rule of the binding effect of a single decision. There is no hierarchy of international tribunals, and even if there were, there is no good reason for allowing the first tribunal in time to resolve issues for all later tribunals. It must be initially for the control mechanisms provided for under the BIT and the ICSID Convention, and in the longer term for the development of a common legal opinion or *jurisprudence constante*, to resolve the difficult legal questions discussed by the *SGS v Pakistan* Tribunal and also in the present decision."

(a) "Fair and equitable treatment" and the international minimum standard

Almost all investment treaties require host states to accord "fair and equitable **11–24** treatment" to investors of the other contracting state. To highlight the significance of this standard of protection, it is frequently addressed at the beginning of the general treatment clauses. For example, Art.II(2)(a) of the US–Argentina BIT provides:

"Investment shall at all times be accorded fair and equitable treatment, shall enjoy full protection and security and shall in no case be accorded treatment less than that required by international law."

It is difficult to reduce the words "fair and equitable treatment" to a precise statement of a legal obligation. They grant considerable discretion to tribunals to review the "fairness" and "equity" of government actions in light of all the facts and circumstances of the case, without necessarily deliberating on the requirements of either national or international law.[75]

International arbitral tribunals called upon to decide cases on the basis of the "fair and equitable treatment" standard have proved unwilling to provide a specific definition of the content of this provision, deciding objectively on a case-by-case basis, in accordance with the "plain meaning" approach, whether the treatment provided by a particular host state to a particular investment was both "fair" and "equitable". Although these notions may be elusive, it is clear from the object and purpose of the treaties that "the fair and equitable treatment" standard is intended to accord foreign investors broad objective protections, including a stable and predictable investment environment, in order to maximise investments.

---

[75] See, *e.g.*, Charles Brower, "Investor-State Disputes under NAFTA: the Empire Strikes Back" (2001) 40 Columbia Journal of Transnational Law 43 at 56; S. Vasciannie, "The Fair and Equitable Treatment Standard in International Investment Law and Practice" (1999) 70 British Yearbook of International Law 99 at 163; and F.A. Mann, "British Treaties for the Promotion and Protection of Investments" (1981) 52 British Yearbook of International Law 241 at 243.

11–25   International arbitral tribunals that are asked to determine if a state's measures violate the "fair and equitable treatment" standard may need to examine "the impact of the measure on the reasonable investment-backed expectations of the investor; and whether the state is attempting to avoid investment-backed expectations that the state created or reinforced through its own acts."[76] It is on this basis that the UNCITRAL ad hoc tribunal in the *CME* case recently found that the Czech Republic's legislative and regulatory changes had unlawfully harmed CME's investment by altering the country's investment framework. It held:

> "[The Government] breached its obligation of fair and equitable treatment by evisceration of the arrangements in reliance upon [which] the foreign investor was induced to invest."[77]

Similarly, in *Técnicas Medioambientales TECMED SA v Estados Unidos Mexicanos*, the tribunal concluded:

> "The Tribunal considers that this [the fair and equitable] provision of the Agreement [the BIT], in the light of the demands of good faith required by international law, requires the Contracting Parties to the Agreement to accord a treatment to foreign investment that does not go against the basic expectations on the basis of which the foreign investor decided to make the investment."[78]

Hence, it has been held that failure to ensure transparency in the functioning of public authorities[79] and the lack of a predictable framework for investment contrary to legitimate expectations of the investor and commitments made by the host state,[80] are breaches of fair and equitable treatment standards.

11–26   This standard has assumed a significant role in the context of NAFTA jurisprudence where arbitral tribunals have found that NAFTA's "fair and equitable treatment" standard was breached by the conduct of public authorities (in the host state) amounting to effective discrimination in favour of domestic entities,[81]

---

[76] J. Paulsson, "Investment Protection Provisions in Treaties" in *Investment Protection/La Protection de l'Investissement* (International Chamber of Commerce, 2000), p.19 at p.22.

[77] *CME Czech Republic BV (The Netherlands) v The Czech Republic*, Partial Award, September 13, 2001, LexisNexis Mealey Publications Doc. No.05-011127-013A, para.611, also available online at: *www.cetv-net.com/arbitration.asp*.

[78] *Técnicas Medioambientales TECMED SA v Estados Unidos Mexicanos*, ICSID Case No.ARB(AF)/00/2, Award, May 29, 2003, (2004) 43 I.L.M. 133 at para.154 (free translation from the Spanish original).

[79] *Emilio Agustín Maffezini v The Kingdom of Spain*, Case No.ARB/97/7, Award, November 13, 2000, (2001) 16 ICSID Review—Foreign Investment Law Journal at para.83.

[80] *CME Czech Republic BV (The Netherlands) v The Czech Republic* (UNCITRAL Rules), Partial Award, September 13, 2001, LexisNexis Mealey Publications Doc. No.05-011127-013A at para.611. Also available online at: *www.cetv-net.com/arbitration.asp*.

[81] *S.D. Myers Inc v Government of Canada*, Partial Award, June 13, 2000. Text available online at: *www.naftalaw.org*.

and threats, denial of reasonable demands and information requests requiring the investor to incur unnecessary expenses and disruption.[82]

There is disagreement over whether "fair and equitable treatment" is merely synonymous with the minimum standard required by customary international law, or whether it represents an independent concept requiring greater protection.[83] Writing in 1981 on British investment treaty practice, F.A. Mann concluded that: "the terms 'fair and equitable treatment' envisage conduct which goes far beyond the minimum standard and afford protection to a greater extent and according to a much more objective standard than any previously employed form of words . . . The terms are likely to be understood and applied independently and autonomously."[84]

This disagreement has become particularly prominent in the context of Art.1105(1) of NAFTA which provides:

"Each Party shall accord to investments of investors of another Party treatment in accordance with international law, including fair and equitable treatment and full protection and security."

A plain reading of the provision would lead to the conclusion that the "fair and equitable treatment" standard has to be interpreted in accordance with "international law". However, in many cases, the tribunals have not restricted the application of the principle to instances of bad faith, wilful neglect, clear unreasonableness or lack of due diligence that are supposedly covered by the customary international law standard.[85] **11–27**

The controversy was given further impetus when the NAFTA Commission (consisting of representatives of the three contracting parties) issued a "binding interpretative statement" of the relevant NAFTA article.[86] The statement provided, *inter alia*, that fair and equitable treatment "does not require treatment in addition to or beyond that which is required by the customary international law minimum standard of treatment of aliens". It is not clear whether this "binding" statement will achieve the desired result. It has been argued that this statement goes beyond "interpretation" and amounts to an unauthorised amendment to

---

[82] *Pope and Talbot Inc v The Government of Canada*, Award on the Merits of Phase 2, April 10, 2001. Text available online at: *www.naftalaw.org*.

[83] See R. Dolzer & M. Stevens, *Bilateral Investment Treaties*, (The Hague, Martinus Nijhoff, 1995), p.59.

[84] F.A. Mann, "British Treaties for the Promotion and Protection of Investments" (1981) 52 British Yearbook of International Law 241.

[85] The content of the international minimum standard is itself open to debate. See UNCTAD, *Series on issues in international investment agreements, Fair and Equitable Treatment* (1999), pp.39–40.

[86] The interpretative statement was issued by the NAFTA Free Trade Commission, composed of one representative of each NAFTA state, under Art.1152(2) of the NAFTA which provides that the Commission may issue binding interpretations of the NAFTA treaty. Text available at: *www.naftalaw.org*.

NAFTA.[87] Certain tribunals have accepted the customary standard whilst noting that such standard is evolutionary, thereby rendering the statement largely ineffective.[88] A recent award of an ICSID Tribunal, however, treats the statement issued by the Commission as binding.[89] According to the Tribunal the effect of the Commission's interpretation is that "fair and equitable treatment" and "full protection and security" are not freestanding obligations and are obligations only to the extent that they are recognised by customary international law. The tribunal referred to certain awards that had expressed a contrary view but held that such views must be disregarded.

(b) Full protection and security

11–28   As in the case of "fair and equitable treatment", it is difficult to give a precise meaning to the notion of "full protection and security". However, its scope may be illustrated by reference to its practical application.

In contrast with most of the other investor protections which impose restrictions on host state activity, the "full protection and security" clause seeks to impose certain positive obligations on the host state to protect investments. The standard applied whilst determining whether there has been a breach of this obligation is one of "due diligence" or an *"obligation de moyens"*, requiring the host state to exercise reasonable care to protect investments, rather than a "strict liability" standard. However, there is no need for the claimant to establish negligence or bad faith. Arbitral tribunals have traditionally found breaches of the "full protection and security" obligation in situations where the host state failed to prevent the physical destruction of property by not taking measures that fell within the normal exercise of governmental functions of policing and maintenance of law and order.[90]

The obligation of the host state to provide full protection and security to investors is independent and not relative to the level of protection provided by the state to its own nationals or to nationals of other states. Therefore, the fact that the state did not protect the property of its own nationals is no defence to a claim by an investor of breach of this obligation.[91]

11–29   Whilst this standard has normally been applied in situations of physical protection of real and tangible property, its scope has been extended to other circumstances. For instance, it has been held that withdrawal of an authorisation

---

[87] *Pope and Talbot Inc v The Government of Canada*, Award on the Merits of Phase 2, April 10, 2001, available online at: *www.naftalaw.org*; also see *Loewen v United States*, ICSID Award, June 26, 2003, (2003) 42 I.L.M. 811 at para.127.

[88] *Pope and Talbot Inc v The Government of Canada*, Award on Damages, May 31, 2002, (2002) 41 I.L.M. 1347 at paras 52 and 55.

[89] *Loewen v United States*, ICSID Award of June 26, 2003, (2003) 42 I.L.M. 811 at para.128.

[90] *Asian Agricultural Products Ltd (AAPL) v Republic of Sri Lanka*, ICSID Case No.ARB/87/3, Final Award, June 27, 1990, (191) 6 ICSID Review—Foreign Investment Law Journal 526; *American Manufacturing & Trading Inc v Republic of Zaire*, ICSID Case No.ARB/93/1, Award, February 21, 1997, 5 ICSID Reports 10.

[91] *American Manufacturing & Trading Inc v Republic of Zaire*, ICSID Case No.ARB/93/1, Award, February 21, 1997, 5 ICSID Reports 10 and 30.

vital to the operation of the investment amounts to a breach of "full protection and security".[92] Similarly, a change in the legal framework, making it impossible to preserve and continue contractual arrangements underpinning the investment, has also been found incompatible with the BITs "full protection and security" provision.[93]

(c) No arbitrary or discriminatory measures impairing the investment

Most investment treaties impose an obligation upon the host state not to impair **11–30** the management or operation of the investment by arbitrary and discriminatory measures. For instance, Art.II(3)(b) of the US–Ecuador BIT provides:

"Neither Party shall in any way impair by arbitrary or discriminatory measures the management, operation, maintenance, use, enjoyment, acquisition, expansion, or disposal of investments . . . "

The concepts of "arbitrary" or "discriminatory" measures are not defined in the treaties. The International Court of Justice formulated the test of "arbitrariness" in the context of investment protection in the *ELSI* case. The court observed:

"Arbitrariness is not so much something opposed to a rule of law, as something opposed to the rule of law . . . It is a wilful disregard of due process of law, an act which shocks, or at least surprises, a sense of juridical propriety."[94]

In relation to "discriminatory" measures, Kenneth Vandevelde explains that it includes measures "that are discriminatory in effect as well as those which are intentionally discriminatory".[95] Thus it is not essential to establish any *mala fides* on the part of the host state.[96] It has been held that, in general, a measure is discriminatory in effect if it results in a treatment of an investor different from that accorded to other investors in a similar or comparable situation.[97] The issue

---

[92] *Antoine Goetz v République du Burundi*, ICSID Case No.ARB/95/3, Award, February 10, 1999, (2000) 15 ICSID Review—Foreign Investment Law Journal 457 at paras 125–131 (in French).

[93] *CME Czech Republic BV (The Netherlands) v The Czech Republic* (UNCITRAL Rules), Partial Award, September 13, 2001, LexisNexis Mealey Publications Doc. No.05-011127-013A, para.613. Also available online at: *www.cetv-net.com/arbitration.asp.*

[94] *Case Concerning Elettronica Sicula SpA (ELSI) (United States of America v Italy)*, Judgment, July 20, 1989, (1989) 15 ICJ Reports 76 at para.128.

[95] K. Vandevelde, *United States Investment Treaties: Policy and Practice* (1992), p.77.

[96] *Loewen v United States*, ICSID Award, June 26, 2003, (2003) 42 I.L.M. 811 at para.127. The tribunal was considering the judgment of a US trial court. The tribunal observed that bad faith or malicious intention is not an essential element of unfair and inequitable treatment and it is sufficient if there is a lack of due process which offends a sense of judicial propriety. Though the tribunal found the trial court proceedings as improper and discreditable, it held against the Claimant due to failure to exhaust all remedies under the US legal system.

[97] *Antoine Goetz v République du Burundi*, ICSID Case No.ARB/95/3, Award, February 10, 1999, (2000) 15 ICSID Review—Foreign Investment Law Journal 457 at para.121.

of whether a particular measure is discriminatory or not is a question of fact and has to be determined in light of the circumstances of each case.

(d) No expropriation without prompt, adequate and effective compensation

11–31 The obligation to compensate for expropriation is among the most crucial protections provided by investment treaties. It is a provision that is frequently relied upon by foreign investors in treaty arbitration. The expropriation provisions in investment treaties are quite similar. A typical provision is, for example, Art.3(1) of the US–Argentina BIT, which reads:

> "Investments shall not be expropriated or nationalized either directly or indirectly through measures tantamount to expropriation or nationalization ('expropriation') except for a public purpose; in a non-discriminatory manner; upon payment of prompt, adequate and effective compensation; and in accordance with due process of law and the general principles of treatment provided for in Article II(2). Compensation shall be equivalent to the fair market value of the expropriated investment immediately before the expropriatory action was taken or became known, whichever is earlier; be paid without delay; include interest at a commercially reasonable rate from the date of expropriation; be fully realizable; and be freely transferable at the prevailing market rate of exchange on the date of expropriation."

Indirect expropriation

11–32 It is now a well-accepted principle of international law that expropriation may occur by a direct and deliberate formal taking, or indirectly, by measures resulting in a substantial deprivation of the use and value of the investment even though the actual title of the asset remains with the investor.

International arbitral tribunals have recognised this principle and upheld claims for indirect expropriation when they have found that government measures had a drastic effect on the value of the investments. For example, the test for indirect expropriation or "*de facto*" expropriation, has been defined in a recent NAFTA case as follows[98]:

> "Expropriation under NAFTA includes not only open, deliberate and acknowledged takings of property, such as outright seizure or formal or obligatory transfer of title in favour of the host State, but also covert or incidental interference with the use of property which has the effect of depriving the owner, in whole or in significant part, of the use or reasonably-to-be-expected economic benefit of property even if not necessarily to the obvious benefit of the host State."

---

[98] *Metalclad Corporation v United Mexican States*, ICSID Case No.ARB(AF)/97/1, Award, August 30, 2000, (2001) 40 I.L.M. 36 at para.130.

In essence, the standard for determining whether government measures amount to an expropriation is the actual effect of the measures on the investor's property. Measures that indirectly, but effectively, deprive an investor of the use or enjoyment of its investment, including deprivation of the whole or a significant part of the economic benefit of property, may be as expropriatory as the seizure of an investor's formal title to its property.

Acts contrary to undertakings and assurances granted to investors may constitute expropriation

States may also expropriate foreign investments through measures that interfere with assurances they offered to investors to induce them to invest. The assurances states offer to create a pro-investment environment may amount to essential conditions for those investments and, as such, form part of the legal framework underlying, and protecting, those investments. A failure by the state to honour those undertakings may give investors who reasonably relied on them a right to compensation.   **11–33**

International arbitral tribunals have held that government assurances and undertakings create "acquired rights" for investors.[99] The rationale for interpreting a state's assurances as giving rise to acquired rights is simple and sensible. Investors looking to invest in developing countries cannot predict with confidence that conditions of stability and security will exist throughout the period of their investment. Thus the state gives core promises to foreign investors in order to underpin the investment, both today and in the future, in order to provide protection against any major changes in local legal or political conditions that would be unfavourable to their interests.[1]

The tribunal in the recent *CME v Czech Republic* case reached such a conclusion when it was asked to consider the expropriation claim of an investor in a joint venture in the Czech Republic. The investor alleged that the joint venture collapsed after the official Czech broadcasting authority forced the investor to give up its exclusive licensing rights and changed other key terms of the joint venture agreement. The tribunal held that the acts of the Czech regulatory authority interfered with the "economic and legal basis of CME's investment" and "destroy[ed] the legal basis ('the safety net') of the Claimant's investment," which ruined the "commercial value of the investment" and, thus, amounted to expropriation.[2]

---

[99] Acquired rights have been defined as follows:
    "Acquired rights are any rights, corporeal or incorporeal, properly vested under municipal law in a natural or juristic person and of an assessable monetary value. Within the scope of such rights fall interests which have their basis in contract as well as in property, provided they concern an undertaking or investment of a more or less permanent character."
    See D.P. O'Connell, *International Law* (2nd ed., 1970), Vol.II, pp.763–764.

[1] A.A. Fatouros, *Government Guarantees to Foreign Investors* (1962).

[2] *CME Czech Republic BV (The Netherlands) v The Czech Republic*, Partial Award, September 13, 2001, LexisNexis Mealey Publications Doc. No.05-011127-013A at paras 551, 554–555 and 591; also available online at: *www.cetv-net.com/arbitration.asp*.

In sum, the paramount concern of tribunals in expropriation cases is whether a state's interference with prior assurances it gave to an investor, be it direct or indirect, express or covert, creeping or not, deprives the investor, in whole or in significant part, of the use or reasonably-to-be expected benefit of its investment.

The purpose of the host state's measures does not affect their characterisation

11–34   The form of measures or their motive may be irrelevant if the effect is to deprive the owner of the expected economic benefit from the asset. This is an enquiry based on effect rather than intention. Arbitral tribunals have held that it is immaterial that the property was expropriated for laudable environmental reasons[3] or as part of the political reorientation of the country.[4]

Although the purpose of an expropriatory measure may affect its legality, it does not affect the host state's obligation to provide the expropriated investor with prompt and adequate compensation. This point was recently affirmed by the ICSID Tribunal in *Compañía del Desarrollo de Santa Elena SA v The Republic of Costa Rica*:

> "While an expropriation or taking for environmental reasons may be classified as a taking for a public purpose, and thus may be legitimate, the fact that the Property was taken for this reason does not affect either the nature or the measure of the compensation to be paid for the taking. That is, the purpose of protecting the environment for which the Property was taken does not alter the legal character of the taking for which adequate compensation must be paid. The international source of the obligation to protect the environment makes no difference.
>
> Expropriatory environmental measures—no matter how laudable and beneficial to society as a whole—are, in this respect, similar to any other expropriatory measures that a state may take in order to implement its policies: where property is expropriated, even for environmental purposes, whether domestic or international, the state's obligation to pay compensation remains."[5]

11–35   The test of whether government measures amount to an expropriation is to measure their actual effect on an investor's ability to use or enjoy its investment. Where government measures interfere with an investor's legitimate expectation that the state will honour the assurances it offered to induce the investment and

---

[3] *Compañía del Desarrollo de Santa Elena SA v Republic of Costa Rica* (2000) 15 ICSID Review—Foreign Investment Law Journal 169 at paras 71–72.

[4] *Philips Petroleum Co Iran v The Islamic Republic of Iran* (1989) 21 Iran–US C.T.R 79 at 115–116.

[5] *Compañía del Desarrollo de Santa Elena SA v The Republic of Costa Rica*, ICSID Case No.ARB/96/1, Final Award, February 17, 2000, (2000) 15 ICSID Review—Foreign Investment Law Journal 169 at paras 71–72.

those measures substantially deprive an investor of the use or enjoyment of its investment, expropriation may be proven. Whilst considering whether there has been expropriation in a particular case, a tribunal need not examine each state measure in isolation. If the cumulative effect of multiple state measures is substantially to deprive the investor of the use, value and enjoyment of its investment, expropriation may still be construed.[6]

Compensation standard

The compensation standard almost universally used in modern treaty practice **11–36** by capital-exporting states reflects that comprised in Art.3(1) of the US–Argentina BIT cited above. The standard dates from 1938 and is known as the "Hull formula" after US Secretary of State Cordell Hull who declared in a dispute between the US and Mexico concerning the expropriation of US oil fields that international law required Mexico to pay "prompt, adequate and effective" compensation. The standard requires the payment of full market value of the expropriated asset speedily in a convertible currency. An alternative formulation of "appropriate compensation" is sometimes seen in BITs and represents a lower standard which permits equitable issues to be taken into account in fixing the compensation.[7] UNCTAD concludes in its report on "Taking of Property" in 2000 that "overall there is a trend in modern BITs towards the Hull standard of compensation".[8] This is echoed in the World Bank Guidelines on the Treatment of Foreign Direct Investment, which state[9]:

"1. Compensation for a specific investment taken by the State will, according to the details provided below, be deemed 'appropriate' if it is adequate, effective and prompt.

2. Compensation will be deemed 'adequate' if it is based on the fair market value of the taken asset as such value is determined immediately before the time at which the taking occurred or the decision to take the asset became publicly known."

---

[6] B.H. Weston, "Constructive Takings Under International Law: A Modest Foray into the Problem of Creeping Expropriation," (1976) 16 Virginia Journal of International Law 103; UNCTAD, *Series on Issues in International Investment Agreements: Taking of Property* (UN, 2000), p.11; Restatement (Third) of Foreign Relations Law of the United States (1987), s.712, comment g; *Compañía del Desarrollo de Santa Elena SA v Republic of Costa Rica*, (2000) 15 ICSID Review—Foreign Investment Law Journal 169 at para.76.

[7] See the discussion of the two formulae in the UNCTAD *Series on Issues in International Investment Agreements: Taking of Property* (UN, 2000), pp.13–14. A rare example of the standard of "appropriate compensation" may be seen in the BIT between China and Thailand which states at Art.5(1)(a): "Only for the public interest and against compensation may either Contracting Party expropriate, nationalize or take similar measures . . . Such compensation shall be equivalent to the appropriate value of expropriated investments . . . "

[8] Above.

[9] Reprinted in Ibrahim Shihata, *Legal Treatment of Foreign Investment: the World Bank Guidelines* (Martinus Nijhoff, 1993), p.193.

(e) National and "most favoured nation" treatment

11–37   Another common protection provided by investment treaties is that the investment must be treated no less favourably than that of nationals and companies of the host state (national treatment) or of any other state (most favoured nation treatment, usually abbreviated to "MFN" treatment). Thus, this protection attempts to ensure "relative" standards of treatment, that is, standards which define the treatment required for covered investment relative to the treatment given to other investments. Article 3(1) of the UK–Egypt BIT is a representative provision:

> "Neither Contracting Party shall in its territory subject investments or returns of investors of the other Contracting Party to treatment less favourable than that which it accords to investment or returns of its own nationals or companies or to investments or returns of nationals or companies of any third State."

Being relative standards of protection, their scope cannot be defined in the abstract, but will vary according to the circumstances of each case. This often requires an analysis of facts including the protections and assurances granted by the host state to other investors. It may be difficult to access the information necessary for such review. The application of national treatment may involve greater problems in cases such as NAFTA which provide that national treatment applies only where the foreign and domestic investor are "in like circumstances".[10]

Traditionally, the MFN clause is relied on in the context of substantive rights. For example, if the host state of the investment provides tax concessions to French investors in the oil industry but not to UK investors in that industry, the UK investor could rely on the MFN clause to claim the same treatment or compensation for the loss suffered as a result of the discrimination. However, as we saw above, in *Maffezini*, the tribunal extended the application of this provision from substantive to procedural matters such as the dispute resolution mechanism between the host state and investors.[11]

11–38   The presence of MFN clauses in investment treaties creates a diffusive effect of investor protection as additional gains obtained by one state flow to other states. This can lead to the creation of a single "highest" standard for all contracting parties to BITs with a particular state.

---

[10] Art.1102(1) of NAFTA, which provides:
> "Each Party shall accord to investors of another Party treatment no less favourable than it accords, in like circumstances, to its own investors, with respect to the establishment, acquisition, expansion, management, conduct, operation and sale or other disposition of investments."

[11] *Emilio Agustín Maffezini v Kingdom of Spain*, ICSID Case No.ARB/97/7, Award on Jurisdiction, January 25, 2000, (2001) 16 ICSID Review—Foreign Investment Law Journal 212.

(f) Free transfer of funds related to investments

Many investment treaties provide guarantees relating to the free movement of **11–39** funds. Article IV of the US–Ecuador BIT provides:

"Each Party shall permit all transfers related to an investment to be made freely and without delay into and out of its territory. Such transfers include: (a) returns; (b) compensation 'pursuant to provisions of the treaty'; (c) payments arising out of an investment dispute; (d) payments made under a contract, including amortization of principal and accrued interest payments made pursuant to a loan agreement; (a) proceeds from the sale or liquidation of all or any part of an investment; and (f) additional contributions to capital for the maintenance or development of an investment.

Transfers shall be made in a freely usable currency at the prevailing market rate of exchange on the data of transfer with respect to spot transactions in the currency to be transferred."

This obligation entitles foreign investors to compensation if suddenly affected by currency control regulations or other host state acts which effectively confine the investor's money in the host state. As is evident from the provision in the US–Ecuador BIT, the free transfer provisions are broad in scope as they are not limited to the invested funds, but cover any amounts derived from or associated with the investment, including profit, dividend, interest, capital gain, royalty payment, management, technical assistance or other fee, or returns in kind.

However, treaties often provide for exceptions to the free movement of funds by allowing host states to restrict transfers during unusual periods of low foreign exchange or balance of payments problems.[12] Further, it is permissible for the host state to maintain laws and regulations requiring reports of currency transfer, or to impose withholding taxes applicable to dividends or other transfers or take measures for protection of creditor interests. Such regulations must nevertheless comply with the other investor treaty provisions requiring equitable and non-discriminatory treatment.

(g) Observance of specific investment undertakings

Treaties often contain a so-called "umbrella clause", *i.e.* the obligation of the **11–40** host state to respect specific undertakings towards investors. Article 2(2), final sentence, of the US–Argentina Treaty sets out an "umbrella clause", whereby the host state is required to observe specific obligations entered into with the investor:

"[e]ach Party shall observe any obligation it may have entered into with regard to investments."

---

[12] See, *e.g.*, para.10 of the Protocol attached to the US–Egypt BIT.

Some commentators have contended that the legal effect of "umbrella clauses" is to elevate to the status of treaty breach any violation of contractual obligations in direct agreements between states and investors. This has, however, recently been rejected by the arbitral tribunal in the *SGS v Pakistan* case, which concluded on the terms of the particular clause in question that it did "not believe that transmutation of SGS's contract claims into BIT claims has occurred" through the operation of such a clause.[13]

The arbitral tribunal concluded that the legal consequences of such an interpretation of the BIT were "so far-reaching in scope, and so automatic and unqualified and sweeping in their apparent operation, so burdensome in their potential impact upon the contracting party",[14] that clear and convincing evidence had to be induced by the claimant, demonstrating that such was the shared intent of the contracting parties to the BIT. In the absence of such evidence, the arbitral tribunal rejected the claimant's interpretation which would, according to the tribunal, amount to "incorporating by reference an unlimited number of state contracts as well as other municipal law instruments setting out state commitments including unilateral commitments to an investor of the other contracting party".[15]

11–41   This limitative interpretation of "umbrella clauses" was rejected in another case brought by the same investor against the Philippines under the Switzerland –Philippines Treaty.[16] That case concerned the following clause:

"Each Contracting Party shall observe any obligation it has assumed with regard to specific investments in its territory by investors of the other Contracting Party".[17]

The tribunal concluded that this clause did make it a breach of the BIT for the host state to fail to observe binding contractual commitments but that the scope of the obligations contained in the investment agreement remained governed by the applicable law of the contract and were not elevated to international law. The practical impact of the decision was, however, limited by their conclusion that the BIT did not override the contractually negotiated exclusive jurisdiction clause in the investment agreement.[18] Since most investment agreements will contain a jurisdiction clause, it is consequently unlikely that the floodgates will open for a rush of purely contractual claims pursuant to BITs.

---

[13] See paras 156 *et seq.* of the decision on jurisdiction in the case of *SGS Société Générale de Surveillance SA v Islamic Republic of Pakistan*, ICSID Case No.ARB/01/13, August 6, 2003, (2003) 42 I.L.M. 1290.

[14] *ibid.*, at para.167.

[15] *ibid.*, at para. 168.

[16] *SGS v Republic of the Philippines*, Decision on Jurisdiction, January 29, 2004. Text available on the ICSID website at: *www.worldbank.org/icsid/cases/awards.htm.*

[17] Art.X(2) of the Switzerland–Philippines BIT.

[18] See above, paras 139–148.

5. REMEDIES UNDER BITS

This issue can be usefully divided into remedies for expropriation and reme- **11–42**
dies for other international law breaches.

(a) Expropriation remedies

The almost universal standard of compensation in expropriation established by **11–43**
BITs in the Hull formula (discussed above) is the "fair market value" of the
investment immediately prior to the expropriatory measure and a reference to
"genuine" or "real" value are generally considered to reflect the same standard
of compensation. The UNCITRAL ad hoc tribunal in the *CME* case, for example,
recently confirmed that "genuine value" equates with "fair market value".[19]

There are various accepted methods of calculating the fair market value of an
asset. However, the fair market value of an income-producing asset or "going
concern" is normally calculated by measuring its future prospects by using the
discounted cash flow analysis ("DCF analysis"), that measures the future cash
flows that would be generated by the business and then discounts them to their
present value. This method is now commonly used by treaty arbitration tribunals
when they have been tasked with valuing a "going concern".[20] This method is
often supported by other valuation tools such as comparative transactions or book
value.

It is, however, an important evidential issue to consider if the asset in question
has a sufficiently reliable history of producing income. In the case of *AAPL v Sri
Lanka*, the tribunal refused to award lost profits since the future profitability of
the firm could not be reasonably established with a sufficient degree of certainty.[21] This approach had been adopted earlier by the Iran–US Claims Tribunal
where a US investor was unable to obtain lost profits from a factory which had
been expropriated before it had started operations.[22] The question becomes more
complex where the asset has been operated for a short period. In the case of
Metalclad v Mexico, the tribunal concluded[23]:

"Where the enterprise has not operated for a sufficiently long time to establish
a performance record or where it has failed to make a profit, future profits
cannot be used to determine going concern or fair market value."

---

[19] *CME Czech Republic BV (The Netherlands) v The Czech Republic*, Final Award, March 14, 2003.
Text of the decision available on the CME website at: *www.cetv-net.com/arbitration.asp.*
[20] For an analysis of damage calculation methods in investment arbitration see M. Ball, "Assessing
Damages in Claims by Investors against States", 16 ICSID Review—Foreign Investment Law
Journal 408.
[21] *Asian Agricultural Products Ltd (AAPL) v Republic of Sri Lanka*, ICSID Case No.ARB/87/3, Final
Award, June 27, 1990,(1991) 6 ICSID Review—Foreign Investment Law Journal 526.
[22] *Phelps Dodge Corp v Iran* (1986) 10 Iran–US C.T.R. 121.
[23] *Metalclad Corporation v United Mexican States*, ICSID Case No.ARB(AF)/97/1, Award, August
30, 2000, (2001) 40 I.L.M. 36 at para.121.

11–44   In *Autopista Concesionada de Venezuela CA v Bolivarian Republic of Venezuela* the tribunal followed the approach developed in, *inter alia*, the *Metalclad* and *AAPL* decisions. The tribunal concluded that lost profits should not be awarded where the Claimant had failed to demonstrate that the investment would have resulted in a profit.[24]

In such circumstances, tribunals will generally look to the amount invested in the project or to the book value of the assets.

The issue of whether an investor can make a successful expropriation claim, but *retain* the assets, has not yet been fully addressed by the case law. This is mainly because the expropriated investment has rarely had any residual value. Recently, however, the *CME* case suggests that a successful expropriation claim is not inconsistent with retaining title to the asset. In calculating compensation for expropriation, the tribunal valued the expropriated investment (the claimant's shareholding in a local company) using, among other methods, DCF analysis. The tribunal applied this method to the remaining period of the licence. From the value resulting from this calculation, the tribunal deducted the residual value of the company, thus implicitly admitting that the claimant's title to the expropriated asset, its shareholding in the company, could remain in the hands of the claimant and need not be relinquished to the respondent state.[25]

11–45   The question may thus turn on how the residual value can be properly calculated. In *CME*, the tribunal focused on the net asset value of equipment, buildings and operation of the company following the adverse governmental measures. There was, however, little prospect for the local company to restart business in the foreseeable future, so the tribunal did not take into account any potential future revenue as part of the residual value. It is possible that, in certain cases, the tribunals may find that the investments such as concession contracts are still going concerns which could generate some positive cash flow in the near future. The residual value of the concessions could be calculated using the DCF analysis on the basis of the tribunal's reasonable projections.

(b) Compensation for other treaty breaches

11–46   BITs usually do not specify the damages to which the claimant would be entitled as compensation for the host state's other treaty breaches, *i.e.* breaches of the "fair and equitable" and other treatment protections provided in the treaties. However, international tribunals have awarded damages for breach of the fair and equitable treatment standard according to the widely accepted principle set out in 1928 by the Permanent Court of International Justice in the *Chorzów Factory* case:

---

[24] Case No.ARB/00/5 at paras 351 and 359–362. Text available on the ICSID website: *www.icsid.org*.
[25] N. Rubins, "Must the Victorious Investor-Claimant Relinquish Title to Expropriated Property?" (2003) 4 Journal of World Investment 481 at 488–89.

"[R]eparation must, as far as possible, wipe out all the consequences of the illegal act and re-establish the situation which would, in all probability, have existed if that act had not been committed."[26]

International tribunals have recently applied the *Chorzów Factory* principle to cases arising under NAFTA, confirming that, under international law, treaty breaches give rise to the obligation to compensate the economic harm they cause (see, *e.g.*, *S.D. Myers v Canada*, *Metalclad v Mexico* and *Maffezini*)[27] in an amount equivalent to the losses that the claimant can prove were caused by the measures in question.

It should be noted that in case of successful claims for expropriation and other treaty breaches, compensation will not be cumulative.

---

[26] *Case Concerning the Factory at Chorzów (Claim for Indemnity) (Germany v Poland)*, Judgment on the Merits, September 13, 1928, Collection of Judgments, Permanent Court of International Justice, Series A, No.17 (1928) 47.

[27] *S.D. Myers Inc v Government of Canada*, Final Award on the Merits, November 13, 2000, (2001) 40 I.L.M. 1408. *Metalclad Corporation v The United Mexican States*, ICSID Case No.ARB(AF)/97/1, Award, August 25, 2000, (2001) 40 I.L.M. 36; and *Emilio Agustín Maffezini v Kingdom of Spain*, ICSID Case No.ARB/97/7, Award, November 13, 2000, (2001) 16 ICSID Review—Foreign Investment Law Journal.

INDEX

Index

Index

Index

Mediation 1–76
Mediation/arbitration 1–83
Meetings. *See* Arbitral tribunal
Mini-trial 1–82
Mistake of fact
  Federal Arbitration Act 9–42
Mistake of law
  Arbitration Act 1996 9–39
  challenging of awards, and. *See*
    Challenging of awards
  Intercantonal Convention on
    Arbitration 1969 9–40
  New York Convention 9–35
  setting aside proceedings 9–40
Multi-party arbitrations 3–73—3–85
  concurrent hearings 3–81
  consolidation by consent 3–84, 3–85
    arbitration agreement, under 3–84
    ICC, and 3–85
    institutional rules, under 3–85
    LCIA Rules 3–85
  court ordered consolidation 3–82,
    3–83
    California 3–82
    English proposals 3–83
    Florida 3–82
    Hong Kong 3–82
    Netherlands 3–82
    New York Convention 3–82
  difficulties 3–73
  Model Law provision 3–76
  several contracts with different parties
    3–77—3–79
    consolidation of proceedings 3–78
    sub-contractors 3–77
  several parties to one contract
    3–74—3–76
    Dutco 3–74
    ICC Arbitration Rules 3–74
    LCIA Arbitration Rules 3–75
    UNCITRAL Model Law 3–76
  string arbitrations 3–80

National courts, role of 7–01—7–42
  beginning of arbitration, and
    7–06—7–09
  challenges to jurisdiction of arbitral
    tribunal, and 7–09
  during arbitral proceedings
    7–10—7–40
  end of arbitration 7–41
  enforcing arbitration agreement 7–07
  establishing arbitral tribunal 7–08
  frontier with arbitral tribunals 7–05

National courts, role of—*cont.*
  increasing independence of
    arbitration, and 7–03
  international agreements on
    jurisdiction 5–62, 5–63
  interim measures: powers of arbitral
    tribunal 7–11, 7–12. *See also*
    Interim measures
    enforcement difficulties 7–16
    inability to act prior to formation
      of tribunal 7–14
    no *ex parte* application 7–17
    no powers 7–13
    order can only affect parties to
      arbitration 7–15
    "recommend" 7–11, 7–12
  interim measures: powers of
    competent court 7–18—7–23
    application to court or arbitrators,
      whether 7–21—7–23
    division of labour 7–22
    incompatibility with arbitration
      agreement 7–19
    prejudice to outcome of arbitration,
      and 7–20
  intervention of 7–06
  judicial control of proceedings and
    award 7–41
  limitations on independence of
    arbitral tribunals 7–04
    Model Law 7–04
  measures aimed at preserving status
    quo 7–28—7–32
  measures relating to attendance of
    witnesses and preservation of
    evidence 7–24—7–27
    Arbitration Act 1996 7–24
    Federal Arbitration Act 7–25
    goods and property 7–26, 7–27
    importance of 7–26
    Model Law 7–24
    UNCITRAL Rules 7–26
  parallel proceedings 7–33—7–38
  partnership with arbitral tribunals
    7–02
  relay race 7–05
National and international laws
  interplay 1–158, 1–159
National law 2–40—2–44
  choice of system 2–41, 2–42
  known legal standard, as 2–40
  precluding unfair treatment 2–43
  stabilisation clauses 2–44